THE
WORLD
SINCE
1945

THE
WORLD
SINCE
1945

A HISTORY OF
INTERNATIONAL RELATIONS

Wayne C. McWilliams and Harry Piotrowski

Lynne Rienner Publishers   Boulder
Adamantine Press Limited   London

Published in the United States of America in 1990 by
Lynne Rienner Publishers, Inc.
1800 30th Street, Boulder, Colorado 80301

Published in the United Kingdom by
Adamantine Press Limited
3 Henrietta Street, Covent Garden, London WC2E 8LU

Library of Congress Cataloging-in-Publication Data
McWilliams, Wayne C.
    The world since 1945: a history of international relations/
by Wayne C. McWilliams & Harry Piotrowski.—2nd ed., fully rev.
and updated.
        Includes bibliographic references.
        ISBN: 1-55587-220-4
        1. World politics—1945-   2. Military history. Modern—20th
century. 3. Developing countries—Economic conditions.
I. Piotrowski, Harry. II. Title.
D843.M34 1990
909.82—dc20   90-33817

British Cataloguing in Publication Data
A Cataloguing in Publication record for this book
is available from the British Library.
(Adamantine International Studies, No. 6)
ISBN: 0-7449-0027-1

Printed and bound in the United States of America

5 4 3 2

Contents

List of Maps   vii
Preface to the Second Edition   ix
Acknowledgments   xi

Introduction   1

Part 1: The Origins of the Cold War   7

1   The End of World War II and the
        Dawn of the Nuclear Age   11
2   The Cold War Institutionalized   29
3   The Cold War in Asia: A Change of Venue   47
4   Confrontation and Coexistence   72

Part 2: Nationalism and the End of Colonialism   99

5   Decolonization in Asia   103
6   Decolonization in Africa   119
7   The Middle East: The Arab-Israeli Wars   138

Part 3: The Shifting Sands of Global Power   157

8   The Communist World After Stalin   161
9   The War in Indochina   187
10   Détente and the End of Bipolarity   210

Part 4: The Third World   227

11   Africa: Political and Economic Disasters   231
12   Revolution and Counterrevolution in Latin America   269
13   Asian Roads to Modernization   304
14   The Third World's Debt: Africa and Latin America   345

Part 5: The End of the Postwar Era   355

15   Militant Islam   359
16   The New Economic Superpowers:
         Japan and the European Community   377
17   The Soviet Empire: A Beleaguered Colossus   403
18   Gorbachev and the Restructuring of Eastern Europe   424
19   The Nuclear Arms Race   456

     Index   479
     About the Book and the Authors   493

☐ Maps

Central and Eastern Europe:
Territorial Changes After World War II   36

East Asia (1945)   49

The Korean War (1950-1953)   63

Europe (1990)   84

Colonial Southern and Southeastern Asia:
European and U.S. Territories in 1900   106

Colonial Africa (1945)   122

The Expansion of Israel   146

Indochina: The Vietnam War   191

Africa After Independence   243

South Africa's "Homelands"   259

South America   273

Central America   286

The Indian Subcontinent   325

The Persian Gulf States   371

☐ Preface to the Second Edition

When we set out in the middle of the 1980s to write about the world since the end of World War II, we treated it as a history of our time. We were, after all, in the midst of it. The events since the first edition went to press, however, have made it clear that the postwar era is over. Changes had occurred in relatively gradual fashion since 1945—European colonization had come to an end, an economic realignment had taken place, Western Europe had begun to resurface as a political force, Islam as a political and social idea had reemerged—but many of the remnants of the postwar era—the division of Europe, the arms race, the extension of the Cold War rivalry into the Third World—continued to linger. The events of the late 1980s, however, have suddenly changed the face of Eastern Europe beyond recognition and have put the logic of the Cold War in question. In sum, what applied to the recent past no longer has much validity. A second edition, therefore, became a necessity long before we had anticipated it. We have taken the story to the historic February 1990 plenum of the Communist party of the Soviet Union, when the party agreed to abandon its monopoly on political power.

Wayne C. McWilliams
Harry Piotrowski

February 1990

☐ Acknowledgments

We wish to express appreciation for the support we have received from many friends and colleagues. We especially appreciate the support and encouragement received from Dean Esslinger and the Faculty Research Committee of Towson State University. We are also indebted to the following colleagues who generously shared their expertise with us and offered us valuable advice and suggestions: David Dent, Edwin Hirschmann, Leroy Johnson, Wayne McKim, Teresa Meade, Myron Scholnick, and Irvin Weintraub. We particularly appreciate the assistance of George Friedman whose careful proofreading of the entire manuscript enhanced its literary quality. We also wish to thank Josephine Ellis, Carolyn Westbrook, and the Instructional Graphics Services of Towson State University for producing the maps for this text.

Last but not least, we wish to express our gratitude to Junko McWilliams and Cristina Piotrowski for their unswerving support, patience, and encouragement, and for the countless ways they assisted us in writing this book.

Wayne C. McWilliams
Harry Piotrowski

☐ Introduction

A survey of current world conditions and a reading of the recent past reveal that the world is neither a fair nor a friendly place. Insurrections and wars abound, and more than half the world's inhabitants live in misery and hunger while others live in comfort and luxury. In this age of modern science and technology, of space exploration and heart transplants, how does one account for the absence of peace and the prevalence of poverty in a world of plenty? What are the roots of the perilous condition of human affairs? Today's students, young and old, must ask and seek to answer these questions. This book, a history of the world since 1945, was undertaken in order to assist them in that endeavor.

Tribal hostility and war between nations have been common throughout history, but in modern times, and especially in the twentieth century with the development of modern military technology, war has become increasingly deadly. World War II brought death and destruction on an unprecedented scale, and it ended with the use of a powerful new weapon of mass destruction, the atomic bomb. From the ruins of that war came a cry, expressed even by military leaders, that there must never be another such war. Yet, even as the ashes of World War II were still smoldering, friction developed among its victors, and they—the United States and Britain on one side and the Soviet Union on the other—became locked in a new power struggle that threatened the very peace they had sacrificed so much to attain. The postwar friction between them rapidly hardened into a political Cold War that soon turned into a military confrontation between East and West marked by mutual mistrust, suspicion, and hostility. Since the end of World War II the Cold War has continued for more than forty years as the major determinant of international affairs. The two superpowers, the United States and the Soviet Union, have aggressively sought to establish and maintain blocs of allies, thus dividing the world into two hostile camps. And since each claimed to be the champion of a superior system, one capitalist and the

1

other Communist, the world became the arena of an enduring ideological conflict.

Meanwhile both superpowers began rearming, and a relentless arms race was soon under way. Each claimed that security—both national and global—lay in military strength, but that the other's armaments threatened world peace. Thus they justified the building of massive arsenals containing thousands of nuclear weapons far more powerful than the ones used against Japan in 1945. Their arsenals have long since been large enough to destroy each other many times over and possibly extinguish human life on this planet, and yet year after year they continue piling up more weapons, spending at a rate of millions of dollars per hour. The military standoff between the nuclear powers has brought about a precarious peace between them, but the world has not been free of war. On the contrary, there have been more than one hundred wars since World War II, and many of these lesser brushfire wars, though contained geographically and limited to conventional weapons, carry the potential of igniting a larger conflagration. Indeed, the combatants are all too often clients of the major powers and are armed by them.

Equally dangerous to the safety and well-being of humanity is the growing gulf between the world's rich and poor, between the industrially advanced nations of the North and the underdeveloped nations of the South. In the South, often referred to as the Third World, one finds the world's lowest standards of living, lowest economic growth rates, lowest levels of education, lowest rates of life expectancy, and the highest population growth rates and infant mortality rates. Thus, millions of the inhabitants of the Third World are dreadfully impoverished, malnourished, disease-ridden, and unable to live productively and in dignity. Governments of Third World nations have struggled, usually ineptly, to lift their countries from such impoverishment, and while some have made marginal progress, many others are merely marking time or slipping even further behind. Many of these countries have contracted enormous foreign debts, which they are unable to pay, and their indebtedness threatens the financial stability of the wealthier nations of the North. Economic failure has made the Third World more volatile politically and more vulnerable to intervention and militarization by the superpowers. Nearly every war fought since World War II has been fought in Third World countries, and they all have been fought with weapons supplied by industrialized nations.

This is the world into which the youth of today were born. Their chances of resolving the immense problems they have inherited, of reducing Cold War tensions and the nuclear threat, and of alleviating the misery of the majority of mankind, thus making this world a safer and more civilized place, depend to a great extent on what they know of the origins of these problems. The clear-eyed vision needed to come to terms with these difficult problems and to progress toward a resolution of them must be based on an understanding of the past. To remain ignorant of that past is to compound the chances of either perpetuating the current problems or committing grievous and possibly irretrievable errors.

It was for the purpose of combatting such ignorance and supplanting it with a knowledge of world affairs that we undertook the writing of this text. Our aim is to provide our readers with an evenhanded, yet critical explanation of the political history of this troubled world and to expose them to more than one viewpoint. We seek to advance our readers' knowledge of the recent past and to develop a better understanding of the difficult issues and dangerous conditions in the world today. Above all, we hope to instill an appreciation of the need for greater objectivity and for careful, critical thinking about political issues. It is, therefore, our hope that this text will serve as a primer for responsible global citizenship.

It should be emphasized that we are primarily dealing with political history in this text, except in certain chapters where economic themes are particularly relevant. We do not address social or cultural dimensions of recent world history, as interesting or important as they may be. We also wish to point out that a text with a scope as broad as the world cannot help but be selective. Obviously, not every political development around the globe is discussed within these pages. We have attempted to provide a balanced coverage of global history, rather than a Western world or U.S.-centered approach. Thus, a substantial portion of the text is devoted to Asia, Africa, and Latin America.

The study of the recent past is no substitute for studying the longer haul of human history. Obviously, World War II had antecedents, the knowledge of which deepens our understanding of that momentous event, its consequences, and the course of events in the postwar period. Nonetheless, because World War II represents a historic watershed, one of the landmarks in history, it is not inappropriate that it be taken as a starting point for the study of recent world history. And because the postwar period is distinctly a new era with many new features—the advent of nuclear warfare, the development of high speed aviation, the emergence of two superpowers, and the end of European colonialism, to name just a few—it makes sense to treat it as a distinct historical period. (To be sure, for certain topics treated in this text, such as the Arab-Israeli conflict or the revolution in China, it will be necessary to trace historical roots further back in time, but our focus remains on the postwar period.)

■ SEVEN MAJOR CONSEQUENCES OF WORLD WAR II

The enormous consequences of World War II gave shape to the postwar world, and they are treated as major themes in this text. We have identified the following as the most important of those consequences:

1. *The end of the European age.* Europe ceased to be the center of international power. At war's end, Europe was in shambles; its nations were prostrate, its cities in ruins, its people exhausted, and its economies shattered. The total defeat and destruction of Germany created a power vacuum in central Europe, and since nature and politics both abhor a vacuum, the victors inevitably filled it.

2. *The rise of the United States to superpower status.* Having played a decisive role in the global war and emerging from it militarily and economically supreme among the nations of the world, the United States shed for good its earlier isolationism and assumed a leadership role in the international arena.

3. *The expansion of the Soviet Union and its rise to superpower status.* Despite its severe war damage and its dire economic condition, the Soviet Union was determined to extend its power, especially in Eastern Europe, and play a major role in world affairs.

4. *The emergence of the Cold War.* Contention, mistrust, and hostility between the two emerging superpowers, the United States and the Soviet Union, developed quickly and produced an ongoing, global, bipolar power struggle.

5. *The beginning of the nuclear age.* The use of the atomic bomb by the United States and the world's failure to achieve international control of atomic energy resulted inevitably in the ever-growing nuclear arms race.

6. *The rise of nationalism and independence movements in Asia and Africa.* Although the roots of nationalism may be traced back to prewar times, it was not until the postwar period that nationalist movements became strong enough to challenge the colonial order in Asia and Africa. The struggle for independence was stimulated by the defeat of Japan and the weakening of the European colonial powers, and, in a remarkably short span of time, many Asian and African states won their independence.

7. *A renewed effort to secure lasting peace through international organization.* The United Nations was created in the hope that it might achieve the global peace and security that the old League of Nations had failed to maintain.

Most of these interrelated themes are discussed in Part 1, "The Origins of the Cold War." In it we examine the global state of affairs at the end of World War II, and analyze the origins of the Cold War and its development in both Europe and Asia. In Part 2, "Nationalism and the End of Colonialism," the sixth theme is taken up. In this part, we also trace the development of Arab and Israeli nationalism and the course of the Mid-East conflict. Part 3,

"The Shifting Sands of Global Power," focuses mainly on the 1960s. In it we examine the changing configuration of the Cold War, the strains within the Eastern and Western blocs, the Sino-Soviet split, and the resulting emergence of multipolarity, which replaced the bipolar confrontation of the earlier Cold War period. This section also includes coverage of the Vietnam War and its consequences. Part 4, "The Third World," takes us back to Asia and Africa to trace their postindependence progress—or lack thereof—and to Latin America as well to examine its similar problems.

In addition to investigating the political and economic patterns on the three Third World continents, we also devote sections to such topics as the problem of the Third World debt, the issue of apartheid in South Africa, the economic progress of certain Asian nations, and the revolution in the Philippines. Part 5, "The End of the Postwar Era," treats the major global developments and issues in the 1980s. We have selected for special attention the rise of militant Islam, especially as manifested in the Iranian revolution, the rise of Japan and the European Community as new economic superpowers, and such Cold War issues as the rise of Solidarity in Poland, the Soviet invasion of Afghanistan, and the nuclear arms race, potentially the most dangerous challenge to modern man. Finally, in Part 5, we analyze the momentous changes in the Soviet Union and Eastern Europe at the end of the 1980s, changes that signal the end of the postwar era.

We urge our readers to join with us in a quest for a fuller, more objective understanding of the world of turmoil in which we live. And we would remind them that history, especially recent political history, is not merely the compilation of dead facts; it is alive with controversy and conflicting ideas. We challenge our readers to confront these controversies, to weigh the conflicting ideas and viewpoints, and to formulate their own opinions.

■ Part 1

THE ORIGINS OF THE COLD WAR

In light of the enormous impact of the Cold War on human life since World War II—the immeasurable human energies it has exhausted, the gargantuan amounts of wealth it has consumed, the shifting of national priorities it has demanded, the attention it has diverted from other global concerns, the civil liberties it has impinged and the intellectual freedom it has strained, the anguish and fears it has caused so many people, and the threat it poses to the earth's inhabitants—it becomes necessary to inquire into its origins and to question whether it was avoidable. If we understand better its causes, it might help us in dealing with it today and aid us in eliminating it in the future.

By its very nature, the Cold War is so divisive a subject that it is all but impossible to study it with detachment and objectivity. So strong are the feelings and so total the commitment of each side to its cause, and so contemptuous and mistrusting is each of the other side, that each has its own self-serving version of the history of the Cold War and of each and every confrontation between East and West.

The United States and the Soviet Union have each perpetuated a series of Cold War myths that have sustained them over the years. On the one hand, the people of the United States generally feel (1) that the Soviet Union broke its postwar promises regarding Eastern Europe and is therefore responsible for starting the Cold War; (2) that its aggressive action in Eastern Europe was a manifestation of the determination of the Soviet Union to capture the entire world for Communism; (3) that so-called "international Communism" is a monolithic (that is, singular) movement centered in and controlled by the Soviet Union; (4) that Communism is enslavement, and is never accepted by any people without coercion; and (5) that the great victory of the United States in World War II, as well as its immense prosperity and strength, attests to the superiority of its values and its system—that, in short, the United States represents humanity's best hope.

On the other hand, the Soviets seem to feel (1) that the United States and the Western allies purposely let the Soviet Union bleed in World War II, and furthermore lacked gratitude for the role that it played in the defeat of Hitler, as well as for the losses it suffered in that cause; (2) that the United States is committed to the annihilation of Communism in general and to the overthrow of the Communist government of the Soviet Union in particular; (3) that the laws of history are on its side, meaning that capitalism is in decline and Communism is the wave of the future; (4) that the U.S. political system is not really democratic but is completely controlled by Wall Street, or at any rate by a small clique of leading corporate interests; and (5) that capitalist nations are necessarily imperialistic and thus responsible for the colonization of the Third World, and that the leading capitalist nation, the United States, is the most imperialistic of them all.[1]

As unquestioned assumptions these myths become a mental straitjacket. They provide only a narrow channel for foreign policy initiatives by either country. When notions such as these are imbedded in the thinking of the two adversaries, it becomes almost impossible for the two countries to break out of the Cold War and equally impossible to analyze objectively the history of the conflict. Nevertheless, we must try.

The myths have come into play throughout the Cold War, and especially in its earliest phase—even before the defeat of Nazi Germany—when the Allied leaders met at Yalta in February 1945. For this reason, in the opening chapter of this book, we examine the wartime relationship between the United States and the Soviet Union, and their respective strengths at the end of the war. We also analyze the U.S. decision to use the atomic bomb against Japan and the impact it had on U.S.-Soviet relations. In Chapter 2, we turn to the Yalta Conference and examine its bearing on the beginning of the Cold War. We then trace the hardening of Cold War positions over critical issues in Europe in the four years following the end of World War II. By 1947, when the U.S. policy of "containment" of Communism was in place, the Cold War myths were firmly entrenched on both sides.

The Cold War quickly became global, and in fact it was in Asia that it became most inflamed in the first decade after the war. In Chapter 3, we pursue the Cold War in Asia by treating the Allied Occupation of defeated Japan, the civil war that brought the Communists to power in China, and the Korean War—all Cold War issues. The Allied Occupation of defeated Japan was thoroughly dominated by the United States over the feeble objections of the Soviets, and eventually the United States succeeded in converting Japan into a major ally in the global Cold War. The Chinese revolution, which brought the Communists to power in 1949, was fought entirely by indigenous forces, but the two superpowers were also involved. The United States responded to the Communist victory in China with still firmer resolve to stem the advance of Communism in Asia. Less than a year later, that resolve was tested in Korea where Cold War tensions grew most intense and finally ignited in the Korean War. The armed conflict between East and West was contained within one Asian country, but it threatened to explode into the dreaded World War III.

After the standoff in Korea, Cold War tensions oscillated during the remainder of the 1950s. During this period, covered in Chapter 4, new leaders—Dwight Eisenhower in the United States and Nikita Khrushchev in the Soviet Union—exhibited a new flexibility, which made possible some reduction in tensions and the solution of a few of the issues that divided the two nations. But the Cold War mentality, the embrace of the Cold War myths, remained undiminished during this period as manifested by sporadic crises and the substantial growth in the nuclear arsenals of both countries. The two superpowers came to the brink of nuclear war in the early 1960s over the deployment of Soviet nuclear missiles in Cuba. The Cuban missile crisis has been the most dangerous of the many confrontations between East and West to date.

■ NOTES

1. These myths are an adaptation of a similar set of Cold War myths presented in Ralph B. Levering, *The Cold War, 1945–1972* (Arlington Heights, Ill.: Harlan Davidson, 1982), pp. 8–9.

☐ 1

The End of World War II and the Dawn of the Nuclear Age

World War II was a cataclysmic event. It was by far the most deadly and destructive war in human history. The war raged on for almost six years in Europe, beginning with Nazi Germany's attack on Poland in September 1939, and ending with the surrender of Germany to the Allied Powers led by the United States, the Soviet Union, and Great Britain on May 9, 1945. The war lasted even longer in Asia, where it began with the Japanese invasion of China in July 1937 and ended with Japan's capitulation to the Allies on August 14, 1945. World War II represented a new dimension in warfare: total war. It was total in the sense that all of the great powers and most of the nations of the world were engaged in it, and in that it involved or affected the entire population of nations, not just the men and women in uniform. Because a nation's military might rested ultimately on its industrial capacity, the civilian work force had to contribute to the war effort; moreover, entire populations, especially urban dwellers, became targets and victims of new and more deadly modern weapons.

Another major dimension of World War II that was of immense importance in ending the war and shaping the postwar world was the introduction of atomic weapons. There are many difficult questions to ponder concerning the U.S. use of the atomic bomb against Japan at the end of World War II, one of the most important and most controversial issues in modern history. But the fundamental question remains: was it necessary or justifiable to use the bomb? It is also important to consider what bearing the emerging Cold War had on the U.S. decision to drop the bomb on Japan, and what bearing its use had on subsequent U.S.-Soviet relations.

After the war, it was the victorious nations—mainly the United States and the Soviet Union—that took the lead in shaping the postwar world. In order to better understand their respective postwar policies, one must consider the impact World War II had on these two nations, which emerged as "superpowers" and as major adversaries in the ensuing Cold War.

The "Grand Alliance" fashioned by the United States, the Soviet Union, and Great Britain during the war hardly lasted beyond it. But before the alliance began to crumble and give way to Cold War hostility, leading political representatives of these and other nations endeavored to create a new international structure for the maintenance of global peace through collective security—the United Nations. Although the founding of the United Nations was attended by great hope, it was from the beginning very severely limited in its capacity to attain its objective of world peace.

■ HISTORY'S MOST DESTRUCTIVE WAR

The carnage of World War II was so great as to be beyond comprehension. Most of Europe and East Asia were in ruins. Vast stretches of both continents were destroyed twice, first when they were conquered and again when they were liberated. Germany and Japan stood in ruins. It is impossible to know the complete toll in human lives lost in this war, but estimates run as high as 50 million people. The nation that suffered the greatest loss of life was the Soviet Union. It lost an incredible 20 to 25 million people in the war, a figure that represents at least half of the total European war fatalities. Poland lost 5.8 million people, about 15 percent of its population. Germany lost 4.5 million people, and Yugoslavia, 1.5 million. Seven other European nations, France, Italy, Romania, Hungary, Czechoslovakia, and Britain each lost more than a half million people. In Asia, approximately 3 million Chinese and 2.3 million Japanese died in the war, and there were large numbers of casualties in various Asian countries from India in the south to Korea in the northeast. In some European countries and in Japan, there was hardly a family that had not lost at least one member in the war.[1]

Over one-half of those who died in World War II were civilians. Never before had warfare taken such a heavy toll of noncombatants. (In World War I only about one-twentieth of the dead were civilians.) An estimated 12 million civilians were killed as a direct result of military action, mainly bombing, and millions more died of starvation or epidemics in Europe and Asia, although we have no way of knowing exactly how many. An estimated 12 million people—Jews, Slavs, Gypsies, the disabled, conscientious objectors, and political opponents (notably Communists)—were systematically exterminated as a result of the policy of Adolf Hitler, the dictator of Nazi Germany. This unspeakable act of barbarism, known as the Holocaust, was aimed primarily at exterminating the Jewish people; it resulted in the reduction of the Jewish population in Europe from 9.2 million to 3.8 million. All mankind was indelibly scarred by this most heinous of crimes committed by the Nazi rulership against the Jewish people.

The main cause for this huge toll of civilian lives was no doubt the development of air power—bigger and faster airplanes with longer range and greater carrying capacity. Indiscriminate bombing of the enemy's cities, populated by noncombatants, became common practice during the war. It began with Hitler's effort to bomb Britain into submission early in the war with a relentless bombing of British cities.[2] Later in the war, British and U.S. bombers retaliated with a massive bombardment of Germany. One Anglo-U.S. bombing raid on the German city of Dresden, in February 1945 (when Germany was all but defeated), killed some 135,000 people, mainly civilians. The Japanese, who also used air power, suffered the destruction of virtually all of their cities by the saturation bombing carried out by U.S. bombers. And the war ended with the use by the United States of a dreadful new weapon of mass destruction, the atomic bomb, which wrought the horrible devastation of Hiroshima and Nagasaki in August 1945. In total war fought with these methods and weapons, there was no place to hide. In the end, the nations that fought in the name of democracy in order to put an end to militarism resorted to the barbaric methods of their enemies. If unrestrained warfare had come to mean sustained, indiscriminate bombing of noncombatants with weapons of mass destruction, what hope was there for mankind should total war ever again occur?

The suffering and sorrow, the anguish and desperation of the survivors of the war lingered long after the last bombs had fallen and the victory celebrations had ended. Never in history had so much of the human race been so uprooted. In Europe alone there were between 20 and 30 million homeless refugees. Many of these displaced persons were people who fled their homelands to escape political persecution and to seek a greater measure of security and freedom elsewhere. Some were fleeing bombed-out cities and others were fleeing the advancing Soviet Red Army. Still others included those who had been forcibly moved to Germany during the war to work in its fields and factories. And then there were those, such as the several million ethnic Germans who had lived in Eastern Europe, whose homelands were transferred to the victors. (Former German territories, which became parts of Poland, Czechoslovakia, and the Soviet Union, have remained among the unresolved issues of the Cold War.) For these millions of homeless people the struggle for survival was especially difficult, and we have no way of knowing how many of them did not survive.

There was also a large refugee problem in Asia, where the Japanese had forced population transfers during the war and where some 6 million Japanese—half of them military personnel—were scattered all over Asia at war's end. After the war, the United States transported most of these Japanese back to safety in Japan and returned Koreans, Chinese, and others to their homelands. However, in Manchuria, which was temporarily occupied by the Soviet Union after the war, several hundred thousand Japanese were never repatriated. They succumbed either to the severity of the Manchurian winter without adequate food, shelter, or clothing or to the brutality of Soviet labor camps in Siberia. Elsewhere in Asia, particularly in China, there were large population movements as millions of people, who had earlier fled from the Japanese invaders, returned to reclaim their lands and homes. In China, cities such as Beijing (Peking) and Shanghai were swollen with weary, desperate people for whom there was no livelihood and insufficient food and other staples. In these places people were plagued by disease, poverty, the black market, inflation, and corruption, all of which ran rampant in China during and well after the war.

The inferno of World War II left many cities gutted and vacant. Dresden, Hamburg, and Berlin in Germany and Tokyo, Yokohama, Hiroshima, and Nagasaki in Japan were virtually flattened, and many other cities in these and other countries were in large part turned to rubble. Some were entirely vacated and devoid of life for a while after the war, and most lost a substantial portion of their people. For example, the huge and once crowded city of Tokyo, which lay mostly in ruins, saw its population dwindle to only a third of its prewar size. In these once bustling cities, survivors scrounged in the debris in hopes of salvaging anything that might help them in their struggle for survival. At war's end homeless people moved into those few buildings that still stood—an office building, a railroad station, a school—and lived sometimes three or four families to a room, while others threw up shanties and shacks made of scraps of wood. Decades later one can still find here and there in many of these cities rubble left over from the war.

The physical destruction wrought by the war—estimated at over $2,000 billion—continued to cause economic and social disruption in the lives of survivors long afterwards. Not only were cities and towns destroyed but so too were industrial plants and transportation facilities. The destruction of factories, farmlands, and livestock and of railroads, bridges, and port facilities made it extremely difficult to feed and supply the needy populations in the war-torn nations of Europe and Asia. Thus, acute shortages of food and scarcity of other life essentials continued well after the fighting was over. In these dire circumstances, many became desperate and demoralized, and some sought to insure their survival or to profit from others' misfortune by resorting to hoarding goods and selling them on the black market. These were grim times in which greed, vengeance, and other base instincts of humanity found expression.

The widespread desolation and despair in Europe bred cynicism and disillusionment, which in turn gave rise to a political shift to the Left. Shaken and bewildered by the nightmarish devastation all about them, many Europeans lost confidence in the old political order and turned to other more radical political doctrines and movements. Many embraced Marxism as a natural alternative to the discredited fascism and as an ideology that offered hope for the future. The renewed popularity of the Left was reflected primarily in postwar electoral victories of the moderate Left, such as the Labour Party in Great Britain and the Socialist Party in Austria. But the Communists, too, were able to make strong showings, particularly in France and Italy. In Asia the political swing to the Left could be seen in China, Indochina, and to a lesser extent in Japan. Alarmed by this resurgence of the Left, U.S. leaders soon came to the view that massive aid was necessary to bring about a speedy economic recovery and thereby eliminate the poverty that was seen as the breeding ground for the spread of Communism.

During the war the United Nations Relief and Rehabilitation Administration (UNRRA) was created to rehabilitate war-torn areas after liberation. Economic aid from this agency as well as from the United States directly not only provided relief for the destitute peoples of Europe and Asia, but also provided much needed credit that made possible the beginnings of economic recovery. By the fall of 1946, many of the transportation facilities and factories in Western Europe had been rapidly repaired, and industrial production began to climb slowly toward prewar levels. But the winter of 1946–1947 brought new economic setbacks with a depletion of food supplies, raw materials, and financial reserves. Economic stagnation and attendant deprivation therefore continued for masses of people throughout Europe, especially in Germany, which had suffered the greatest physical destruction in the war, and in Great Britain, one of the victors. A similar situation prevailed in the war-ravaged nations of Asia, especially China and Japan.

When we consider all the death, destruction, suffering, and social dislocation that it caused for so many people, we realize that World War II was much more than a series of heroic military campaigns, and more than a set of war games to be played and replayed by nostalgic war buffs. It was human anguish and agony on a scale unprecedented in the history of mankind. And nowhere were the scars any deeper than on the two Japanese cities, Hiroshima and Nagasaki.

■ THE ATOMIC BOMBING OF JAPAN

On August 6, 1945, the United States dropped an atomic bomb on Hiroshima, and three days later it used another one on Nagasaki. In each instance a large city was obliterated and tens of thousands of its inhabitants were either instantly incinerated, or left to succumb to radiation sickness weeks, months, or even years later. According to Japanese estimates, about 140,000 people were killed in Hiroshima by the atomic bomb strike, and about 70,000 in Nagasaki.[3] Thus, World War II ended and the nuclear age began with the use of this new weapon of unprecedented destructive power, a weapon that one scientist later called "a magnificent product of pure physics."[4]

The people of the United States and their wartime president, Franklin

Roosevelt, were determined to bring about the earliest possible defeat of Japan. The costly war in the Pacific had been raging for almost three-and-a-half years by the time Germany surrendered in May 1945. President Roosevelt, who had commissioned the building of the atomic bomb, was prepared to use it against Japan once it was ready, but he died in April 1945. The decision to employ the revolutionary new weapon fell to the new president, Harry S. Truman, who had not even been informed of its existence before he took office. In consultation with the secretary of war Henry Stimson, Truman set up an advisory group known as the Interim Committee, which was to deliberate on the matter of introducing the new weapon into warfare. Ultimately, the Interim Committee recommended that the atomic bomb be used against Japan as soon as possible, and without prior warning, on a dual target (meaning a military or war plant site surrounded by workers' homes, that is, a Japanese city).[5] The rationale for this strategy for the use of the bomb was to enhance its shock value. The atomic bomb was successfully tested in a remote New Mexico desert on July 16, just as Truman was meeting British Prime Minister Winston Churchill and Soviet leader Joseph Stalin at Potsdam, Germany. Nine days later, on July 25, Truman, elated by the news of the test, approved the military orders for its use. The following day he issued the Potsdam Proclamation, which contained the final surrender terms for Japan and warned of "prompt and utter destruction" for noncompliance, but which made no specific reference to the new weapon. The proclamation was rejected by the Japanese government, and thus the orders for the first atomic bomb strike were carried out as planned.

On the official level, the Japanese government dismissed the proclamation, for it was silent on the most important question, a guarantee that the victors would retain the most sacred of Japanese institutions, the emperor. The U.S. intelligence community, which from the very beginning of the war had been able to decode Japanese diplomatic cables, had become well aware that the Potsdam Proclamation had a "magnetic effect" on the emperor, Prime Minister Suzuki, and the army. Some Japanese officials thought that Article 10 of the Potsdam Proclamation implied the retention of the emperor and thus could be used as the basis of a Japanese surrender; others wanted a clarification. The Potsdam Proclamation, far from triggering an expression of Japanese intransigence, had the earmarks of the terms of surrender of the armed forces of the empire of Japan. Only one question remained: Would the U.S. government clarify Article 10 and accept a Japanese surrender before or after atomic weapons were used?[6]

Many people have since questioned the use of the atomic bomb, and opinions differ sharply. The orthodox view, presented by U.S. officials after the event and generally shared by the U.S. public, is that, by cutting short the war and sparing the casualties that would have occurred in the planned invasion of Japan, the atomic bomb actually saved many lives, Japanese as well

Hiroshima, Japan, Aug. 1945. Located near ground zero, this building with its "A-Bomb Dome" has been preserved as a peace monument.

as U.S. This explanation concludes that, although use of the bomb was re-grettable, it was nonetheless necessary. Japan's die-hard military leaders were determined to fight to the bitter end, as they had in the Pacific islands, and they were prepared to fight even more fanatically on their own soil to prevent defeat. Thus, in order to bring about the earliest possible surrender of Japan and an end to the long and costly war,[7] the United States was com-pelled to use the revolutionary, powerful new weapon its scientists and en-gineers had secretly produced.

However, this interpretation, basically a justification of the atomic bombing of Japan, neglects many important historical facts. First, Japan was all but defeated. Its home islands were defenseless against the sustained naval and air bombardment they were undergoing, its navy and merchant marine were sunk, its armies were weakened and undersupplied, and it was already being strangled by a U.S. naval blockade. U.S. leaders, who had underestimated the Japanese at the beginning of the war, were now over-estimating Japan's remaining strength. Although the die-hard determination of its military leaders kept Japan from surrendering, the nation's capacity to wage war was virtually eliminated.

Second, before the the United States had tested the atomic bomb in mid–July, the Japanese were already attempting to begin negotiations to end the war through Soviet mediation. (Direct communication between Tokyo and Washington was not possible because of the state of war between the two countries, but Japan was not at war with the Soviet Union.) The U.S. government was fully aware of these efforts and of the sense of urgency voiced by the Japanese in their communications to Moscow. U.S. decision makers chose to ignore these diplomatic overtures, which they dismissed as unreliable and possibly a trick. The major obstacle to Japan's effort to achieve a diplomatic settlement to the war was the U.S. insistence upon unconditional surrender. (Unconditional surrender calls for the enemy's acceptance of complete submission to the will of the victor, as opposed to a negotiated settlement to end the war.) This was entirely unacceptable to the Japanese, who wanted at least a guarantee of the safety of their sacred imperial institution—which is to say, they insisted on the retention of their emperor, Hirohito, in whose name the imperial forces had fought the war. The United States government steadfastly refused to offer any such exception to the unconditional surrender policy. The Potsdam Proclamation, the final Allied ultimatum, issued on July 26, 1945, did not offer Japan any guarantees regarding the emperor, and thus the Japanese could not accept it as a basis for surrender. This condition was the only one the Japanese insisted upon, and eventually it was granted by the United States, after the nuclear destruction of Hiroshima and Nagasaki. On August 11, the Japanese government agreed to surrender provided that it "does not comprise any demand which prejudices the prerogatives of His Majesty as a sovereign ruler."[8] This was a condition the United States accepted in its reply when it demanded the unconditional surrender of the Japanese forces. If this condition had been granted beforehand, the Japanese may well have surrendered and the atomic bombs been unnecessary to attain that objective.

Third, the Japanese might have been spared the horrendous fate of Hiroshima and Nagasaki had the U.S. government provided them with an explicit warning about the nature of the new weapon and possibly an actual demonstration of an atomic blast as well. If they had still refused to accept the surrender terms after such a warning or demonstration, the use of the atomic weapons might have been morally justifiable. The Japanese were given no warning of the atomic bombing outside of the threat in the Potsdam Proclamation of "prompt and utter destruction." The Interim Committee ruled out the idea of providing Japan with either a warning or a demonstration of the bomb in favor of its direct use on a Japanese city in order to shock the Japanese into surrender. It was also argued that a demonstration would be risky because of the possibility of the bomb's failing to work, thus causing the United States to lose credibility and the Japanese military leaders to gain confidence.

Fourth, an unquestioned assumption of most of those who defend the use of the two atomic bombs is that it produced the desired results: Japan quickly surrendered. But questions do arise. Did the atomic bombings actually cause the Japanese to surrender? And was the second bomb necessary to bring it about? (It should be pointed out that there was no separate set of orders to drop a second atomic bomb on Japan. Instead, the plan was to use a "one-two punch" using both bombs in rapid succession, and, if necessary, a third, which was to be ready within ten days, so as to maximize the new weapon's shock value and force Japan to capitulate as rapidly as possible.)

Those who specifically protest the bombing of Nagasaki as unnecessary, and therefore immoral, assume that the bombing of Hiroshima was sufficient to cause Japan's surrender, or that Japan should have been given more time to assess what had hit Hiroshima. One may indeed question whether the interval of three days was long enough for the Japanese military leaders to assess the significance of the new force that had destroyed one of their cities. But a more fundamental question is whether the atomic bombings—the first or both—actually caused Japan's surrender. Japanese newspapers, the testimony of Japanese leaders, and U.S. intercepts of Japanese diplomatic cables provide reason to believe that the Soviet entry into the war against Japan on August 8 was as much a cause for Japan's surrender as the dropping of the two atomic bombs. The Soviet Union was the only major nation in the world not at war with Japan, and the Japanese leaders were still desperately hoping for Soviet neutrality or possible Soviet mediation to bail them out of the war. They took heart in the fact that the Soviet Union had not signed the Potsdam Proclamation or signified its support for it, even though Stalin was meeting with Truman and Churchill when it was issued. But with the Soviet attack the last shred of hope was gone, and Japan could no longer avoid admitting defeat. As for the effect of the atomic bombings on Japanese leaders, Japan's inner cabinet was divided three-to-three for and against accepting the Potsdam Proclamation before the bombing of Hiroshima, and it remained so afterward. And it remained equally divided after the Soviet entry into the war and the bombing of Nagasaki, until finally the emperor himself broke the deadlock in favor of ending the war.

What were the thoughts of the U.S. leaders about the role of the Soviet Union in bringing about Japan's defeat? Clearly, at the Yalta Conference in February 1945, President Roosevelt and his military advisers strongly desired the early entry of the Soviet Union into the war against Japan and he was willing to concede much to Stalin to attain this. But five months later, after the atomic bomb was successfully tested, leading figures in the Truman administration were not so sure they wanted the Soviet Union to enter the war against Japan. Nor did they want the Soviets to know anything about the atomic bomb. In fact, both Roosevelt and Truman pointedly refused to inform Moscow about the development of the new weapon and the plans to use it against Japan, despite the advice of some of the leading atomic scientists to do so in order to prevent a nuclear arms race after the war.

This last point raises intriguing and important questions about the connection between the U.S. use of the bomb and its policies toward the Soviet

Union at the end of the war. One historical interpretation asserts that the United States used the atomic bomb on defeated Japan not so much as the last attack of World War II, but as the first attack in the Cold War. In other words, the bomb was used in order to coerce the Soviet Union into behaving itself in Europe, Asia, and elsewhere. This explanation would explain the hurried use of the bomb before the Soviet Union had entered the war against Japan and nearly three months prior to the planned invasion of Japan by U.S. forces. And it would explain Truman's refusal to inform Stalin officially about the new weapon before (or even after) its use against Japan. In this way it is argued that the United States sought to maintain its nuclear monopoly (shared with Britain) and to use it as a means to curb Soviet expansion. This has been referred to as nuclear diplomacy.

Although this interpretation by revisionist historians is based on rather substantial evidence and logic, it remains speculative, and those who hold the orthodox view, of course, reject it and offer counterarguments. They emphasize the fanaticism and intransigence of the Japanese military leaders, who even resorted to suicidal *kamikaze* airplane attacks on U.S. ships. And they argue that the atomic bomb was needed to subdue an irrational enemy who seemed determined to fight suicidally to the bitter end. Therefore, they conclude, it was solely for military purposes that President Truman decided to use the atomic bomb. They also argue that President Truman, as commander in chief, had the responsibility to use the military power at his command to produce the earliest possible defeat of Japan, and that, if he had not used the atomic bomb and more U.S. military personnel had died in the continuing war, he would surely have been condemned as being politically and morally liable for their deaths.

Those who hold this view also point out that Truman could hardly have decided against use of the atomic bomb. As a new occupant of the White House following the popular Roosevelt, Truman inherited Roosevelt's cabinet, his policies, and specifically his resolve to treat the new weapon as a legitimate one of war. General Leslie Groves, head of the Manhattan Project (the code name of the secret program to build the atomic bomb), certainly assumed and fully expected that it would be used as soon as it became operational. The military planning for its use was well under way. There was, among the scientists and military personnel involved in the project, a rising anticipation of the successful deployment of the weapon they had brought into being after four years of herculean effort. It is argued that Truman, who had only learned about the new weapon when he took office in April, could hardly have stemmed the momentum. The military leaders, and General Groves in particular, seemed especially determined to deploy the new weapon in order to know its destructive force. They had decided upon a set of Japanese cities as targets and had ordered that these cities be spared from conventional bombing so that they would remain unspoiled targets for the new weapon.

■ THE POLITICAL FALLOUT

Historians are also in disagreement over the impact of the atomic bomb on the Cold War. Did the Truman administration actually attempt to employ nuclear diplomacy after the war? If it did, it is safe to say that it did not work. The nuclear threat, implicit in the exclusive Anglo-U.S. possession of the atomic bomb, did not seem to produce any significant change in Soviet behavior and policies anywhere. But it did, no doubt, affect attitudes on both sides that contributed to Cold War mistrust. U.S. possession of the bomb caused its leaders to be more demanding and less flexible in dealing with the Soviet Union, and the U.S. possession and use of the bomb surely caused the Soviet leaders, in turn, to increase their suspicions of the West.

It is fairly certain that the secretive manner of the United States in building and then using the atomic bomb made a postwar nuclear arms race likely, if not inevitable. Truman's secretary of state, James Byrnes, who also served on the Interim Committee, contended that it would take the Soviet Union at least ten years to develop an atomic bomb and that in the interval the United States could take advantage of its "master card" in dealing with the Soviet Union. However, leading U.S. nuclear scientists, including Robert Oppenheimer, predicted that the Soviet Union could build the bomb within four years.[9] Several of the Manhattan Project scientists attempted to warn the Truman administration that the atomic monopoly could not be maintained for long and that a nuclear arms race would surely follow and threaten the peace of the world if the U.S. government did not share information about this revolutionary new weapon of mass destruction with its ally, the Soviet Union, and did not attempt to bring it under international control. This advice, given both before and after the Hiroshima and Nagasaki bombings, went unheeded, and the result was exactly what the scientists had predicted. Indeed, Oppenheimer's prediction that the Soviets would have their own atomic weapons in four years was right on target.

The U.S. government did, however, after months of careful study of the complicated issues involved, offer a proposal for international control of atomic power. This proposal, the Baruch Plan, presented to a committee within the United Nations in June 1946, was unacceptable to the Soviet Union because, among other reasons, it permitted the United States to retain its nuclear arsenal indefinitely, while restricting Soviet efforts to develop one. The Soviets countered by proposing the immediate destruction of all existing nuclear weapons and the signing of a treaty outlawing any future production or use of them. The United States, understandably unwilling to scuttle its atomic monopoly, flatly rejected this. Talks continued for the next three years at the United Nations, but they proved fruitless. In the meantime, the Soviet Union's frantic effort to build an atomic bomb did bear fruit as early as the U.S. atomic scientists had predicted—July 1949. The nuclear arms race was joined.

■ THE UNITED STATES AND THE
SOVIET UNION AT WAR'S END

The two nations that emerged from the war as the most powerful shapers of the postwar world, the two new superpowers, the United States and the Soviet Union, had very different wartime experiences. No nation suffered as many casualties as the Soviet Union, and no major nation in the war suffered as few as the United States.

In June 1941, the Soviet Union was invaded by a German army of more than 2 million soldiers. Immense areas of the Soviet Union were devastated by the ensuing war, leaving some 1,700 cities and 70,000 villages in ruins and some 70 percent of its industries and 60 percent of its transportation facilities destroyed. During the war, the Germans took several million Soviet prisoners, many of whom did not survive their ordeal, and several million others were forcibly conscripted to labor on German farms during the war. The horrors of the German invasion and occupation policies and the siege of Soviet cities aroused the patriotism of both the Russian and non-Russian peoples of the Soviet Union who fought heroically to defend the nation in what is still called the Great Patriotic War. Ultimately, these people endured, and the Soviet Red Army drove the shattered German armies off their land and across Eastern Europe back to Germany where they were finally defeated. But the cost in lives was enormous: an estimated 7.5 million military deaths and twice—possibly three times—as many civilian lives. Any discussion of postwar policies of the Soviet Union and its relations with the United States must begin with a recognition of the incredible losses it suffered in its war against Nazi Germany and its insistence that there be no repetition of this history.[10]

In contrast, the United States emerged from the war virtually unscathed. Except for the Japanese attack on Pearl Harbor at the outset of the war, it had not been invaded or bombed and there had been no bloody battle lines across its terrain. In comparison with the huge Soviet death toll, the number of U.S. soldiers killed in the war—approximately 330,000—was small. For every U.S. death resulting from the war there were 85 to 90 Soviet deaths. The Soviet Union lost more people in the siege of Leningrad or in the battle of Stalingrad than the United States did in the entire war.

In contrast to the immense physical destruction sustained by the Soviet Union, the United States suffered very little damage. On the contrary, the U.S. economy experienced a great wartime boom, which brought it out of the Great Depression. While the Soviet Union's industrial output fell by 40 percent during the war years, that of the United States more than doubled. And while the Soviet Union sorely needed economic rehabilitation to recover from the ravages of war, the United States possessed unparalleled economic power. Indeed, no nation has ever achieved such economic supremacy as that achieved by the United States at the end of World War II. In a war-ravaged world where every other industrial nation had suffered extensive damage and declining production, the U.S. economy, with its wartime growth, towered over all others like a colossus. What is more, the United States had the capacity to greatly extend its huge lead. It possessed in great abundance every resource necessary for sustained industrial growth in the postwar era: large, undamaged industrial plants, skilled labor, technology, raw materials, a sophisticated transport system, and, last but not least, a huge supply of capital for investment.

The United States emerged from the war with another important although intangible asset: a greatly inflated national ego. The nation was brimming with renewed confidence and optimism. The pessimism spawned by the Great Depression was a thing of the past. The U.S. people saw their victory in war as proof of the superiority of their way of life. With their nation standing tall at the pinnacle of power in the war-torn world, the people exhibited what has been called an "illusion of American omnipotence."[11] Bolstered by this new confidence and sense of supremacy, the United States now displayed a new determination to play the role of a great power and to exercise its leadership in shaping the postwar world.

■ THE QUEST FOR COLLECTIVE SECURITY

The task of establishing a new world order after the defeat of Germany and Japan fell, of course, to the victors, especially the most powerful among them, the United States, the Soviet Union, and to a lesser degree Great Britain. During the war, the leaders of these countries—the "Big Three," Franklin Roosevelt, Joseph Stalin, and Winston Churchill—met not only to coordinate war plans but also to lay plans for the postwar settlement. These men, especially Roosevelt, were confident that the harmony and trust developed during the war would endure and that through personal diplomacy they could settle the enormous problems of the postwar world, such as the future of Germany, Eastern Europe, Japan, and the rest of Asia. However, before the war ended, two of the three were no longer in power: Roosevelt died in April 1945, and Churchill was defeated in the British election of July of that year. But it was already apparent before Roosevelt's death that the wartime alliance would not outlast the war. In retrospect, it is clear that the Big Three had little more in common than a common enemy, and once Nazi Germany was defeated their conflicting interests came to the fore.

The wartime solidarity attained by the personal diplomacy of the Big Three could not be counted on to guide the postwar world to safety and security, and would not in any case endure beyond the war; however, they did endeavor, albeit cautiously, to erect a new international structure of peace. While sharp differences arose among the Big Three over a number of issues as the war was coming to an end, they were in general agreement on the concept of maintaining peace through collective security. President Roosevelt was most ardent in advocating the creation of a new international peacekeeping organization to replace the defunct League of Nations. Early during the war years, Roosevelt began sounding out Churchill on this idea and then found occasion to discuss it with Stalin as well. All three were concerned about maintaining a postwar working relationship among the "united nations," as the allied powers were sometimes called. Roosevelt wished to avoid a return of his country to isolationism, and Stalin seems to have had a similar concern; he did not want the Soviet Union to be isolated as it had been prior to World War II.

Within each of the three governments there was much discussion about the shape the new collective security organization should take, its structure, functions, and authority. The most difficult issue was that of internationalism versus nationalism, or more concretely, whether member nations were to surrender part or all of their own sovereignty to the new supranational body in the interest of maintaining world peace. How would it be possible to provide the international organization with enough authority to enforce its decisions on member nations and yet permit each nation the right to pursue and protect its national interests? Another key question was the relationship of the major powers to the many smaller nations in the international body. From the outset the Big Three were in agreement that they would not sacrifice their power to majority rule. They insisted that their own nations, which had played the major role in defeating the aggressor nations in World War II, should be entrusted with the responsibility to maintain the postwar peace, and that the new international organization should invest authority in them to exercise leadership unobstructed by the collective will of the more numerous, smaller member states.

These issues were resolved among the Big Three at a series of wartime conferences. At a meeting in Moscow in October 1943, the Allied foreign ministers agreed in principle to the creation of the organization that would come to be known as the United Nations (or simply the UN). In August 1944, as victory in the war approached, representatives of the Big Three, now joined by China, met at Dumbarton Oaks (in Washington) to hammer out the shape of the new international body. At the Yalta Conference in February 1945 (see Chapter 2), the Big Three came to terms on the matter of securing for each of the major powers the right to veto decisions of the new international body. This cleared the way for convening a conference at San Francisco in April 1945, where the United Nations Charter, which spelled out the principles and the powers of the new organization as well as its organizational structure, was signed by representatives of the 51 founding nations. In September 1945, the United Nations officially opened at its headquarters in New York City.

The principal organs of the United Nations were the Security Council, the General Assembly, the Economic and Social Council, the International Court of Justice, and the Secretariat. The most powerful and important of these was the Security Council, which was given the responsibility to keep the peace. It was empowered to determine whether an action such as armed aggression by a member nation constituted a breach of the United Nations Charter and to recommend corrective measures or sanctions, including the use of force under the principle of collective security. The Council was composed of five permanent members (the five great powers: the United States, the Soviet Union, Great Britain, China, and France) and six other nations elected for two-year terms. The permanent members were given veto power, which is to say the Council could not act (pass a binding resolution) unless there was unanimity among the five. It was in this manner that they intended to protect themselves against actions by the world body against their individual interests. It must be noted that both the United States and the Soviet Union insisted on this veto power, and without it they would not have joined the United Nations. And it should also be noted that it was this same provision that soon rendered the United Nations Security Council ineffective, because in the ensuing Cold War unanimity among the major powers was all but impossible to attain. In the early years of the United Nations, the Soviet Union, which often stood alone against the other four major powers, resorted again and again to the veto.

The UN General Assembly was composed of all of the member nations, each of which had an equal voice and a single vote. It acted as an open forum in which international problems and proposed solutions were discussed. The Assembly passed resolutions by majority vote, but these were treated merely as recommendations and were not binding on the member nations. This body was important mainly for giving the smaller nations a greater voice in world affairs. The UN Secretariat was the permanent administrative office concerned primarily with the internal operations of the organization. It was headed by a secretary general, who was the highest and most visible officer of the United Nations.[12] Although actual authority was limited, the secretary general was able to exert considerable diplomatic influence owing to the prestige of the office. The other bodies of the United Nations, especially the specialized agencies under the Economic and Social Council (e.g. the World Health Organization), functioned more effectively than the Security Council precisely because they were more operational than political in nature, and the problems they addressed could be separated from Cold War polemics. This also was essentially true for such UN bodies as the International Court of Justice, UNESCO (United Nations Educational, Scientific, and Cultural Organization), and UNRRA (United Nations Relief and Rehabilitation Administration).

The founding of the United Nations was an expression of hope by the survivors of catastrophic World War II, and it was greeted by them as the fulfillment of dreams for an organization that would ensure international peace and order. The political leaders who actually took part in its creation also had high hopes for it. It was not long, however, before the United Nations proved unable to fulfill those dreams and even became an object of derision for many. The United Nations did on several occasions intervene to settle or moderate international disputes in such places as Iran, India, Malaya, and the Middle East, when and where the interests of both the United States and the Soviet Union were either minimal or not in conflict. However, the veto power that both superpowers had insisted on and the Cold War contention between them rendered the Security Council all but powerless to keep the peace in the postwar era.

■ RECOMMENDED READINGS

☐ World War II

Calvocoressi, Peter, and Guy Wint. *Total War: Causes and Courses of the Second World War.* New York: Pantheon Books, 1972.
  A comprehensive account of the war both in Europe and Asia.
Dower, John W. *War Without Mercy: Race and Power in the Pacific War.* New York: Pantheon, 1986.
  A frank analysis of the racial nature of the war.
Hart, B. H. Liddell. *History of the Second World War.* New York: Putnam, 1971.
  One of the most highly regarded single-volume studies of World War II.
Saburo, Ienaga. *The Pacific War: World War Two and the Japanese, 1931–1945.* New York: Pantheon Books, 1978.
  A strong indictment of Japanese militarism.
Toland, John. *The Rising Sun.* New York: Random House, 1971.
  The best book on Japan's war.
Werth, Alexander. *Russia at War, 1941-1945.* New York: Dutton, 1964.
  Excellent on the Soviet Union's wartime experience, by a British war correspondent, a native of Leningrad.
Wright, Gordon. *The Ordeal of Total War.* New York: Harper & Row, 1968.
  A classic study of the war.

☐ The Atomic Bomb

Alperovitz, Gar. *Atomic Diplomacy: Hiroshima and Potsdam.* New York: Simon and Schuster, 1965.
  The foremost revisionist interpretation of the atomic bomb decision.
Bernstein, Barton J., ed. *The Atomic Bomb: The Critical Issues.* Boston: Little, Brown, 1976.
  An excellent anthology, which provides excerpts from the writings of some of those involved in the atomic bomb project and by various other writers.
Committee for the Compilation of Materials on Damage Caused by the Atomic Bombs in Hiroshima and Nagasaki. *Hiroshima and Nagasaki: The Physical, Medical and Social Effects of the Atomic Bombs.* New York: Basic Books, 1981.
  The definitive study on these subjects.

Feis, Herbert. *The Atomic Bomb and the End of World War II*. Princeton: Princeton University Press, 1966; originally published as *Japan Subdued*, 1961.
> A standard work that focuses on both the military and diplomatic aspects of the atomic bomb decision.

Herken, Gregg F. *The Winning Weapon: The Atomic Bomb in the Cold War, 1945–1950*. New York: Knopf, 1981.
> One of the best works on atomic diplomacy and the role of the atomic bomb in immediate postwar diplomacy.

Hersey, John. *Hiroshima*. New York: Bantam Books, 1959.
> A classic on the death and destruction caused by the first atomic bomb attack.

Sherwin, Martin J. *A World Destroyed: The Atomic Bomb and the Grand Alliance*. New York: Knopf, 1975.
> Among the best studies of the politics and diplomacy involved in the decision to drop the atomic bomb on Japan.

■ NOTES

1. The magnitude of the slaughter was such that no exact figures are possible. For a breakdown of the figures, particularly in Asia, see John W. Dower, *War Without Mercy: Race and Power in the Pacific War* (New York: Pantheon, 1986), pp. 295–301.

2. Aerial bombardment actually began before World War II. Its effectiveness was demonstrated by the German bombing of Spanish cities in the Spanish civil war and the Japanese bombing of Chinese cities in Manchuria. In World War II, Britain carried out bombing raids on Berlin before Germany began its bombardment of Britain, but the latter represents the first sustained, large-scale bombing attack on the cities of another country.

3. U.S. estimates of the death toll from the atomic bombings are 70,000 in Hiroshima and 40,000 in Nagasaki. The discrepancy in the fatality figures apparently results partly from different methods of calculation and partly from differing intentions of those doing the counting.

4. Dr. Yoshio Nishina, "The Atomic Bomb" Report for the United States Strategic Bombing Servey (Washington, D.C.: National Archives), p. 1, Record Group 243, Box 56.

5. Notes of the Interim Committee," Record Group 77, Manhattan Engineering District Papers, Modern Military Branch, National Archives (Washington, D.C.: National Archives, May 31, 1945), pp. 9–10.

6. Pacific Strategic Intelligence Section, intelligence summary of August 7, 1945, "Russo-Japanese Relations (28 July–6 August 1945)," National Archives, Record Group 457, SRH–088, pp. 3, 7–8, 16. For the Japanese attempts to surrender, beginning on July 13, 1945, see "Magic Diplomatic Extracts, July 1945," MIS, War Department, prepared for the attention of General George C. Marshall; National Archives, Record Group 457, SRH-040, pp. 1–78.

7. One commonly finds the figure of 1 million as the estimate of Allied (mainly U.S.) soldiers who would have been killed in the invasion of Japan if the atomic bomb had not been used, but this figure seems grossly exaggerated. It is more than three times the total number of U.S. military deaths resulting from World War II—both in Europe and in the Pacific in four years of warfare. The 1 million figure was used by Secretary of War Stimson after the war in an article intended to justify the use of the atomic bomb on Japan. In point of fact, at a meeting of top U.S. military officials to discuss the planned invasion of Japan on June 18, 1945, General George C. Marshall, the Chair of the Joint Chiefs of Staff, expressed the view that it was impossible to give an estimate of the casualties in such an invasion, but he said that in the first month they would probably not exceed those suffered in the invasion of Luzon—31,000. See Herbert Feis, *The Atomic Bomb and the End of World War II* (Princeton: Princeton University Press, 1966), pp. 8–9.

8. Harry S. Truman, *Memoirs, I, 1945: Year of Decisions* (New York: Signet, [orig. 1955] 1965), p. 471.

9. "Notes of the Interim Committee," May 31, 1945, pp. 10–12; Gregg Herken, *The Winning Weapon: The Atomic Bomb in the Cold War, 1945–1950* (New York: Random House, 1981), pp. 109–113. Byrnes was apparently less influenced by the views of the scientists than he was by General Groves, who speculated that it would take the Soviet Union from ten to twenty years to produce an atomic bomb.

10. It is estimated that there were about as many Soviet deaths in the Battle of Stalingrad alone as the United States suffered in the entire war (330,000), and it is estimated that over one million died in the seige of Leningrad.

11. Sir Denis Brogan cited in Louis Halle, *The Cold War as History* (New York: Harper & Row, 1967), p. 25.

12. The secretary general was appointed by the General Assembly on the recommendation of the Security Council. In effect, this meant finding a neutral candidate from a neutral country acceptable to the two sides in the Cold War. The first secretary general was Trygve Lie of Norway, who was followed by Dag Hammarskjold of Sweden, U Thant of Burma, Kurt Waldheim of Austra, and Javier Perez de Cuellar of Peru.

□ 2

The Cold War
Institutionalized

At the end of 1944, it became clear that it was only a matter of time until the Allies would defeat Nazi Germany. It also became evident that the reason for the wartime alliance—always a marriage of convenience—was coming to an end. Postwar considerations were beginning to play an ever increasing role in the relations between the Allies. Throughout the war, the Allies had made it clear repeatedly that they fought for specific aims and not merely for the high-sounding principles of liberty and democracy. In 1945, the moment thus came to consider the postwar world, to present one's claims. For these reasons the Allied heads of state—Franklin Roosevelt of the United States, Joseph Stalin of the Soviet Union, and Winston Churchill of Great Britain—met in February 1945 in the Soviet resort of Yalta on the Crimean Peninsula in the Black Sea. It was here that the Big Three attempted to sort out four central issues.

■ THE YALTA CONFERENCE

The main topic at Yalta was the status of postwar Eastern Europe, and mainly that of Poland, which had been—and still was at the time of the conference—an ally in the war against Germany. It had been on behalf of the government of Poland that Great Britain and France had declared war on Germany in 1939. This action by the Western powers had transformed the German-Polish war into a European conflict, which then spilled over into the Atlantic, the Mediterranean, and North Africa, and with the Japanese attack on Pearl Harbor in December 1941, into Asia and the Pacific. In short, the governments of France and Great Britain had taken the momentous decision to go to war—and thus risk the welfare and the independence of their own nations, not to mention their people's lives and fortunes—to prevent the German conquest of a nation in Eastern Europe.

The Big Three. Soviet Marshal Joseph Stalin, U.S. President Franklin D. Roosevelt and British Prime Minister Winston Churchill at the Tehran conference in Nov. 1943. The second of the two wartime meetings of the Big Three was at Yalta in Feb. 1945. (*National Archives*)

President Harry S. Truman and General Dwight Eisenhower, Jan. 1951. Two years later the general would succeed Truman as president. (*National Archives*)

As the war drew to a conclusion and the Germans were expelled from Poland, the fate of that nation became the overriding political concern of the Allies. To complicate matters for the West, the government of Poland, virulently anti-Russian and anti-Communist, had fled Warsaw in the wake of the German invasion and had taken up residence in London, waiting to return to power at the end of the war. The Poles in London now insisted that the West had an obligation to facilitate their return to Warsaw as the legitimate government of Poland. The Western leaders, Churchill and Roosevelt, wanted to oblige, but it was the Red Army of the Soviet Union that was in the process of occupying the country. It became increasingly clear that Stalin, not Roosevelt or Churchill, held the trump cards.

The second issue at Yalta was one of prime importance for the U.S. armed forces, which at that time were still engaged in a bitter war with Japan that promised to continue perhaps into 1946. Japanese resistance was as fierce as ever. The sustained bombing of Tokyo and the Battle of Okinawa (where the United States first set foot on Japanese soil) had not yet taken place. For the U.S. Joint Chiefs of Staff, therefore, Yalta was primarily a war conference with the aim of bringing the seasoned Red Army into the Pacific war.

The third question was the formation of the United Nations to replace the old League of Nations, a casualty of World War II. Roosevelt sought an organizational structure for the United Nations acceptable to Churchill and Stalin, as well as to the U.S. people back home. Roosevelt firmly believed that there could be no effective international organization without U.S. and Soviet participation.

Finally, there was the question of what to do with the German state, whose defeat was imminent. The Allies, after all, would soon be in control of a devastated land, whose uncertain future was in their hands.

☐ The Polish Question

The first question, the status of Poland, proved to be the thorniest. It came up in seven of the eight plenary (full, formal) sessions. Roosevelt and Churchill argued that Poland, an ally, must be free to choose its own government. Specifically, they sought the return of the prewar government of Poland, which had gone into exile in London during the war.

But there was a problem. This "London government" consisted of Poles who did not hide their strong anti-Russian and anti-Communist sentiments, the result of age-old struggles between the Russians and Poles. Their animosity toward the socialist government in Moscow was so great that on the eve of the war with Germany they had refused even to consider an alliance with the Soviet Union. Stalin then made his famous deal with Hitler whereby the two agreed to a Non-Aggression Pact,[1] by which Stalin hoped to sit out the war. As part of the bargain, Hitler offered Stalin the eastern portion of Poland, a large piece of territory that the victorious Poles had seized from a devastated Soviet state in 1921. The Polish conquest of what the Soviets considered part of their empire and the Soviets' reconquest of these lands with Hitler's complicity were but two events in the long and bloody relationship between these two peoples. In 1941, Hitler used Poland as a springboard to invade the Soviet Union and at the end of the war the Soviets returned to Poland once more.

Stalin understood only too well the nationalistic and bitterly anti-Russian attitudes of the Poles, particularly that of the prewar government, which had sworn eternal hostility to his government. As the Soviet soldiers moved into Poland they became targets of the Polish resistance, which took time out from fighting the Germans to deal with the invader from the east. Stalin had no difficulty understanding the nationalistic and religious divisions in Eastern Europe. He himself, an ethnic Georgian, was after all a product of the volatile ethnic mix of the old tsarist empire. He knew, as he told his Western allies at Yalta, that the Poles would be "quarrelsome."[2]

Hitler had used Poland as a staging area for the invasion of the Soviet Union, and the subsequent war cost the Soviet Union between 20 and 25 million lives. At Yalta, Stalin was determined to prevent the reestablishment of a hostile Poland along his western border. Stalin had no intentions, therefore, of permitting the London Poles to take power in Warsaw. This was a major concern Stalin repeatedly conveyed to his allies who grudgingly accepted in principle the reality that Eastern Europe in general, and Poland in particular, had already become part and parcel of the Soviet Union's sphere of influence. To this end, even before Yalta, Stalin had created his own Polish government, with its seat in the eastern Polish city of Lublin, which consisted primarily of Communists and socialists.

Roosevelt and Churchill faced a dilemma. World War II had been fought for the noble ideals of democracy and self-determination. But in postwar Poland there would be neither. Britain, moreover, still had a treaty obligation with the London Poles.[3] Yet, Stalin held the trump card; the Red Army controlled Poland. At the end of the talks at Yalta, Stalin offered a "concession" to his Western allies. He agreed to permit "democratic" elections in Poland after the war. This promise made it possible for Roosevelt to claim, however lamely, that he had been able to obtain something for the Poles and the cause of democracy in Eastern Europe. But Stalin's definition of a democratic election was so narrow that the promise became meaningless. When elections took place the slate of candidates was restricted to safe politicians who posed little threat to the Soviet presence in Poland.

At Yalta, Stalin apparently was under the impression that the Western powers had essentially yielded to the Soviet Union's presence in Poland and that their complaints were largely cosmetic and for domestic consumption. He thus considered the question resolved. But in Britain, and in particular the United States, the Soviet Union's control of Poland never sat easily. After all, Stalin had violated the letter of his promise of free elections, his control of Poland was in direct conflict with the Western war aims, such as freedom and democracy, and the Red Army in Poland had pushed Stalin's political and military influence toward the center of Europe.

From these events came the following arguments, which Roosevelt's Republican critics often made: (1) Roosevelt had yielded Poland (as well as the rest of Eastern Europe) to Stalin; and (2) Stalin had broken his promise at Yalta to hold free elections, and this act of infidelity precipitated the Cold War. The Democrats, stung by these charges, replied that Roosevelt had not ceded Eastern Europe to the Soviets. Geography and the fortunes of war, they contended, had been responsible for putting the Red Army into Eastern Europe, not appeasement on the part of Roosevelt or of his successor, Harry Truman, who became president upon Roosevelt's death on April 12, 1945.

The Ghost of Munich   At this juncture the two major allies in World War II became locked into positions that were the result of their peculiar readings of the lessons of history—particularly, the "lessons of Munich." This refers to the event that many politicians and historians have considered the single most important step leading to World War II.

In the autumn of 1938, Adolf Hitler insisted that a part of western Czechoslovakia—the Sudetenland with a population of 3 million ethnic Germans—must be transferred to Germany on the basis of the principle of national self-determination, a principle ostensibly dear to the victors who, after World War I, had created the sovereign state of Czechoslovakia. Germans must live in Germany, Hitler threatened, otherwise there will be war. France had a treaty of alliance with Czechoslovakia that committed France to war in case Germany attacked that country. But the French government was psychologically and militarily incapable of honoring its treaty and sought a way out to resolve the crisis Hitler's threats had created. At this point England's Prime Minister, Neville Chamberlain, stepped in. The result was the Munich Conference, by which the Western powers avoided war, if only for the time being, and Hitler obtained the Sudetenland. Hitler promised that this was his last demand in Eastern Europe. Chamberlain returned to London proclaiming that he had "brought peace in our time."

Events quickly showed that Hitler had lied. In March 1939, he annexed the rest of Czechoslovakia and then pressured the Poles to yield on territorial concessions. When the Poles refused to budge, the British, and later the French, determined that the time had come to take a stand and offered the Poles a treaty of alliance. Hitler then invaded Poland, and a European war was in the making.

The lessons for the West were clear. A dictator can never be satisfied. Appeasement only whets his appetite. In the words of the American Secretary of the Navy, James Forrestal, there were "no returns on appeasement."[4] When Stalin demanded his own sphere of influence in Eastern Europe, the West quickly brought up the lessons of Munich and concluded that Western acceptance of the Soviet Union's position would inevitably bring further Soviet expansion and war. Western leaders, therefore, proved to be psychologically incapable of accepting the Soviet Union's presence in Eastern Europe: there could be no business-as-usual division of the spoils of victory.

The Soviets had their own reading of these same events. To them, Munich meant the first decisive move by the capitalist West against the Soviet Union. The leaders in the Kremlin always believed that they, and not the West or Poland, were Hitler's main target. Throughout the latter half of the 1930s, the Soviet Union had repeatedly pleaded for an alliance with the West against Germany, but the pleas had always fallen on suspicious ears. Instead, the West's deal with Hitler at Munich appeared to have deflected Hitler toward the East. In rapid order Hitler then swallowed up Czechoslovakia and a host of other East European nations, confirming the Soviet leaders' deep suspicions. By June of 1941, when Hitler launched his invasion of the Soviet Union, he was in control of all of Eastern Europe—not to mention most of the rest of Europe as well—and proceeded to turn it against the Soviet Union.

For the Soviets the lessons of Munich were obvious. Eastern Europe must not fall into the hands of hostile forces. Stalin would not tolerate the return to power of the hostile Poles in London, nor of the old regimes in Hungary, Romania, and Bulgaria, which had cooperated with the Nazis. No foreign power would have the opportunity to do again what Hitler had done and turn Eastern Europe against the Soviet Union. The old order of hostile states aligned with the Soviet Union's enemies must give way to a new reality that served Moscow's interests.

From the same events the two antagonists in the Cold War thus drew diametrically opposed conclusions. The Western position held that its containment of the Soviet Union and its unwillingness to legitimize the Kremlin's position in Eastern Europe kept the peace. A lack of resolve would surely have brought war. The Soviets in their turn were just as adamant in insisting that the buffer they had created in Eastern Europe kept the capitalist West at bay and preserved the security of the nation. These opposing visions of the lessons of history are at the core of the conflict between the West and the Soviet Union.

Polish Borders   At Yalta, Stalin also insisted on moving Poland's borders. He demanded a return to the Soviet Union of what it had lost to the Poles in the Treaty of Riga in 1921 (after the Poles had defeated the Red Army). At that time Lord Curzon, the British foreign secretary, had urged the stubborn Poles to accept an eastern border 125 miles to the west since that line separated more equitably the Poles from the Belorussian and Ukrainian populations of the Soviet empire. But in 1921, the victorious Poles rejected the Curzon Line and, instead, imposed their own line upon the defeated Soviets. In 1945, it became Stalin's turn to redraw the border.

To compensate the Poles for land lost to the Soviet Union, Stalin moved Poland's western border about 75 miles farther west into what had been Germany, along the Oder and Western Neisse rivers. At Yalta, Stalin sought his Allies' stamp of approval for the Oder-Neisse Line but without success.

A third readjustment of Poland's border called for the division between the Soviets and the Poles of East Prussia, Germany's easternmost province. Stalin intended that East Prussia become part of the spoils of war. His reasoning was simple. The Soviet Union and Poland had suffered grief at the hands of the Germans and the peoples of both nations felt that they deserved compensation. The West reluctantly acceded to Stalin's demands.

Since 1945, the Soviets and Poles have considered the border changes at the expense of Germany as a *fait accompli*. Germans, however, have been reluctant to accept these consequences of the war. When, after World War II, the Western powers and the Soviet Union failed to reach an agreement on the political fate of Germany, the result was the division of that nation into the U.S.-sponsored Federal Republic of Germany (commonly known as West Germany) and the Soviet creation, the Democratic Republic of Germany (or East Germany). The East German government had little choice but to accept the new German-Polish border. The West German government has always insisted that it was the sole legitimate German government and that it spoke for all Germans, East and West. The original West German government of Chancellor Konrad Adenauer—the champion of German territorial integrity—bitterly opposed Soviet expansion westward and refused to accept the consequences of the war. In the late 1960s, the West German government, under the leadership of Willy Brandt, began to acknowledge that new borders exist in fact; but more than forty years after the conclusion of the war, no West German government has formally accepted the legality of the transfer of German territory. It remains one of the unresolved consequences of the war.

☐ The Japanese Issue

The second issue at Yalta was more straightforward. The U.S. Joint Chiefs of Staff wanted the Soviet Red Army to enter the war against Japan. The Soviets, as it turned out, needed little prodding. Stalin promised to enter the Japanese war ninety days after the end of the war in Europe. The Japanese had handed Russia a humiliating defeat in the Russo-Japanese War of 1904–1905. In the wake of the Bolshevik Revolution of 1917 and the civil war that followed, the Japanese had invaded eastern Siberia and remained there

PRE–WORLD WAR II BOUNDARIES

POST–WORLD WAR II BOUNDARIES

TERRITORIAL CHANGES
RESULTING FROM WORLD WAR II

FINLAND

*PORRKALLA,
LEASED TO U.S.S.R.
1946–1956*

NORWAY

SWEDEN

Leningrad

*ESTONIAN
S.S.R.*

NORTH

SEA

LATVIAN S.S.R.

DENMARK

*OCCUPATION ZONES
IN GERMANY*

*ADMINISTRATION
U.S.S.R*

*LITHUANIAN
S.S.R*

SOVIET

*EAST
PRUSSIA*

U.S.   *U.S.S.R*

NETH.

BR.   Berlin

*ADMINISTRATION
POLAND*

UNION

BELG.

GERMANY

SILESIA

POLAND

*EASTERN
PRE-WAR POLAND*

LUX.

SAAR   *FR.*

CZECHOSLOVAKIA

U.S.

FRANCE

FR.

U.S.S.R.   •Vienna

U.S.

BESSARABIA

*OCCUPATION
ZONES IN
AUSTRIA*

SWITZ.   *FR.*   AUSTRIA

HUNGARY

BR.

ROMANIA

•Trieste

ITALY

ADRIATIC SEA

YUGOSLAVIA

BULGARIA

300 MI.

ALBANIA

(TURK.)

GREECE

TURKEY

*DODECANESE IS.
(GR.)*

BALTIC SEA

CENTRAL AND EASTERN EUROPE:
TERRITORIAL CHANGES AFTER W. W. II

until 1922.[5] In the 1930s, it seemed for a while as if the Soviet Union might become Japan's next target after the Japanese annexation of the northern Chinese province of Manchuria. In fact, in late summer 1939, the Red Army and the Japanese clashed along the border at Khalkin Gol. Only Japan's thrust southward—which ultimately brought it into conflict with the United States—and the Soviet Union's preoccupation with Nazi Germany kept the two from resuming their old rivalry. When the Soviets attacked the Japanese army in Manchuria at the close of World War II, it marked the fourth Russo-Japanese conflict of the twentieth century. From the Soviet point of view, here was a golden opportunity to settle past scores and to regain lost territories.

☐ The UN Question

The third major topic at Yalta dealt with the organization of the United Nations. Roosevelt proposed, and Churchill and Stalin quickly accepted, the power of an absolute veto for the world's great powers of any United Nations action they opposed. In 1919, when President Woodrow Wilson unsuccessfully proposed the U.S. entry into the League of Nations, his opponents argued that in doing so the foreign policy of the United States would be dictated by the League. A U.S. veto would prevent such an eventuality. Naturally, however, the United States could not expect to be the only nation with a veto. Roosevelt proposed that any one of the "Big Five"—the United States, the Soviet Union, Great Britain, France, and China—have the power to veto a UN action. It also meant that the United Nations could not be used against the interests of any of the big powers. The United Nations, therefore, could act only when the Big Five were in concert, and that has proven to be a rare occasion. The weakness of the United Nations is thus built into its charter.

An example of what this sort of arrangement meant in practice may be seen in this exchange between Stalin and Churchill at Yalta (concerning the issue of Hong Kong, a colony Great Britain had taken from China in the 1840s):

Stalin: Suppose China . . . demands Hong Kong to be returned to her?

Churchill: I could say "no." I would have a right to say that the power of [the United Nations] could not be used against us.[6]

☐ The German Question

The fourth question, the immediate fate of Germany, was resolved when the Big Three decided that as a temporary expedient the territory of the Third Reich—including Austria which Hitler had annexed in 1938—was to be divided into zones of occupation among the participants at the conference.

Shortly, the French insisted that as an ally and a major power they, too, were entitled to an occupation zone. Stalin did not object to the inclusion of another Western, capitalist power but he demanded that if France were to obtain a zone it must come from the holdings of the United States and Great Britain. The result was the Four-Power occupation of Germany and Austria, as well as of their respective capitals, Berlin and Vienna.

As the Big Three returned home from Yalta, they were fairly satisfied that they had gotten what they had sought. But, as events would show, Yalta had settled little. Instead, it quickly became the focal point of the Cold War. The issues under discussion at Yalta—Poland and its postwar borders, the United Nations, the Red Army's entrance into the war against Japan, and the German and Austrian questions—became bones of contention between East and West in the months ahead.

■ THE POTSDAM CONFERENCE

By mid-summer 1945, with Berlin in ruins and the defeat of Japan all but a certainty, the Grand Alliance of World War II fell apart with remarkable speed. The first signs of tension had appeared upon the conclusion of the war in Europe when both the Western powers and the Soviet Union sought to carve out spheres of influence in Eastern Europe. Whatever cooperation had existed during the war had turned into mutual suspicion. Still, the two sides were consulting with each other and they were slated to meet again in July 1945, this time for a conference in Germany at Potsdam (not far from Berlin, the bombed-out capital of Hitler's Third Reich).

The Big Three at Potsdam were Joseph Stalin, Harry Truman (who had succeeded Roosevelt in April 1945), and Winston Churchill (who later in the conference would be replaced by Britain's new premier, Clement Attlee). This meeting accomplished little. The Polish question came up at once, particularly the new border drawn at the expense of Germany, but the conference did not manage to resolve this issue. The Western leaders grudgingly recognized the new socialist government in Poland, but they repeatedly voiced their objections to other client governments Stalin had propped up in Eastern Europe, particularly those of Romania and Bulgaria. The Soviets considered the transformation of the political picture in Eastern Europe a closed issue, comparing it to the creation of the new government in Italy under Western supervision, replacing the previous fascist government that had been an ally of Nazi Germany. The sharp exchanges at Potsdam only heightened suspicions and resolved nothing.

Another source of disagreement was the issue of reparations, which the Soviets demanded from Germany. They insisted on $20 billion from a nation that was utterly destroyed and could not pay. This demand would therefore mean the transfer of whatever industrial equipment Germany still possessed to the Soviet Union. Such measures would leave Germany impoverished, weak, and dependent on outside help. Such a scenario presented several disadvantages to the West: a helpless Germany was no physical deterrent against potential Soviet expansion westward; it might succumb to Communism; and it could become neither an exporter of the goods it produced, nor an importer of U.S. goods. Moreover, the United States was already contemplating economic aid to Germany, and thus the Soviet demand meant that U.S. money and equipment would simply pass through Germany to the Soviet Union as reparations.

The Soviets insisted that at the Yalta Conference in February 1945 their allies had promised them the large sum of $20 billion. U.S. representatives replied that this figure was intended to be the basis of discussion depending upon conditions in Germany after the war. The devastation of Germany at the very end of the war, therefore, meant that the Soviets would have to settle for far less.

To Truman the solution was simple. He would exclude the Soviets from the Western zones of occupation, leaving the Soviets to find whatever reparations they could come up with in their Eastern zone. They did so by plundering the eastern part of Germany. The reparations question marked the first instance of the inability of the wartime allies to come to an agreement on how to govern Germany. It established the principle that in each zone of occupation the military commander would have free reign. As such, the occupation powers never came up with a unified policy for Germany. A consequence was the permanent split of Germany. Within three years there was no point in pretending that a single German state existed.

The only thing on which Truman and Stalin seemed to agree at Potsdam was their position on Japan. Neither, it seems, was willing to let the Japanese off the hook. Surrender could only be unconditional. While at Potsdam, Truman was notified that the first atomic bomb had been successfully tested at Alamogordo, New Mexico. Truman knew of Japanese efforts to end the war, but with the atomic bomb he could now end the conflict on his own terms. Stalin, too, did not want a quick Japanese surrender. At Yalta he had pledged to come into the war with Japan ninety days after the war against Germany had ended, and he had every intention of doing so. It would give him the chance to settle old scores with the Japanese and to extend his influence in the Far East. Apparently, there was no way out for the Japanese.

The defeat of Japan, however, brought no improvement in East-West relations. Both sides constantly voiced their grievances and suspicions of each other. Each point of disagreement was magnified, each misunderstanding became a weapon; each hostile act was positive proof of the other side's evil intentions. But one could not yet speak of a full-blown Cold War. This came in 1947, when the conflict reached a new plateau. In fact, many historians, in the Soviet Union as well as in the West, see that year as the true beginning of the Cold War. It was then that the United States declared its commitment to contain—by economic as well as military means—all manifestations of Communist expansion wherever it occurred. In the same year a Soviet delegation walked out of an economic conference that concerned itself with the rebuilding of Europe. With this act all East-West cooperation came to an end and the battle lines were clearly drawn.

■ THE TRUMAN DOCTRINE

"The turning point in American foreign policy," in the words of President Truman, came early in 1947 when the United States was faced with the prospect of a Communist victory in a civil war in Greece.[7] The end of World War II had not brought peace to Greece. Instead, it saw the continuation of a bitter conflict between the Right and the Left, one which in early 1947 promised a Communist victory. The British, who for a long time had played a significant role in Greek affairs, had supported the Right, but they were determined to end their involvement in Greece. The British were exhausted; they could not go on. Unceremoniously, they dumped the problem into Truman's lap: If the United States wanted a non-Communist government in Greece it would have to see to it, and it would have to go it alone. Truman, a man seldom plagued by self-doubt, quickly jumped into the breach. But he also understood that the U.S. public would be slow to back such an undertaking. At the end of World War II, the U.S. public had expected that within two years the U.S. military presence in Europe would end. Truman's involvement in Greece promised to extend it and postpone the U.S. disengagement from Europe indefinitely. In fact, it meant an increased, continued U.S. presence in Europe. To achieve his aim, Truman knew he would have to "scare the hell out of the American people."[8] And he succeeded admirably.

In March 1947, Truman addressed a joint session of Congress to present his case. In his oration, one of the most stirring Cold War speeches ever made by a U.S. political leader, Truman expounded his views: the war in Greece was not a matter between Greeks; rather, it was caused by outside aggression. International Communism was on the march and the orders came from its center, Moscow. It was the duty of the United States "to support free peoples who are resisting attempted subjugation by armed minorities or by outside pressures." The United States must play the role of the champion of democracy and "orderly political processes."[9] Truman argued that there was even more at stake here than the upholding of political and moral principles. A Communist victory in Greece threatened to set off similar events in other countries, like a long chain of dominoes. "If Greece should fall under the control of an armed minority, the effect upon its neighbor, Turkey, would be immediate and serious. Confusion and disorder might well spread throughout the entire Middle East. . . . "[10] This speech, which became known as the Truman Doctrine, firmly set U.S. foreign policy on a path committed to suppressing radicalism and revolution throughout the world.

But there was no clear evidence that the guiding hand of Stalin was behind the Greek revolution. Stalin, it seems, kept his part of the bargain made with Churchill in October 1944, by which the two agreed that after the war Greece would fall into Britain's sphere of influence. Churchill later wrote that Stalin adhered to this understanding.[11] If anything, Stalin wanted the Greek revolt to "fold up . . . as quickly as possible" because he feared precisely what ultimately happened.[12] He told the Yugoslav vice president, Milovan Djilas: "What do you think? That . . . the United States, the most powerful state in the world will permit you to break their line of communications in the Mediterranean Sea? Nonsense, and we have no navy.[13]" But to Truman and most of the U.S. public it was a simple matter: all revolutions in the name of Karl Marx must necessarily come out of Moscow.[14] The Republican Party, not to be left behind in the holy struggle against "godless Communism," quickly backed Truman. Thus, a national consensus was forged, one which remained intact until the divisive years of the Vietnam War.

The first application of the Truman Doctrine worked remarkably well. U.S. military and economic aid rapidly turned the tide in Greece. And it was achieved without sending U.S. troops into combat. There appeared to be no limits to U.S. power. This truly appeared to be, as Henry Luce, the influential publisher of *Time* and *Life* had said earlier, the "American Century."[15] Yet, at about the same time, events in China showed that there were in fact limits on the ability of the United States to affect the course of history, when the position of the U.S.-supported government there began to unravel.

■ THE MARSHALL PLAN

Three months after the pronouncement of the Truman Doctrine, the United States took another step to protect its interests in Europe when the Truman administration unveiled the Marshall Plan, named after General George Marshall, Truman's secretary of state, who first proposed the program. The program was intended to provide funds for the rebuilding of the heavily damaged economies of Europe. The Marshall Plan was in large part a humanitarian gesture for which many Europeans have expressed their gratitude. Because of it, the United States is still able to draw on a residue of good will forty years after the war. The Marshall Plan was also intended as a means to preserve the prosperity the war had brought to U.S. society. At the very end of the war, the United States had taken the lead in establishing an international system of relatively unrestricted trade. But international commerce demanded a strong and prosperous Europe. The United States proved to be extremely successful in shoring up the financial system of the Western, capitalist world. In this sense, the Marshall Plan became a potent political weapon in the containment of Soviet influence.[16] It well complemented the Truman Doctrine. The Marshall Plan, Truman explained, was but "the other half of the same walnut."[17]

The United States was willing to extend Marshall Plan aid to Eastern Europe, including the Soviet Union, but not without a condition. The money would have to be administered by the United States, not by its recipients. Several Eastern European states were receptive to the plan, particularly Czechoslovakia, which was governed by a coalition of Communist and non-Communist parties. The Soviet Union, too, at first appeared to be ready to participate in the rebuilding of Europe under the auspices of the Marshall Plan.[18] Its foreign minister, Viacheslav Molotov, came to Paris with a large entourage of economic experts to discuss the implementation of the plan. But shortly afterward, he left the conference declaring that the Marshall Plan was unacceptable to the Soviet Union since its implementation would entail the presence of U.S. officials on East European and Soviet soil and would, therefore, infringe upon his country's national sovereignty. Molotov did not say publicly that the presence of U.S. representatives in Eastern Europe would reveal the glaring weaknesses of the Soviet Union and its satellites. The Marshall Plan was a gamble Stalin apparently felt he could not afford. Stalin then pressured the governments of Poland and Czechoslovakia to reject the Marshall Plan.

In February 1948, Stalin went beyond merely applying pressure on Czechoslovakia. A Communist coup in that country ended the coalition government and brought Czechoslovakia firmly into the Soviet orbit. This act regenerated in the West the image of an aggressive, brutal, and calculating leadership in Moscow. The Communist coup in Czechoslovakia, only ten years after Hitler had taken the first steps to bring that nation under his heel, did much to underscore in the West the lessons of Munich.[19] The coup had a deep impact on public opinion in the West and it became *prima facie* evidence that one could not do business with the Soviets.

Stalin's rejection of Marshall Plan aid also meant that the East European countries would have to rebuild their war-torn economies with their own limited resources and without U.S. aid and Western technology. In fact, Stalin's economic recovery program for Eastern Europe was exploitative since it favored the Soviet Union. As Churchill had remarked in his speech in Fulton, Missouri in 1946, an "Iron Curtain" had descended across Europe from Stettin on the Baltic Sea to Trieste on the Adriatic Sea.

■ LIMITS OF SOVIET POWER

Yet, immediately after Stalin appeared to have consolidated his position in Eastern Europe, the first crack appeared in what had been a monolithic facade. The Yugoslav Communist leadership, under the direction of Joseph Tito, broke with the Kremlin over the fundamental question of national sovereignty. Moscow insisted that the interests of a foreign Communist party must be subordinate to those of the Soviet Union, officially the center of an international movement. The Yugoslavs insisted, however, on running their own affairs as they saw fit. In the summer of 1948, the bitter quarrel became public. Tito refused to subordinate the interests of his state to those of Stalin and the result was the first Communist nation in Eastern Europe to assert its independence from the Soviet Union.

Stalin understood only too well that "Titoism" (that is, a nationalist deviation from the international Communist community) was no isolated phenomenon. Other East European nations could readily fall to the same temptation. In order to forestall such an eventuality, Stalin launched a bloody purge of East European "national Communists." The purge was so thorough that until Stalin's death in March 1953, Eastern Europe remained quiet. The prevailing—and, as events later showed, incorrect—view in the West was that Titoism had proven to be an isolated incident.

In 1948, it also became evident that the division of Germany and Berlin would become permanent. All talks on German reunification had broken down and the West began to take steps to create a separate West German state, with Berlin, a city 110 miles inside the Soviet sector, becoming a part of West Germany. When the Soviets had agreed on the division of Berlin among the allies, Stalin had not bargained on such an eventuality. The last thing he wanted was a Western outpost in his zone. Berlin always had little military value for the West since it was trapped and outgunned. But it served as a valuable political, capitalist spearhead pointing into Eastern Europe. Most importantly, Berlin was invaluable as a center of espionage operations. In July 1948, Stalin took a dangerous, calculated risk to eliminate the Western presence in that city. He closed the land routes into Berlin in the hope of convincing the West to abandon Berlin. The West had few options. It wanted neither World War III nor the abandonment of Berlin. The result was the "Berlin Airlift," by which the West resupplied the city for nearly a year until Stalin yielded in May 1949 by reopening the highways linking the city with West Germany. Stalin had lost his gamble and there was no point in perpetuating the showdown. This crisis, which had brought both sides to the edge of war, was over if only for the time being.

Throughout the late 1940s, the U.S. assumption was that the Soviet Union was preparing for an attack on Western Europe, an assumption based largely on fear rather than on fact. The image of an expansionist, aggressive

Soviet Union was the result of three conditions. First, the Red Army had pushed into the center of Europe during the war. Second, in the West, this act was regarded not so much as the logical consequence of the war but as the fulfillment of Soviet propaganda stressing the triumph of socialism throughout the world. Third, the differences of opinion between the Soviet Union and the West quickly took on the character of a military confrontation, and people began to fear the worst.

Once the specter of an inevitably expansionist Soviet state gripped the Western imagination, it became almost impossible to shake this image. This view of Soviet intentions buttressed the U.S. arguments that the Soviet Union must be contained at all cost. The "containment theory," first spelled out in 1947 in a lengthy essay by George Kennan, a State Department expert on the Soviet Union, seemed to be working reasonably well with the application of the Truman Doctrine and the Marshall Plan. But Kennan never made clear the nature of the containment of the Soviet Union he had in mind. Later, he insisted that he had meant the political, and not the military, containment of the Soviet Union. Yet, the central feature of Truman's containment policy was its military nature. In 1949, the United States created NATO, the North Atlantic Treaty Organization, an alliance that boxed in the Soviet Union along its western flank. One person's containment theory is another person's capitalist encirclement. Stalin responded by digging in.

■ RECOMMENDED READINGS

Andrzejewski, Jerzy. *Ashes and Diamonds*. London: Weidenfeld & Nicholson, 1962; orig. 1948.
    The classic novel on life in Poland at the very end of World War II.
Clemens, Diane Shaver. *Yalta*. New York: Oxford University Press, 1970.
    The best monograph on the Yalta Conference, which sees Yalta not as an ideological confrontation but an exercise in horse-trading.
de Zayas, Alfred M. *Nemesis at Potsdam: The Anglo-Americans and the Expulsion of the Germans; Background, Execution, Consequences*. 2d rev. ed. London: Routledge & Kegan Paul, 1979.
    Focuses on the refugee problem after the war, a topic generally ignored in Cold War histories.
Fleming, D. F. *The Cold War and Its Origins, 1917–1960*. 2 vols. Garden City: Doubleday, 1961.
    By one of the first practitioners of the revisionist school of history of the Cold War.
Halle, Louis J. *The Cold War As History*. New York: Harper & Row, 1967.
    One of the few books on the Cold War that puts it into a historical perspective.
Ulam, Adam B. *Expansion and Coexistence: Soviet Foreign Policy 1917–1973*. 2d ed. New York: Frederick A. Praeger, 1974.
    The most useful treatment of Soviet foreign policy.
Ulam, Adam B. *The Rivals: America and Russia Since World War II*. New York: Viking, 1971.
    Discusses the first phase of the East-West confrontation.

■ NOTES

1. Often called the Molotov-Ribbentrop Pact, after the foreign minister of Nazi Germany, Joachim Ribbentrop, and the Soviet Union's commissar for foreign affairs, Viacheslav Molotov, who worked out the details of the arrangement.

2. Winston S. Churchill, *The Second World War, VI, Triumph and Tragedy* (New York: Bantam, [orig. 1953] 1962), p. 329.

3. The treaty with the Polish government in London consisted of an obligation on the part of Britain to defend its ally only against Germany, not the Soviet Union, a point the British government stressed in April 1945 when it released a secret protocol of the 1939 treaty. With this release, Britain's legal obligation to the Polish government came to an end. But there was still the moral duty to defend a former ally against the aspirations of a totalitarian ally of convenience.

4. A cabinet meeting of September 21, 1945 in Walter Millis, ed., *The Forrestal Diaries* (New York: Viking, 1951), p. 96.

5. The U.S. president, Woodrow Wilson, too, sent troops into eastern Siberia at that time, ostensibly to keep an eye on the Japanese. Earlier, at the end of World War I, Wilson also sent troops into European Russia, ostensibly to protect supplies that had been sent to the Russian ally—led at the time by Tsar Nicholas II—to keep them from falling into German hands. The Soviets have always rejected this explanation and have argued that U.S. intentions were to overthrow the fledgling Communist government.

6. James F. Byrnes, *Frankly Speaking* (New York: Harper & Brothers, 1947), p. 37.

7. Harry S. Truman, *Memoirs, II, Years of Trial and Hope* (Garden City: Doubleday, 1956), p. 106.

8. The words are Senator Arthur Vandenberg's, cited in William A. Williams, *The Tragedy of American Diplomacy* rev. ed. (New York: Delta, 1962), pp. 269–270.

9. "Text of President Truman's Speech on New Foreign Policy," *New York Times,* March 13, 1947, p. 2.

10. Ibid.

11. Churchill's report to the House of Commons, February 27, 1945, in which he stated that he "was encouraged by Stalin's behavior about Greece." *The Second World War, VI,* p. 334. In his "iron curtain" telegram to Truman, May 12, 1945, Churchill expressed concern about Soviet influence throughout Eastern Europe, "except Greece"; Lord Moran, *Churchill: Taken From the Diaries of Lord Moran, The Struggle for Survival, 1940–1965* (Boston: Houghton Mifflin, 1966), p. 847. Churchill to the House of Commons, January 23, 1948, on Greece: "Agreements were kept [by Stalin] when they were made." Robert Rhodes James, *Winston S. Churchill: His Complete Speeches, 1897–1963, VII, 1943–1949* (New York: Chelsea House, 1974), p. 7583.

12. Milovan Djilas, *Conversations with Stalin* (New York: Harcourt, Brace & World, 1962), pp. 181–182.

13. Ibid., p. 182.

14. After World War II, the most militant Communist head of state was Joseph Tito of Yugoslavia. It was Tito, rather than Stalin, who openly supported the Greek Communist insurgency by providing them weapons and refuge in Yugoslavia. Tito's actions were seen in the West as evidence of Stalin's involvement via a proxy; yet, even Tito, once he broke with Stalin in 1948, shut his border to the Greek Communists and abandoned them.

15. Henry Luce, "American Century," W. A. Swanberg, *Luce and His Empire* (New York: Dell, 1972), pp. 257–261.

16. The political move to the Left in Western Europe after World War II had in fact largely burned itself out by 1947, at the time the Truman administration proposed the Marshall Plan. The Soviet Union's influence in Western Europe was dependent on the strength of the Com-

munist parties. After initial strong showings, particularly in France and Italy, the Communist parties' fortunes declined. The Marshall Plan then helped to accelerate the swing to the Right.

17. Quoted in Walter LaFeber, *America, Russia, and the Cold War, 1945–1984* , 5th ed. (New York: Knopf, 1985), pp. 62–63.

18. At the end of World War II, after the U.S. wartime Lend-Lease program to the Soviet Union had come to an end, Moscow had applied for economic assistance from the United States, but nothing came of it. Lend-Lease, a massive wartime assistance program to U.S. allies, provided the Soviet Union with $11 billion in aid. Subsequent U.S. aid to the Soviet Union, however, was dependent upon proper Soviet behavior in Eastern Europe.

19. During the coup, Czechoslovakia's foreign minister, Thomas Masaryk, was murdered under mysterious circumstances, an act generally attributed in the West to Stalin.

☐ 3

The Cold War in Asia:
A Change of Venue

The Cold War, which had its origins in Europe where tensions mounted between East and West over the status of Germany, Poland, and other Eastern European countries, became even more inflamed in Asia. In 1945, U.S. policy in East Asia was focused primarily on the elimination of the menace of Japanese militarism and on support of the Nationalist government of China under Jiang Kaishek (Chiang Kai-shek)[1] as the main pillar of stability in Asia. But within five short years the United States was confronted with a set of affairs very different from what its people had envisioned just after the war.

The Nationalist regime in China was defeated by the Chinese Communists who, under the leadership of Chairman Mao Zedong (Mao Tsetung), proclaimed the founding of the People's Republic of China on October 1, 1949. The largest nation on earth was now under Communist rule. Only nine months later the Communist forces of North Korea invaded the U.S.-supported, anti-Communist regime in South Korea, and in the Korean War, for the first time, the rivals of the Cold War, East and West, clashed in the field of battle. These two major events had a profound effect on the military occupation of defeated Japan, which had begun immediately after Japan's surrender. All three of these interrelated events developed in the context of the Cold War and contributed toward making Cold War tensions ever more dangerous in this area of the world. The contention between East and West, evident from the very outset of the military occupation of defeated Japan in 1945, hardened by the early 1950s.

■ THE ALLIED OCCUPATION OF JAPAN

The Allied Occupation of Japan, which lasted almost seven years (from September 1945 to May 1952), is unique in the annals of history, for, as the his-

47

torian Edwin Reischauer says, "Never before had one advanced nation attempted to reform the supposed faults of another advanced nation from within. And never did the military occupation of one world power by another prove so satisfactory to the victors and tolerable to the vanquished."[2] From the outset, the U.S. policy in Japan was benevolent and constructive, although it would also have its punitive aspects as well. The Japanese, who had never in their long history been defeated and garrisoned by foreign troops, expected the worst. Not only did their fears of U.S. brutality prove unfounded, but so also did U.S. fears of continued hostility by Japanese die-hards. The two nations, which had fought each other so bitterly for almost four years, made amends, and in a remarkably short time they established enduring bonds of friendship and cooperation. This was partly the result of the generous treatment by the U.S. occupation forces, and partly the result of the receptivity and good will of the Japanese themselves. They welcomed the opportunity to rid themselves of the scourge of militarism that had led their nation into the blind alley of defeat and destruction. And they appreciated the sight of U.S. GIs brandishing, not rifles, but chocolate bars and chewing gum. Even more important for securing the active support of the Japanese was the decision by U.S. authorities to retain the emperor on the throne rather than try him as a war criminal, as many in the United States had demanded. Indeed, one important reason why the Japanese were so docile and cooperative with the U.S. occupation forces was that their emperor, whom they were in the habit of dutifully obeying, had implored them to be cooperative.

Prior to the defeat of Japan, officials in Washington were already planning a reform program to be implemented under a military occupation. The Allied Occupation of Japan was, as the name implies, supposedly an allied affair, but it was in fact dominated by the United States, despite the desire of the Soviet Union and other nations to play a larger role in it. General Douglas MacArthur was appointed Supreme Commander of Allied Powers (SCAP), and under his authority a broad-ranging reform program was imposed on Japan. The government of Japan was not abolished and replaced by a military administration as was the case in defeated Germany; rather, the Japanese cabinet was maintained as the instrument by which the reform directives of SCAP were administered. Also, unlike the case of Germany, Japan was not divided into separate occupation zones, largely because of the insistence of the United States on denying the Soviet Union its own occupation zone in Japan.

The principal objectives of the U.S.-controlled occupation program were demilitarization and democratization. Demilitarization was attended to first and was attained promptly. Japan's army and navy were abolished, its military personnel brought home from overseas and dismissed, its war

EAST ASIA (1945)

plants dismantled, and its weapons destroyed. Some 3 million Japanese soldiers were repatriated to Japan from all over Asia and the Pacific by U.S. ships, as were almost as many Japanese civilians. Also as a measure to rid Japan of militarism, Japanese wartime leaders were put on trial at an international military tribunal in Tokyo. In court proceedings similar to the Nuremberg trials of Nazi war criminals, certain leading figures were accused of "planning a war of aggression" and "crimes against humanity," found guilty, and given severe sentences. (Seven were sentenced to death and 17 were sentenced to prison for life.) Additionally, several thousand other Japanese military officers were tried and found guilty of a variety of wartime atrocities.

The occupation reformers also sought to rid Japan of its ultranationalist ideology, often referred to as emperor worship. On New Year's Day 1946, the emperor was called upon to make a radio speech to the nation renouncing imperial divinity. Steps were also taken to abolish "State Shinto," the aspect of the religion native to Japan that promoted the belief in the divine descent of Japan's imperial ruler. Textbooks were censored to rid them of such ideas and other content considered militaristic.

Democratization of Japan was a more complex matter and would take longer to achieve, but the first major step in that direction was taken with the writing of a new constitution for Japan in 1947. The new constitution, which was actually drafted by MacArthur's staff, provided for a fundamental political reform. It provided Japan with a parliamentary system similar to that of Britain, and consistent with Japan's own prewar political experience. The people of Japan were made sovereign (meaning, in effect, that government power ultimately rested on the consent of the governed, the people). The emperor, who had been sovereign in the old constitution, became no more than a symbol of the state (which is to say, he would no longer have any political authority). All laws were to be passed by a majority in the popularly elected House of Representatives in the Diet (Japan's parliament). The 1947 constitution also included extensive Bill of Rights provisions spelling out the civil rights of Japanese citizens in great detail. The most striking feature of the new constitution—one in keeping with the demilitarization objective—was Article Nine, which outlawed war and forbade Japan to maintain land, sea, or air forces. MacArthur himself ordered that this provision be put into the constitution, but the idea was enthusiastically endorsed by the political leaders and the common people of war-weary Japan.

As the occupation continued under the watchful eye of MacArthur, a host of other reforms were imposed upon the Japanese. The economic reforms included the dismantling of the old *zaibatsu,* (the huge financial cartels that dominated Japan's prewar economy), a land reform that redistributed farmland for the benefit of poor farmers and at the expense of wealthy landowners, and a labor reform creating Japan's first genuine trade union movement. There were also far-reaching social and educational reforms, all of which were intended to make Japan a more democratic society. Generally, these various reform programs were remarkably successful, largely because they addressed real needs in Japan and because the Japanese themselves desired the reforms. Indeed, the Japanese genuinely rejected past militarism and wholeheartedly embraced the new democracy.

One of the anomalies of the occupation is that democracy was being implanted in Japan by a military command, that is by General MacArthur and his staff. SCAP's mode of operation was military. It censored the Japanese press, disallowing free speech, and it ruled by fiat, its directives to the Japanese government not being arrived at by democratic means. Also anomalous was the character of General MacArthur as a reformer. In Japan he was aloof, arrogant, and almighty. The defeated Japanese seemed to need an august authority figure, and the imperious MacArthur seemed destined to play just such a role. Although he claimed to like the Japanese people, his manner toward them was condescending, and he often expressed contempt for their culture. In his view the Japanese were but twelve-year-old children who must be shown the way from "feudalism" to democracy.[3] But despite MacArthur's arrogance and the military cast of the occupation, he and his staff possessed a genuine reformist zeal, and their sense of mission contributed greatly toward the successful rooting of democratic ideas and institutions in Japan.

The menace of Japanese militarism was thus eliminated and supplanted by democracy, but U.S. minds soon perceived a larger menace looming on the Eastern horizon: the spread of Communism in Asia. The Communist victory in the civil war in China in 1949, and Communist aggression in Korea in the following year, caused the U.S. government to recast its policy in Japan reflecting Cold War exigencies. Safely under U.S. control, Japan was to be prepared to play a key role in the U.S. policy of containment of Communism.

It is difficult to arrive at a final assessment of the occupation of Japan, for opinions differ greatly according to one's ideology and nationality. That the occupation program, with its various reforms, was in every instance a grand success is certainly debatable. Many Japanese historians as well as revisionist historians in the United States argue that the U.S. exercise of power in postwar Japan was excessive, that the "reverse course" policies (discussed later) negated the democratic reforms, and that Japan was victimized by zealous U.S. anti-Communist policies. But there is little question that Japan emerged from the experience with a working democratic system of government and a more democratic society, a passionate pacifism, the beginnings of an economic recovery, and a large measure of military security. And the United States emerged with a new, potentially strong, ally strategically located in a part of the world confronted with the spread of Communist revolution.

■ THE CIVIL WAR IN CHINA

The victory of the Chinese Communists over the Nationalist government of
China in 1949 was the culmination of a long struggle between two revolutionary parties—the Communists and the Nationalists—that began back in
the 1920s. After winning the first round of that struggle and coming to power
in 1928, the Nationalist party, under its domineering leader Jiang Kaishek,
sought to exterminate the rural-based Communist party led by Mao Zedong.
In 1935, the Communists barely escaped annihilation by embarking on the
epic "Long March," a trek of over 6,000 miles, after which they secured themselves in a remote area in northwest China. When the war with Japan began
in mid–1937, Mao persuaded Jiang to set aside their differences and form a
united front for the purpose of defending China from the Japanese invaders.

During the war against Japan (1937–1945), the Chinese Communist
Party (CCP) and its army grew enormously while the Nationalist regime deteriorated badly. The Communists' success was the product of inspired
leadership, effective mobilization of the peasantry for the war effort, and
skillful use of guerrilla warfare tactics against the Japanese. By the end of the
war the Communists controlled nineteen "liberated areas," rural regions
mainly in northern China, with a combined population of about 100 million,
and the size of their army had increased ten-fold from about 50,000 to over
half a million. In contrast, the Nationalist government and army retreated
deep into the interior to Chungking during the war and failed to launch a
successful counteroffensive against the Japanese. Meanwhile, wartime inflation became rampant, as did corruption within Jiang's Nationalist government and army. Growing political oppression was met by growing public
discontent and declining morale. The Nationalist Army, supplied and trained
by the United States, was hardly used against the Japanese, but rather was
deployed to guard against the spread of Communist forces or languished in
garrison duty. Thus, military morale sank as well.

When World War II ended with the U.S. defeat of Japan, civil war within
China was all but a certainty as the two rivals, Nationalists and Communists,
rushed to fill the vacuum created by the defeated Japanese. Both sought to
expand their areas of control, and particularly went after the major cities in
northern China. Jiang Kaishek issued orders sanctioned by the United States
that Japanese commanders were to surrender only to Nationalist military officers rather than turn over areas under their control to the Communists.
Moreover, the United States landed some 53,000 marines to take and hold
several key cities in northern China until the Nationalist forces arrived.

While the United States continued to support Jiang's government as it
had during the war, it wished to avert the impending civil war and thus
urged Jiang Kaishek to find a peaceful solution to his conflict with the Communists. Before World War II had ended Washington had sent a special

envoy, Patrick Hurley, to China to serve as a mediator between the two sides. He was successful only in bringing the rivals Mao and Jiang to the negotiating table in August 1945, but not in finding a solution to their feud. After his efforts ended in failure, President Truman sent General George C. Marshall to China in December to mediate the dispute. Despite Marshall's initial success in getting the two sides to agree—on paper at least—to an immediate cease-fire and to a formula for mutual military demobilization and political cooperation, he too ultimately failed as the conflict escalated into a full-fledged civil war in the spring of 1946. The U.S. efforts to mediate between the CCP and Jiang's regime were destined to failure largely because Jiang refused to share power with the Communists. Essentially, Mao demanded the formation of a coalition government, followed by the mutual reduction and integration of Communist and Nationalist military forces; whereas, Jiang insisted on the reduction of Communist forces and their integration into the Nationalist Army as the precondition for sharing power with the Communists. The U.S. position as mediator was weakened by its lack of neutrality, for continued U.S. military and economic aid to the Nationalists served to alienate the Communists. However, the civil war that the United States had tried so hard to prevent was not initiated by Mao, but rather by Jiang, who was convinced that the only solution to the problem was a military one, and that it was obtainable.

At the outset of the Chinese civil war, the Nationalists had good reason to be confident of victory. Despite Communist gains the Nationalist Army still had a numerical superiority of three to one over the Communist forces. The Nationalist Army was much better equipped, having received huge amounts of U.S. military aid, including artillery pieces, tanks, and trucks, as well as light arms and ammunition. Moreover, the Nationalists benefitted by having the use of U.S. airplanes and troop ships for the movement of their forces. In contrast, the Communist army, reorganized as the People's Liberation Army (PLA), was relatively poorly equipped and had practically no outside support. Given the Nationalist edge, it is not surprising that Jiang's armies were victorious in the early months of the war, defeating the PLA in almost every battle in northern China. But within a year of fighting the tide began to shift.

The battle for China took place mainly in Manchuria, the northeastern area of China, which had been under Japanese control since the early 1930s. It was prized by both sides for its rich resources and as the most industrialized area of China (thanks to the Japanese and to the earlier imperialist presence of Russia). Immediately after World War II, Manchuria was temporarily under the control of the Soviet Union, whose Red Army had attacked the Japanese forces there in the closing days of the war and "liberated" the area. On August 14, 1945, the Soviet Union concluded with the Nationalist government of China a treaty of friendship, which included provisions for the withdrawal of Soviet forces from Manchuria to be completed within three months of the surrender of Japan. Before the Nationalists could occupy the area with their forces, the Soviet Red Army hastily stripped Manchuria of all the Japanese military and industrial equipment it could find and shipped it, together with Japanese prisoners of war, into the Soviet Union, thus depriving the Chinese of a valuable industrial base. Meanwhile, Chinese Communist forces had begun entering Manchuria immediately after the surrender of Japan. A poorly equipped PLA force of about 100,000 troops was rapidly deployed in rural areas surrounding the major cities of Manchuria. Jiang Kaishek was determined to maintain Nationalist military control of Manchuria, and he decided—against the advice of his U.S. military advisers—to position his best armies in that remote area, where they could be supported or reinforced only with great difficulty. Thus, when the battle for Manchuria began, Jiang's Nationalist forces held the major cities, railways, and other strategic points, while the PLA held the surrounding countryside. The Chinese Communists were not assisted by the Soviet Red Army in Manchuria (or elsewhere), but before the Soviets left Manchuria they did provide the PLA with a much-needed cache of captured Japanese weapons (mainly light arms—machine guns, light artillery, rifles, and ammunition).

In the major battles in Manchuria in late 1947 and 1948, the Chinese Communists were big winners. Not only did the Nationalist Army suffer great combat casualties, running into the hundreds of thousands, but it lost almost as many soldiers to the other side either as captives or defectors. Moreover, the PLA captured large amounts of U.S. weapons from the retreating Nationalist Army. The Communist forces, which were better disciplined and had stronger morale, used their mobility to advantage, since they were not merely trying to hold territory as were the Nationalists. In the end, it was they, not the Nationalists, who took the offensive. With their greater maneuverability they were able to control the time and place of battle and to inflict great losses on their less mobile enemy. The Nationalists, on the other hand, had spread their forces too thin to maintain defensive positions and were unable to hold open the transportation lines needed to bring up reinforcements and supplies.

After the last battle in Manchuria in 1948, the momentum in the civil war shifted to the Communists. The last major engagement of the war was fought in the fall of 1948 at Xuzhou (Hsuchow), about a hundred miles north of the Nationalist capital of Nanjing (Nanking). In this decisive battle Jiang deployed 400,000 of his best troops, equipped with tanks and heavy artillery. But after two months of fighting, in which the Nationalists lost 200,000 men, the larger and more mobile Communist army won a decisive victory. From that point it was only a matter of time before the Nationalist collapse. During the spring and summer of 1949, Jiang's forces were rapidly retreating south in disarray, and in October Jiang fled with the remainder of his army to the Chinese island of Taiwan. There the embattled Nationalist leader continued to claim that his Nationalist regime (formally titled the Republic of China) was the only legitimate government of China, and he promised to return to the mainland with his forces to drive off the "Communist bandits." In the meantime, on October 1, 1949, Mao Zedong and his victorious Communist Party proclaimed the founding of the People's Republic of China (PRC) with Beijing (Peking) as its capital.

The Chinese civil war, however, was not entirely over, but instead became a part of the global Cold War. The new Communist government in Beijing insisted it would never rest until its rival on Taiwan was completely defeated; conversely, the Nationalist government was determined never to submit to the Communists. The continued existence of "two Chinas," each intent on destroying the other and each allied to one of the superpowers, would remain the major Cold War issue and source of tension in East Asia for the next three decades.

The outcome of the Chinese civil war was the product of many factors, but direct outside intervention was not one of them. Neither of the superpowers, nor any other nation, became engaged militarily in the conflict once it began in 1946. By that time the United States had pulled its troops out of China. Nor was indirect foreign assistance a major factor in determining the

Mao Zedong (Mao Tse-tung) Chairman of the Chinese Communist Party, Oct. 1, 1950, the first anniversary of the founding of the People's Republic of China. (*National Archives*)

outcome of the conflict. If military aid had been a major factor, the Nationalists surely should have won, for the United States provided them far more assistance, military and otherwise, during and after World War II than the Soviet Union provided the Chinese Communists. The United States had provided Nationalist China with a massive amount of military and economic aid since 1941, amounting to more than $2 billion.[4]

The postwar policy of the Soviet Union toward China was ambivalent, as was its attitude toward the Chinese Communists. It is noteworthy that at the end of World War II Stalin signed a treaty with the Nationalist government of China and publicly recognized Jiang's rulership of China. The Soviet Red Army did little to deter the takeover of Manchuria by Jiang's Nationalist Army, and it withdrew from Manchuria not long after the date to which the two sides had agreed.[5] The Soviet Union's looting of Manchuria for "war booty" was of benefit to neither of the combatants in China and was objectionable to both. Moreover, Stalin made no real effort to support or encourage the Chinese Communists in their bid for power in China, except for turning over the cache of Japanese arms in Manchuria. On the contrary, Stalin is known to have stated in 1948, when the victory of the Chinese Communists was all but certain, that from the outset he had counseled the Chinese Communist leaders not to fight the Nationalists because their prospect for victory seemed remote. Indeed, when we take all this into account and take note of how guarded Moscow was in its dealings with the Chinese Communists after their victory, we can speculate that Stalin might have been happier with a weak Nationalist government in China rather than a new and vigorous Communist government. Jiang's regime could more readily be exploited than could a strong fraternal Communist regime.

More important as a determinant of the civil war's outcome than outside support (or the lack of it) were domestic factors: the popular support of the peasantry for the Communists, the high morale and effective military strategy of the Communist forces, the corruption of the Nationalist regime, the low morale and ineffective strategy of its army, and the inept political and military leadership of Generalissimo Jiang Kaishek. Still another factor was the deteriorating situation on the Nationalist home front, where runaway inflation, corruption, and coercive government measures combined to demoralize the Chinese population. The Communists, by contrast, enjoyed much greater popular support, especially from the peasantry (which made up about 85 percent of the population), because of its successful land redistribution programs. The Nationalists had alienated themselves from the peasantry for lack of a meaningful agrarian reform, having provided neither a program of land redistribution nor protection for tenant farmers against greedy and overbearing landowners.

The turn of events in China had immediate political repercussions in the United States. Shortly before the civil war ended, the United States Senate Foreign Relations Committee heard the testimony of U.S. teachers, business people, journalists, and missionaries who had lived in China for years. They were unanimous in their criticism of Jiang's regime and warned that any additional aid would only fall into the hands of the Communists. The Truman administration understood this, but it nevertheless continued to provide aid. It knew that to cut off aid to its client promised to invite the inevitable political charges that Truman had abandoned a worthy ally, albeit a hopelessly corrupt one, in the struggle against international Communism. The Republicans, of course, who had been sharpening their knives for several years, did not disappoint him. No sooner had the civil war ended in China than they were blaming the Democratic administration of President Truman for "losing China." Republican Senator Joseph McCarthy went so far as to blame the "loss of China" on Communists and Communist sympathizers within the State Department. Although McCarthy's charges proved unfounded, the Democrats were nonetheless saddled with the reputation of having lost China to Communism.

The loss of China to international Communism, as perceived by the U.S. public, and the intensified Cold War mentality it engendered within the United States, served to drive the Truman administration still further to the Right in its foreign policy. Consequently, Truman became ever more vigilant to check the spread of Communism to other parts of Asia, and when, soon afterward, he was faced with Communist aggression in Korea and the prospect of losing Korea, it is little wonder that he responded immediately and forcefully.

■ THE KOREAN WAR

On June 25, 1950, only nine months after the Communist victory in China, the armed forces of Communist North Korea launched a full-scale attack on South Korea. The United States and its major allies responded swiftly and decisively to halt what they perceived to be the forceful expansion of international Communism and a blatant violation of the United Nations Charter. Korea thus became the first real battleground of the Cold War and the first major threat of an all-out war between the East and West. Even though it remained a limited war, it proved to be a bitter and bloody conflict that lasted over three years, produced over 1 million fatalities, and left Korea devastated and hopelessly divided. The Korean War was a product of the Cold War and had profound effects on its continuation.

The roots of the Korean conflict go back to the last days of World War II when the United States and the Soviet Union divided the Korean peninsula at the 38th parallel. The division, which was agreed to by U.S. and Soviet diplomats at Potsdam in July 1945, was meant to be a temporary arrangement for receiving the surrender of Japanese military forces in Korea after the war. The Soviet military occupation of northern Korea after Japan's defeat and the U.S. occupation of the southern half of Korea were to last only until a unified Korean government could be established—an objective agreed to by both parties. However, before any steps were taken to achieve that objective, Soviet-trained Korean Communists, who had been in exile in the Soviet Union during the war, established in the north a Soviet-styled government and speedily carried out an extensive land reform program. Meanwhile, in the south, U.S. occupation authorities attempted to bring order to a chaotic situation. Korean nationalists opposed continued military occupation of their country and agitated for immediate independence. Rival nationalist parties, some of whom were virulently anti-Communist, contended with each other in a political free-for-all. Political disorder, which was exacerbated by economic problems—namely, runaway inflation and the demand for land redistribution—continued in the south, even after an authoritarian and staunchly anti-Communist regime was established in 1948 by the Korean nationalist Syngman Rhee.

Under these circumstances, unification of the north and the south proved impossible. U.S. and Soviet diplomats had agreed in late 1945 to set up a provisional Korean government, which for five years would be under a joint U.S.-Soviet trusteeship, and a joint commission was set up in Seoul to implement this plan. However, the first session of this commission in March 1946 produced a typical Cold War scene with the U.S. and Soviet delegates hurling accusations at one another. The Soviet side accused the U.S. military command in South Korea of fostering the development of an undemocratic anti-Communist regime in the south, and the U.S. side similarly accused the Soviets of implanting an undemocratic Communist regime in the north. The Soviets insisted that no "anti-democratic" (meaning anti-Communist) Korean political party be allowed to participate in the political process, while U.S. representatives insisted on the right of all parties to participate. The Soviets also proposed the immediate withdrawal of both Soviet and U.S. occupation forces from Korea; but the United States, concerned about the Soviet advantage of having a better organized client state in the north, insisted on a supervised free election to be carried out in both the north and the south prior to troop withdrawal.

Failing to solve the impasse in bilateral talks, the United States took the issue of a divided Korea to the United Nations in September 1947. As a result, the UN General Assembly passed a resolution calling for free elections throughout Korea and set up a commission to oversee these elections. In May 1948, the National Assembly elections were held under UN supervision, but in the south only, since the Communist regime in North Korea refused to permit the UN commission into the north. On the basis of his party's victory in the UN-sanctioned election, Syngman Rhee proclaimed the founding

of the Republic of Korea, which purported to be the only legitimate government of all of Korea. Less than a month later, in September 1948, the Communist regime in the north, led by Kim Il Sung, formally proclaimed the
founding of the People's Democratic Republic of Korea, and it too claimed
to be the rightful government of all of Korea. With the peninsula now divided between two rival regimes there seemed little prospect of unification.
Despite this and despite the steadily mounting tensions between the two
opposing regimes, both the Soviet Union and the United States began withdrawing their forces from the peninsula, and by mid–1949 the withdrawal
was completed. (There remained in North Korea a 3,500-troop Soviet military mission and in South Korea a 500-troop U.S. Military Advisory Group.)

Not only were tensions mounting in Korea, but elsewhere in the global
Cold War struggle. By the end of the 1940s, the U.S. policy of containment of
the Soviet Union began to show signs of weakness, especially when, in 1949,
the U.S. public was hit with twin shocks. First, the Soviet Union exploded an
atomic bomb, thus breaking the U.S. monopoly in four short years. Second,
the civil war in China came to an end with a Communist victory and with it
the world's most populous nation had fallen to what the West perceived to
be militant, expansionist Communism. (Predictably, the people of the
United States believed that the Communist triumph in China somehow had
been engineered by Moscow.)

As noted previously, the loss of China to Communism had immediate
political repercussions in the United States. The Republican charge that Truman had lost China to the Communists just as Roosevelt had lost Eastern
Europe to the Soviets served to create a perception of dominoes falling one
after another. The relentless Republican criticism of the Democrats for
being "soft on Communism" caused the Truman administration (and especially Secretary of State Dean Acheson, a favorite target of McCarthy) to
strengthen even more its resolve to stand up to the Communists.

In April 1950, President Truman received and accepted a set of recommendations from his National Security Council, the president's own advisory committee.[6] These recommendations, known as NSC-68, were based
on the premise that there could be no meaningful negotiations with the
Kremlin until it "changed its policies drastically." According to NSC-68, Stalin
understood only force. It recommended, therefore, that the United States
develop the hydrogen bomb to offset the Soviet Union's atomic bomb, and
that it rapidly increase its conventional forces. The cost of such a program
would have to be borne by a large increase in taxes. The U.S. people would
have to be mobilized; the emphasis must be on "consensus," "sacrifice," and
"unity."

NSC-68 urged the creation of regional alliances, similar to NATO, to
create global positions of strength. NSC-68 also expressed the hope of making "the Russian people our allies in this enterprise" of ridding the world of

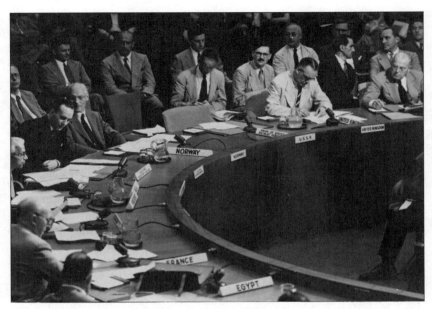

United Nations Security Council Session, New York, June 27, 1950, at which the resolution condemning North Korean aggression was discussed in the absence of the Soviet representative who was then boycotting the UN. (*National Archives*)

"Communist tyranny." This hope, however, was based on the questionable assumptions that people never willingly accept Communism, that it is always forced on them, and that they will always welcome U.S. forces as liberators. This set of assumptions later produced fatal consequences for U.S. foreign policy in Cuba and in Vietnam where the local populations refused to rally to the U.S. cause.

The first test of the mobilization of the U.S. people came two months after the president approved NSC-68, when the Korean War broke out and, as a consequence, the remilitarization of the United States began in earnest. It should be noted, however, that earlier in the year top U.S. military leaders (including the Joint Chiefs of Staff and Generals Dwight Eisenhower and Douglas MacArthur) had concluded that Korea was not of sufficient importance to U.S. national interests to be included within its defensive perimeter. This assessment was based mainly on the higher priority given to defending Europe and Japan and on the insufficiency of U.S. ground forces at the time. Secretary of State Acheson stated publicly in January 1950 (as MacArthur had done earlier) that the U.S. defense perimeter stretched from Alaska through Japan to the Philippines, and that Korea was outside that perimeter. In making this statement Acheson can hardly be blamed for inviting the North

Korean attack on the south as his critics would later charge, because he was merely stating what was already quite clear to the Soviet Union. Moscow was well aware of America's strategic priorities and troop limitations. U.S. military doctrine at the time emphasized preparation for "total war" and focused primarily on resisting the Soviet threat in Europe, not in Asia. Neither Acheson, MacArthur, nor anyone in the Truman administration had anticipated Communist aggression by a relatively small Asian nation, and when the attack came in June 1950, they were all caught completely off guard.

It is not altogether clear, even today, what roles the Soviet Union and Communist China played in the decision of North Korea to attack the south, but neither Soviet nor Chinese troops were involved initially. However, North Korea was a Communist state that received substantial Soviet political, economic, and military support and was considered to be under its influence. The United States and its allies concluded, therefore, that this was another case of Soviet aggression, and they were quick to lay the blame at Joseph Stalin's feet. Whether the decision was made in Moscow or in Pyongyang, the capital of North Korea, the decision makers assumed that the United States lacked either the will or the means to come to South Korea's assistance, and this proved to be a serious miscalculation.

Far from ignoring or standing by idly while its former client was being overrun by a superior Communist force, the U.S. government rapidly swung into action. First, President Truman immediately ordered U.S. naval and air support from bases in nearby Japan to bolster the retreating South Korean army, and, secondly, he immediately took the issue of North Korean aggression to an emergency session of the United Nations Security Council. In the absence of the Soviet delegate, who was boycotting the United Nations in protest against its refusal to seat the People's Republic of China in the world body, the Security Council passed a resolution on June 25 condemning the invasion by North Korea and calling for the withdrawal of its forces from South Korea. Two days later the Security Council passed a second resolution calling for member nations of the United Nations to contribute forces for a UN "police action" to repel the aggression.

By virtue of this resolution, U.S. military involvement in Korea was authorized by the United Nations. But in point of fact, Truman had already, the previous day, ordered U.S. ground troops (in addition to air and naval support) into action in Korea. The Soviet Union made use of this point to argue that U.S. military action in Korea was an act of aggression. Moreover, Moscow contended that the war in Korea was started by South Korea and that the deployment of UN forces in Korea was in violation of the UN Charter because neither the Soviet Union nor the People's Republic of China was present at the Security Council session to cast a vote. The Soviets protested that the UN operation in Korea was actually a mask for U.S. aggression. Clearly, the UN engagement in Korea was largely a U.S. operation. Although some sixteen nations ultimately contributed to the UN forces in Korea, the bulk of its troops, weapons, and material were from the United States; its operations were largely financed by the U.S. government; the UN forces were placed under the command of U.S. Army General Douglas MacArthur; and the military and diplomatic planning for the war was done mainly in Washington.

The swift and resolute U.S. response to halt Communist aggression in Korea belies the Acheson statement of January 1950. It instead reflects the thinking of NSC-68. The Truman administration, which had been ready to write off Korea earlier in the year, decided that the United States must meet the Communist challenge to the containment policy. On second look, it determined that South Korea's defense was vital to the defense of U.S. interests in Asia, especially since the prospect of a Soviet-controlled Korea would threaten the security of Japan, which had suddenly become the major U.S. ally in Asia. Moreover, President Truman saw the defense of Korea as important to the maintenance of U.S. credibility and defense commitments elsewhere in the world, and thus to the maintenance of the Western alliance. Indeed, he likened the situation in Korea in June 1950 to the Nazi aggression in the late 1930s and invoked the lesson of Munich: appeasement to an aggressor does not bring peace but only more serious aggression. Korea represented a test of U.S. will. Thus, the United States must not fail to stand up to that test.

The South Korean army, which lacked tanks, artillery, and aircraft, was no match for the heavily armed North Korean forces, and it therefore took a beating in the early weeks of the war. It was barely able to hang on to keep from being driven off the peninsula. The first units of U.S. ground troops to come to its rescue were also undermanned and ill-equipped, but still they succeeded in holding the Pusan perimeter in the southeastern corner of Korea. Then, in September 1950, MacArthur engineered a dramatic reversal of the war with his successful landing of a large U.S./UN force at Inchon several hundred miles behind the Communist lines. Taken by surprise by this daring move, the North Koreans then beat a hasty retreat back up the peninsula. By early October the North Koreans were driven across the 38th parallel; the U.S./UN forces had gained their objective in a spectacular fashion.

At this juncture the U.S. government had a critical decision to make: whether or not to pursue the retreating enemy across the 38th parallel. General MacArthur, riding the wings of victory, was raring to go, and so, of course, was Syngman Rhee, who hoped to eliminate the Communist regime in the north and bring the whole of the country under his government. But the use of military force to achieve the unification of Korea had not been the original purpose of the UN engagement; the June 27th resolution called only for repelling the North Korean invasion. Moreover, U.S./UN military action in North Korea ran the risk of intervention by Communist China and possibly the Soviet Union as well in an expanded conflict. At the United Nations,

THE KOREAN WAR (1950–1953)

the United States rejected proposals by the Soviet Union and by India aimed at achieving an over-all peace in Asia including both an armistice in Korea and the seating of the People's Republic of China in the United Nations. Instead, the United States succeeded in getting a resolution passed in the UN General Assembly that called for nationwide elections in Korea after "all appropriate steps [are] taken to ensure conditions of stability throughout Korea." The United States had opted for a UN General Assembly resolution because the Soviet Union would surely have vetoed any Security Council resolution sanctioning the use of UN forces to unify Korea. (No nation has veto power in the General Assembly.)

Tentatively, Washington then decided first to authorize the entry of the South Korean Army into the north and then to give the go-ahead to MacArthur, on the condition that the UN forces would halt their advance northward if either Chinese or Soviet forces entered the war. Nonetheless, the U.S. war objective was now significantly altered; the goal was no longer limited to repelling an attack but was extended to eliminating the Communist regime in the north and militarily unifying the whole of Korea. Despite the caution manifested in Washington, General MacArthur, sensing the imminent collapse of the North Korean army, pressed on, rapidly advancing his forces toward the Yalu River, the boundary between Korea and China. In doing so he ignored the repeated warnings from Washington and those from Beijing, which threatened intervention by Chinese forces if its territory were threatened. To Beijing, the prospect of a hostile "imperialist" military presence across the border from the most industrialized area of China was intolerable.

MacArthur's aggressive pursuit of the enemy caused Washington and its allies qualms. In mid-October President Truman met with his field commander on Wake Island in the Pacific in order to urge caution against provoking the Chinese or Soviet entry into the war, but at that meeting MacArthur confidently predicted an imminent victory and assured Truman that if the Chinese dared to intervene they could get no more than 50,000 troops across the Yalu and the result would be "the greatest slaughter."[7] Back in Korea, MacArthur launched a major offensive, which, he predicted, would have the U.S. soldiers back home in time for Christmas.

With U.S. forces rapidly advancing toward the Chinese border, the Chinese did exactly as they had warned they would; they sent their armed forces (which they insisted were "volunteers") into battle in Korea. After an initial surprise attack on October 25, the Chinese made a strategic retreat for about a month only to come back in much greater numbers. MacArthur's intelligence reports badly underestimated the number of Chinese troops involved and China's capacity to greatly increase the size of its forces. Suddenly, on November 26, a vast Chinese army of over 300,000 soldiers opened a massive counteroffensive. Overwhelmed by this superior force, Mac-

Arthur's UN forces beat a hasty retreat southward over 250 miles to below the 38th parallel.

The Chinese intervention with a force much larger than MacArthur thought possible made it an entirely new war, and it also provoked a sharp dispute between President Truman and General MacArthur over political and military policy. MacArthur, frustrated by having an imminent victory denied him and by the limitations placed on him by his superiors in Washington, favored widening the war, including using Chinese Nationalist forces from Taiwan, bombing Chinese Communist bases in Manchuria, and blockading the coast of China. The president, his advisers, and his European allies feared that such steps might touch off World War III—a nuclear war with the Soviet Union—or that the overcommitment of U.S. forces in an expanded Korean War would leave Europe defenseless against a possible Soviet attack. MacArthur publicly criticized the policy of limited warfare that he was ordered to follow. In March 1951, he clearly exceeded his authority by issuing a public statement threatening China with destruction if it refused to heed his demand for an immediate disengagement from Korea. It was this unauthorized ultimatum that caused President Truman to dismiss the general from his command. Truman, who later stated that this was the most difficult decision he had ever made, felt it necessary to reassert presidential authority over the military and make it clear to both enemies and allies that the United States spoke with a single voice. Moreover, there was good reason to fear that continued insubordination by MacArthur, in his quest for total victory, might indeed instigate an all-out war between East and West. For his part, MacArthur minimized such prospects and argued that the West was missing an opportunity to eliminate Communism not only from Korea but from China as well.

The dismissal of MacArthur on April 11, 1951, brought no change in the war, however. His replacement, General Matthew Ridgeway, held against a new Chinese offensive in late April, and several weeks later he was able to force the Chinese to begin a retreat. Soon thereafter the war stalemated with the battle line remaining in the general vicinity of the 38th parallel. The war dragged on for two more years without a major new offensive by either side. Still, the toll of casualties mounted as patrol action on the ground continued, as did dogfights in the air between U.S. jet pilots and Chinese and North Korean pilots flying Soviet jet fighters.

The military deadlock of the spring of 1951 brought about the beginning of peace talks. In June of that year, Moscow and Washington agreed to begin negotiations for a cease-fire in Korea, and both Beijing and Pyongyang concurred. Talks began in July and continued on-again-off-again for the next two years at Panmunjom, a town situated along the battle line. Two main questions divided the negotiators: the location of the cease-fire line and the exchange of prisoners. The Communist side insisted on returning to the

38th parallel, but finally agreed to the current battle line, which gave the South Koreans a slight territorial advantage. On the second issue, the Communists insisted on a complete exchange of all prisoners, but the U.S. negotiators called for allowing the prisoners to decide for themselves if they wished to be returned to their homelands. The truce talks remained deadlocked on this issue, which carried great propaganda value for the United States. In point of fact, many North Korean captives—perhaps as many as 40,000—did not wish to be repatriated, and the United States wanted to exploit this matter as much as the Communists wanted to prevent this mass defection, and thereby deny the United States a major propaganda victory.

After the emergence in 1953 of new leadership in Moscow with the death of Stalin and in Washington with the election of Eisenhower, the two sides finally exhibited the flexibility necessary to break the impasse in Korea and to end the costly stalemated war. On June 8, 1953, the negotiators at Panmunjom signed an agreement that made repatriation of prisoners voluntary, but allowed each side the opportunity (under the supervision of a UN commission) to attempt to persuade their defectors to return home. However, a truce settlement was delayed because of a drastic attempt by South Korean president Syngman Rhee to sabotage it. Rhee, who desired to continue the fight to unify the country under his regime, released some 25,000 North Korean prisoners, who allegedly rejected repatriation to the north. The Chinese responded with a new offensive against South Korean units. Finally, after U.S. negotiators offered assurances to pacify and restrain Rhee, the two sides signed a truce on July 23, 1953. The fighting ended with the final battle line as the truce line, which was widened to become a two-and-a-half-mile-wide demilitarized zone (DMZ). The truce, however, did not mean the end of the war; it merely meant a halt in the fighting by exhausted adversaries. Officially, a state of war has continued, and the truce line between North and South Korea has remained the most militarized border anywhere in the world. For over thirty years it has remained a potential flash point in the Cold War.

Even though the Korean War ended at about the same place it began, both its costs and its consequences were enormous. The United States lost over 33,000 men in the conflict; South Korea, an estimated 300,000; North Korea, 52,000; and China, 900,000 (Washington estimates). While its outcome represented something short of victory for either side, both could claim important achievements. The United States succeeded, with the help of its allies, in standing firm against Communist aggression. This brought greater security to Japan and it contributed to the strengthening of NATO as well. The Chinese emerged from the Korean conflict with greatly enhanced prestige, especially insofar as its now battle-hardened army had stood up to technically superior Western armies in a manner that no Chinese army ever had.

For the Koreans, both in the north and in the south, the war was disastrous. In addition to the great death and destruction suffered by the Koreans, the division of their country was made permanent, and there would be no reduction of tensions and bitterness between the Communist regime in the north and the anti-Communists in the south. The war produced millions of refugees, and when the fighting ended several hundred thousand Korean families were left separated. The Cold War thus remained deeply entrenched in Korea.

■ THE UNITED STATES AND THE COLD WAR IN ASIA

The Communist victory in China represented a major setback for U.S. foreign policy. The threat to U.S. power in East Asia was made all the greater when the new Communist government of China promptly cemented its relations with the Soviet Union with a thirty-year military alliance aimed at the United States, and vehemently denounced U.S. "imperialism." The United States was then confronted by what seemed to be a global Communist movement that had suddenly doubled in size and now included the world's most populous nation. The turn of events in China meant that the United States's immediate postwar Asian policy, which had envisioned the emergence of a strong, united, democratic China to serve as the main pillar of stability in Asia, was completely shattered. Now the U.S. government fashioned a new Asian policy that called for the containment of Communism and featured Japan, the United States's former enemy, in the role of its major ally and base of operations.

In 1948, when it became apparent that the Chinese Communists would defeat the Nationalists in the civil war raging in China, the U.S. occupation policy in Japan took a strong turn to the Right. The new policy, often called the "reverse course," called for rebuilding the former enemy, Japan, so that it would play the role of the United States's major ally in Asia, acting as a bulwark against the spread of Communism in that part of the world. Beginning in 1948, Washington, which heretofore had made no effort to assist Japan economically, now began pumping economic aid into Japan and assisting Japan's economic recovery in other ways. The reverse course was evidenced by a relaxation of the restrictions against the *zaibatsu,* a new ban on general labor strikes, and the purge of leftist leaders. And with the outbreak of war in nearby Korea in 1950, the security of Japan became an urgent concern to the United States. In order to maintain domestic security within Japan, General MacArthur authorized the formation of a 75,000-person Japanese National Police Reserve, thus reversing his earlier policy for an unarmed Japan. This step was the beginning of the rearmament of Japan, and it was bitterly disappointing to many Japanese who were sincere in their conversion to pacifism.

In the midst of the intensified Cold War, the United States not only groomed Japan to become its ally, but also took the lead in framing a peace treaty with Japan in 1951 that would secure the new relationship. The treaty, which formally ended the Allied Occupation and restored full sovereignty to Japan, was crafted by the U.S. diplomat John Foster Dulles in consultation with major U.S. allies. The Communist bloc nations, which were not consulted, objected to the final terms of the treaty and they chose not to sign it. Tied to the treaty, which went into effect in May 1952, was a U.S.-Japan Mutual Security Pact, which provided that the United States would guarantee Japan's security. It also allowed U.S. military bases to remain in Japan to provide not only for Japan's security but also for the defense of U.S. interests in Asia, or, more specifically, for the containment of Communism. Moreover, the United States retained control of the Japanese island of Okinawa, on which it had built a huge military installation. The reborn nation of Japan thus became a child of the Cold War, tied militarily and politically as well as economically to the apron strings of the United States.

Within Japan the Cold War was mirrored by political polarization between the Right and the Left. The Right (the conservative political parties, which have governed Japan throughout the postwar period) accepted the Mutual Security Pact and favored the maintenance of strong political and military ties with the United States. It recognized the threat that the war in nearby Korea represented and the advantages provided by the security arrangement with the United States. Moreover, it was fully aware of Japan's economic dependence on the United States and did not wish to jeopardize these vital economic ties. The Left (comprised of the opposition parties, affiliated labor unions, and many—probably most—of Japan's intellectuals and university students) was bitterly opposed to the Security Pact, to U.S. military forces remaining on Japanese soil, and to the rearmament of Japan. It favored instead unarmed neutrality for Japan, rather than its becoming a party to the Cold War. But since the conservative party remained in power, Japan continued to be a close partner of the United States in the international arena, and U.S. military bases have remained.

The Korean War had a great and lasting impact on the global Cold War. Beyond the fact that the two sides fought to a standstill in Korea, the war occasioned a large general military build-up by both East and West, and this meant the militarization of the Cold War. "Defense" budgets of both the United States and the Soviet Union skyrocketed during the Korean War to record peacetime levels, and they were to remain high thereafter. The military budget of the People's Republic of China also grew commensurately, and that nation remained on a war footing in the years that followed.

A less tangible, but no less important, consequence of the Korean War was the great intensification of hostility between the United States and the

People's Republic of China. The possibility for accommodation between them, which still existed before they crossed swords in Korea, vanished. Both continued to accuse each other of aggression, and both increased their vigil against each other. For the PRC, the increased U.S. military presence in Asia meant a rising threat of U.S. "imperialism," and for decades to come this perceived threat remained the central point of Chinese diplomacy and security policy. For the United States, the continuing threat of "Chinese Communist aggression" required a greatly strengthened commitment to the containment of Communist China, and this became the central feature of the U.S. Asian policy for the next twenty-five years. This was reflected in the policy of making Japan the United States's major ally and base of operations in Asia, a decision to guarantee the security of South Korea and maintain U.S. forces there, a commitment to defend the Nationalist Chinese government on the island of Taiwan against an attack from the mainland, and a growing U.S. involvement in Vietnam in support of the French in their efforts to defeat a Communist-led revolutionary movement. The United States thus locked itself into a Cold War position in Asia in its endeavor to stem the spread of Communism, and its Communist adversaries in Asia strengthened their own resolve to resist U.S. intervention and "imperialism." The Cold War . battle lines were thus drawn by the early 1950s, and for the next two decades, the two sides maintained their respective positions in mutual hostility.

■ RECOMMENDED READINGS

□ Japan

Dower, John W. "Occupied Japan and the American Lake, 1945–1950." In *America's Asia,* edited by Edward Friedman and Mark Selden. New York: Pantheon Books, 1971.
　　Condemns the United States for coercing Japan to serve U.S. anti-Communist policies in Asia.
Kawai, Kazuo. *Japan's American Interlude.* Chicago: Chicago University Press, 1960.
　　A critical "inside view" of the occupation is offered by a Japanese-American scholar who edited an English language newspaper in Japan during the period.
Minear, Richard. *Victor's Justice: The Tokyo War Crimes Trials.* Princeton: Princeton University Press, 1971.
　　Argues that the war crimes trials were unjust.
Perry, John C. *Beneath the Eagle's Wings: Americans in Occupied Japan.* New York: Dodd, Mead, 1980.
　　A popular account, which lauds the benevolent role played by the United States in the occupation of Japan.

□ China

Bianco, Lucien. *The Origins of the Chinese Revolution, 1915–1949.* Stanford: Stanford University Press, 1971.
　　A lucid analysis of the Communist revolution in China that stresses the strengths of the Communists and the failures of the Nationalists.

Fairbank, John K. *The United States and China.* 4th ed. Cambridge, Mass.: Harvard University Press, 1979.
    A standard work, which contains an excellent annotated bibliography of modern Chinese history.
Purifoy, Lewis M. *Harry Truman's China Policy: McCarthyism and the Diplomacy of Hysteria, 1947–1951.* New York: New Viewpoints, 1976.
    Strongly critical of the U.S. policy of supporting Jiang Kaishek.
Tsou, Tang. *America's Failure in China, 1941–1950.* Chicago: Chicago University Press, 1963.
    A thorough and critical analysis of the political struggle in China and of the U.S. role in it.
Tuchman, Barbara. *Stilwell and the American Experience in China, 1911–1945.* New York: Macmillan, 1970.
    An award-winning account of the difficulties the United States experienced in dealing with Jiang Kaishek during the war, offering a strong condemnation of Jiang and his government.

☐ Korea

Cumings, Bruce. *The Origins of the Korean War: Liberation and the Emergence of Separate Regimes, 1945–1947.* Princeton: Princeton University Press, 1981.
    Perhaps the best scholarly analysis on the background of the Korean conflict.
Rees, David. *Korea: The Limited War.* Baltimore: Penguin, 1964.
    A military history focusing on the uniqueness of this conflict as the United States's first limited war.
Spanier, John W. *The Truman-MacArthur Controversy and the Korean War.* New York: W. W. Norton, 1965.
    The definitive study of the Truman-MacArthur rift.
Stone, I. F. *The Hidden History of the Korean War.* New York: Monthly Review Press, 1952.
    A controversial account of the war that argues, for example, that the attack by North Korea on South Korea was neither a surprise nor unprovoked.
Whiting, Alan S. *China Crosses the Yalu: The Decision to Enter the Korean War.* New York: Macmillan, 1960.
    An excellent historical analysis of the Chinese entry into the war.

■ NOTES

1. One finds in English language materials on China two quite different spellings of Chinese names depending on when they were published. The pinyin system of romanization of Chinese names and words, the method used in the People's Republic of China, was adopted by American publishers in 1979 in place of the Wade-Giles system that had been standard previously. Prior to 1979, Jiang Kaishek's name was rendered Chiang Kai-shek, and Mao Zedong's name was rendered Mao Tse-tung. In this text the pinyin system is adopted, but in most instances, the old spelling of a Chinese name will also be provided in parentheses. Also note that personal names for Chinese, Japanese, and Koreans are given in the manner native to their countries, i.e., the surname or family name precedes the given name.

2. Edwin O. Reischauer, *Japan: The Story of a Nation* (New York: Knopf, 3rd ed., 1981), p. 221.

3. MacArthur referred to the Japanese as twelve-year-olds in his testimony to the joint committee of the U.S. Senate on the military situation in the Far East in April 1951. Cited in Rinjiro Sodei, "Eulogy to My Dear General," in L. H. Redord, ed., *The Occupation of Japan:*

Impact of Legal Reform (Norfolk, Va.: The MacArthur Memorial, 1977), p. 82.

4. After Jiang Kaishek launched a full-scale civil war in mid–1946, General Marshall made it clear to him that the United States would not underwrite his war. Thereafter, Washington turned down Jiang's urgent requests for additional military aid and provided only a reduced amount of economic aid after the end of 1946.

5. Soviet withdrawal from Manchuria was completed in May 1946, four months later than called for in the initial agreement with Nationalist China, but this was partly because Jiang Kaishek actually requested the Soviets to postpone their withdrawal until the Nationalist forces were prepared to take control.

6. The National Security Council duplicates much of the work of the State Department and since the days of the Kennedy administration (1961–1963) there has been the tendency of presidents to consult the NSC rather than the professionals in the State Department. The discussion in 1950 on the nature of the Soviet threat proved to be one of the first instances where the professionals in the State Department played second fiddle to the National Security Council. The State Department's experts on the Soviet Union, Charles Bohlen and George Kennan, both of whom later served as ambassadors to Moscow, challenged the argument that Stalin had a master plan of conquest. They saw the Soviet threat largely as a potential political problem in Western Europe. But they were overruled by Dean Acheson, who sided with the hard-liners on the National Security Council who argued that the United States must create order throughout the world.

7. Quoted in Richard Rovere and Arthur Schlesinger, Jr., *The General and the President* (New York: Farrar, Straus, 1951), pp. 253–262.

Confrontation and Coexistence

For centuries the nations of Europe have struggled against one another. France and Britain were often enemies in past centuries, and in modern times the strife between France and Germany has been even bloodier. They have fought each other in three major wars within the span of seventy-five years. Twice in the first half of the twentieth century, the nations of Europe divided into warring camps and fought each other furiously with ever more destructive consequences. During and immediately after World War II, leading political representatives of war-ravaged Europe spoke fervently of the necessity of burying the violent past and embarking on a new future of peace, friendship, and unity among Europeans. For these reasons, as well as to counter the Soviet Union's hegemony in Eastern Europe, the United States and its allies began to take steps in the late 1940s to secure the integration of Western Europe.

The onset of the Cold War and the closing of the Iron Curtain by Stalin over Eastern Europe meant that Western designs for European unity would be limited to Western Europe. Indeed, the East-West division of Europe and the perceived threat posed by the Soviet Union to the security of Western European nations served to reinforce the need for greater unity among them. And in its turn, Moscow set out to create its own unified empire in Eastern Europe. The result was a rigid political division of Europe.

■ WEST EUROPEAN ECONOMIC INTEGRATION

The division of Europe into hostile East-West camps and the subsequent development of unity within each was the product of the Cold War, and from the outset the United States, no less than the Soviet Union, was involved in a major way. From the beginning of the postwar era, the focal point in the East-West power struggle in Europe was Germany, which had been divided into four occupation zones. Disagreements over reparations to be extracted from Germany and other issues led to a closing off of the Russian zone in East Germany from the U.S., British, and French zones in West Germany. By early 1947, less than two years after the conclusion of the war, it had become clear to Washington that the chances for a settlement of the German question had vanished in the Cold War climate of acrimony, suspicion, and fear. The time had come to consolidate the U.S. position in Western Europe, a position centered around a North Atlantic community of nations with common economic and political systems and security interests. In essence, it meant an attempt to integrate the parliamentary, capitalist nations of Western Europe, such as Great Britain, France, Italy, Belgium, the Netherlands, Luxembourg, Denmark, and Norway (but excluding the dictatorial states of Spain and Portugal). Shortly, West Germany, by virtue of its location, size, and economic potential, was also to be integrated into this community and it was destined to play a major role in it. Thus, in the late 1940s, West Germany became, like Japan in East Asia, the first line of defense for the United States against Soviet expansion.

The creation of a separate West German state and its economic recovery were matters of high priority in U.S. foreign policy in the late 1940s. The United States (with the concurrence of Britain and France) took the lead in creating a West German parliamentary government, officially known as the Federal Republic of Germany. From the very moment of its formation, the West German government insisted that it spoke for all of Germany, including what at the time was still the Soviet zone of occupation.[1] In rapid order, the United States integrated West Germany into a system of international trade, supplied it with generous amounts of economic aid (through the Marshall Plan), introduced a new currency, and eventually brought West Germany into the U.S.-led military alliance, NATO. Under such circumstances, West German democracy flourished as did the economy of the rebuilt nation. Indeed, West Germany was the first of the world's war-torn industrial nations to attain a complete economic recovery, and by the late 1950s its postwar growth was considered an economic miracle, or *Wirtschaftswunder.*

When the United States and West Germany introduced the new German mark into West Berlin, the Soviets realized that not only had the United States created a new German state, but that this state now had an outpost 110 miles inside the Soviet zone. When, during the war, the Soviets had agreed to the allied occupation of Berlin, they had not bargained for a permanent Western outpost in their zone. This U.S. and West German action triggered a Soviet response. In July 1948, the Soviets attempted to force the West to abandon Berlin by closing the overland routes into West Berlin from West Germany. The allies responded with the Berlin Airlift, an operation involving daily flights of U.S., British, and French transport planes over East Germany delivering food and other goods to the West Berliners. For political, psychological, and practical reasons, the West was in no mood to yield.[2] When Stalin finally relented by lifting the overland blockade in May 1949, it was a tacit recognition that West Berlin would remain part of West Germany.

The notion of creating a fully integrated, supranational union of Europe—a "United States of Europe"—faded as the emotional idealism generated by the war gradually gave way in the postwar period to a more realistic and pragmatic approach toward integration. In May 1948, some 750 political leaders met at The Hague to create the Council of Europe, designed to be a permanent European assembly. However, this organization floundered from the beginning largely because Britain objected to joining a supranational integration of Europe. At Britain's insistence, the Council's Assembly was not given legislative authority, and its only decision-making body, the Council of Ministers, was comprised of the foreign ministers of the member states. As such it was merely the sounding board for each nation's interests. The failure of this attempt at European political integration was signalled by the resignation of its first president, Paul-Henri Spaak, in 1951. When resigning, Spaak, one of the Council's founders and ardent supporters, strongly denounced the nationalism of those who obstructed its efforts to achieve a meaningful integration of Europe. Although the idea of European political integration was revived from time to time thereafter, the only significant progress toward European unity came with the creation of a set of economic and military organizations, which addressed more pragmatic concerns.

Western European economic integration had its beginnings in the Marshall Plan, the U.S. economic aid program announced in June 1947, which was intended primarily to rescue Europe from the economic devastation of the war. However, insofar as the Marshall Plan was rejected by Moscow for all of Eastern Europe, the aid and the integrative impact of the program was limited to Western Europe.

After the initial impulse from the Marshall Plan, the countries of Western Europe took bold steps toward greater economic integration. In May 1950, France proposed the creation of a European Coal and Steel Community, and in April 1951 six nations—France, West Germany, Italy, and the Benelux countries (Belgium, the Netherlands, and Luxembourg)—signed a treaty establishing this joint venture. This program, designed primarily by the French economist Jean Monnet and French Foreign Minister Robert Schuman, called for the pooling of the coal and steel resources of the member nations. It created a High Authority, which on the basis of majority vote was empowered to make decisions regulating production and development of coal and steel in the six countries. In effect it internationalized the highly industrialized Saar and Ruhr regions of West Germany. Not only did this program eliminate a source of national contention and greatly raise production, but it was considered at the time as the platform on which to build both the economic and political integration of Europe.

So well did the integrated coal and steel program work that in 1955 the same six nations decided to form a European Economic Community (EEC), and in March 1957 they signed the Treaty of Rome, which brought this more comprehensive organization into existence on January 1, 1958. In addition to coordinating economic production, the EEC (commonly referred to as the Common Market) established a customs union, which involved the lowering of tariffs among the member states and the erecting of one common tariff rate on imports from outside countries. This easing of trade restrictions greatly increased the flow of trade, which in turn stimulated production, provided jobs, and increased personal income and consumption. Thus, the Common Market contributed significantly to the economic growth and higher standards of living of its member states, and it allowed Europe to reemerge as one of the thriving economic regions of the world. In fact, the economic growth rate of the Common Market countries surpassed that of the United States by the end of the 1940s and remained significantly higher thereafter.

Great Britain did not share in the benefits of the Common Market because it initially chose not to join. Britain already enjoyed the benefits of a preferential tariff system within its own community of nations—the Commonwealth—and it could not reconcile its Commonwealth trade interests with those of its European neighbors in the Common Market. Other reasons for Britain's rejection of the Common Market included its conservative inclination to retain the old order rather than join in the creation of a new one, its reliance on its strong ties with the United States and Commonwealth friends, and its reluctance to give up a measure of its national sovereignty to a supranational body whose decisions were binding on member nations. However, after both its economy and its international status faltered in the 1950s, Britain saw fit in 1961 to apply for membership in the Common Market, only to find that admission now was not for the mere asking. The issue of Britain's entry was hotly debated both within Britain, where the Labour Party opposed it, and in France, where President Charles de Gaulle had his own terms for British admission. After over a year of deliberation, de Gaulle, who had attempted in vain to draw Britain into a European military pact, suddenly announced in January 1963 his firm opposition to British membership in the Common Market. Since voting within the Common Market structure was not by majority but required unanimity—a point de Gaulle insisted upon—the French president's veto unilaterally kept Britain out. When Britain renewed its application to join the Common Market in 1966, de Gaulle—who was critical of Britain's close political and economic ties with the United States and with the Commonwealth nations in other parts of the world—still objected, and it was only after de Gaulle's resignation as president of France in 1969 that Britain gained entry. Although the heads of the six Common Market states declared their approval of Britain's entry in December 1969, negotiations among them and the British government were protracted by technical complications, and it was not until January 1973 that Briain (together with Denmark and Ireland) finally entered the Common Market.[3]

The success of the Common Market revived the hopes of some of its members for achieving political as well as economic integration, and efforts were made to make use of its organizational machinery for that purpose. From its inception there existed a division between the "supranationalists," who desired total integration, and the "federalists," who wished to retain for each nation essential decision-making power. Within the Common Market structure the primary decision-making body was its Council of Ministers, comprised of the foreign ministers of each member state. It voted on proposals brought to it by the Commission, an elected body made up of delegations from each of the member nations according to their size. Since decisions on key issues were binding for all member states, certain members (most notably France and later Britain) insisted on consensus rather than majority voting on such issues. Also, within the EEC structure was the European Parliament, a deliberative body that best represented the supranationalist interests, but this body was given only a consultative role. Because it had no power over decisions made by the executive branch of the EEC, it remained toothless and thus has not been an effective vehicle for political integration.

■ NATO: THE MILITARY INTEGRATION OF WESTERN EUROPE

While the efforts to achieve meaningful political integration did not achieve results commensurate with the progress toward the economic integration of Western Europe, more was accomplished in the realm of military affairs. But here, too, efforts to bring about an integrated military establishment ran up against formidable obstacles. Nonetheless, a significant degree of military coordination, if not unity, was achieved. Once again the main obstacle to military integration was the force of nationalism, especially as personified by France's Charles de Gaulle.

In April 1949, the United States took the lead in the formation of the North Atlantic Treaty Organization (NATO) as a collective security system for Western Europe and North America. It was the military equivalent of the Marshall Plan, designed to extend U.S. protection to its allies in Western Europe. The ten European countries that originally joined NATO (Britain, France, Iceland, Norway, Denmark, Belgium, the Netherlands, Luxembourg, Portugal, and Italy), with the United States and Canada, attained a twenty-year guarantee of their security against attack by the Soviet Union. Ultimately, it brought U.S. air power and nuclear weapons to bear as the primary means to prevent the Soviet Union from using its large land forces against West Germany or any of the member states. Each of the NATO nations was to contribute ground forces to a collective army under a unified command.

The first serious question facing NATO was whether to include West Germany. Its territory was covered by the initial NATO security guarantee, but it was not a treaty member; in fact, it was still under allied military occupation until 1952 and had no armed forces of its own. As early as 1950, after the outbreak of the Korean War, U.S. officials began encouraging the rearmament of Germany and integration of its forces into NATO. But the French and other Europeans, fearing the return of German militarism, were reluctant to see the rearmament of Germany. As an alternative, France proposed in 1952 the creation of the European Defense Community (EDC), a genuinely integrated military force in which German soldiers could serve together with those from other European countries in multinational units placed under a multinational European command center. For four years the EDC was under debate among the NATO members, but ultimately it failed mainly because of Britain's refusal to join it and France's own opposition to an EDC without Britain.

The fear of a reappearance of German militarism was, however, overshadowed by the fear of Soviet aggression. Moreover, German troops were badly needed to beef up the under-strength NATO ground forces. Therefore, at the urging of the United States, Britain, and West Germany itself, the NATO members agreed by the end of 1954 on West Germany's entry into NATO—on the conditions that it supply twelve divisions of ground forces and that it be prohibited from the development of nuclear, bacteriological, and chemical weapons; warships; or long-range missiles and bombers.

The Soviet Union, too, opposed the rearmament of Germany and it made an eleventh-hour attempt to block West Germany's entry into NATO. It proposed the immediate and total evacuation of all occupation forces from Germany—East and West—the reunification of Germany, and the creation of a security pact to defend it as a neutral nation. It is idle to speculate whether such a generous proposal would have received a better reception in Western capitals had it been made earlier, but the plan was rejected out of hand as a Soviet propaganda ploy aimed merely at disrupting the strengthening of the Western military alliance.

In its first decade the weak link in the NATO collective security system was France, which lacked political stability until the emergence of General Charles de Gaulle as president of the newly established Fifth French Republic in 1958. France was unable to supply its share of ground troops to NATO because they were needed first in Indochina and later in Algeria where France was engaged in struggles to retain its colonial empire. The new

French president was intent on cutting France's losses abroad and regaining for France a dominant position in Europe. De Gaulle, France's great World War II hero and always the supreme nationalist, wished to remake Europe in his own way. His vision of a powerful Europe was not one of political integration as suggested by the Common Market, but rather an association of strong nations. He was staunchly opposed to any notion of supranationalism, for his real objective was to elevate the role of France in a reinvigorated Europe. His determined pursuit of French domination of the new Europe was the cardinal point of what came to be called Gaullism.[4]

De Gaulle's boldly assertive nationalism was also reflected in his view of the security needs of France (and Europe). Because he sought the strengthening of the posture of France within Europe and the reassertion of European power in global affairs, de Gaulle wished to put the United States at a greater distance from Europe. He felt that Europe, especially NATO, had been dominated in the postwar period by the United States and, secondarily, by its closest ally, Great Britain. Specifically, de Gaulle questioned the commitment of the United States to the defense of Europe and, therefore, he considered NATO to be flawed. He thought that, while the Untied States might enter a nuclear war in defense of its West European allies if they came under a nuclear attack from the Soviet Union, it could not be counted on to risk its own destruction in nuclear warfare in order to defend Western Europe from an invasion by conventional ground forces. After rejecting a U.S. offer to place nuclear weapons in France, de Gaulle went ahead with the development of France's own *force de frappe* (nuclear arsenal). Not only did he wish to enhance France's international prestige by joining the exclusive club of nuclear powers, but his idea was that, even if France's nuclear force were far smaller than that of the superpowers, it still might serve as a deterrent. In the 1960s, de Gaulle turned a deaf ear to foreign critics who castigated France for its refusal to join other major powers in signing a series of nuclear arms control agreements and for its refusal to halt its atomic bomb testing program in the Pacific Ocean.

Charles de Gaulle persistently challenged U.S. leadership of the Western alliance as he sought to assert France's independence. In 1964, he broke ranks with the United States by extending diplomatic recognition to the People's Republic of China. Later, in 1966, de Gaulle again challenged U.S. dominance of the Western alliance when he decided to withdraw all French troops from NATO (although he did not formally withdraw France from the NATO alliance) and when he called for the withdrawal of all U.S. forces from French soil. French security, the general insisted, must remain in French hands.

De Gaulle disliked the confrontational approach taken by the United States in the Cold War, especially in the Cuban missile crisis (to be discussed later), and he did not want to be left out of diplomatic meetings between the superpowers where decisions might be made affecting the security and interests of France. He sought to counter U.S. Cold War diplomacy and its domination of the Western allies by conducting his own diplomacy with the Soviet Union and Communist China, and by strengthening France's ties with the most powerful continental West European state, West Germany.

The entente (understanding) between France and West Germany was achieved by the political skill of de Gaulle and West Germany's aged chancellor, Konrad Adenauer. After Adenauer accepted an invitation to meet with de Gaulle in Paris in July 1962, de Gaulle made a triumphant tour of West Germany two months later. This exchange of visits was followed by the signing of a Franco-German treaty aimed at strengthening their relations and thereby making it the cornerstone of Western European solidarity. This act served to check the Anglo-U.S. domination of the Western alliance. The entente proved to be short-lived, however, for neither Adenauer nor de Gaulle remained in power much longer. Nor did it result in putting greater distance between West Germany and the United States, as de Gaulle had wished. It did, however, symbolize the marked improvement in the postwar era of the relations between these two major European nations, which had been hostile for so long.

■ EASTERN EUROPEAN INTEGRATION

In Eastern Europe, Moscow had its own program of political and economic integration. What had begun in 1944–1945 as a military occupation by the Red Army shortly became a social, political, and economic revolution with Stalin's Soviet Union serving as the model. In 1949, in response to the Marshall Plan, Stalin's foreign minister Viacheslav Molotov introduced the Council of Mutual Economic Aid, commonly known as COMECON. Its purpose was to integrate the economies of the East European nations of Poland, Hungary, Romania, Czechoslovakia, and Bulgaria (and later Albania) with that of the Soviet Union. It was designed to aid in the postwar reconstruction of the Soviet Union and in the industrial development of Eastern Europe, which was still largely an agricultural region. It also supplemented the Kremlin's political control of Eastern Europe by giving it an economic lever.

The transformation of the East European economies took place along Soviet lines. The emphasis was on heavy and war industries, with consumer goods taking a back seat. Expropriation decrees, issued as early as September 1944 in Poland, led to the confiscation of the estates of nobles and the churches. These measures eliminated the "landlord" classes and paved the way for collectivization of agriculture.

The economic transformation of Eastern Europe was accompanied by sweeping political changes. In Bulgaria, Albania, Yugoslavia, and Romania the monarchies were officially abolished. Moscow's East European satellites followed the Soviet example by adopting constitutions similar to Stalin's Constitution of 1936. Everywhere, parties in opposition to the new political order were declared illegal.

With the Red Army in occupation of much of Eastern Europe, Stalin's hold on the region appeared secure. The Soviet bloc appeared for all intents and purposes to be a monolith, one and indivisible. But as early as 1948, nationalism once again reared its head in Eastern Europe when arch-Communist Joseph Tito of Yugoslavia asserted his independence from Moscow. The split between Tito and Stalin was the result of heavy-handed, clumsy Soviet attempts to intervene in the internal affairs of Yugoslavia. The upshot of the Tito-Stalin split was a series of terrible purges of East European Communists suspected of Titoism or "nationalist deviation." When Stalin completed his cleansing of the East European Communist parties, he left them in the hands of functionaries loyal to Moscow who, upon Stalin's death in March 1953, were immediately challenged by the remaining "nationalists."

The dominant force in Eastern Europe since the end of World War II has been the Soviet Army, augmented by the forces of the new socialist regimes. In 1955, the Soviet Union, ostensibly in response to the inclusion of West Germany into NATO, created its own military alliance, the Warsaw Treaty Organization, commonly known as the Warsaw Pact. Its membership included Albania, Bulgaria, Czechoslovakia, East Germany, Hungary, Poland, Romania, and the Soviet Union. Unlike NATO, its members did not have the right to withdraw from the organization, an act the Kremlin considered the supreme political sin its satellites could commit. Albania, by virtue of its geographic position and relative lack of importance, did manage to leave the Warsaw Pact in 1968, but Hungary's flirtation with neutrality in 1956 met with an attack by the Red Army. When Czechoslovakia in 1968 and Poland in the early 1980s moved dangerously close to a position similar to that of Hungary in 1956, the Soviet leadership made it clear that it would not tolerate the disintegration of its military alliance. The Soviet empire, although plagued by recurrent cracks, must retain its socialist solidarity.

The most interesting manifestation of the force of nationalism in Eastern Europe is that of Romania, which since the mid–1960s has sought to carve out a measure of independence from Moscow. Under the leadership of Nicolai Ceausescu, the Romanian Communist Party has successfully maneuvered to secure a limited economic and political independence, particularly in its dealings with Western Europe. Over the years, Ceausescu has rejected his nation's role in agricultural and petrochemical production as allocated by COMECON, retained diplomatic ties with Israel after all other East European nations broke relations with Israel in the wake of the 1967 "Six Day" war (see Chapter 7), refused to participate in Warsaw Pact maneuvers, maintained correct relations with the People's Republic of China at a time of ever-increasing hostility between Moscow and Beijing, given warm receptions to visiting U.S. presidents, and sent his athletes to the 1984 Olympic Games in Los Angeles in defiance of the Soviet boycott of the games. Throughout, the Kremlin has cast a weary eye on the Romanian maverick but has refrained from taking drastic action. After all, there has been no pressing need to discipline Ceausescu since he remains a loyal member of the Soviet Union's military alliance and, perhaps even more importantly, has shown absolutely no tendency toward any sort of reform. Moscow has always considered political reform in Prague and Warsaw as a greater threat to its hegemony in Eastern Europe than Ceausescu's actions, which, although an irritant, do not pose a major problem. As long as Ceausescu retains the most harshly repressive political system in Eastern Europe, the Kremlin has been willing to tolerate his unorthodox behavior in foreign policy matters.

Despite the Kremlin's insistence on maintaining its hegemony over Eastern Europe, the forces of nationalism have repeatedly made it clear that Eastern Europe contains restless populations with whom the Kremlin's control does not sit easily. In the face of repeated Soviet pronouncements that consider Eastern Europe a closed issue (notably General Secretary Leonid Brezhnev's statement in 1968 that the Soviet Union's defensive borders were at the Elbe River separating East and West Germany), the region remains a potentially volatile problem.

■ THE FIRST ATTEMPTS AT DÉTENTE

The Korean War, one of the most dangerous moments in the Cold War, brought about the remilitarization of both the United States and the Soviet Union. Immediately upon the conclusion of World War II, the two nations had reduced their armed forces despite the shrill accusations in Washington and Moscow focusing on the evil intentions of the other. U.S. intelligence records show that a Soviet attack was not in the cards—unless an uncontrolled chain of events led to miscalculations on the part of the leaders in the Kremlin. By early 1947, U.S. forces had dwindled from a wartime strength of 12 million to fewer than 1 million soldiers under arms. Because of this reduction, Western Europe was exposed to a possible assault by the Soviet Army. If that occurred, U.S. troops in Western Europe were under orders not to fight but to find the quickest way across the English channel.

But the Soviets showed no inclination to initiate World War III on the heels of the just-concluded, bloody conflict. The Soviet Army had been reduced to its prewar level of about 3.5 million soldiers, much of the Soviet Union was in ruins and in need of rehabilitation, and there was always the U.S. trump card, the atomic bomb. If the leaders in Washington did not consider it likely that Stalin would direct his armed forces across the Iron Curtain, similarly, those in the Kremlin did not contemplate a U.S. attack. For the next five years the protagonists maintained their forces at a level just sufficient to repel a potential attack. But by 1950 the arguments were in place to transform the political Cold War into a military confrontation. The Korean War proved to be the catalyst for this transformation.

In the United States in April 1950, nine weeks prior to the outbreak of the war in Korea, National Security Council directive NSC-68 recommended to President Truman a drastic increase in the military budget. The prospects of attaining this were slim, for popular sentiment was against it. Yet, the opportunity to implement NSC-68 came in June 1950 when, according to Secretary of State Dean Acheson, "Korea came along and saved us."[5]

In the Soviet Union a similar process was taking place. Stalin long ago had demanded unity and sacrifice from his people. In the late 1940s, he renewed his insistence that the socialist, Soviet fatherland must be defended at all cost. There could be no deviation from this principle. A renewed emphasis on ideological rigidity and conformity became the order of the day, and with it purges of individuals suspected of ideological nonconformity. When the war in Korea broke out, Stalin rapidly increased the size of the Red Army from 3.5 million to about 5 million troops, the approximate level the Soviet armed forces have retained ever since. The five-year period during which both sides had reduced their armed forces and curtailed their military expenditures was at an end. Both sides had begun to think that, if diplomacy and compromise could not resolve the issues of the day, perhaps elemental force could.

Truman's retirement from political life took place in January 1953, and Stalin's death came six weeks later. The exit of the two chief combatants in the Cold War made it possible for the new leaders to try a different tack, for they were not locked into the old positions to the same degree their predecessors had been. (In late 1952, there had been a brief flurry of speculation that Stalin and Truman might meet for the first time since 1945. Nothing came of it for apparently they had nothing to talk about.)

President Dwight Eisenhower and the new Soviet premier Nikita Khrushchev, who had emerged as one of the Soviet Union's leading figures by September 1953, began a dialogue that resulted in the lessening of tensions. It was in this context that the word *détente* (relaxing the strain) first entered the vocabulary of the Cold War.[6] Eisenhower, the hero of World War II, had no need to establish his anti-Communist credentials. He had, therefore, greater latitude in dealing with the Soviets than did Harry Truman or his secretary of state, Dean Acheson, whom the Republicans (notably Joseph McCarthy and Richard Nixon) had berated time and again for being "soft on Communism." There was nothing they could do to shake off the Republican charges and, in fact, McCarthy had gone far beyond charging Truman with a lack of vigilance. He went so far as to allege that Truman's State Department was filled with Communist subversives.

Khrushchev and his colleagues began to move away from the Stalinist pattern of conduct at home and abroad shortly after they buried Stalin. Khrushchev was determined to avoid a military showdown with the West and declared, by dusting off an old Leninist phrase, that peaceful coexistence with the West was possible. With it he rejected the thesis of the inevitability of war between the socialist and capitalist camps.

At Geneva in 1954, the great powers convened to deal with the central problems of the day. The more relaxed climate, the "Spirit of Geneva," made possible the disengagement of the occupying powers from Austria. It proved to be the first and only political settlement of any significance by the belligerents of the Cold War.[7] In May 1955, Austria, under four-power occupation since the end of the war, gained its independence as a neutral state. Austria became a nonaligned buffer in the heart of Europe, separating the armies of the two superpowers. The Iron Curtain shifted eastward, to the borders of Czechoslovakia and Hungary, which also brought about the disengagement of Western and Soviet troops along a line of about 200 miles. In return, Austria pledged its neutrality in the Cold War, a condition that suited the Austrian temperament perfectly. Austria quickly became a meeting ground between East and West. Its capital city, Vienna, became a neutral site for great-power meetings—and it now has one of the largest concentrations of foreign spies of any city in the world.

A solution similar to the Austrian settlement had earlier been envisioned for Germany. But in contrast to Austria, by 1955 two Germanies already existed. Austria's good fate was that at the end of the war it was treated not as a conquered, but a liberated nation. Also, it had a relatively small population of just over 7 million and was insignificant as an economic and military power. Yet, the latter may be said of Korea and Vietnam, while no political solution was ever found for these nations. One of the main reasons why a solution for Austria ultimately proved to be feasible was Stalin's unilateral action in April 1945. He appointed the moderate socialist Karl Renner as the new head of Austria and in this fashion Austria, unlike Germany, Korea, and Vietnam, was under one government, which all of the occupying powers eventually recognized. Churchill and Truman were unhappy with Stalin's action, not because they objected to Renner, but because it was unilateral, high-handed, and accomplished without their consultation. Nevertheless, they grudgingly accepted Stalin's choice. Renner then proceeded to guide his nation carefully on a middle course between the superpowers. When the time came to disengage in 1955, Austria already had a neutral government ten years in existence. The German experience had been quite different. At the end of the war the allies had spoken of creating a German government that all sides could accept but it never happened.

The partial rapprochement between the United States and the Soviet Union made possible Nikita Khrushchev's visit to the United States in 1959. Khrushchev's itinerary took him to New York City, a farm in Iowa, Los

EUROPE (1990)

Angeles, and the presidential retreat of Camp David in the hills of western Maryland, where he and Eisenhower conferred in private. The "Spirit of Camp David" produced recommendations for disarmament and a decision for the two men to meet again at a summit meeting in Paris in May 1960, to be followed by Eisenhower's visit to the Soviet Union.

The Austrian settlement and talks between the heads of state did not mean that the Cold War was over. Nor did it mean that a process of disengagement had begun. Détente was always tempered by a heavy residue of mistrust and a continued reliance on military might. (The leadership in Washington and Moscow has always been divided on which approach to take—diplomacy or force.) At the high-point of détente in the 1950s, the Cassandras were always in the wings warning of dire consequences.

The Soviets spoke of peaceful coexistence—as they called détente—but the ideological struggle and the preservation of the empire continued. Nikita Khrushchev always had his critics at home, particularly the old Stalinist, Viacheslav Molotov, who remained foreign minster until Khrushchev replaced him in 1956.[8] Détente did not mean, therefore, the abandonment of influence and power. The Soviets were unwilling to abandon an inch of territory within what they considered their sphere of influence vital to their security. When they were challenged in Eastern Europe they did not hesitate to act. They quickly suppressed rebellions in East Germany in 1953 and in Hungary in 1956. The empire, the Soviet bloc, remained one and indivisible.

A similar conflict between détente and Cold War aspirations was also evident in the United States. The Republican president Eisenhower pursued the high road of compromise and negotiations; his secretary of state, John Foster Dulles, was an uncompromising anti-Communist. Dulles went beyond the stands his Democratic predecessors (Dean Acheson and George Marshall) had taken. Containment of the Soviet Union was not enough, for it suggested tolerance of an evil, Godless system. To Dulles, the Cold War was not merely a struggle between two contending economic and political orders; it was also a clash between religion and atheism. Dulles, therefore, proposed the "rollback" of the Soviet Union's forward position and the "liberation" of lands under Communist rule. Officially, U.S. foreign policy abandoned what had been a defensive position, and took on a "new look," an offensive character.[9] But as events showed, particularly in Hungary in 1956, it is the president who ultimately determines foreign policy, and Eisenhower had no desire to start World War III by challenging the Soviets in their sphere. Despite Dulles's rhetoric, U.S. foreign policy had to settle for containment.

Dulles acted vigorously to preserve and protect the U.S. presence throughout the world. When in 1954 the Communist Viet Minh of Vietnam triumphed over the French, he moved to preserve the southern half of that country for the Western camp. When the United States felt its interests threatened in Iran in 1953 and in Guatemala in 1954, the CIA, under the guidance of Allen Dulles, John Foster's brother, quickly moved into covert action and accomplished some of its most successful coups. In Iran, the CIA returned the shah to power when it engineered the overthrow of Premier Mohammed Mossadegh, who had sought to nationalize the nation's oil industry in order to take it out of the hands of British and U.S. companies. In Guatemala, the CIA replaced the socialist Jacobo Arbenz, who had proposed the nationalization of lands held by U.S. corporations, with a military junta.[10]

■ MOSCOW'S RESPONSE TO CONTAINMENT

In the mid–1950s, the Kremlin's foreign policy underwent a significant transformation when Khrushchev took the first steps to negate the U.S.-led system of alliances designed to contain the Soviet Union. Until that time the country had resembled a beleaguered fortress, defying what it perceived to be an aggressive West, a view not without foundation. The United States was in the process of implementing one of the provisions of NSC-68, the creation of regional alliances directed against the Soviet Union. In 1954, the United States created the Southeast Asia Treaty Organization (SEATO) and in 1955, the Bagdad Pact. In conjunction with NATO and its military ties in the Far East (South Korea, Japan, and Taiwan), the United States was about to close a ring around the Soviet Union.

The Bagdad Pact was intended to be a Middle Eastern alliance, consisting largely of Arab states, led by the United States and Great Britain. Yet, the only Arab state to join was Iraq; the other members were Turkey, Pakistan, and Iran. In March 1955, Egypt's Gamal Abdel Nasser created an Arab alliance, which included Syria and Saudi Arabia, to counter the West's influence in the Middle East. In this fashion, Nasser sought to establish his independence from the West. Nasser's act of defiance and his anti-Western rhetoric contributed to the rapid deterioration of relations. The United States sought to bring Nasser to heel by withdrawing its funding for the Aswan High Dam on the upper Nile. Nasser then turned to the Soviet Union to complete the dam. By that time he had already concluded an arms agreement with the Soviet Union (its first with a non-Communist state). When, in the summer of 1956, Nasser nationalized the Suez Canal, which had been in British hands since 1887, the stage was set for a retaliatory strike by the West. In October 1956, France and Britain joined Israel in an attack on Egypt (see Chapter 7). The Cold War once again had spilled over into the Third World.

In 1954, when Kremlin leaders took the first steps in arming a client beyond the Communist world,[11] this change in Soviet foreign policy did not come without intense debate in the high echelons of the Soviet Union's ruling circle. From the end of World War II until Stalin's death, the Soviet Union had conducted a relatively conservative foreign policy. To be sure, Stalin had refused to yield to the West on a number of central issues, notably Eastern Europe, but he had not challenged the West outside the confines of his own empire. The successful Communist insurgencies in Vietnam and China, for instance, were not of his making. Stalin had dug into his fortress behind his massive land army. Shortly after Stalin's death, the CIA, in a special report to President Eisenhower and the National Security Council, described Stalin as a man "ruthless and determined to spread Soviet power," who nevertheless "did not allow his ambitions to lead him to reckless courses of action in his foreign policy."[12] The CIA warned, however, that Stalin's successors might not be as cautious.

Events quickly bore out the CIA's prediction. In 1954, a bitter debate took place in the Kremlin over the nation's foreign policy. One faction, led by Prime Minister Georgi Malenkov and Foreign Minister Viacheslav Molotov, urged caution, favoring a continuation of the Stalinist pattern of defiance and rearmament. The majority in the Presidium of the Central Committee of the party, led by Nikita Khrushchev, who was the first secretary of the party and thus its leader, argued for a more active foreign policy, calling for a breakout from what they called capitalist encirclement.[13] This argument stressed that those who accept the status quo and merely stand still will suffer defeat at the hands of the capitalists. (Interestingly, this position echoes that of John Foster Dulles, who could not tolerate the mere containment of the foe. The conflict, both sides argued, must be taken to the enemy.)

Molotov and his allies warned that involvement in the Middle East was bound to fail. After all, British and U.S. navies controlled the Mediterranean Sea and were bound to stop all shipments, as the United States had intercepted a Czechoslovak arms shipment to Guatemala earlier in 1954. But Khrushchev and his faction prevailed and the Soviet Union began early in 1955 to arm Nasser in secret, a *fait accompli* revealed to the world later that year.

In return for its support of Nasser, the Soviet Union obtained a client in the Middle East, and it was thus able partially to offset the effects of the Baghdad Pact.[14] For the first time the Soviet Union was able to establish a foothold in a region beyond the Communist world. The person largely responsible for this significant departure in Soviet foreign policy and who reaped handsome political dividends at home was Nikita Khrushchev. He had begun to challenge the West in what had formally been a Western preserve. The monopoly of Western influence in the Third World was no more. It marked the beginning of a contest for the hearts and minds of the nonaligned world. With this in mind, Khrushchev undertook in 1955 a much-publicized journey to South Asia. He visited India and on his way home stopped in Kabul, the capital city of Afghanistan, to forestall apparent U.S. designs on that country. "It was . . . clear that America was courting Afghanistan," Khrushchev charged in his memoirs. The U.S. penetration of that country had "the obvious purpose of setting up a military base."[15] In 1960, Khrushchev paid a second visit to Asia. Eisenhower, concerned with the growing Soviet influence in southern Asia, followed in Khrushchev's footsteps when in 1960 he visited India and several other nonaligned nations.

In May 1960, relations between the Soviet Union and the United States took a sudden turn for the worse when a U.S. spy plane, a U-2, was shot down deep inside the Soviet Union. The Soviet Rocket Force Command had finally been able to bring down a high-flying U.S. spy plane, which had been periodically violating Soviet air space since 1956. This event wrecked the summit between Khrushchev and Eisenhower later that month, and it canceled Eisenhower's scheduled goodwill visit to the Soviet Union. Khrushchev's vehement denunciation of Eisenhower overstepped the boundaries of both common sense and good manners.[16] Western historians have often speculated that Khrushchev had to placate the hardliners at home who had never been happy with his rapprochement with the West.

Nineteen-sixty was also a presidential election year in the United States. Presidential election campaigns have never been known for elevated discussions of the issues, and this was no exception. The "outs," in this case John Kennedy and his Democratic Party, accused the "ins," Richard Nixon (Eisenhower's vice-president) and the Republicans, of having fallen asleep on their watch. The Soviets had (supposedly) opened up a "missile gap" that endangered the security of the United States. The Cold War was back in full bloom.

■ THE CUBAN MISSILE CRISIS

The division of Europe and its integration into two distinct blocs was both the result of the Cold War and a source of the continuation of the conflict. The belligerents remained in place and proceeded to arm for a military showdown that no one wanted. The main feature of the Cold War during the 1950s was the arms race, both conventional and nuclear. In conventional forces, the Soviet bloc always held the lead, while the West relied upon the U.S. nuclear umbrella. The U.S. nuclear monopoly, however, was short-lived. In 1949 the Soviet Union tested its first atomic weapon; in the early 1950s it exploded its first thermonuclear bomb; and in 1955 it obtained the capability of delivering these weapons by means of intercontinental bombers. By the end of the 1950s, Washington and Moscow had successfully tested intercontinental missiles. The stage was set for the escalation of the arms race and the dangers inherent in it.

The Cold War reached its most dangerous stage in a most unlikely place. It was over Cuba in 1962 that the first and only direct nuclear confrontation between the United States and the Soviet Union took place. The showdown came in the wake of the Cuban revolution of the late 1950s, a revolution by which Fidel Castro took Cuba out of the U.S. orbit and gave it a new political and economic direction. Castro's revolution made Cuba another arena for the superpowers.

Castro's direct challenge to the existing Cuban order and its president Fulgencio Batista began on July 26, 1953, when he led an unsuccessful attack on the Moncada army barracks. Castro spent eighteen months in prison and then went to Mexico, only to return to Cuba for a second attempt in December 1956. On May 28, 1957, Castro and his band of 80 guerrillas scored a significant psychological victory with an attack on the garrison at Uvero. For the next year and a half, Castro's forces, which never numbered more than 300 soldiers under arms, remained in the field as a visible challenge to the bankrupt Batista government, which at the end could count on no one to come to its defense. Because of Castro's small force and the fact that Batista's support rapidly began to crumble, the revolution never did reach the magnitude of a civil war in the proper sense of the word. Castro himself admitted that had Batista enjoyed a measure of popular support, his revolution would have been easily crushed. Instead, whatever support Batista had melted away and on January 1, 1959, Fidel Castro and his small band triumphantly entered Havana. Batista then fled the country. It was not so much that Castro had won political power as that Batista had lost it.

Castro was by no means the first Cuban to seize power by force, but he certainly was the first to take steps to challenge the unequal relationship between the United States and his country, one which had been in existence since the days of the Spanish-American War of 1898 when the United States gained a foothold in Cuba. Castro demanded the nationalization of U.S. property in Cuba and its transfer into Cuban hands. At first Castro appeared to be willing to offer compensation to U.S. companies, but not at the high level that the U.S. businesses demanded. The result was a deadlock with severe repercussions. It was not so much the differences in opinion over the value of U.S. property as it was ideological principles that led to the impasse. The United States became the champion of the right to private property of U.S. citizens in Cuba; Castro became the defender of Cuban national sovereignty.

Shortly, high-ranking U.S. officials in the Eisenhower administration became convinced that Castro was a Communist. At what point he did in fact become a Communist is difficult to say. His brother Raul had long been a Communist; Fidel's conversion apparently came sometime after the revolution. Because the United States had dealt successfully (that is, forcefully) with radical Latin American leaders before, most recently in Guatemala in 1954, it subsequently took steps to put pressure on Castro.

Thus far, events in Cuba had paralleled those in Guatemala in 1954, after Jacobo Arbenz had won an electoral victory. President Arbenz had proceeded to take steps to limit the power of foreign corporations, notably that of the United Fruit Company, a U.S. concern, which owned 10 percent of the nation's land. Arbenz nationalized uncultivated land and supported strikes against foreign businesses. The U.S. secretary of state, John Foster Dulles, raised the specter of Communism, but he obtained no support of his interpretation of events from other Latin American nations. The actions of Arbenz did not sit well with John Foster or his brother Allen, the director of the CIA, for reasons of national security, ideology, and the fact that both owned stock in the United Fruit Company and had previously provided legal services for the company. The Dulles brothers went into action. The CIA organized and outfitted disaffected elements of the Guatemalan army. The successful coup took place in June 1954. For Washington, the crisis was over. For Guatemala, a succession of military regimes—some of them of extraordinary brutality—became the order of the day.

There was little reason to believe that the United States could not repeat the Guatemalan scenario and reestablish its economic and political position in Cuba. The first weapon Washington employed was economic; if needed, other weapons would be employed later. The United States closed its market to Cuba's main source of income, the export of sugar cane. The U.S. market previously had taken half of Cuba's exports and provided nearly three-quarters of its imports. Predictably, the U.S. trade embargo had severe repercussions on the Cuban economy.

At this point events began to move rapidly. Castro refused to yield to U.S. pressure. Instead, he turned to the Soviet Union for economic, political, and military support. He saw his revolution as a model for other revolutionaries throughout Latin America and as such posed a direct challenge to U.S. hegemony in Latin America. His reform program at home acquired a Marxist flavor and it resulted in the exodus of thousands of Cubans who opposed the accompanying political and economic restrictions and sweeping changes. They settled mainly in Florida, waiting to return to their native land. In March 1960, a frustrated Eisenhower administration turned the Cuban problem over to the CIA and subsequently to the new president, John Kennedy.

Cuba became Kennedy's first foreign policy adventure. In the spring of 1961, Allen Dulles assured Kennedy that Castro could be removed with little difficulty. After all, the CIA had dealt with similar problems before and had handled them successfully. Dulles then put together a plan for Cuba. It called for Cuban exiles, trained and supplied by the CIA, to land on the beaches of Cuba and call upon the Cuban population to rise up against Castro. The Marxist regime of Cuba, according to policy makers in Washington, had no popular support and would collapse. All that was needed was a push, they said, and the corrupt house of cards would come down.

President Kennedy decided to put the CIA plan into operation in April 1961. But something went wrong. The population did not rise against Castro and his armed forces destroyed the force of 1,500 Cuban exiles who had landed on the beaches of the Bay of Pigs. It was all over in forty-eight hours.

French President Charles de Gaulle and visiting U.S. President John F. Kennedy, Paris, June 2, 1961. (*National Archives*)

A vague understanding between the CIA and the Cuban exiles had led the exiles to believe that the United States would not abandon them on the beaches. They expected direct U.S. military intervention in case they ran into difficulty. When Kennedy did not respond militarily to the fiasco at the Bay of Pigs, many Cubans in the United States considered his inaction an act of betrayal. But Kennedy never had contemplated the need for such a contingency. Moreover, such an action would have been in violation of international law and promised international and domestic repercussions. Kennedy had planned only for a covert operation.

Kennedy, stung by this defeat, blamed Allen Dulles for the fiasco. Castro's Cuba then became an obsession with him. Three days after the Bay of Pigs, he offered Castro a warning: "Let the record show that our restraint is not inexhaustible. . . . I want it clearly understood that this Government will not hesitate in meeting its primary obligations which are to the security of our Nation."[17] Kennedy's obsession, coupled with domestic politics and questions of national security, made it difficult for him to accept the presence of Castro in nearby Cuba.

The Soviet Union could do little to aid Castro. It could not readily challenge the United States in the Caribbean in an attempt to protect a client. The United States enjoyed a vast naval superiority, particularly in the Gulf of

Soviet leader Nikita Khrushchev and
Cuban President Fidel Castro, at the
United Nations, New York, Nov. 1960.
(*National Archives*)

Mexico, not to mention a large advantage in delivery systems of nuclear
weapons. When John Kennedy entered the White House, the United States
possessed over 100 intercontinental and intermediate-range ballistic missiles, 80 Polaris missiles, 1,700 intercontinental bombers, 300 nuclear-
armed airplanes on aircraft carriers, and 1,000 land-based fighters with
nuclear weapons. In contrast, the Soviets possessed 50 intercontinental
ballistic missiles, 150 intercontinental bombers, and an additional 400
intermediate-range missiles capable of reaching U.S. overseas bases.[18]

In the presidential election of 1960, Kennedy had charged that the
Eisenhower administration had been responsible for a "missile gap" to the
detriment of the United States. But that political myth was laid to rest shortly
after Kennedy became president. In October 1961, Deputy Secretary of Defense Roswell Gilpatric announced that there was no missile gap; on the contrary, there was a gap favoring the United States. "We have a second-strike
capability," Gilpatric stated, "which is at least as extensive as what the Soviets
can deliver by striking first."[19]

The Soviet premier, Nikita Khrushchev, understood this all too well. His
boasts of Soviet military might had only masked the reality. There seemed to
be little he could do about this state of affairs. But one day in 1962, a solution
came to him in a flash. He reasoned that if he could establish a Soviet nuclear
presence in Cuba he could solve several problems in one bold stroke.[20] The
implementation of such a plan promised three dividends. First, Khrushchev
would be able to present himself as the defender of a small and vulnerable
state. Secondly, and more importantly, medium-range missiles in Cuba
would essentially give the Soviet Union nuclear parity with the United States.

The missile gap, which favored the United States, would be no more. Thirdly, nuclear parity with the United States would greatly enhance the international prestige of the Soviet Union.

Khrushchev quickly decided to act. His memoirs suggest that he never spent much time considering the consequences of this rash act. (He was after all always a man of action, not of reflection.) There is no evidence he sought the advice of other Communist Party members or military experts. In the past, Khrushchev had several times taken decisive, yet potentially dangerous steps which, however, had brought him political rewards. Now the stakes were higher than ever before. Success promised to bring great rewards; failure promised to contribute to the early end of his political career. And in fact, two years after the Cuban missile crisis, when his party turned him out, he was accused of "hare-brained" and "wild schemes, half-baked conclusions and hasty decisions," none too subtle reminders of what had gone wrong in the Caribbean.[21]

When the CIA became aware of the construction of Soviet missile sites in Cuba, Kennedy had to act. Military and domestic political considerations demanded it. The Joint Chiefs of Staff understood that the presence of 90 Soviet intermediate-range missiles in Cuba, while posing a formidable threat to much of the eastern part of the United States, did not change the balance of terror whereby both sides were capable of annihilating the other. But when Kennedy and his advisers met, they knew that theirs was first and foremost a domestic political problem. At the height of the crisis, Secretary of Defense Robert McNamara told National Security Advisor McGeorge Bundy: "I'll be quite frank, I don't think there *is* a military problem here. . . . This is a domestic, political problem. . . . We said we'd *act*. Well, how will we act?"[22]

One option was to launch preemptive air strikes against the missile sites, which could bring about the deaths of Soviet military personnel and which would mean the humiliation of a great power. Such an action could touch off a nuclear war. The Joint Chiefs of Staff and the CIA felt that in an all-out war the Soviet nuclear arsenal was capable of destroying the United States without the Cuban missiles. This bleak assessment had a sobering impact on Kennedy and his advisors who met around the clock in an effort to find a solution to the crisis.

A second possibility was an invasion of Cuba, but such action was as dangerous as similar to the first option. The destruction of Soviet forces on Cuba would leave Khrushchev with few options. He could accept a defeat, contemplate a nuclear exchange, or attack the West's isolated and vulnerable outpost in Berlin where the Red Army had a marked advantage.

Kennedy decided on a third option, a blockade of Cuba (which he called a "quarantine" since a blockade is an act of war) that would give both sides additional time to resolve the issue. The blockade was a limited one since its purpose was only to intercept ships carrying missile components. Khrushchev, in the face of U.S. action, was prepared to back down. But he, not unlike Kennedy, had his own political problems at home. Since he could not afford to come away from the confrontation empty-handed, Khrushchev demanded concessions from Kennedy. First, he insisted on the Soviet Union's right to place defensive missiles in Cuba. After all the United States had done the same when it had placed missiles in Turkey, along the Soviet Union's southern border. At the least, therefore, the U.S. missiles should be removed from Turkey. But Kennedy refused to publicly discuss this demand. He, too, could not afford to appear to back down, despite the fact that the U.S. missiles in Turkey were obsolete and already had been scheduled for removal. Second, Khrushchev wanted a pledge from the United States not to invade Cuba and to respect the sovereignty of that nation. For several days the standoff continued. A false move would mean disaster for everyone involved.

Eventually, Kennedy saw the absurdity of his position. He was at the verge of bombing a small nation, an act that could touch off a nuclear war, over the issue of obsolete missiles in Turkey—missiles that he had already ordered to be removed. Kennedy ignored Khrushchev's belligerent statements and instead decided to reply to a conciliatory letter from the Soviet prime minister in which Khrushchev expressed his desire to resolve the dilemma:

> We and you ought not to pull on the ends of the rope in which you have tied the knot of war, because the more the two of us pull, the tighter that knot will be tied. And a moment may come when that knot will be tied too tight that even he who tied it will not have the strength to untie it. . . . Let us not only relax the forces pulling on the ends of the rope, let us take measures to untie that knot. We are ready for this.[23]

Robert Kennedy, the president's brother and closest adviser, met with Soviet Ambassador Anatoly Dobrynin to tell him that the United States was prepared to pledge not to invade Cuba in the future and that after a sufficient interval it would remove the missiles from Turkey. But there would be no official U.S. acknowledgement of this second concession. On the next day, Dobrynin told Robert Kennedy that the Soviet missiles would be withdrawn. The crisis was over.

In the wake of the crisis, after the first Soviet ships were turned back by the U.S. blockade, Secretary of State Dean Rusk said: "We looked into the mouth of the cannon; the Russians flinched." But it was not merely the Soviets who had flinched.[24] The United States had reacted in a similar fashion. The Cuban missile crisis had a profound, sobering effect on the nuclear powers. Both the United States and the Soviet Union realized that the constant state of confrontation had been in part responsible for the nuclear showdown. The time had come for a constructive dialogue. And, in fact, relations between the United States and the Soviet Union improved markedly shortly thereafter. The most notable, immediate achievement was the partial Nuclear Test Ban Treaty of 1963, which forbade nuclear testing in the atmosphere. It set the stage for further East-West discussions and the beginning of the détente of the 1960s.

In the aftermath of the crisis, historians, politicians, and soldiers have sought to determine the lessons of this confrontation. A view commonly held in the United States emphasizes that the crisis showed that the Soviets will yield in the face of determination and will. Force, after all, is the only thing they understand. On the surface, Khrushchev had surrendered to Kennedy's demands by removing the Soviet missiles from Cuba. But this explanation has several serious flaws. On balance, the victory did go to Kennedy. But it came at a price. Until the very end, Khrushchev always insisted on a *quid pro quo* (something in return) and he continued to hold out for concessions until he received them. In the meantime, his government granted Kennedy nothing. As long as the deadlock persisted, the Soviets continued to work on the Cuban missile sites and they challenged the U.S. U-2 spy planes that continued their surveillance flights. A Soviet missile—fired by Cubans at the express order of Fidel Castro—shot down and killed Major Rudolph Anderson, one of the pilots who had initially brought back the information on the missile sites. And when, during the crisis, a U.S. intelligence plane took off on a routine flight over the Soviet Union, the Soviet air force met it and chased it back.

The Cuban missile crisis was first and foremost a political test of wills. Nothing that either side did or contemplated doing would have changed the military balance of power. The crisis was political in nature, one that called for a political solution, namely, a *quid pro quo*. And that is how, in fact, it was resolved, not by one side dictating a settlement to the other. It ended only after Kennedy gave assurances on the missiles in Turkey and a pledge of noninterference in Cuban affairs. As Khrushchev emphasized in his memoirs, the crisis had been settled by political compromise, and he spared no words in thanking John Kennedy for settling it in that fashion rather than going to war.[25]

The Cuban missile crisis sobered up the belligerents and ushered in a climate of cooperation and the reduction of tension. But it also sowed the seeds for the destruction of détente. The crisis revealed the Soviet Union's relative weakness in the face of U.S. military might. This imbalance in favor of the United States was in part the result of a modest build-down on the part of the Soviets, which had begun in the late 1950s. But after Kennedy's demand for an increase in the U.S. nuclear arsenal, Kremlin leaders committed themselves to the quest for nuclear parity with the United States. The Soviet Union's rearmament program, however, did nothing to change the balance of power by the time of the Cuban crisis of October 1962. The Soviets then vowed that the United States would never again humiliate them. The result was a renewed Soviet effort to close the gap or, at the least, to create the illusion of parity between the two nuclear powers.

■ RECOMMENDED READINGS

☐ Western Europe

Calmann, John. *The Common Market: The Treaty of Rome Explained*. London: Blond, 1967.
    An analysis of the origins of the Common Market.
Hiscocks, Richard. *The Adenauer Era*. Philadelphia: Lippincott, 1966.
    A study of the accomplishments of the architect of West Germany.
Sampson, Anthony. *Anatomy of Europe: A Guide to the Workings, Institutions, and Character of Contemporary Western Europe*. New York: Harper & Row, 1968.
    A readable analysis of postwar Europe.
Williams, Philip, and Martin Harrison. *Politics and Society in de Gaulle's Republic*. New York: Doubleday, 1971.
    A book that focuses on the politician responsible for the political orientation of postwar France.

☐ The Cold War, 1953–1962

Beschloss, Michael R. *Mayday: Eisenhower, Khrushchev and the U-2 Affair*. New York: Harper & Row, 1986.
    A detailed analysis of the U-2 incident and its impact on U.S.-Soviet relations.
Dallin, David. *Soviet Foreign Policy After Stalin*. Philadelphia: Lippincott, 1961.
    A scholarly treatment of Soviet foreign affairs during the 1950s.
Ra'anan, Uri. *The USSR Arms the Third World: Case Studies in Soviet Foreign Policy*. Cambridge, Mass.: The M.I.T. Press, 1969.
    A valuable account of the debates in the Kremlin over foreign policy.

☐ Cuba

Abel, Elie. *The Missile Crisis*. Philadelphia: Lippincott, 1966.
    A journalist's scholarly account of the nuclear confrontation.
Kennedy, Robert F. *Thirteen Days: A Memoir of the Cuban Missile Crisis*. New York: W. W. Norton, 1969.
    By the president's brother and close adviser, who presents what may be called the official view.
Szulc, Tad. *Fidel: A Critical Portrait*. New York: Morrow, 1986.
    A detailed biography that offers the thesis that Castro was already a Communist before seizing political power.
Walton, Richard J. *Cold War and Counterrevolution: The Foreign Policy of John F. Kennedy*. New York: Viking, 1972.
    Contains two chapters highly critical of Kennedy's handling of the Bay of Pigs and the missile crisis.
Weyden, Peter. *Bay of Pigs: The Untold Story*. New York: Simon and Schuster, 1979.
    Contains a most detailed account of the CIA's ill-fated attempt to overthrow Fidel Castro.

■ NOTES

1. West Germany's choice of a capital, the small provincial city of Bonn, signified the capital's provisional and temporary status. The traditional German capital, Berlin (which was also divided into East and West German sectors), was within East German territory. Over the years, Bonn has been transformed and now contains a large complex of government office buildings befitting a capital city.

2. West Berlin's main practical/strategic value to the West was that it was a most important center of intelligence operations. One psychological benefit was that the steadily improving standard of living in West Berlin stood in sharp contrast to that of East Germany by which it was surrounded.

3. The Common Market later expanded to include Greece in 1981 and Spain and Portugal in 1986, bringing the membership to twelve nations.

4. Gaullism also entailed the vigorous assertion of executive power within France and the build-up of France's military forces, specifically its nuclear arsenal.

5. Quoted in Walter LaFeber, *America, Russia, and the Cold War,* p. 98.

6. *Détente* is a French word meaning an unbending or relaxing; specifically, in the case of the Cold War, the relaxation of strained international relations.

7. A bold and sweeping statement, to be sure. Other agreements on trade, arms limitations, travel, and the like, must not be lightly dismissed. Yet, none of them settled a major political problem. The stubborn fact that it took the two sides ten years and new leaders to agree on the Austrian solution—and on little else in the succeeding thirty years—is testimony to the intensity of the Cold War.

8. The man who replaced Molotov was Dimitri Shepilov. In early 1957, Andrei Gromyko, who retained his post until July 1985, was kicked upstairs to take the ceremonial post of president of the Soviet Union. Gromyko's replacement was Eduard Shevardnadze, the coice of the new leader of the Communist party, Mikhail Gorbachev.

9. Dulles's "rollback" and "liberation" and Eisenhower's "New Look" are discussed in Stephen E. Ambrose, *Rise to Globalism: American Foreign Policy, 1938–1970* (Baltimore: Penguin, 1971), pp. 221–225.

10. Peter Wyden, *Bay of Pigs: The Untold Story* (New York: Simon and Schuster, 1979), pp. 94–99.

11. Charges in the West that Nasser was a Communist were incorrect. In fact, Nasser outlawed the Egyptian Communist Party. The Soviet Union turned a blind eye to Nasser's actions in order not to jeopardize its new relationship with the Arab world. Similarly, when the Soviets began to sell arms to the Sukarno government of Indonesia, the powerful Indonesian Communist Party complained bitterly. The party's fears were well founded; in October 1965, the Indonesian army launched a bloodbath that destroyed the Communist Party.

12. CIA special estimate, advance copy for National Security Council, March 10, 1953, "Probable Consequences of the Death of Stalin and of the Elevation of Malenkov to Leadership in the USSR," p. 4, in Paul Kesaris, ed., *CIA Research Reports: The Soviet Union, 1946–1976* (Frederick, Md.: University Publications of America, 1982), Reel II, frames 637–648.

13. Today, the Presidium is known as the Politburo of the Central Committee of the Communist Party, the decision-making body, which consists of approximately a dozen individuals. The number is not fixed; it varies frequently.

14. The Bagdad Pact, at any rate, did not last long; nor did it accomplish much. Similarly, the Soviet Union's national interests were hardly served by supplying arms to Nasser. The actions of the superpowers had little more than symbolic value.

15. N. S. Khrushchev, *Khrushchev Remembers: The Last Testament* (Boston: Little, Brown, 1974), pp. 299–300.

16. The event had embarrassed Eisenhower who had first lied about it and then had to

acknowledge that he had approved the spying mission. It had also proven to be an embarrass-
ment for Khrushchev, whose military and scientific establishment had launched the first earth
satellite and the first intercontinental missile, and yet had been unable to bring down a U.S.
plane at 75,000 feet until engine troubles forced it to a lower altitude.

17. Quoted in Richard J. Walton, *Cold War and Counter-Revolution: The Foreign Policy of
John F. Kennedy* (Baltimore: Viking, 1972), p. 50.

18. David Horowitz, *The Free World Colossus: A Critique of American Foreign Policy in
the Cold War* (New York: Hill and Wang, rev. ed., 1971), pp. 342–345. Also, Edgar M. Bottome, *The
Balance of Terror: A Guide to the Arms Race* (Boston: Beacon Press, 1971), pp. 120–121 and
158–160.

19. "Gilpatric Warns U.S. Can Destroy Atom Aggressor," *New York Times,* October 22, 1961,
pp. 1, 6.

20. In 1955, Khrushchev had argued for a secret arms shipment to Nasser's Egypt and it
had proven to be a bold and successful plan of action. In Cuba, he could perhaps do the same.

21. "Nezyblemaia leninskaia general'naia linia KPSS," *Pravda,* October 17, 1964, p. 1.

22. Kai Bird and Max Holland, "Dispatches," *The Nation,* April 28, 1984, p. 504.

23. Robert F. Kennedy, *Thirteen Days: A Memoir of the Cuban Missile Crisis* (New York:
Norton, 1969), pp. 89–90.

24. Ibid., p. 18.

25. *Khrushchev Remembers: The Last Testament,* pp. 513–514.

Part 2

NATIONALISM AND THE END OF COLONIALISM

After World War II a wave of nationalism swept across Asia and Africa, and in its wake a host of new nations proclaimed independence from their European colonial masters. Within two decades about one-third of the world's population was freed from colonial rule. The scope and the speed of the dismantling of the colonial empires were unforeseen. But by 1960, it had become clear to even the more conservative rulers of the colonial powers that they could no longer resist the demands rising from the colonized peoples of Asia and Africa for independence and nationhood. None stated it better than British Prime Minister Harold Macmillan in his famous "Wind of Change" speech delivered at the end of a tour of Africa in January 1960:

> We have seen the awakening of national consciousness in peoples who have for centuries lived in dependence upon some other power. Fifteen years ago this movement spread through Asia. Many countries there of different races and civilisations pressed their claim to an independent life. Today the same thing is happening in Africa and the most striking of all the impressions I have formed since I left London a month ago is the strength of this African national consciousness. The wind of change is blowing through the continent, and whether we like it or not this growth of national consciousness is a political fact, and our national policies must take account of it.[1]

Several historical developments merged to bring about this rise of nationalism and rapid decolonization in the postwar period. First, the war itself caused strains on the European colonial powers, which caused them to lose grip on their overseas colonies. Some of them had lost their colonies during the war and found it difficult to restore control of them afterward, while others were so exhausted by the war that they came to view the maintenance of a colonial empire as a burden greater than it was worth. Another factor was the emergence of a Western-educated elite among the natives of the colonies who took seriously the lessons they had learned in the Western universities and demanded democracy, self-government, and nationalism. In some cases the colonial peoples took part as allies in the war and, having contributed to the victory of freedom, they now demanded a measure of that freedom for themselves.

Still another factor with relevance to Asia, as we shall point out in Chapter 5, was the role of Japan in bringing an early end to European colonialism. On the one hand, Japan lost its own colonies, and on the other hand, it had promoted and provoked in various Asian countries nationalist movements, which opposed the return of the colonial powers after the war. Britain responded with greater alacrity than did France and the Netherlands to the strength of the independence movement in Asia and took the lead in decolonization. Once it granted independence to India, long the most important of its colonies, the grounds for maintaining its rule over lesser colonies vanished. France, however, resisted granting independence to its colonies, for it seemed to find in the restoration of the French empire a means of compensating for its humiliating defeat in World War II. In Chapter 5, we relate the frustrations of France in Indochina, where it was met and ultimately defeated by a determined Vietnamese nationalist movement led by Ho Chi Minh.

In Africa, decolonization came later than in Asia largely because national consciousness and strong nationalist movements were slower to develop. There are several historical reasons for this, but as we explain in Chapter 6, the persistence of tribalism in Africa was a major obstacle to the development of nationalism. As in Asia, the pattern of decolonization in Africa was determined, to a great extent, by the policy of the European colonial nations. In general, Britain did more to prepare its African colonies for self-rule and independence than did France or the other European powers. In fact, the abrupt departure of France and Belgium from Africa left their former colonies particularly ill-prepared for either political or economic independence. France, in addition, refused to abandon Algeria, which many French citizens called home and which their government considered a province of France and not a colony. But the Muslim majority among native Algerians was determined to win independence from France, and the result was that France had on its hands another long and bitter revolutionary struggle.

Nationalism was a key ingredient in the postwar struggles in the Middle East as well. Here, two peoples, Jews and Arabs, clashed over claims to the same land on which to establish their nations. The Jews, fortified by their particular brand of nationalism—Zionism—returned to settle a land they had parted from centuries before, while the Palestinians, who had occupied this same land for centuries, were determined not to make room for the Jews who came in greater and greater numbers after the war. Chapter 7 provides a review of the long historical background to their conflicting claims, without which their postwar feud cannot be understood. The state of Israel came into being in 1948, at the expense of the Palestinians, and ever since it has been embattled by its Arab neighbors, none of whom (with the exception of Egypt since 1978) have been willing to accept its right to exist.

The continuing struggle for national self-determination in Vietnam is treated in Chapter 9 in the following section, and the postindependence drive of the new nations of Asia and Africa for political and economic modernization is taken up in Part 4, "The Third World."

■ NOTES

1. James H. McBath, ed., *British Public Addresses, 1828–1960* (Boston, Houghton-Mifflin Co., 1971), pp. 75–83.

□ 5

Decolonization in Asia

Independence movements in Asian nations had been brewing since about the beginning of the twentieth century, and by the end of World War II they had become boiling cauldrons, the contents of which the lid of colonialism could no longer contain. The demand for self-determination and national independence was sounded by ardent nationalists throughout Asia, in India and Burma, in Vietnam and Malaya, in Indonesia and the Philippines. In some cases, independence was achieved peacefully, because the imperial nation became resigned to the termination of its colonial rule, as was the case of the United States in the Philippines and Great Britain in India and Burma. In other cases, imperial powers were determined to resist the national independence movements in their colonies and ultimately granted independence only after engaging in a long and bloody struggle, as was the case of the French in Indochina and the Dutch in the East Indies.

The primary ingredient in all independence movements was nationalism. The beginnings of nationalist resistance to European colonial rule in Asia may be traced to the turn of the century. Gradually, the colonized peoples awakened to their precolonial traditions and developed a sense of national consciousness. Their quests for national independence were mixed with strong anti-imperialist and anti-white racial sentiments. They were outraged by imperialist domination, by being treated as inferior citizens in their own native lands. They could point out to the Europeans the blatant contradiction between their own professed ideals of democracy and self-government and their denial of the same to their Asian colonies. After witnessing the destruction European nations had wrought upon one another in World War I, the Asian colonial peoples began to doubt the superiority of their colonial masters. By the end of World War II, Asian

103

nationalist movements had become quite strong, and they were determined to fight for an end to colonial rule and for full national independence.

■ THE IMPACT OF WORLD WAR II

World War II, and especially the role played by Japan in the war, greatly stimulated the national independence movements in Asia. During the war, several of the imperial powers of Europe were either defeated by Nazi Germany, as were France and the Netherlands, or were fighting desperately for survival, as was Great Britain. These nations were unable to maintain their colonial regimes in Asia, or did so only with difficulty. Moreover, Japan quickly took advantage of this situation and filled the power vacuum by its own conquest of most of Southeast Asia at the outset of the war. The Japanese claimed that they came not as enemies of the Asian peoples but as their liberators, fighting to free Asia from the chains of Western imperialism and to make it safe for Asians. While it is true that the Japanese merely replaced the former colonial regime with one of their own, they nonetheless did much to generate nationalism and independence movements in the various countries they occupied in Southeast Asia—the Philippines, Indochina, the Dutch East Indies, Malaya, and Burma. The swiftness and apparent ease with which the Japanese defeated the European forces in Asia signaled to the Vietnamese, Indonesians, Burmese, and others that their former European masters were not as powerful as they had thought.

In Indonesia the Japanese released native political prisoners from the jails and threw the Dutch colonial officials into the same cells. They banned the use of the Dutch language and promoted the use of native languages. They granted nominal independence to the Philippines and to Burma in 1943, and promised it to others. In some cases, such as in India and Burma, Japan helped arm and train national armies to fight the British. By the end of the war, when Japan was forced out, the nationalist organizations Japan had assisted stood ready to oppose the efforts by the European powers to reimpose their colonial rule. This was especially the case in Indonesia, where nationalist leaders immediately issued a declaration of independence at the time of Japan's surrender.

The United States, too, played a role in hastening the end of colonialism in Asia. During the war U.S. leaders, especially President Roosevelt, had been outspoken in their opposition to the continuation of European colonialism in postwar Asia. The United States became the first Western nation to relinquish its colonial power there after the war. The U.S. government had long before promised independence to the Philippines, a U.S. colony since 1898, and no sooner was the war over than plans for the transfer of power were made. In 1946, with great fanfare, the Republic of the Philippines was pro-claimed on an appropriate date, July 4th.

■ INDEPENDENCE AND THE PARTITION OF INDIA

The decolonization of British India has deeper historic roots. The nationalist resistance to British rule began back in the nineteenth century with the founding of the Indian National Congress (a political party usually known as Congress). Prior to World War II, the British were already committed to even-tual self-government and independence for India, but the war speeded up the timetable. In May 1942, the British government sent a special envoy, Sir Stafford Cripps, to India on a mission aimed at placating the Indian nationalists (and world opinion). In what became known as the Cripps pro-posal, he promised India dominion status (self-government but continuing membership in the British Commonwealth) and an election for a native con-stituent assembly to draft an Indian constitution—after the war. This pro-voked a negative reaction from Indian nationalist leaders, notably Mahatma Gandhi and Jawaharlal Nehru, who were determined to turn Britain's dis-advantage—the war emergency—into India's advantage. Their firm rejec-tion of the Cripps proposal and their inspirational rhetoric aroused the nationalism of their fellow Indians, which found expression both in Gandhi's passive resistance movement as well as in violent political demon-strations. Gandhi had become a unique force to be reckoned with because of his long-suffering and selfless pursuit of national independence using such nonviolent methods as organizing work stoppages and fasting until near death.[1] Flushed with the heady wine of nationalism, Congress, in Au-gust 1942, not only rejected the British offer for eventual independence but passed the Quit India Resolution, which demanded instead the immediate departure of the British from India.

The British response to the Quit India Resolution was to arrest Gandhi, Nehru, and the entire Congress Working Committee. Congress followers re-belled but were suppressed in several weeks. One expatriate Indian nationalist leader, Subhas Chandra Bose, went so far as to put an army in the field (with Japanese assistance) to fight the British. Toward the end of the war, the British viceroy, the crown's representative in India, repeatedly ad-vised London that the demand for independence in India was so strong that it could be postponed no longer. Prime Minister Winston Churchill, the guardian of Britain's empire, had little tolerance for the Indian nationalist movement and had no intention of granting independence. His public reac-tion to the Quit India Resolution was:

COLONIAL SOUTHERN AND SOUTHEASTERN ASIA:
EUROPEAN AND U.S. TERRITORIES IN 1900

We intend to remain the effective rulers of India for a long and indefinite period. . . . We mean to hold our own. I have not become the King's First Minister in order to preside over the liquidation of the British Empire. . . . Here we are, and here we stand, a veritable rock of salvation in this drifting world.[2]

Churchill reduced the issue in India to two clear-cut alternatives: the British could either stand and rule or they could cut and run, and he never seriously considered the latter. He did, however, consider adopting a policy aimed at undermining the Indian National Congress by enlisting the support of the impoverished rural masses of India with a land reform program that would benefit them at the expense of wealthy landowners, who were identified with Congress.[3]

In June 1945, in anticipation of the end of the war, British authorities in India convened a conference of Indian leaders (several of whom were released from prison so that they could take part) aimed at creating an interim coalition government pending the granting of independence after the war. These talks, however, were complicated by the presence of a third party, the Muslim League. The Muslims made up a large religious minority in India, and they feared being swallowed up by the far more powerful Hindu majority. They did not wish to become a helpless minority in an Indian nation in which the Hindu-Muslim population ratio was about five to one. Therefore, the Muslim League, led by Mohammed Ali Jinnah, insisted on nothing less than a separate state for the Muslims. Gandhi and the Congress leaders were staunchly opposed to such a division, and they tried to reassure Jinnah and the British that Muslim autonomy and safety would be guaranteed within the new Union of India. The British, too, wished to preserve the unity of India, but Jinnah remained adamant in his demands for a separate Muslim nation.

In London, the new prime minister, Clement Attlee, whose Labour Party had unseated Churchill's government in July 1945, declared that the goal of his government was to transfer power to the Indian people as soon as possible, and at the same time to preserve the unity of India. However, these two goals were in conflict because of the Muslim insistence on a partition of India. In an effort to resolve the partition/unity issue, Attlee dispatched, in March 1946, a cabinet mission to India, where tensions were rapidly mounting. Indian nationalist aspirations for independence clashed with Muslim aspirations for nationhood. Indian nationalism was made manifest in a mutiny by Indian sailors against their British naval officers, by expressions of popular support for Indians who were put on trial for having taken up arms against the British during the war, and by the outpouring of the inspired nationalist rhetoric of Gandhi and Nehru. The Muslim leader, Jinnah, was equally articulate and passionate in his demand for the creation of a separate nation for the Muslims. After conducting a two-month-long investigation in

India, the cabinet mission released its report, rejecting partition as impractical but favoring instead a formula for assuring the autonomy of Muslim provinces within a greater Indian unity. But efforts to implement this plan were forestalled by mutual mistrust and quarreling. With the outbreak of communal violence between Hindus and Muslims (and among other minorities), there was too little time to work out a peaceful solution.

The tense situation developing in India caused the British to advance the timetable for independence. A new initiative was made with the appointment of Lord Louis Mountbatten, the popular wartime hero, to the post of viceroy of India. On his arrival there in March 1947, Mountbatten announced July 1948 as the new deadline for the transfer of power from the British to the Indians. Instead of pacifying the Indians—both Hindus and Muslims—as he had intended, his announcement excited them all the more. As violence mounted and thousands of people were being killed in the strife, negotiations among the three parties intensified. Although Mountbatten at first reaffirmed the British desire to preserve the unity of India, he could not satisfy the Muslim League with anything less than partition, and he therefore decided to settle the matter speedily on the basis of establishing two successor states. The result was a hasty agreement in June 1947 on the division of India

Indian Prime Minister Jawaharlal Nehru, addressing an audience in the United States, Oct. 11, 1949, two months after independence was granted to India. (*National Archives*)

Muhammed Ali Jinnah, President of the Moslem League and later the first President of Pakistan, Aug. 9, 1945. (*AP/Wide World Photos*)

to go into effect on the new, earlier date set for independence, August 15, 1947.

On that day, not one but two nations came into being: India and Pakistan, the new Muslim state. This event, known as the partition, was followed by the movement of some 15 million people from one area to another, mainly the flight of Muslims from various regions of India to their new nation. A commission was set up to define the boundaries of the new state of Pakistan, half of which was to be in the northwest and half in the northeast (the Bengal region). The agreement on the partition of India did not specify the future status of the Sikhs, another religious minority, and the 560 small, independent princely states scattered throughout the Indian subcontinent. It was presumed, however, that they would look to one or the other of the two new governments for protection and thus be integrated into either India or Pakistan.

While the partition met the nationalist aspirations of the Muslims, who were jubilant over the birth of Pakistan, it was a disappointment to both the Indian nationalists and the British, who would have preferred the preservation of a united India. But none of the three could be pleased by the terrible brutality that attended the partition. Under the best of circumstances, hardship always accompanies the dislocation of peoples. Instead of putting an end to the civil strife between Hindus and Muslims, partition led to much greater bloodletting. Hysterical mobs of Hindus, Muslims, Sikhs, and others savagely attacked one another in acts of reprisal, bitterness, and desperation. In many cities terrorism raged out of control for many days when arson, looting, beatings, murder, and rape became common occurrences. Numerous villages became battlegrounds of warring groups and massacres were frequent along the highways clogged with poor and usually unprotected migrants. Before it was over, almost 1 million people lost their lives. The British, in fact, had warned the two impatient and obstinate sides of this possible result of moving too hastily on partition, but it had been to no avail. Indeed, the British laid themselves open to charges of moving with excessive haste and without adequate planning for an orderly population transfer.

■ THE BRITISH AND DUTCH IN SOUTHEAST ASIA

The process of decolonization in Southeast Asia varied from country to country but, in general, it was more orderly in the U.S. and British colonies (excepting, of course, the violence involved in the partition of India) than it was in the French and Dutch colonies.[4] The British granted independence to Ceylon (now known as Sri Lanka) in 1947 and to Burma in 1948. They were prepared to transfer power to a Malayan union in 1948, but this was delayed for a decade by internal strife between the Malays, the Muslim majority, and the Chinese, who were in the minority except in the city of Singapore.[5] An unsuccessful ten-year-long Communist insurgency complicated matters further. Finally, in August 1957, after the Communist movement was suppressed and a greater degree of ethnic harmony between the Malays and the Chinese was attained, the British granted full independence to the Federation of Malaya.

Britain also relinquished control of its other colonies on the periphery of Malaya. Singapore remained a British crown colony until it became an independent nation in 1959. Sarawak and North Borneo, British colonies located on the northern side of the island of Borneo (the southern part of which belonged to the Dutch East Indies), were granted independence in 1963 and, together with Singapore, joined Malaya to form the new state of Malaysia.[6]

In contrast to the British, the Dutch had no intention of granting independence to the Dutch East Indies, a colony made up of many Southeast Asian islands, which the Dutch had exploited for three centuries. But Dutch intransigence was met by equally strong resistance on the part of the Indonesian nationalists. During World War II, the Japanese military rulers who controlled the Dutch colony gave their active support to an anti-Dutch, nationalist organization known as Putera. By the end of the war, this organization, under the leadership of Achem Sukarno, had developed a 120,000-troop army. When news of Japan's surrender reached Jakarta, the capital, Sukarno, who had been under intensive pressure from the more radical student element in Putera, quickly drafted a declaration of Indonesian independence. He read it on August 17, 1945, to a huge crowd that had gathered to celebrate the event. At about the same time the British landed an occupying force to receive the Japanese surrender and to maintain order until Dutch forces could arrive.

The Dutch returned with a design to restore colonial rule, only to be confronted by a strong nationalist movement with a large, well-equipped army and by an even more hostile Communist movement. Negotiations produced a suggested compromise settlement in late 1946 whereby the Dutch would recognize Indonesian independence only on the islands of Java and Sumatra, on the condition that this new Indonesian republic remain within the Dutch colonial empire in a "Union of Netherlands and Indonesia." Indonesian leaders, however, rejected this plan, and when the Dutch resorted to police action to quell demonstrations in July 1947 they were met by armed resistance. Despite United Nations efforts to arrange a cease-fire and diplomatic pressures by the United States and Britain on the Dutch, the Indonesian war of independence continued for another two years, with thousands of casualties on both sides. Finally, in 1949 the Dutch conceded, and a fully independent Federation of Indonesia came into being with Sukarno as its president.

■ THE FRENCH IN INDOCHINA

The French, not unlike the Dutch, were also opposed to granting independence to their Asian colony in Indochina, and their efforts to reimpose colonial power there would also meet with failure.

France's colonial presence in Vietnam dates back to 1858, when its troops occupied the Mekong River delta in the south. By 1883, when the native ruling dynasty submitted to French rule, the French had extended their rule to the Red River delta in the north. The conquest of Vietnam was then complete. But, according to the Museum of the Revolution in Hanoi, the struggle against this latest manifestation of foreign domination of Vietnam began on the very day the French had extended their dominion over all of Vietnam.[7] At first, defiance consisted of unorganized peasant uprisings, which the French quickly suppressed. At the turn of the century, French rule, not unlike that of other colonial powers elsewhere, appeared to be secure. Vietnamese nationalists, humiliated by the French presence, found themselves incapable of challenging the colonial power. Imprisonment and the public use of the guillotine had their intended impact.

The early career of Ho Chi Minh is a case in point. Later in life he fought and defeated the French, but as a young man he could do no more than humbly request justice for his native land. In 1919, he happened to be living in Paris, where the victors of World War I were meeting to decide the fate of the losers. The U.S. president Woodrow Wilson had came to the conference as the champion of national self-determination, the one who spoke for the rights of all subjugated peoples. Ho Chi Minh submitted a petition to the U.S. delegation in the hope that Wilson would intervene on Vietnam's behalf. But the delegates had more pressing issues to consider, and the French, whose overriding concern was the punishment of Germany, were in no mood to discuss with a U.S. president (with whom relations were strained as it were) their colonial rule in a faraway land. Ho's calls for amnesty for all political prisoners, equal justice, freedom of the press, and "the sacred right of all peoples to decide their own destiny" fell on deaf ears.[8]

In the following year, Ho became one of the founders of the French Communist Party. His attraction to Communism, he wrote later, was because he saw it as the only political movement in France that concerned itself "a great deal with the colonial question." Communism, for Ho Chi Minh, thus became a vehicle for national liberation of his native land from a succession of French governments that professed the sacred principles of liberalism and democracy. Ho's identity as a Marxist and anticolonialist made it impossible for him to return to Vietnam and took him to Moscow in 1924, at a time when the Kremlin began to officially focus on domestic problems and all but abandoned its ideological commitment to international revolution. By the late 1920s, he made his way to China, where revolutionary ferment promised to spread to the rest of Asia. For nearly twenty years, he remained a man without a country, living in exile and waiting for a chance to return to Vietnam to challenge the French.

The opportunity came in 1941, during the early years of World War II. The French army, the world's best on paper, had collapsed in the face of the German attack in the spring of 1940. In the following year, when the Japanese swept over Southeast Asia, the French again offered little resistance. Japan had humbled one of Europe's great powers, but this proved to be little solace for the Vietnamese since they merely exchanged one master for another. The Japanese conquest of Southeast Asia, however, put into sharp focus the vulnerability of the European colonial presence in Asia, a lesson that was not lost on the Vietnamese, who at the end of the war demanded the end of French colonial rule.

In the meantime, Ho Chi Minh returned to Vietnam in 1940 to create a native resistance movement, the Viet Minh (the League for the Independence of Vietnam), and turned against the Japanese, who now controlled Vietnam. Thus, by a strange twist of fate, Ho and the United States became allies during World War II in their common struggle against the Japanese empire. The United States recognized the usefulness of the Viet Minh, and in fact the OSS (the U.S. Office of Strategic Services, the forerunner of the CIA) provided Ho with weapons and supplies.

When the war ended in 1945, it was Ho and his men who controlled much of Vietnam. France's colonial ambitions in Southeast Asia seemed to be at an end. Toward the end of the war, President Roosevelt had urged the French to follow the U.S. example in the Philippines and grant Vietnam its independence. But the French, humiliated in World War II and insisting on the restoration of France as one of the world's great powers, refused to accept the loss of a prized colony. They sought refuge in a page out of the nineteenth century, which equated colonialism with national pride and prestige. They insisted on reasserting their authority as they had done in the past.

In the meantime, Ho Chi Minh declared the independence of Vietnam in Hanoi on September 2, 1945. He drew on hallowed French and U.S. political documents to justify a Vietnam free from colonial rule. Ho made use of The Declaration of the Rights of Man and Citizen from the French Revolution of 1789 and the U.S. Declaration of Independence, a copy of which was given to him by an OSS official. Talks between Ho and the French came to nothing. At a minimum, the Vietnamese insisted on a genuine measure of autonomy within the context of the French empire. The French, however, were not interested in coming to the conference table to oversee the dissolution of their empire. The French navy eventually replied with a classic example of gunboat diplomacy. In November 1946, the French fleet bombarded the Vietnamese sector of the port of Haiphong. According to French estimates, 6,000 civilians died in the shelling of the city. The French then marched into Hanoi, and the first Indochina War began.

■ THE FIRST INDOCHINA WAR

Initially, the Viet Minh proved to be no match for the French army, which possessed superior equipment as well as more troops. The French were able to put airplanes, tanks, trucks, and heavy artillery into battle. In a conventional head-to-head clash the French were destined to win. The Viet Minh, therefore, had no choice except to pursue the tactics of the weak against the strong: guerrilla warfare.

Guerrillas (from the Spanish meaning "little war") have no chance of defeating their more powerful enemy in a decisive battle, because they simply do not have the means to do so. They rely instead on a series of small campaigns designed to tie down the enemy army without engaging it directly. Once the enemy forces bring their superior power into play, the guerrillas break off the fight and withdraw, leaving the battlefield to the conventional forces who then plant their banners and proclaim victory. Armies fighting guerrillas can often point to an uninterrupted string of "victories," in the traditional sense of the word. The guerrillas are almost always "defeated."

But such a scenario is frequently misleading. Ché Guevara, who was one of the better known practitioners of guerrilla warfare and who fought with Fidel Castro in Cuba in the 1950s, compared a guerrilla campaign to the minuet, the eighteenth century dance. In the minuet, the dancers take several steps forward and then back. The "steps back" are of central importance to the guerrillas. They cannot afford to hold their ground since they know they will be decimated; therefore, they must always retreat after going forward. They must gather their dead and wounded and their supplies, and then reorganize to fight another day. Little wonder that the conventional forces are always able to claim that they are winning the war and that it will only be a matter of time until the guerrillas suffer their "final" defeat.

The guerrillas' victory comes only after a prolonged struggle that wears down the enemy physically and psychologically. Of utmost importance for the guerrillas is the conduct of political action necessary to gain recruits for their cause. For conventional forces, the conflict is frequently of a purely military nature; in contrast, successful guerrilla movements always focus on the psychological and political nature of the conflict. French Colonel Gabriel Bonnet reduced this to a quasi-mathematical formula: $RW = G + P$ (revolutionary warfare is guerrilla action plus psychological-political operations)."[9]

In Vietnam, the French forces generally held the upper hand, and with it came repeated predictions of victory. But they were unable to suppress the insurrection. The Viet Minh always managed to reappear and fight again. And, thus, what was intended as a short punitive action by the French turned into a long and costly war of attrition. And because all wars have political and economic repercussions, successive French governments were beginning to feel the heat. At the outset of the war, the French public had supported the efforts to suppress an anti-colonial rebellion, but as the years went by and the financial burden became increasingly heavier, public dissatisfaction grew.

In 1950, the United States became involved in the Korean War, which it considered part of a general Communist offensive in Asia across a wide front. Its view of the Viet Minh insurgency was no different. President Harry Truman became concerned with the French position in Vietnam, and he thus became the first U.S. president to involve the United States in that region when he offered the French financial aid. (When the war ended in 1954, most of the French expenditures in Vietnam were being underwritten by the U.S. taxpayer.)

But the U.S. line of reasoning that revolutions have no indigenous causes but are fomented instead from the outside (a view that lies at the core of Washington's view of the Cold War) proved to be a questionable one in this case. The Soviet Union offered the Viet Minh no aid, and when the Chinese Communists came to power in 1949, Ho Chi Minh emphatically rejected the idea of using Chinese troops against the French although he did accept Chinese supplies, particularly artillery. Chinese-Vietnamese enmity is age-old, and Ho feared the Chinese, their Communism notwithstanding, as much as he did the French. But once the Truman administration took the position that the struggle in Indochina was part of a global Communist movement, the anti-colonial rebellion in Southeast Asia was destined to become a focal point of the Cold War.

After years of fighting, the French public grew tired of the war. Predictions of victory by French generals and politicians had proven to be hollow promises. In desperation, the French military command hoped to find a solution to the elusiveness of the Viet Minh guerrillas, to entice the Vietnamese to stand up and wage a conventional battle. The bait was the enticement to attack the remote outpost of Dien Bien Phu, near the border of Laos. If the Viet Minh took the bait, it would result in a conventional showdown and they would be crushed. The French, after all, possessed superior firepower and they controlled the air and the roads leading to Dien Bien Phu.

General Vo Nguyen Giap, the military genius of the Viet Minh, decided to oblige the French, but only after he had made adequate preparations for the battle. With great difficulty he managed to bring into combat heavy artillery, which the Viet Minh had not used previously to any great extent. To the surprise of the French, Giap managed to place the artillery on the hilltops overlooking the valley of Dien Bien Phu, and the decisive battle of the war began. The French soon realized their position was doomed and they appealed for U.S. intervention. Some of President Eisenhower's advisors urged a nuclear strike, but Eisenhower rejected this option because he understood that nuclear weapons are tools of destruction, not war. It made no sense to incinerate Dien Bien Phu—French and Vietnamese alike—to "save" it. Eisenhower refused to become involved in Vietnam, particularly after the Senate majority leader, Lyndon Baines Johnson, told him that the U.S. people would not support another war in Asia, particularly in light of the fact that the cease-fire in Korea had been signed only the previous year.[10]

The Battle of Dien Bien Phu ("hell in a very small place," in the words of the French historian Bernard Fall) took place in the spring of 1954. In early May the French garrison finally fell and with it some of France's finest soldiers. Two thousand of the French forces died; 10,000 were taken prisoner, and only 73 managed to escape.[11] The French defeat was total and the French role in Indochina was over. The French government and the public both welcomed the end.

By coincidence, the world's leading powers—both Communist and capitalist—were engaged at that time in discussing several issues in Geneva. The French and Vietnamese agreed, after the battle of Dien Bien Phu, to take their dispute to this forum. At the conference, however, the Vietnamese Communists received precious little support from the other Communist powers, the Soviet Union and China, both of whom were more interested in other issues. As a consequence, the talks produced a strange agreement. The Geneva Agreement called for a Vietnam temporarily divided along the 17th parallel, but only until a nationwide election, scheduled for July of 1956, could be held. The election was intended to give the country a single government and president and to bring about the "unity and territorial integrity" of Vietnam. In the meantime, the agreement demanded the neutrality of both regions of Vietnam, north and south.[12]

The U.S. delegates at Geneva were hypnotized by a vision of a monolithic Communism. But they need not have worried. Both the Communist Chinese and the Soviets were more interested in cutting a deal with the French than in coming to the aid of their Vietnamese comrades. It appears that it was the Chinese foreign minster, Zhou Enlai (Chou En-lai), much to the surprise of the French, who first proposed a division of Vietnam. The Vietnamese, under Chinese and Soviet pressure, finally yielded, but they insisted on a dividing line along the 13th parallel, which would leave the Viet Minh two-thirds of the country. The French insisted on the 18th parallel; under Chinese and Soviet pressure, the Vietnamese backed down and accepted the 17th parallel, which cut the country roughly in half. At the farewell banquet, Zhou hinted to the South Vietnamese delegation that he favored a permanent partition of Vietnam. This suggestion reflects China's centuries-old animosity toward Vietnam rather than solidarity among Communist nations.

The Viet Minh also yielded on the question of the timetable for the scheduled election. They wanted an election as soon as possible to cash in on their stunning defeat of the French. It was the Soviet foreign minster, Viacheslav Molotov, who asked rhetorically: "Shall we say two years?"[13] The French and the U.S. delegates quickly endorsed Molotov's proposal. It was the best deal the U.S. delegation could hope to obtain. Secretary of State John Foster Dulles had never been happy with the prospect of pitting a candidate hand-picked by the United States against the popular Ho Chi Minh. He knew full well that a free election throughout all of Vietnam would bring Ho to power. Earlier in the conference, Dulles had cabled the U.S. ambassador in Paris:

> Thus since undoubtedly true that elections might eventually mean unification Vietnam under Ho Chi Minh this makes it all more important that they should be held only as long after cease-fire agreement as possible and in conditions free from intimidation to give democratic elements best chance. We believe important that no date should be set now. . . .[14]

As it was, losing half a nation to Communism did not sit well with Dulles. It was for this reason that the United States refused to sign the Geneva Agreement. In a separate statement, however, the U.S. negotiator General W. Bedell Smith, on behalf of President Dwight Eisenhower, pledged U.S. adherence to the agreement.

The postponement for two years of the creation of a single government for Vietnam had predictable consequences. In a development reminiscent of Korea and Germany, two separate governments came into being: a pro-Western regime in the south (with its capital city of Saigon) and a Communist dictatorship in the north (with the capital in Hanoi). The United States soon began to prop up the anti-Communist government in the south, which it dubbed as "democratic," and which refused to abide by the Geneva Agreement calling for free elections. The elections were never held. Instead, the United States became increasingly tied to the unpopular and repressive regime of Ngo Dinh Diem in South Vietnam. From the very beginning, the United States provided military assistance, as well as economic aid, thus sowing the seeds for direct U.S. intervention once the very existence of the Diem regime was threatened.

For U.S. government leaders, South Vietnam became the gate guarding the "free world," and the United States became "the guardian at the gate." Once that metaphor took root in popular thought, the anti-Communist regime in South Vietnam became identified with the very survival of the United States. For psychological, geopolitical, and domestic political reasons, therefore, U.S.-South Vietnamese relations became a Gordian knot that a succession of U.S. presidents did not dare to cut. When Diem was challenged by an insurgency in the late 1950s, the second Indochina War began.

■ RECOMMENDED READINGS

☐ India and Pakistan

Brown, W. Norman. *The United States and India, Pakistan, Bangladesh.* 3d. ed. Cambridge, Mass.: Harvard University Press, 1972.
    A lucid treatment of Indian independence and partition and the subsequent division of Pakistan.
Hutchins, Francis G. *India's Revolution: Gandhi and the Quit India Movement.* Cambridge, Mass.: University Press, 1973.
    An excellent analysis of Gandhi's role in the Indian nationalist movement.
Merriam, Allen H. *Gandhi vs Jinnah: The Debate Over the Partition of India.* Calcutta: Minerva, 1980.
    Recreates the debate between Gandhi and Jinnah over partition, with many quotations from the speeches and writings of each man.
Thorne, Christopher. *Allies of a Kind: The United States, Britain, and the War with Japan.* Oxford: Oxford University Press, 1978.
    An authoritative study of Britain's wartime and immediate postwar policies regarding its colonies in Asia.

☐ Vietnam

Fall, Bernard. *Hell in a Very Small Place: The Siege of Dien Bien Phu.* Philadelphia: Lippincott, 1966.
    The definitive history of the battle by a recognized French expert.
Fall, Bernard, ed. *Ho Chi Minh on Revolution: Selected Writings, 1920–66.* New York: Praeger, 1967.
    A valuable collection.
The Joint Chiefs of Staff and the War in Vietnam: History of the Indochina Incident, 1940–1954. Washington, D. C.: Joint Chiefs of Staff, 1955; declassified 1981.
    The Pentagon's critical assessment of why the French lost.
Lacouture, Jean. *Ho Chi Minh: A Political Biography.* New York: Random House, 1968.
    The standard biography of the Vietnamese revolutionary.
Patti, Archimedes. *Why Vietnam? Prelude to America's Albatross.* Berkeley: University of California Press, 1980.
    An account of immediate postwar Vietnam by a U.S. OSS officer who established a working relationship with Ho Chi Minh in 1945.

■ NOTES

1. Gandhi's career of passive resistance to the laws of Britain that he considered immoral drew upon the writings of the nineteenth-century U.S. writer Henry David Thoreau, and in turn Gandhi's philosophy influenced the U.S. civil rights leader, Martin Luther King, Jr.

2. As quoted in Francis G. Hutchins, *India's Revolution: Gandhi and the Quit India Movement* (Cambridge, Mass.: Harvard University Press, 1973), p. 143.

3. Churchill once expressed the view that the Indian National Congress represented hardly anybody except lawyers, moneylenders, and the "Hindu priesthood." Ibid., p. 284.

4. Southeast Asia refers to the area of Asia stretching from Burma to the Philippine Islands, and including such countries as Thailand, Vietnam, Indonesia, and Malaysia.

5. Given the large Chinese population in Singapore, the Chinese would have been the majority population in the new Malaysian union that Britain proposed, and it was for this reason that Muslim leaders opposed its creation.

6. Brunei, another British protectorate in northern Borneo, was scheduled to join its neighbors, Sarawak and North Borneo, in becoming members of the new union of Malaysia, but, prompted by Indonesia, it refused to do so at the last minute. It remained a source of contention among Britain, Malaysia, and Indonesia until it attained self-government under British tutelage in 1971. Singapore separated from Malaysia in 1965 and became a sovereign state.

7. Harrison E. Salisbury, *Behind the Lines—Hanoi: December 23, 1966–January 7, 1967* (New York: Harper & Row, 1967), pp. 52–53.

8. Jean Lacouture, *Ho Chi Minh: A Political Biography* (New York: Random House, 1968), pp. 24–25; Chalmer M. Roberts, "Archives Show Ho's Letter," *Washington Post,* September 14, 1969, p. A 25.

9. Bernard B. Fall, *The Two Vietnams: A Political and Military Analysis,* 2nd rev. ed. (New York: Frederick A. Praeger, 1967), pp. 349–350. For an analysis of Bonnet's formula, Bernard B. Fall, *Last Reflections on a War* (Garden City: Doubleday, 1967), pp. 209–223.

10. David Halberstam, *The Best and the Brightest* (New York: Random House, 1969), p. 141; also Stanley Karnow, *Vietnam: A History* (New York: Viking, 1983), p. 197.

11. Bernard B. Fall, "Dienbienphu: A Battle to Remember," in Marvin E. Gettleman, ed., *Vietnam: History, Documents, and Opinions* (Greenwich, Conn.: Fawcett, 1965), p. 107.

12. The text of the Geneva Agreement may be found in several anthologies, as well as in Appendix 2, in George McTurnan Kahin and John W. Lewis, *The United States in Vietnam,* rev. ed. (New York: Delta, 1969), pp. 422–443, particularly the Final Declaration, pp. 441–443.

13. Stanley Karnow, *Vietnam: A History* (New York: Viking, 1983), pp. 198–204.

14. Neil Sheehan, et al., *The Pentagon Papers* (New York: Bantam, 1971), p. 46. Dulles also sent a copy of the cable to the U.S. delegate at Geneva, Bedell Smith. Eisenhower wrote in his memoirs that Ho Chi Minh would have won an election with 80 percent of the vote.

☐ 6

Decolonization in Africa

Africa was the last frontier of white colonialism. At the close of World War II, the European powers—Britain, France, Belgium, Portugal, and Spain—still held firmly to their African colonies, which collectively encompassed virtually the entire continent. But this was soon to change with the awakening of African nationalism. In 1945, there were only three independent nations on the African continent (Ethiopia, Liberia, and South Africa), but by 1970 there were no less than fifty-two independent African nations.

By the mid–1950s the British government recognized the inevitability of decolonization and began preparing for it rather than resisting it. By the end of that decade the French, too, had resigned themselves to the new reality, and they, too, willingly handed over political power to the nationalist leaders in all of their African colonies, except Algeria. The 1960s in Africa were full of excitement and expectation as power changed hands from the white colonial rulers to new black African rulers who were flushed with nationalistic pride and eager to face the new challenges of nationhood. The transition was remarkably smooth and was achieved faster and with far less bloodshed than an earlier generation—black or white—dreamt possible.

The decolonization process in Africa differed from region to region and colony to colony, and it is therefore difficult, if not impossible, to generalize about it. Africa has two distinct regions: North Africa, bordering the Mediterranean Sea, and sub-Saharan Africa, consisting of the remainder of the continent south of the Sahara Desert. And there are distinct areas within the sub-Saharan region, namely, West Africa, East Africa, Central Africa, and Southern Africa. The colonial system and the pattern of decolonization varied not only according to region but also according to the European nation involved. British colonial rule differed substantially from the French or Belgian colonial systems. There were also great differences in native populations from colony to colony, and from tribe to tribe within a colony.

The bloodiest struggle for national independence in Africa took place in Algeria, where the French made their last stand for colonial empire. The revolution in Algeria, which lasted for eight years, was an especially violent one, and it may be considered an archetype of an armed struggle for national liberation that features terrorism as a means toward a political end.

■ THE RISE OF NATIONALISM

The tribal make-up of the African population had an important bearing on the decolonization process. The various colonies that sought nationhood had boundaries that had been artificially created by the Europeans in the past century. The black African inhabitants of any given colony were not usually all of the same tribe, and in some cases one tribe's area was in more than one colony. The growth of nationalism required that loyalty to tribe be shifted to loyalty to nation. The timing of decolonization in the various colonies therefore depended, to a great extent, on the growth of national consciousness and the development of a sense of political unity in the native population. This was a slow process and was still far from complete in the 1950s. The persistence of tribal loyalties retarded the growth of nationalism and the birth of independent nations in Africa, and it continued to plague the new African nations once independence was granted.

Prior to World War II, European colonial rule was hardly challenged by the subject peoples of Africa. The colonial administrations seemed so secure that they needed little military force to protect them. In some cases, especially in British colonies, this was achieved by use of the protectorate system, whereby local African rulers were allowed to retain considerable autonomy and were protected by the colonial "overlords." Local rulers were made more secure by the military, political, and financial support supplied by their colonial masters. Also, the European rulers used the divide-and-rule method, whereby they retarded or blocked the development of African unity, or even tribal unity, that might threaten their colonial rule. In general, the Africans, the majority of whom were illiterate, viewed the Europeans with mixed awe and fear, and they were hesitant to attempt armed insurrection. And since political consciousness remained relatively low, there seemed little prospect of an effective, organized anti-colonialist action by the African blacks.

Gradually this situation changed as more Africans received an education—ironically, at the hands of the Europeans—and gained more experience in and exposure to the world of the Europeans. The very presence of Europeans in Africa fundamentally altered African society, particularly in the cities. On the one hand, the Europeans created a labor class among the blacks, whose cheap labor was exploited; and on the other hand, the Europeans created new educational and economic opportunities as well as new models for the Africans. One might say that colonialism carried within it the seeds of its own destruction, especially when the colonial powers were nations that espoused democracy and civil liberties. Some Africans, the more privileged and able among them, became well educated, urbanized, and Westernized. Thus, after several generations under colonial rule, a native elite emerged, marked by its Western education and values. It is this class that first developed a sense of grievance and frustration, and then a political consciousness marked by a strong desire to liberate black Africans from colonial rule. It was from this class that the new leaders of the independence movements emerged: leaders who educated their fellow Africans and aroused in them a political consciousness and who established bonds with nationalist leaders of other colonies to strengthen their mutual endeavor for independence. The bond among these new nationalist leaders developed into a pan-Africanist movement in which they found unity in the cause of liberating the whole of Africa from colonial rule.

Although some signs of African restiveness appeared in the prewar period, especially as African businesspeople and workers felt the effects of the Great Depression of the 1930s, it was not until World War II that nationalism and the demand for independence gained strength in Africa. Some African leaders pointed out that their people, who had been called upon to participate in that war to help defeat tyranny and defend liberty, deserved their just reward, a greater measure of that liberty. Their military experience in the war suggested a means of gaining national independence —the use of armed force. They were also stimulated by the example of colonies in other areas of the world, mainly in Asia, winning their independence from the same Europeans who ruled them. These new nations, especially Nehru's India, vigorously championed the cause of decolonization in the United Nations and other forums. The founding of the United Nations also gave heart to the African nationalists, who looked forward to the day when their new nations would join its ranks as full-fledged member nations. It may be added that initially the two superpowers, the United States and the Soviet Union, both urged early decolonization. All these factors contributed to the growing force of nationalism in Africa in the postwar period.

As important as the growth of nationalism in Africa was in preparing the way for independence, that objective would not have been achieved so swiftly or smoothly had Britain, France, and the other colonial nations not come to the realization that it was not in their interest to perpetuate their colonial empires on that continent. Economically underdeveloped colonies were increasingly viewed as both an economic and political liability. The British were the first to come to that realization, but within the decade of the 1950s the French and Belgians also came to the same view.

POLITICAL AFFILIATION

FRANCE

BRITAIN

PORTUGAL

ITALY

BELGIUM

SPAIN

INDEPENDENT

OTHER (or MIXED)

COLONIAL AFRICA (1945)

■ THE BRITISH DEPARTURE

The British colonial system after the war envisioned eventual independence for its colonies. In a gradual, step-by-step manner, the British permitted greater participation by the native peoples in the governing of their colonies. They established executive and legislative councils to advise the governors of the colonies, and began to appoint a few well-educated, black Africans to these councils. Next, black political leaders were permitted to seek election to the legislative council. Once this was granted, the nationalist leaders began convening national congresses and organizing political parties, which, of course, became organs of nationalistic, anti-imperialist propaganda. They also began agitating for expanding the right to vote in the legislative council elections. The granting of universal suffrage (extending the right to vote to native populations) was the turning point, for it paved the way for the nationalist, pro-independence parties to gain power. According to the parliamentary system that operated in British colonies, the party that won the election and gained the majority in the legislative council earned a majority of seats in the executive council. The leader of the majority party was then chosen to fill the post of chief minister. That person was usually a charismatic figure who had long been recognized as the leader of the national independence movement. Typically, the one chosen was an able and articulate leader, who had a Western education, had spent many years as a political organizer and agitator, and had spent not a few years in the jails of the British colonial administration before gaining the opportunity to lead the independence party to power. Finally, when the British authorities judged that the new ruler could maintain order and govern responsibly, they prepared for a transfer of power to this responsible leader and party and granted the colony self-rule and ultimately full independence.

This procedure took place first in the Gold Coast, which became the first of Britain's African colonies to gain independence. In this West African colony, the able nationalist leader, Kwame Nkrumah, organized an effective political organization and aggressively fought for independence. He took advantage not only of the legal political process, but also of various forms of illegal political pressure, including "positive action"—namely, strikes and boycotts. In 1951, in the first election under universal suffrage, Nkrumah managed his party's campaign while sitting in a British prison. His party won a large majority, and on the basis of this electoral victory, the British governor released Nkrumah, now a national hero, and granted him a seat on the executive council. Three years later the colony, now renamed Ghana, was made self-governing under Nkrumah's leadership, and in March 1957 Nkrumah, now prime minister, was able to announce that Ghana had won its full independence.

Kwame Nkrumah, on a visit to the United States addresses a New York audience. (*National Archives*)

Kenyan Prime Minister Jomo Kenyatta, Nov. 1964. Ruler of Kenya from independence in 1963 until death in 1980. (*National Archives*)

Ghana immediately became the model for other African independence movements, and Nkrumah became the continent's most outspoken champion of liberation. In 1958 Nkrumah invited leading African politicians, representing African peoples from the entire continent, to a series of two conferences at Accra, the capital of Ghana. These conferences (the first in April and the second in December 1958) greatly promoted the cause of pan-African unity. It was at these conferences that the Organization of African Unity was created. The delegates at the December 1958 conference unanimously endorsed Nkrumah's pronouncement that all Africans must work together for the complete liberation of all of Africa.

The demand for independence thus spread rapidly across Africa. In general, the British were more responsive to these demands than were the other Europeans. The British attempted to institute a decolonization process similar to that employed in Ghana in its other colonies in Africa, but the timing differed according to the particular circumstances involved. For example, in Nigeria, the most heavily populated British colony whose nationalist leaders were among the earliest and most vocal in demanding liberation, the process was delayed by serious tribal conflicts. And in East Africa, Kenya's independence was forestalled by other, very different problems.

Kenya, like some other British colonies in Eastern and Southern Africa (but unlike those in Western Africa), was a settlers' colony, meaning that there were European settlers on the land. These white settlers, numbering about 50,000, lived in the Kenyan highlands, possessed the best lands, and discriminated against the black population in numerous ways. They were, of course, opposed to any independence movement based on majority rule. Instead, they insisted upon the creation of a multiracial state that would permit them to maintain their land, wealth, power, and privilege. The largest tribe in Kenya, the Kikuyu, reacted against the domination of the white settlers, and in 1952 it launched a movement known as the Mau Mau. The primary aim of the Mau Mau was to return the land to the black population, which had become overcrowded on reservations. The Mau Mau uprising terrorized the British settlers, but it in fact directed most of its violence toward other blacks who collaborated with the British. The Mau Mau were forcibly suppressed by 1955, but the threat of continued violence remained long afterward to hamper the decolonization process.

The Kikuyu and other tribes eventually formed a national party under the able leadership of Jomo Kenyatta. Kenyatta, a Western-educated member of the Kikuyu tribe, had languished in a British jail for over seven years as a political prisoner. After he was released in 1959, he led his party to electoral victories and eventually to independence in December 1963. Kenyatta's party and the outgoing British colonial authorities worked out a political formula, embodied in a new constitution, designed to provide for majority rule and yet protect the white minority. Still, fear caused most of the settlers to leave. But those who remained in the country were not victimized by Kenya's black majority nor by the new government. Under Kenyatta's enlightened rule, Kenya became one of the most politically stable of Africa's new nations—at least until the mid–1970s.

In South-Central Africa there remained three British settler colonies: Nyasaland, Northern Rhodesia, and Southern Rhodesia. These three joined together to form a federation in 1953, partly for economic reasons and partly as a means of retaining rule by the white minorities. However, in response to increasing pressure by the majority black populations, the British dissolved the federation and imposed on Nyasaland and Northern Rhodesia constitutions guaranteeing majority rule, thus ending white minority rule. In 1961 Nyasaland under black rule became independent Malawi, and in 1963 Northern Rhodesia became the African-ruled state of Zambia. In Southern Rhodesia, however, a white minority regime, led by Ian Smith, defied the British government and its own black majority by rejecting its British-made, majority-rule constitution and by unilaterally declaring its independence in 1965. Only after prolonged guerrilla attacks by African nationalist parties from bases in neighboring countries and sustained international pressure did Smith finally relent, accepting a plan in 1976 to allow majority rule two years afterward. Continued fighting among rival nationalist parties delayed until 1979 the creation of a black majority government in the country, now known as Zimbabwe.

■ THE FRENCH DEPARTURE

The French colonial system was different from the British, and this meant that the decolonization process was also different, even though the timetable was similar. The aim of French colonial policy had been the assimilation of its African colonies into the French empire and the transformation of the African natives into French citizens. The blacks were enjoined to abandon their own culture in favor of the "superior" French civilization. They were taught the French language and culture, and the elite among them received their higher education at French universities. No attempt was ever made to prepare the native Africans for independence; however, because the colonies were part of the French empire, they were permitted to send elected representatives to Paris where they held seats in the French National Assembly.

There always was a problem with the French program of assimilation in that it assumed that the population of the French African colonies wanted to become and in fact were somehow capable of becoming "French." In the case of Algeria, the assimilation of Muslim Arabs proved to be impossible, as the French settlers and the Arabs both rejected it. The Arabs always understood that they were, first and foremost, conquered subjects. The lot of the Africans south of the Sahara was little different. There was no point for black schoolchildren to recite the lessons written for their counterparts in Paris: "Our ancestors the Gauls had blue eyes and blond hair." At its worst, assimilation as Paris envisioned it was racist; at its best, it was unabashedly ethnocentric. A greater French union of France and the former colonies could only have succeeded on the basis of equality and on the recognition of cultural and racial diversity.

Until the mid–1950s none of the short-lived cabinets in postwar France responded to the African demands for self-rule. However, at this juncture, shortly after abandoning its colonial empire in Asia, France was faced with a revolutionary movement in Algeria and a growing demand for independence in its other African colonies. With the exception of Algeria, where the French refused to budge, the African colonies of France were surprised to find a new French receptiveness to change. The French no longer insisted upon assimilation; instead, they began to search for a workable alternative.

African nationalists who desired the liberation of their people still found it necessary to work within the French system. The most politically successful of the black African leaders from the French colonies was Félix

Houphouët-Boigny, a medical doctor from the Ivory Coast. Shortly after World War II, he had taken the lead in forming an African political party, which championed the cause of the blacks. As a member of the French National Assembly, Houphouët-Boigny played a leading role in drawing up a new colonial policy that set in motion the movement for colonial self-government. The effect of this bill, which was passed by the assembly in 1956, was to permit greater autonomy for the separate French colonies, which heretofore were under one centralized colonial administration. Each colony was now to have a French prime minister and African vice-ministers, and elections for legislative assemblies under universal suffrage. Meanwhile, in the various French colonies, Houphouët-Boigny's party established branches, which began organizing for elections under the banner of nationalism.

Still, it remained the intention of France to maintain some form of indirect control over its African colonies. A plan for continued association was endorsed by President Charles de Gaulle, after he came to power in Paris in May 1958. Later that year he offered the twelve separate sub-Saharan colonies the option of membership in the French Community or immediate and full independence. The former meant autonomy, but continued association with France; more importantly, it meant continued French economic and military aid. This was the preference of all of the colonies except Guinea, which courageously and perhaps foolishly opted instead for independence. In response to Guinea's decision, France immediately pulled out all of its personnel and equipment and terminated all economic aid in hopes of forcing the maverick back into the fold. Guinea, however, stuck with its decision.

The example of Guinea, and nearby Ghana as well, inspired the nationalist leaders in the neighboring French colonies in West Africa. In 1960, after two years of agitation and negotiations, President de Gaulle granted independence to all of the remaining French colonies in sub-Saharan Africa. These new nations were relatively unprepared either politically or economically for independence, and consequently they tended to remain politically unstable, remaining therefore economically dependent on France for years to come.

■ THE FRENCH STRUGGLE IN ALGERIA

France's determination to retain control over Algeria must be viewed in the historical context of its prior struggle in Vietnam. The long war in Vietnam had drained the French people emotionally, physically, and economically. When defeat came in 1954, most of the French accepted the loss of Vietnam without bitter recrimination. They yielded to fate. At the outset of the Vietnamese conflict in 1946, French society had supported the suppression of the Vietnamese independence movement; eight years later, Vietnam had become a burden to be lifted from their shoulders. When in the spring of 1954 Prime Minister Pierre Mendès France promised to end the war by granting the Vietnamese independence, there were few dissenting voices. With the Geneva Conference of July 1954, the French colonial presence on the Asian mainland came to an inglorious end.

Yet, within a few months of the Geneva settlement, the French were once more faced with the prospect of losing a colony. This time it was Algeria. The same people, however, who had been willing to abandon Vietnam, now took a different position. Having lost one colony, they were in no mood to contemplate another seeming humiliation—another defeat at the hands of a colonized people, a people of a different color and religion. At stake were France's honor, its role as a great power, and its position in Africa. On the Algerian question, therefore, they refused to yield.

The French, however, were in no position to invoke any of the traditional justifications for restoration of order in Algeria. Great power politics (where "the powerful exact what they can, and the weak grant what they must" [Thucydides]), colonialism, and racism had all been discredited in the war against Adolf Hitler. The French, therefore, insisted that Algeria was not a colony but an integral part of France, a province across the Mediterranean, in the same manner that Brittany, Alsace, Lorraine, and Provence were provinces of France. France's control of Algeria was more than one hundred years old. More importantly, Algeria was the home of 1 million French citizens who considered themselves to be living in France. The provinces "of Algeria are part of the republic," Premier Pierre Mendès France insisted, "they have been French for a long time. Between it and the mainland, no secession is conceivable. . . . Never will France . . . yield on this fundamental principle." The minister of the interior, François Mitterand, added: "Algeria is France."[1]

France's presence in Algeria dates back to 1830 when its first troops landed. It took the French seventeen years to complete the conquest of the population, which consisted of people who spoke Arabic and professed the faith of Islam, a religion remarkably impervious to Christian missionaries. (For a summary of Islam, see Chapter 15.) In 1848 the first French, Roman Catholic settlers arrived. The French quest for empire in this section of the world thus became a bitter struggle between two cultures and two religions. In 1870–1871, in the wake of France's losing effort in its war with Germany, the Arab population rose in rebellion. This was at last the Algerians' opportunity to rid themselves of French rule. But the rebellion was put down in blood and was followed by the widespread confiscation of Muslim lands. Algeria then became a land divided between the immigrant French, who had seized the best lands along the coast and who enjoyed the rights and protection of French citizenship, and the native Algerians for whom the law

offered little protection. The French have always justified their colonial conquest as part of their civilizing mission. Yet, the blessings of French democracy were meant only for Europeans in Algeria, not for the indigenous Arab
and Muslim population. Democracy and imperialism, after all, never mix
very well.

In the years between the two world wars (1918–1939), the French government repeatedly grappled with the question of the status of native Algerians. Liberals, both French and Algerian, urged the integration of the Muslim Algerians into French society by granting them citizenship without their
first having to convert to Catholicism. To that effect, in 1936 France's premier,
Léon Blum, proposed a bill granting a number of select Arabs—soldiers
with distinguished records in World War I, teachers, graduates from French
institutes—the privilege of French citizenship even though they continued
to profess the faith of their ancestors.² Bitter and unrelenting opposition
killed the bill—and with it the opportunity of integrating Algeria with
France. As a consequence, the fiction of the 1950s that Algeria was a province
of France clashed with the reality of a Muslim, Arabic Algeria distinct from
French civilization.

Algerian integration into French society clearly was a pipe dream pursued by a liberal minority. The French settlers in Algeria refused to even consider it. And the same may be said for most Muslims. They, too, could not
envision themselves as French; instead, they were Arabs and Muslims. As
one Muslim scholar put it: "The Algerian people are not French, do not wish
to be and could not be even if they did wish."³ Children in Muslim schools
were taught to recite: "Islam is my religion. Arabic is my language. Algeria is
my country."⁴

World War II was fought for the noblest of reasons: against fascism, racism, and colonialism, and for democracy and human rights. It was little wonder that upon the conclusion of this war the colonial peoples in Asia and
Africa demanded the implementation of the ideals for which the war had
been fought. To complicate matters for the Europeans, natives of these colonies had been recruited to fight precisely for these ideals. Inevitably, after
the war the Algerians presented the bill for their services to the French.

The first manifestation of the new Algerian attitude became apparent
even before the guns fell silent in Europe. On May 1, 1945, during the May
Day celebrations in Algiers, demonstrators staged an unauthorized march
in which Algerians carried banners denouncing French rule and demanding
Algerian independence. The French attempt to halt the demonstration led
to the deaths of ten Algerians and one Frenchman. The French then boasted
that they had ended all disorder. But several days later, on May 8, 1945, the
V-E (Victory-in-Europe) day celebrations in the Algerian town of Sétif turned
into a riot. The French had hoisted the *tricolor* in honor of the victory of the
Allies. Algerian participants in the celebrations, however, had their own

agenda. They came again with banners calling for the independence of Algeria—and one young man defiantly carried Algeria's forbidden green and white flag with the red crescent. A police officer shot him to death.

This act touched off an anti-colonial rebellion in Algeria. The heavy-handed French response brought into combat the police, troops, airplanes to bomb and strafe villages, and warships to shell coastal settlements. The British, as they did later that year in Vietnam when they secured that colony for the French upon the defeat of the Japanese, came to the assistance of the French colonial administration when they provided airplanes to carry French troops from France, Morocco, and Tunisia. When the fighting was over, the French conducted wholesale arrests—the traditional French policy after colonial outbreaks. The French killed between 1,165 (according to the official French count) and 45,000 Arabs (according to Algerian estimates).[5] The OSS (the Office for Strategic Services), the U.S. wartime intelligence-gathering organization, put the number of casualties between 16,000 and 20,000, including 6,000 dead.[6] The rebellion claimed the lives of 103 Europeans. On May 13, the French staged a military parade in Constantine to impress upon the Algerians the decisive nature of their victory. The Algerians quickly found out that World War II had been a war for the liberation of the French from German occupation, not for the liberation of the French colonies from French domination.

French society was unanimous and determined in its response to Algerian defiance. In Paris, politicians of all stripes, including the Communist Party—whose official position was one of anti-colonialism and which later opposed the war in Indochina—strongly supported the suppression of the revolt in Algeria. The French colonial authorities admitted that the violence had been in part the result of food shortages. But they did not acknowledge that the rebellion had been fueled by a deep-seated opposition to French rule in Algeria.

For the next nine years relative stability prevailed in Algeria. But four months after France had signed the Geneva Agreement (July 1954), which extricated it from Vietnam, it faced another anti-colonial rebellion in Algeria.

The ensuing struggle in Algeria was a war of extraordinary brutality. The revolution was organized by the FLN (*Front de libération nationale*), which turned to the traditional weapon of the weak—terror.[7] Terrorists have little hope to defeat an adversary whose military strength is formidable. Instead, they seek to intimidate and to keep the struggle alive in the hope of breaking the other side's will. The FLN resorted to bombing attacks against European targets; the Europeans then, logically and predictably, bombed Muslim establishments. The French military responded with its own version of terror by executing and torturing prisoners in order to uncover the FLN's organizational structure. In 1956, Parliament—with the express support of the Communist Party—granted General Jacques Massu of the Tenth Parachute

Division absolute authority to do whatever was necessary, and with this the "Battle of Algiers" began. It ended with the destruction of the FLN's leadership. Brute force had triumphed over brute force and seemed to have settled the issue. Within a year the colonial uprising appeared to be over.

But the rebellion continued, nevertheless, as new leaders emerged. Algerians, such as Ferhat Abbas, who had devoted their lives to cooperation with the French, joined the rebellion. The 1 million French settlers in Algeria demanded an increase in military protection and they received it. French military strength, initially at 50,000, rose to 400,000. The bloodletting and the atrocities continued. At the end, about 2 million Arabs (out of a population of 9 million) had been driven from their villages to become refugees, and perhaps 1 million had died.

Gradually, many in France began to comprehend the unpalatable truth that Algeria would never be French. By the late 1950s, the French, who had been unified on the Algerian question in 1954, began an intense debate on the subject. (The French in Algeria always remained adamant that there could be no surrender. For them, this was not a subject for consideration.) The war had become too costly, both in economic and political terms. It divided French society to the point that it threatened to touch off a civil war. One of the telling arguments against the continued French occupation of Algeria was that it corrupted the young people who were serving in a French army guilty of repeated atrocities. Many French citizens (not unlike many of their U.S. counterparts during the war in Vietnam) became more concerned about the effect the killing, the brutality, and the torture had on their own society than the impact of such actions on the Arab victims. The costs of the continuing struggle were outweighing the benefits. Many of the French, therefore, came to the conclusion that the time had come to quit Algeria.

It took an exceptional political leader to take France out of Algeria because the nation, which had been united in its desire to get out of Vietnam only four years earlier, remained bitterly divided on this question. The colonials in Algeria, who as French citizens insisted on the protection of what they perceived to be their rights, and the army remained determined to stay. By 1957, the greatest peril to France was not the Algerian uprising, but a sequence of "white rebellions," which threatened to topple the constitutional government of France itself. Only a politician of the stature of General Charles de Gaulle was able to accomplish the difficult task of resolving the Algerian dilemma without plunging France into civil war. Charles de Gaulle had emerged in World War II as the sacred symbol of French resistance to Nazi Germany and had thus salvaged France's honor. In May 1958, he announced that he was ready to serve his nation once again. After he was installed as the new French president in June 1958, he sought at first to resolve the conflict by offering the Algerians what all previous French governments had refused. He announced the rectification of inequalities between Arabs and Europeans and a plan to hold elections on the basis of equal voting power for all Algerians. In this way, Algeria was to remain a part of France. But this solution, which might have worked before the rebellion began in 1954, was now rejected by the Arab nationalists. An elementary revolutionary logic was at work, and nothing short of full independence would do. De Gaulle's choices were now narrowed down to two. He could either crush the rebellion or withdraw. Courageously he chose the latter. In the summer of 1960, de Gaulle began talking publicly of an *"Algérie algérienne,"* which, he declared would have "its own government, its institutions and its laws."[8] De Gaulle and many of his people understood at last that the time had come to put to rest the myth that native Algerians could be French and that Algeria was part and parcel of France.

In July 1962, de Gaulle quit Algeria in the face of intense opposition within his own army and from the settlers in Algeria, many of whom left for France and never forgave de Gaulle for his act of betrayal. When de Gaulle took an inspection trip to Algeria in December 1960, the Europeans organized a general strike to protest his policies. The demonstrators demanded an *"Algérie française!"* But it was to no avail. De Gaulle made a point of addressing Algerian gatherings only. It was only a matter of time until the French authorities withdrew from Algeria. Only 170,000 French residents remained when Algeria formally declared its independence in July 1962. This event essentially marked the end of France as a colonial power.

■ THE BELGIAN AND PORTUGUESE DEPARTURES

The Belgian government paid even less attention than France to preparing its colonial possession, the Congo, for self-government, and yet it quite abruptly granted independence to that huge colony in June 1960. The Belgian Congo, which had once been the private domain of King Leopold, was one of the largest and richest of the African colonies. The Belgian colonial policy of enlightened paternalism was designed to allow the African workers a modicum of material advancement while denying them political rights. In response to the wave of nationalism that had spread over the continent, and especially to the outbreak of insurrection in the city of Leopoldville in early January 1959, the Belgian government hastily issued plans for the creation of what was meant to be a new democratic order for the Congo. The new government in Leopoldville was to be based on universal suffrage and was to guarantee the liberties of all of its people and eliminate any further racial discrimination. In January 1960, the Belgian government made the stunning announcement that in only six months it would formally transfer power to the new sovereign state of the Republic of the Congo.

However, the turbulent events that followed independence suggest that the Congo was ill-prepared for self-rule and that it had been too hastily abandoned by Belgium. The explosion of tribal rivalry and separatist wars was, in part, the consequence of the lack of development of a nationalism sufficient to pull its approximately two hundred tribes into a national union. Even before the Belgians exited, a rift had developed between the two most noted nationalist leaders: Patrice Lumumba, who favored a unitary state with a strong central government, and Joseph Kasavubu, a long-time nationalist leader who insisted upon a loose federation of autonomous regions based on tribal affiliation. No sooner had these two leaders established rival regimes than Moise Tshombe, the separatist leader of the rich copper-mining province of Katanga, announced the secession of that province from the new republic. The result was not only a complicated three-sided political struggle, but a tragic war that soon involved outside forces, including UN forces, the CIA, and Soviets. It was an extraordinarily violent war that lasted over two years and left tens of thousands dead.

The Congolese army, weakened by the mutiny of black soldiers against their white officers and divided in loyalty between the contending leaders, Lumumba and Kasavubu, was unable to maintain order or prevent savage attacks by blacks against the white settlers. Nor could either leader match the Katanga forces of Tshombe, whose army remained under the command of Belgian officers. Tshombe, who had the support of the Union Minière, the huge corporation that controlled the copper mines, and of the white settlers, invited Belgian reinforcements into Katanga to defend its independence. Desperate to maintain Congolese national unity, Lumumba requested military assistance from the United Nations. The UN Security Council called upon Belgium to withdraw its forces from the Congo and dispatched a peacekeeping force with instructions to prevent a civil war. The UN intervention, however, proved unsuccessful, as its member states were in disagreement about its role in the Congo.[9] Frustrated by the UN's failure to act decisively against Katanga, and still unable to defeat Katanga's Belgian-led forces, Lumumba then turned to the Soviet Union for support. This complicated the situation all the more as the Western powers sought to make use of the UN presence in the Congo as a means to check Soviet influence. Lumumba was then overthrown by a military coup (supported by the CIA) and delivered to his Katangan enemies, who murdered him.

After a long and costly struggle, the Republic of the Congo, later renamed Zaire, managed to survive with the province of Katanga included, but only after Kasavubu brought Tshombe and his followers into the government on their own terms. About a year later, in November 1965, both Kasavubu and Tshombe were overthrown in a military coup by General Joseph Mobutu, who then established a lasting, brutal, and dreadfully corrupt regime. In addition to having a ruinous effect on the political and economic development of Zaire, the Katangan war and its aftermath severely damaged the credibility of African nationalists who had insisted on the readiness of Africans for self-government. It also had the effect of tarnishing the reputation of the United Nations as a neutral, peacekeeping body, and of draining its resources as well. Moreover, the conflict in the Congo proved to be a forerunner of recurrent East-West power struggles now shifting into the arena of the Third World.

Not all of Africa was liberated from colonial rule by the end of the 1960s. In Northern Africa, Algeria was the scene of a bloody revolution for independence from France, and in Southern Africa, Portugal still stubbornly held onto its colonies, Angola and Mozambique. Portugal, a very small country that had remained under the dictatorship of Dr. Oliveira Salazar from 1929 to 1969, regarded its African possessions—which together amounted to twenty times the size of Portugal itself—as "overseas provinces." Thus, they were considered an integral part of the nation and not colonies at all. Portugal savagely suppressed a nationalist insurrection in Angola in 1961, killing about 50,000 people, and quashed a similar uprising in Mozambique in 1964. The Salazar regime ignored the UN condemnation of its colonial policies and continued its use of military force to subdue guerrilla resistance in the colonies. Not until the autocratic regime was overthrown in Portugal in April 1974 did that country take steps to grant independence to its African colonies. The transfer of power to an independent Angola in 1975 was accompanied by the eruption of warfare between rival nationalist parties, each of which had international supporters, and the country remains a scene of domestic turmoil and East-West contention. The Portuguese, exhausted by the conflict in Angola, decided in June 1975 to grant independence to Mozambique as well.

After most of Africa was liberated by the early 1960s, the remaining remnants of colonialism and white minority rule in Southern Africa served as an impetus for pan-Africanism. African leaders sought an early end not only to colonialism but to the white supremacist rule in the independent nation of South Africa (see Chapter 11). Although they persisted in their quest for black African solidarity, the goal remained elusive, partly because the concept itself remained vague and ill-defined. While all the black African leaders affirmed that the liberation of the entire African continent was their first order of business, they in fact lacked the military power and the economic leverage, either singularly or in unison, to achieve that objective. In reality the various leaders were forced to direct their immediate attention to the very difficult tasks of nation building awaiting them in their own countries. They were confronted with a host of political, economic, and military problems, which came with independence. The greatest political challenge was that of creating and maintaining an effective central government whose authority was accepted and whose power was sufficient to enforce its laws throughout the entire nation.

The African nationalist leaders who had led in the struggle for independence also championed the cause of democracy, but it soon became clear that the attainment of the former did not guarantee the success of the latter. Even where genuine efforts were made to establish democratic institutions and to operate according to declared democratic principles, those who gained power by the democratic electoral process were, all too often, loath to risk their positions in another election. As a result the principle of a loyal opposition (that is, a multiparty system) never became firmly entrenched. Eventually, most elected African governments gave way to dictatorships, the notable exceptions being Senegal, the Ivory Coast, Tanzania, and Botswana.

The rulers of the newly independent African nations, especially the former French colonies, also found it extremely difficult to maintain a sound economy and raise their people's standard of living—as they had earlier promised. They were soon to find that independence itself brought no magic solution to the struggle against poverty, and that they would remain far more dependent economically on their former colonial rulers than they had hoped. One unanticipated financial burden on the new governments of Africa was the ever-increasing cost of building armed forces that were deemed necessary to guard the borders and maintain internal security. Eventually, such armies everywhere became the major threat to the security of African rulers and their governments.

Yet, despite the numerous problems that lay ahead (see Chapter 11), the liberation of Africa stands as a momentous historical event. The peoples of the new nations of Africa and their proud leaders were swept up in the wave of nationalism and were understandably euphoric about the future of nationhood. In retrospect, however, the tasks of nation building, economic growth, and the maintenance of democratic institutions proved to be more difficult than anyone had anticipated.

■ RECOMMENDED READINGS

□ Black Africa

Cameron, James. *The African Revolution.* New York: Random House, 1961.
    A stirring contemporary account of the independence movement in Africa by a British journalist.
Cartey, Wilfred, and Martin Kilson, eds. *The African Reader: Independent Africa.* New York: Random House, 1970.
    A useful anthology of writings by participants in the African independence movement.
Oliver, Roland, and Anthony Atmore. *Africa Since 1800.* 3rd ed. New York: Cambridge University Press, 1981.
    A survey focusing mainly on former British colonial regions.
Mazrui, Ali A. *The Africans: A Triple Heritage.* Boston: Little, Brown, 1986.
    An introduction to the culture and politics of Africa by a native of Kenya whose emphasis

is on the European colonial heritage; a companion volume of the BBC/WETA television series.

Mazrui, Ali A., and Michael Tidy. *Nationalism and New States in Africa*. London: Heineman Educational Books, 1984.
 A recent survey of the decolonization process in Africa, focusing on Ghana.

☐ Algeria

Fanon, Frantz. *A Dying Colonialism*. New York: Monthly Review Press, orig. 1959; English edition, 1965.
 By a native of the West Indies, a psychiatrist, whose focus is the psychological oppression and disorientation French colonialism created in Algeria.

Fanon, Frantz. *The Wretched of the Earth*. New York: Grove Press, 1963.
 Fanon's most influential book on the impact of colonialism.

Horne, Alistair. *A Savage War of Peace: Algeria, 1954–1962*. New York: Viking Press, 1977.
 Another fine explanation of a brutal anticolonial conflict.

Talbott, John. *The War Without a Name: France in Algeria, 1954–1962*. New York: Random House, 1980.
 A fine history of the Algerian war.

■ NOTES

1. Pierre Mendès France and François Mitterand cited in John Talbott, *The War Without a Name: France in Algeria, 1954–1962* (New York: Knopf, 1980), p. 39.

2. During the first year, 21,000 Moslems were to be admitted to French citizenship. In later years the list was to be increased.

3. Abdelhamid Ben Badis, one of the founders in 1931 of the Society of Reformist Ulema, in Tanya Matthews, *War in Algeria: Background for Crisis* (New York: Fordham University Press, 1961), p. 20.

4. Ibid., p. 20.

5. Frantz Fanon, *A Dying Colonialism* (New York: Monthly Review Press, 1965), p. 74.

6. "Moslem Uprisings in Algeria, May 1945," Record Group 226, OSS Research & Analysis Report 3135, May 30, 1945, pp. 1–6, National Archives, Washington, D.C.

7. The distinction between terrorism and guerrilla tactics has always been blurred, particularly in the last few years when the charge of terrorism has become a political buzzword. Guerrilla action is a type of warfare (which frequently uses terror); terror is a form of political propaganda. The FLN in Algeria was primarily a terrorist organization (similar to the PLO). The guerrillas of the NLF in Vietnam, no stranger to the uses of terror, went into combat. (All guerrilla movements have been labeled by their opponents as terrorists, bandits, and the like.) We would like to point out that all the studies on contemporary terror have yet to come up with a generally accepted definition of the term. Richard E. Rubenstein, *Alchemists of Revolution: Terrorism in the Modern World* (New York: Basic Books, 1987) defines it as "politically motivated violence engaged in by small groups claiming to represent the masses." That would include the FLN and the French government. To complicate matters further, no one ever admits to being a terrorist.

8. The political discussions revolved around the fate of Algeria: *Algérie française* or *Algérie algérienne*. In 1947, de Gaulle had tied the fate of Algeria to the "sovereignty of France! This means that we must never allow the fact that Algeria is our domain to be called into ques-

tion in any way whatever from within or from without." For de Gaulle's position in 1960, see Samuel B. Blumenfeld's epilogue in Michael Clark, *Algeria in Turmoil: The Rebellion, Its Causes, Its Effects, Its Future* (New York: Grosset & Dunlap, 1960), pp. 443–454.

9. Secretary General of the United Nations Dag Hammarskjold made great eforts to resolve conflicts among the disputants in the Congo and among member states of the United Nations disputing the Congo issue. In this effort, he made frequent trips between the UN headquarters in New York and the Congo, and on a trip to Katanga in September 1960 he was killed in an airplane crash.

7

The Middle East:
The Arab-Israeli Wars

The Middle East did not escape the anti-colonial rebellions of the twentieth century. There, however, the resistance to foreign domination was first directed not against a European power, but the Ottoman Turkish empire, which had been in control of the region for several centuries. But with the defeat of Turkey in World War I, the Middle East fell under the dominion of other outside forces, namely, Britain and France. Thus, the Arab states merely exchanged one master for another and, predictably, the anti-colonial movement continued. The result was the gradual weakening of the hand of the European colonial overlords who slowly began to understand that ultimately they would have to leave. The Arab world had always been impervious to European cultural penetration, a lesson hammered home to the French during their bloody attempt to suppress the Algerian revolution. Arab nationalism and culture steeped in the Islamic tradition undermined, gradually yet irrevocably, the French and British positions in the Middle East.

Yet, by a twist of fate, at the same time that Arab cultural and political nationalism began to assert itself, the Middle East saw the introduction in the 1880s of another cultural and political element: the first attempts to recreate a home for the Jews, to reestablish the Biblical Zion in Jerusalem, in a region populated largely by Arabs. The Zionists, primarily of European background, thus launched their experiment at a time when the European presence in the world beyond Europe was under direct challenge and retreat. The subsequent political, religious, and cultural conflict between Arabs and Jews remains a volatile and unresolved issue more than a century later.

■ THE REBIRTH OF ZIONISM

Contemporary Zionism has its origins in the rebirth of European nationalism, which soon became transformed—in Germany and elsewhere—into a virulent manifestation of racism. The late eighteenth and early nineteenth centuries witnessed the revival of romantic national consciousness among Europeans who sought to define their histories, origins, and unique contributions to civilization. The result was an increased fragmentation of what is commonly called European civilization. The Germans, Italians, Russians, and Irish, just to mention a few, discovered in their ancient histories their uniqueness and professed cultural superiority over their neighbors. They all had this in common: they sought to find their proper places in the context of European civilization.

The Jews of Europe were another case in point. Their religion set them apart from the rest of Christian Europe and generally made it impossible for them to achieve cultural and political assimilation. Moreover, the nineteenth century was an extraordinarily race-conscious age. The relative toleration of Jews during the previous century, the Age of Reason, was no more. The legal status of Jews was beginning to deteriorate, particularly in Eastern Europe. As a consequence, a number of European Jews began to contemplate the recreation of the ancient Jewish state in the Biblical land of Zion. The result was the rebirth of the concept of Jewish nationalism.[1] It was intended to become an escape from the destructive fury of a rejuvenated anti-Semitism during the last decades of the nineteenth century.

Appropriately, the father of the concept of a Jewish state was Leon Pinsker, a Jew from Russia, a nation where anti-Semitism had become a state policy. The *pogroms* (anti-Jewish riots) of 1881, in the wake of the assassination of Tsar Alexander II, convinced Pinsker that self-preservation demanded the creation of a Jewish state. Jews made up a large percentage of the revolutionary movement, and, although ethnic Russians carried out the murder of the tsar, the assassination let loose anti-Semitic passions of unprecedented scope and intensity. It produced an exodus of Jews—some went to Palestine, although a much larger number of Jews went to the United States and other nations overseas. In 1882 Pinsker published his pamphlet, *Auto-Emancipation: An Appeal to his People by a Russian Jew.* The book was instrumental in the creation of a Zionist organization (the "Lovers of Zion") that launched the first wave of emigrants to Palestine. By the end of the 1880s, the Jewish population of Palestine was between 30,000 and 40,000, about 5 percent of the population.

In 1897 an Austrian Jew, Theodor Herzl, became the best known publicist of the Zionist cause when he organized the First World Zionist Congress and published his pamphlet, *The Jewish State*. The creation of such a Jewish state, however, faced numerous obstacles. Palestine, as well as nearly the entire Middle East, was in the hands of Turkey, a power that sought to suppress manifestations of Jewish nationalism, as well as resurgent Arab nationalism. It was little wonder that Herzl called the first Zionists "beggars . . . with dreams."[2] The nationalist movements of modern times (that is, since the end of the Middle Ages) have grown up in the main as reactions to foreign imperialism. The Napoleonic Wars gave birth to German nationalism; the Mongol invasion of Russia gave rise to Russian nationalism; American nationalism came with the struggle against the British. Modern Jewish nationalism was the product of an assault on the culture and ultimately the very existence of the Jews. Similarly, the resurgence of Arab nationalism came with the struggle against the Turkish Ottoman empire. Jewish and Arab nationalism thus reappeared at about the same time. Arabs sought to reclaim their lands; desperate Jews sought a safe haven from the gathering fury of anti-Semitism. In the process, both sought the same piece of land.

The early Zionists were slow to grasp the fact that their struggle would ultimately be against the Arabs. Eventually, it became clear to them that the defeat of Turkey would be but the first step of a long journey. David Ben Gurion, one of the early Zionist settlers and later Israel's first prime minister, had overlooked the Arabs until 1916. It was a friend, a Palestinian Arab, who awakened him to the prospect of an Arab-Jewish conflict. The Arab expressed his concern over Ben Gurion's incarceration when he visited the Zionist in a Turkish military prison. "As your friend, I am deeply sorry," he told Ben Gurion, "but as an Arab I am pleased." "It came down on me like a blow," Ben Gurion later wrote, "so there *is* an Arab national movement *here*."[3]

The possibility of a Jewish state came during World War I when Great Britain launched a drive against Turkey, an ally of imperial Germany. In December 1916, the British advanced from Egypt, and in the following month they entered Jerusalem. By this time, the British and their French allies had already decided to carve up the Middle East after Turkey's defeat. By this arrangement, the secret Sykes-Picot Agreement of May 1916, Britain was to extend its influence into Palestine, Iraq, and what shortly became Trans-Jordan while France claimed Lebanon and Syria.

The British did not foresee the troubles ahead. While fighting the Turks, they had enlisted Arab support and had promised them nationhood after the war. These pledges had contributed to anti-Turkish rebellions in

Jerusalem, Damascus, and other cities long controlled by the Turks. At the same time, however, the British government also enlisted Jewish aid, and in return promised a "national home for the Jewish people." This pledge came in 1917 in the Balfour Declaration (named after the British foreign secretary) in a one-page letter to Lord Rothschild, a representative of the Jewish community in England. (The declaration also insisted, however, that "nothing shall be done which may prejudice the civil and religious rights of the existing non-Jewish communities in Palestine.")[4] The declaration and its endorsement later by the League of Nations gave international sanction to what since 1881 had been a haphazard experiment to create a homeland for Jews.

The Arabs have always rejected the Balfour Declaration. The promises made by the British, they argue, were at best limited and conditional. A Jewish "national home" in Palestine, they insist, did not constitute a Jewish state. Moreover, Great Britain had no right to give away Palestine over the heads of its inhabitants, particularly at a time when Britain had not yet gained possession of Palestine. If anything, Britain earlier had promised Palestine to the Arabs in the Hussein-McMahon Letters of 1915–1916. This exchange of letters led to the Hussein-McMahon Agreement of 1916 (between Sherif Hussein, emir of Mecca, and Sir Henry McMahon, Britain's high commissioner in Egypt) whereby the Arabs, in exchange for Britain's recognition of a united Arab state between the Mediterranean and Red Seas, joined Britain in the war against Turkey.

The best that can be said about the British policy is that the authorities in London did their best to satisfy all claimants to the lands of the Middle East that were a part of the British postwar mandate. First, to satisfy the Arabs, they granted Abdullah, the second son of Sherif Hussein, a stretch of territory east of the Jordan River. With this action, the British transferred the easternmost portion of Palestine to what became the Emirate of Trans-Jordan, today's Kingdom of Jordan. The creation of this artificial realm constituted the first partition of Palestine. The remainder of Palestine west of the Jordan River, with its restless Arab and Jewish population, remained under British rule.

The British soon found out, however, that one cannot serve two clients with conflicting claims. Arabs and Jews both suspected that the British were backing away from the commitments they had made to them. Arabs feared that the British were in the process of creating a Zionist state; Jews feared that the British favored the numerically superior Arabs and thus had no intentions of honoring the Balfour Declaration. The British had no clear policy except to try and keep the antagonists apart. The consequences of British fencestraddling was that they were destined to come under a cross fire when they incurred the enmity of both Jews and Arabs.

After World War I, both Jews and Arabs were determined to create their own national states in Palestine. In this age of rejuvenated nationalism, the clash between Zionists and Palestinians became a conflict fueled by passion, anger, and hatred between two nationalist movements insisting on their historic and religious rights to the same land. The Balfour Declaration had asserted the rights of two peoples whose claims and aspirations clashed. The result was that Jews and Arabs acted out a tragedy of classic proportions in which the protagonists became victims of inexorable forces over which they had but little control.

During the 1920s, Jews and Arabs were engaged in mortal combat. Each side engaged in acts of violence, which in turn led to additional violence. Particularly bloody were the riots of 1929, the first instance of large-scale bloodshed between Jews and Arabs. In Jerusalem, in a dispute over the Wailing Wall, 133 Jews and 116 Arabs lost their lives. In Hebron, the Jewish inhabitants, a people with an ancient linear connection to Biblical times, were driven out of the city in a riot that claimed 87 Jewish lives. The British authorities sought to keep the peace but with limited success. Both sides felt that the British had betrayed them for not fulfilling the promises made during the war. In 1939, Britain, in order to placate the Arabs, who had risen in bloody rebellion (1936–1939), issued its controversial White Paper, or position paper. With it the British authorities sought to limit the Jewish population of Palestine to one-third and severely curtail the transfer of land to Jews. (The Jewish population at that time was already at 30 percent, up from 10 percent in 1918.)

The new British directive came at a time when life in Nazi Germany had become unbearable for the Jews. Yet, no country would take them in, and later Hitler initiated his program for the extermination of the Jews. Militant Zionists began to suspect collusion between the British and the Nazis. The British decision created a legacy of bitterness. After the war it led to violence between the British army and militant Jewish organizations, such as the Irgun (*Irgun Zvai Leumi,* or National Military Organization) headed by Menachem Begin.

The destruction of the European Jews at the hands of Nazi Germany during World War II, all too frequently with the collusion of peoples—Poles, Ukrainians, French, and others—who themselves had been conquered by the Germans, seared the consciousness of Jews everywhere. The recreation of the state of Israel now became more than a spiritual quest to return to one's ancient home; it became a matter of self-preservation. Such a state seemed to be the only place where a Jew could be assured a safe haven against the fury of anti-Semitism. Israel would be created by the survivors of the Holocaust, whose actions were constantly marked by the remembrance of that cataclysmic event. (When Egyptian President Gamal Abdel Nasser several years later spoke of the destruction of Israel, its citizens could not help but invoke the memory of Hitler's attempt to annihilate the Jews.)

After World War II, the British decided to wash their hands of Palestine. It was at this point that the United Nations agreed to take its turn in trying to solve this problem. It was clear by then that a single Palestinian state consisting of Arabs and Jews, as the Balfour Declaration had suggested, was an impossibility. Few Zionists and Arabs were interested in such a solution. Both saw themselves as the legitimate heirs to the land of Palestine. Moreover, too much blood had already been shed between them. In November 1947, the United Nations, therefore, called for the creation of separate Israeli and Arab states. Jerusalem, a holy city for both Jews and Muslims, was to have international status with free access for all worshippers. The United Nations decision marked the second partition of Palestine. It divided what was left after the British had initially granted the east bank of the Jordan River to the king of Trans-Jordan.

Nearly all Arabs rejected the UN resolution. They were in no mood for such a compromise with what they considered to be a foreign presence in their land. The Arabs also harbored the suspicion that Zionism in control of only half of Zion—not to mention the fact that the very heart of Zion itself, Jerusalem, was slated to remain a separate entity, apart from the state of Israel—would ultimately satisfy few Israelis and inevitably lead to a renewal of Zionist expansion. In 1947, however, most Jews were generally willing to accept the borders that the United Nations had drawn, despite the fact that they fell far short of what the Zionist movement originally had envisioned. David Ben Gurion, Israel's first prime minister, who once had argued that Israel's eastern border must reach the Jordan River, rejected all pressure for expansion in the hope of gaining Arab recognition of what in his youth had been but a dream, the state of Israel. The early Zionists, particularly people such as Begin whose *Irgun* had as its logo a map of Israel with borders beyond the Jordan River, had a much different map of Israel than the one that came into existence in 1948. The territorial confines of Israel in the wake of the 1948 war were at the heart of the conflict between Ben Gurion and Begin.

The Arabs remained adamant in their refusal to recognize Israel's existence. At best, some were willing to accept the presence of a Jewish minority in an Arab state. More significantly, most Arabs were convinced that they could prevent the establishment of the Israeli state by military means and drive the Zionists into the sea. The UN resolution and the Arab rejection of the partition of Palestine were but the last of a series of events that made the first Arab-Israeli war inevitable.

In 1947, the Zionist dream finally had borne fruit. The state of Israel (no longer merely a homeland for Jews) had obtained international sanction. The first state to extend diplomatic recognition to Israel was the United States; the Soviet Union and several Western nations quickly followed suit. No Arab state, however, recognized Israel.[5] Arab intransigence—coupled with the threat of another holocaust a scant three years after Hitler's defeat—made it clear that Israel's right to exist would have to be defended by the sword.

■ THE ARAB-ISRAELI WARS

Inevitably, an escalation of violence took place. The British were slated to withdraw from Palestine in May 1948 and both sides prepared for that day. Violence between Arabs and Jews, already endemic, escalated. On April 9, 1948, Begin's Irgun killed between 116 and 254 Palestinians (depending upon whose account one credits) in the village of Deir Yassin, and three days later an Arab reprisal caused the deaths of 77 Jews. These and other acts of violence became etched into the collective memory of both peoples. Each massacre had its apologists who defended the bloodletting as a just action in a just war. In this fashion the first Arab-Israeli war began.

The 1948 war was over in four weeks. A number of Arab states—Jordan, Syria, Egypt, Lebanon, and Iraq—invaded Israel, but their actions were uncoordinated and ineffectual. The Israeli victory was accompanied by the third partition of Palestine. The Israelis wound up with one-third more land than under the UN partition plan when they seized West Jerusalem, the Negev desert, and parts of Galilee. Jordan in its turn carried out the fourth partition of Palestine when its King Abdullah made the best of his defeat at the hands of the Israelis by annexing the West Bank and the rest of Jerusalem. As a result of this joint action by Israel and Jordan, the UN-designated Palestinian state never came into being. The Palestinians had been defeated by the state of Israel and betrayed by the kingdom of Jordan.

The war also produced a refugee problem that continues to plague the Middle East four decades later. By the end of April 1948, before the outbreak of the first Arab-Israeli War, 290,000 Palestinian Arabs had become refugees. The war itself produced another 300,000 refugees. By 1973, the number was over 1.5 million. Most of the refugees fled across the Jordan River into Jordan.[6] The flight of the Arabs settled the nature of the new state. It guaranteed that Israel became a Zionist state dominated by a Jewish majority at the expense of what was now an Arab minority left behind. Whatever land the Arabs had abandoned, if only to seek shelter elsewhere during the war, was confiscated.

Neighboring Arab nations did not want the refugees; moreover, most refugees did not want to leave the refugee settlements, which in any event they considered temporary. Migration to other Arab lands, the Palestinians reasoned, was tantamount to the acceptance of the permanent loss of Palestine and the recognition of the triumph of Zionism. After four decades, the Palestinian problem remains.

When the war ended, the Israelis considered the armistice lines, which gave them the additional lands, as permanent and they refused to permit the return of the refugees whose lands were now confiscated. To the Arabs, the new borders and the refugees were a humiliating reminder of their defeat and they proved to be incapable of accepting the consequences of the war. These factors, coupled with Arab intransigence on the question of Israel's right to exist, have been at the core of the continuing deadlock in Arab-Israeli relations.

The partitions of Palestine were the result of actions taken by Great Britain, the United Nations, Israel, and Jordan with the complicity of the nations of Europe, both capitalist and Communist. The United States and other major Western powers had from the beginning offered the Israelis their diplomatic support, while the Soviet Union provided most of the weapons for the Jewish victory in the first Arab-Israeli war.

It was only a matter of time until the second war between Jews and Arabs. The 1948 war between Israel and Palestine had been a bitter blow to the pride and national consciousness of the Arabs. The war had exposed their weaknesses and their inability to unite. Throughout the war Israeli forces outnumbered those of the Arabs by a ratio of roughly two to one. Arabs spoke of Arab unity and another war against Israel to drive them into the sea, but their rhetoric only masked their impotence and frustration.

A palace revolution in Egypt in 1952 swept aside the ineffectual King Farouk and in 1954 brought to power one of the conspirators, Gamal Abdel Nasser, who promised the regeneration of both Egypt and the rest of the Arab world. He envisioned a pan-Arab movement uniting all Arabs, and for a short time Egypt and Syria were in fact merged into one nation, the United Arab Republic. This show of unity, however, did not last long. Nasser's rejuvenation of Arab pride and ethnic consciousness called for the ouster of the Western presence, notably that of the British, French, and Jewish, which in the past had been responsible for the humiliation of the Muslim world. Another war between Israel and the Arabs now became inevitable. Nasser, instead of coming to grips with the reality of Israel, was busy putting another Arab-Israeli war on the agenda. All that was needed was a spark to touch it off.

As tensions in the Middle East increased, so did the arms race. Nasser turned to the Soviet Union and in September 1955 announced a historic

Extent of Israel as proposed
under the U.N. partition plan
for the   establishment
of a Jewish State — 1947

Occupied by Israel in 1948
and 1949 in excess of the U.N.
recommended partition plan

Territories occupied by Israel
in June 1967

Beirut

Damascus

LEBANON

SYRIA

Golan Heights

Tel Aviv

West Bank

Amman

MEDITERRANEAN SEA

Jordan River

DEAD SEA

Gaza Strip

Jerusalem

JORDAN

"Palestine"
claimed by World
Zionist Organization
1919

Cairo

SUEZ CANAL

E G Y P T

Sinai Peninsula
(returned to Egypt by 1982)

SAUDI ARABIA

RED SEA

THE EXPANSION OF ISRAEL

weapons deal by which he became the recipient of Soviet MIG-15 fighter planes, bombers, and tanks. The Soviet Union, in its turn, gained for the first time a client outside of its Communist sphere of influence. Israel immediately renegotiated an arms agreement with France. The Middle East was now on a hair trigger alert waiting for a crisis to unfold. The wait was not long. In July 1956, Nasser decided to nationalize the Suez Canal to eliminate British and French management of that waterway.

The British and French prepared a counterattack. They were joined by the Israelis who had their own reasons to enter the fray. For a number of years Israelis had listened to Nasser's bloodcurdling rhetoric promising the destruction of their state. They now saw their chance to deal with Nasser and to halt the border raids by the Arab *fedeyeen* (literally "those who sacrifice themselves"). These raids had produced an unbroken circle of violence, a series of "little wars" consisting of incursions and reprisals, which in turn led to other raids and reprisals. These actions produced a small but deadly momentum with a life of its own.

In October 1956, Britain, France, and Israel signed the secret treaty of Sèvres in preparation for the second Arab-Israeli war. Israel attacked in the Sinai Desert and, with the support of French planes, swept all the way to the Suez Canal and the southern tip of the Sinai at Sharm-el-Sheikh. The war lasted only a few days, from October 29 until November 2, 1956. Egypt's defeat on the battlefield—not to mention its humiliation—was complete.

President Eisenhower's opposition, Soviet threats, and UN condemnations forced Britain, France, and Israel to back down and retreat. Israel eventually agreed to withdraw from the Sinai while Egypt pledged not to interfere with Israeli shipping through the Straits of Tiran, which gave Israel an outlet to the Red Sea. The United Nations then sought to patrol the border between Egypt and Israel and in this fashion helped to preserve an uneasy truce for more than ten years.

The 1956 war resolved none of the grievances that the belligerents had accumulated over the years. Officially, the state of war between the Arabs and the Jews continued. Israel still was unable to obtain recognition from any of the Arab governments and the Arabs continued to seek the destruction of the Israeli state. Both sides had no illusions that another war was in the offing and they took steps to prepare for it.

By the spring of 1967, Nasser, in an attempt to negate the consequences of the 1956 war, closed the Straits of Tiran to Israeli shipping in the face of Israeli warnings that such an action constituted a *casus belli,* a cause for war. Inevitably, tensions rose rapidly. Nasser then demanded that the UN forces leave Egyptian territory along the Israeli border, and concluded a military pact with King Hussein of Jordan. When Iraq also joined the pact, the Israelis struck, initiating the inevitable third war, the Six Day War of June 1967. It was a classic case of a preventive war. The Israelis claimed that theirs had been an attack to counter an intended Arab offensive.

As its name suggests, the war was over in less than a week. Israel defeated the forces of Egypt and Jordan in a matter of days. Once again—as it had done in the 1956 war—Israel conquered the Sinai all the way to the Suez Canal. It then turned against Syria and took from that country the Golan Heights, a strategic plateau rising 600 feet above Galilee and from which the Syrian army had fired repeatedly on the settlements below. But more important, Israel also took what had been Jordanian territory west of the Jordan River and the Dead Sea—a region that is generally known as the West Bank (west of the Jordan River). With it, Israel came into possession of the entire city of Jerusalem, which immediately became the nation's new capital. The Six Day War rearranged the map of the Middle East and its political repercussions still haunt the region. All the conquered territories—the Sinai Peninsula, the Golan Heights, the West Bank, and Jerusalem—became Israeli-occupied lands, and as such they became the source of still further contention between Arabs and Israelis.

In November 1967, the great powers once again sought to make use of the United Nations to resolve the conflict. The United States and the Soviet Union were fearful of being increasingly drawn into the Arab-Israeli wars, each backing one of the belligerents. In a rare display of U.S.-Soviet cooperation, the UN Security Council sought to resolve the crisis by passing Resolution 242, which called for an Israeli withdrawal from territories conquered in the Six Day War, accompanied by a political settlement that would include an Arab recognition of Israel and a fair deal for the Palestinian refugees. After some hesitation, Egypt and Jordan accepted Resolution 242, but Syria and the militant Palestinians rejected it. The Israelis were not readily inclined to give up all the spoils of victory, and they too rejected it. For two decades, leaders of various political and national persuasions have repeatedly reached for Resolution 242 as a potential answer to this deadly dispute. But the overwhelming strength of Israel's military in effect negated the resolution. The Israeli government had no pressing need to return to its pre–1967 borders, particularly because it never contemplated the return of Jerusalem. And the Arabs have always insisted that in Resolution 242, "*the* territories occupied [by Israel] in the hostilities" meant "*all* territories."[7] General Moshe Dayan, the architect of Israel's victory in the Six Day War, expressed the extremist conviction when he said: "I would rather have land than peace"; to which King Hussein of Jordan replied: "Israel can have land or peace, but not both."[8] The resultant deadlock became but another manifestation of how in the Middle East the militants have nearly always carried the day.

With the acquisition of the West Bank, Israel now came into possession of a territory containing 750,000 hostile Arab inhabitants. For the next ten years the Israeli government remained by and large undecided over what to do with this territory. And when no solution acceptable to both Arabs and Jews was found, the status quo prevailed. In 1977, a general election in Israel brought to power Menachem Begin, who had always insisted that the West Bank was not merely conquered Arab territory or a bargaining card eventually to be played in exchange for Arab recognition of Israel's right to exist. It consisted instead of the Biblical lands of Judea and Samaria, an integral part of Israel's religious heritage. For Begin there was no question that these lands should ever be returned to the Arabs. He proceeded to treat them as a natural part of Zion, and for that reason he urged that Israelis settle in the region. Despite the objections of Arab states, the United Nations, the United States, and other nations, Begin considered the annexation a closed matter. His government also considered the question of the Golan Heights a closed matter when it officially annexed it.

The problem of the West Bank is complicated by the fact that its largest city, Hebron, contains the tomb of Abraham, who is revered by both Jews and Muslims. Both consider Abraham God's messenger and their spiritual and physical patriarch. The Jews consider themselves the direct descendants of one of Abraham's sons, Isaac; the Arabs see themselves as children of the other son, Ishmael. Today Jews and Muslims worship at the tomb of Abraham—separated by a single rope.

The Arab defeat of 1967 had another, unexpected, result. It strengthened the hand of Palestinian liberation/terrorist organizations, which now operated under the aegis of an umbrella organization, the Palestine Liberation Organization (PLO) led by Yassir Arafat. It is these organizations, rather than the armies of the Arab nations generally, which since 1967 have kept the Middle East in turmoil by conducting their private wars against the Israelis. During the 1972 summer Olympic Games in Munich, for instance, Palestinian terrorists dramatized their cause before a worldwide audience by the kidnapping and killing of 15 Israeli athletes. It was an act that propelled the Palestinian question into the consciousness of the Western world. But this example of "propaganda by the deed" (to use a phrase from the Russian revolutionary movement of the nineteenth century) only strengthened the hands of the extremists on both sides and continued to impede any and all efforts to resolve the questions. It should not have been surprising, therefore, that the consequence of the inability to resolve Arab-Israeli differences was another war.

The fourth Arab-Israeli conflict, the Yom Kippur War, took place in October 1973, when Egyptian President Anwar Sadat (who had succeeded Nasser in 1970) initiated an offensive against the seemingly impregnable Israeli position across the Suez Canal. Egypt enjoyed some initial successes, but Israeli forces successfully counterattacked and threatened to destroy the Egyptian army. The United Nations and the two superpowers, the United States and the Soviet Union, intervened to stop the war. Neither Israel nor Egypt were to be permitted to destroy the other. Egypt was permitted to retain a foothold on the east side of the Suez Canal and the United Nations then created a buffer zone to keep the two sides apart.

This Egyptian offensive proved to be the first time that an Arab state had been able to wrest any territory at all from the Israelis. After suffering one humiliation after another for a quarter of a century, an Arab army had finally proven its battleworthiness. Sadat felt that now he could negotiate with Israel as an equal. He began to take steps to recognize the existence of the state of Israel and in this fashion became the first and only Arab head of state to do so. In an act of supreme courage, Sadat responded to an invitation from the Israeli government and flew to Jerusalem in 1977 to address the Knesset, Israel's parliament.

Sadat's actions set the stage for the Camp David Agreement of September 1978, signed by Begin, Sadat, and U.S. President Jimmy Carter, which led directly to the Egyptian-Israeli Peace Treaty. The treaty ended a state of war of thirty years' duration between Egypt and Israel and brought about the diplomatic recognition of Israel by Egypt. In its turn, Israel pledged to return the Sinai to Egypt and did so by April 1982. This marked the first and only instance whereby an Arab state managed on its own to regain territory lost to Israel. Sadat had achieved through negotiation what no other Arabs had achieved by war. For their efforts, the three leaders were nominated for the Nobel Peace Prize. In the end, Begin and Sadat, former terrorists turned diplomats, shared the prize; inexplicably, Jimmy Carter was excluded.

But the Camp David talks of 1978 did not adequately address the thorny questions of Jerusalem, the West Bank, and the Palestinian refugees. Sadat wanted Palestinian independence from Israel; Begin spoke vaguely of Palestinian "autonomy" within the state of Israel. Begin was more interested in peace with Egypt and diplomatic recognition than in discussing the fate of the inhabitants of what he considered to be an integral part of Israel and thus an internal matter. Nor did the Camp David Agreement settle the issue of Jerusalem, Israel's capital city. On this issue, virtually no Israelis are willing to compromise. Jerusalem must remain one and indivisible. But the Palestinians, too, envisioned Jerusalem as the capital of their future state.

The PLO was not consulted in these negotiations. Begin refused to talk to the PLO, which he considered a terrorist organization. Nor was the PLO's leadership interested in joining the talks. Participation in the negotiations, after all, would have meant the *de facto* recognition of Israel. The PLO instead continued its attacks against the Israelis.

Inevitably, many Arabs saw Sadat as a man who had betrayed the Palestinian and Arab cause. His dealings with Israel contributed to his domestic problems. As his critics became more vocal, his regime became increasingly dictatorial and his opponents in their turn became increasingly embittered. He was assassinated in 1981.

The festering Palestinian problem continued to rile up the region. In 1970 King Hussein of Jordan had driven the PLO leadership from his country after it had become clear that its presence in Jordan posed a threat to his

Egyptian President Anwar Sadat, U.S. President Jimmy Carter and Israeli Prime Minister Menachem Begin, after signing the Middle East peace treaty at Camp David (Maryland), Mar. 27, 1979. (*AP/Wide World Photos*)

regime.[9] Searching for a home, the PLO found a new base of operation in southern Lebanon, a nation already divided between a politically dominant Christian minority and the majority Muslim population. In the early 1970s, Lebanon was a country on the edge of civil war with a government incapable of maintaining order. Lebanon's political factions operated private armies in an unrestricted manner. It was into this volatile environment that the Palestinians introduced their own private armies. And it was from Lebanon that the PLO launched its raids into Israel.

The Israelis, predictably, responded in kind. Raids and reprisals were the order of the day along the Lebanese-Israeli border. In July 1981, however, the PLO and Israel agreed on a "cessation of all armed attacks."[10] The ceasefire for the next ten months was in part the work of the special U.S. envoy to the Middle East, Philip Habib. Both sides abided by the terms of the agreement until June 1982, when the government of Menachem Begin attempted to eliminate the Palestinian threat in Lebanon once and for all by launching an invasion into southern Lebanon.

The Israeli government's official explanation for the resumption of war against the Palestinians was to secure "Peace for Galilee" and to root out the Palestinians across the border. This rationale for the invasion always had a hollow ring to it since there had been no Palestinian attacks across that border for nearly a year. The scope of the operation, the Begin government announced, would be limited. The Israeli army would go no farther than forty kilometers (twenty-five miles) into Lebanon. Events proved, however, that Begin and in particular his defense minister Ariel Sharon had more ambitious plans.

In December 1981, Sharon outlined the following scenario to Philip Habib. Sharon contemplated a strike into Lebanon in the hope of quickly resolving several problems at once. He sought to dislodge the Syrians, who had been invited several years earlier by the Lebanese government to restore order at a time when the country was beginning to disintegrate into civil war. Once invited, however, the Syrians stayed. Sharon considered the Syrians, with whom the Israelis had been on a war footing since 1948, to be the real masters of Lebanon. Second, Sharon intended to destroy the Palestinian base in southern Lebanon and with it to subdue the restless Palestinian population of about half a million. "What can be done," Sharon told Habib, "and this is not actually a plan, but it is practicable, is a swift and vigorous strike of 24 to 48 hours, which will force the Syrians to retreat and inflict such heavy losses on the PLO that they will leave Lebanon." Sharon also expected the Lebanese government to regain control of the Beirut-Damascus highway, driving the Syrians further north.[11]

In this fashion the PLO, a "time bomb" in Sharon's words, would be destroyed. When Habib asked of the fate of the 100,000 Palestinians directly across the border in Lebanon, Sharon told him that "we shall hand them over to the Lebanese. . . . Fifty-thousand armed terrorists won't remain there, and the rest will be taken care of by the Lebanese." Habib protested the impending violation of a cease-fire he had worked out. Shortly afterward, President Reagan warned Prime Minister Begin against any moves into Lebanon, but it was to no avail.

The invasion of Lebanon did bring about the military (although not necessarily political) defeat of the PLO, the Israeli bombardment and destruction of parts of Beirut containing Palestinian populations, and the massacre of Palestinian civilians by Lebanese Maronite Christian Phalangist (right-wing) militia forces who had long been engaged in bitter conflict with the Palestinians. Israeli forces did achieve the destruction of Syrian forces and the military hardware the Soviets had provided, but the Syrians quickly recovered their losses and have remained as deeply entrenched in Lebanon as ever. Egypt recalled its ambassador from Jerusalem in protest over Israeli action in Lebanon.

The cost of the invasion is incalculable. The greatest losers were the Palestinians, who suffered first at the hands of the Israelis, then the Christian Phalangists, and finally the Shiite Muslims. The war also pitted the Israelis against the Shiites; the Shiites against the Maronite Christians and their army, the Phalangists; and a faction of the PLO (the rebels being supported by the Syrians) against Arafat's faction. It produced the evacuation of the PLO guerrillas; the deaths of over 600 Israeli soldiers; the *de facto* partition of Lebanon between Syria and Israel; and a deep emotional split among the population in Israel. The volatile political debates in Israel centered on whether the invasion had been necessary, for this was the first war initiated by Israel in which the survival of the state had not been an immediate issue.

The invasion of Lebanon did not resolve the central issues of the region. Instead, it added fuel to the fire of the civil war in that country. More than five years later the bloodletting has continued. A U.S. peacekeeping force ran head-on into an opposition of fury and anger few U.S. citizens were able to understand when a truck filled with explosives blew up a marine encampment killing 240 marines. And at the fifth anniversary of the invasion of Lebanon, Israeli forces were still trying to extricate themselves from southern Lebanon and were launching reprisal raids against Lebanese Shiites who were hard on the heels of the retreating Israeli forces. Moreover, the questions of the Palestinian refugees and the West Bank are no closer to being resolved, and the state of war continues in the Middle East.

■ THE ISRAEL-PALESTINIAN IMPASSE

In the mid-1980s the PLO was no closer than before to achieving its stated goals—the creation of a Palestinian state and the destruction of Israel. After the 1982 expulsion from Lebanon, the PLO was in disarray, as PLO fighters were now openly split, various Arab countries supported contending factions, and morale was low. For the next several years the nominal leader of the PLO, Yassir Arafat, now based in Tunisia, struggled to maintain the unity of the organization. His main conflict was with Syrian president Hafez Assad, with whom some of the more radical elements of the PLO became linked. Arafat gravitated toward more moderate Arab leaders, Hussein of Jordan and Mubarak of Egypt, and began to explore the possibility of a negotiated settlement with Israel, as opposed to a military one.

As the PLO floundered for lack of unity and a policy, and Arab nations remained divided over policy toward Israel, Israel itself was immobilized by its own political problems. The leading parties, the right-wing Likud and the left-of-center Labor party, were unable to find a consensus on how to deal with the PLO. They shared power in an awkward coalition after an inconclusive parliamentary election in 1984.

Nothing changed until December 1987, when the Palestinian population in Gaza and in the West Bank took matters into their own hands and by doing so stirred the other parties to move off dead center. Their uprising, the *intifada* (literally, "shaking off" the Zionist yoke), began in Gaza when an Israeli truck collided with two cars, killing four Palestinian refugees. The protests escalated and spread to the West Bank. Israel was put into the uncomfortable position of using soldiers against stone-throwing Palestinians. By early 1990, more than 600 Palestinians had been killed by Israeli soldiers. Israeli hard-liners tried to deflect criticism by blaming the violence on the PLO.

The *intifada* spurred a debate within Israel over the future of Gaza and the West Bank, and within the PLO over strategy and tactics. Israel's problem was compounded by the fact that it had built settlements on the West Bank for some 70,000 of its citizens. Moreover, the fate of Jerusalem was not negotiable. In Israel, the Likud and the Labor party squared off in another parliamentary election in November 1988, the central issue being the future of the occupied territories. Yitzhak Shamir, incumbent prime minister and head of the Likud, took a hard line, insisting on no mercy for the *intifada*, no talks with the PLO, no Israeli participation in an international conference on the Middle East, and no trading land for peace (the last two ideas supported by Washington by this time). His opponent, Shimon Peres, took a more flexible approach, favoring an international conference to resolve the conflict. In short, Shamir held that, to survive, Israel must keep the West Bank and Gaza, whereas Peres held that Israel must trade land for peace. The election produced another deadlock, with neither party winning a majority in the Knesset. Once more, no consensus was possible.

Meanwhile, the PLO decided to take advantage of the opportunity presented by the *intifada*. It convened in Algiers a meeting of the Palestinian National Council in November 1988, at which it passed a resolution proclaiming its willingness to recognize the state of Israel on the condition that Israel officially endorse UN resolutions 242 and 338, which called for Israeli withdrawal from the occupied territories and for the right of all parties in the Middle East to live in peace and security.

For the PLO this was a remarkably conciliatory position, as it had never previously acknowledged the right of Israel to exist or live in peace. Arafat went so far as to "repeat for the record that we totally and absolutely renounce all forms of terrorism."[12] Washington then announced that it would for the first time enter discussions with the PLO to prepare for an international conference. After more than 30 years, the PLO was now willing to accept what it had always rejected.

Israel was now virtually isolated. The major Western powers, the dominant elements in the PLO, key Arab countries, and the Soviet Union too were all in essential agreement on the need for an international peace conference that would lead to the creation of an autonomous Palestinian state on at least part of the occupied territories. But Shamir stood firm. He did not believe the peaceful protestations of his mortal enemies; there would be no international conference, no talks with the PLO, and no Palestinian state. He could not forget that the PLO had vowed in the past to destroy the state of Israel and that, in fact, several of its factions still held this position.[13] He offered, instead, a proposal to conduct an election in the occupied territories to produce a Palestinian leadership with which he could negotiate the future of the West Bank and Gaza. Neither the PLO nor other Arab nations found this acceptable, nor did Washington. The political deadlock remained.

■ RECOMMENDED READINGS

Avineri, Shlomo. *The Making of Modern Zionism: The Intellectual Origins of the Jewish State.* New York: Basic Books, 1981.
　　An explanation of the intellectual climate of the nineteenth century that produced the Zionist movement.

Elon, Amos. *The Israelis: Founders and Sons.* New York: Holt, Rinehart and Winston, 1971.
　　A classic treatment of the roots of Zionism as well as the first two decades of the existence of Israel.

Lilienthal, Alfred M. *The Zionist Connection: What Price Peace?* Rev. ed. New Brunswick, N.J.: North American, 1982.
　　A critical explanation of the Zionist movement.

Oz, Amos. *In the Land of Israel.* New York: Random House, 1983.
　　By an Israeli novelist who dwells on Israel's dilemma.

Peters, Joan. *From Time Immemorial: The Origins of the Arab-Jewish Conflict Over Palestine.* New York: Harper & Row, 1984.
　　An ambitious and controversial attempt to prove that the Jews did not displace the Arabs in Palestine, but instead that Arabs had displaced Jews.

Reich, Walter. *A Stranger in My House: Jews and Arabs in the West Bank.* New York: Henry Holt, 1984.
　　An evenhanded and judicious attempt by a U.S. psychiatrist to understand the historical, sociological, and theological arguments of the inhabitants of the West Bank.

Said, Edward W. *The Question of Palestine.* New York: Random House, 1980.
　　By a U.S. scholar of Palestinian descent, it is the classic study championing the Palestinian cause.

Segev, Tom. *1949: The First Israelis.* New York: Free Press, 1985.
　　A controversial, best seller in Israel, a reinterpretation by an Israeli journalist of the early history of the state.

Shehadeh, Raja. *Samed: Journal of a West Bank Palestinian.* New York: Adama Publishers, 1984.
　　Life on the West Bank from a Palestinian's perspective.

Shipler, David K. *Arab and Jew: Wounded Spirits in a Promised Land.* New York: Times Books, 1986.
　　By a correspondent of the *New York Times.*

Tuchman, Barbara W. *Bible and Sword: England and Palestine from the Bronze Age to Balfour.* New York: New York University Press, 1956.
　　A discussion of England's age-old fascination and ultimate involvement in the Holy Land.

■ NOTES

1. Jewish nationalism has existed ever since the diaspora, the dispersion of the Jews that began in the sixth century B.C. with the destruction of Solomon's temple and culminated with the destruction of the second temple in Jerusalem in 70 A.D. and the defeat of Bar Kochba in A.D. 135. The British philosopher Bertrand Russell, in reminding his readers that modern nationalism is a relatively new concept, pointed out that at the end of the Middle Ages "there was hardly any nationalism except that of the Jews."

2. Quoted in Amos Elon, *The Israelis: Founders and Sons* (New York: Holt, Rinehart and Winston, 1971), p. 106.

3. Palestinian Arab and Ben Gurion cited in ibid., p. 155 (emphasis in the original).

4. Balfour Declaration, Ruddock F. Mackay, *Balfour: Intellectual Statesman* (Oxford: Oxford University Press, 1985), pp. 315–316.

5. In fact, when King Abdullah of Jordan, the grandfather of the current King Hussein, sought to come to terms with the state of Israel (he met in secret with several of the Zionists in 1949), it cost him his life at the hand of an assassin. The first, and only, Arab nation to exchange ambassadors with Israel was Egypt in 1977. For this, as well as for domestic reasons, the Egyptian president Anwar Sadat suffered the fate of Abdullah when he, too, was assassinated.

6. As a result, 70 percent of the population of the Kingdom of Jordan consists of Palestinians, from which comes the argument in some quarters in Israel that a Palestinian state already exists.

7. UN Resolution 242, Abba Eban, *Abba Eban: An Autobiography* (New York: Random House, 1977), pp. 451–453.

8. Moshe Dayan and King Hussein quoted in Dana Adams Schmidt, *Armageddon in the Middle East* (New York: John Day, 1974), p. 249. For a discussion of the positions of Dayan and Hussein, see Bernard Avishai, *The Tragedy of Zionism: Revolution and Democracy in the Land of Israel* (New York: Farrar, Straus, Giroux, 1985), pp. 275–278.

9. Despite King Hussein's bloody suppression of the PLO in 1970, the king and the PLO made common cause in 1985 in an uneasy alliance, which proposed a Jordanian-Palestinian federation that would include the West Bank. President Hosni Mubarak of Egypt sought to peddle the plan to Washington but with no success. Israel rejected the proposal outright.

10. This information and that in the following paragraph is from a report of a U.S. diplomatic summary of the conversation between Sharon and Habib, published by the Israeli Labour Party newspaper, *Davar.* The U.S. ambassador to Israel, Samuel W. Lewis, and the State Department confirmed the basic outlines of the conversation. Thomas L. Friedman, "Paper Says Israeli Outlined Invasion," *New York Times,* May 26, 1985, p. 15.

11. Ibid.

12. Text of Arafat Statement, *Baltimore Sun,* December 15, 1988.

13. Yitzhak Shamir, "Israel at 40: Looking Back, Looking Ahead," *Foreign Affairs,* 66, 3 (1988), pp. 585-586.

■ Part 3

THE SHIFTING SANDS OF GLOBAL POWER

From the outset the Cold War created a bipolar world in which the two contending superpowers pulled other nations toward one pole or the other. But gradually this bipolar East-West confrontation underwent a transformation marked by divisions within each camp and the emergence of other centers of power. In the first decade of the Cold War there existed a straightforward adversary relationship featuring the hard-nosed diplomatic combat of Joseph Stalin and Harry Truman. It also featured the Soviet Iron Curtain, the U.S. containment policy, a tense standoff in Europe, the creation of two military alliances (NATO and the Warsaw Pact), a war in Korea, persistent ideological attacks and counterattacks, and the massive rearmament of both sides. Despite the conciliatory gestures by the successors of Stalin and Truman and talk of peaceful coexistence, the bipolar struggle carried over into the 1960s and grew even more intense as the two superpowers squared off in the Cuban missile crisis.

However, by that time, it was becoming clear to both superpowers that they had lost the capacity to make military use of their huge nuclear arsenals and that the day of direct confrontation had ended. Also by the early 1960s, the two superpowers could no longer take for granted the solidarity of their respective alliances. The bipolar world of the 1950s began to give way to multipolarity in the 1960s.

In order to understand this process, the political legacy of Joseph Stalin in the Soviet Union is our point of departure in Chapter 8. Here we trace the efforts of his successor, Nikita Khrushchev, to put to an end the excesses of Stalinism, the terror and the arbitrary and abusive use of state power, and to institute reforms aimed at restoring orderly and legal procedures to Soviet rulership and revitalizing the economy. The consequences of this reform effort and the pattern of Soviet politics under Khrushchev's successors are also discussed. Additionally, we examine the stresses and strains within the Communist bloc and particularly the impact of Khrushchev's reforms in Eastern Europe. The impact of de-Stalinization was controlled within the Soviet Union, but that was not the case in the satellite countries, especially in Poland and Hungary, where it rekindled nationalist sentiments and unleashed pent-up desires for political liberalization and liberation from Moscow's control.

But if the resulting revolts in Poland and Hungary and later in Czechoslovakia could be snuffed out by the Soviet Union, a recalcitrant Communist China could not be so easily dealt with. In Chapter 8, we analyze the causes and the course of the Sino-Soviet split, which divided the Communist world. Their bitter and long-lasting feud signified that ideological bonds are not stronger than national interests and that international Communism was not the monolithic movement it was generally thought to be.

Meanwhile, in the 1960s, the United States government, still convinced that Communism was monolithic, went off to war in distant Asia to stop its spread. In Chapter 9, we explain how and why the United States took up the fight in Vietnam. We argue that the staunch anti-Communist logic of U.S. leaders caused them to misread the revolution in that country, its causes and strengths, and come up with the erroneous conclusion that its source was Beijing-based Communist aggression rather than Vietnamese nationalism. We next offer an explanation of the prolongation and expansion of the war in Indochina and the difficulty the United States had in extracting itself from that war. We also examine the tragic consequences of U.S. involvement in Vietnam, the trauma of its defeat, and the impact of its departure on the remainder of Indochina, especially Cambodia, and the tragedy of the boat people refugees.

In the late 1960s, when the United States was still mired in Vietnam, progress was made in lowering East-West tension on other fronts. New leadership in West Germany, specifically that of Chancellor Willy Brandt, took bold steps seeking to break up the twenty-year-old Cold War logjam in Central Europe. In Chapter 10, we examine Brandt's conciliatory policy toward the Communist nations of Eastern Europe and the role it played in bringing détente—the relaxation of tension—to East-West relations. By the early 1970s détente became the basis of Soviet-U.S. diplomacy.

The new relations between Washington and Moscow left Beijing isolated as an enemy of both. In fact, the U.S.-Soviet détente at first brought jeers from China, which suspected an anti-Chinese conspiracy. But as we relate in Chapter 10, Chinese leaders came to realize the dangers of China's continued isolation and judged that it had more to gain in terms of economic development and national security by normalizing its relations with the United States. In a dramatic diplomatic turnabout the United States and Communist China, two nations that had been the most intransigent of ideological foes for two decades, suddenly in 1972 buried the hatchet.

With U.S.-Soviet détente and the normalization of U.S.-Chinese relations, a new era of delicate tripolar power relations had arrived. Moreover, with the resurgence of Western Europe and the emergence of an economically powerful Japan, the international arena was now multipolar with at least five centers of power. The simpler world of East versus West, of the struggle between the "free world" and the "Communist world," gave way to a more complex world of power-balancing diplomacy, one calling for greater political flexibility.

□ 8

The Communist World After Stalin

When Stalin died in March 1953, he had ruled the Soviet Union for nearly thirty years and in the process left his imprint on the Communist party and the nation. In the late 1920s, Stalin and his party had set out to initiate a program of rapid industrialization with a series of Five-Year Plans. In order to feed the growing proletariat (the industrial work force), he introduced a program of rapid collectivization whereby the small and inefficient individual farms were consolidated into larger collectives, which in effect made the Soviet peasant an employee of the state. The state set the price the collective farms received for their agricultural commodities, a price kept low so that the countryside wound up subsidizing the cities where an industrial revolution was taking place. Agriculture became one of the "stepchildren" of the Communist revolution in the Soviet Union.

At the time of the Communist revolution of 1917, the peasants had realized an age-old dream, the private and unrestricted ownership of their land. Predictably, they resisted the Stalinist drive toward collectivization. Stalin, faced with intense opposition, had two choices: curtail the program of collectivization and industrialization or pursue it with force. He chose the latter. Collectivization became a bloody civil war during the late 1920s and early 1930s in which several million peasants perished and which witnessed widespread destruction of equipment and livestock. In such wasteful and brutal manner, the countryside subsidized the industrial revolution and the growth of the city.

Stalin subordinated Soviet society to one overriding quest, to create an industrial state for the purpose of bringing to an end Russia's traditional economic backwardness, the root cause of its military weakness. In 1931, Stalin spoke to a conference of factory managers on the question of whether the mad dash toward industrialization could be slowed. He offered his audience a capsule history of Russia:

To slacken the tempo would mean falling behind. And all those who fall behind get beaten. . . . One feature of the history of old Russia was the continual beatings she suffered because of her backwardness. She was beaten by the Mongol khans. She was beaten by the Turkish beys. She was beaten by the Swedish feudal lords. She was beaten by the Polish and Lithuanian gentry. She was beaten by the British and French capitalists. She was beaten by the Japanese barons. All beat her—because of her backwardness, military backwardness, cultural backwardness, political backwardness, industrial backwardness. . . . Such is the law of the exploiters, to beat the backward and the weak. . . . Either we do it [catch up with the capitalist West], or we shall be crushed. . . . In ten years we must make good the distance which separates us from the advanced capitalist countries. . . . And that depends on us. *Only* on us![1]

Stalin's Five-Year Plans gave the Soviet Union a heavily centralized economy capable of withstanding the supreme test of fire, the German attack on the Soviet Union in 1941. In fact, during World War II the Soviet war economy, despite massive destruction at the hands of the Germans, outproduced that of Germany. Studies conducted after the war for the U.S. Joint Chiefs of Staff repeatedly paid tribute to Stalin's industrial revolution, which had transformed the Soviet Union from a weak, backward country into a formidable opponent that all too soon broke the U.S. nuclear monopoly (1949) and later was first to venture into the frontiers of space (1957).

All of this did not come without a heavy price. Stalin contributed to the transformation of what initially had been meant to be a "dictatorship of the proletariat"[2] into a dictatorship of the party over the proletariat and the peasantry, and eventually into a dictatorship of the secret police over the proletariat, the peasantry, and the party itself. In 1937, Stalin initiated the last of a series of purges of the party by which he eliminated all opposition within the Communist party to his regime. The Bolshevik Revolution of 1917, which had begun as an uprising by the proletariat, rank-and-file soldiers, and peasants, had become a monument to the triumph of the secret police.

■ KHRUSHCHEV AND STALIN'S GHOST

When Stalin died, the party immediately took steps to reassert the position of preeminence it had enjoyed in the days of Vladimir Lenin, the architect of the Bolshevik Revolution, who had led the Soviet Union until his death in 1924. Within a week after Stalin's death, the party forced Stalin's designated successor, Georgi Malenkov, to give up one of the two posts he held. The party told him to choose between the post of first secretary of the party (that is, the head of the party) or that of prime minister. Malenkov, inexplicably, decided to hold on to the position of prime minister. As a result a lesser member of the Politburo, Nikita Khrushchev, took charge of the daily opera-tions of the party. The party then took another step to prevent the consolida-tion of power in the hands of one person. It officially established a collective leadership, a *troika* (Russian for a sled pulled by three horses) consisting of Malenkov as prime minister, Viacheslav Molotov as foreign minister, and Lav-rentii Beria as the head of the secret police. Beria, who had been an agent of Stalin's terror, remained a threat to the party. In the summer of 1953, the party, with the help of the leadership of the Red Army (which also had suf-fered greatly during the secret police's unchecked reign of terror), arrested Beria. It charged him with the abuse of power and then shot him.

The party then continued to attempt to come to terms with the Stalinist legacy. The reformers repeatedly clashed with those who sought to prevent meaningful changes. Gradually, the reformers gained the upper hand and some of the shackles of the Stalinist past were cast off. A general amnesty freed political prisoners. Writers, many of whom had been "writing for the desk drawer," succeeded in seeing their works in print. The first version of détente with the West now became a possibility. Western visitors began to arrive in Moscow.

The most dramatic assault on the status of Stalin came in February 1956, at the Communist party's Twentieth Congress, when Nikita Khrushchev de-livered a scathing attack on Stalin's crimes. It became known as the "Secret Speech," but it did not remain secret for long—since an address before an assembly of several hundred delegates, many of whom had much to gain by making it public, would certainly reach the light of day. The speech was the result of a commission the party had set up to report on Beria's and Stalin's crimes, mostly those committed against the party itself. The Communist party announced through Khrushchev that Stalin's terror, including the de-struction of its role in the affairs of the state, had been an act of lawlessness, one which the party now sought to prevent in the future. "Socialist legality" was to take the place of one-person rule.

The speech was essentially an attempt by the party at self-preservation. And it was limited to just that. It did not address the larger question of Stalin's terror directed against the peasants, religious organizations, writers and composers—in short, the public at large. As one of Khrushchev's Western biographers has written, the Secret Speech was a smokescreen as well as an exposure.[3] It did not tackle the question of one-party rule by the "vanguard of the proletariat," namely the Communist party. Neither did it challenge the Stalinist system of agriculture, which the party admitted at the time was in ruin, nor the system of industrial production, which still worked reasonably well. Instead, Khrushchev's speech focused on the dictatorship of the police over the party.

The Secret Speech signaled the end of the arbitrary terror of Stalin's time. The secret police was brought under the party's control and its wings were clipped, particularly in dealing with party members. Arbitrary arrests were largely ended. Censorship restrictions were partially lifted, breathing new life into the Soviet Union's intellectual community. Throughout his tenure Khrushchev repeatedly waged war against the memory of Stalin, particularly in 1957 and then in 1961 when he went so far as to remove Stalin's body from the mausoleum he shared with Lenin and to rename cities and institutions that had been named in Stalin's honor. The City of Stalingrad, for example, the supreme symbol of the Soviet Union's resistance to Hitler, where an entire German army found defeat, became merely the "city on the Volga," or Volgograd.

After Khrushchev's ouster in October 1964, the party made no concerted effort to rehabilitate Stalin's image, although overt criticism of Stalin was brought to an end. It was clear, however, that one day Soviet society had to come to grips with Stalin's legacy. The transformation of Stalin's image from a hero and generalissimo, to a murderous tyrant in violation of "Leninist legality," and finally to a shadowy figure who appears scarcely to have existed, simply would not do. In 1961, the party published the long-awaited second edition of its *History of the Communist Party of the Soviet Union*. The first edition had been published in 1938 under Stalin's direct editorship and as such had heaped voluminous praise on Stalin. The second edition, in contrast, was an example of revisionist history with a vengeance. It never mentioned Stalin's name. It was Mikhail Gorbachev who in 1987 forced Soviet society once again to come to grips with its past and reopened the discussion of Stalin's role.

To many observers in the West, these changes were of little consequence. The Communist party still retained its control and the economy remained unchanged. But in the context of Russian and Soviet history, these liberalizing changes were nothing short of revolutionary. This is something on which both the Soviet opponents and defenders of Khrushchev agreed. What Khrushchev needed to do was continue to introduce innovations without major repercussions, for, as Alexis de Tocqueville (the French political writer of the nineteenth century) has written, the most difficult time in the life of a bad government comes when it tries to reform itself. Khrushchev soon found that out.[4]

Philosophically, Khrushchev expressed the view that art must not be censored. But the flood of writings that sought to portray Soviet reality as it in fact existed, warts and all, soon overwhelmed the party, and Khrushchev himself became a censor. In 1962, Khrushchev permitted the publication of Alexander Solzhenitsyn's exposé of Stalin's labor camps, *One Day in the Life of Ivan Denisovich,* the literary sensation of the post-Stalin age; yet, several years earlier, Khrushchev had supported "administrative measures" to prevent the publication of Boris Pasternak's *Doctor Zhivago,* admittedly without having read it. Late in life, a repentant Khrushchev wrote that "readers should be given a chance to make their own judgments" and that "police measures shouldn't be used."[5] As the first secretary of the party, however,

Soviet leader Nikita Khrushchev, flanked by Foreign Minister Andrei Gromyko and Marshal Rodion Malinovski at press conference, Paris, May 16, 1960. (*National Archives*)

Khrushchev never did manage to come to grips with his contradictions. The result was that he was unable to bring the restless writers under control. This task fell to his successor, Leonid Brezhnev.

By the early 1960s, Khrushchev had worn out his welcome. The majority of the party was increasingly beginning to view his erratic moves and innovations as hare-brained schemes. The classic case in point was the attempt to place nuclear missiles in Cuba in 1962, a rash impulsive act. Poorly thought-out and hasty reforms in the areas of agriculture and industry came back to haunt Khrushchev. In October 1964, Khrushchev contemplated a shake-up in the party. It proved to be the last straw for it threatened the exalted positions of many. It was clear that by then Khrushchev had lost the support of the majority in the Central Committee, officially the major decision-making body of the Communist party. The party, in a vote of no confidence, sent him out to pasture with the stipulation that he stay out of politics. Leonid Brezhnev succeeded him as the head of the party.

Khrushchev's demise proved to be his finest hour. He had dealt with his opponents within the bounds of "socialist legality," that is by using the rules and procedures written into the party's statutes and by using the support many in the party at one time gave him enthusiastically. But when his behavior became increasingly irrational, embarrassing, and reckless, the party then turned against him. Once he faced the cold, hard fact that he had lost the support of the majority, he stepped down. There was never a question of using the military or the secret police.

Khrushchev's successors gave the Soviet Union twenty years of stability, a significant increase in the standard of living, and rough military parity with the West. At the same time, this was an era when the status quo was maintained. A free-wheeling discussion of Stalin's role in Soviet history, therefore, had no place in the scheme of the Brezhnev vision of Soviet society. The intellectuals were eventually brought under control by intimidation, jailing, and, in several cases, notably that of Solzhenitsyn, expulsion from the country. Brezhnev, the first secretary of the party, and particularly his prime minister, Alexei Kosygin, contemplated economic reforms but they were soon shelved when it became apparent that all too many factory managers had their fill of reforms under Khrushchev and fought for the retention of the *status quo*.

By the time Brezhnev died in 1982, the party was beginning to accept the need for another round of reform, this time primarily in the field of industry and agriculture. Yuri Andropov and Konstantin Chernenko initiated the first modest steps, but both were hampered by what turned out to be incurable illnesses. In 1984, Mikhail Gorbachev, the new first secretary of the party, took on the nation's problems.

The Communist party stands to come full circle. Nikita Khrushchev began the attack on Stalin's political legacy, the terror against the party and people. Mikhail Gorbachev inherited the unenviable task of tackling Stalin's economic legacy, top-heavy industrialization and collectivized agriculture. For more than three centuries, successive rulers of Russia have repeatedly introduced significant departures from the policies of their predecessors. Gorbachev, in a direct challenge to Breshnev's political, economic, and intellectual inertia, committed his nation to a free-wheeling discussion of its shortcomings, to the restructuring of the economy, and to the acceleration of the process of transformation (see Chapter 19).

■ EASTERN EUROPE: THE SATELLITES

As the Communist party in the Soviet Union wrestled with Stalin's ghost, a similar drama began to unfold in Moscow's East European satellites. There, the conflict was fought with much more intensity and conviction. The reformers were willing to go much further than their counterparts behind the Kremlin walls. Although much of Eastern Europe subsequently moved further from the Stalinist model than the Soviet Union, Moscow has always made it clear that the reforms must remain within certain perimeters which, although not rigidly defined and constantly shifting, must nevertheless not be transgressed. Moscow's position vis-à-vis Eastern Europe follows along the classic lines of the carrot, in the shape of a tolerance of reforms, and the stick, wielded by the Soviet Army to maintain control.

The Cold War of the late 1940s effectively split Europe in half. The Western part fell under U.S. influence and most of Eastern Europe became a Soviet sphere of influence. The West immediately considered the expansion of Soviet political and military power as a threat to its security and saw this development as a source of Soviet strength. But Stalin saw it in a different light. He understood that the East European buffer offered his state security, but that it was also a potential source of headaches. At the Yalta Conference he had described the Poles as "quarrelsome." He well understood the volatile mix of nationalism, religion, and anti-Russian sentiments in Eastern Europe. Soviet occupation of Eastern Europe had given him a measure of military strength in any future confrontation with the capitalist West, but it also promised to bring problems.

By 1948, Stalin appeared to have consolidated his position in Eastern Europe. The Communist parties of that region were for the most part the creation of the Soviet Union and on the surface loyal members of the socialist camp lined up in solidarity against the capitalist threat. But the Communists of Eastern Europe were soon showing nationalist tendencies whereby they were more interested in championing the causes of their own nations instead of serving the interests of the Soviet Union.

☐ Yugoslavia

The classic example of such "nationalist deviation" was the case of Joseph Tito, the Communist ruler of Yugoslavia. In the 1930s Tito had spent time in Moscow under Stalin's tutelage, and during World War II he had fought with the allies against Nazi Germany. His loyalty to Stalin and the cause of international Marxist solidarity appeared beyond reproach. Soon after the war, however, at the very moment the West and the Soviet Union were taking steps to consolidate their respective positions, the Yugoslav and Soviet Communists had a falling out over the question of who was to play the dominant role in running Yugoslavia. The upshot of this quarrel was that Tito established his independence from Moscow. He did not, however, move into the capitalist camp. He accepted aid from the West, but always maintained a position of neutrality in the struggle between East and West.[6] The Tito-Stalin split pointed to a central problem the Soviets faced in Eastern Europe, the volatile force of nationalism.

The immediate consequence of Tito's defection was Stalin's reorganization of the Communist governments of Eastern Europe. He executed and jailed Communists (such as Poland's Wladyslaw Gomulka, of whom we will hear more later) whom he suspected of nationalist (or Titoist) tendencies.

Foreign Communists were to have one loyalty and that was to be to the Soviet Union, not their native lands. Stalin's definition of a loyal Communist was one who faithfully served the interests of the Kremlin. An international *"revolutionary,"* Stalin wrote in 1927, is one "who is ready to protect, to defend the U.S.S.R. without reservation, without qualification."[7] In short, the interests of the Soviet Union outweigh the considerations of all other socialist governments. Stalin never budged on this definition of an international revolutionary. Only one Marxist was permitted to be a nationalist, namely, Stalin himself.

The damage Stalin did to Communist movements beyond the Soviet Union has seldom been adequately appreciated in the West. Not only did he subordinate the Communist parties to the interests of his state, but in doing so he tainted them with a brush wielded by a foreign power. As such, these movements found themselves struggling for support. That was particularly true in Europe after both world wars. Within two to three years after the wars, the radical shifts for which the wars and subsequent disillusionment had been largely responsible had burned themselves out. All that remained were Communist parties struggling to survive, their association with Moscow having become a millstone dragging them down, and their thunder stolen by reformist socialists. In short, the shifts to the Left were not the creation of Stalin; the Left's demise, however, was in part Stalin's responsibility.

Stalin's brutal cleansing ("purging") of the East European Communist parties did have its desired effect. Until Stalin's death in March 1953, these parties were outwardly loyal to the Soviet Union, and Eastern Europe remained calm.

☐ Poland

But soon after Stalin's death the East European Communist parties began to work toward partial independence from Moscow. This did not mean that they sought to leave the socialist camp or legalize capitalist political parties, but they did insist on dealing with their own internal problems without direct intervention by Moscow. An element of self-preservation played a large part in the restructuring of the relationship between the East European Communist parties and Moscow. The East Europeans sought to do away with Moscow's repeated and arbitrary purges of their ranks and interference in their internal affairs. The Polish party took the lead when it quietly released (December 1954) and later readmitted (August 1956) into the party the nationalist Wladyslaw Gomulka whom Stalin had jailed in 1948.

The return to power of East European Communists who had been driven from power by Stalin was greatly speeded up when the new Soviet leader, Nikita Khrushchev, denounced Stalin's "mistakes" and "excesses," namely his crimes against members of the Communist party in the Soviet

Union itself. Khrushchev sought to discredit his Stalinist political opponents at home, but his action had unforeseen and important repercussions in Eastern Europe.

When Khrushchev's first attack on the dead Stalin took place in his Secret Speech at the Twentieth Congress of the Communist party of the Soviet Union in February 1956, the Polish Communist party, which had sent delegates to the congress, leaked a copy of the speech to the West. Khrushchev later wrote in his memoirs: "I was told that it was being sold for very little. So Khrushchev's speech . . . wasn't appraised as being worth much! Intelligence agents from every country in the world could buy it cheap on the open market."[8] If Khrushchev could denounce Stalinism at home, the Poles reasoned, then they ought to be able to do the same. The Poles then used the speech to justify their attempt to travel their own road toward socialism without, however, leaving the Soviet camp.

At home the Polish Communist party had its work cut out. The summer of 1956 saw rioting by workers, particularly in Poznan where 75 workers lost their lives in confrontations with police, and the country became unmanageable. To deal with this crisis, the party convened in October 1956 to initiate a program of reform and to elect Gomulka as its first secretary. Upon his election, Gomulka delivered a speech in which he affirmed Poland's right to follow a socialist model other than the one the Soviet Union offered. He also insisted on his country's "full independence and sovereignty," as part of every nation's right to self-government. Polish-Soviet relations, he said, must be based on equality and independence.

What particularly had galled the Poles was that their defense minister, Konstantin Rokossovsky, was a Soviet citizen. Rokossovsky, a native of Poland, had left his country for the Soviet Union and had risen to the highest rank, that of marshal of the Red Army. As Poland's minister of defense he thus served a foreign master. Understandably, Rokossovsky became one of the first casualties of Poland's peaceful "October Revolution."

The behavior by the Polish Communists alarmed their Soviet comrades. A high-level Soviet delegation, led by Khrushchev, arrived uninvited at the October 1956 congress in Warsaw. In the resulting confrontation the Poles refused to back down. They made it clear that they would travel the socialist road, yet at the same time they insisted on the right to take care of their own internal problems. In addition, they pledged their loyalty to the Warsaw Pact, the Soviet-led military alliance. They eventually convinced the Soviets to return to Moscow.

The Soviet Union, here, gave tacit assent to the principle that there exist several different roads to socialism, that the Soviet model was not the only one and thus not necessarily the correct one. In effect, the Kremlin yielded and accepted the legitimacy of what once was a heresy, the right to nationalist deviation. If the Soviets had the right to find their own path to socialism, so did the other socialist countries. It was in fact at this time that the Soviets buried the hatchet in their ideological dispute with Tito. Khrushchev went to Belgrade on a state visit and when he and Tito embraced it signalled an end to the intra-Marxist feud. The Soviet Union's monopoly on interpreting the writings of Marx and Engels was no more. The Italian Communist Palmiro Togliatti coined a word to describe the new reality, "polycentrism."[9] This term made it clear that the world now has not one but many centers of Marxist orthodoxy.

The Poles, although still in the shadow of the Soviet Union, embarked on their own road to socialism, and the Communist party took steps to placate the restless population. Workers gained concessions, and the gradual process of collectivizing farm land was halted and then reversed. (Unlike the Soviet Union where the state owns all land, most farmland in Poland is in the hands of private farmers.) Political parties other than the Communist party were permitted to exist and they received subordinate representation in the government. Gomulka released from jail the prelate of the Roman Catholic Church in Poland, Stefan Cardinal Wyszynski, and the church regained the traditional right to administer its own affairs. In turn, Gomulka received the church's endorsement.

Resistance Fighters in the Hungarian Revolt, Budapest, Oct. 11, 1956. (*National Archives*)

☐ Hungary

Across the border, the Hungarians watched the developments in Poland with increasing intensity. If the Poles could eliminate some of the effects of Stalinism, why could not they? Heated discussions took place in intellectual circles and within the Hungarian Communist party. The upshot was that the Stalinists were forced to resign and Imre Nagy, Hungary's "Gomulka," took over.

Initially, events in Hungary paralleled those in Poland. But Nagy could not control the rebellious mood that was building up in his country. It was not enough to rid the nation of the Stalinists; nothing short of independence from Moscow would do. A reformed Communist party was not enough; the Communist party was, after all, a creation of the Russians. Deep-seated Hungarian animosity toward the Russians has its historic roots in the intervention by the Russian army during the revolution of 1848 when Hungarians had sought to free themselves of Austrian domination. Also, the Stalinist secret police had bred deep resentment. These factors, as well as economic grievances, led to Nagy's announcement on November 1, 1956, that Hungary was an independent nation. With this declaration came the pledge to hold free elections—elections that promised to end Communist party rule in Hungary.

The events in Hungary left Nikita Khrushchev few choices, particularly when Radio Free Europe, a station operating out of Munich under the aegis of the CIA, encouraged the Hungarians by offering vague promises of U.S. aid. In this highly charged moment in the Cold War, a neutral Hungary was out of the question. John Foster Dulles, the U.S. secretary of state, had said earlier that neutrality in this holy war against the forces of absolute evil was the height of immorality.[10] The leaders in the Kremlin held a similar view. Hungary was thus destined to be but a pawn in an ideological and military tug-of-war. Its fate was to serve either the interests of Washington or those of Moscow. With the Soviet position in Eastern Europe beginning to disintegrate, Khrushchev acted.

The Red Army attacked Budapest three days after Nagy's proclamation. After a week of savage fighting the Soviets reestablished their control over Hungary. The Kremlin executed Imre Nagy and installed Janos Kadar as the Hungarian party's new first secretary. Kadar, who came to power with blood on his hands, proved in time to be a cautious reformer.[11] Gradually over the next three decades he introduced the most sweeping economic reforms anywhere in the Soviet bloc, culminating in the legalization of private enterprises in the early 1980s. This combination of the carrot (tolerance of reforms) and the stick (the Red Army) has lifted many restrictions, raised the standard of living, and kept Hungary quiet since.

The United States could do little but watch with indignation the Soviet suppression of the Hungarian uprising and offer political asylum to many of the nearly 200,000 Hungarians who fled their country. John Foster Dulles, who in the past had repeatedly stated that the aim of the United States was the liberation of Eastern Europe and the roll-back of the Soviet presence there, could do no more than watch in frustration. The events in Hungary seemed to offer him the opportunity to put his policy into operation, but President Eisenhower's cautious response revealed that Dulles's rhetoric was just that. The Hungarian rebellion also revealed that the United States would not challenge the Soviet Union in Eastern Europe; it would not start World War III over Poland or Hungary. The lesson was not lost on the Soviets when they had to deal with Czechoslovakia in 1968.

☐ Czechoslovakia

Events in Poland and Hungary did not affect Czechoslovakia during the 1950s. The country continued to be ruled by Antonin Novotny, whom Stalin had placed in power in 1952. In the late 1960s, Czechoslovakia, therefore, appeared to be the least likely candidate for social and political reform. Yet, the unreconstructed Stalinist Novotny was bitterly resented by many in Czechoslovakia, particularly the writers and including members of his own party. When a writers' rebellion began late in 1967, Novotny found himself unable to deal with it because his own party did not support him. In fact, in short order the party asked him to resign, and he did so in January 1968. The party then elected Alexander Dubcek as its first secretary.

The writers, many of whom were Communists, had raised a number of basic questions—those of civil rights, censorship, and the monopoly of the Communist party in the political, economic, and social affairs of the nation. Under Dubcek's stewardship, the Communist party introduced numerous reforms at breakneck speed. It attempted to create a "Communism with a human face," one that sought to combine Eastern-style socialism with Western-style democracy. One restriction after another was lifted. The results were freedom of the press, freedom to travel, freedom from fear of the police. An intense and open debate of the nature of the reforms took place in the uncensored pages of the press. In the spring and summer of 1968, euphoria swept a nation that became oblivious to the inherent dangers of such radical reforms. Soon there was the inevitable talk of neutrality and the possibility of leaving the Soviet bloc.

Both the United States and the Soviet Union watched these developments intensely. Several high-ranking delegations arrived from Moscow and other East European capitals. The Communist parties of Eastern Europe urged Dubcek and his party to bring the movement under control before it completely got out of hand. Several of the East European governments (particularly those of Yugoslavia and Hungary) did not want to give the Soviet Union an excuse for intervention. But it was to no avail. Dubcek neither wanted to nor was he able to put an end to the discussions and experiments. The hopeful "Prague Spring" continued unabated. The border between Czechoslovakia and Austria became but a line on a map that Czechs—and visitors from the West—crossed without restriction. The Iron Curtain had ceased to exist in this part of Europe.

Until August 1968, the Soviet leadership appeared to be divided on what course to take. But by that time the hard-liners in Moscow became convinced that Dubcek and his party were no longer in control. Moreover, events in Czechoslovakia threatened to create repercussions at home. The non-Russian population of the Soviet empire—approximately half of the population—watched the events in Czechoslovakia with growing interest. The party chiefs in the non-Russian republics, particularly those of the Ukraine and Lithuania, took the lead in urging strong action. They convened a plenary session of the party's Central Committee to decide on a course of action. On August 20, 1968, the Communist Party of the Soviet Union ordered the Red Army to put its contingency plans into operation. When the Red Army's tanks and troops rolled into Prague, the Czechs, as expected, did not resist to any appreciable degree. The Soviets then proceeded to replace Dubcek with Gustav Husak.

The Soviets justified their invasion of Czechoslovakia by claiming that they had to protect that nation against a counterrevolution. Moreover, they declared they had an inherent right to intervene in all socialist countries similarly threatened. This Soviet right of intervention in Eastern Europe became known in the West as the Brezhnev Doctrine. In 1979, Brezhnev used it anew to justify intervention in Afghanistan when he sent the Red Army to bail out a bankrupt socialist government. And in 1980, Brezhnev resurrected it to warn Poland's Solidarity movement against going too far.

Ironically, the Soviet Union had been able to count on a certain measure of good will among the population of Czechoslovakia until the invasion of 1968. After all, it had been the Soviet army in 1945 that had liberated Prague from the Germans, and only the Soviets had appeared to be willing to come to the aid of Czechoslovakia when Hitler had carved it up in 1938. But whatever good will had existed before 1968 became a thing of the past.

* * *

On paper the forces of the Warsaw Pact have always looked formidable. But the Soviet could never actually rely on most of the East European armies. Yugoslavia and Albania left the Soviet camp during the late 1940s and early 1960s respectively. Romania conducted its own foreign policy since the mid-1950s. The East Germans, Poles, Czechs and Slovaks, and

Hungarians were never as reliable as the Kremlin wanted them to be. Only Bulgaria appeared to be a loyal ally. In the West, Communist Eastern Europe was generally viewed as a potential forward base for the Soviets. At the same time it served as a defensive barrier protecting the Soviet Union's borders. But increasingly, as the events of 1989 showed, it also became a glacier protecting Western Europe through which the Red Army could cross only at its peril.

■ THE SINO-SOVIET SPLIT

As if the challenges emanating from Eastern Europe were not enough for the Soviet leadership, they faced simultaneously another crisis within the Communist world. By the mid–1950s, those who ruled the People's Republic of China, once a seemingly loyal member of an international Communist movement, began to strike out on their own. Before long, it became apparent that the two Communist giants were at loggerheads and that the split was irrevocable. Polycentrism in the Communist world had truly become a fact of life and no force could put Humpty Dumpty together again.

The partnership between the Soviet Union and the People's Republic of China, established immediately after the Communists came to power in China in 1949, appeared to rest on a solid foundation. At the time Moscow and Washington were engaged in a potentially deadly rivalry, which already had turned into a nuclear confrontation. As early as 1950, Beijing sent its troops against the U.S.-led forces of the United Nations in Korea. Moscow and Beijing thus faced a common foe and professed a common ideology. There was little reason to believe that their alliance would be short-lived. Yet, only six years later the two began to pull apart. The rift between them became more serious with each passing year, and by the early 1960s, relations were openly hostile. The feud between the two Communist giants, which has continued ever since, had of course a great impact on international relations. As the Sino-Soviet feud emerged, the Cold War, initially a bipolar struggle between East and West, became more complicated. It gave way to a triangular pattern of relations among the Soviet Union, China, and the United States.

In 1949, there were good reasons to believe that the new China, the People's Republic of China (PRC), would establish and maintain close relations with the Soviet Union. Many observers in the West felt that the Soviet Union in some manner had been involved in the Communist victory in China. Moreover, Chairman Mao Zedong's mission to Moscow in early 1950 seemed to confirm the suspicion that Mao and Stalin were comrades united in the cause of international Communism and mutually dedicated to the defeat of the capitalist world. In Moscow, in February 1950, they signed a thirty-year military alliance aimed at the United States, and the Soviet Union took up the cause of seating the PRC in the United Nations to replace the Republic of China (Nationalist China). The Soviet Union also provided much needed economic assistance to China in the form of loans, technicians, and advisers. The two nations also rallied in support of Communist North Korea during the Korean War. And of course they spoke the same Marxian language, which denounced U.S. imperialism. They certainly seemed united.

It was little wonder then that the United States was skeptical about the early reports of difficulties between the two Communist states. The U.S. assumption, fostered by the Cold War, was that Communism was a monolith, a single, unitary movement directed by Moscow. This assumption was much slower to die than the reality of Communist unity.

In retrospect, we can recognize signs of friction between Beijing and Moscow from the very outset. The Chinese could hardly be pleased by the rather cavalier manner in which Stalin treated them. The terms of the Moscow agreements were not at all generous. Stalin offered Mao a development loan of no more than $300 million to be spread over five years and to be repaid by China in agricultural produce and with interest. As a price for that loan China agreed to continued Soviet use and control of the principal railroads and ports in Manchuria and to the creation of joint Sino-Soviet stock companies to conduct mineral surveys in Xinjiang (Sinkiang), the innermost province of China. The paucity of Soviet aid and the concessions Stalin demanded from China suggest that Stalin's purpose was to accentuate Soviet supremacy and Chinese dependency. Indeed, it would seem that Stalin was wary of this new Communist friend and that he would have preferred dealing with a weaker, more vulnerable Nationalist China than with a vigorous new Communist regime in China. If the Chinese harbored ill feelings toward Stalin or resented the continued Soviet presence in Manchuria and Xinjiang, they prudently remained silent, publicly accepting Stalin's leadership and extolling the fraternal relationship with the Soviet Union. The backwardness of China's economy was such that Chinese leaders considered Soviet economic assistance and diplomatic support too important to sacrifice on the altar of national pride.

The unspoken misgivings between Moscow and Beijing of the early 1950s did not lead directly to the Sino-Soviet split of the late 1950s. Nor is that feud to be explained as a direct consequence of earlier Sino-Russian troubles. One can surely trace the historical roots of animosity between the two countries back in time, to tsarist imperialism in the nineteenth century, or even to the Mongol invasions of Russia in the thirteenth century. But it would be too simple to argue that the conflict in the late 1950s was, therefore, the inevitable result of that history. The troubled past may have been an underlying factor that conditioned the attitudes of the two adversaries, but it did not cause their dispute. The two sides dredged up the conflicts of the past, such as territorial claims, only after the dispute began to develop over other contemporary issues in the mid–1950s.

The first strains of conflict between Moscow and Beijing came in consequence of Soviet leader Nikita Khrushchev's famous Secret Speech in February 1956. The Chinese leaders were caught by surprise by this sudden, scathing attack on Stalin and by Khrushchev's call for peaceful coexistence with the capitalist world. Chinese Communists had no particular reason to defend the departed Stalin, but they did question the wisdom of peaceful coexistence, and more importantly, they disputed the right of Moscow to unilaterally make such a major ideological shift with important global implications. The Chinese leaders chafed at Khrushchev's boldly reinterpreting Marxist-Leninist doctrine, without so much as consulting with Mao Zedong in advance. Mao, who had led the Chinese Communist party (CCP) since 1935, was the world's senior ranking Communist leader, and he had reason to object to being ignored by the brash new leader of the Soviet Union. The Chinese were beginning to question not only Khrushchev's authority to dictate policy to the Communist world but also the substance of his ideological pronouncements.

The new Soviet line of peaceful coexistence was soon to become the major bone of contention between Moscow and Beijing. The Soviet leadership had become alarmed about the nuclear arms race and came to the conviction that the Soviet Union must avert a devastating nuclear war with the United States, whose burgeoning nuclear arsenal posed a serious threat to the survival of their country. Khrushchev, therefore, concluded that it would be necessary to coexist peacefully with the capitalist superpower. However, at the same time that they were offering the olive branch to the other side, the Soviets worked feverishly to close the gap in the arms race, and in 1957 they made two remarkable technological breakthroughs. The Soviet Union launched its first ICBM (intercontinental ballistic missile) in August, and in October it stunned the world with Sputnik, the first satellite sent into orbit around the earth. The enormous strategic significance of this Soviet advance in military technology was not lost on the Chinese. Mao Zedong, attending a meeting of world Communist leaders in Moscow in November 1957, contended that the international situation had reached a new turning point and that the Communist world had stolen the march on the capitalist world in the contest for global power. Mao asserted that "at present, it is not the west wind which is prevailing over the east wind, but the east wind prevailing over the west wind."[12] He argued that the Communist camp should put its newfound military superiority to work to attain the final victory over capitalism. Khrushchev strongly rejected these ideas and concluded the meeting with a reaffirmation of peaceful coexistence.

This was the origin of a dispute over global strategy that ultimately split the two Communist giants. The Chinese argued that, by making peace with the capitalists, the Soviet Union was departing from essential Marxist-Leninist doctrine. Peaceful coexistence might suit the Soviet Union because it was already an industrialized nation with secure borders and nuclear weapons, but it was unsuited to China, which had none of these. Mao argued that Communist nations should continue the international struggle, for example, by assisting Communist forces engaged in wars of national liberation. Moreover, the PRC sought assurances of Soviet support in its own unfinished war of national liberation: the civil war against Jiang Kaishek's regime, which controlled the island of Taiwan. In 1958, Beijing intensified the pressure on Taiwan by launching a sustained artillery barrage against two off-shore islands, Quemoy and Matsu, which were occupied by the Nationalist forces. It seems that Mao's purpose was to test the resolve of the United States to defend Nationalist China and to test Soviet willingness to provide active military support to the PRC. The United States made clear its commitment to the defense of Taiwan, but the Soviets, instead of pledging support, denounced China's actions as reckless. The Soviet Union would not allow itself to be drawn into a nuclear war with the United States over Taiwan. Moreover, in 1959, Moscow rescinded an earlier agreement to provide China nuclear technology to build an atomic bomb.

In addition to disputing global strategy, the two Communist powers also disagreed on the means to attaining Communism. The Chinese had adopted the Soviet model for economic development when, in 1953, they put into operation a Soviet-style Five-Year Plan. But by 1957, the leaders in Beijing were beginning to question the appropriateness of the Soviet model for China, and Mao in particular became very critical of its top-heavy, bureaucratic nature. In early 1958, Mao called for scrapping the Second Five-Year Plan and replacing it with a new program known as the Great Leap Forward. Mao thus abandoned the Soviet model in favor of his own program designed to achieve industrial development and the collectivization of agriculture simultaneously. Boldly, Mao proclaimed that China had overtaken the Soviet Union in the quest to build a Communist society. But Mao was too quick to trumpet success, for within a year the Great Leap Forward, with its hastily created communes, produced an economic disaster (see Chapter 13). The Soviet leadership, concerned about the implications for the Eastern European satellites of China's departing from the Soviet model, was from the beginning critical of the new experiment in China. Indeed, Khrushchev heaped scorn on Mao's heralded Great Leap all the more when it failed.

The growing feud with Moscow was reflected in a political crisis that occurred in Beijing in the summer of 1959. Chairman Mao, who had championed the Great Leap Forward, was chagrined by its failure and was compelled to accept blame for it. While Chinese party leaders deftly worked to repair the damage and yet not embarrass Mao, one high ranking official dared openly to condemn Mao for his failures. Chinese defense minister,

Peng Dehuai, who had just returned from a visit to the Soviet Union, spoke out strongly against Mao's policies and in favor of retention of the Soviet model, which he regarded necessary for China's military modernization. Mao led a blistering counterattack against Peng, charging him with conspiring with Moscow against the Chinese revolution and denouncing him as a traitor. Mao suspected that Peng was being used by Khrushchev in a maneuver to oust him (Mao) as chairman of the CCP. At a meeting of the Central Executive Committee of the CCP in August 1959, Mao accepted criticism of the Great Leap Forward failures, but he secured the party's support for the expulsion of Peng from the government and the party. Peng was replaced as defense minister by Lin Biao, a supporter of Mao, who immediately declared that China was in no need of Soviet technical or military assistance for its national defense.

Only a month later, Khrushchev gave Mao added reason to suspect that the Soviet Union was plotting against China. At the invitation of President Eisenhower, Khrushchev made a two-week visit to the United States. Mao, who remained adamantly opposed to peaceful coexistence, obviously took a dim view of this diplomatic venture, and he was left to speculate on what had transpired in the private talks between Khrushchev and Eisenhower. He suspected that his Soviet counterpart was making concessions at China's expense. The Chinese suspected that Khrushchev was in Washington to strike a bargain that would trade Western concessions on the Berlin question for a Soviet commitment to block the PRC's use of force to settle the Taiwan question. When Khrushchev subsequently announced intentions of reducing the size of the Soviet army and seeking a general disarmament, the Chinese could only think that the Soviet Union had abandoned the Marxist-Leninist cause of combating "capitalist imperialism."

In 1960, the polemical feud between Moscow and Beijing became an open confrontation as each side, for the first time, made public their attacks on the other. The Chinese struck first, in April 1960, with an article titled "Long Live Leninism" in *Red Flag,* an official organ of the Chinese Communist party. It argued that peaceful coexistence was contrary to the precepts of Leninism:

> We believe in the absolute correctness of Lenin's thinking: War is an inevitable outcome of systems of exploitation and the source of modern wars is the imperialist system. Until the imperialist system and the exploiting classes come to an end, wars of one kind or another will always occur.[13]

The Soviet government responded with both words and actions. In July 1960, Moscow abruptly pulled out of China its 1,300 economic advisers and military technicians who took their blueprints with them and left behind many unfinished projects. This was a serious blow to China's industrialization efforts.

Khrushchev's purpose was not to terminate the alliance but to force Beijing back into line and to coerce its acceptance of Moscow's policies and position of leadership. In the year that followed, Beijing seemed to acquiesce to an extent while a more conciliatory Moscow seemed to be backing away from détente with the United States.[14] But this proved to be but a brief respite, for in October 1961, at the Twenty-second Party Congress of the Communist party of the Soviet Union, Khrushchev again lashed out at the Chinese. He attacked China's economic policies and ideology and argued that modern industrial development must precede experiments with creating communes. Communism was to be achieved by following the Soviet lead. In response, Chinese Foreign Minister Zhou Enlai led the entire Chinese delegation out of the congress and back to Beijing.

In 1962, new diplomatic issues divided Moscow and Beijing and exacerbated their conflict. China and India went to war in October over a border dispute, and, Moscow, instead of supporting China (with whom it had a military alliance), offered diplomatic support to India while joining the United States in condemning China for its reckless aggression. And in October, in the wake of the Cuban missile crisis, in which the United States and the Soviet Union came perilously close to a nuclear war, the Chinese scorned Khrushchev as weak-kneed for caving in to U.S. demands to pull out the Soviet missiles from Cuba. Moreover, the year that followed the Cuban missile crisis brought a new thaw in Soviet-U.S. relations with ominous consequences for China. In August 1963, the two superpowers signed a treaty banning atmospheric testing of nuclear weapons. For Beijing this was devastating, for it signified that China was being abandoned by its Communist comrades in favor of the capitalist world. It meant more than diplomatic isolation; it also meant strategic isolation.

The Chinese originally had hoped to draw from the strength of the Soviet-led Communist movement and specifically to attain from Moscow a firm commitment to provide military support for the "liberation" of Taiwan. Having failed in this, Beijing then sought to strengthen its position by cultivating its relations with other Communist and national liberation movements in Asia, Africa, and Latin America—areas that are referred to collectively as the Third World. China had already made a major step in identifying itself with the nonaligned nations of these parts of the world by its participation in the Bandung Conference in Indonesia in 1955.[15] Increasingly in the 1960s, the PRC sought to befriend leaders of revolutionary movements and those of newly independent nations in the Third World even to the point of providing economic aid that China, with its own economic problems, could ill afford. Additionally, Beijing engaged in a propaganda program aimed at convincing Third World nations that the Maoist revolution was the correct path to Communism and was, in any case, more appropriate to developing countries than the Soviet model, which China had tried and found wanting.

In the early 1960s, when the breach with China became wide open, Khrushchev seems to have become as obsessed with the recalcitrant China as Mao had become obsessed with what he regarded as Soviet treachery. After publishing an open letter demanding Beijing's submission to Soviet leadership, Khrushchev began formulating plans for a meeting of world Communist leaders at which he would either force China back into the fold or force it out. Several Communist parties, however, declined invitations because they opposed Khrushchev's confrontational approach. Before this meeting could be arranged, Khrushchev himself was suddenly ousted from power in Moscow. And on the very day that this was reported in the world press, October 16, 1964, the PRC announced it had successfully tested an atomic bomb. Proudly, the Chinese proclaimed that the PRC too was now a superpower. They had defied Khrushchev's efforts to dictate policy and his efforts to deny them nuclear weapons.

No significant change occurred in Sino-Soviet relations in consequence of the fall of Khrushchev and his replacement by Leonid Brezhnev. Nor did the escalation of the U.S. involvement in the Vietnam War in 1965 bring the two Communist powers together; instead, they rivaled one another for influence over the Communist regime in North Vietnam. In April 1965, Moscow proposed to Beijing that the two nations cooperate in support of North Vietnam. It asked the Chinese to allow Soviet aircraft use of Chinese airports and airspace. After lengthy debate within ruling circles in Beijing, Chairman Mao, who opposed any cooperation with the Soviets, rejected the proposal. Mao and his comrades in Beijing feared not only a Soviet military presence in China but also a full-scale war with the Soviet Union. The specter of a preemptive nuclear strike against the PRC and its fledgling nuclear arsenal caused great alarm in China.

Mao Zedong's bombastic attack on the Soviet Union reached new heights in the summer of 1966, when he launched the Great Cultural Revolution, a campaign designed to revitalize the Chinese revolution by mass mobilization (see Chapter 13). This political program contained a strong anti-Soviet aspect, for Mao called upon the Chinese people to purge the party of leaders whom he condemned for trying to establish a Soviet-type Communism in China. He pronounced them guilty of the same crimes that he pinned on Soviet leaders: bureaucratic elitism, revisionism, sabotage of the Communist movement, and taking it down the capitalist road. The political and economic chaos caused by his Cultural Revolution gave the Soviet Union still more reason to ridicule Mao and Maoism. Nevertheless, despite the upheaval it caused, Mao proclaimed that he had set the revolution back on the track to true Communism, and he called upon all Communists and would-be Communists throughout the world to abandon the revisionist Soviets and turn instead to China for their model.

Tensions between the two Communist giants mounted even higher on yet another front: the Sino-Soviet border. From time to time during their feud, Mao had called into question the Soviet claim to territory north of the Amur River boundary between the two countries in Eastern Asia.[16] During the 1960s, as their feud heated up, both the Soviets and the Chinese fortified their common border with larger and larger forces. Within the Ussuri River, which separates China and the Soviet Maritime Province, were several disputed islands, and in March 1969 a skirmish between Chinese and Soviet armed forces suddenly broke out on the island of Damanski. After the Chinese launched an assault, the Soviets struck with artillery, tanks, and aircraft and drove the Chinese back. The warfare left about 800 Chinese troops dead as compared with about 60 Soviet dead. Although a cease-fire was arranged, a war of nerves continued throughout the year. A full-scale war between China and the Soviet Union seemed imminent. It was in this context that leaders in Beijing began to consider ending their diplomatic isolation and improving their relations with the United States. Tension along the border continued on into the 1980s as both sides reinforced their border security with greater military force. Ultimately, the Soviet Union deployed an estimated 1 million troops along its long China borders and armed them with the most modern of weapons, including tactical nuclear weapons. China's border forces are thought to be as large as the Soviets, but not as well equipped.

One of the major consequences of the Sino-Soviet split, and specifically of the near war between the two Communist nations, was the normalization of relations between the PRC and the United States in the early 1970s. This had a profound effect on global power relations, supplanting the bipolar Cold War with what has been called the strategic triangle. Throughout the 1970s and on into the 1980s, the PRC has moved closer to the United States and still further away from the Soviet Union. It charges the latter with "socialist imperialism" and "hegemonism." In fact, "anti-hegemonism" became the main pillar of China's foreign policy in the 1970s, when it endeavored to attain the active support of the United States, Japan, and other nations in its struggle against Soviet global expansion. Its fears of Soviet aggression largely account for its great efforts since the late 1970s to speed up its retarded industrialization and to close the technology gap.

■ THE THIRTY-YEAR FEUD IS ENDED

The open estrangement between the two Communist giants continued into the 1980s. Although Moscow showed signs of desiring a thaw, the Chinese hunkered down with an inflexible policy. Deng Xiaoping's government identified three specific paramount issues on which it insisted on a change in Soviet policy before relations could be normalized. It wanted a withdrawal (or at least a substantial reduction) of Soviet forces from the Chinese border, an end to the Soviet invasion of Afghanistan, and an end to Soviet support for the Vietnamese army in Cambodia. Although bilateral trade and diplomatic exchanges were gradually restored, further progress was blocked by Chinese intransigence on the "three obstacles."

As both Beijing and Moscow focused their attention on economic reform in the 1980s, the prospects for Sino-Soviet rapprochement improved. Mikhail Gorbachev, who came to power in the Kremlin in 1985, brought a dynamic new pragmatism to Soviet diplomacy. Determined to regenerate the faltering Soviet economy, Gorbachev saw it necessary to reduce the size of its military establishment, including the large deployment of Soviet forces in Asia, and toward that end to take steps to reduce tensions in Asia. With these ideas in mind, in July 1986 Gorbachev went to Vladivostok, the largest Soviet city in East Asia, to deliver a speech that boldly proclaimed a new Soviet initiative to establish peaceful relations with China and other Asian nations. In this conciliatory speech, Gorbachev addressed Beijing's three burning issues, declaring Soviet readiness to seek accommodation on all three. He indicated that steps were already being taken toward the evacuation of Soviet forces from Afghanistan, that Soviet troops would be withdrawn from Mongolia on the Sino-Mongolian border, and that Moscow was prepared to discuss the issue of mutual reduction of military forces on the Sino-Soviet border and the Vietnam-Cambodia issue.

Deng Xiaoping reacted positively. In April 1987, for the first time since 1978, Chinese and Soviet negotiators began addressing "regional issues" (i.e., border disputes) and the Cambodian question. Negotiations continued on various levels through the following year as both parties reciprocated with confidence-building gestures and agreements. They entered into an agreement, for example, on barter trade across the border, which resulted in a vast increase in mutually beneficial contacts between the two peoples along their 4,000-mile-long boundary. Between 1981 and 1988, trade between the Soviet Union and China expanded tenfold. A new bridge built across the Amur River not only served the practical needs of the Chinese and Soviets on each side, but also served as a symbol of their renewed ties. By 1989, substantial improvement had been made toward the restoration of peaceful relations. The Soviet Union withdrew from Afghanistan, reduced its troops along the Chinese border,[17] and pressured Vietnam to begin evacuation of its troops from Cambodia. Placated by these conciliatory measures, Deng accepted Gorbachev's proposal for a summit meeting, and extended an invitation to come to Beijing in May 1989.

Gorbachev's visit to China signaled the end of the thirty-year-long rift. He arrived in Beijing, however, in the midst of the mammoth student demonstrations in the Chinese capital, and his historic visit was upstaged by this tumultuous event (see Chapter 13). The summit meeting was, nonetheless, a success. Gorbachev, who acknowledged that the Soviet Union was partly to blame for the deep split between the two countries, proclaimed the summit a "watershed event." The two sides pledged to continue talks aimed at mutually reducing military troop strength along their long shared border "to a minimum level commensurate with normal, good-neighborly relations," to seek expanded trade and cultural relations, and to restore relations between the Communist parties of the two countries.[18] On Cambodia, they acknowledged a lack of agreement but pledged to continue efforts to avert a civil war in that country and to help it become independent and nonaligned. On the whole, the summit meeting advanced the new rapprochement between China and the Soviet Union and reflected their mutual objectives of lessening tensions and improving economic relations.

■ RECOMMENDED READINGS

Bethell, Nicholas. *Gomulka: His Poland, His Communism.* New York: Holt, Rinehart and Winston, 1969.
>An explanation of the Polish road to socialism.
Clubb, O. Edmund. *China and Russia: The "Great Game."* New York: Columbia University Press, 1971.
>A comprehensive, detailed, and evenhanded analysis of the Sino-Soviet split by a U.S. diplomat-turned-scholar.
Crankshaw, Edward. *Khrushchev: A Career.* New York: Viking Press, 1966.
>The standard Western biography of Khrushchev.
Deutscher, Isaac. *Stalin: A Political Biography.* Rev. ed. New York: Oxford University Press, 1966.
>The classic biography by a Trotskyite.
Hinton, Harold C. *China's Turbulent Quest.* 2nd ed. New York: Macmillan, 1973.
>An analysis of the Sino-Soviet rift.
Kecskemeti, Paul. *The Unexpected Revolution: Social Forces in the Hungarian Uprising.* Stanford, Calif.: Stanford University Press, 1961.
>An explanation of the Hungarian uprising.
London, Kurt, ed. *Eastern Europe in Transition.* Baltimore: Johns Hopkins University Press, 1966.
>An explanation of the force of nationalism in Eastern Europe.
Medvedev, Roy A. *Let History Judge: The Origins and Consequences of Stalinism.* New York: Knopf, 1971.
>An indictment of Stalin by a Soviet "Leninist" historian.
Shipler, David K. *Russia: Broken Idols, Solemn Dreams.* New York: Times Books, 1983.
>An attempt to explain Soviet society by a correspondent of the *New York Times.*
Solzhenitsyn, Alexander. *One Day in the Life of Ivan Denisovich.* New York: Praeger, 1962.
>An exposé of Stalin's forced labor camps, the novel that brought Solzhenitsyn international acclaim.

Tatu, Michel. *Power in the Kremlin: From Khrushchev to Kosygin*. London: William Collins Sons, 1968.
A well-received study of Soviet politics by a French expert.
Ulam, Adam. *Stalin: The Man and His Era*. New York: Viking Press, 1973.
A highly readable, detailed biography written from a Western perspective.
Valenta, Jiri. *Soviet Intervention in Czechoslovakia in 1968*. Baltimore: Johns Hopkins University Press, 1979.
A detailed explanation of the Kremlin's reasons for ending the Czechoslovak experiment in liberalization.

■ NOTES

1. J. V. Stalin, "The Tasks of Business Executives," February 4, 1931, J. V. Stalin, *Works* (Moscow: Foreign Languages Publishing House, 1955), XIII, pp. 40–41.

2. A proletarian—a member of the proletariat—is a wage earner, or more commonly, a factory worker. In Marxist jargon, the words "proletarian" and "worker" are used interchangeably.

3. Edward Crankshaw, *Khrushchev: A Career* (New York: Viking, 1966), p. 228.

4. De Tocqueville, quoted in Bernard B. Fall, *The Two Vietnams*, p. 253.

5. N. S. Khrushchev, *Khrushchev Remembers: The Last Testament*, p. 77.

6. Tito's independence of both the Soviet Union and the West led him to take a "third" road. Tito, Nehru of India, and Nasser of Egypt became the early leaders of the Third World, that is, nations that refused to align themselves with either the Western or socialist blocs. The term has lost its original meaning, for it is used primarily to designate the poverty-stricken nations of the tropical regions.

7. J. V. Stalin, "The International Situation and the Defence of the U.S.S.R.," speech delivered on August 1, 1927, to the Joint Plenum of the Central Committee and Central Control Commission of the C.P.S.U. (b), J. V. Stalin, *Works*, (Moscow: Foreign Languages Publishing House, 1954), X, pp. 53–54.

8. N. S. Khrushchev, *Khruschchev Remembers* (Boston: Little, Brown, 1970), p. 351; for the full text, pp. 559–618.

9. Adam B. Ulam, *Expansion and Coexistence: The History of Soviet Foreign Policy, 1917–67* (New York: Praeger, 1968), pp. 578–579.

10. For a summary of Dulles's views on Communism, see his testimony before Congress, January 15, 1953, Walter LaFeber, ed., *The Dynamics of World Power: A Documentary History of United States Foreign Policy, 1945–1973, II, Eastern Europe and the Soviet Union* (New York: Chelsea House, 1973), pp. 465–468.

11. "Blood on his hands" is a reference to Kadar granting safe conduct to Nagy (who nevertheless was executed) and the bloody suppression of the rebellion. Kadar then became known as the "butcher of Budapest."

12. Mao: "At present it is not the west wind," *Survey of the China Mainland Press*, U.S. Consulate General, Hong Kong, no. 1662. December 2, 1957, p. 2.

13. Mao on Lenin, *Current Background*, U.S. Consulate General, Hong Kong, No. 617, April 26, 1960.

14. The U.S.-Soviet détente suffered a setback in May 1960 when the Soviets shot down a U.S. U-2 spy plane over the Soviet Union, and Khrushchev, after demanding a U.S. apology, declined to meet President Eisenhower at a scheduled summit meeting in Paris and withdrew an earlier invitation for Eisenhower to visit Moscow. In 1961, Khrushchev rescinded earlier plans for a Soviet arms reduction and resumed testing of nuclear weapons after a three year moratorium. Also, that year the Berlin Wall was erected.

Since the outset of the Cold War, the Soviet Union had found the political, military, and espionage presence in West Berlin unacceptable. East Germans had used Berlin as a means to resettle in West Germany by merely taking the subway to the Western sectors of the city. By the early 1960s, as the West German economy was undergoing its economic miracle, the flow of East Germans—many of them highly skilled—became an unacceptable hemorrhage of the East German economy. The Berlin Blockade (1948–1949) and Khruschev's saber-rattling proved to be ineffective in dislodging the Western powers. The Berlin Wall solved East Germany's most pressing problem when it sealed off the last remaining gap in the Iron Curtain. It also removed Berlin as one of the focal points of the Cold War.

15. At this conference of twenty-nine Afro-Asian nations, China's representative, Zhou Enlai, shared the spotlight with India's neutralist prime minister, Nehru. China joined with these Third World nations in pledging peace and mutual noninterference.

16. In two separate treaties in 1858 and 1860, China relinquished to tsarist Russia territory north of the Amur River and east of the Ussuri River (the latter territory known as the Maritime Province). But Mao now contended that these were ill-gotten gains and that, since the treaties were forced on China by an imperialist government, they should not be honored or considered binding.

17. Gorbachev pledged in December 1988 at the United Nations to cut Soviet military forces by half a million, 200,000 of which would be from military units in Asia. He also announced plans to withdraw three-quarters of the Soviet troops in Mongolia, and indicated that the first contingent of 12,000 soldiers were already being taken out.

18. Scott Shane, "Gorbachev Returns Home from 'Watershed' Summit," *Baltimore Sun*, May 19, 1989.

The War in Indochina

The Vietnam War, the United States's longest war, was one of the most tragic experiences in the history of the United States. It was even more tragic for Vietnam, the country in which it was fought. The United States became engaged in a conflict in a distant Asian nation, confident that its great military capability could produce a victory and stop the spread of Communism in that part of the world. By getting involved in a war against an Asian people fighting in defense of their homeland, the United States ignored the lessons of the past—the Chinese resistance against an overpowering Japan in the 1930s and 1940s, and the success of the Viet Minh guerrillas in their eight-year-long battle against the French in Vietnam.

The massive U.S. intervention began in 1965, but continued to escalate until U.S. troops numbered well over half a million by 1968. This huge armed force with its modern weaponry was, however, denied victory by a resilient, determined Vietnamese enemy. In time, Washington learned that piling up the dead higher and higher would not necessarily bring victory. However, for political reasons, it would prove much more difficult to get out of Vietnam than it was to get in. In this chapter, our first concern is how and why the United States became involved in this war. Secondly, we will examine U.S. difficulties in getting out of the war and the war's costs and consequences.

■ THE ESCALATION OF U.S. INVOLVEMENT

The Geneva Conference of 1954 called for the withdrawal of France from Indochina after the French defeat at Dien Bien Phu. The agreement established the independent states of Laos and Cambodia, and made a temporary separation of Vietnam into two zones divided at the 17th parallel. In the north a Communist government, the Democratic Republic of Vietnam, was already established with Hanoi its capital and Ho Chi Minh its president. In the south, the French transferred power to the native monarch, Bao Dai, in Saigon. The Geneva Accords called for the unification of Vietnam on the basis of an internationally supervised election to be held two years later, in July 1956. It also provided that, until unification, the people in Vietnam would be free to relocate across the dividing line, and that neither part of Vietnam would introduce foreign troops or make any military alliances. French troops were to remain in the south until the unification process was completed.

The United States sought from the start to strengthen the Saigon regime and weaken the Hanoi regime. The United States, which had already assumed the greater part of the financial burden of France's war in Vietnam, now took up the task of supporting a client state in South Vietnam, financially, politically, and militarily. Even before the Geneva Accords had been signed (the United States never signed them, but did pledge to abide by them), U.S. Army officers arrived in Saigon to establish a military mission and prepare for "paramilitary operations."

In Saigon, the most effective political leader was not the playboy king, Bao Dai, known to some as the "emperor of Cannes," but his prime minister, Ngo Dinh Diem. Diem, a Roman Catholic from North Vietnam, was not in his homeland during its struggle for independence against the French but was instead in the United States where he cultivated some important friendships, particularly with influential clergy. In October 1955 Diem deposed Bao Dai in a referendum and with it he became the president of the newly created Republic of Vietnam. It was a smashing electoral victory for he won an incredible 98 percent of the votes cast, and in the city of Saigon he received 130 percent of the registered vote.[1] The French had little faith in Diem's ability to unify the country, but U.S. leaders saw in him the strongman needed to govern and defend South Vietnam. He was the "Churchill of Southeast Asia," a decisive, staunchly anti-Communist leader who was determined to prevent the unification of Vietnam under Ho Chi Minh's Communist government and to smash any resistance to his own government in the South.[2] So determined was he that he willfully ignored the terms of the Geneva Agreement regarding the nationwide elections. With the silent support of Washington, Diem defied the Geneva Accords on the matters of the elections and military alliances, and went on to entrench himself in the South with ever more U.S. aid.

Ngo Dinh Diem soon encountered an opposition movement in the villages of South Vietnam, and his own policies and authoritarian style gave it cause. First, his rejection of the elections in 1956 stirred protests, especially by former Viet Minh soldiers who had remained in the South in expectation of the reunification of the country. Diem sought to silence this protest by conducting a campaign of terror against the Viet Minh involving arrests, beatings, torture, and execution of suspected Viet Minh members. A second cause of the growing unrest in rural areas was the peasants' demand for land reform. A radical redistribution of landholdings was being instituted in North Vietnam, and Diem's government had promised one in the South. The peasantry, which made up 85 percent of the population, felt betrayed by Diem's refusal to carry out a genuine land reform program. This discontent was exploited by the Communist party, which was formed mainly by Viet Minh veterans. It took the lead in organizing the anti-government elements in the countryside and preparing them for a program of forceful resistance, which is to say, insurrection. Diem's increasingly repressive policies played into its hands. When Diem began rounding up suspected dissidents—Communist and non-Communist alike—and placing them into detention camps, the new Communist-led revolutionary movement began to wage guerrilla warfare against his regime. Government terror was met with guerrilla terror, and the level of violence steadily increased in the late 1950s and early 1960s.

In December 1960 various opposition groups and parties, including the Communist party, formed the National Liberation Front (NLF), and this organization directed the revolutionary movement in South Vietnam thereafter. The guerrilla forces of the NLF were commonly known as the Viet Cong, short for Vietnamese Communists. It was a derisive term Diem used to label his enemies. The more brutal Diem's regime became in its efforts to root out and destroy the insurrection, the more popular and active the NLF revolutionaries became and the larger their forces grew. When Diem replaced local village headmen with his own bureaucrats in an attempt to control the countryside, these new leaders became targets for assassination by the Viet Cong. After trying several schemes to reorganize and secure the villages of South Vietnam, Diem finally resorted to the drastic measure of resettling the villagers in compounds called strategic hamlets. Although these met with the approval of U.S. advisers who financed them, the peasants were strongly opposed to them and the NLF condemned them as concentration camps.

Diem's government was no more popular in the cities. He adopted the style of a benevolent dictator, which he rationalized by his own doctrine, called "personalism." According to his Confucian-like doctrine, individual freedom must take second place to the collective betterment of society, which is achieved by dutiful loyalty to the morally superior ruler. In practice this meant absolute obedience to Diem, even to the point of requiring all citizens to hang official photographs of him in their homes. Meanwhile, he gathered around himself a tightly knit clique of loyal supporters, several of whom were his own brothers. The most notable among these was Ngo Dinh Nhu, who matched his brother in arrogance and who gained notoriety as the ruthless head of Diem's secret police. The Diem regime resorted to forceful measures to demand the active support of the various Buddhist organizations in the country, and when they resisted, Nhu used brute force against them. In protest, several Buddhist priests resorted to self-immolation. In a public square they doused themselves with gasoline, and while seated in the posture for meditation they ignited themselves. This spectacle, seen around the world on television, signaled the degree to which Diem's government had alienated South Vietnamese society. Even the South Vietnamese army turned against him and made an unsuccessful attempt to topple him. Despite—and because of—the brutal methods used by Diem and his brother Nhu, the opposition grew stronger. And the stronger the insurrectionist movement grew the more repressive Diem's regime became. It became a vicious circle.

Finally, U.S. observers in Saigon came to the conclusion that, because Diem had become so ruthless, especially in his attacks on the Buddhists, and because his regime was so weak both in the countryside and in Saigon itself, he should be replaced by a new regime more capable of defeating the Communist-led insurrection. A group of South Vietnamese army officers, encouraged by the U.S. embassy, staged a coup d'état in November 1963, murdering Diem and his brother Nhu in the process. They then formed a junta (a military ruling group) to govern in Saigon and to direct the military effort to crush the NLF.

The new government had the blessing of the United States from the outset, but it proved to be no more effective than the previous one. When it became apparent in the following year that the NLF was winning the struggle for control of South Vietnam, the Pentagon and State Department planners began laying plans for a greatly increased U.S. role in the conflict. During the Kennedy administration, the U.S. presence grew from several hundred advisers to 18,000 "special forces" troops. Lyndon Johnson, who succeeded the slain Kennedy as president in November 1963, confronted the prospect that the South Vietnamese government, one which the United States had propped up for ten years, would soon be overthrown by a Communist-led insurrection. President Johnson inherited the commitment to defend Vietnam against that fate, and he committed himself fully to that cause.

The thinking in Washington at this time was that the NLF was completely controlled by the Communist regime in Hanoi, which in turn was under the control of Communist China. If South Vietnam were to fall to Communism, then other neighboring states would also fall one by one to this Beijing-directed Communist aggression. (This scenario was referred to as the domino theory, a term that had been widely used in Washington since the Eisenhower administration.) Therefore, the U.S. commitment in South Vietnam was to defend this "free" (non-Communist) nation against "Communist aggression from outside." The Johnson administration always saw the war in Vietnam as an international conflict, never a civil war among the Vietnamese.

INDOCHINA: THE VIETNAM WAR

President Johnson told the nation in October 1964 that "We are not going to send American boys nine or ten thousand miles away from home to do what Asian boys ought to be doing for themselves," but at the same time he declared that the United States would "defend freedom" in South Vietnam and stop the "Communist aggression" from the north.[3] He was determined to prevent his administration from being charged with losing the battle against Communism in yet another Asian country. Moreover, he feared that such a major foreign policy setback would do political damage to his presidency and thus endanger the Great Society program that he had launched at home.

The United States's Communist opponents in Vietnam, whose voice was generally not heard in Washington, had a very different view of the realities in that country. The NLF disputed the legitimacy of the Saigon government, protesting that the Diem regime and its successors in Saigon were merely puppets of U.S. forces in Vietnam. It called for the implementation of the 1954 Geneva Accords, the withdrawal of U.S. military forces from the country, and the creation of a coalition government in South Vietnam. Ho Chi Minh's government in Hanoi took the same position. In April 1965, it set forth a four-point proposal, which called for (1) withdrawal of U.S. forces, (2) an end of hostilities against North Vietnam, (3) honoring the Geneva Accords, and (4) allowing the Vietnamese to solve their own problems. Hanoi did not sway from this position throughout the war.

Critics of President Johnson's policy—and they were still rather few at this stage—disputed the claim that the Saigon government was the victim of foreign aggression and raised the key question of the relationship between

Ngo Dinh Diem, President of the Republic of Vietnam from 1955 to Nov. 1963 when he was killed in a coup d'etat. (*National Archives*)

the NLF and the Communist government in Hanoi. The official U.S. position was that the NLF was a puppet of Hanoi, and thus Johnson consistently refused to recognize it in any formal capacity. His critics argued that the NLF was neither created nor controlled by Hanoi, but was the organized center of the revolution within South Vietnam and was essentially independent of Hanoi. The relationship between the two is still not clearly known to historians. As noted above, they had similar objectives and had the same enemies, and the NLF no doubt looked for and received guidance and supplies from Hanoi. However, it is fairly clear that the NLF fought its own battle against the Saigon regime and its U.S. supporters, at least until the massive intervention by U.S. troops in 1965. In June 1966, Senator Mike Mansfield (D-Montana) revealed that when sharp U.S. escalation began in early 1965, only 400 of the 140,000 enemy forces in South Vietnam were North Vietnamese soldiers. The defense department confirmed these figures.[4] *The Pentagon Papers* point to similar such low estimates of North Vietnamese forces during the years 1963–1964. Washington's panicky reaction to developments in South Vietnam was not a response to North Vietnamese strength in that country, but to the weakness of South Vietnam and the fear of a Viet Cong victory.[5] It was not until 1965, after the sustained U.S. bombing of North Vietnam began in February of that year, that North Vietnam regulars entered the war in the south with military units.

In its effort to prepare the U.S. public for the escalation of the war, the U.S. State Department, under the hawkish Dean Rusk, sought to prove that the war in South Vietnam was the result of Communist aggression from the north. In early 1965 it published, with great fanfare, its famous White Paper (or position paper) in which it sought to prove its case. For that purpose it produced evidence that, among weapons captured from the NLF, a number were of Communist origin. But the number—179 out of 15,100—only proved that the NLF was depending more on weapons captured from the inept and demoralized South Vietnamese army than on outside Communist sources.[6]

■ THE "AMERICANIZATION" OF THE WAR

In early August 1964, during the U.S. presidential election campaign, President Johnson found the pretext he needed for the United States to intervene directly in the war in a major way and to do so with Congressional support. This was the Gulf of Tonkin incident. The U.S. government reported that one of its naval ships, the destroyer *Maddox,* had been attacked by North Vietnamese torpedo boats. Although Johnson claimed that the attack took place on the high seas (that is, in international waters) and that it was unprovoked, the destroyer was in fact within the twelve-mile limit of North Vietnam gathering intelligence electronically and providing support for covert military operations against North Vietnam by South Vietnamese commandos. After an alleged second North Vietnamese "attack" two days later—one that was never confirmed by an investigation—President Johnson ordered retaliatory air strikes against selected targets in North Vietnam. But more importantly, he also went to Congress for authorization to use military force in Vietnam. The result was the Gulf of Tonkin Resolution, which authorized the president to take "all necessary measures to repel any armed attacks against the forces of the United States and to prevent further aggression." This resolution was passed unanimously by the House of Representatives and by a ninety-eight to two vote in the Senate. Supporters of the war called it a "functional equivalent of a declaration of war."[7] Both President Johnson and his successor, Richard Nixon, used it as the legal basis for massive military operations in Vietnam and in neighboring countries.

Not until he was elected and inaugurated for a new term of office did President Johnson actually use these new powers. During the election campaign he had wanted to appear as a "dove" compared to his "hawkish" Republican opponent, Barry Goldwater. Thus, he repeatedly vowed that he was against committing American boys to fighting a war in Vietnam. But, after the election, on the advice of his political and military advisers, a group of men who had served under Kennedy, Johnson decided to step up the U.S. involvement in the war. He ordered sustained bombing raids on North Vietnam in February 1965, and in the weeks that followed U.S. combat troops landed in large numbers on the shores of South Vietnam to take up the battle.

Meanwhile, in June 1965, another military coup in Saigon brought to power a new set of officers who were more strongly committed to the anti-Communist cause in which the United States was so heavily engaged. The leaders of the new ruling group were Air Marshal Nguyen Cao Ky and Army General Nguyen Van Thieu. Their regime was quite willing to use force against any and all political opposition, and did so against the Buddhists in Hue in May 1966. They resolutely refused any negotiations or compromise with the NLF. In September 1967, a controlled election was held and Thieu was elected president and Ky vice-president. The election served to provide the semblance of democracy that Washington needed to support its case that the United States was fighting in defense of a government that represented the will of the people of South Vietnam.

The continued bombing of North Vietnam and its supply routes into the south (nicknamed the Ho Chi Minh Trail) and the heavy commitment of U.S. forces in search and destroy missions seemed to promise certain victory. In late 1966, General William Westmoreland, the commanding officer of U.S. forces in Vietnam, felt confident enough to state "we have reached an important point, when the end begins to come into view."[8] The United States introduced an incredible amount of firepower into the war, and inflicted an ever

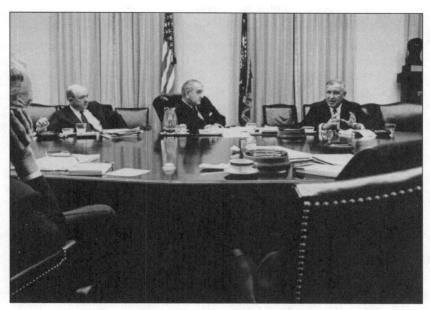

President Lyndon Johnson meets with General Creighton Abrams and key cabinet members at the White House for discussion of the Vietnam War, Oct. 29, 1968. (*National Archives*)

Vietnamese President Nguyen Van Thieu and Vice President Nguyen Cao Ky meet with U.S. President Lyndon Johnson, Honolulu, Hawaii, Feb. 7, 1966. (*National Archives*)

increasing number of casualties on its enemy. Every week U.S. television viewers were treated to higher and higher body counts of dead Communist soldiers. However, despite their increasing losses, the Communists forces seemed to grow ever stronger. Hanoi continued to infiltrate more supplies to arm the Viet Cong, who were able to recruit more soldiers to fight and die for their cause against the foreign army. Nationalism was surely on the side of the NLF, as their appeals to avenge the dreadful toll of Vietnamese deaths and the devastation of their country were answered by hundreds of thousands of their own people. The more that the United States bombed and strafed and napalmed, the more that it killed and captured, the stronger its Vietnamese enemy grew.

And so the weary war went on through 1966 and 1967. No longer did South Vietnam carry the chief burden of the war; it had become the United States's war. And with North Vietnam engaged in the fight in South Vietnam it became an entirely different conflict, one which belied President Johnson's 1964 campaign promise that he sought no wider war. By the beginning of 1968, the optimism in Saigon and in Washington began to give way to pessimism. The war was proving to be "an escalated military stalemate." By this time, after three full years of large-scale warfare and increasingly volatile political protests at home, Lyndon Johnson could hear voices within his own administration and his own party urging him to consider getting out of Vietnam.

The Vietnam War had become a dreadful nightmare that went on and on. It grew more and more costly to both sides. For the Vietnamese the cost was death and destruction on an unprecedented scale. For the United States the cost was, in addition to the increasing number of war dead, a huge drain on the U.S. economy, strained relations with U.S. allies who opposed the U.S. position, and loss of influence in the Third World. The war also caused serious political and social upheaval in the United States itself. In fact, it was one of the most divisive issues in U.S. history. It ruined the political career of President Lyndon Johnson, and contributed to the downfall of the next president, Richard Nixon. In 1968, both men—Johnson as he was leaving the presidency and Nixon as he campaigned for and prepared to assume the office—came to the realization that the United States must pull out of this costly war.

That realization came to President Johnson in the wake of the February 1968 Tet Offensive. After a lull in the fighting, which the United States interpreted as a sign that the enemy had finally been worn down, the Viet Cong and the army of North Vietnam launched a surprise offensive throughout South Vietnam during Tet, the lunar New Year holiday. At the outset, they were able to take thirty-six of the forty-four provincial capitals in the country, and most surprising of all, they staged a major attack on Saigon, where suicide commandos even penetrated the grounds of the U.S. embassy. The impact of the Tet Offensive, as Communist forces had calculated, shattered the popular illusion the U.S. leaders had created, that the United States was on the verge of victory. However, the U.S. military command in Vietnam, in an effort to demonstrate its supremacy, launched a furious counterattack making full use of its massive firepower.

The Communist losses were staggering as they were driven out of Saigon and the other cities and towns they had taken. Within a month General Westmoreland could claim that the Tet Offensive was a disaster for the enemy, that it had wasted its remaining strength. This was not an empty claim, for subsequent evidence has made it clear that the U.S. counterattack all but eliminated the Viet Cong as a fighting force, leaving North Vietnamese forces to fight the war from this point on.

Particularly harsh were the fates of the old imperial city of Hue and of Ben Tre, a provincial capital in the Mekong Delta. After the North Vietnamese conquered Hue, they immediately rounded up and executed an estimated 3,000 residents of the city suspected of collaboration with Saigon and U.S. forces. The United States military command, in an effort to drive the North Vietnamese out of Hue, subjected the city, particularly its huge citadel, to sustained bombardment. In all, 10,000 soldiers and civilians died in the battle for Hue. In late February 1968, U.S. marines reoccupied a city largely in ruins.

Ben Tre suffered a similar fate. U.S. artillery destroyed it completely. When asked why the city had been levelled, a U.S. major offered what became his country's epitaph in Vietnam: "We had to destroy it in order to save it."[9] It was the only answer he could give. The U.S. military involvement in Vietnam no longer made sense.

The Tet Offensive was a military setback for the Communists. It was, however, a psychological and political victory for them, because of its impact on the people of the United States and on the Johnson administration. Hanoi was well aware that 1968 was an election year in the United States. In addition to seeking a sudden military victory, Hanoi's purpose seems also to have been to give notice that the war was far from over, despite the optimistic pronouncements by U.S. generals and politicians alike. In this the Communists were quite successful. President Johnson, faced with mounting opposition to his Vietnam policy even in his own party, was forced to reassess the entire war effort. At about this time, he received from General Westmoreland in Vietnam a request for 206,000 more soldiers. This request would have surprised the U.S. public if it had known of it, for General Westmoreland had consistently maintained that his troops were winning the war. President Johnson, who had also promised victory, could not in this election year meet this request. Instead, after making a reappraisal of the situation in Vietnam, he made a televised address to the people of the United States, announcing that he would call a halt to the bombing of North Vietnam as an inducement to Hanoi to seek a negotiated settlement and—the real surprise—that he would not seek reelection. Lyndon Johnson wanted to wash his hands of Vietnam.

The winner of the 1968 presidential election, Richard Nixon, proclaimed during the campaign that he had a secret plan to end the war. Several years later he admitted that he had no specific plan, but once in office he devised a war strategy that was designed to gradually end the U.S. involvement in Vietnam, but which in fact kept U.S. soldiers in the war for four more years. Nixon's plan called for the "Vietnamization" of the war, a plan whereby the United States would gradually disengage itself from the war while strengthening the ARVN (the Army of South Vietnam). This would allow him to placate his domestic opponents of the war by announcing periodic withdrawals of U.S. troops, and yet was intended to produce a victory against the Communists. But this plan took time to implement, and in the meantime the war raged on, as did opposition to it at home. Subsequently, thousands more U.S. and Vietnamese soldiers died in battle during the years of Vietnamization, from 1969 to 1973. Ultimately, the Vietnamization scheme failed, despite the enormous amount of military provisions supplied by the United States, mainly because, no matter how well equipped, the corrupt and undisciplined ARVN was no match for its more determined Communist foes.

■ THE U.S. EXIT

President Johnson had tried persistently to persuade Hanoi to come to the bargaining table, but Hanoi just as persistently refused his terms. North Vietnam had presented its peace plan in April 1965, a four-point proposal calling for the withdrawal of U.S. forces from Vietnam, the end of hostilities against North Vietnam, adherence to the Geneva Accords, and allowing the Vietnamese alone to settle their problems. They also insisted, as a condition for negotiations, that the NLF be recognized and be allowed to take part in the negotiations. But the Johnson administration and the Thieu-Ky government in Saigon steadfastly refused to have any dealings with the NLF. This remained the main obstacle to starting negotiations until the very end of the Johnson administration. Finally, in October 1968, the two sides agreed to begin peace talks in Paris with the NLF and Saigon represented as well as Hanoi and Washington.

The four-party peace talks began in January 1969, just as the Nixon administration took office in Washington, but they were immediately deadlocked. The Communist side demanded a commitment by the United States on a timetable for the complete withdrawal of U.S. forces from Vietnam and the replacement of the Saigon regime by a coalition government made up of all parties, including the NLF. The Nixon administration rejected these demands, and further talks were postponed indefinitely. However, in 1971 the U.S. negotiator, Henry Kissinger, and the North Vietnamese representative, Le Duc Tho, met in Paris to conduct secret negotiations. Still, the two sides refused to make the kind of concessions or compromises that were necessary to end the war. Neither wished to give up at the bargaining table that for which they had been fighting so long. Neither side wished to dishonor its war dead by compromising the cause for which they had died in battle.

And so the war dragged on. Even though U.S. troop levels were reduced from 542,000 soldiers in February 1969 to 139,000 in December 1971, the warfare did not diminish; in fact, it was expanded into Laos and Cambodia. Richard Nixon, as Lyndon Johnson before him, was determined not to be the first president to lose a war. He counted on the destruction of North Vietnam's sanctuaries and supply routes in the neighboring countries to bring victory in Vietnam.

The prelude to the entry of ARVN and U.S. forces into Cambodia[10] was the overthrow of the ruler of that country, Prince Norodom Sihanouk, in March 1970. Prince Sihanouk had managed to keep his country out of the Vietnam conflict by professing a policy of neutrality while in fact allowing Vietnamese Communist forces to make use of Cambodian jungle areas along the eastern border and accepting U.S. retaliatory air strikes against them. He was overthrown by his own prime minister, General Lon Nol, who then turned to the United States for military aid. In response to reports of the spreading military operations of Vietnamese Communists in Cambodia, President Nixon, in April 1970, authorized joint U.S.-ARVN attacks into that country to clean out the Communist bases. For over a month U.S. and ARVN troops, numbering over 50,000, searched the jungles of eastern Cambodia in a futile effort to find the headquarters for the Communist operations in South Vietnam (COSVN).[11] This widening of the war caused an uproar of protest from anti-war activists in the United States. It was at this juncture that anti-war students at Columbia University and other colleges in the United States sought to forcibly shut down their schools in protest. They were intent on "bringing the war home," and in a sense that is what happened on the campus of Kent State University, where four anti-war student protesters were shot to death by the National Guard on May 4, 1970.

A similar incursion into Laos in early 1971 demonstrated the failure of the Vietnamization plan, because the ARVN forces that entered Laos with U.S. air support were badly routed. Television crews sent back images of panic-stricken ARVN troops hanging on the skids of evacuation helicopters in a desperate effort to escape the North Vietnamese counterattack.

As the 1972 election rolled around, the Vietnam War was still raging; 15,000 additional U.S. soldiers had died since Nixon had come to office. Nixon intensified his effort to achieve a negotiated settlement. Secret talks between Kissinger and Tho resumed in Paris in April 1972. Meanwhile, both sides sought to strengthen their bargaining positions, as Hanoi launched an offensive on the ground and U.S. jets pounded North Vietnam with the heaviest bombing yet, and U.S. ships blockaded and mined the Haiphong harbor. On the eve of the U.S. election, Kissinger was able to announce that "peace is at hand."[12] He and Le Duc Tho had secretly hammered out a preliminary agreement for ending the war. Its main terms were that within sixty days after the cease-fire the United States would complete the withdrawal of all of its troops from Vietnam, Hanoi would release all U.S. prisoners, and the political settlement in South Vietnam would be left for the Vietnamese to work out. The contending Vietnamese factions were to form a "National Council of Reconciliation and Concord" with equal representation for the Thieu regime, the NLF, and neutralists. But one major problem remained. President Thieu, Washington's man in Saigon, refused to accept these terms. To win him over Kissinger traveled to Saigon carrying with him President Nixon's pledge of continued U.S. protection for his government and a billion dollars worth of additional armaments for his armed forces. Thieu, however, remained opposed to the peace terms.

Before the peace agreement was reached, the United States delivered one final, savage punishment to North Vietnam. In an effort to break a new deadlock in the Paris peace talks and to demonstrate his continuing commitment to defend Thieu's government, President Nixon, who had recently been reelected in a landslide victory, ordered another bombing of Hanoi and Haiphong. The around-the-clock bombing raids (called the Christmas bombings), which began on December 18 and continued until the end of the month, turned large parts of these two cities into rubble. This final act of war gave a hollow ring to Nixon's insistence on "peace with honor." Curiously, the bombings did not bring any significant change in the terms of the peace agreement finally signed in January; its terms were essentially those agreed to by Kissinger and Tho in October.

With the signing of the peace agreement on January 27, 1973, the United States finally exited from the Vietnam War. This long-awaited event brought great relief to the United States, but it did not bring an end to the war in Vietnam. Saigon staged a new offensive of its own, seemingly in order to sabotage the peace agreement and keep the United States in the war. But as the battle raged on, the ARVN forces with all of their U.S. arms proved to be no match for the North Vietnamese army. Reintervention by the United States was impossible, for once the troops had been withdrawn surely the U.S. people would not have allowed their return. Moreover, the Nixon administration was by this time in shambles over the Watergate affair,[13] and Congress, reflecting the will of the nation, cut off further aid to South Vietnam. Finally, in January 1975, ARVN collapsed when a North Vietnamese attack in the northern highlands produced a panic that spread throughout the country. The expected battle for Saigon never took place. Instead, North Vietnamese forces entered the city unopposed and in triumph, and South Vietnam fell to the Communists. The U.S. embassy in Saigon was the scene of a frantic airlift of the remaining U.S. citizens in the country and as many of their Vietnamese cohorts and friends as they could crowd onto the last helicopters.

The full dimensions of the U.S. defeat in Vietnam are still to be learned. The final cost of the war for the United States includes nearly 58,000 soldiers killed and more than 300,000 wounded. Economically, the war cost an estimated $165 billion. The indirect economic cost is beyond estimation, but the huge expenditures for the prolonged war surely contributed to the inflation, the deficit, and the balance of payments problems that have plagued the United States since the early 1970s. The social, political, and psychological damage of the Vietnam tragedy is also incalculable. U.S. society was divided as it had not been since the Civil War. Vietnam aroused intense feelings and bitter struggles among the people and brought them the frustration of defeat. It also brought on strong-arm police action against anti-war protesters and the use of armed force against student demonstrators. The war generated a political awakening for the country's young people—a new activism and a heightened political consciousness. But later, as it dragged on and on, the war, together with the Watergate scandal, caused deep feelings of mistrust, apathy, and skepticism toward government. Thus, sadly, another of the casualties of the war was the credibility of the U.S. government.

The cost of the war to the peoples of Indochina was also enormous and incalculable. The U.S. estimate of the military deaths of the South Vietnamese Army is over 200,000, and for the Communist Vietnamese almost 500,000 (including both NLF and North Vietnamese forces). We will never know how many civilian casualties there were or how many refugees, but in both cases the numbers are in the millions. The physical mutilation of the country was staggering. The United States dropped three times more bombs on Indochina than it dropped on its enemies in World War II. In addition, it defoliated over five million acres with chemicals such as Agent Orange. Yet, as great as the physical destruction was, it could eventually be repaired. Less visible and less readily repaired was the serious damage done to the social order, to the Vietnamese way of life.

■ THE CONTINUING TRAGEDY OF INDOCHINA

In the short term the outcome of the "fall of Vietnam" to Communism was not as grim as the U.S. government had predicted, but in the long term it was even worse. Vietnam was, of course, unified under the Communist rule of Hanoi, but the idea that a Communist victory in

Vietnam would be a victory for Communist China proved entirely wrong. After the war, Chinese-Vietnamese relations deteriorated, becoming so hostile that the two nations became engaged in war four years after the fall of Saigon. Predictions of a dismal future for the people of Vietnam proved correct; however, not all the blame is to be placed on the Communist rulers of the country. The causes for the ensuing tragedy in Vietnam and in neighboring Laos and Cambodia are more complex.

In the wake of the Communist military victory, the South Vietnamese braced themselves for the terrible, vengeful "bloodbath" that President Nixon had predicted, but it did not come. Hanoi initially allowed South Vietnam to retain its separate identity under a Provisional Revolutionary Government. The government in Hanoi adopted a policy of gradualism in imposing its system on the people of the south and was much less forceful and heavy handed than anyone expected. To be sure, those identified as high-ranking former government or military officers of the overthrown Saigon regime were singled out for severe punishments, usually involving confiscation of property, arrest, and long sentences to hard labor in remote rural "re-education" camps.

The new order in the south meant, of course, a transformation of the city of Saigon, renamed Ho Chi Minh City. Quickly, the bars and dance halls were closed and the prostitutes disappeared, as did other traces of the twenty-year-long U.S. presence in that city. But beyond this and the introduction of revolutionary broadcasts and music over street loudspeakers, change in the city was rather minimal. The city was grossly overpopulated as a result of the influx of refugees during the war years, and its economy had been almost entirely dependent on the U.S. presence. The U.S. departure left almost two-thirds of the 3 million people in the city unemployed. The dire lack of goods and housing to provide for this huge unproductive population gave rise to rampant inflation and black marketeering.

Within a year, severe economic problems gripped Vietnam, and conditions steadily worsened year after year. The government's plan to quickly restore the agricultural productivity of the south to complement the industrial development of the north proved too optimistic. In part, the failure at economic recovery was the result of legacies of the war. Not only were the cities blighted, but vast areas of the countryside were no longer under cultivation due to the flight of the peasants and the defoliated and bomb-cratered land. And there were many other problems. The government lacked trained administrators to carry out policies; machinery, draft animals, fertilizer, and irrigation systems were are all lacking; and the transport system was in shambles. The army, instead of being demobilized, was put to work reclaiming wastelands and developing irrigation. Hundreds of thousands of unemployed city dwellers were lured to rural New Economic Zones with promises of houses, land, and food. Many of these people would soon flee from the harsh, almost primitive conditions of these rural developments back to the cities, causing the government to resort to forced relocation and detention in the New Economic Zones. To compound matters, southern Vietnam experienced three successive years of natural disasters, including both droughts and devastating floods, causing crop failures. As a result, the country was left desperately short of rice by early 1978. The agricultural failure was ruinous for the nation, as it now required large imports of food, lacked capital for industrial development, and was forced to resort to still more austere measures, which caused still greater despair for the people.

Nor was there international deliverance. Vietnam was unable to attract foreign investment, without which its hopes of economic recovery were dim. It had hoped for reparation payments from the United States, such as President Nixon had once offered, but Washington was not so forgiving or generous. Instead, it refused to provide either economic aid or investment, and pressured international lending agencies to reject Vietnam's pleas. Other Western nations were also unsympathetic. Hanoi's efforts to court favor with members of ASEAN (Association of Southeast Asian Nations—Malaysia, Thailand, Brunei, Indonesia, Singapore, and the Philippines) were also unsuccessful. Increasingly, Hanoi was forced to turn to the Soviet Union for economic assistance, and as it did so, aid from other sources diminished. Moreover, reliance on the Soviet Union contributed to a worsening of relations with China, which until 1978 had provided a modicum of aid to Hanoi. Vietnam's economic and diplomatic difficulties worsened in 1979, when it sent its military forces into Cambodia.

* * *

In the aftermath of the Vietnam War, the anticipated bloodbath occurred not in Vietnam but in neighboring Cambodia, and it is to the historical background of that part of the Indochina tragedy that we must now turn. When the United States disengaged from Vietnam in early 1973, it also terminated its military support for the Lon Nol government in Cambodia, which was embattled by the Khmer Rouge, a native Communist force. But in a final effort to deny the Cambodian Communists a victory, the United States unleashed its heaviest yet B-52 bombing raids on Communist-held areas of Cambodia, disregarding its neutrality. The Khmer Rouge, which had the support of North Vietnam at this time, battled with renewed intensity and seized much of the countryside. In April 1975, at the same time that Saigon fell to the North Vietnamese, the Khmer Rouge defeated Lon Nol's forces and swept into Phnom Penh, the Cambodian capital.

Cambodia braced itself for a new order under the Communist government led by Pol Pot, who immediateiy began a horrendous reign of revolutionary terror. Pol Pot, unlike most other revolutionaries, did not merely advocate a revolutionary transformation; he was willing to eradicate completely the old order, root and branch, and to reorganize society to a degree no revolutionary regime had ever attempted. The entire urban population was evacuated to the countryside, where they were placed in armed work camps. His ideal was to create a nation of workers and peasants who would modernize industry and agriculture. All other classes were to be transformed, and if they resisted they would be exterminated. In the space of three years, at least 1.5 million Cambodians—almost one-fifth of the population—were murdered. Pol Pot and the Khmer Rouge directed their fury against the old order, the Western-educated elite, city dwellers, and all real or suspected "enemies" of the revolution.

Not only did Pol Pot employ brutal force against his own people, but he initiated attacks against neighboring countries: Thailand on the western border and Vietnam, his former ally, on the east. Pol Pot was vehemently anti-Vietnamese, regarding Vietnam as the greatest threat to the independence of the Cambodia revolution. He perceived a rebellion against his regime developing in the eastern part of the country, which had a substantial ethnic Vietnamese population. In 1978, he unleashed a furious attack against the suspected rebels in the east, slaughtering thousands of people, Cambodians and Vietnamese alike, and driving many of the latter across the border into Vietnam. In pursuit of rebel forces, the Khmer Rouge army attacked Vietnamese forces in the Parrot's Beak border area. The purpose of these attacks was not only to eliminate native resistance, but also to settle old scores with Vietnam and assert Cambodia's claim to certain disputed borderlands.

In retaliation, Vietnam, with its superior, battle-tested army, drove into Cambodia in January 1979, scattered the forces of the Khmer Rouge, took control of Phnom Penh, and installed a former Khmer Rouge officer, Heng Samrin, as head of a new pro-Vietnamese government of Cambodia. The Vietnamese conquest of Phnom Penh, however, did not bring peace to Cambodia. A Vietnamese army of about 170,000 occupied the country and continued to battle remnants of Pol Pot's forces as well as other resistance forces. The war threatened to spill over into Thailand as thousands of the fleeing rival

Cambodian forces and civilians took refuge in camps across the border. The military occupation of Cambodia and the continuing struggle against its opponents in remote jungle encampments near the Thai border put an enormous strain on an already exhausted Vietnamese nation. It meant withdrawing its army from food production and reconstruction and diverting dwindling treasury funds to the military. It also meant still greater reliance on Soviet economic assistance to prop up its stagnant economy.

The international consequences of Vietnam's military occupation of Cambodia and the increased dependence of Vietnam on the Soviet Union were profound. Even though Hanoi publicized the genocide of the Pol Pot regime in Cambodia and used this to legitimize its military intervention, it was roundly rebuked by the United States, by other Western countries, by the ASEAN countries, and most strongly by China. In response to Vietnam's "invasion" of Cambodia, China invaded Vietnam in February 1979 in order to "teach it a lesson." This warfare was quite costly for both sides, but proved inconclusive, because the Chinese withdrew within a month, leaving Vietnam in control of Cambodia and Laos. The Chinese continued to support the deposed Pol Pot regime as a means to force Vietnam to withdraw its army from Cambodia. The United States, too, condemned Vietnam for its invasion of Cambodia. Mainly because of this issue, Washington strengthened its resolve not to extend official recognition to the government of Vietnam or to provide it desperately needed economic assistance. Meanwhile, Hanoi turned to the Soviet Union not only for continuing economic assistance but for military support as well. The Soviet Union signed a twenty-year defense agreement with Vietnam, and thereby gained unlimited access to Cam Ranh Bay, the enormous naval base that had been built up by the United States during the Vietnam War as one of the largest naval supply depots in the world. Both China and the United States were, of course, disturbed by the increased Soviet presence in Indochina. Ironically, the United States, which had entered Vietnam initially to stem Chinese Communist aggression in Indochina, found itself several years after that war on the side of China in the ongoing struggle in that region. And China, which had earlier feared the U.S. military presence in Indochina, now had to contend with the extension of Soviet power in that very same region on its southern border.

The tragedy of Cambodia continued through the 1980s as it remained a cockpit of international struggles. Determined to dislodge both the Vietnamese from Cambodia and the Soviets from the region, China persisted in its aid to the Khmer Rouge, which remained under the command of the mass murderer Pol Pot. In 1982, the Khmer Rouge formed a coalition with two other resistance forces in order to keep up the fight against the Vietnamese-backed regime in Phnom Penh. The two groups (supporters of the deposed Lon Nol and Sihanouk governments respectively) were aided by neighboring ASEAN countries and by the United States. (Critics of U.S. policy in Cambodia pointed out that this U.S. military aid was, in effect, support for the Khmer Rouge, the dominant member of the coalition.) Even with foreign support, the coalition of resistance forces was not able to mount a serious threat to the Vietnamese forces in Cambodia in the fighting that continued through the 1980s. At the end of the decade, when the Soviet Union finally pressured Vietnam to end its occupation of Cambodia, the prospects of victory by the resistance forces were only slightly improved because they remained weak. Moreover, much uncertainty remained about the shape that a new coalition government might take, for many feared that it might bring back to power the Khmer Rouge and Pol Pot, whose forces were the strongest within the resistance movement.

■ THE REFUGEES OF INDOCHINA

Another dimension of the continuing tragedy of Indochina is the desperate flight of millions of people from Vietnam, Cambodia, and Laos. Driven to escape by the hardships and dangers that confronted them, hundreds of thousands of people attempted to flee from their homelands, even at great risk to their lives. From Cambodia and Laos they trekked overland to Thailand, and in Vietnam, many thousands of people managed to escape the country by boarding vessels and taking to the sea. The risk was great, for many of those attempting to flee were arrested and punished, and many of those who did escape on overcrowded makeshift boats perished before finding safe harbor. Even if these "boat people" did succeed in reaching the shores of neighboring countries, there were no guarantees that they would be sheltered or would find their way to other nations where they could settle and begin new lives.

It is estimated that since the fall of Saigon in April 1975 over 1.5 million refugees fled Vietnam by boat, and of this number some 200,000 died on the South China Sea from exposure, drowning, and attacks by pirates while attempting their perilous voyage. The first wave of boat people came at the time of the fall of Saigon, when about 100,000 people fled the country. The exodus diminished during the next three years, but in 1978 and 1979, when the war between Cambodia and Vietnam occurred, a second and much larger wave of refugees fled Vietnam. The new flood of boat people, reaching the shores of neighboring countries at the rate of over 12,500 a month, quickly caused an international crisis as such nations as Malaysia (where most of them landed), Thailand, and Singapore refused to accept them and began driving them away forcibly. In July 1979, a UN Conference on Refugees was called at Geneva to attempt to bring the problem of the boat people under control. It secured an agreement from Vietnam to limit the refugee outflow, provided relief to the nations of "first asylum" such as Malaysia, and received promises from other nations to open their doors to the refugees.

The majority of those who left Vietnam were ethnic Chinese who were virtually forced to leave. The ethnic Chinese, who had long dominated private business in southern Vietnam, fell victim to government policies in early 1979, which abolished "bourgeois trade" and introduced a currency reform that rendered their accumulated savings almost worthless. Deprived of much of their wealth and livelihood, they saw no better choice than to flee the country. Curiously, many were assisted in their flight by the Communist authorities, who collected exit fees of $2,000 in gold from each departing refugee. In northern Vietnam the exodus of the Chinese amounted to expulsion. In the wake of the Chinese invasion of Vietnam in February 1979, ethnic Chinese were dismissed from Vietnamese military and government posts and were deprived of work and business opportunities. About 250,000 of the approximately 300,000 ethnic Chinese in northern Vietnam trekked northward to find sanctuary in the People's Republic of China.

Still another sad refugee drama unfolded in Laos, Cambodia, and Thailand. After the Communist takeover in Laos in 1978, some 250,000 Hmong tribesmen, who had earlier fought on the U.S. side, fled overland into Thailand. And from Cambodia came at least 150,000 survivors from the scourge of Pol Pot and the Vietnamese invasion in 1979. The entry of these thousands of pathetic refugees presented the Thai government an enormous problem. Not all those who crossed over into Thailand were refugees; at times Pol Pot's guerrilla troops also found it expedient to take refuge there. In any case, there was a limit to Thailand's ability to accommodate this influx of people in its already swollen refugee camps, and it resorted to driving newcomers away. For the vast majority of the Laotian and Cambodian refugees, the temporary asylum in Thailand would last many years while the war in Cambodia went on interminably. For them and the refugees who continued to flee from Vietnam at the end of the 1980s, the Indochina tragedy still goes on.

■ RECOMMENDED READINGS

Caputo, Philip. *A Rumor of War.* New York: Holt, Rinehart and Winston, 1977.
> The reminiscences of a loyal marine who, by the end of his tour of duty, questioned the purpose of the U.S. involvement.

Fall, Bernard B. *Vietnam Witness, 1953–1966.* New York: Praeger, 1966.
> By the French historian who while alive was widely considered the West's leading authority on Vietnam.

FitzGerald, Frances. *Fire in the Lake: The Vietnamese and the Americans in Vietnam.* New York: Random House, 1972.
> An award-winning study that places the U.S. intervention in a context of Vietnamese history.

Halberstam, David. *The Best and the Brightest.* New York: Random House, 1972.
> A classic account of how the leaders in Washington drifted into a war on the other side of the globe.

Herring, George C. *America's Longest War: The United States and Vietnam, 1950–1975.* New York: John Wiley & Sons, 1979.
> A solid, evenhanded account of the war.

Herrington, Stuart A. *Peace With Honor: An American Report on Vietnam, 1973–75.* Novato, Calif.: Presidio Press, 1983.
> A critical view of U.S. responsiblity for the fall of Saigon to North Vietnamese forces.

Hersh, Seymour. *My Lai Four: A Report on the Massacre and its Aftermath.* New York: Random House, 1970.
> An excellent piece of investigative journalism.

Isaacs, Arnold R. *Without Honor: Defeat in Vietnam and Cambodia.* Baltimore: Johns Hopkins University Press, 1983.
> A newspaper correspondent's eyewitness account and analysis of U.S. failings in Vietnam and Cambodia.

Karnow, Stanley. *Vietnam: A History.* New York: Viking, 1983.
> A major work by a noted journalist who served as the consultant for a thirteen-part television documentary on the Vietnam War.

Shawcross, William. *Sideshow: Kissinger, Nixon and the Destruction of Cambodia.* New York: Simon and Schuster, 1979.
> An analysis of the widening of the war into Cambodia, faulting the policy of President Nixon and Henry Kissinger for causing the bloodbath that occurred subsequent to the U.S. withdrawal from that country.

Sheehan, Neil. *A Bright Shining Lie: John Paul Vann and America in Vietnam* (New York: Random House, 1988.)
> A critical account of the U.S. conduct of the war in Vietnam

Sheehan, Neil, et al. *The Pentagon Papers.* New York: Bantam, 1971.
> The most useful collection of primary sources on the U.S. involvement in the Vietnam War, revealing the plotting and planning of Washington decision makers.

Summers, Harry G. *On Strategy: A Critical Analysis of the Vietnam War.* Novato, Calif.: Presidio Press, 1982.
> A provocative military history of the Vietnam War which argues that the United States lacked a strategy for victory.

■ NOTES

1. Bernard B. Fall, *Last Reflections on a War,* p. 167. In Saigon, Diem received 605,025 votes from 450,000 registered voters.

2. Vice President Lyndon Johnson's characterization of Diem, cited in Frances FitzGerald, *Fire in the Lake: The Vietnamese and the Americans in Vietnam* (Boston: Little, Brown, 1972), p. 72; also, John Osborne, "The Tough Miracle Man of Vietnam: Diem, America's Newly Arrived Visitor, Has Roused His Country and Routed the Reds," *Life,* May 13, 1957, pp. 156–176.

3. Quoted in Richard J. Barnet, *Intervention and Revolution: The United States in the Third World* (New York: New American Library, 1968), p. 216.

4. Theodore Draper, "The American Crisis: Vietnam, Cuba & the Dominican Republic," *Commentary,* January 1967, p. 36.

5. Neil Sheehan, et al., *The Pentagon Papers* (New York: Bantam, 1971), documents 61–64, pp. 271–285.

6. For the White Paper, "Aggression From the North" and I. F. Stone's reply, see Marcus G. Raskin and Bernard B. Fall, eds., *The Viet-Nam Reader: Articles and Documents on American Foreign Policy and the Viet-Nam Crisis,* rev. ed., (New York: Vintage, 1967), pp. 143–162.

7. First used by President Johnson's acting Attorney General Nicholas Katzenbach, Karnow, *Vietnam,* p. 362.

8. General Westmoreland, ibid., p. 479.

9. Frances FitzGerald, *Fire in the Lake,* p. 393.

10. In 1975, the government of Cambodia adopted an alternate spelling of the nation's name, Kampuchea, but for consistency we have retained the spelling that continues to be most commonly used in the West.

11. President Nixon was already conducting a secret war in both Laos and Cambodia prior to the entry of U.S. ground forces into Cambodia in April 1970—secret only in the sense that the Nixon administration did not make public U.S. military operations (mainly heavy bombing by B-52s) in these two countries, and in fact repeatedly denied reports of these military operations.

12. Transcript of Kissinger's news conference, *New York Times,* October 27, 1972, p. 18.

13. Watergate was a direct outgrowth of the war in Vietnam. In June 1971 Daniel Ellsberg, who had once served as a zealous administrator of official U.S. policy in Vietnam and who had since become an equally zealous opponent of the war, leaked to the *New York Times, The Washington Post,* and other newspapers copies of a study of the war, the "Pentagon Papers" as they became popularly known, which had been commissioned by President Johnson's secretary of defense, Robert McNamara. President Nixon, furious at this and other leaks of classified information, created a group, the White House "plumbers," whose task it was to plug intelligence leaks and to investigate Ellsberg and other subversives undermining his presidency and conduct of the war. For reasons still not clear, in June 1972, the "plumbers" broke into the national headquarters of the Democratic party at the Watergate apartment complex in Washington, D.C. As evidence of wrongdoing began to implicate Nixon himself, he ordered his subordinates to commit perjury, or lying under oath. Unfortunately for Nixon, he had taped his own crime and, for reasons also still not clear, he had not destroyed all the evidence. The upshot was the preparation for an impeachment trial in the Senate. When it became obvious to Nixon that his removal from office was all but a certainty, he resigned; Vice President Gerald Ford then became the nation's chief executive.

14. During the Vietnam War, the United States turned Saigon's Tan Son Nhut Airport into one of the busiest in the world and Cam Ranh Bay into one of the largest naval supply bases in the world, but, ironically, in the 1980s they were both used mainly by the Soviet Union to supply its needy ally.

☐ 10

Détente and the
End of Bipolarity

Ironically, the years of direct U.S. involvement in Vietnam, 1965–1973, which represented a crusade against international Communism, saw a gradual improvement in relations between Washington and the two great Communist states. Toward the end of that period, the Cold War took on several unexpected turns. First, détente eased, if only for a short time, the tensions between Moscow and Washington. Secondly, the early 1970s saw the normalization of relations between the United States and the People's Republic of China. In the end, President Richard Nixon, the quintessential anti-Communist who had always urged strong measures against the Vietnamese Communists (commonly perceived as proxies of the Soviet Union and Communist China), visited Moscow and Beijing. The bipolar world, with Moscow and Washington at center stage, was no more.

■ THE UNITED STATES AND CHINA:
THE NORMALIZATION OF RELATIONS

The split between the Soviet Union and the People's Republic of China gave the United States a golden opportunity. Monolithic Communism, or "international socialist solidarity" as its proponents frequently called it, proved to be an ideological quest that ran aground on the shoals of nationalist interests. A succession of governments in Washington, tied down to the principle of an international Communist conspiracy, were slow in taking advantage of the falling out between the two most important of Communist states. But by the early 1970s, the time had come to cash in on what clearly had become a windfall for Washington.

Rapprochement between the United States and the vast Chinese empire could only give the Soviets a headache. At first, it had been Moscow that had been able to play the "China card." With it, the Soviet Union's first line of defense in the East had been on the shores of the Yellow Sea. Washington's ability to play the same card promised to pay immeasurable dividends. The Chinese in their turn, a proud and ancient people, had no intentions of playing the pawn and instead sought to carve out their own niche as a major player in the superpower game. When Beijing and Washington took the first steps toward the normalization of relations in the early 1970s, the result was an end to great-power bipolarity and a renewed complexity in international relations.

For more than twenty years the United States and the People's Republic of China (PRC) had no official relations; instead, they were hostile adversaries. Successive U.S. presidents denounced "Red China" as a menace to the peace-loving peoples of Asia, as a reckless, irresponsible, aggressive regime, unworthy of diplomatic recognition or United Nations membership. The United States maintained relations instead with Jiang Kaishek's regime on Taiwan, adhering to the fiction that it was the only legitimate government of China and pledging to defend it against "Communist aggression." Meanwhile, the United States effectively blocked the PRC from gaining admission into the United Nations, surrounded it with a ring of military bases, maintained a rigid embargo on all trade with China, and permitted no one from the United States to travel to China.

The hostile relations between the two countries had originated at the very time that the PRC was established in October 1949. Washington withheld recognition of the new Communist government in Beijing (then called Peking), and instead maintained official ties with the government of Jiang Kaishek, which had been driven from the mainland to the island of Taiwan. Mao Zedong, the ruler of Communist China, rebuked the United States for interfering in China's civil war, and promptly went to Moscow to sign a thirty-year military alliance. To most observers in the West this was proof of the unity of the two Communist giants and of their complicity in international Communist aggression. In response, the United States extended its containment policy to Asia. It did not immediately commit itself to the defense of the government on Taiwan, but it did so in 1954, after having engaged Chinese Communist forces in battle for three years in Korea. Beijing denounced the U.S. military alliance with Jiang's Nationalist government and the U.S. military presence on Taiwan as "imperialist aggression" and as interference in the internal affairs of China.

Nor was this merely a bilateral feud, since both antagonists called upon their respective Cold War allies for support. Supporting China, at least in the first decade of the Beijing-Washington clash, was the Soviet Union, its satellite states in Eastern Europe, and Communist parties in other parts of the world. The Soviet Union had supported from the outset the PRC's bid to replace the Republic of China (as Jiang's government was called) in the United

Nations. The United States, which perceived itself as leading and speaking for the "free world," applied diplomatic pressure on its allies for support of its uncompromising China policy. Washington realized that a trade embargo against China would not be effective unless most, if not all, of the allies of the United States adhered to it. And Washington also pressured its friends to stand united against diplomatic recognition of the PRC and against its entry into the United Nations. The United States reacted negatively, for example, when in 1964 the independent-minded French government decided to break ranks and extend formal recognition to the PRC.

While Washington tirelessly denounced "Red China" and condemned Mao and the Chinese Communists for their brutal enslavement of the Chinese people, Beijing regarded the United States, the most powerful capitalist nation in the world, as its Number One enemy and argued persistently that U.S. imperialism was the major threat to world peace. The United States pointed to the Chinese intervention in the Korean war and China's border war with India in 1962 as examples of Chinese aggression. But Beijing (and some observers in the West) countered that in both cases China acted legitimately to protect its borders. The Chinese pointed to the ring of U.S. military positions on China's periphery—from Japan and Korea in the northeast, through Taiwan and the Philippines to Vietnam and Thailand in the south—as proof of the aggressive imperialism of the United States. So intense was this ideological conflict between the two countries that any reduction of tensions seemed impossible.

The Sino-Soviet split that became manifest in the late 1950s did not bring about an improvement in Sino-U.S. relations. Instead, relations worsened since it was China, not the Soviet Union, that argued for a stronger anti–United States line. When the United States and the Soviet Union began to move toward détente in the late 1960s, Beijing's anti-imperialist, anti–United States rhetoric became even more shrill as it sought to make its point: The Soviet Union had grown soft on capitalism, while China had not. China complained bitterly of Soviet "socialist imperialism" arguing that it was linked with U.S. "capitalist imperialism" to encircle China. Mao spoke fervently of China's support for the revolutionary peoples of the world and support for wars of national liberation such as that waged by the Communist forces in Vietnam. He even taunted the United States to make war on China, saying that the atomic bomb was merely a paper tiger and that China would prevail in the end. Mao's inflammatory rhetoric made it easy for both superpowers to condemn China as a reckless warmonger and as the major threat to world peace.

The seemingly interminable hostility between China and the United States ended quite suddenly in the early 1970s, in one of the most dramatic turnabouts in modern diplomatic history. On July 15, 1971, President Richard Nixon made an unanticipated announcement that stunned the world. He stated that he intended to travel to China within six months, at the invitation of the Chinese government, for the purpose of developing friendly relations with that government. He revealed that his Secretary of State, Henry Kissinger, had just returned from a secret trip to Beijing where he and Chinese Premier Zhou Enlai had made arrangements for this diplomatic breakthrough.

The Nixon administration had begun making subtle overtures to the PRC in the previous year. In Warsaw, Poland, where the U.S. and Chinese ambassadors had periodically engaged in secret talks, the U.S. side intimated its desire for improved relations. In his State of the World speech before Congress in February 1971, President Nixon referred to the Beijing government as the People's Republic of China, instead of the usual Red China or Communist China, and Chinese leaders took note of the fact that for the first time the U.S. government had publicly used the proper name of their government. Meanwhile, the U.S. government announced its intention to ease restrictions against travel to China. This opened the door to what became called "ping-pong diplomacy." A U.S. table tennis team was invited to play an exhibition tournament in Beijing, and Premier Zhou gave them a warm reception and noted that their visit "opened a new page in the relations between the Chinese and U.S. peoples."[1] President Nixon responded by announcing a relaxation of the U.S. trade embargo with China, and this was followed by Kissinger's secret trip to Beijing in early July 1971 that prepared the ground for President Nixon's dramatic announcement.

The following February, President Nixon made his heralded two-week visit to China. He was welcomed by Chinese leaders with great fanfare. At the Beijing airport he extended a hand to Premier Zhou, the same Chinese leader whom John Foster Dulles had pointedly snubbed eighteen years earlier by refusing to shake hands. In addition to his own large staff, Nixon was accompanied by a large retinue of journalists and television camera crews who recorded the historic event and gave the U.S. people their first glimpse of life in Communist China. For two weeks the United States was treated to pictures of China and its friendly, smiling people, who seemed equally curious about the people of the United States. And they were treated to the spectacle of the U.S. president, a man known for his trenchant anti-Chinese Communist pronouncements in the past, saluting the aged and ailing Chairman Mao Zedong and toasting the new bond of friendship with China's most able diplomat, Premier Zhou Enlai. For the United States and China alike, it was a mind-boggling 180 degree turnabout.

It was ironic that Nixon, a conservative, Communist-hating Republican, would be the one to go to China and establish friendly relations with its Communist government. But the task required just such a politician. A Democratic president would have found it impossible to do so, because the Democratic party still carried the scars of allegedly having "lost China" to Communism in the first place. But a Republican president like Nixon, whose

U.S. President Richard Nixon and Chinese Premier Zhou Enlai, at reception banquet in Beijing, Feb. 21, 1972. (*National Archives*)

anti-Communist credentials were beyond question, would encounter much less opposition for reversing U.S. policy toward Communist China, when any Democratic president would surely be charged again with being soft on Communism and for that reason be unable to gain political support for taking such a step.

In any case, the normalization of U.S.-PRC relations was an event whose time had come. Indeed, it was long overdue. Both sides finally came to the realization that they had much more to gain by ending their mutual hostility than by continuing it. The Chinese needed to end their isolation in the face of a growing Soviet threat after the Ussuri River border clash in February 1969. The Soviets had greatly increased their ground forces along the Chinese border and equipped these forces with tactical nuclear weapons. Menaced by a superior Soviet force on their border, the Chinese leaders came to view closer ties with the United States as a means to decrease the possibility of a preemptive nuclear attack on China by the Soviet Union. By ending its isolation and reducing tensions between itself and the United States, the PRC stood to gain greater security from becoming engaged in a war with either of the two superpowers, much less with both of them in a two-front war. Normalization of relations with the United States was also seen as a means to finally gain entry into the United Nations and to solve the

Taiwan question. China's international prestige would be greatly enhanced by its new relationship with the United States, while that of its rival, the Nationalist government on Taiwan, would be undermined. In addition, China had much to gain economically from the new trade opportunities that would come with normalization of relations with the United States and its allies.

The United States stood to benefit from normalization as well. President Nixon and his ambitious secretary of state, Henry Kissinger, had developed a grand design for achieving a new global balance of power. They postulated that the bipolar world dominated by the two opposing superpowers was giving way to a world with five major power centers: the United States, the Soviet Union, Western Europe, Japan, and China. In order to achieve an international power balance it was necessary to end the isolation of one of those new centers of power, the PRC. Détente with the Soviet Union was already well under way, but now the United States sought to "play the China card" when dealing with Moscow. By cautiously drawing closer to China the United States sought to gain greater leverage in its diplomacy with Moscow. The Nixon administration saw that détente with the Soviet Union and normalization of relations with China were possible at the same time and that together these policies would constitute giant steps toward ending the Cold War and attaining world peace. The result would be greater national security for the United States at a reduced cost. Nixon and Kissinger also calculated— incorrectly it turned out—that Beijing could bring influence to bear on Hanoi to negotiate an end to the Vietnam War. The opportunity for trade with China was also a motivating factor, but not as important as the diplomatic factors.

The major obstacle to improvement of relations between the two countries was—as had always been the case—Taiwan. The United States had stood by the Nationalist regime on Taiwan, recognizing it as the sole government of China, and had made a commitment to defend it. The only compromise solution to the Taiwan question that U.S. leaders had ever been willing to discuss was the so-called "two China" formula, which called for formal diplomatic recognition of two separate Chinese governments, one on the mainland, the other on Taiwan. But this proved to be an impossibility since both Chinese governments firmly refused to accept that formula. Neither would give up its claim as the sole legitimate government of the whole of China.

When President Nixon first communicated his desire for talks aimed at improving relations with the PRC, Zhou Enlai replied that he was ready to join in that effort only on the condition that the United States was prepared for serious negotiations on the Taiwan issue. Beijing was not willing to bend on that question, but the U.S. government was finally willing to do so. The first step toward a solution of this issue came with the U.S. government's ending its objection to the PRC's entry into the United Nations.[2] In October 1971, the PRC was admitted to the United Nations on its terms, namely, as the sole government of China and as the rightful claimant of the seat that had been occupied by the Republic of China in that body.

It was a test of the diplomatic skills of Henry Kissinger and Zhou Enlai to arrive at an agreement on Taiwan that would recognize the PRC's claim to Taiwan and yet would be less than a complete sell-out of the Nationalist government on Taiwan by its U.S. ally. A tentative agreement on the Taiwan issue was reached in the carefully worded Shanghai Communiqué at the end of Nixon's visit to China. In it, the United States acknowledged that all Chinese maintain that "there is but one China and that Taiwan is part of China" and stated that the United States does not challenge that position. In the communiqué, the U.S. side reaffirmed "its interest in a peaceful settlement of the Taiwan question by the Chinese themselves." The United States also agreed to reduce its military forces on Taiwan "as tension in the area diminishes." (This was in reference to the war in Indochina from which U.S. forces were gradually withdrawing.) The PRC obtained important concessions on the Taiwan issue—namely, the U.S. acknowledgement that the island is part of China proper and a U.S. promise to withdraw its military force from that island. The United States, which seems to have conceded more than it gained, came away with an understanding that the PRC would not attempt to take over Taiwan by military means and with the satisfaction that its new friendship with China would serve to enhance security in Asia.

This was not the end, but the beginning of the normalization process. Full normalization of relations, involving the formal recognition of the PRC by the United States and the breaking off of U.S. diplomatic ties with Nationalist China was yet to be achieved. However, in accordance with the Shanghai Communiqué, the two countries respectively established liaison offices in each other's capital, began a series of exchanges in the fields of science, technology, culture, journalism and sports, and initiated mutually beneficial trade relations that grew steadily in subsequent years.

It was not until January 1979 that full diplomatic relations between the two countries were achieved. There were two main reasons for the seven-year delay: the political leadership problems in both countries in the mid–1970s, and the still unresolved Taiwan issue. In the United States, President Nixon was suffering from the Watergate scandal and finally resigned in disgrace in August 1974. And in China, both Chairman Mao and Premier Zhou died in 1976, leaving a succession problem that was not resolved until Deng Xiaoping consolidated his leadership in 1978. It was left to new political leaders, Deng and President Jimmy Carter, to settle the Taiwan question. Deng came to the view that establishing diplomatic ties with the United States was of greater importance than liberating Taiwan and that a formula could be found to achieve the former by postponing the latter. Secret negotiations produced an agreement in December 1978, the terms of which included restoration of full diplomatic relations between the two nations and termination of the United States's official relations and defense pact with the Republic of China. It did allow, however, for continued U.S. commercial and cultural ties with Taiwan and continued U.S. arms sales to Taiwan. On that point, the Chinese government agreed to disagree, which is to say that it did not formally agree to such arms sales, but would set aside that issue so that the normalization agreement could be made without further delay. In effect, the U.S. government now recognized the PRC's title to Taiwan even though the island remained in the hands of the anti-Communist Nationalist government now headed by Jiang Jingguo (Chiang Ching-kuo), son of Jiang Kaishek, who had died in 1975. The U.S. government attempted to soften the blow to Taiwan by passing the Taiwan Relations Act, which affirmed the resolve of the United States to maintain relations with the people (not the government) of Taiwan and to consider any effort to resolve the Taiwan issue by force as of "grave concern to the United States." To further strengthen the new diplomatic relations, Deng Xiaoping accepted an invitation to visit the United States, and he was given a warm reception during his nine-day visit that began less than a month after the normalization agreement went into effect on January 1, 1979.

The consequences of the normalization of Chinese-U.S. relations were immense. The United States ended the anomaly of recognizing a government that ruled only 17 million Chinese in favor of one that governed over 900 million. Normalization resulted in a great reduction of tension between the two nations and it provided greater stability in Asia. Both countries attained greater security, and at the same time they gained greater maneuverability in dealing with other powerful nations, notably the Soviet Union. Normalization opened the way to a vast increase in trade, which provided China with much-needed capital and technology for its ongoing economic modernization and provided the United States with a large market that would serve to offset its mounting trade deficit in other world markets.

One of the most important consequences of the normalization of Sino-U.S. relations was the ending of China's diplomatic isolation. Not only did the PRC gain a permanent seat in the UN Security Council, but many nations of the world that had formally withheld formal ties with PRC now followed the U.S. lead by breaking off official ties with Taiwan and recognizing the PRC instead. In 1969, sixty-five countries recognized Taiwan as the legal government of China, but by 1981 only twenty countries did so.

The breakthrough in Sino-U.S. relations brought in its wake an equally abrupt turnaround in Sino-Japanese relations, which was of great significance to both countries and for peace and stability in Asia. Initially, the Japanese were stunned by President Nixon's surprise announcement in July 1971, not because they opposed the move but because they were caught off guard by it and felt that they should have been consulted beforehand.[3] But once they got over the "Nixon shock," as they referred to it, the Japanese hastened to achieve their own rapprochement with China. Japan's newly elected prime minister, Tanaka Kakuei, responded to mounting public pressure within Japan for normalization of relations with China by arranging a visit to Beijing at the invitation of the Chinese government. His trip to China, which took place in September 1972, was also of great historical importance, being the first visit to China ever made by any Japanese head of state and coming after almost a century of hostile Sino-Japanese relations. In Beijing, the Japanese prime minister contritely expressed his regret over the "unfortunate experiences" between the two nations in the past and stated that "the Japanese side is keenly aware of Japan's responsibility for causing enormous damage in the past to the Chinese people through war and deeply reproaches itself."[4]

The product of Tanaka's talks with Zhou Enlai in Beijing was an agreement on the restoration of full diplomatic relations between the two countries on the following terms: Japan affirmed its recognition of the PRC as the sole legal government of China and agreed to the claim that Taiwan was an inalienable part of the territory of the PRC. China waived its claim to a war indemnity amounting to several billion dollars and agreed to discontinue its protest against the U.S.-Japan Mutual Security Pact and to drop its insistence that Japan end its trade relations with Taiwan. The two countries also agreed to negotiate a new treaty of peace and friendship in the near future. (It was implicitly understood that Japan would then abrogate its existing peace treaty with the Republic of China.) Japan was thus able to achieve full normalization of relations with China much more rapidly than the United States, which had initiated the process. Both China and Japan reaped enormous benefits from their improved relations particularly from the huge volume of two-way trade that developed between them in the following years. The two countries are natural trading partners. China has various raw materials to offer resource-poor Japan in exchange for Japan's technology, machinery, and finished goods. The diplomatic rewards of the Sino-Japanese détente are probably even greater, for relations between these two major Asian nations have never been better than since 1972, and the new friendship between these once hostile neighbors has brought an era of stability and security to this previously inflamed part of the world.

The country most disaffected by the PRC's new diplomatic achievements was, of course, the Republic of China on Taiwan. It bitterly denounced its former allies—the United States, Japan, and others—for abandoning a friend and argued that leaders in Washington and Tokyo had been duped by the Communist government in Beijing, toward which Taiwan leaders directed their strongest attacks. Although it was becoming isolated diplomatically, Taiwan carefully sought to retain ties with the United States, Japan, and other Western nations with whom it still maintained a lucrative commercial trade. And despite its diplomatic setback, Taiwan has continued to maintain a high rate of economic growth, which has produced a much higher standard of living for its people than the Chinese on the mainland have achieved. Stubbornly, its government, still dominated by the Nationalist Party, has rebuffed every overture by the PRC for a peaceful reunification. Meanwhile, the PRC, careful not to risk damaging its good relations with the United States, has patiently refrained from forceful gestures toward Taiwan and has waited for a softening of Taiwan's position. But, insofar as the very *raison d'être* of the Nationalist government on the island is to overthrow the Communist rulers of the mainland, it has neither wavered in its resolute anti-Communist policy nor moderated even to the slightest degree its strident anti-Beijing propaganda. The spirit of the Cold War has remained very much alive on the island of Taiwan.

■ DÉTENTE BETWEEN EAST AND WEST

The rapprochement between Washington and Beijing took place in an era of thawing of frozen relations across a wide front. It pointed to significant changes in the Cold War mentality in both camps. Originally, both sides had taken the position that there could be no improvement of relations until such grievances as Taiwan, Germany, and the like, had been resolved. In the mid–1960s, however, the belligerents backtracked when they took the position that a normalization of relations—such as in the areas of trade, international travel and contact, and arms limitations—could ultimately resolve the greater issues—the unification of nations, the nuclear arms race, and perhaps even put an end to the Cold War. The result was a period of lessening tensions in international relations.

As we have described previously, the Cold War of the late 1940s had created two German states—a West German state aligned with the West and ultimately with the North Atlantic Treaty Organization (NATO), and an East German state whose government had been installed by the Red Army and which later joined the Soviet Union's military organization, the Warsaw Pact. The conservative anti-Communist West German governments of the 1950s and the early 1960s, particularly that of Chancellor Konrad Adenauer, considered the Soviet creation of East Germany as illegitimate and refused to recognize and deal with it. The West German leaders insisted that only they spoke for all Germans, in East Germany as well as in West.

Adenauer stated his position forcibly when his government issued the Hallstein Doctrine (named after the state secretary of the West German Foreign Office) in 1955. The Hallstein Doctrine made it clear that West Germany would not recognize any state (with the exception of the Soviet Union) that had diplomatic relations with East Germany. In practical terms it meant that West Germany would have no dealings with the Soviet client states of Eastern Europe. West Germany would make no attempt to raise the Iron Curtain.

But in 1966, Willy Brandt, West Germany's new foreign minister, reversed Adenauer's stand when he took the first steps to establish contact with the socialist nations of Eastern Europe. He was willing to recognize the political realities now that more than two decades had elapsed since the Red Army had rolled into the center of Europe. The old maps of Eastern Europe were no more. The president of the United States, Lyndon Johnson, anticipated Brandt's new position when he stated that the reunification of Germany could only come about as a result of détente. In other words, Brandt and Johnson took the position that détente was a precondition for a unified Germany, whereas Adenauer and Hallstein had earlier argued that there must first be a unified Germany before there could be talk of improved relations with the Soviet bloc. Brandt and Adenauer sought the same end; they only differed over the means.

Brandt's departure from Adenauer's stance also meant that he was willing to grant *de facto* recognition to the existence of East Germany, as well as to the new borders of the two Germanies resulting from Germany's defeat in World War II. To achieve the normalization of relations between East and West, Brandt's government was willing to recognize the Oder-Neisse Line as the border between East Germany and Poland. The new border had been in existence since the end of the war, when the Soviet Union moved Poland's western border about 75 miles (into the region of Silesia, which before the war had been German territory) to the Oder and Western Neisse rivers. Of the 6 million former German inhabitants of the area lost to Poland, many had been killed during the war, others had fled before the advancing Red Army, and the remaining 2 million were expelled. The Germans also had lost East Prussia, the easternmost province of the German Reich, to the Soviets, who took the northern half, and to the Poles, who took the southern. And in Czechoslovakia, the Germans had lost the Sudetenland, which the British and the French had granted Hitler in 1938. The Czechs, of course, wasted little time after the war in expelling what was left of the 3 million Sudeten Germans.[5]

The Adenauer government had been most adamant in its refusal to accept the loss of German territory to Poland. Willy Brandt, however, was willing to accept the Oder-Neisse Line, which in 1966 was after all over twenty years old and had virtually no Germans living east of it. Brandt also stopped believing that his government could ever hope to reclaim East Prussia. Any attempt to do so would lead to another war in Europe and only drive Poland and the Soviet Union into each other's arms. (In 1945, the Poles and the Soviets had been able to agree on only one thing, that Germany must pay for the war with the loss of territory.) Brandt also abandoned all claims to the Sudetenland. This was the least controversial of the steps Brandt was willing to take, for the region had been Czechoslovakia's before the war and its transfer to Hitler's Reich was generally seen as one of the most significant events leading to World War II. That the Sudetenland would be returned to Czechoslovakia after the war had been a forgone conclusion.

The Soviet Union and East Germany, however, wanted more than a mere West German recognition of what after all had been a reality for two decades. They wanted a formal West German recognition of the East German government which, of course, would legitimize the Soviet Union's creation of and the permanence of two Germanies. Such recognition would also undermine the West German government's claim that it spoke for all Germans. This, however, Brandt—or any other West German leader—was not willing to do.

But the two German governments did begin to talk to each other. On March 19, 1971, a historic meeting took place in Erfurt, East Germany, between Willy Brandt, who by now was West Germany's chancellor, and the head of the East German Communist party, Walter Ulbricht. These events led to the Basic Treaty of 1972 between the two German states. East Germany did not obtain full diplomatic recognition from West Germany. But the treaty did call for "good neighborly" relations and it led to increased contacts of a cultural, personal, and economic nature. The Iron Curtain was therefore partially lifted.

Brandt's attempts to establish contacts with Eastern Europe became known as *Ostpolitik* (an opening toward the East, literally "eastern politics"). It included a partial thaw in relations with the Soviet Union and other East European countries. In 1968, West Germany established diplomatic relations with Yugoslavia. In 1970, the governments of West Germany and the Soviet Union signed a non-aggression treaty in Moscow. Later that year, Brandt went to Warsaw to sign a similar treaty with the Polish government and his government accepted the Oder-Neisse Line.

But Brandt's recognition of that line merely meant that he would not permit it to stand in the way of better relations with the East. A central feature of the West German position—one spelled out during the early 1950s—had not changed. There could be no adjustment of Germany's borders until Germany signed peace treaties with the nations involved. The Helsinki Agreement (see below) was not a legally valid substitute for such treaties and until such treaties were ratified there could be no *de jure* recognition of the post-war borders. With the later deterioration of East-West relations, West German conservatives, including Chancellor Helmut Kohl, have dusted off this argument. They refuse to consider Germany's borders a closed issue.[6]

Détente and Brandt's *Ostpolitik* made possible a series of arms limitation talks, including SALT I and SALT II (of which more later), which led di-

West German Foreign Minister Willy Brandt received by U.S. Vice President Hubert Humphrey, Washington, D.C., Feb. 1967. (*National Archives*)

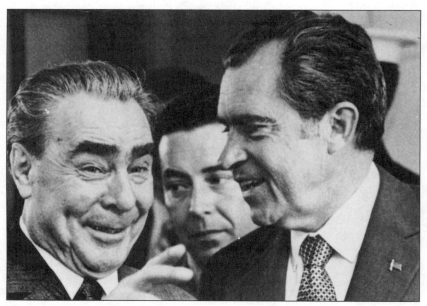

Soviet leader Leonid Brezhnev and U.S. President Richard Nixon, at the White House, Washington, D.C., June 19, 1973. (*AP/Wide World Photos*)

rectly to the European Security Conference of August 1975 in Helsinki, Finland. The Soviets had proposed such a conference as early as 1954 and again in the late 1960s to ratify the consequences of World War II. The Soviet proposals were to no avail. Since no formal treaty or conference had recognized the redrawn map and the new governments of Eastern Europe, the Soviet leaders continued to press for such a conference. At Helsinki in 1975, thirty years after the fact, they hoped to obtain such recognition.

The participants at Helsinki included all European states (except Albania) as well as the United States and Canada. The agreement signed at Helsinki recognized the postwar borders of Europe, but it left open the prospect that the borders could be changed, although only by peaceful means. West Germany renounced its long-standing claim as the sole legitimate German state. East and West agreed to observe each other's military exercises to avoid the misreading of the other's intentions. Lastly, all signatories of the Helsinki Agreement promised greater East-West contact and to guarantee the human rights of their citizens. In Eastern Europe the rights of citizens are defined differently than in the West, and this point later become a central issue when détente was shelved by the United States during the late 1970s.

Détente between East and West also produced the first steps down the road to limit the unchecked nuclear arms race. Until 1972, there were no limits on the nuclear arsenals of the United States and the Soviet Union. Both had more than enough firepower to destroy each other several times over and there was little point in adding to stockpiles already of grotesque proportions. By 1970, the Soviet Union had concluded its concerted effort to catch up with the United States and had achieved in this fashion a rough sort of parity. The U.S. nuclear arsenal consisted at that time of 3,854 warheads; the Soviet total was 2,155.[7]

The year 1975 with its Helsinki Agreement saw the high point of détente. After that relations between the United States and the Soviet Union began to deteriorate, and by 1980, détente was a thing of the past. A number of factors contributed to the new climate.

Détente had never set well with a number of U.S. policymakers. To them, détente was always a snare and a delusion. One cannot do business, they warned, with an ideological system that professes world revolution. They wasted no time seizing every opportunity to sabotage détente. Eventually, a number of liberals joined their chorus.

With the intensification of the Cold War came a reassessment of Soviet military strength and intentions. In 1976, George Bush, as the head of the CIA, brought in a group of Cold War warriors (better known as the B Team) who overruled a CIA estimate of Soviet military spending. The professionals in the CIA, the B Team declared, had misunderstood the nature of the Soviet threat, for according to the B Team's interpretations, the Soviets were spending nearly twice as much on their military as the CIA had reckoned. These ominous interpretations placed Soviet intentions and capabilities in a new light. The new figures were quickly accepted by reporters and editorial writers and became part of the new orthodoxy of the latest phase of the Cold War.[8]

With these new estimates of Soviet military spending came a reevaluation of the nuclear arms race and the charge that the Soviets had opened up a lead on the United States. Between 1976 and 1980, presidential candidate Ronald Reagan got considerable mileage out of this argument. He also promised to restore U.S. military might, a pledge that, probably more than anything else, gained him the presidency in 1980 after the incumbent Jimmy Carter proved impotent in gaining the release of the U.S. hostages in Iran (see Chapter 15). Most of the U.S. public had taken the defeat in Vietnam stoically; it had been clear for a number of years that Vietnam was a losing proposition. The seizure of the hostages and the burning of U.S. flags in full view of television cameras had a more profound effect. A new militancy set in.

The Soviets, in their turn, appeared to be doing everything in their power to scuttle détente. Their definition of détente had always been different than that of the West. They insisted on the right to continue to conduct their foreign and domestic affairs as they had in the past. For example, what they did in Africa, they insisted, had nothing to do with Soviet-U.S. relations. But many in the United States perceived the Soviet activities in Africa differently. In 1975, the Soviet Union began sending arms to clients in Angola, Somalia, Ethiopia, and Mozambique, and Cuban soldiers arrived in Soviet planes in Angola and Ethiopia to train African soldiers. In the early 1970s, the Soviet Union had established close ties with the Marxist leader of Somalia, Siad Barre. Then in late 1976, the Soviet Union began to send arms shipments to the Marxist head of Ethiopia, Mengistu Haile Miriam. In 1978, the governments of Somalia and Ethiopia went to war over a stretch of desert in the Somalian border province of Ogaden. The Soviets had to choose, and they decided to stay with Ethiopia. The United States then became the supplier of weapons to Siad Barre. In addition, Moscow had a client in Vietnam who, in 1978, marched into Phnom Penh, the capital of Cambodia. And in December 1979 the Red Army moved into Afghanistan to prop up a bankrupt and brutal Communist government. Then, in 1981 the head of the Polish state invoked martial law in an attempt to destroy the only independent labor union in the Soviet bloc. To many in the West, Moscow's surrogates appeared to be on the march. In reality, until the Soviets invaded Afghanistan in late 1979, most major conflicts during the second half of the 1970s were between contending Marxist factions. In Angola, the Horn of Africa, and in Cambodia, the Soviet Union supported one Communist side, the United States the other.

At home, the Soviets also undermined the spirit of détente. Jewish emigration from the Soviet Union was drastically curtailed. Jews who wished to leave the Soviet Union were always bargaining chips in East-West relations during the 1970s. In all, about 270,000 Jews emigrated. The numbers rose steadily between 1975 and 1979, when over 50,000 Jews were granted permission to leave. Since then, emigration has slowed to a trickle. Dissidents, the most famous of whom was the nuclear physicist Andrei Sakharov, were either jailed or exiled in violation of the Helsinki Agreement. Under these conditions, détente had little chance of survival.

■ RECOMMENDED READINGS

Bueler, William M. *U.S. China Policy and the Problem of Taiwan.* Boulder, Colo.: Colorado Associated University Press, 1971.
    A discussion of the Taiwan issue on the eve of Nixon's visit.
Fairbank, John K. *The United States and China.* 4th ed. Cambridge, Mass.: Harvard University Press, 1981.
    A standard work that provides a historical account of Sino-U.S. relations as well as a survey of Chinese history.
Garthoff, Raymond. *Détente and Confrontation: American-Soviet Relations From Nixon to Reagan.* Washington, D. C.: The Brookings Institution, 1985.
    The most detailed and best analysis of the topic to date.
Griffith, William E. *Peking, Moscow, and Beyond: The Sino-Soviet Triangle.* Washington, D. C.: Center for Strategic International Studies, 1973.
    Discusses the implications of Nixon's visit to Beijing.
Hersh, Seymour M. *The Price of Power: Kissinger in the Nixon White House.* New York: Summit Books, 1983.
    A devastating analysis of Kissinger's foreign policy; second volume promises to take the story to 1977.
Schaller, Michael. *The United States and China in the Twentieth Century.* New York: Oxford University Press, 1979.
    A useful study that takes the story well beyond the Nixon visit to China.
Ulam, Adam B. *Dangerous Relations: The Soviet Union in World Politics, 1970–1982.* New York: Oxford University Press, 1983.
    Discusses the problems of and the end of détente.

■ NOTES

1. Immanuel C. Y. Hsu, *The Rise of Modern China,* 3rd rev. ed. (New York: Oxford University Press, 1983), p. 373.

2. In fact, the United States voted against the PRC replacing the Republic of China in the United Nations, but made it known that it would not block this move as it had for over two decades. The U.S. vote was essentially a face-saving gesture.

3. The Japanese prime minister, Sato Eisaku, had for years stressed the mutual trust between his government and Washington, and, in order not to jeopardize the strong ties with the

United States, he had consistently resisted the popular pressure within his own country for normalization of relations with China. For the United States to suddenly reverse its China policy without consulting its major Asian ally was considered by the Japanese as a diplomatic slap in the face and was referred to as the "Nixon shock."

4. As quoted in Hsu, p. 751.

5. For a map of the transfer of land after World War II, see the one in Chapter 2, "The Cold War Institutionalized."

6. Bernt Conrad, "How Definite is the Oder-Neisse Line?", *Die Welt,* December 24, 1984; reprinted in *The German Tribune: Political Affairs Review* (a publication of the West German government), April 21, 1985, pp. 15–16. See also, *The Week in Germany,* a weekly newsletter of the West German Information Center, Washington, D.C., June 21, 1985, p. 1.

7. For details of negotiations between Washington and Moscow, see Chapter 17, "The Nuclear Arms Race: The March of Technology."

8. In 1983 the professionals in the CIA, in a report to a Congressional committee, cast off the shackles of Bush and the B Team when they restated the validity of their original estimates of Soviet military spending. They cut the B Team's estimates by more than half. While the B Team's findings had received much publicity, the CIA's declaration of independence from meddling outsiders received scant attention. In January 1984, a NATO study concluded that Soviet military spending since 1976 had been at less than 2.5 percent of the nation's GNP, as compared to 4–5 percent during the early 1970s.

■ Part 4

THE THIRD WORLD

The East-West confrontation has surely been the dominant theme in international relations in the postwar period, but in the past decade another cleavage, the North-South divide, has become increasingly important. "North" refers to the modern industrialized nations, most of which happen to be located in the temperate zones of the northern hemisphere, and "South" signifies the poorer nations, most of which are in the equatorial region or in the southern hemisphere. The nations of the South, scattered through Asia, Africa, and Latin America, have not yet developed industrial economies. They are sometimes euphemistically called "developing countries," even though some of them are hardly developing at all, and sometimes called "underdeveloped countries." More commonly they are referred to collectively as the "Third World." [1]

There has been much discussion about the meaning or the validity of the concept, the Third World. Originally, the term had a political definition, signifying neutrality—that is, not being aligned with either the capitalist nations (First World) or with the Communist bloc (Second World). But it later came to be used more loosely designating economically underdeveloped nations, whatever their political orientation, or even more loosely meaning simply the three continents, Asia, Africa, and Latin America. The concept of the Third World continues to carry a political connotation to the effect that it is comprised of nations that reject the notion that the world is divided between the two superpowers and that all nations must choose between the two. Third World nations have needs and concerns that take precedence over political or ideological alignment. Moreover, there has developed a sense of identity among Third World nations and a degree of solidarity. They have in common a shared past—most were former colonies of European powers—

and their contemporary conditions, concerns, and needs are similar. There are over one hundred Third World nations, and in the General Assembly of the United Nations they comprise about two-thirds of the voting membership. In that and other forums they have made their collective voice heard, for example in demanding better treatment in international trade relations and a fairer share of the world's wealth.

The principal identifying characteristic of Third World nations is their poverty. In the dispossessed nations of the Third World live almost three-quarters of the world's population, but they possess less than one-quarter of the world's wealth. The economic dilemma of the Third World is a major theme of Chapter 11, in which we examine the reasons for the relative lack of economic progress in the Third World and point out that the gulf between the prosperous North and the impoverished South is growing at an alarming rate.

Economic development and political development are inter-related, one being a function of the other. It is necessary, therefore, to seek political reasons for the economic problems in the Third World and economic reasons for its political problems. In Chapter 11, we focus on the political patterns of postindependence Africa, where the demise of fledgling democratic governments and the increase in political instability has gone hand in hand with economic difficulties. South Africa stands apart from its northern neighbors, not so much because it is more prosperous but because it alone among African nations continues to be ruled by a white minority. The policy of apartheid in South Africa and the movement to overturn that racist policy is traced through the end of the 1980s in Chapter 11.

The militarization of politics, new to Africa after independence, has long been a reality in Latin America. In South American countries, large and small, postwar economic development has been disappointing, and the disaffected classes in these countries, mainly landless or land-short farmers and laborers, continued to be victimized by an elitist system that has endured for centuries. In Chapter 12, we will examine the patterns of politics—the swings between democratic rule and militarism in South America, particularly in Argentina, Brazil, and Chile. Economic and political problems in Central America are even more acute than in South America. Indeed, several Central American nations have become hotbeds of revolution, and in this chapter our attention is directed toward them, particularly Nicaragua and El Salvador. We also treat the U.S. intervention in Panama and the issue of the Latin American drug trade.

In Chapter 13, we turn to Asia and examine the modernization efforts of two major Third World nations: the People's Republic of

China and India. China and India, by far the two largest nations in the world, present an interesting contrast, for although they share common problems—how to feed a burgeoning population, for example—they have approached their problems quite differently; India with a democratic form of government and a mixed economy, and China with a Communist form of government and a socialist economic system upon which Deng Xiaoping grafted an element of capitalism. In great contrast to them are the smaller nations on the periphery of China, specifically the "four tigers" (South Korea, Taiwan, Hong Kong, and Singapore), whose success in economic modernization has been phenomenal. This chapter also examines the overthrow of the corrupt Marcos dictatorship in the Philippines.

In China, one is confronted with a unique case, a massive Third World country whose Communist government sought to develop a Communist society and achieve rapid economic development at the same time. After we examine the revolutionary program of Mao Zedong and its failures, we then chart the course taken by China since Mao's death in 1976—the dramatic political and economic changes instituted by his successor, Deng Xiaoping, who ultimately turned on his own creation when he crushed the "democracy movement" in Beijing in June 1989.

In Chapter 14, our focus is on an increasingly serious global economic problem: the world debt crisis. Many of the nations of the Third World, even those with relatively industrialized economies such as Brazil, Mexico, and Argentina, have amassed foreign debts so large that they are unable to pay either the principal or the interest on their loans. Their precarious position threatens not only the economic structures of these nations but also the international monetary system as a whole. The dimensions of this crisis and its causes are examined in this chapter.

■ NOTE

1. The Third World concept may be traced to the early 1950s when it was sometimes called the Afro-Asian bloc. The most influential figure in the early years of the Third World movement was Jawaharlal Nehru, the leader of India, one fo the largest Third World nations. Also important in the launching of the Third World movement were Joseph Tito of Yugoslavia and Gamal Abdel Nasser of Egypt.

□ 11

Africa: Political and Economic Disasters

In the early 1960s, when most African nations gained their independence, proud African leaders heralded the dawn of a new age for their continent. Freed from the shackles of European colonialism, they looked confidently to a new political and economic order that promised an end to the continent's economic backwardness and dependence on the West. But the euphoria of the early 1960s soon gave way to a more somber reality, for as years went by their shared goals of economic growth, of national self-reliance and dignity, and of African unity remained elusive. Indeed, twenty-five years later those dreams were in shambles as most African countries became increasingly impoverished and more dependent on foreign aid than ever before. Across the continent one finds declining economies, grinding poverty, crop failures, starving and hungry people, spreading disease, overcrowded and deteriorating cities, massive unemployment, and growing numbers of desperate refugees. Many of those hopeful leaders of Africa's new nations did not live to see the dashing of their dreams, for they would become victims of military revolts, which became common throughout the continent.

The plight of Africa must be understood in terms of the larger context of global economics. Therefore, we will first examine the growing disparity between the developed nations of the North and the underdeveloped nations of the South and the reasons for the disparity. Most of the various obstacles to industrialization discussed here are present in Africa, especially in sub-Saharan Africa. The economic problems of African nations are particularly acute, and these are exacerbated by the political turmoil that has become common throughout Africa. In one African country after another, democratic rule has given way to military rule, and in several countries there have been a series of military coups. After examining the militarization of African politics, we turn to South Africa and its unique policies and problems.

■ THE DISPARITY BETWEEN NORTH AND SOUTH

Among the nations of the world, there has always existed a gulf between the rich and the poor, but never has that gulf been as wide as it became in the postwar era. Most of this world's wealth is produced and consumed by a relatively small proportion of its people, those of the North. Conversely, the large majority of the earth's people, those in the South, produce and consume but a small proportion of the world's wealth. This disparity in wealth between the North and South is revealed by the figures on per capita GNP (Gross National Product)[1] in Table 11.1.

The alarming increase in the gap between the impoverished South and the more prosperous North was the focus of an international conference convened in Cancun, Mexico, in September 1981. Figures presented at this conference indicate that the 140 nations that classified themselves as "developing nations" comprised 75 percent of the world's population but had only 20 percent of the world's income. More recent figures indicate that the gap between the North and South continued to grow larger in the 1980s.

The statistical average of $700 annual per capita income for the Third World masks the great disparity of wealth among Third World nations. In fact, the per capita income for most sub-Sahara African countries is far below $700. According to World Bank figures, in 1984 Ethiopia had a per capita income of only $110, the lowest among African nations, followed by Mali ($140), Zaire ($140), and Burkina Faso ($160).[2] Moreover, most of the nations of Africa have very low economic growth rates. Indeed, several—at least fourteen—African nations have registered "negative growth" or decline of per capita GNP in recent years. World Bank figures reveal that Zaire, for example, had a negative growth rate of –1.2 percent and Uganda one of –3 percent for the decade between 1972 and 1982. This means that in those

Table 11.1 Per Capital Gross National Product, 1987–1988

North	
North America (U.S. and Canada)	$18,210
Switzerland	21,330
Japan	15,760
West Germany	14,400
European Community (12 members)	10,730
Eastern Europe (Poland, Romania, East Germany, Czechoslovakia, Hungary, and Bulgaria), 1988	8,210
South	
Sub-Saharan Africa (excluding Namibia and South Africa)	330
China	290
South Asia (including India)	290
Latin America and Caribbean	1,790

Sources: World Bank, *World Development Report 1989*, pp. 164–165 and CIA, Population Reference Bureau, in *New York Times*, January 7, 1990, p. E3.

Table 11.2 North vs. South

	North	South
Population	1.18 billion	3.76 billion
Annual per capita GNP	$9,510	$700
Life expectancy	73 years	58 years
Annual rate of population growth	0.6%	2.0%

Source: Population Reference Bureau, *1986 World Population Data Sheet.*

countries the population was growing faster than the economy. And in real terms this can only mean continued dismal poverty, hunger, and misery for their inhabitants.

Within each impoverished nation of the South, there exists a great disparity between the relatively wealthy and the poor. The maldistribution of wealth in the underdeveloped nations of the Third World is greater than in industrialized nations of the North.[3] The majority of the people in Third World nations, mainly peasants but many city dwellers as well, have far less than the national average per capita income. Taking this into account, as well as the increasing population and low per capita income figures for the poorest nations, we can begin to fathom the dimensions of poverty and hunger in the Third World. It is estimated that approximately 1 billion people—perhaps as many as one-quarter of planet earth's inhabitants—live in abject poverty and suffer from chronic hunger and malnutrition.

■ THE POPULATION FACTOR

Unquestionably, population growth is a major factor in the persistence of poverty in the world. The population of the world has grown at an increasing rate and at an especially alarming rate in the twentieth century. It took about five million years for the world's population to reach 1 billion, around 1800. The second billion mark was reached in about 130 years, by 1930; the third billion, in 30 years, by 1960; the fourth billion in 15 years, by 1975; and the fifth billion in 11 years, by 1986. (See Figure 11.1.) The rate of growth of world population peaked at 2.4 percent annually in 1964, and has since fallen to about 1.7 percent, a drop that is mainly attributable to the population controls that have been instituted in China and in many developed countries.

The pressure of overpopulation is much greater in the developing nations of the Third World, where population growth rates remain very high compared to the developed nations of the North. Since World War II, Third World population has grown at a historically unprecedented rate. Many Third World nations, especially in Africa, have growth rates of more than 3 percent, and some have risen to more than 4 percent. In contrast, the industrialized nations have a much lower rate of growth, and some of them, notably East Germany, West Germany, and Austria, have attained a stable population (no growth at all) or even a negative growth rate. (See Figure 11.2.)

Because of their huge population growth rates, many of the Third World nations are on a treadmill. Africa is a case in point. The increase in its economic output, never large to begin with, has all too often been swallowed up by the relentless growth in population. In the past decade, Africa's population growth rate at just under 3 percent is about nine times that of Europe and about three times that of the United States and Canada. These ominous statistics mean that unless the trend is reversed, the continent's population of 500 million will double in only 23 years. The growth rate in Kenya throughout the 1970s stood at 3.5 percent and by the mid–1980s it had risen to 4.2 percent. Its fertility rate (the average number of children born to a woman) is 8.0. These figures are among the highest in recorded history. But Kenya is not alone, for all of the following African countries have population

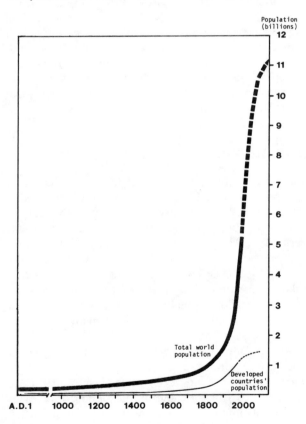

Figure 11.1   Past and Projected World Population, A.D. 1–2150

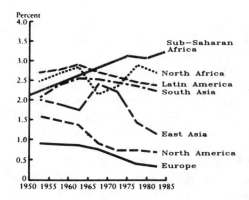

Figure 11.2   Population Growth Rates, Selected Regions, 1950–1985. (Source: *Population Growth and Policies in Sub-Saharan Africa*, World Bank, 1986)

growth rates approaching 4 percent: Rwanda, Zimbabwe, Tanzania, Uganda, Ghana, and Libya.

How is the population explosion in the Third World to be explained? In briefest terms, the death rate has fallen while the birth rate either has risen or remained constant. Demographers explain that the introduction of modern medicines, the eradication of communicable diseases (such as smallpox), and improved public health and education have all contributed to a reduced rate of infant mortality and an increased life expectancy. But there has been no corresponding decrease in fertility. In most developing countries, most families have at least four children, and in rural areas often more than five. In these countries, not unlike the developing European countries of the nineteenth century, the larger the number of children in a family, the greater the number of hands in the fields or in the factories where they were able to earn an income to supplement the parents' meager income. For this reason having a large family is a means to escape poverty and is therefore considered economically rational. The responsibility in the Third World often lies with men, who tend to distrust all artificial birth control methods and to whom many children are signs of virility and moral rectitude. Yet, it is the women who bear the children and wind up caring for the large families. But it is also true that in most of the Third World, women typically share the desire for many children.

Programs of local governments and international agencies to control population growth in the Third World have met with mixed success. The most dramatic reduction of birthrate has occurred in China, where the Communist government instituted a stringent birth control program including paramedical services, free abortions (even at near full term), public education, social pressure, and economic sanctions. Government-supported family planning programs have been moderately successful in other Third

World countries, notably South Korea, Colombia, Mauritius, Sri Lanka, Argentina, Uruguay, and Egypt. In many other countries governments have been less active in, or have only recently begun, birth control efforts. In India, birth control programs have had mixed results, but have generally been more effective in regions where public education is more widespread. As yet, birth control programs, whether those of Third World governments or international agencies, have had little or no effect on many countries in Latin America (especially Central America) and in sub-Saharan Africa.

The problems of overpopulation in the Third World are compounded by an ongoing exodus of people from the surrounding countryside migrating into the city. Where land cannot support large populations, millions have flocked to the already overcrowded cities in quest of a better life.[4] The result has been a phenomenal growth of Third World cities, many of which are among the largest in the world, for example, Mexico City, Sao Paulo, Buenos Aires, Seoul, Calcutta, and Cairo. In Africa there were only three cities with a population of 500,000 in 1950, but now there are twenty-nine cities of at least that size. The urban population of Kenya doubled in a decade. The population of Lagos, Nigeria grew incredibly from 300,000 in 1970 to over 3 million in 1983.

While the cities typically offer more and better employment opportunities, medical services, and education than the villages, they cannot accommodate the massive numbers of newcomers. It is impossible for these cities to provide adequate employment, housing, sanitation, and other services for the numerous new inhabitants, many of whom remain unemployed, impoverished, and homeless. Mexico City is the most extreme case. Its population doubled in the last decade to over 18 million. More than one-third of these people live in squatter settlements in the world's largest slum. This scene is duplicated in most other Third World cities, such as Cairo, where many thousands live in the city's refuse dump, and Calcutta, where nearly 1 million of the city's 10 million inhabitants live in the streets. The concentration of such huge numbers of disaffected peoples, living in the shadows of the edifices of the more opulent class and often within marching distance of the centers of political power (many of the largest Third World cities are capital cities), heightens the potential for massive political revolts.

One of the most critical problems associated with overpopulation is feeding the people. In recent years, television has brought home to people in the North the tragedy of mass starvation in Ethiopia, but most viewers remained unaware that the problem was not limited to Ethiopia, that hundreds of thousands of people in other African countries—Sudan, Kenya, Mozambique, Chad, Mali, Niger, and others—were also suffering from starvation. Estimates of the extent of world hunger vary greatly, depending in part on how hunger is defined, but there is little doubt that an enormous number of Third World people—perhaps 1 billion—are chronically malnourished.

■ THE AGRARIAN DILEMMA

Food production in the South has actually increased at about 3.1 percent annually since the late 1960s, but population increase has eaten up this increase almost entirely. Although most Asian nations have made considerable progress in agricultural production, fifty-five Third World nations, again most of them in Africa, registered a decline in food production per capita in the last two decades. In the early 1970s, the nations of the South were collectively net exporters of agricultural produce, but by the early 1980s they were net importers of food.

Why is it that the nations of the Third World, almost all of which are agrarian nations, are unable to increase their agricultural production to a level of self-sufficiency? This complex question defies a simple explanation, but several major causal factors are presented in the following.

1. *Natural Causes.* Most Third World nations are in the tropics, close to the equator, where the climate is often very hot and where both extended droughts and torrential rain storms occur. Desertification is a major problem in Africa, where the Sahara has pushed its frontier southward into West Africa and eastward into Sudan. Indeed, much of that continent has suffered from prolonged droughts. Other Third World areas also suffer from drought and various other natural catastrophes such as excessive heat, flooding, cyclones, and earthquakes.

2. *Abuse of the Land.* Great amounts of topsoil are lost to wind and water erosion every year, and this is partly due to human causes such as deforestation and overcultivation. In Africa, the problem is often one of overgrazing, that is, too much of the land is devoted to herd animals. Other land has been overcultivated and its nutrients exhausted.

3. *Primitive Farming Methods.* Most Third World peasants work with simple tools, many with nothing more than a hoe, and most plowing is still done with draft animals. Peasants are usually too poor to afford modern equipment. In some instances intensive farming with traditional methods and tools is very efficient, especially in the case of paddy farming in Asia, but in many other areas, especially in Africa, toiling in parched fields with hand tools is an ineffective mode of production. In some parts of Africa much of this toil is done exclusively by women.[5]

4. *Inequality of Land Holdings.* Throughout the Third World, agricultural production suffers because the majority of the peasants have too little land to farm and many are tenants burdened with huge rent payments. The impoverished, debt-ridden peasants are often forced to become landless laborers. According to one international study, in Latin America 80 percent

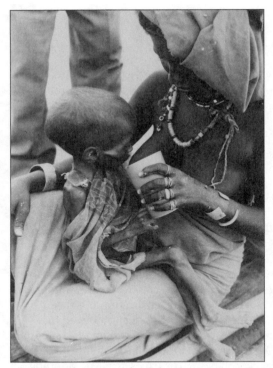

Ethiopian famine victims, 1984. (*AP/Wide World Photos*)

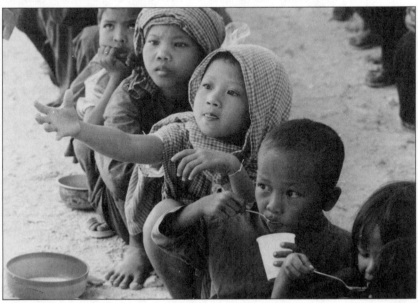

Hungry Cambodian children receiving relief food in refugee camp in Trat, Thailand, June 4, 1979. (*AP/Wide World Photos*)

of the farmland was owned by 8 percent of landowners, while the poorest peasants—66 percent of all owners—were squeezed onto only 4 percent of the land.[6] Land reform, that is, redistribution of land, has paid off with significantly increased agricultural output for nations such as Japan and Bulgaria, and it would no doubt benefit many Third World nations.

5. *Lack of Capital for Agricultural Development.* Third World food producing farmers need irrigation works, better equipment, chemical fertilizers, storage facilities, and improved transport, none of which they can afford, nor have their governments been willing or able to supply the capital needed to provide these essentials.

6. *One-crop Economies.* In many of the Third World nations the best land with the best irrigation belongs to wealthy landowners (and sometimes to multinational corporations) who grow cash crops—peanuts, cocoa, coffee, and so on—for export rather than food for consumption. Generally, Third World leaders have accepted the dogma that the progress of their country depends on what they can produce for sale to the developed countries. Dependence on a single cash crop for export places the developing nations at the mercy of the world market where prices fluctuate greatly. It has proven disastrous for Third World countries in recent years when prices of their agricultural exports have dropped sharply while prices of necessary imports (especially petroleum, fertilizers, and finished goods) have risen. Meanwhile, Third World leaders have neglected the needs of the majority of the farmers, that is, the food-producing peasantry, in favor of support for the cash crop farmers. In many cases these leaders have deliberately kept food prices artificially low to the benefit of the growing number of city dwellers and to the detriment of the food-growing peasantry.

The list could be extended with still other reasons for the lack of growth of agricultural output in the Third World, some of which are peculiar to specific regions, but it is apparent that many of the problems lie at the doorstep of the political leaders rather than the farmers. The solution to these problems would seem to lie in land reform, diversification of agriculture, and the building of irrigation systems, roads, storage facilities, fertilizer plants, and agricultural schools. But these efforts require a large amount of capital, political stability, and strong and able political leadership, all of which are frequently lacking.

The nations of the Third World have been provided relief in the form of large shipments of food to feed starving people. However, while such aid is beneficial and humane, it does not go to root of the problem (and in fact it often does not reach those who need it most). Increasingly, donor nations and international financing institutions have channeled their aid into long-term agricultural development programs for which they provide expertise, training, and incentives as well as capital. There is little question that larger amounts of well-directed developmental aid from nations of the North and such agencies as the World Bank are greatly needed by the developing nations.

■ PREREQUISITES FOR INDUSTRIALIZATION

Upon gaining independence from Europe, Third World nations tended to blame their economic backwardness on their former colonial masters. They looked forward to rapid progress as independent nations, hoping to close the gap that separated them from the economically advanced nations of the world. The leaders of these nations usually viewed industrial development as the primary road to economic modernization. By giving priority to industrial growth, however, these countries tended to neglect agriculture and its role in economic development. Moreover, their efforts at rapid industrialization were often met with frustrations and failures. They expected the dynamics of change to bring them rapid progress, but they have found, to their dismay, that industrial development is a tortuously difficult process. Economists have long argued over the prerequisites for industrial development, but the following are generally considered minimal necessary conditions.

1. *Capital Accumulation.* Money for investments to build plants and buy equipment has to come from somewhere: the World Bank, foreign powers (which usually seek to gain political or military influence), heavy taxation (often falling upon people who can least afford it), or the export of cash crops or raw materials. This last method of capital accumulation has often led to the following anomaly: the agrarian nations of the Third World find themselves importing expensive food, often from the developed nations, in ever-increasing amounts, and thus money tends to flow out of their economies, rather than in.

Third World nations are in great need of foreign aid, but such aid is not necessarily the answer to their problems. They have been receiving vast amounts of aid from abroad for many years, but all too often the money is mismanaged, misdirected, squandered on unproductive projects, or simply siphoned off by corrupt leaders. Moreover, there are hazards involved in overreliance on financial aid from outside. On the one hand, Third World leaders are wary of political strings attached to foreign loans and intrusions into their national sovereignty or threats to their own personal power. On the other hand, there are problems of excessive indebtedness. Many Third World countries have already borrowed beyond their ability to repay (see Chapter 14). After having struggled to win their political independence from the developed nations of the North, they are loath to become economic dependencies of those same nations.

2. *Technology.* To compete with the highly sophisticated industries of the economically advanced nations, developing nations must rapidly incorporate new technology. But technology transfer is a complicated matter, and its acceptance and implementation in tradition-bound societies is at best a slow process. Meanwhile, technological change in developed nations is rapid, and the developing countries, even when making progress, fall further behind.

3. *Education.* Technology, even when borrowed from abroad, requires educated technicians and workers. An industrialized society requires a literate working class as well as educated managers and engineers. Industry needs skilled labor, and literacy is essential for training such a work force. The attainment of mass education is a long-term and costly undertaking.

4. *Favorable Trading Conditions.* In general, the system of free trade erected by the industrially advanced nations of the world after World War II has served both developed and developing nations well, but the latter need preferential treatment in order to compete with the former in the international market place. The Third World nations have sought new trade agreements that will, in some manner, underwrite their exports with guaranteed minimum purchases at prices not to fall below a fixed level. They also want to be allowed to maintain higher tariffs on imports to protect their native industries. As yet, the club of industrially developed nations has been unresponsive to these demands.

5. *Political Stability.* Capital accumulation and the conduct of business require safety and stability. Domestic strife and international wars are disruptive and costly, draining off the meager resources for industrial development. (Nearly all of the wars since 1945 have been fought in Third World countries. The list is endless: China, Korea, Vietnam, Iran, Iraq, Ethiopia, Chad, Nigeria, Lebanon, India, Pakistan, El Salvador, Nicaragua, and so on.) Even those developing nations not engaged in external or civil wars spend an extraordinary amount of currency on sophisticated weapons, which they cannot afford and which are purchased from the industrialized powers, primarily the United States and the Soviet Union.

6. *Capital Investment.* The economies of the Third World tend to be exploitative of their own people. Available capital, from whatever source, is often spent on luxury imports for the elite, the building of showcase airports and hotels, and the like, and not on the development of the economic substructure for industrial and agricultural growth, an activity that would benefit the population as a whole. Thus, we see in Third World cities great contrasts of wealth coexisting side-by-side with grinding poverty—elegant mansions in one part of town and tin roof hovels in another.

After independence the hard realities of economic development began to set in as Third World countries struggled to overcome their economic deficiencies and to come to terms with the problems of feeding their people and improving the quality of life in their countries. In this endeavor, some countries, mainly in Asia, have met with considerable success, but others, mainly in Africa and Latin America, continue to find themselves in a perilous condition.

■ AFRICA'S ECONOMIC PLIGHT

In Africa we find the world's worst poverty, lowest economic growth rates, highest infant mortality rates, and highest rates of population growth. The population of Africa is growing at about twice the rate of increase in food production in the last decade. Chronic malnutrition and starvation have become more common in recent years. Perhaps as many as 200,000 people succumbed to starvation in the Ethiopian famine in the early 1970s,[7] and another famine a decade later, more publicized than the earlier one, took an equally large toll. Media attention focused on Ethiopia diverted attention from the hundreds of thousands of people malnourished and on the verge of starvation in Sudan, Chad, Niger, and Mali. These nations as well as Ethiopia are most affected by the relentless expansion of the Sahara desert. Further south, such countries as Kenya, Uganda, Gabon, and Mozambique are also drought-stricken. The Economic Commission for Africa, a UN agency, reported that from 1960 to 1975 there was no significant improvement in most African nations' economies and it suggested that, if trends continued, Africa will be even worse off in the year 2000 than it had been in 1960. In 1960, Africa was about 95 percent self-sufficient in food, but twenty-five years later every African country except South Africa was a net importer of food.

The nations of sub-Saharan Africa are not equally impoverished. By far the most prosperous nation on the continent is South Africa, which stands as an exception to the economic decline characteristic of the remainder of sub-Saharan Africa.[8] Of all black African nations, the Ivory Coast has had the best economic performance and the highest standard of living, which may be

DATE OF INDEPENDENCE: *(19 . . .)*

AFRICA AFTER INDEPENDENCE

explained in part by the contribution of some 60,000 French residents in that small country. Nigeria, burdened with Africa's largest population and yet blessed with large deposits of oil, has prospered greatly since independence, only to find its economy in collapse as a result of political corruption and plummeting world oil prices in the early 1980s. An examination of per capita GNP growth rates since 1973 reveals that black African nations are either struggling to maintain marginal economic progress, marking time, or actually declining. According to World Bank figures on GNP per capita growth rates, those showing marginal growth include Benin, Botswana, Cameroon, The People's Republic of Congo, the Ivory Coast, and Rwanda; those marking time include Angola, Ethiopia, Guinea, Kenya, Malawi, Mali, Namibia, Niger, and Zimbabwe; and those with declining per capita GNP growth rates include the Central African Republic, Chad, Gabon, Ghana, Guinea-Bissau, Liberia, Mozambique, Nigeria, Senegal, Sierra Leone, Tanzania, Uganda, Zaire, and Zambia.[9] Most tragic are those states that have the potential for economic growth and that actually made considerable progress in the first decade of independence only to slide backwards since then. Ghana, Nigeria, Kenya, Uganda, and Zaire particularly come to mind.

■ POLITICAL INSTABILITY IN SUB-SAHARAN AFRICA

The miseries of Africa are both economic and political. Indeed, there exists an interrelationship between the economic and political problems. Political chaos often follows in the train of economic disaster, and conversely, political problems often contribute to the economic woes of African nations.

Since independence, Africa has witnessed the steady erosion of democratic institutions and the steady militarization of politics. After initial trial runs in parliamentary democracy, elected governments all too often retained their powers by eliminating the electoral process and political opposition. Subsequently, military coups—not popular elections—have been the primary vehicle for the transfer of power. Authoritarianism is common throughout Africa, where about three-quarters of the governments are controlled either by one-party regimes or militarists. Only about a half-dozen states in sub-Saharan Africa permit opposition parties to engage in the political process, and not a single African head of state has ever been voted out of office. Political repression has seemed to be the order of the day, especially in such countries as Uganda and Guinea where political leaders have massacred many thousands of opponents. And more often than not African leaders have been as corrupt as they were repressive.

How and why did the political chaos in Africa come about? Many African leaders are quick to answer that a century of European colonialism was responsible for many of Africa's problems. There is little question that colonialism was exploitative and disruptive and its impact on Africa enormous, but the nature of the impact is not so easily determined. This is not the place to reexamine the legacy of European colonialism in Africa, the mix of positive and negative aspects of that long experience on African society. Still, it is possible to discern certain consequences of colonialism that left Africans ill-prepared for the tasks of nation building. One may well question whether the political and economic models that Europeans provided Africa and that many of the westernized African elites adopted were suitable for African society. In retrospect, it also might be argued that the Europeans left too abruptly, leaving the Africans with political institutions for which few Africans, beyond a small circle of educated elites, had appreciation or understanding. The colonial powers did little in the way of developing national economies in their colonies; instead, they had mainly built up enterprises focused on a single export product, whether an agricultural product such as coffee, or raw materials such as copper. The economic system inherited by the new African nations was hardly designed for delivery of goods and services to its own people. Moreover, the export-oriented economy of each colony was directly linked with the former colonial power instead of being linked with its African neighbors, and this would remain a major obstacle to regional trade and economic development.

Perhaps the most baleful legacy of European colonialism was the artificiality of the national boundaries it had created. In the nineteenth century, the European imperialists often hastily drew straight-line boundaries as they divided Africa into colonies, and these arbitrary boundaries, drawn with little or no appreciation of the ethnic make-up of Africa, have been the root of many of Africa's problems since independence. It is not so much that the new African nations have disputed the boundaries or have clashed over them, for border conflicts have not been as serious a problem as tribal conflicts and secessionist wars within the new African nations. As a result of the political boundaries created by the Europeans, most African states are much larger than the precolonial political units and contain within them many tribal groups. Only two countries in sub-Saharan Africa have ethnic uniformity (Lesotho and Swaziland). All others have populations made up of several tribes. In the most extreme cases, Nigeria includes within its borders some 250 distinct ethnic groups, and Zaire approximately 200. The new nations of Africa were in many instances artificial constructs, and their rulers had the task of superimposing over the existing tribal configuration a new national identity. In most instances, however, tribalism has prevailed over nationalism—a relatively new and foreign concept—to the detriment of the process of nation building. The result has been frequent tribal conflict ranging from tribe-affiliated political contention to bloody civil wars, secessionist wars, and even genocide.

The first and one of the most tragic instances of postcolonial tribal warfare was the Katanga separatist movement in the Congo (now Zaire) just as independence was attained in 1960. Tribalism also claimed a frightful toll of lives in the two small central African nations of Rwanda and Burundi in the 1960s and 70s.[10] Even more lives were lost in Nigeria in the 1960s in tribal strife known as the Biafran War (discussed later).

Tribalism is of course a legacy not of colonialism but of African history. It persisted through the colonial era, in some places strengthened by colonial policy, in others diluted, and remained strong after independence. Typically, an African's strongest loyalties are to family and tribe. Given the relative lack of geographic mobility in Africa, people of one tribe maintain local roots and mix very little with people of other tribes. Governments in Africa often represent but one dominant tribe to the exclusion of others, and the discontent of the excluded tribes is often the source of both political instability and political repression. In countries ruled by political leaders from a minority tribe, such as Kenya, Uganda, or Zambia in the mid–1980s, the ruler can maintain political order only as long as the country's largest tribes can be satisfied.

Tribalism relates to another aspect of African heritage that has plagued African politics: corruption. In kinship-based societies such as those in Africa, communal elders are entrusted not only with authority to make decisions binding for the group but to divide the wealth among its members. This entails a communal sense of property with little distinction between personal and public possession, which gives rise to a pattern of self-indulgence by leaders and public acceptance of the same. It also entails a patronage system whereby gifts and favors are parceled out by the leader who expects to be favored with gifts in return, and this too lends itself to practices that elsewhere are viewed as graft and corruption. Once a tribal leader attains rulership of a nation and gains access to its wealth and control of its instruments of power, self-aggrandizement and corruption on an immense scale are often the result. There is usually little dissent, except from members of other tribes whose opposition to the corruption is largely based on jealousy. Thus, African politics has often degenerated into tribal contests for the spoils of power.

The combination of unbridled corruption and the cult of personality in Africa has produced some of the world's most outrageous displays of extravagance. Not a few African rulers live in regal splendor in fabulous palaces, own fleets of Mercedes-Benz cars, and stash vast amounts of money in Swiss banks. Many have been excessive, but none has exceeded Colonel Jean-Bedel Bokassa, the erstwhile emperor of the Central African Republic, in bizarre extravagance. He spent about $20 million—one-quarter of his nation's revenue—on his coronation ceremony in 1977. For that occasion, this dictator of a country that has no more than 170 miles of paved roads, wore a robe bedecked with 2 million pearls and costing $175,000, and donned a $2 million crown topped with a 138-carat diamond. Two years later Bokassa was deposed.

The demise of democratic government and the militarization of African politics did not happen overnight, but rather evolved in several stages. Most of the newly independent nations of Africa began with an inherited parliamentary system of government in which executive power was in the hands of a prime minister who was elected by and responsible to a popularly elected legislative body. The challenges of rapid nation building were such that strong personal leaders were called for. Moreover, many of the new rulers had already affected a charismatic style of leadership prior to becoming prime ministers of the new nations. Typically, the African prime ministers revised the constitution in order to become presidents with broadened executive powers and longer terms of office. (A prime minister is elected by the parliament and is responsible to it, and may be called to resign at any time by a vote of no confidence in the parliament. But a president is elected by the people for a fixed, usually longer, term and is not so easily expelled from office.) Without an effective check on their new powers, the presidents began exercising them in a dictatorial manner and no longer tolerated political opposition. They argued that opposition parties were divisive, a threat to political stability, even unpatriotic, and on these grounds the presidents abolished them. Thus, one-party states were created. The notion of the "loyal opposition," an out-of-power political party opposed to the current party in power but loyal to the nation and qualified to govern if elected, was still foreign to Africans, especially to those in power. Moreover, as noted above, most often the opposition parties did not represent different policies but rival tribes, and as such they were all the more targeted for suppression.

Thus, the African presidential dictators entrenched themselves in power by eliminating parliamentary procedures and political opponents. They also took steps to strengthen the central governments by bringing local governments and all levels of civil service under their direct control. They replaced local officials with party members and cronies personally loyal to themselves. They made use of state wealth, especially foreign loans, to buy off or secure the loyalties of others. In order to win popular support, they used other instruments of modern state power, such as media control and propaganda, in which loyalty to nation and loyalty to the ruler were equated. They also relied on military force to guard their power, to suppress dissent, and sometimes to terrorize the population.

■ THE MILITARIZATION OF AFRICAN POLITICS

Presidential dictators in Africa, however, could not be certain of the loyalty of the military, and this proved to be the Achilles heel for many of them. In many African nations military revolts supplanted presidential dictators with military dictators. With some notable exceptions, many of Africa's first line of rulers were overthrown by their own armies.[11] The forceful overthrow of Ghana's Nkrumah in 1966 gave rise to a wave of military coups across Africa, and by 1980, no less than sixty successful coups had taken place. Military officers with their own *esprit de corps* and their own political ambitions had little difficulty in finding cause to overthrow corrupt rulers who had destroyed democratic institutions and wrecked the economy. Some of the new military rulers promised to restore rule to civilian politicians, but few actually did so. Some, like Zaire's Joseph Mobutu, retired their military uniforms and became presidents; while others became victims of later military coups. Most of the earlier coups were carried out by high-ranking officers, but as time went on, lower-ranking officers and even noncommissioned officers thrust themselves into power by the barrel of a gun. In Sierra Leone, army generals took power in 1967 but were overthrown several months later by other army officers, who were in turn soon ousted by a sergeants' revolt. And in Benin (formerly Dahomey), there were five military coups and ten attempted coups between 1963 and 1972.

New military regimes were often welcomed by a disillusioned people, but, because the military rulers were usually less prepared than the ousted politicians to cope with the problems of poverty, economic stagnation, and political unrest, they seldom succeeded. As their regimes became more tyrannical and as corrupt as those of the civilian rulers they had overthrown, they quickly lost popular support and became ripe for overthrow by still other ambitious military officers.

Many of Africa's military leaders have been brutal, but none exceeded Idi Amin of Uganda. In 1971, Amin, an army officer, staged a coup overthrowing the government of Milton Obote. Soon Amin found scapegoats for the economic and social ills of Uganda in several minority tribes and in the community of Asian (mainly Indian) residents of the country. In 1972, Amin forcefully expelled some 50,000 Asians from Uganda, an act which caused great harm to the economy. As conditions worsened in the country, Amin resorted to torture, public executions, and assassinations to enforce his rule. He meanwhile launched an attack on neighboring Tanzania and used the pretext of war to further terrorize his own people. After surviving a number of plots on his life, he was finally overthrown in 1979 by a force from Tanzania, which then installed a civilian government of native Ugandans. Before his removal from power, Amin, the crazed dictator, had massacred an estimated 250,000 of his own people, caused about as many to flee the country as refugees, and left Uganda in shambles. In 1980, Milton Obote returned to power as dictator of Uganda. His regime's continued military "clean-up operations" never succeeded in restoring order but instead eventually killed almost as many people as Amin had and caused another wave of refugees to flee the stricken country.

The process of militarization in African politics is demonstrated by the experience of Ghana, a nation that was once looked upon as the pacesetter in Africa's drive for modernization. The charismatic Kwame Nkrumah, who had led the fight for independence, provided vigorous leadership as prime minister of the hopeful nation, which in the early 1960s had the second highest per capita income in Africa. As the most outspoken champion of pan-Africanism, Nkrumah was involved in the struggle to liberate other African colonies at the same time that he was guiding his own nation's progress. He adopted a socialist program for Ghana that entailed nationalization of industries and state planning, but he did not attempt a social revolution involving land redistribution. Nkrumah was an inspirational nationalist who placed special emphasis on education as a vehicle for Ghana's development. But before his reorganization programs produced any significant economic progress, Ghana was victimized by the drastic decline in the world price in cocoa, its principal cash crop and source of earnings. In the decade following independence the price fell to a third of its previous level. The declining economic fortunes of the country in combination with the rising expectations of its people stirred discontent. Nkrumah's own corruption and extravagance were also targets of criticism. But President Nkrumah, who did not tolerate dissent, became increasingly repressive. With the pressures of a bankrupt economy and popular unrest mounting higher, the volatile Nkrumah, now a dictator, jailed the opposition and silenced dissent. Finally, in February 1966, when he was away on a visit to China, his regime was toppled by the army.

In the years that followed, Ghana became the epitome of political instability as coup followed coup. The military officers who grasped power in 1966 made good their promise to restore civilian rule, but after a brief period of democratic government, a group of junior officers staged another coup in 1969 eliminating former government leaders by firing squads. After still another coup in 1972, Ghana remained under military rule through the 1970s. In 1979, a youthful flight lieutenant named Jerry Rawlings shot his way into power and carried out another wave of executions. However, in 1980, he made good his promise to give democracy another chance in Ghana. This, too, proved short-lived, for at the end of 1981, Rawlings once again took power. Like others before him, he promised an end to corruption, sweeping political and economic reforms, and a brighter future for the blighted country. All the while, however, during the two decades of political instability since 1966, Ghana's economic and social woes have continued to worsen.

Nigeria provides another case of the militarization of and a good example of the problems of tribal conflict within countries. No African nation has spilled more blood in tribal strife than Nigeria, and perhaps none has made greater efforts to overcome tribal disunity. Nigeria, Africa's most populous nation and one of its wealthiest, was at the time of its independence a federal republic made up of three self-governing regions, each of which was dominated by one major tribe—the Hausa-Fulani in the Northern Region, the Yoruba in the Western, and the Ibo in the Eastern. In January 1966, military officers, mainly of the Ibo tribe, staged a coup, murdering political leaders and establishing a military regime under General J. T. Ironsi. Ironsi prepared a new constitution supplanting the federal system with a unitary state. Northerners were suspicious of Ibo intentions of dominating the new state, and one of them, Lt. Col. Yakubu Gowon, led a military revolt overturning Ironsi and setting up a new regime. In the north some 20,000 Ibo were massacred and hundreds of thousands of them fled from other parts of the country, returning to the Eastern Region. Gowon sought to bring national unity with a reorganization of Nigeria into twelve states, a scheme designed to reduce the status of the three largest tribes and increase that of the lesser tribes. The Ibo rejected the new plan and instead declared themselves an independent nation, Biafra, and in the summer of 1967 civil war began. The Biafran War was the bloodiest in African history, costing over 1 million lives. The Ibo, although initially successful, were driven back village by village until they finally capitulated in January 1970. Magnanimous in victory, Gowon sought to heal the wounds of the bitter war and to reintegrate the Ibo into the nation, which in 1976 was divided into nineteen states.

Despite the enormous costs of that war, Nigeria began the 1970s on a strong economic footing. Nigeria's production and export of oil was growing rapidly, and its income from oil multiplied with the OPEC price increases in the 1970s. But many of the country's problems went unresolved—inequalities of wealth, agricultural failures, urban unemployment, and the like—and dissatisfaction with the government grew. In July 1975, Gowon was overthrown by a coup led by General Murtala Muhammed, who instituted reforms aimed at strengthening the central government. But before he could proceed very far with his program he was slain in an unsuccessful coup. He was succeeded by his chief of staff, Olusegun Obasanjo, a Yoruba army officer. Obasanjo provided Nigeria with a new constitution modeled on that of the United States with a popularly elected president, a bicameral legislature, and locally elected state governments. Also, political parties were reorganized on a national rather than local or tribal basis. The new election laws were carefully designed to break down old tribal cleavages. On the basis of an election in 1979 in which 48 million Nigerians voted, many of them across tribal lines, Shehu Shagari was elected as the nation's first president, and military government was ended for the time being.

Although the new presidential government got off to a good start, regionalism began to resurface, especially as Shagari, in the face of the worsening economy (caused mainly by the collapse of oil prices in the early 1980s) began abusing his governmental powers to entrench himself and his party in power. He was re-elected in 1983 in a rigged election. By this time the

Nigerian economy was devastated by the crash in oil prices, and the majority of its people were driven into desperate poverty. In early 1983, some 2 million Ghanaian workers were forcefully expelled from Nigeria. Amidst new cries of political corruption and incompetence, the military once again intervened at the end of 1983. The new strongman, General Buhari, suspended the constitution and attempted to restore political order to his chaotic country only to be overthrown by yet another military coup in August 1985.

■ FOREIGN INTERVENTION

The political instability and the widespread economic disaster make African nations ripe for exploitation and intervention by outside powers. From the outset of independence, African leaders sought to eliminate dependence on foreign powers, and then as now, they have insisted on "African solutions to African problems." It was largely in quest of this ideal that the Organization of African Unity was formed in 1963. This body has never achieved a meaningful concert of Africa, as the individual nations have tended to pull apart rather than together and most of them have maintained closer ties with their former colonial masters in Europe than with their neighbors. They have continued to rely on the Europeans for economic aid and sometimes military assistance as well, and the Europeans continue to invest in Africa and protect their investments. France, in particular, maintained in the early 1980s a military presence of more than 15,000 troops, including its highly mobile *force d'intervention*.[12] As the gap between African economic development and that of the industrialized nations widened, especially after the oil crises in the 1970s, the Africans were forced all the more to depend on foreign aid and became all the more vulnerable to meddling by outside powers. These outside powers were not limited to the former colonial powers of Europe but came to include the superpowers, which, in their global contest for power, were eager to make themselves indispensable to new African friends and to check the spreading influence of the other. In addition to the East-West rivalry, there was competition between the Soviet Union and China for influence as well.

China's boldest undertaking in Africa was the building of the twelve-hundred-mile Tanzam "Great Freedom" railroad in the mid–1970s linking land-locked Zambia with the Tanzanian port city of Dar-es-Salaam. The $500 million project, which employed some 20,000 Chinese and 50,000 African workers, was undertaken after Britain, Canada, and the United States declined the project. The United States had earlier missed an opportunity to expand its influence in Northern Africa when, in 1956, it rejected Egypt's request for financial backing to build the Aswan Dam on the Nile River. The Soviet Union moved in within a year to build it and temporarily won Egypt as a client state.

East-West power rivalry on the African continent was relatively mute during the 1960s when the two superpowers contended mainly for influence over the newly independent nations, but without direct military involvement. The United States sought to extend its sphere by offering security arrangements and arms as well as economic aid to needy African clients, and the Soviet Union sought to pull African states into its orbit by generously supplying weapons, especially to those nations whose leaders espoused Marxism. Although the United States has provided much more developmental aid to African nations than has the Soviet Union, it did not win more friends. Nowhere is this more evident than in the United Nations, where African nations and the Soviet Union, sharing an anticolonialism standpoint, often vote the same way, while the United States is seldom able to count on the votes of these nations.

Advocacy of Marxism by an African leader did not necessarily signify successful Soviet intervention, however. To some extent Marxism-Leninism was in vogue in the early postindependence years as new African leaders were attracted to the ideology for its explanation of past colonial exploitation and neocolonialism (continuing economic domination by the capitalist nations). They also found in Marxism-Leninism a model for political organization and state planning for economic modernization. But nations, such as Guinea and Angola, which adopted Marxism and established close ties with Moscow, found developmental aid from the Soviet Union to be disappointingly meager. Some African leaders, such as Nkrumah of Ghana and Nyerere of Tanzania, conjured up their own brands of "African socialism," a blend of Marxist ideas and indigenous African notions, which were usually rather fuzzy and had little resemblance to either Marxism or the Soviet system. In actuality, it is difficult to distinguish between those African states that were nominally socialist and those that claimed to be capitalist, for in all of them state planning and control of the economy were common, and none of them has shed elitism for genuine egalitarian reforms. "The distinction between socialist and capitalist states in Africa," two noted African specialists explain, "has often proved to be more one of rhetoric than reality. . . . In the last resort, the socialist or capitalist jargon employed in any individual state is often a reflection of where external aid was coming from at a particular time."[13]

It was not until the mid–1970s, with the end of Portuguese colonial rule in Southern Africa, that a direct confrontation between the superpowers occurred in Africa. The departure of Portugal created a volatile situation across Southern Africa, not only because power was up for grabs in its former colonies but because the buffer between black African nations and the white supremacist regime of South Africa was removed. South Africa had previously gained security by supporting a white minority government in Rhodesia and by providing valuable trade and aid, as well as employment opportunities, to its black-ruled northern neighbors. But South Africa found itself threatened in the late 1970s with the accession of a Marxist regime in Mozambique in 1975, the transfer of power to a black government in Zimbabwe (formerly Rhodesia) in 1980, and the increasing resolve of Botswana, Zambia, and other black African nations to oppose its racist regime. As a consequence, South Africa resorted increasingly to military force, intervening in Angola, Mozambique, and Lesotho.

In defiance of the United Nations and the major powers of the World—East and West—South Africa has continued to dominate Namibia, occupying it militarily and thwarting its demand for independence.[14] South Africa installed a puppet black government in Namibia in 1975 and promised to grant it independence, but the left-leaning South-West Africa People's Organization (SWAPO), the largest Namibian party, was left out of the government. SWAPO, which is supported by black African nations, has continued its guerrilla resistance in its fight for Namibian independence.

The focal point of international struggle in Africa in the past decade has been Angola, where the largest build-up of foreign military forces in Africa since the colonial era occurred. The outside forces were from such nations as the United States, the Soviet Union, the People's Republic of China, Cuba, and Zaire, in addition to South Africa. When Portugal finally decided to withdraw in April 1975, three separate Marxist Angolan revolutionary groups rivaled each other for power: the Popular Movement for the Liberation of Angola (MPLA), a group founded in 1956 and longest engaged in the fight for independence, in control of the capital city; the National Front for the Liberation of Angola (FNLA), established in 1962, holding control of the mountainous region in the north; and the National Union for the Total Independence of Angola (UNITA), founded in 1966, representing the Ovimbundu, the largest tribe in Angola, and in control of the central and southern regions. The transitional government established by the Portuguese collapsed in June 1975, and foreign powers, instead of supporting the accords drawn up by Portugal for the transfer of power, intervened in support of rival revolutionary groups in Angola.

Typically, the United States and the Soviet Union have accused each other of intervention in Angola and claim that their own involvement was justified by the aggression of the other. By the time that fighting began in mid–1975, the MPLA had received Soviet financial support and was being assisted by Cuban advisers and a Zairean military unit, and the FNLA and UNITA were receiving financial support and covert military assistance from the CIA. By September the MPLA won a decisive victory against the FNLA, and it then battled a UNITA force fortified by South African troops. When South Africa entered the fray, the Chinese, who had supported opponents of the Soviet-backed MPLA, withdrew. Another result of the South African entry into the conflict (which led to stepped-up CIA action in Angola) was a huge increase in Soviet and Cuban assistance for the MPLA. In November, the scales were tipped heavily in favor of the MPLA with the arrival of a massive amount of Soviet and Cuban armaments and several thousand Cuban troops. By the end of the year, the MPLA's victory appeared complete, and it formed a new Angolan government.

Continued U.S. military aid to UNITA rebels and continued South African military involvement in the years that followed, however, has served to keep the Angolan situation alive as an international issue. Indeed, this inflamed issue was one of several that brought an end to the era of détente between the United States and the Soviet Union. In the mid–1980s the two superpowers were still feuding over Angola, while pressures continued to mount against the increasingly isolated South African regime and the remainder of sub-Saharan Africa continued to seethe with political tensions and worsening economic woes.

■ THE WORSENING PLIGHT OF SUB-SAHARAN AFRICA

The 1980s saw in general an increase in the living standard throughout much of the globe, except for the nations at war, such as Afghanistan, Nicaragua, El Salvador, and most certainly Cambodia, Iran, and Iraq, for which no figures are available. The most important exception, however, is sub-Saharan Africa (SSA), the region that covers the whole of Africa with the exception of the Arabic-speaking belt along the shores of the Mediterranean Sea in the north and South Africa and Namibia in the south. It is a heterogeneous region—some of the nations are doing relatively well (Botswana and Mauritius); others cling to the bottom rung of the world's economic ladder (Ethiopia, Chad, and Zaire.) Its population in 1990 was just under 10 percent of the world's total, nearly 500 million.

Since 1965, that is, since shortly after independence, per capita income in SSA has grown a mere 0.6 percent. Overall, its economic growth averaged 3.4 percent per year, but only a fraction above the increase in population. From independence until 1973, SSA's economies saw slight improvement and grew along the lines of other developing countries, but then began to fall behind. Since then, thirteen SSA countries, with one-third of the region's population, became poorer per capita than they had been in 1960.

The 1980s, in particular, saw the further deterioration of an already bleak picture. In November 1989, the World Bank published a detailed account of SSA's past economic performance.[15] Per capita income and food production decreased; the share of SSA's exports in world markets declined from 2.4 percent in 1970 to 1.3 percent in 1987; and the region witnessed, in the terse language of the World Bank report, "accelerated ecological degradation." In some countries school enrollment declined and urban unemployment rose. Several countries—among them Ghana, Liberia, and Zambia—slipped from the middle income to the low income group. In 1987, SSA's population of 450 million produced only as much as Belgium's 10 million. The world's per capita GNP in 1987 stood at $3,010; for SSA, the figure was $330,[16] a ratio of over 9:1.

The causes for the miserable economic performance are many. For one, the newly independent governments sought to industrialize as rapidly as possible. In the process, they neglected the agricultural sector. In the 1960s, farm production increased by nearly 3 percent, thus generally keeping up with population growth. Since 1970, however, the rate of growth of agricultural production declined by nearly 50 percent; it grew at a pace at less than half of the unchanged rate of population growth, 1.4 percent against 3.3 percent. Droughts and the increasing drying up of the Sahel, the belt directly south of the Sahara, were in part to blame for the decline in agricultural production. The result was that SSA suffered from both a decline in world agricultural prices and falling volume. To add to SSA's problems, its share in the world's oil market declined from 7 percent to 4 percent, a drop of over 40 percent of its previous share. In addition, manufacturing grew a scant 2 percent since 1965, from 9 percent to 11 percent of total SSA economic activity.[17]

Whatever economic gains SSA enjoyed during the past 30 years were eaten up by the phenomenal rise in population. "Never in human history has population grown so fast," the World Bank concluded. By the year 2010, SSA's population is expected to more than double, to over 1 billion. Often the result is hunger. Nearly one-quarter of the population faces "chronic food insecurity." Family planning is necessary not only to reduce the threat of hunger, but also for improved health care. SSA has the highest rates of maternal and infant mortality. In the poorest countries (Burkina Faso, Ethiopia, and Mali) one-quarter of the children die before they reach the age of five.

Another problem is the high level of public expenditures for government, schools, and the military. A direct link exists between low military spending and good economic performance, as in Botswana and Mauritius. The World Bank addressed for the first time the question of official corruption, although only briefly and gingerly. "Bad habits," it noted, "are hard to undo," such as the siphoning of millions of foreign aid dollars into private accounts outside of SSA. An unfettered and vigilant press, which could play the role of a watchdog, is all too rare, however. The two nations with the best economic performances—Botswana and Mauritius—both have parliamentary democracies and a free press.

The outlook is bleak; should current trends continue, SSA will "increasingly be unable to feed its children or find jobs for its school leavers." The region is overburdened by an external debt that totaled nearly $106 billion in 1987, up from $5.3 billion in 1970 and $41.2 billion in 1980. It had to reschedule its foreign debt payments, and several lenders have written off debts. But the World Bank did see a faint glimmer of hope. With sustained and increased external support and, more importantly, by internal reform, the trends can be reversed. But the road promises to be long and hard.

■ APARTHEID: THE SOUTH AFRICAN SOLUTION

South Africa stands apart from the rest of Africa, not only as the most economically developed nation on the continent, but as the only nation ruled by a white minority. In defiance of world opinion, of the expressed will of the remainder of Africa, and of the demands of the black majority within the country, the rulers of South Africa have maintained political power by means of a racist policy known as *apartheid*. Apartheid defines the basic laws of the Republic of South Africa. Literally, it means apartness; in reality it is a legal system that demands the most rigid form of racial segregation anywhere. The laws forbid the most elementary contact between the four racial groupings in South Africa: the blacks (also known as Bantus); the whites (mostly of English and Dutch descent); the coloureds (of mixed black-white parentage); and the Asians (largely Indians).

The whites of Dutch descent are today the primary factor in South African political and economic affairs. Since 1948, they have replaced another group of European settlers, the English, as the dominant political force in shaping the destiny of a country they consider to be theirs. The Dutch, having settled on the South African coast as early as 1652, consider it their native land. In fact, they call themselves *Afrikaner,* Dutch for Africans. (They also call themselves *boers,* or farmers, and are often referred to by that name.) They claim that they had arrived in South Africa no later than the Bantu-speaking blacks whom they conquered in the 1830s. They argue that their claim to the land rests on discovery, conquest, economic development, and ultimately on the will of God.

Apartheid is steeped in the teachings of the Dutch Reformed Church, which sees the Afrikaner as God's chosen people, destined to dominate the land as well as other peoples who inhabit it. Apartheid, the Afrikaner have argued, is the word of God and is specifically sanctioned in the Bible. The most fervent defenders of apartheid are frequently ministers of the Dutch Reformed Church.

Apartheid is also based on the primitive principle of racial superiority. The Bantus, the Afrikaner argue, have contributed nothing to civilization; their existence has been one of savagery. The twin pillars of apartheid—religious determinism and racial superiority—are the consequence of the Afrikaner's long struggle against heresy, Western liberalism, and the black, native population of South Africa.

By the end of the eighteenth century, the Dutch had set deep roots in the South African soil. In 1795, however, the British conquered the South African cape. The result was a struggle for political and religious supremacy between the established Dutch and the newly arrived, victorious English who had settled largely around the Cape of Good Hope. It was a contest the Afrikaner could not win and brought about their decision to move into the hinterlands to escape the discriminatory English laws. Moreover, the Afrikaner opposed the English ban of slavery, which in 1833 became the law of the empire. In 1835, the boers set out on the Great Trek northward into the high plains of Natal and Transvaal. It was a journey filled with bitterness and determination, coupled with a religious fervor seldom matched. The trek became a triumphant religious procession by which God's elect, a people with a most narrow view of salvation, set out to build a new Jerusalem. And God's favor seemed clearly to shine on the "righteous" when, on December 16, 1838—in a scene straight out of the Old Testament—470 boers decisively defeated a force of 12,500 Zulu warriors, killing 3,000 of them, on the banks of what became known as the Blood River.[15] December 16 is celebrated today as a national holiday, the Day of Covenant between God and the Afrikaner.

When later in the century the British once again encroached on boer territory, the boers stood and fought two wars; however, it was the British who emerged victorious by 1902. This was a bloody and brutal struggle in which the Afrikaner were defeated in what they considered to be their own country. Ever since that day, they prepared for the day of liberation to redress their defeat and to reestablish the social and religious principles of the Great Trek. That day came in 1948, when their party, the Nationalist party, under the leadership of D. F. Malan, a former minister of the Dutch Reformed Church, won a narrow electoral political victory.

It was at this juncture that British efforts to maintain racial harmony in South Africa were abandoned and the South African segregation laws came into being. Between 1937 and 1948, the British authorities had attempted to create a form of representative government for South Africa only to find that little harmony existed among black, white, coloured, and Asian politicians. World War II generated conflicting ideological tendencies among whites— one trend leaning toward interracial cooperation, the other toward extreme racism. Still, the decade before the Afrikaner electoral victory of 1948 saw a growing interdependence among the races, particularly in the economy, but also in churches, welfare organizations, schools, and universities.[16]

In 1948, however, the Afrikaner, driven by an intense sense of religious and cultural self-preservation, rejected all previous proposals for social and racial integration. Instead, at a time when Hitler's brutality and defeat in World War II had just managed to discredit thoroughly once-respected racial theories, they insisted that the races must be kept apart by law and that no one had the right to cross the color line. The upshot of this militant position in the wake of World War II was the political isolation of South Africa. Yet, such isolation has only bred defiance and has strengthened and reinforced the outlook of a people long accustomed to adversity and determined to go it alone. A stiff-necked people, the boers have stood up to the British, the blacks, and now the world.

The first of the segregation laws, enacted in 1949, forbade miscegenation—the marriage or cohabitation of persons of a different color. Another law, passed in 1953, barred interracial sex,[17] and other segregation laws followed in rapid succession. Schools, jobs, pay scales were all determined by the segregation laws. The Population Registration Act listed individuals on the basis of race; another law demanded residential segregation and limited the rights of blacks to remain in designated cities. Political organizations and strikes by non-whites were outlawed. All public facilities—from hospitals to park benches to beaches—became segregated. Whites and non-whites were not permitted to stay under the same roof for the night. Every aspect of sexual, social, religious, and economic intercourse between the races was regulated, both among the living and the dead, for even the cemeteries were segregated. The number of apartheid laws, now runs well over three hundred.

The question of race and segregation became obsessions in South Africa. But to separate the races, a classification board must first assign a category for each and every individual. In many cases that is not an easy task. Deliberations can take months and years, for the science of distinguishing facial features, skin color, and hair texture is not an exact one. Ultimately, however, the board renders its verdict. Often the result is as follows:

> In one typical twelve-month period, 150 coloreds were reclassified as white; ten whites became colored, six Indians became Malay; two Malay became Indians; two coloreds became Chinese; ten Indians became coloreds; one Indian became white; one white became Malay; four blacks became Indians; three whites became Chinese.[18]

In 1959, the Nationalist party set aside eight regions (Bantustans, or homelands), comprising 13 percent of the nation's land, for the black population. One writer has called them an "archipelago of misery." The Bantustans are the centerpiece of apartheid, for they deny native blacks legal access to the rest of South Africa. They were designed to establish the legal principle that blacks merely enjoyed temporary residence in South Africa proper. This is part of what the government euphemistically calls "separate development," or "plural democracy," words that sound more appealing than apartheid, which has acquired a stigma throughout the world. The Bantustans are the sole legal residences for the nation's black population. The significance of their creation lies in the argument that the black population, the nation's essential work force, consists of strangers who have no right to be in, let us say, the city of Johannesburg. It also means that although black fathers may find work in an area set aside for whites, their families must remain behind. Thus not only blacks and whites are divided but black families as well, frequently for eleven months at a stretch. They are but visitors at the pleasure of the host, the whites of that city. The blacks of South Africa have thus become aliens in their native land.

The laws of apartheid were designed to preserve the dominant position of the whites and to preserve racial purity. They have turned the once oppressed Afrikaner into oppressors of the majority of the population. In this nation of 28 million, the blacks outnumber the whites by a ratio of three to one, 18 million to 6 million. The coloureds number about 3 million; the Asians nearly 1 million. It is little wonder that a siege mentality permeates white society. And, in fact, white settlements are frequently referred to as *laagers,* literally camps, a term taken from the Great Trek of the 1830s.

SOUTH AFRICA'S "HOMELANDS"

The segregation laws are also the linchpin of economic exploitation. The laws exclude nonwhites from the better paying jobs and positions of authority. In the construction industry, for instance, whites earn twice the salary of Asians, three times that of coloureds, and five times that of blacks. A white miner earns $16,000 a year; a black miner, $2,500. And this pattern of exploitation and discrimination exists throughout the entire economy. The combination of rich natural resources, industrial planning, and cheap labor provided by the black work force has turned the nation into the African continent's only modern, industrialized state, but only for the white population. The defenders of apartheid have pointed out that the wealth of the nation has also trickled down to the black population, whose standard of living is the highest of any blacks in Africa. The blacks regard this argument as irrelevant.

Apartheid is a philosophy of psychological oppression, economic exploitation, and political domination. It is a way of life that only force can maintain. And the white minority has shown time and again a willingness to go to any length to maintain the status quo. Political observers, both in South Africa and abroad, have frequently raised the question of how long such conditions can prevail. Black activists have repeatedly called for the repeal of all apartheid laws, insisting that nothing short of equal pay for equal work, political representation, and equal protection under the law will do. For years, the clouds have been gathering on the horizon, but the storm has not yet broken.

Black-white violence thus far has been sporadic. There have been no major uprisings, certainly nothing that has been organized. Students of revolution know that sporadic and spontaneous action can only succeed against a government that no longer has the will to govern. In 1960, black political agitation led to demonstrations, which the police quickly suppressed in the Sharpeville massacre by killing 69 persons. And more recently, highly publicized disturbances have taken place in Soweto (short for South-West Township), a black ghetto of 1 million people, thirty minutes from the elegant financial capital of South Africa, Johannesburg. In 1985, during demonstrations commemorating the twenty-fifth anniversary of the Sharpeville massacre, the police killed 19 at one demonstration alone and scores of people died in other clashes. The funeral processions for those killed served as still more demonstrations, which brought still more violence. The summer of 1985 saw the deaths of over 700 blacks as well as that of several whites. At summer's end white residential areas became for the first time the scenes of racial confrontations.

Predictably, the government has repeatedly charged that any resistance to authority is the handiwork of Communists. It is a charge that serves to legitimize the suppression of all dissent. A future black-white civil war in South Africa will most certainly become another attempt by a discredited government to suppress "Communism." In fact, the most influential political force challenging apartheid is the African National Congress (ANC), which, during the past two decades has embraced both violence and Marxism as vehicles for change. Among the most visible symbols in opposition to apartheid is Nelson Mandela, sentenced in 1964 to a life term for his association with the ANC. To complicate matters for the government, Mandela refused a deal in early 1985 whereby he would be granted freedom on condition that he pledge to refrain from violent activity and live in the tribal homeland for Xhosa-speaking people, the Transkei.

On the other side of the revolutionary spectrum stands Episcopalian Bishop Desmond Tutu, who in 1985 received the Nobel Prize for Peace in recognition for his attempts to work out a peaceful solution to his country's political dilemma. Yet, President Botha's government has shown no inclination to reach an accord with Desmond Tutu, let alone with Nelson Mandela.

South Africa has remained largely impervious to the cries of the leaders of the newly independent nations on the African continent who have appealed to the world's powers and the United Nations for a united effort against the white supremacist regime in Pretoria. They have called for economic sanctions and the diplomatic isolation of South Africa. But their efforts have had only limited success. The leading Western nations have been slow in giving their support for a total boycott, presumably because their professed outrage against apartheid is outweighed by vested economic interests in doing business with South Africa. It appears that pressure from inside, rather than outside, is what the South African whites have to fear.

The pressure has been building since the Soweto riots of 1976. The accompanying violence has thrust South Africa into the international spotlight. It has led to an intense discussion within the nation, one that seeks to come to grips with the future of apartheid. The debate has been taken up by the highest officials in the government. Such action points to a new mood among the white population, particularly those of Dutch descent. The mood is radically different from that of 1960, at the time of the Sharpeville massacre, when the intransigent government of Henrik Verwoerd reaffirmed the principles of apartheid with guns blazing.

In 1984, the government granted limited representation in Parliament to coloureds and Asians without, however, granting them political power, of which the whites retained a monopoly. Most critics have stated that this concession is therefore meaningless and, moreover, it is only designed to drive a wedge between groups of people hitherto subjected together to discrimination and humiliation. Its purpose, they argue, is to provide for the white society a buffer consisting of Asians and coloureds against the black majority. As things stand in the mid–1980s, that assessment is largely correct. But parliamentary representation, even without direct political participation, does give Asians and coloureds a forum to voice their grievances. Access to

Protesting South African workers, Johannesburg, South Africa, Aug. 13, 1986.
(*AP/Wide World Photos*)

the throne—the right to petition, the right to be heard—has in the past been the first step toward political participation for colonized peoples.

In early 1985, President P. W. Botha took the heretical position of acknowledging the reality of the permanence of blacks in "white" South Africa, a permanence that ultimately would have to be granted legality. Demographics alone, in a nation where the black population is growing more rapidly than its ruling white population, would seem to demand such a concession. With this position, Botha brought into question the very essence of apartheid. Its logical extention would grant a segment of the black labor force a legal existence beyond the borders of the Bantustans.

Botha's statements reflected a split in his government between the *verligte,* or "enlightened," ministers and the conservatives, who were fearful of any and all change. In short, the Afrikaner community became confused. What was at stake was the very survival of Afrikaner society as it had been known up til then. Botha's slogan of early 1985 was "adapt or die." His opponents vowed to take not a single step backward. In the wake of widespread riots in the summer of 1985, Botha delivered a major address. Many throughout South Africa and elsewhere expected him to propose cautious steps for reform. But they were to be disappointed for Botha succumbed to pressures from his Right. The initial worldwide response to the wave of unrest in South

Africa, in which 700 blacks died by summer's end, provoked the traditional response by the boers. They retreated to their *laager* in defiance of the black majority and world opinion.

The anti-apartheid movement would not, however, be silenced, and in 1986 blacks continued to defy government restrictions against protest marches. Time and again they were met by police equipped with a vast arsenal of riot control weapons. Determined to quell the racial disturbances and to put an end to worldwide press and television coverage of the carnage occurring in its streets, the Botha government imposed a nationwide state of emergency on June 12, 1986. Under this decree a black protestor could be imprisoned without trial for up to ten years for statements interpreted to "weaken or undermine" confidence in the government.

Under persistent pressure at home and from abroad, the Botha government continued efforts to defuse the racial unrest in the country. International pressure on Pretoria increased, and it began to have a telling effect on Botha's policies despite his persistent denials. The United States and most European governments imposed trade sanctions, and many foreign corporations began withdrawing capital from South Africa. Between 1986 and 1988, the country suffered a net capital outflow of nearly $4 billion; consequently, unemployment, inflation, and interest rates all increased and the economic growth rate declined from 5 to 2 percent. The price of apartheid had become too high.[22] In reaction, a growing number of whites, especially in the business community, began urging a change in the apartheid program. Many whites also felt a sense of isolation in the world's community. The changing mood among whites was reflected in the increased popularity of the liberal Democratic party, which openly advocated an end to the old policies of racial oppression.

Thus it was as much to placate whites as blacks that President Botha began gradually to moderate the apartheid system in 1988 and 1989. Some of the more superfluous apartheid restrictions were lifted. Certain public facilities, such as drinking fountains, movie theaters, and public parks and swimming beaches, were desegregated, and mixed residency was permitted in certain previously segregated urban residential sections.

Botha was confronted also by demands for moderation within the ruling Nationalist party. He was, in fact, outmaneuvered in the party by the more flexible leader of the moderate faction, Frederik W. de Klerk, who was sworn in as South Africa's president in September 1989. In his inauguration speech, de Klerk pledged to work for "a totally changed South Africa . . . free of domination or oppression in whatever form."[23] He went on to declare his intentions of bridging the deep gulf of distrust and fear among the races to find a "completely new approach" to negotiations with black leaders and of developing a new constitution to include all South Africans. Anti-apartheid leaders and the Democratic party welcomed the new vision expressed by the new president, but waited to see whether he would deliver on his promises.

A major sign of the changing attitudes in the country under the leadership of de Klerk was the remarkably conciliatory policy toward the outlawed African National Congress (ANC), the largest and most militant anti-apartheid organization in the country. Several leaders of the ANC, which had been banned for over three decades, were released from prison, and negotiations for the release of Nelson Mandela, the 71-year-old titular leader of the organization, were begun. Anti-apartheid protestors were permitted to hold a mammoth rally in Soweto at which the released ANC leaders were allowed to address the throng of some 60,000 people. The lack of police interference and the coverage of the event by government-controlled television were noteworthy changes. Still more surprising were the lifting of the ban of the ANC and the release of its heralded leader, Nelson Mandela, in February 1990. At the same time, de Klerk promised to free all political prisoners and ended the state of emergency that Botha had declared in June 1986. De Klerk also took steps to reduce the power of the security forces by reining in the once all-powerful State Security Council and making it subordinate to his cabinet. It was a tacit admission on the part of de Klerk that more than forty years of apartheid had not worked.

De Klerk gave hope to anti-apartheid leaders, but they still awaited more substantial reforms necessary to bringing an end to apartheid. Meanwhile, international investors lost no time in making money available to the South African economy. The Johannesburg Stock Exchange industrial index rose 7.2 percent in two days.[24] But at the same time, the right wing of de Klerk's party promised demonstrations and strikes to bring him down. Black leaders insisted he had not gone far enough. In the days leading up to de Klerk's historic speech, demonstrators were still dying in the streets. And after the speech, they were still dying.

As the newly freed Nelson Mandela began to take the first tentative steps seeking to negotiate an end to apartheid with the de Klerk government, other old issues came to the fore. One of them was the continued political rivalry between the tribal Zulu *Inkbata* movement, led by their Chief Mangosuthu Buthelezi, and Mandela's ANC. In contrast to Buthelezi, Mandela, although a descendant of Xhosa kings, had moved long ago beyond tribal politics. The ANC has always been an umbrella political organization of all opponents of racial injustice:

whites, coloreds, Asians, and blacks—and it included both Zulus and Xhosa. The *Inkhata*–ANC conflict was fueled in part by the fact that Buthelezi was also the chief minister of the Kwazulu Bantustan while the ANC was committed to the abolition of all Bantustans.

To complicate matters, physical conflict among blacks escalated, and between 1987 and early 1990, the bloodletting had cost 2,500 lives. Much of the violence was between young radical blacks, the "Young Lions," who sought to establish bases of economic and political power in the townships. The "Young Lions" had gained notoriety by "necklacing" their victims (by pinning their arms with burning tires). Mandela's highly publicized release from prison had no effect on them. Many of them were still unemployed and they continued to face the consequences of decades of legal, social, and economic discrimination. They were beyond the control of and impervious to the pleas for moderation by all the established leaders, as well as the radical Zeph Mothopeng, the head of the Pan-Africanist Congress. Even Mandela, upon release from prison, appealed to them unsuccessfully to throw their guns and knives into the sea.

To complicate matters still further, white society, too, became polarized between the diehards who circled the wagons in defiance of the winds of change blowing out of Pretoria and those who wanted to rid the nation of apartheid. De Klerk's problems thus went beyond the abolition of apartheid laws. His first order of business after Mandela's release was to bring South Africa's civil violence to an end.

■ RECOMMENDED READINGS

☐ Third World—General

Barnet, Richard J. *The Lean Years: Politics in the Age of Scarcity.* New York: Simon and Schuster, 1980.
   A study of the political factors involved in sharing limited global resources.
Brown, Lester R., et al. *State of the World, 1986.* New York: W. W. Norton, 1986.
   An up-to-date reference on food and environmental issues around the globe.
George, Susan. *How the Other Half Dies: The Real Reason for World Hunger.* Montclair, N.J.: Allanheld, Osmun, 1977.
   A thoughtful analysis of the problem.
Harrison, Paul. *Inside the Third World.* 2d ed. New York: Penguin, 1984.
   An excellent comprehensive description and analysis of the dilemmas of the Third World.

☐ Africa

Crowder, Michael. *The Story of Nigeria.* New York: Frederick A. Praeger, 1978.
   Examines the troubled history of this major African nation.

Gavshon, Arthur. *Crisis in Africa: Battleground of East and West.* New York: Penguin, 1981.
A study of superpower intervention and rivalry in Africa.

Lamb, David. *The Africans.* New York: Random House, 1982.
An eye-opening account of today's Africa and its various problems by a journalist who spent four years in Africa visiting and reporting from forty-eight of its countries.

Leys, Colin. *Underdevelopment in Kenya: The Political Economy of Neo-Colonialism.* Berkeley, Calif.: University of California Press, 1975.
An interpretive study of Kenya's economic dilemma.

Mazrui, Ali A. *Africa's International Relations: The Diplomacy of Dependency and Change.* London: Heineman, 1977.
A study by a noted African specialist who presents his case from the Africans' viewpoint.

Neuberger, Ralph Benyamin. *National Self-Determination in Postcolonial Africa.* Boulder: Lynne Rienner Publishers, 1986.
A theoretical and comparative analysis of the impact of colonial experience on postcolonial African nationalism and secession issues.

Oliver, Roland, and Anthony Atmore. *Africa Since 1800.* 3d ed. New York: Cambridge University Press, 1981.
A succinct and judicious treatment of post-independence African history.

☐ South Africa

Breytenbach, Breyten. *The True Confessions of an Albino Terrorist.* New York: Farrar, Straus, Giroux, 1984.
An autobiographical account by a poet from a well-known Afrikaner family who became a revolutionary activist.

Lelyveld, Joseph. *Move Your Shadow: South Africa, Black and White.* New York: Times Books, 1985.
A *New York Times* reporter explains the racial realities of South Africa.

Thompson, Leonard. *The Political Mythology of Apartheid.* New Haven: Yale University Press, 1985.
An account of the origins of and a justification for that racial policy.

Woods, Donald. *Biko.* New York: Paddington Press, 1978.
A white South African's sympathetic account of the racial issue in his country, focusing on the role of Steve Biko, founder of the "black consciousness" movement, who died in police custody in 1977.

■ NOTES

1. GNP, or Gross National Product, is the wealth—the total goods and services—a nation produces per year. The per capita GNP is calculated by dividing the figure for wealth generated (calculated in U.S. dollars) by the nation's population.

2. World Bank, *World Development Report, 1986* (Washington, D.C.: World Bank, 1986), p. 180. Actually, the African nation with the lowest per capita GNP is Chad. No GNP figures were available for war-torn Chad in this report, but an earlier World Bank report indicates that in 1982 it had a mere $90 per capita GNP.

3. See Paul Harrison, *Inside the Third World* (New York: Penguin, 2d ed., 1984), pp. 414–415. Harrison provides figures to illustrate that the gap in income between the richest and the poorest people in Third World countries is, on average, greater than the income gap between rich and poor in the world's developed countries.

4. Harrison, p. 145, notes that 185 million people lived in Third World cities in 1940, but by 1975 the number had risen to 770 million, and that, in the early 1970s, 12 million people a year—33,000 a day—were arriving in these cities.

5. Traditionally, African men were primarily hunters and herdsmen, and women were left to work in the fields. The tradition has changed only to the extent that, with the depletion of wild game, few men still hunt. But still too proud to toil in the fields, men either supervise women who do that work, seek other employment, or loaf in the towns. Exact figures are difficult to obtain, but a United Nations report, *State of the World's Women,* 1985, estimated that between 60 and 80 percent of farm work in Africa was still done by women. Barber Conable, the president of the World Bank, at a joint World Bank–International Monetary Fund meeting, stated that women do two-thirds of the world's work, earn ten percent of the world's income, and own less than one percent of the world's property. "They are the poorest of the world's poor." (Clyde Farnsworth, "World Bank Chief Outlines Strategy," *New York Times,* October 1, 1986, p. D 23)

6. Harrison, p. 455.

7. Ethiopia's aged emperor, Haile Selassie, did little to avert the earlier famine, but instead went to great lengths to suppress news of it. After he was overthrown in 1974, a new Marxist regime attempted to carry out an extensive land reform program, only to reap another agricultural disaster, which was not so much the consequence of the reforms as of past years of deforestation, overcultivation, and the hostile forces of nature. In 1984, Ethiopia's plight was given broad television coverage around the world, resulting in a great outpouring of food relief from various nations, with the United States alone providing several hundred thousand metric tons of emergency food.

8. Since 1980 South Africa has had a per capita income of more than $2,650, far higher than that of any other African country. It should be pointed out, however, that the blacks, who outnumber the whites by three to one, earn only about one-sixth of what white workers are paid. In contrast to the standard of living of the South African whites, whose standard of living is among the highest in the world, that of the blacks is substantially lower.

9. *The World Bank Atlas,* 1985.

10. In Rwanda, in the early 1960s the majority Hutu tribe massacred some 100,000 people of the Watusi tribe; a decade later, in neighboring Burundi, the ruling Watusi gained revenge, when, in the span of three months in 1972, they killed over 200,000 of the Hutu tribe. Watusi rulers hauled captured Hutus by the truckload to open pits where they were buried alive by bulldozers. See David Lamb, *The Africans* (New York: Random House, 1982), pp. 318–319.

11. The most notable exceptions include such rulers as Leopold Senghor of Senegal, Felix Houphouët-Boigny of the Ivory Coast, Jomo Kenyatta of Kenya, Julius Nyere of Tanzania, Kenneth Kaunda of Zambia, Sekou Toure of Guinea, and Seretse Khama of Botswana, all of whom remained in power for fifteen years or more.

12. Arthur Gavshon, "French Troops in Africa," *Crisis in Africa: Battleground of East and West* (New York: Penguin, 1981), p. 175.

13. Roland Oliver and Anthony Atmore, *Africa Since 1800* (New York: Cambridge University Press, 1981), p. 330.

14. Namibia had been a German colony known as South-West Africa until World War I when it was conquered by South African forces. After that war it was placed under a League of Nations mandate administered by South Africa. The mandate was assumed by the United Nations after World War II, but by that time the South African presence in Namibia was deeply entrenched politically and militarily.

15. *Sub-Saharan Africa: From Crisis to Sustainable Growth: A Long-Term Perspective Study* (Washington, D.C.: The World Bank, 1989). All data from this source.

16. The figures are for all "reporting countries," which excludes the Soviet Union and most of its bloc—an inclusion of which, however, would not appreciably change the

figures. See World Bank, *World Development, Report 1989* (Washington, D.C.: World Bank, 1989), p. 165.

17. Mining, oil, and construction make up 17 percent; farming, 33 percent; and services (including the public sector), another 40 percent.

18. C. F. J. Muller, ed., *Five Hundred Years: A History of South Africa* (Pretoria, South Africa: Academia, 1969), pp. 166–167.

19. Leo, Kuper, "African Nationalism in South Africa, 1910–1964," in Monica Wilson and Leonard Thompson, eds., *The Oxford History of South Africa, II, South Africa, 1870–1966* (New York: Oxford University Press, 1971), pp. 451–459.

20. The South African government, in order to appease its critics at home and abroad, repealed this law in the wake of violent and bloody demonstrations in 1985. The supporters of the South African authorities pointed to the repeal as a sign of meaningful change toward a more egalitarian society; its critics declared the concession as meaningless because it did not address the core of the matter, the legally inferior status of people of color. Moreover, it was a law that was difficult to enforce, and it was not worth the while of the police to do so.

21. Lamb, *The Africans,* pp. 320–321. The official absurdity knows no end. Chinese are classified as a white subgroup and Japanese, mostly visiting business representatives, are bestowed the questionable title of "honorary whites."

22. World Bank, *World Development Report, 1989*, pp. 165, 167, and 179, has the following figures: percentage of average annual growth rate, 1965–1987, stood at mere 0.6 percent; average rate of inflation, 1980–1987, at 13.8 percent. During the years 1980–1987, there has been a decline in average annual growth rate in industry and manufacturing of -0.1 and -0.5, respectively. Gross domestic investment, 1980–1987, was down by 7.3 percent.

23. Peter Honey, "De Klerk Sworn in, Promises `Totally Changed' S. Africa," *Baltimore Sun*, September 21, 1989.

24. Floyd Norris, "Hopes Run High For South Africa," *New York Times*, February 6, 1990, p. D10.

☐ 12

Revolution and Counterrevolution in Latin America

Latin America is of the Third World and shares many of its features: economic underdevelopment, massive poverty, high population growth rates, widespread illiteracy, political instability, recurrent military coups, autocratic regimes, intervention by outside powers that seek to further their own causes, and fervent nationalistic pride.[1] In contrast to other Third World regions, however, there is a greater range of economic development and modernization within the Latin American region. For example, several large nations such as Mexico, Brazil, and Argentina have in the past sustained impressive industrial growth and have attained GNP and standard of living levels that qualify them as "middle-income nations." The causes for Latin American economic and political problems are similar to those of other Third World nations. But unlike most other parts of the Third World, the nations of Latin America are not newly independent states struggling to meet the challenges of nationhood after World War II. On the contrary, most of these countries, having won their independence from Spain early in the nineteenth century, have experienced almost a century and a half of nationhood by the postwar period.

■ THE COLONIAL HERITAGE

But if Latin America's colonial experience lies in the distant past, it still conditions the present, much as other Third World nations are conditioned by their colonial past. The legacy of Spanish rule has persisted over the centuries and is still embodied in the culture and social fabric of Latin American countries.

They inherited from their distant Spanish past complex multiracial societies with pronounced social cleavages between a traditional aristocracy and the underprivileged lower classes. The prosperous and privileged elite, mainly the white descendants of the European conquerors, preserved for themselves vast wealth and power and have thoroughly dominated the remainder of the population, which consists mainly of mestizos (racially mixed peoples), native Indians, descendants of black slaves imported from Africa, and newer immigrants from Europe. The traditional social structure continues, even in the post–World War II period, to influence political and economic patterns.

The great gulf between the privileged class, whose tight aristocracy may be thought of as an oligarchy, and the dispossessed lower classes is best seen in the landholding patterns in Latin America. Nowhere in the world is the disparity in land ownership as great. Traditionally, in Latin America over two-thirds of the agricultural land is owned by only 1 percent of the population. The *latifundia,* or huge estates owned by the elite, are so large—often over a thousand acres—that they cannot be fully cultivated, and as a result much of that land lies fallow. One 1960 study reveals that in Colombia, for example, 70 percent of the agricultural land is *latifundia,* and only 6 percent of it is actually cultivated. In contrast, the *minifundia,* the small farms of most farmers, are too small to provide subsistence. In fact, the majority of the rural population own no land at all; they are peons whose labor is exploited by the owners of the *latifundia.* Even after years of land reform efforts, the imbalance remains. Statistics for the late 1960s show that, on the one end, about 70 percent of the land is owned by the mere 1.5 percent of the landowners whose farms are over 2,000 acres in size, and on the other end, only 3.7 percent of the agricultural land is in the hands of that 73 percent of farmers whose farms are smaller than 8 acres.[2] Nor is this traditional inequity in landholding a thing of the past. Among all Latin American countries only Mexico and Nicaragua have carried out a genuine land reform. Other countries in the region have enacted modest land reform programs, but these have hardly been implemented, and consequently very little agricultural land has been redistributed.

Many of Latin America's persistent economic problems stem from this inequity of land ownership and the inefficiencies inherent in it. It is the direct cause for the dreadful poverty throughout rural Latin America. And the wastefulness of the *latifundia* is a major cause of the failure of Latin American agriculture to meet the food needs of its people. Other reasons include the primitive methods of farming and use of the best land to raise crops for export. On average, over 20 percent of Latin America's imports are foodstuffs, and this has had a baleful effect on the economies of the region. Moreover, the depressed state of agriculture and the impoverishment of the rural population militate against industrial development not only because of the lack of agricultural surplus for investment but also because the majority of the people are too impoverished to be consumers of industrial products.

■ "YANQUI IMPERIALISM"

The colonial heritage is but one of two major outside influences on the economic and political life of contemporary Latin America; the other is the "Colossus to the North," the United States. Ever since Spain quit the continent in the early 1800s, the United States has cast its long shadow over its neighbors to the south and has especially been a dominant force in Latin American affairs in the twentieth century. In many ways, the role played by the United States in Latin America is analogous to that played by the European colonial powers in other parts of the Third World. Where the nationalism of Asian and African countries was directed against their former European colonial masters, nationalism in Latin America has characteristically been focused on "Yanqui imperialism," an emotive term referring to the pattern of U.S. (Yankee) domination and interference in Latin America.

With the Monroe Doctrine of 1823, the United States claimed for itself a special role in the Western Hemisphere as the protector of the weaker countries to the south. Early in the twentieth century, Washington extended its claim with the Roosevelt Corollary by which it asserted the right to intervene in Latin American countries in order to maintain political order. By the 1920s, the Corollary was invoked several times and a pattern of military intervention to prop up tottering regimes and protect U.S investments was firmly set. Inevitably, Latin American leaders bristled with fear and resentment at "Yanqui" interventionism. The strains in U.S.–Latin American relations were, however, ameliorated somewhat by President Franklin Roosevelt's "good neighbor" policy and by the exigencies of World War II during which they cooperated as allies.

After the war, Washington sought to strengthen its bonds with Latin American countries by plying them with military and economic aid, taking the lead in forming an organization for regional collective security, and making bilateral defense agreements. Latin leaders welcomed U.S. aid, but were disappointed at being left out of the generous Marshall Plan that pumped far greater amounts of aid into the United States's European allies. Meanwhile, Washington's increasing preoccupation with the Cold War gave a distinct anti-Communist ideological cast to its hemispheric relations, and consequently it pressured Latin American governments to cut ties with the Soviet Union and outlaw local Communist parties, and it altered its aid program to give greater priority to bolstering the armies in Latin American countries than to economic development. While Latin American military leaders stood to gain by this shift, politicians, who were generally more interested in economic assistance, especially modern technology, had misgivings about it. The United States, however, became all the more vigilant in its Latin American policy as a result of Cuba's turn to Communism in 1959 under Fidel Castro.

Thus, Latin American leaders were placed in a bind; while they sought to reduce their dependence on their powerful neighbor to the north, they still needed its economic assistance. The United States readily exploited that need, for it had long understood the utility of economic aid as an effective tool for achieving political ends. The dollar dangled before needy governments was more effective and less likely to prompt outcries than was military intervention. Political use of economic aid caused friction only when the political aims of the United States were contrary to those of Latin governments. Generally, democratic leaders in Latin America were willing to accept U.S. aid programs directed at fostering democracy as well as economic growth, and generally Washington professed such aims. And when an economic aid package was as generous as President Kennedy's 1961 Alliance for Progress program, they were eager to accept it, even with its political and military components.

The Alliance for Progress offered $20 billion to Latin American governments over ten years conditional on their instituting fundamental social and economic reforms, including land reform, and on their developing counterinsurgency programs designed to thwart Cuban-type revolutionary movements. Despite the initial enthusiasm for this program, it soon proved a failure. The Alliance produced an increased financial dependency and indebtedness of Latin American countries, confusion over priorities (social reform, relief to the poverty stricken, industrial projects, or others), and political/administrative confusion (would aid be administered before, during, or after a reform program was undertaken?).

Direct governmental aid was but one level of increased U.S. influence in the Southern Hemisphere. In addition, corporate U.S. business interests continued to invest heavily, buying Latin American lands, mines, oil fields, establishing industries (exploiting cheap labor), and selling arms. As a consequence, one finds that in Brazil, for example, 31 of the 55 largest business firms in the 1960s were owned by foreigners, mainly from the United States. In the 1970s, 8 of the 10 largest firms in Argentina and 50 percent of its banks were foreign-owned.[3] U.S. business interests assumed that, as in the past, the U.S. flag follows the dollar, and they lobbied for and expected United States diplomacy to protect their investments. Business interests usually coincided with Washington's ideological and strategic interests insofar as both gave priority to the maintenance of political stability and the suppression of revolutionary movements that threatened their investments. And if support for military dictators was deemed necessary to achieve these ends, military dictators would be supported. And if political intervention—overt or covert—was deemed necessary, this too would be done.

■ ECONOMIC AND POLITICAL PATTERNS

Industrialization became an obsession for Latin American countries after World War II, and the postwar industrial progress of several of the larger

SOUTH AMERICA

countries was indeed impressive. The governments of these countries began playing an important role in this endeavor, investing in heavy industry, erecting high import tariffs, and in other ways fostering industrialization. Argentina particularly exhibited a strong economic nationalism aimed at ending foreign dependency. Industrial progress was, however, limited to only a few countries (Argentina, Brazil, and Mexico alone accounted for 80 percent of Latin America's industrial output in the late 1960s) and to only a few cities in those countries, with most industry concentrated in Buenos Aires, São Paulo, and Mexico City. Aside from the problems incurred by this imbalance, the postwar industrial surge was stymied by a number of serious problems. In general, the new industries were mainly import substitution industries, designed to produce consumer goods that once had to be imported, and as such they depended on a growing domestic market, which failed to develop, mainly because the majority of the population lacked purchasing power. Moreover, even the larger industrializing countries lacked sufficient capital and soon found themselves again relying heavily on foreign investments. By the early 1960s, they became even more dependent on outside sources, mainly the United States, for capital, technology, and markets.

Although industrial growth did produce higher GNP figures and contributed to a modest increase in the standard of living, it also produced frustration as it failed to meet expectations. It engendered the growth of the middle class and an urban working class, both of which sought a larger share of the nations' wealth and a larger role in the political process. The middle class, finding political expression through political parties, provided support for democratic government. However, the growth of the middle class was stunted by the lagging industrial growth. It remained too weak to challenge the traditional landowning elite. Its attempts to institute meaningful social and political change, for example, land reform, through democratic reform were frustrated by the entrenched oligarchy, and it was powerless to protect democracy from the military. Indeed, the middle class often could do little better than to acquiesce in the status quo and to ape the social status of the traditional elite. The new urban working class grew in size but remained largely impoverished. It sought to advance its cause for higher wages both through trade unions and political parties. Growing radicalism by organized labor, however, tended to arouse fears of the middle class and cause it to side with the more conservative elements, the traditional oligarchy and the military.

Given the frailties of the middle class, the entrenchment of the oligarchy, the lack of political involvement of the impoverished rural masses, and the potential radicalism of the growing labor class, it is little wonder that democratic governments were never firmly rooted in Latin America. They became all the more vulnerable when they failed to achieve promised economic development after World War II and to lift their countries from economic dependency. And thus, having proved unable either to meet the rising expectations of their people or to quell growing unrest, democracies were ripe for military takeover.

Military intervention in politics has a long history in Latin America. Since World War II there have been scores of military coups, and in the short span of less than three years (1962–1964) eight countries fell victim to military takeovers. The military in Latin America, with few foreign wars to fight, tended to assume a domestic role as the guardian of the state. Military personnel, traditionally nationalistic and conservative, could be counted on to defend the status quo and maintain order. Military rule, or at any rate authoritarian rule, was reinforced by still another enduring legacy: autocratic rulership by a "strong man." In modern times, Latin America has seen a number of powerful, charismatic demagogues such as Getulio Vargas of Brazil and Juan Peron of Argentina.

The political pattern of postwar Latin America, with its pendulum swings from civilian to military rule, begs certain questions: Is social revolution a necessary condition for the achievement of democracy and economic development? Or to put it another way, can democratic government and economic modernization occur without causing a degree of social and political disruption unacceptable to the stubborn oligarchy and the military? And what of the middle class? It has yet to exhibit either the will or the power to bring significant social change to Latin American countries. Or, is the military itself capable of being the agent of social reform? By examining more closely the postwar political experiences of selected South American countries, we will be in a better position to answer these questions and to observe the various political forces at work. In Argentina, Brazil, and Chile we see variations of the pattern of the alternating civilian and military rule in particular national settings.

☐ Argentina

Postwar Argentina has gone through four distinct political phases: a decade of the dictatorship of Juan Peron, a decade-long experiment in democratic government, seventeen years of military dictatorship, and a new period with the return to democracy in 1983. The rule of Peron was quite distinctive yet difficult to characterize for it contained elements of populism and autocracy, and of capitalism and national socialism, at the same time. Peron, a former army officer, was elected to the presidency in Argentina in 1946 largely on the strength of the votes of the working class, whose support he had cultivated in his previous post as labor minister. Peron's nationalistic policies aimed at ridding his country of foreign domination and attaining

Argentine self-sufficiency were initially quite successful, and as a result his popularity soared. He bought out foreign businesses with wartime profits, created a government board for marketing agricultural produce, subsidized industrial development, extended social services, expanded education, and strengthened labor's rights. Meanwhile, he took steps to greatly increase his personal power by impeaching the Supreme Court, enacting a new constitution that broadened the powers of the president, and purchasing the support of the army by vastly increasing the military budget. He also benefitted from the immense popularity of his wife, Eva Peron, who was given a large budget for building hospitals and schools and dispensing food and clothing to the needy.

Peron's economic program, however, began to sputter by 1950 and within a year he was confronted with an economic crisis marked by falling agricultural and industrial production, wage reductions, worker layoffs, and runaway inflation. In response to the economic woes and protests, Peron became more dictatorial, silencing the press and political opposition. Frustrated by his loss of public support (occasioned in part by the death of Eva in 1952) and the mounting economic chaos, he became more erratic. He feuded with the Roman Catholic Church, which caused him a still greater loss of support.[4] Finally, in September 1955, the military, too, abandoned him and forced him into exile.

The army made good its promise to restore democracy but only after struggling for over two years to root out Peronists from the government, the army itself, and the powerful General Confederation of Labor (CGT). The Peronist constitution was scrapped, the Peronista party was outlawed, and its leaders arrested. Elections were held in February 1958 and a democratically elected president, Arturo Frondizi, took office. His government inherited a politically fragmented country with a still bankrupt, inflation-ridden economy. Although Peron himself remained in exile in Spain for the next seventeen years, he continued to cast a shadow over Argentine politics, and his Peronista party, although officially outlawed, remained a force to be reckoned with, as did the CGT, still dominated by Peronists. So strong were the Peronists that it was only by wooing them that Frondizi was able to stay in power. But his economic policies, specifically his inviting foreign interests to take control of the stalled oil industry, provoked a nationalistic outcry, especially from the Peronists. All the while, his relations with the military were strained, and when he began looking to the Left for support, a section of army leaders known as the *gorillas* began to stir. In desperate need of support during the election in 1962, he once again tried to enlist Peronist support by legalizing the Peronista party. The result was a smashing electoral victory for the Peronists. The army, however, rejected this verdict, seized power once again, arrested Frondizi, and again banned the Peronists.

A similar round of events followed: A newly elected president found it necessary to curry favor with the Peronists, ultimately legalizing their party, only to be unseated by them in the next election (1965), and this was followed by an inevitable military coup in June 1966. Thus began an extended period of military dictatorship in Argentina. The military regime, first headed by General Juan Carlos Ongania, ruled by fiat, arrested the Peronists and other political dissenters, muzzled the press, controlled the unions, and imposed an economic austerity program in order to curb inflation and stabilize the economy. This time there were no promises of a return to democracy. But as the economic malaise continued and political disorders broke out, General Ongania was forced aside by other generals, who proved no more successful.

The parade of military rulers was broken momentarily in 1972 by none other than Juan Peron, whose party once again won an electoral victory. Peron's return was triumphant, but the Peron spell was insufficient to the task of remedying the country's economic ills. He died in office in July 1974, leaving power in the hands of his third wife, Isabel, who was his vice-president. But she too proved unequal to the immense task of governing this troubled nation, and in 1976 her government was overthrown by the army.

The new military regime, headed by General Jorge Rafael Videla, was more ruthless than any of its predecessors. Determined to force compliance with its dictates and to eliminate terrorism and political disorders caused mainly by leftists, it imposed a reign of terror that not only filled the jails but also took many lives. The army engaged in a witch hunt against its political enemies, rounding them up by the thousands and killing them, sometimes pushing them off airplanes over the Atlantic Ocean. Nearly 10,000 Argentines were killed or simply disappeared. Meanwhile, inflation continued and the standard of living declined. As if to draw the people's attention from their woes and to arouse their patriotism, the militarists in 1982 took the nation to war in defense of Argentina's historical claim to the Falkland Islands (a British possession known in Argentina as the Malvinas), located some 300 miles off its coast. The costly defeat suffered by the Argentine forces at the hands of the British further discredited the military, and consequently it was forced to call elections and relinquish power to a new civilian government in October 1983.

Argentina's new president, Raul Alfonsin, head of the Radical party, was the first to defeat the Peronists in an open election, and his election was considered a mandate to restore order and civility to the country. Courageously, yet cautiously, he set in motion criminal proceedings against his military predecessors. The generals were put on trial and convicted of various crimes committed in the "dirty war" they had waged against leftist enemies. Alfonsin also had to face an even greater challenge—one that had doomed all of his predecessors—to reverse the downward slide of the Argentine economy. He inherited an economy with one of the world's highest rates of inflation and one of the world's highest foreign debts.

☐ **Brazil**

Brazil stands out among the nations of South America partly because of its Portuguese background, but even more because of its immense size. In both population (now approaching 140 million) and size (one-third of the continent) it dwarfs the other nations of South America. Its vast resources and economic potential make it a giant among them. The political pattern in Brazil, however, is strikingly similar to that of other South American countries. Its problems are also similar: the quest for industrialization while trying to meet the demands of militant workers for higher wages, and the flagrant inequality of land ownership with its inherent waste and its oppression of the peasantry. Brazil, like Argentina, experimented with democracy (after a long rule by a charismatic dictator), and after democratically elected governments proved unable to cope with economic decline and popular unrest, they gave way to military leaders who used harsh autocratic methods to tackle these problems. In both Argentina and Brazil military rule lasted from the mid–1960s until the early 1980s, and finally yielded to popular pressure for the return to democracy. The major differences between the two countries' experiences are that the Brazilian military regimes proved more successful in dealing with economic problems and they were somewhat less brutal than those in Argentina.

Brazil was under the paternalistic dictatorship of Getulio Vargas from 1930 to 1945. Vargas had done much to centralize political power in the nation and promote industrial growth, and under his rule the middle class grew in size. His regime became increasingly dictatorial as he sought to quash both rightist and leftist movements, and by the end of World War II, the nation, especially the middle class, demanded liberalization. In October 1945, the military ousted Vargas, and elections were scheduled. Most of the candidates for president were former officials in the Vargas regime, and the most conservative of them, General Eurico Dutra, was elected. His five-year administration hardly represented a clean break with the past; it enacted a conservative constitution and it made no attempt to institute social reform. Its economic policies of heavy government borrowing and spending were ruinous, causing a huge trade deficit and serious inflation. An election victory in 1950 returned Vargas to power, but his presidency proved no more successful in solving the economic problems. His austerity program slowed inflation only slightly, but at the cost of losing the support of the urban workers whose wages were held down. But the main opposition to his government came from the military. In August 1954, when the army demanded that he step down, he committed suicide.

The new president, Juscelino Kubitschek, aggressively pursued the goal of economic modernization in Brazil with lavish spending programs. His most extravagant project was the building of a spectacular new capital city, Brasilia, located in the interior of the country. This project was designed to spur the development of the interior region, stimulate national pride, and divert attention from the ever more serious problems of soaring inflation and national debt. Kubitschek was defeated in the 1960 election largely because of the worsening economic conditions, but his successor, Janio Quadras, fared no better. After only seven months in office, he resigned when his austerity measures met bitter opposition.

Brazil's new president, Joao Goulart, brought a fresh approach to the nation's problems, for, unlike any of his predecessors, he attempted fundamental reforms. Goulart proposed an extensive land reform, an election reform to enfranchise the nation's illiterate (40 percent of the population), and a tax reform to increase government revenues. When his reforms were blocked by Congress, he tried to achieve them by presidential decree. In March 1964, he ordered the expropriation of certain types of the nation's largest estates. These programs earned him the support of the peasantry and the working class but also the wrath of the landowning elite, the middle class, and the military. Goulart also proclaimed a neutralist foreign policy, established diplomatic relations with the Soviet Union, legalized the Brazilian Communist party, and began to woo its support. This shift to the left in both domestic and foreign policy placed him in greater difficulty with conservative elements. Goulart overplayed his hand when he supported efforts of enlisted personnel in the armed services to unionize, and granted amnesty to several who had been found guilty of mutiny. It should be added that Goulart's free-spending policies, like those of Kubitschek, caused runaway inflation, and this too resulted in an erosion of support from the middle class. Army leaders, who secured the support of the United States in advance, forced his resignation in April 1964.

This time the military came to stay; military officers governed Brazil with a heavy hand for the next twenty years. Blaming civilian politicians, and especially the cashiered left-leaning Goulart, for all of Brazil's ills, the military was determined to purge them from the government, silence all opposition, and forcefully impose its austerity program on the nation. The new ruling junta (a military group in power after overthrowing a government) banned the Communist party and carried out mass arrests of suspected Communists. It then issued a series of "institutional acts," which incrementally restricted the powers of the Congress, arrogated greater powers to the presidency, disenfranchised politicians and their parties, repressed political freedoms, and crushed the labor unions. Under the military presidencies of Castello Branco and Arturo da Costa e Silva during the late 1960s, Brazil moved steadily toward totalitarian government. The strong-arm methods were relaxed only slightly by their successors in the 1970s.

Repression tends to breed revolutionary violence, for when legal opposition is suppressed, only illegal and violent means of opposition are possible. The polarization of Brazilian politics had begun before the military came to power, but with military rule the struggle between the Right, entrenched in power, and the outlawed Left became nasty and brutal, as it had in Argentina. (To the extent that the military rulers were engaged in a battle to quash Communist terrorism, they had the blessings and material support of the United States.)

To the credit of the military rulers, the Brazilian economy responded to the stringent austerity program and, in fact, during their rule Brazil realized its highest economic growth rates. In 1966, Brazil's annual rate of growth of the GNP was 4 percent, but this rose steadily to reach 10 percent in the early 1970s, which was higher than any Latin American country has ever achieved. The growth of both agricultural and industrial production made possible for the first time since World War II a favorable balance of trade. But there was a dark side to this economic success story. On the one hand, it could not be sustained partly because of the severe impact of the oil crises of the 1970s and partly because of the gigantic foreign debt that the military leaders ran up (a problem discussed in Chapter 14). On the other hand, the growth of the GNP had not produced a higher standard of living for the Brazilian people. Industrial growth was made possible by keeping wages low, and the rise in the cost of living continued to exceed the growth in wages. In addition, no land reform was undertaken and nothing at all was done to improve the lot of the rural poor.

☐ Chile

In Chile we see still another variation of the theme of oscillation between civilian and military governments. Military rule in Chile had little in common with the reformism of the Peruvian generals, but instead resembled that of Argentina and Brazil in its conservatism and strong-arm methods. However, unlike those two countries, Chile did not succumb to military rule until the 1970s. Until then, democracy prevailed; the army had stayed out of politics until 1973, when it entered with a vengeance. As the historian Arthur Whitaker points out, "Chile's political system was the most orderly and democratic in Latin America from World War II to 1970," and "the Chilean armed forces were [until then] exceptionally apolitical by Latin American standards."[5]

Chile also stands out as one of the most flagrant examples of the United States's interference in South America in order to further its ideological and strategic ends, not to mention its business interests. Nowhere in South America were U.S. business interests more substantial. Since early in the twentieth century, Chile was the main source of copper for the United States, and its copper mines and many of its industries were owned by U.S. firms. Thus, when Chilean politics moved further to the Left, it was not only conservative elements within Chile that were alarmed. Washington would not sit still while another Latin American country, especially one as economically and strategically important as Chile, edged closer to Communism.

In 1964, the presidential election in Chile was a contest between two left-of-center candidates seeking to succeed Jorge Alessandri, whose six-year term in office had come to an end. Eduardo Frei, head of the Christian Democratic party, campaigned for extensive reforms and defeated Salvador Allende, the candidate of a leftist coalition. Frei's campaign was supported by the CIA and by Chilean conservatives, both of whom sought to head off an electoral victory by Allende and the Marxists. His administration instituted a moderate agrarian reform, fostered industrial development, expanded the education program to reduce illiteracy, and advanced the government's social services. Under Frei, Chile received generous amounts of Alliance for Progress aid, which financed industrial expansion but also greatly increased the nation's indebtedness. His gradualist reform program was opposed as too radical by the Chilean elite and conservative parties, and it also drew fire from the working class and the parties on the Left for being too modest. Only the middle class and Washington seemed to be happy with it.

The polarization of Chilean politics was evident in the 1970 election. The battle lines were drawn between the conservative Jorge Alessandri on the Right, and Allende, who headed a leftist coalition known as Popular Unity, on the Left. (Frei was ineligible for a second term, and his party's candidate was not a strong contender.) Allende squeaked by with a very narrow victory, but his election was confirmed by the Chilean Congress in accordance with Chilean law. It was the Western Hemisphere's first elected Marxist government. Allende, whose cabinet consisted mainly of socialists and Communists, called for a peaceful transition to socialism. But he went right to work to achieve that end, nationalizing both U.S. and Chilean copper and nitrate companies, many other industries and banks, implementing and extending the land reform begun by Frei, and placing a ceiling on prices while raising workers' wages. These measures were immensely popular with the great majority of the people in Chile, but they alarmed his opponents and policy makers in Washington. Spurred by his initial success and by the Communists in his government, Allende pushed on to even more radical reforms. Initially, Allende had the tentative support of the military, but his efforts to retain its loyalty were frustrated by the worsening economic problems and political strife stirred by his policies.

Ultimately, Allende's regime failed for both economic and political reasons. Chile was already in a depression caused by declining copper prices when Allende took office. By the second year of his term the economy was in a tailspin with inflation running out of control. To a considerable extent his own policies had contributed to these problems, but beyond doubt the major blow to the Chilean economy was a drastic fall in the international price of copper. By mid–1972, the economy was in dire straits, and Allende's base of support had dwindled down to little more than the working class and the poor. The middle class and other conservative elements began or-

Chilean President Salvador Allende, who was slain in the presidential palace during the Sept. 1973 military coup. (*Organization of American States*)

General Augusto Pinochet, who led the military coup against Allende in 1973 and remained in power in Chile afterward. (*Organization of American States*)

ganizing in opposition to Allende and carried out such actions as a crippling nationwide trucking industry strike, an action that was secretly supported with CIA funds. The polarization of the nation became extreme, and a violent clash seemed imminent. Allende and his Communist supporters began arming workers, as the army began plotting a military coup. That anticipated coup took place in September 1973, when the air force bombed the presidential palace where Allende was gunned down.

There is considerable debate about the role of the United States in the overthrow of Allende's government, but there is no question that it was heavily involved in efforts to prevent him from coming to power in the first place and, having failed that, to destroy his government. President Nixon and his National Security Adviser, Henry Kissinger, treated Allende as a pariah and regarded his regime as a Communist threat to the entire region. In addition to working to isolate Allende diplomatically, the Nixon administration used two levers to force his downfall: it funneled some $8 million through the CIA to Allende's opponents in Chile, and it took steps to cut off all loans, economic aid, and private investments to Chile. It argued that this was justifiable retaliation for Allende's nationalization of U.S. properties in Chile, but clearly these measures amounted to an attempt at the economic strangulation of Allende's government. Some have argued that there was direct involvement or at least complicity by the United States in the military coup. But while this appears likely it remains to be proven. It is true that the Chilean military officers who led the coup, like many others from Latin American countries, had received training at the School for the Americas, a facility in Panama established by the U.S. Army to train Latin American military officers. Washington was, of course, delighted by the coup and quickly came to the support of the new military regime.

The military regime, headed by General Augusto Pinochet, swiftly carried out a relentless campaign against leftists and people suspected of having been associated with the deposed regime. Thousands were killed and the jails were crammed with political prisoners. Pinochet invited back U.S. copper companies, halted the land reform program, broke up labor unions, dissolved Congress, banned all leftist parties, and in general conducted a wholesale attack on civil liberties in the name of national reorganization. His regime steadily became ever more savage in its crushing of political opposition as years went by. By the mid–1980s, there was no let-up in the strong-arm tactics of the Pinochet regime nor any indication that it intended to return the country to civilian rule. Although anti-government demonstrations remained outlawed, courageous protesters by the thousands went into the streets to demand political change. All the while, the Pinochet government continued to enjoy the support of the United States, which preferred the secure climate for investment and the anti-Communist partnership it provided over the political instability that its overthrow might bring.

Meanwhile, however, the mid–1980s have witnessed a comeback for democracy elsewhere in South America. We have already noted the end of military rule in Brazil and the election of Alfonsin in Argentina and his efforts to rein in the Argentine military. (The criminal proceedings against the Argentine generals begun by Alfonsin represent a dramatic new endeavor to rid Latin American politics of militarism.) The coming of a new political order in both Brazil and Argentina may be the harbinger of a swing to civilian rule in Latin America. It appears, at this writing, that Latin America may no longer be the graveyard for democracies that it was a decade earlier.

■ REVOLUTION IN CENTRAL AMERICA

The twentieth century has been one of extraordinary violence, death, and destruction. It has witnessed the most devastating wars in history; it is also an age of unmatched revolutionary upheavals. It has produced a leftist challenge to the status quo, a challenge to the dominance of the bourgeois governments that had seized power in another age. Central America is no exception to this pattern of revolutions. Political struggles, recurrent ever since the days of colonial occupation, have resurfaced with a vengeance during the late 1970s and have attracted worldwide attention. The conflicts in Latin America between the Left and the Right have become a focus in the global struggle between the United States and the Soviet Union.

Central American societies have long been separated into classes and it is these deep social divisions that have fueled the region's revolutions. On one side are the landowners who enjoy political power and generally have the backing of the army. Opposing them are the majority of the population who have little land, few political rights, and are impoverished.

Students of revolutionary movements are well aware that the side that commands the loyalty of the army will ultimately hold power. In Central America, those in power have generally been able to call on the army. The notable exception took place in Cuba, in the late 1950s, when Fulgencio Batista found that at the end he had little support in the army, not to mention the population, and in 1959 Fidel Castro took Havana by default. The army, from whose ranks Batista had risen to power, ultimately had no desire to save his corrupt regime. But such a pattern is the exception to the rule. In 1932, in El Salvador, General Hernandez massacred 30,000 *campesinos* (field workers) and effectively eradicated whatever revolutionary movement existed in that country. More recent instances of intervention on the part of the military in Latin America took place in 1954 in Guatemala, when the army overthrew the reformist government of Jacobo Arbenz, and in 1973 in Chile, when General Augusto Pinochet ousted and murdered President Salvador Allende. In each case, the armed forces determined the political fate of the nation. And in the cases of Chile and Guatemala, the armies overthrew democratically elected governments.

Direct U.S. involvement in Central America began in the 1890s, particularly since the days of the Spanish-American War of 1898 when the United States took upon itself the role of police officer of the Western Hemisphere, especially the Caribbean region. The United States, in the words of Teddy Roosevelt, would not permit "chronic wrongdoing" in the region.[6] Successive U.S. administrations repeatedly intervened to suppress political unrest and prop up governments tolerant of a U.S. presence in Central America. The Caribbean Sea became a U.S. sphere of influence where the protection of U.S. interests—political, economic, and military—became of paramount concern.

On the official level, the U.S. goal in Central America has always been to introduce the local populations to the blessings of democracy. In 1913, President Woodrow Wilson commented that he would "teach the South American Republics how to elect good men."[7] But democracy has always been defined differently in Central America than in the United States. For the latter, democracy entails activities that have to be conducted according to certain, well-defined rules that no one may transgress. The outcome of an election is final and no one, least of all the military, has the right to circumvent the electoral process. Yet, no one has been able to teach the Central American military to stay out of political affairs. Thus, military dictatorships, rather than democracies, have been the rule there. Also, U.S. attempts to champion the cause of democracy tended to take a back seat to what became the primary quest: political stability and the protection of U.S. interests. In the early 1960s, President John Kennedy, in describing the U.S. dilemma in Central America, offered this well-known explanation:

> There are three possibilities in descending order of preference: a decent democratic regime, a continuation of the Trujillo regime [a right-wing dictatorship] or a Castro regime [a left-wing dictatorship]. We ought to aim at the first, but we really can't renounce the second until we are sure that we can avoid the third.[8]

Washington's problem, therefore, has always been the absence of "decent democratic regimes" in Central America. Successive U.S. administrations have had to choose between the likes of a Trujillo or a Castro. The real trick, however, has been to reconcile the official U.S. political creed of liberty and justice for all with its support of right-wing dictators who had come to power with the help of armies and who used the military to retain that power. Washington, in its quest for stability in the region, has embraced many such dictatorial governments, and to justify its support for these military regimes has resorted to labeling them "democracies." And in opposition to its official stance, the U.S. government has done little to assist such democratically elected, reformist governments as that of Goulart in Brazil.

The first significant change in Latin America came with the Cuban revolution of 1959. Fidel Castro, unlike other revolutionaries in Latin America—and Latin America has had its share of revolutionaries who have seized power—refused to accept the unequal relationship between his country and the United States, one which dates back to 1898 when the United States seized Cuba from Spain. A large portion of the Cuban economy was in U.S. hands and the U.S. ambassador to Havana wielded great power. To rectify this condition, Castro insisted on the nationalization (governmental takeover) of U.S. property—with compensation[9]—and the reorganization of the Cuban economy along socialist lines. In addition, Castro worked out a trade agreement with the Soviet Union trading Cuban sugar for Soviet oil and machinery.

The United States, unaccustomed to such a brazen show of defiance, initiated economic warfare against the Castro regime and broke off diplomatic relations. It then moved to overthrow Castro, which resulted in a fiasco in the Bay of Pigs in 1961 (for details, see Chapter 4). Other attempts followed, but Castro survived and with the help of the Soviet Union he consolidated his power. The Cuban missile crisis in 1962 led to a U.S. pledge not to invade Cuba, but successive U.S. governments, whether Democratic or Republican, were in no mood to tolerate other radical regimes in their "backyard." One Cuba was enough.

CENTRAL AMERICA

UNITED STATES

MEXICO

Mexico City

GULF OF MEXICO

Yucatan Peninsula

BAHAMA ISLANDS

Havana

CUBA

Guantanamo

JAMAICA

CARIBBEAN SEA

HAITI

DOMINICAN REPUBLIC

PUERTO RICO

LESSER ANTILLES

GRENADA

Caracas

VENEZUELA

BELIZE

Belize City

GUATEMALA

Guatemala City

San Salvador

EL SALVADOR

HONDURAS

Tegucigalpa

NICARAGUA

Managua

San Jose

COSTA RICA

Panama Canal

Panama City

PANAMA

COLOMBIA

Bogota

PACIFIC OCEAN

0   350   700

miles

☐ **Nicaragua**

The next serious outbreak of revolutionary violence in Central America took place in Nicaragua during the mid–1970s. It came in the wake of a devastating earthquake in 1972 that leveled Managua, the nation's capital. Nicaragua was ruled by the Somoza family, which had come to power in the early 1930s with the help of the U.S. Marines (an occupation force in Nicaragua—off and on—from 1911 to 1932). President Franklin Roosevelt remarked of Anastasio Somoza Garcia, the founder of the dynasty that he was an "s.o.b., but our s.o.b."[10] The greed of the Somozas became legendary. Exact figures of their wealth are not available. But while opponents have always overestimated it, when Anastasio Somoza said that "Nicaragua is my farm," he was only stating a fact. When the last of the Somozas, Anastasio, Jr. ("Tachito"), fled the country in 1979, he took with him an estimated $100 to $400 million, most of it from the national treasury.

The earthquake of 1972 brought into sharp focus the greed of Anastasio Somoza and the National Guard, his private army. Both had long been involved in the seizure of land and the control of many sectors of the economy—prostitution, construction kickbacks, gambling, taxation. When the devastation hit the capital all discipline in the National Guard broke down. Rank-and-file soldiers looted publicly; Somoza and his officers did so in private. They handled all U.S. contributions for the relief of the victims of the earthquake, siphoning off large sums of money and selling relief supplies for their own benefit.

By 1974, Somoza had created powerful enemies—the Roman Catholic Church and the middle class—the latter of which had not forgiven him for his conduct after the earthquake. In January 1978, *Somocista* killers assassinated Pedro Joaquin Chamorro, an outspoken critic and the editor of the newspaper *La Prensa*. This act sparked the first mass uprising against Somoza. After Jimmy Carter became president in 1977, the U.S. government officially became the champion of human rights throughout the world. Somoza now stood alone; he could no longer count on the United States to bail him out (although it continued to sell him arms). The National Guard systematically executed thousands, but it was too late. The rebellion gathered in strength; no amount of bloodshed could save Somoza's regime.

The violence in Nicaragua was brought home to the U.S. public in June 1979 when the National Guard arrested ABC newsman Bill Stewart, forced him to kneel, and executed him. Stewart's camera crew recorded the murder on film and hours later the scene was reproduced on U.S. television screens. It was only then that the Carter administration cut off arms sales to Somoza's government.

A month later, in July 1979, Somoza fled, leaving behind a devastated country. The death toll was between 40,000 and 50,000; 20 percent of the population was homeless; and 40,000 children were orphaned. The industrial base was in ruins. The Somocistas had plundered the country, leaving behind a foreign debt of $1.5 billion.

In Somoza's place, the *Sandinistas,* a coalition of revolutionaries, seized power. The Sandinistas had taken their name from the revolutionary Augusto Sandino, whom the first Somoza had murdered nearly fifty years previously. The United States did not intervene in the civil war, despite the fact that the administrations of President Gerald Ford and Jimmy Carter did not like the leftist orientation of the Sandinistas. In the late 1970s, the U.S. public, in the wake of the withdrawal from Vietnam, did not have the inclination to attempt to suppress another revolutionary movement. Moreover, President Carter, the advocate of human rights, had little choice but to turn his back on Somoza for the human rights record of the Somozas had been a dreadful one. Later, Carter went so far as to provide a modest amount of foreign aid to the Sandinistas in order to retain a bit of leverage in the internal politics of Nicaragua. But the Nicaraguan revolution, to the dismay of Washington, continued to shift to the left and brought itself into conflict with its own middle class. Shortly before he left office, a disillusioned Carter suspended all economic aid to the Sandinistas.

The Sandinistas then proceeded to solidify their position. With it came the establishment of a new order. Its features included the nationalization of land, press censorship, political prisoners, the nationalization of segments of industry, a militarized government, and a restricted electoral process. But it also included extended health care for the population, a literacy campaign, the redistribution of land, an economy half of which still is in private hands, and a fair measure of freedom of speech. In short, the Sandinista government became a typical example of a revolution seeking to consolidate its power, while at the same time seeking to resolve the nation's most pressing social and economic problems.

The war of nerves between Washington and Managua had escalated in 1981, after President Reagan was sworn in. Reagan halted all aid to Nicaragua and launched an ideological war, as well as covert (secret) CIA actions, against the Sandinistas. The Sandinistas had become an affront and an obsession to President Reagan and his first secretary of state, Alexander Haig. They had committed the unpardonable sin of becoming recipients of aid from the Communist states of Eastern Europe, notably the Soviet Union (but also from West European states such as France and West Germany). With this aid they had reversed Nicaragua's traditional dependence on Washington. And prior to March 1981, they had sent a small amount of arms to the rebels in El Salvador. In the eyes of the Reagan administration the Sandinistas had become a spearhead of Soviet expansionism in the United States's own backyard.

The CIA then proceeded to organize and arm the counterrevolutionary opponents of the Sandinistas, the Contras. Headed by former members of the National Guard, Somoza's private army, who were tainted by their past association with Somoza and therefore have little support in Nicaragua itself. The Reagan administration had a difficult time selling its policy of aiding the Contras to Congress and the U.S. people, who were leery of becoming drawn into another civil war in a land of which they knew little. But after Daniel Ortega, the dominant figure in the Sandinista government, flew to Moscow seeking economic aid, the links between Moscow and Managua promised to become closer; up to that point the Soviets had provided only military aid. Congress reacted to Nicaragua's tightening of its ties with Moscow by voting approval for financial aid to the Contras, aid that was to be used for "humanitarian," rather than military purposes. As President Reagan had promised earlier in the year, the screws were going to be tightened until the Sandinistas "cried uncle."

In reaction to the Reagan administration's military solution, the Contadora group (the various "dominoes" Washington was ostensibly protecting) called for a political settlement. The Contadora group—Mexico, Panama, Colombia, and Venezuela—was named after an island off the coast of Panama where its representatives initially met in September 1983. It called for a mutual disengagement of all foreign advisers and soldiers—Cubans, Soviet, and U.S.—from Central America; in short, for the political neutralization of the region. The Contadora group pointed to the counterproductive nature of Washington's Central American containment program: the Salvadoran revolutionaries had tripled their forces since 1981 and the Sandinista army had doubled in size. Cuban advisers in Nicaragua had increased from some 2,000-3,000 in 1983 to over 7,000 three years later, and they had been joined by military advisers from the Soviet Union, East Germany, Libya, and the PLO. Washington had conducted its own escalation when it allowed the CIA to carry on its own war against Nicaragua, increased the number of military advisers in El Salvador, and began to conduct military exercises in Honduras. Central America was on the threshold of becoming another Third World battleground in the East-West confrontation. The Sandinistas proclaimed their willingness to abide by the Contadora solution; the Reagan administration, however, rejected this solution because it would permit the Sandinista regime to remain intact and because it contained an implicit understanding that the time-honored U.S. interpretation of the Monroe Doctrine—the right to intervene in Central America—had become an anachronism.

The Reagan administration went through several arguments explaining its opposition to the Sandinistas. First, it tried to prove, with little success as it turned out, that the Sandinistas were continuing to channel Soviet-bloc weapons to the rebels in El Salvador. Throughout this initial phase, the administration was at pains to insist that it had no intentions of overthrowing the Sandinista government. However, the CIA proceeded in secret to arm and train the Contras, who in fact sought nothing less than the destruction of the Sandinistas. This "covert" CIA operation soon became public, and since it was in violation of international—as well as U.S. domestic—law, another, less direct, approach had to be found. Washington's hope rested with the Contras, whom President Reagan called "freedom fighters," comparing them to the American revolutionaries of 1776. Although the U.S. Congress in 1985 had restricted assistance to the Contras to humanitarian aid, CIA-sponsored "private" gunrunners continued to supply them with weapons.

Second, the Reagan administration repeatedly came back to the specter of U.S. security and credibility being at risk. In his address to Congress in April 1983, President Reagan tied the fate of the Nicaraguan revolution to the global Cold War between the United States and the Soviet Union:

> If Central America were to fall, what would be the consequence for our position in Asia and Europe and for alliances such as NATO? If the United States cannot respond to a threat near our own border, why should Europeans and Asians believe we are seriously concerned about threats to them? . . . The national security of all the Americas is at stake in Central America. If we cannot defend ourselves there, we cannot expect to prevail elsewhere. Our credibility would collapse, our alliances would crumble. . . .[11]

When in May 1985 President Reagan declared an embargo on trade with Nicaragua, he did so under emergency powers Congress had granted the president in 1977, the International Emergency Economic Powers Act. In his

Daniel Ortega, Sandinista leader and president of Nicaragua. (*Organization of American States*)

message to Congress, the president declared that because "the policies and actions of the Government of Nicaragua constitute an unusual and extraordinary threat to the national security of the United States," it had become necessary to declare a national state of emergency to deal with that threat.[12] In one sentence, the president tied events in Nicaragua to the very survival of the United States and therefore declared a state of emergency. Once again, events in a small and distant land were linked to the very existence of the United States. It was little wonder that many in the United States heard the echoes of Vietnam. In April 1985, Secretary of State George Shultz did little to defuse the situation when he openly compared Nicaragua to Vietnam:

> Broken promises. Communist dictatorship. Refugees. Widened Soviet influence, this time near our very borders. Here is your parallel between Vietnam and Central America.[13]

Shultz's remarks touched a responsive chord among the convinced, those who had always defended the U.S. involvement in Vietnam. But they also reawakened for many the memory of a divisive and costly war of dubious import to U.S. interests.

☐ El Salvador

In El Salvador, a repetition of the Nicaraguan scenario appeared to be unfolding in the early 1980s. A rebellion in the countryside threatened to oust the oligarchy (government by the privileged few) who governed the country. This oligarchy was composed largely of *las catorce familias,* the Fourteen Families. Jorge Sol Costellanos, an oligarch and a former minister of the economy, defined the class structure in El Salvador as follows:

> It's different from an aristocracy, which we also have. It's an oligarchy because these families own and run almost everything that makes money in El Salvador. Coffee gave birth to the oligarchy in the late 19th century, and economic growth has revolved around them ever since.[14]

Sol went on to say that, in fact, the fourteen Families (or, more accurately, clans) controlled 70 percent of the private banks, coffee production, sugar mills, television stations, and newspapers. In contrast to the wealth of the Fourteen Families, were the landless poor. The impoverished peasantry of El Salvador made up the bulk of the population, but they received a disproportionately small share of the nation's meager wealth. In 1984, the annual per capita GNP of El Salvador was around $710, about 6 percent of the U.S. figure. (The U.S. government has generally ignored such maldistribution of wealth and the lack of social justice that are the actual roots of revolution in Central America.)

The revolutionary violence that broke out in El Salvador in the early 1970s had its roots in the events of the early 1930s. In 1932, deteriorating economic conditions—brought about by the Great Depression and falling farm prices—and Communist activities under the leadership of Augustin Farabundo Marti led to peasant uprisings. A lack of organization and arms proved to be fatal for the peasants, for machetes were no match against a well-equipped army. In a matter of days, the armed forces, led by General Maximiliano Hernández, slaughtered 30,000 *campesinos* (peasants). Marti was captured and executed. The revolution was over but its impact remained deeply etched into the collective memory of the nation. Hernández became the symbol of both deliverance and oppression. His ghost still haunts El Salvador today.

The massacre of 1932 produced an uneasy stability in El Salvador until the national elections of 1972 when the candidates of the Christian Democratic party (PDC)—Jose Napoleon Duarte and his running mate Guillermo Ungo—defeated the candidate of the military. The PDC had called for reforms to forestall a revolution, but the oligarchy and the military shrank from the prospect of reforms, particularly those calling for the redistribution of land and wealth. The military therefore arrested Duarte, tortured him, and sent him into exile. It then terrorized the country. These acts in turn spawned left-wing terror. The oil crisis of 1973 added to the nation's economic problems. Duarte in exile continued to hold out hope for electoral reforms. Others in the PDC, notably Guillermo Ungo, joined the revolutionary cause.

Violence reached a new level when right-wing "death squads" went on a rampage of indiscriminate killings. These assassination squads summarily killed thousands of men, women, and children. In March 1980, the Roman Catholic Archbishop of San Salvador, Oscar Arnulfo Romero, a critic of the government, was gunned down by rightists while saying mass at the altar. This act of sacrilege was but a reflection of that nation's violent past.

The assassination of Romero put into focus a major change in the political life of Latin America that had been occurring during the past two decades. The Roman Catholic Church, traditionally the champion of the status quo, had begun to reexamine its mission. Portions of it moved toward a renewed commitment to improve the lot of its faithful on this earth. Village priests in particular found they could not preach eternal salvation and at the same time ignore the violence visited on their parishioners. The upshot was a split between the traditional wing of the clergy and those, such as Romero, who championed what became known as "liberation theology." (This approach accepts a view of the world similar to that of the Marxists to redress traditional social injustices.)

Unlike the Latin church, Washington continued to be more concerned about violent revolution in El Salvador than right-wing violence. And U.S. policy makers continued to insist that revolutionary violence was being inspired from the outside, by Nicaragua, Cuba, and ultimately the Soviet

Union. Thus, for Washington, a key to the suppression of the revolution in El Salvador lay in going to the alleged outside source, primarily Nicaragua.

The Reagan administration's stance on El Salvador rested on three pillars. First, it provided much needed economic aid to a nation wracked by a civil war. Second, it became the source of the military hardware the Salvadoran army employed in its attempt to suppress the revolution. Third, it emerged as the champion of Salvadoran electoral democracy. Under U.S. supervision, elections returned Duarte to power in 1979, but clearly at the pleasure of the military who needed him, because without Duarte the Reagan administration could hardly justify its support of the Salvadoran military. Duarte's election made it possible for Washington to argue that reforms were taking hold and that the army's human rights record was improving. The violence, however, continued after Duarte's election.

In this fashion another small country became the focus of the East-West struggle. The argument is a simple one: From the United States's point of view, a leftist victory, no matter where, is a defeat for the West and a victory for the Soviet Union. Thus, any change in the status quo is seen as altering the balance of power. Moscow holds a similar view of the world. It sees the establishment of regimes hostile to the United States as an improvement of its own international position. Logically enough, the Soviet Union took advantage of the revolutionary cauldron in Central America by providing economic and military aid to Fidel Castro, the Sandinistas, and other revolutionaries. It claimed to be the champion of revolutionary justice and liberation from Yanqui imperialism. And, of course, all of this only reinforced the view from Washington that it's all a Communist plot. This in turn drove the Central American revolutionaries into closer cooperation with the Kremlin.

■ NEW INITIATIVES IN CENTRAL AMERICA

In the 1980s, the Sandinista regime in Nicaragua became an obsession for President Reagan. He remained convinced that it was a conduit for international Communism and that unless the Sandinistas were overthrown the Soviet Union would soon establish a beachhead in Central America. He was impervious to the logic that said that support for the Contras resulted in increased Soviet military aid for Nicaragua and to the evidence that the Contras had not made any significant military progress, had no base of popular support in Nicaragua, and had virtually no prospect of defeating the Sandinista army. When Congress suspended further military aid to the Contras in 1984 and again in early 1985, Reagan resolved to find other ways to support the Contras and win a proxy war against the "Communist" regime in Nicaragua.

Thus began what came to be known as the "Iran-Contra affair." Officials in the president's National Security Council worked out a complex scheme whereby profits from the covert and illegal sales of arms to Iran through intermediaries would be turned over to the Contras. Col. Oliver North, who conducted this operation from the basement of the White House, also sought money for the same purpose from political donors within the United States and from friendly foreign governments. All this was in violation of laws passed by Congress prohibiting further military aid to the Contras. These covert operations were not detected until November 1986, by which time, ironically, Congress had authorized another $70 million in military aid to the Contras. The Iran-Contra scandal remained the national focus for over a year—much like the Watergate scandal in the Nixon era—for it raised many questions about ethics, law, and power, as well as foreign policy. Where Nicaragua was concerned, it had a ruinous effect on Reagan's policy. Congress, which had earlier vacillated on the issue of Contra aid, now firmly rejected any further military support, despite Reagan's persistent pleas.[15]

Another setback for the Reagan administration's Nicaraguan policy came in June 1986, when the World Court (the International Court of Justice in The Hague, Netherlands) ruled that the United States had violated international law by mining Nicaraguan harbors (in 1984) and in providing military support to the Contras for the purpose of overthrowing the government of Nicaragua. The United States had not participated in the court's proceedings because, as the Reagan administration explained, the United States did not recognize the World Court's jurisdiction in this case.

The Contadora peace process, begun in 1983, had virtually expired by 1987, but a new peace initiative was then launched from within Central America. In February 1987, Costa Rican President Oscar Arias presented a proposal that won the endorsement of the rulers of all five Central American nations, including Sandinista leader Daniel Ortega. The Arias plan committed the Central American nations to a cease-fire, a general amnesty, a national dialogue with civilian political opposition, the promotion of democracy through freedom of the press and political parties, free elections, the suspension of all foreign military aid, reduction in the level of arms, and prohibition of the use of national territories to attack neighboring countries.

Daniel Ortega signed the Arias peace plan and pledged to uphold its provisions. The plan offered him a diplomatic victory over Washington, and it spelled doom for the Contras, who were in any case deteriorating because of a lack of U.S. funding. The prospect of ending the war was welcomed in Nicaragua also because the Sandinista regime needed to address the problems of a rapidly deteriorating economy. Ortega's government moved quickly to comply with the Arias plan's requirements. In September 1987, less than a month after the peace plan was signed, Ortega authorized the reopening of the opposition newspaper *La Prensa* and the repeal of the policy of prior censorship of the media. He also agreed to mediation between the Sandinista regime and the Contras by Cardinal Miguel Obando y Bravo.

Ortega's "peace offensive" had a telling effect in Washington where Congress in February 1988 turned down yet another presidential request for Contra aid. Six weeks later, President Reagan dispatched 3,200 elite troops to Honduras to defend that nation from an "invasion" by Nicaragua, after the Sandinista army had crossed the border to destroy a Contra base in Honduras and then withdrew after the one-day operation. Reagan apparently hoped that the dispatch of troops would persuade Congress to restore Contra aid, but it did not. One week later, Ortega, setting aside his standing refusal to negotiate directly with the Contras, signed a temporary cease-fire agreement with them. The Contras, still about 18,000 strong and still based in Honduras, were now a lost cause. Humanitarian aid from Washington kept them alive, but this aid was due to expire in March 1989. One month before that date, the presidents of the five Central American nations agreed to a plan calling for the disbanding of the Contras and their expulsion from Honduras.

But Ortega's problems were by no means over. The same agreement called for the implementation of further reforms in Nicaragua in preparation for fair and free elections to be held in February 1990. Ortega's government had hoped that his adherence to the Arias plan and his coming to terms with the Contras would bring improved relations with Washington, an end of the economic embargo, and a grant of reconstruction aid. Neither the Reagan administration nor that of his successor, George Bush, was so forgiving, but rather in 1989, Bush continued the barrage of criticism against Ortega and provided support for his political opponents. The Sandinista regime endeavored to silence its critics at home while it grappled with a crisis far more threatening to its survival than either the Contras or political opponents: the economy. The war, the U.S. trade embargo, the loss of foreign credit, and its own mismanagement had caused an economic disaster for Nicaragua. Nicaragua's per capita GNP had fallen from over $1,000 in 1980 to $830 in 1987, and fell still lower in 1988. During the same period, annual exports fell from $600 million to a mere $200 million. Even more ruinous was hyperinflation, which seemed in 1989 to be beyond the control of the government. At the end of the decade, the fate of the Sandinista government hung in the balance as the nation languished in poverty.

In 1989, the Sandinistas took a calculated risk when they agreed to hold free elections in February 1990 and to abide by the population's decision. The Sandinistas reasoned they would not only win, but an election would also make it even more difficult for Washington to continue to arm the Contras. The Sandinistas, however, lost the gamble when UNO, a coalition of anti-Sandinista parties, led by Violeta Chamorro, the widow of the publisher of *La Prensa* who in 1978 had been murdered by Somoza, won 52 of the National Assembly's 90 seats. Nearly a dozen years of war and deprivation took their toll on the Sandinista revolution when the voters cast their ballots for a change. Ortega hesitantly and grudgingly accepted defeat and agreed to transfer his movement's base of power, the 70,000 troops of the army, to the authority of the new government. At the same time, however, he and Chamorro kept a weary eye on the Contras who, although now more isolated than ever before, still had the power to disrupt society.

* * *

In neighboring El Salvador, civil war continued. By 1989, after nine years of fighting, the loss of some 70,000 Salvadoran lives, and the absorption of some $3.3 billion of U.S. economic and military aid, little had changed. The leftist guerrillas, regarded by one observer as "the best trained, best organized and most committed Marxist-Leninist rebel movement ever seen in Latin America,"[16] controlled about one-third of the country and made their military power felt with periodic attacks in the remainder of the country. President Duarte remained Washington's best hope for political reform, but he was never able to control the army. Duarte's U.S.-backed Christian Democratic party lost ground to the right-wing ARENA (Nationalist Republican Alliance) which had won control of the legislative assembly in elections in March 1988. ARENA staunchly opposed political change, and its paramilitary death squads continued to work with the army in murdering political opponents and terrorizing the nation. Duarte, whose health was deteriorating, prepared to step down after elections scheduled for March 1989.

In anticipation of those elections, the rebels, known as the FMLN (Farabundo Marti National Liberation Front), announced in February 1989 that they were willing to take part in the election, but requested that it be postponed for six months to give them time to prepare. The FMLN also proposed a cease-fire and declared its willingness to recognize the army as the sole legitimate military force in the country, but only on the condition that army officers responsible for massacres such as the murder of Archbishop Romero and four U.S. nuns be tried and punished. It made other conditions, but this one was critical, for no senior military officer had ever been brought to trial, even though many had been linked to the killings. At the urging of Washington, leaders of Duarte's party and ARENA held talks with FMLN leaders, but although the atmosphere was peaceable, ARENA and the army ultimately rejected the rebels' proposals. The army argued that the 1987 Amnesty Law absolved the security forces of past crimes. It was plainly unwilling to submit to civilian and judicial control.

The presidential elections and a peaceful transfer of power brought a semblance of political progress, but violence soon returned to El Salvador. ARENA candidate Alfredo Cristiani won the election and took office on June 1, 1989. To allay U.S. fears, Cristiani promised democratic reforms and pledged to control ARENA and army extremists. The FMLN proposed a new round of talks in September, and as a sign of good will it unilaterally agreed to suspend its sabotage raids and the use of mines. The Cristiani government, which pointed to recent acts of brutality by the rebels, rejected the proposal and retaliated with its own violence. On October 31, a bomb destroyed the headquarters of a militant labor union aligned with the FMLN, killing 10 people and wounding 30 others. Ten days later, the rebels launched a military offensive that turned San Salvador, the capital, into a battlefield. For almost a week they held a large section of the city and claimed control of 8 of the country's 14 provinces. The army resorted to aerial bombing and strafing in order to drive the rebels out of the capital, and in the process more than 100 civilians were killed, 680 were wounded, and many homes were destroyed.

While the battle still raged, the army committed yet another atrocity, which would, in effect, lift the shadow from the rebels and cast it over the ARENA government. On November 16, 1989, right-wing death squads burst into the rooms of six Jesuit priests who taught at the Catholic University and brutally beat and murdered them, their cook, and her daughter. Cristiani, whose government was still receiving U.S. military aid, was pressured by Washington to conduct a thorough investigation and bring the killers to justice.[17] In mid-January 1990, his government arrested and officially charged 8 military men, including a colonel who allegedly ordered the murder of the priests. This represents an important first, for no military officer had ever been charged with—let alone convicted of—a human rights abuse crime in the Salvadoran civil war. Only by breaking the army's death lock on the country and asserting civilian control of the military could Cristiani (or any ruler in Central America) put an end to political violence and war, for not until the military is reined in can the roots of revolution—poverty, despair, and social injustice—be dealt with effectively.

■ PANAMA'S NORIEGA

The first year of the Bush presidency saw a puzzling war of words with Manuel Noriega, the military strongman of Panama. It was a strange spectacle because Noriega, after all, only a few years previously had been a valuable ally of the United States. In fact, he had been on the payroll of the CIA, which paid him $250,000 per year for Caribbean intelligence. As head of intelligence in Panama during the 1970s, Noriega had risen rapidly through the ranks of the National Guard of the Panamanian dictator Omar Torrijos. After the death of Torrijos in 1981, and after Noriega had consolidated his hold on power, the United States used him in the war against Nicaragua. Throughout, the Reagan administration turned a blind eye to human rights abuses on the part of Noriega. Torture, murder,[18] rape, plunder, prostitution, drug trade, and the theft of elections, such as that in 1984, did not faze Washington. It continued to fund the army, now renamed the Panamanian Defense Forces (PDF), as it contemplated the military withdrawal from the Canal Zone by the year 2000 stipulated by the treaty of 1979. Under Noriega, the PDF grew from 10,000 to 21,000 troops.

But in 1987 Washington became aware that Noriega had transgressed the bounds of propriety as he was also dealing with Cuban intelligence. Noriega's military headquarters had become a brokerage house where intelligence was bought and sold as just another commodity. Ambler Moss, President Carter's envoy to Panama, explained that Noriega was "dealing with everybody—us, the Cubans, other countries. We used to call him the rent-a-colonel."[19] The seemingly loyal ally in the cause against hemispheric Communist subversion proved to be a man of neither scruples nor morals. The feeling of betrayal by the Reagan-Bush forces became too much to bear. They accused Noriega, quite correctly, of being part of the international drug cartel. But it was reminiscent of Claude Rain's discovery of gambling in Rick's place in *Casablanca*. Knowledge in Washington of Noriega's drug connections go back to the Nixon administration.[20]

Noriega resisted all U.S. pressure to step down and presented himself as the champion of small Latin American nations once again bullied by the "colossus of the North." In 1987, grand juries in Tampa and Miami indicted Noriega on drug trafficking charges. Just before Christmas 1989, Bush sent a posse of 20,000 soldiers to bring Noriega to justice. Operation "Just Cause," as Bush chose to call the U.S. military intervention, got its man, but the cost was high. Several hundred Panamanians—mostly civilians—and 23 U.S. soldiers died in the fighting. In addition, the "collateral damage" of property and subsequent looting of stores in Panama City resulted in losses of $1 billion to small businessmen, presumably the chief beneficiaries of "Just Cause."

The invasion may have served the cause of democracy, but the Bush adminstration appeared well on its way to repeating the mistakes of the past when it insisted on rebuilding the shattered Panamanian army. When the new president of Panama, Guillermo Endara, visited President Oscar Arias of Costa Rica in January 1990, Arias urged him to forgo an army. Arias advocated, instead, the Costa Rican solution of 1948, when it had abolished its army and as such has become the only viable democracy between the Rio Grande and the Straits of Magellan.

The invasion of Panama was also perhaps the first instance of U.S. military intervention abroad in which the anti-Communist theme was not used. As such, it was a sign of the times as the Cold War was winding down. Bush instead defended his action as part of his war on drug dealers and said that it was his duty to defend the Panama Canal and to protect the lives of U.S. citizens. But as another sign of the times, he stood in direct contrast to Soviet leader Mikhail Gorbachev, who had declared that no nation had a legal or moral right to interfere in the internal affairs of another nation.

In Miami, before a federal judge, Noriega presented himself in his general's uniform as a prisoner of war. The judge, however, thought he was dealing with a common criminal. U.S. foreign policy was acquiring a new focus, the international drug connection, and Noriega's arrest became Exhibit A of the federal prosecution's commitment to a new war.

■ LATIN AMERICAN DRUG TRAFFIC

In the late 1980s, the increasing volume of illicit drugs flowing from South America to the United States and the rising level of violence attendant to this drug traffic became a major issue in the relations between Washington and several South American countries. In 1989, President Bush proclaimed an all-out war against drugs to be waged both within the United States and in Latin America, aimed at eliminating the demand in the former and the supply in the latter. The drug problem in the United States and the policies drawn up in Washington to counter it have been the subject of considerable controversy, particularly because the so-called war on drugs, despite the resounding fanfare with which it was proclaimed, has had very little success to date.[21]

The heart of Latin American drug traffic is in Colombia, where several powerful drug cartels manage operations that are responsible for about 80 percent of the cocaine entering the United States. Marijuana and coca plants, from which cocaine is extracted, grow abundantly in the equatorial climate of Colombia, Bolivia, and Peru. The farmers on the western slopes of the Andes mountains and the Amazon valley in these countries are paid far more to grow and harvest these plants than they could possibly earn from growing food crops. The infusion of drug money is the salvation of farmers and a windfall for local police and politicians, who point with pride to the new houses and newly paved roads in their once poverty-stricken towns and villages.

The largest drug operation, the Medellin cartel, was founded in 1981 in the Colombian city of Medellin. It operates like a large multinational corporation with a multibillion dollar business. U.S. Drug Enforcement Agency officials estimate that its profits may be as high as $5 billion a year and that it has tens of thousands of people on its payroll. It is rivaled by the Cali cartel, based in the smaller city of Cali.[22] Both cartels are well prepared to offer enormous bribes to Colombian military, political, and judicial officers to protect their operations, and when bribes fail to achieve their purpose, they have readily resorted to violence. Medellin drug lords have been particularly violent.

The Colombian government launched its own war on the drug cartel in August 1989, shortly after presidential candidate Luis Carlos Galan, who pledged to eradicate the drug cartels, was assassinated by drug thugs. Colombian President Virgilio Barco Vargas ordered military forces into action against the drug cartel, setting their crops ablaze, destroying production facilities, and seizing the homes and properties of several of the major drug kingpins. The drug cartels, particularly the Medellin, responded with a counteroffensive of terrorism. They carried out hundreds of bombings and gunned down opponents in cold blood. Among their victims were 43 judges and elected officials. In December 1989, they bombed the headquarters of the Department of Security, the agency most involved in the effort to destroy the drug operations. A half ton of dynamite destroyed the six-story building, killing 52 people and injuring 1,000. They also claimed responsibility for the bombing of a Colombian jetliner ten days earlier, killing all 107 people aboard. In terms of property and lives lost, the drug cartel appeared to be winning the war in Colombia. Barco's government was, however, able to claim some success: the flow of drugs from Colombia was, at least temporarily, reduced by about 30 percent, and in January 1990 his security forces killed Jose Gonzalo Rodriguez Gacha, reputed to be the principal Medellin leader responsible for the recent violence.

A central issue in the drug war within Colombia was the extradition treaty signed with the United States in 1979, according to which a captured Colombian drug boss would be sent to the United States to stand trial. Extradition is what the drug lords feared most, and it was therefore the main weapon of the United States and the Colombian governments in fighting the drug cartels. In February 1987, Carlos Lehder, a major drug figure, was captured and extradited to the United States, where a year later he was found guilty for drug smuggling and sentenced to life plus 135 years. Later in 1987, the Colombian Supreme Court, probably cowing to Medellin pressure and terrorism, nullified the extradition law. But after the murder of Galan in August 1989, President Barco exercised his executive authority to resurrect the extradition treaty, and the Colombian Supreme Court upheld his action. The drug lords exerted enormous pressure on judges and politicians to overturn the law, offering them in some cases a choice between a fantastically large bribe or death. They attempted to persuade politicians to legalize the drug trade by promising an end to further violence as well as by the usual bribery and threats. It remains to be seen whether the government of Colombia or the drug industry controls the nation and its drug policies. But even if the government wins this battle and drives the cartels out of Colombia, the highly profitable drug traffic is not likely to disappear, for the powerful drug lords can readily relocate to neighboring Bolivia or Peru, where other smaller drug organizations are already operating. As long as the economy of the region remains depressed and the farming of legal crops remains unprofitable, the prospect of eradicating the drug industry in the region seems remote.

■ RECOMMENDED READINGS

□ Latin America – General

Burns, Bradford. *Latin America: A Concise Interpretive History.* Englewood Cliffs, N.J.: Prentice-Hall, 3d ed., 1982.
> Offers an excellent analysis of modern Latin America's progress and problems.
Lewis, Paul H. *The Governments of Argentina, Brazil, and Mexico.* New York: Crowell, 1975.
> A useful comparative study of politics in three major Latin American nations.
Skidmore, Thomas E., and Peter H. Smith. *Modern Latin America.* New York: Oxford University Press, 1984.
> An excellent survey by two noted specialists.
Wolf, Eric R., and Edward C. Hansen. *The Human Condition in Latin America.* New York: Oxford University Press, 1974.
> A penetrating analysis of the dilemmas of poverty in Latin America.

☐ South America

Alexander, Robert J. *Juan Domingo Peron: A History.* Boulder, Colo.: Westview Press, 1979.
    An authoritative biography of the most important political figure in modern Argentine politics.
Alexander, Robert J. *The Tragedy of Chile.* Westport, Conn.: Greenwood Press, 1978.
    The tragedy is the overthrow of Allende by the militarists.
Blanco, Hugo. *Land or Death: The Peasant Struggle in Peru.* New York: Pathfinder Press, 1972.
    A longtime revolutionary argues strongly his case for radical land reform.
Burns, E. Bradford. *A History of Brazil.* New York: Columbia University Press, 2d ed., 1980.
    A survey of Brazilian history with good coverage of its recent politics.
Valenzuela, Arturo. *The Breakdown of Democratic Regimes: Chile.* Baltimore: Johns Hopkins University Press, 1978.
    Strongly critical of the militarist intervention in Chile.
Wesson, Robert. *The United States and Brazil: Limits of Influence.* New York: Frederick A. Praeger, 1981.
    A study of U.S.-Brazilian relations.
Whitaker, Arthur P. *The United States and the Southern Cone: Argentina, Chile, and Uruguay.* Cambridge, Mass.: Harvard University Press, 1976.
    An interpretive history of the three countries, as well as U.S. involvement in them.

☐ Central America

Berryman, Phillip. *Inside Central America: The Essential Facts Past and Present on El Salvador, Nicaragua, Honduras, Guatemala, and Costa Rica.* New York: Pantheon, 1985.
    The observations of a man who for four years served as Central American representative for the American Friends Service Committee.
Chace, James. *Endless War: How We Got Involved in Central America—and What Can Be Done.* New York: Vintage, 1984.
    Offers a brief but insightful historical analysis.
Diedrich, Bernard. *Somoza and the Legacy of U. S. Involvement.* New York: Dutton, 1981.
    A history of the impact of Somoza on Nicaraguan society.
LaFeber, Walter. *Inevitable Revolutions: The United States in Central America.* New York: W. W. Norton, expanded ed., 1984.
    A detailed and informative account by a well-known revisionist historian of the role of the United States in the Cold War.
Langley, Lester D. *Central America: The Real Stakes, Understanding Central America Before It's Too Late.* New York: Crown, 1985.
    A critical analysis by a professional historian of Latin America.
Montgomery, Tommie Sue. *Revolution in El Salvador.* Boulder, Colo.: Westview Press, 1982.
    An account of the recent political history of El Salvador.
Schlesinger, Stephen, and Stephen Kinzer. *Bitter Fruit: The Untold Story of the American Coup in Guatemala.* Garden City, N.Y.: Doubleday, 1982.
    The best seller on the CIA's 1954 coup in Guatemala.

■ NOTES

1. Latin America embraces the thirteen countries of the South American continent, the seven countries that make up Central America, and the various islands that dot the Caribbean Sea. In the first part of this chapter generalizations will be made about the entire region of Latin America; then the focus shifts to South America specifically, and then to Central America.

2. Richard P. Schaedel, "Land Reform Studies," *Latin American Research Review,* I, 1 Fall (1965), p. 85.

3. E. Bradford Burns, *Latin America: A Concise Interpretive History.* Englewood Cliffs, N.J.: Prentice-Hall, 3d ed., 1982), p. 214.

4. Peron was angered by the Catholic Church's refusal to canonize the departed Eva as a saint. The church in turn opposed his efforts to require the teaching in schools of his ideology that deified the state and himself as its head. He accused the church of organizing a mass movement against him, and responded by censoring Catholic newspapers, arresting priests, and forbidding church processions. The Pope, Pius XII, retaliated by excommunicating Peron.

5. Arthur P. Whitaker, *The United States and the Southern Cone: Argentina, Chile, and Uruguay.* (Cambridge, Mass.: Harvard University Press, 1976), pp. 301, 309.

6. Theodore Roosevelt, "Annual Message to Congress," December 1904, in Robert H. Farrell, *American Diplomacy: A History* (New York: Norton, 1959), p. 251.

7. A conversation with Sir William Tyrell, a representative of Britain's Foreign Office, November 13, 1913. Wilson explained his position on the civil strife in Mexico with this comment: "I am going to teach the South American republics to elect good men!" Arthur S. Link, *Wilson, II, The New Freedom* (Princeton: Princeton University Press, 1956), p. 375.

8. John F. Kennedy, quoted in Arthur M. Schlesinger, Jr., *A Thousand Days: John F. Kennedy in the White House* (Boston: Houghton Mifflin, 1965), p. 769.

9. Castro offered to pay for U.S. property, but only on the basis of a low assessment the companies themselves had submitted for tax purposes. The U.S. companies insisted on full value. Stephen E. Ambrose, *Rise to Globalism: American Foreign Policy, 1938–1970* (New York: Penguin, 1971), p. 269n.

10. "I'm the Champ," *Time* (cover story on Somoza), November 15, 1948, p.43.

11. Ronald Reagan to a joint session of Congress, reported in the *New York Times,* April 28, 1983, p. A 12.

12. Ronald Reagan, "Executive Order and Message to Congress," *New York Times,* May 2, 1985, p. A 8.

13. Don Oberdorfer, "Central America Could Share Vietnam's Fate, Schultz Warns," *The Washington Post,* April 26, 1985, pp. A 1, A 16; George P. Schultz, excerpts from a speech to State Department employees on the tenth anniversary of the fall of Vietnam, "The Meaning of Vietnam," ibid., p. A 16.

14. Paul Heath Hoeffel, "The Eclipse of the Oligarchs," *New York Times Magazine,* September 6, 1981, p. 23.

15. Congress approved continued "humanitarian," or non-lethal, aid to the Contras in 1987 and 1988, and this expired in March 1989.

16. James Le Moyne, "El Salvador's Forgotten War," *Foreign Affairs,* Summer 1989, p. 106.

17. One month later a witness to the murders complained to church officials of "coercive interrogation" by Salvadoran and U.S. officials, who allegedly were attempting to get her to change her story. Apparently neither Christiani nor the Bush administration wanted the Salvadoran army to be found responsible for this atrocity, for it might cause Congress to suspend further military aid to the country.

18. Guillermo Sanchez Borbon, "Hugo Spadafora's Last Day: A murder in Panama undoes a regime," *Harper's,* June 1988. pp. 56–62.

19. Tim Collie, "Noriega played all angles in ascent," *The Tampa Tribune,* December 25, 1989, p. 22A.

20. *Ibid.,* pp. 22A, 25A.

21. For a scorching criticism of President Bush's war on drugs see Lewis H. Lapham, "A Political Opiate: The War on Drugs is a Folly and a Menace," *Harper's Magazine,* December 1989, pp. 43–48

22. Medellin is the main supplier of drugs to Miami, and Cali had control the cocaine traffic in New York City, until the fall of 1988 when the Medellin dealers invaded the drug market in New York City, touching off an underground drug war.

□ 13

Asian Roads to Modernization

Most of the countries of Asia may be characterized as Third World nations, and several of them, such as Bangladesh, Cambodia, Burma, and Laos, are among the world's poorest. Certainly the two giant Asian nations, the People's Republic of China and India, each with a per capita GNP under $400, qualify as Third World nations. There are, however, other countries in Asia, all on the rim of China, which have far higher GNPs and growth rates and cannot at all be considered Third World or underdeveloped nations. Japan immediately comes to mind, but certain other Asian countries are following Japan's footsteps and rapidly becoming highly industrialized nations.

The twentieth century has been an age of social experimentation and upheavals, and China, the world's largest nation, has had its share of both. The Chinese Communist government's efforts to transform and modernize China warrant an examination, not only because of the magnitude of the task, but also because of the great lengths to which the Chinese Communists have gone to apply Marxism to the task. The endeavor to put Marxism into practice in this huge country has, however, caused enormous political and economic upheavals. Only after the passing of Mao Zedong in 1976 did China attain a significant measure of both political stability and economic growth.

India, the other Third World giant of Asia, has maintained a democratic form of government and has enjoyed a greater degree of political stability than China, but its economic performance has been no better than China's. India, too, has engaged in social/economic experimentation, mixing elements of capitalism and socialism, while avoiding radical shifts in policy. In their own ways, both India and China have struggled to come to terms with a massive population and massive poverty, and not until the 1980s have they both been able to register substantial economic gains.

In stark contrast with either China or India is Japan and four other East Asian countries that have had remarkable economic development in the past two or three decades. In this chapter our attention will be on the "Four Tigers of Asia," namely South Korea, Taiwan, Hong Kong, and Singapore (leaving Japan aside for a later chapter). South Korea, Taiwan, and Singapore were by all means poor Third World countries in the 1950s, but they have achieved spectacular growth and economic modernization, and, like Hong Kong (technically a British colony rather than a nation), they became newly industrialized countries (NICs). We treat one other Third World Asian nation which has not kept pace with the four tigers: the Philippines. Our main focus there is on the Marcos dictatorship and the revolution that toppled him.

■ MAO AND THE POLITICS OF MODERNIZATION

The enormity of China is the starting point of any inquiry into China's economic progress, for its great size alone sets China apart. Never in history has there existed a nation of over a billion people. China has always been an agrarian nation with a mass of poor peasants, but in the twentieth century this nation has struggled to modernize. The Communist government of China has stressed industrialization, economic growth, and improvement of the standard of living. At the same time it has given priority to building a revolutionary Communist society. The interplay of the economic and political objectives, and especially the question of priorities, is key to understanding revolutionary China and its efforts to achieve economic growth.

But first one must take note of the objective conditions in China and of its past efforts to deal with those conditions. China's overriding problem in modern times (for at least the past two centuries) has been how to feed itself. The population continued to grow rapidly both before and after the Communists came to power in 1949. At that time it was about 535 million; by 1960 it was 680 million; by 1970, 840 million; and in the early 1980s, it pushed past the 1 billion mark. Traditionally, over 90 percent of the population were peasants engaged in subsistence agriculture. Despite the great size of the country, there was never enough land to support the people on it. Only about 20 percent of the land is arable, the remainder being either too mountainous or too arid for agriculture. Therefore, China's huge population is heavily concentrated in the areas with arable land, mainly the coastal plains. But even in these areas there is not enough land for all the people. And because of unequal distribution of land the bulk of the peasants in the past either owned too little land or none at all. This set of conditions—the plight of the impoverished peasantry and their exploitation by the landown-ing class—gave rise to Mao Zedong's Communist movement, and his regime was committed to putting an end to these conditions.

China had made very little progress toward modernization of its econ-omy prior to Communist rule. The Nationalist regime in the 1930s made an attempt to industrialize, but this endeavor was cut short by the eight-year-long war with Japan. The Communists inherited a country in 1949 that had suffered the destruction of that war as well as three years of civil war. It was a country that had only a very meager industrial development, that was wracked with uncontrolled inflation and economic chaos, that had an im-poverished and illiterate peasantry, and that had cities swollen with jobless, desperate people. It was a huge, backward country that lacked many of the basic elements for modernization: capital, technology, and an educated working class.

Under the rule of Communist party Chairman Mao, politics, which is to say Marxist revolution, had greater priority than did economic growth. Mao's often quoted dictum, "politics take command," meant that everything, every activity, in China was to be defined politically in Marxist terms. Thus, to study economic development in Mao's China is to study the Marxist poli-tics of Mao Zedong and his comrades in the Chinese Communist party (CCP).

Initially, upon coming to power in 1949, however, the Communists stressed economic rehabilitation and postponed their socialist objectives. In the first three years they managed to establish economic and political order, control inflation, and restore production in the existing industries to their prewar level. Major industries were nationalized, foreign enterprises were confiscated, and only gradually was private enterprise eliminated as state control of the economy was increased. The new regime also addressed the peasant question—an issue that could not wait—by instituting a wholesale land reform. The redistribution of land was carried out swiftly and ruthlessly, resulting in the transfer of millions of acres of land to over 300 million peasants and in the elimination of the "landlord class." Estimates of the loss of life involved in the latter vary greatly, but no doubt several mil-lion Chinese met their deaths in this revolutionary process.

By 1953, the Chinese government was ready to institute the first Five-Year Plan, which was modeled on that of the Soviet Union and guided by Soviet economic advisers. Economic assistance from the Soviet Union was of great importance to China—the technical aid more so than the monetary loans, which were rather meager (but more than China obtained from any-where else). As in the Soviet Union, the Five-Year Plan stressed rapid development of heavy industry. It was successfully implemented, and as a result China's production of steel, electricity, and cement increased remarkably.

As the second Five-Year Plan was about to be launched, Mao Zedong questioned the effect that this method of economic modernization was having on the Chinese revolution. Mao feared that it would result in the entrenchment of a powerful bureaucracy, a new elite that would exploit the Chinese masses. In early 1958, he suddenly called a halt to the second Five-Year Plan, thereby rejecting the Soviet model for development, and called instead for a "Great Leap Forward." It called for tapping the energies of the masses of people—China's greatest resource—and making a massive joint effort to industrialize and collectivize at the same time. In the countryside the agricultural collectives, which had been formed in the mid–1950s, were to be reorganized into larger units, communes, which would embody the basic Marxian principle: "From each according to his abilities, to each according to his needs." Mao's approach was to mobilize the masses with the use of ideology in order to develop a revolutionary fervor. However, this frenzied pace could not be maintained, and the excess of zeal, lack of administrative ability, and poor planning produced an economic disaster. The economic collapse was made worse by Khrushchev, who withdrew from China all Soviet technicians in 1960, and by three consecutive crop failures (1959, 1960, and 1961). The Great Leap Forward was, in fact, a disastrous leap backward, and it cost China dearly, taking a huge toll in lives and causing untold hardship as well as crippling the economy.

From this point on, one can clearly detect the contention between two conflicting strategies in Communist China, or as the Chinese refer to them: "two lines toward socialism." The one we can label Maoist, or radical, the other moderate. The radical approach is reflected in the manner in which Mao built the Communist movement in China in the 1930s, in the Great Leap Forward, and later in the Great Cultural Revolution. It stresses the "mass line," meaning the power of the people and their active engagement in the revolution. It calls for the intense ideological training of the CCP cadre, those dedicated party leaders who stimulate and serve as a model for the masses. The cult of Mao was an important tool for politicizing the masses. It was not an end in itself, but a means to the end: a thoroughly revolutionary society, a society that is egalitarian and free of exploitation of the masses.

The moderate line deemphasized ideology and revolutionary zeal and stressed instead state planning, bureaucratic leadership, and the development of the skills and expertise necessary for the advancement of China. Its main feature is pragmatism—a rational, problem-solving, do-what-works approach. It is therefore less political, less ideological, and less emotional than the Maoist line, and gives higher priority to bureaucratic management and economic modernization than to ideology.

After the Great Leap Forward fiasco, the moderates took charge of cleaning up the mess Mao had made of things. Gradually, during the first half of the 1960s, the economy recovered under the guiding hand of such moderate leaders as Liu Shaoqi (Liu Shao-ch'i) and Deng Xiaoping (Teng Hsiao-p'ing). But once again Mao became disturbed about the trend toward bureaucratic elitism. Using his immense prestige as "The Great Helmsman," Mao bypassed the CCP structure and initiated in July 1966 a new political upheaval aimed at purging the CCP of its elitist leaders: the "Great Proletarian Cultural Revolution."

Chairman Mao was determined once and for all to eradicate bureaucratism in the Chinese revolution. He charged his opponents not only with elitism, meaning that they were guilty of selfishly guarding and advancing their own personal power and privilege, but also with revisionism, meaning that they were guilty of revising (distorting) Marxist-Leninism, just as Mao felt current Soviet leaders had. He claimed that many party leaders were taking the "capitalist road" and thus destroying the Communist revolution. Mao enlisted the active support of the youth of China, who were dismissed from colleges and schools, organized into the "Red Guard," and instructed to go out and attack all those who were guilty of selfish elitism. "Serve the people" was the slogan and Mao's writings were the guidelines. Throughout China the Red Guards enjoined all people high and low—officials, soldiers, peasants, and workers—to study arduously the thought of Mao Zedong as presented in capsule form in the "Little Red Book."

Mao's Cultural Revolution was a unique event, a revolution within a stagnant revolution, a people's revolt against the revolutionary party, ordered by the head of that party. Mao, the great revolutionary leader, purposely instigated a political upheaval by calling upon the masses to purge their leaders—even in his own Communist party—in order to put the revolution back on the right track.

The results were similar to the earlier failure of the Great Leap Forward. The Red Guards, who rampaged throughout the country on their Maoist crusade, met considerable resistance, and numerous clashes occurred. As the disruption and violence continued, Mao had to call in China's military forces, the People's Liberation Army (PLA), to quell the storm and restore order. The PLA, which was Maoist in political orientation, was hence given a much greater political role in China.

It took several years for the Cultural Revolution to wind down. It was never formally ended or denounced until after Mao's death in 1976, but in fact, it was being abandoned quietly by the beginning of the 1970s. As Mao was by then aged and ill, leadership passed into the hands of the very able leader Zhou Enlai (Chou En-lai). Zhou was actually a moderate but had never been attacked by the Maoists as such, and now, more than ever, he was trusted and relied upon by Mao. Gradually, Zhou reinstated moderates who had been expelled from the CCP and put China back on the track toward economic development. It was Zhou who engineered the new foreign policy of rapprochement with the United States in the early 1970s.

But the tensions between radicals (Maoists) and moderates was mounting under the surface of calm maintained by Zhou and Mao. It erupted in 1976, the eventful "Year of the Tiger," when both Zhou and Mao died. Mao's designated successor, Hua Guofeng (Hua Kuo-feng), was able to quash an attempt by the radicals to gain control of the CCP and the government. Hua arrested the ringleaders, who were collectively labeled "the Gang of Four." One of the principal culprits was none other than Mao's wife, Jiang Qing (Chiang Ch'ing). For the next several years, Hua and the resurrected moderate leader, Deng Xiaoping, conducted a political campaign of denunciation of the Gang of Four, as a means of attacking the radicalism that the Gang (and the departed Mao) had stood for. By the end of the 1970s, Deng was in full control of the party, having gently nudged Hua aside, and the Gang was put on trial for their crimes. Cautiously, the new leadership undertook the de-Maoization of China as even Mao was denounced for his "mistakes" in the Cultural Revolution. Clearly, the moderates were now back in the saddle again. It was their turn to reorganize Chinese society.

■ DENG XIAOPING'S MODERNIZATION DRIVE

Under Deng's leadership the march toward economic modernization gained momentum. China normalized relations with the United States and with Japan, with the objective of developing trade relations, attracting foreign capital, and purchasing technology. These and other programs, such as providing bonuses as material incentives for production and restoring a capitalistic market mechanism, stimulated economic growth and modernization. In their drive to close the technology gap, Chinese leaders welcomed foreign visitors, especially scientists, technicians, and industrialists, and meanwhile they began sending large numbers of Chinese students abroad, especially for study in scientific fields.

In an effort to increase agricultural production within China, and thus increase surpluses for investment in the industrial sector, the new leadership instituted in 1979 a new agrarian program called the "responsibility system" or "contract system." According to this new system, the peasants contract for (or rent) a given amount of land, seeds, tools, and the like, from the state, and then, at harvest time, they meet their contract obligations (pay their rent) and are allowed to keep as personal income all that they earn over and above what they contracted for. They then sell their surplus production on the open market. The incentive for personal profit makes for efficient farming and serves to increase overall agricultural production. The very able farmer may in fact rent a large amount of land and hire other workers, and thus become an entrepreneur.

The new system, which has worked quite well, strikes observers as being more like capitalism than Communism. It surely represents a radical departure from Mao's brand of Communism with its emphasis on egalitarianism. However, Deng, the dauntless pragmatist, remained determined to pursue whatever will speed up China's modernization and strengthen its economy. The new pragmatism was guided by Deng's two principles: "Practice is the sole criterion of truth" and "Seek truth from facts."[1] Soviet leaders, who once criticized Mao for going too far to the left, condemned Deng's programs as going too far to the Right. A Soviet visitor to China is said to have remarked, "If this is Marxism, I must reread Marx."[2] The following commentary, which appeared in the authoritative *People's Daily* in December 1984, made it abundantly clear that the Chinese leaders indeed adopted a new view of Marxism:

> [In addition to Marx] we must study some modern economic theories, as well as modern scientific and technological know-how. Studying Marxism means a study of universal laws, elaborated by general writings and opinions on how to solve problems. We can never rigidly adhere to the individual words and sentences or specific theories.
>
> Marx died 101 years ago. His works were written more than 100 years ago. There have been tremendous changes since his ideas were formed. Some of his ideas are no longer suited to today's situation, because Marx never experienced these times, nor did Engels or Lenin. And they never came across the problems we face today. So we cannot use Marxist and Leninist works to solve our present-day problems. . . . If we continue to use certain Marxist principles, our historic development will surely be hampered.[3]

Deng's regime put a new face on China. Economic liberalization transformed China almost overnight from a drab proletarian society, in which individual expression was suppressed, into a lively new consumer society in which individuality is expressed much more freely. This transformation was even more dramatic than the one instituted by Mao's revolution. In today's China private enterprise, profit seeking, capital investment, consumerism, and the pursuit of private wealth were no longer taboo but were instead encouraged. In recent years some enterprising Chinese have been extremely successful in business ventures and have displayed their newfound wealth in conspicuous ways, purchasing large homes and automobiles and taking trips abroad. While authorities are concerned about the jealousy that this behavior causes, they nonetheless encourage the people to seek their fortunes in the confidence that it is for the betterment of the individual and the advancement of China's economic modernization. Deng went so far as to proclaim as a new credo for the Chinese people, "to get rich is glorious," an utterly outlandish notion by Maoist standards, but one welcomed by the new entrepreneurs.

Deng's economic reform program, launched in 1979, represented a bold and far-reaching attempt to restructure the economy of the world's largest nation. In the short term it was remarkably successful. By 1987, eight years after his ascent to power, the nation's GNP had grown substantially; rural incomes tripled and urban incomes doubled; foreign trade doubled, reaching $10 billion by 1987; and direct foreign investment in China rose dramatically.

Between 1981 and 1987 China sustained an average annual growth rate of almost 10 percent, the highest among major nations. The rapid rise in agricultural output in the first half of the 1980s resulted in self-sufficiency and even a modest surplus in food production. This feat, previously considered impossible for this nation of 1.1 billion people, was the result of both the new capitalistic farming system and new population control measures enacted by the government.

The great persistent problem of modern China has been overpopulation, but the Communist regime has addressed this problem effectively. It instituted a stringent birth control program, which rewards families that have no more than one child (increased food rations and employment and education benefits, for example) and penalizes families that have more than one child (decreased food rations and increased taxes, among other hardships). This policy and its related family-planning program, including coerced abortions, had a significant

Chinese leader Deng Xiaoping, Chairman of the Chinese Communist Party Central Advisory Commission, Dec. 14, 1985. (*Courtesy of the Embassy of the People's Republic of China*)

effect on reducing the rate of population growth. This program has served to hold in check a population explosion that otherwise would swallow up any increased economic output. (One can only wonder about its social consequences. One result has been an increase in infanticide, the killing of unwanted children. And it remains to be seen what a society without brothers and sisters will be like.)

The economic modernization program, so successful in the early 1980s, began to falter when it encountered new problems in 1987. Agricultural output fell in the mid-1980s as many farmers sought enrichment in other more profitable economic enterprises now open to them. The resulting grain shortage caused havoc for the economic modernization program. Moreover, the efforts to institute price reforms resulted in sharply rising inflation.

Deng and his protégé, premier Zhao Ziyang, the most vigorous of the economic reformers, regarded price reform the key to the continued success of the economic reform program. Heretofore, prices of consumer goods were rigidly controlled and kept artificially low by government subsidies. These subsidies placed a huge financial burden on the state, which sought to increase budget outlays for capital improvements and other projects necessary to China's economic modernization. In addition to addressing that problem, price reform was aimed at bringing production more in line with demand. However, when the government began removing price controls on such basic commodities as food and fuel, prices soared. By 1988 the inflation rate climbed by about 30 percent. Only those whose income had increased significantly as a result of new business opportunities or those willing to take advantage of their government or Communist party connections could afford the new prices. The vast majority of people whose incomes were fixed and relatively low—factory workers, intellectuals, professionals, lower and middle level government workers—were not so fortunate. The new inflation inevitably brought an increase of corruption and of resentment .

It also brought a government decision to slow down the economic modernization program. Li Peng, newly appointed as premier in early 1988, emerged as the leading proponent of retrenchment. As prices continued to soar upward during the year, Li and Zhao vigorously debated the price reform program and the pace of economic modernization, and the more conservative Li was the victor. Under his influence, the government in September 1988 called for a two-year program of austerity, renewed centralized planning, reinstatement of state trading monopolies, and postponement of further price reform. The aim was to curb the inflation, cool off the "overheated" economy, and maintain a "reasonable" economic growth rate.

■ POLITICAL REFORM IN DENG'S CHINA

The program of economic liberalization, which constituted a departure from Marxism and a rejection of the Stalinist-type economic system, represented ideological flexibility, but it was not attended by as radical a program of political liberalization. Deng's regime, however, did embark on a program of cautious political reform, which gradually offered a greater degree of openness and accountability in reporting governmental affairs, permitted freer access to information and ideas, reduced censorship, and allowed for a greater freedom of personal expression for the people. The reform plans drawn up by Deng and Hu Yaobang, head of the Communist party since 1981, specifically called for (1) administrative reforms that separated more clearly the functions of the ruling Communist party and the government, decentralized decision making, and made individual political leaders more accountable for their decisions; (2) legal reforms aimed at replacing arbitrary and personal power with rule by law and establishing for the first time a legal basis for political and economic activity in China; (3) election reforms offering more than one candidate in National People's Congress elections; and (4) a greater role of public opinion in the governing of China through such means as opinion polling, public forums, and encouragement of suggestions and criticism in letters to editors of newspapers.

These political reforms were attended by considerable rhetoric about "democratization." Deng and his fellow reformers employed this term loosely in reference to reforms they had enacted in order to make the political system less arbitrary and more accountable. The democratization reforms were never intended to introduce a democratic political system characterized by free elections contested by rival political parties vying for power. Deng strongly rejected the notion that "bourgeois liberalism" was appropriate to China. Instead, he consistently reaffirmed the following as China's "four cardinal principles:" (1) the socialist road, (2) rule by the Chinese Communist party, (3) the "people's democratic dictatorship," and (4) Marxist-Leninist and Maoist thought. By invoking these principles, Deng made it clear that there were limits to "democratization" and to dissent in the People's Republic.

If Deng's regime, reformist though it was, had no intention of power sharing, its rhetoric of democratization as well as the greater political and personal freedoms that it had already permitted whetted the appetite of the Chinese for a greater measure of democracy or political liberalization. The new freedoms permitted in the economic sector could not, of course, be neatly limited to that sector, and the call for creativity, resourcefulness, and unrestricted inquiry in scientific and technological fields could not help but influence people's thinking toward social and political matters. Since the early 1980s, hundreds of thousands of Chinese had gone abroad to study and were exposed to democratic institutions and ideas and to social values that gave greater rein to individual rights and liberties. The ideas and impressions they brought back and communicated freely to other Chinese, as well as ideas and images found in foreign magazines and books now readily accessible in Chinese bookstores, stirred the imagination of young Chinese, especially university students. The increased knowledge of democratic societies, together with new economic liberalization, contributed to the emergence of a freer, more individualistic life-style in China, characterized by greater pursuit of pleasure and privileges as well as profit. By the mid-1980s, however, the government began condemning the new Western-influenced behavior and thinking as "spiritual pollution." Not only did it prohibit some of the more visible forms of Western culture, such as rock music, but it also began to crack down on the more vocal proponents of democratic reform.

The growing demand for democratic change was suddenly made manifest by university students in large political demonstrations in December 1986 and January 1987. First in Shanghai, then in Beijing, students turned out in the hundreds of thousands to register their demand for greater democratic reform in China. These demonstrations, by far the largest to date in the People's Republic, continued almost two weeks before being broken up the government—not by force, but with a very distinct threat of force. The students, tentative and lacking resolve and organization, bowed to the government, which had showed considerable restraint and now offered vague promises of addressing the students' concerns. In reprisals that followed, however, Deng underscored the Communist party's position as the final arbiter of all political matters. The specific sacrificial lamb was party chief Hu Yaobang, the most outspoken advocate of reform in the government. More conservative party leaders such as Li Peng attacked Hu as being too radical and reckless in the pursuit of democratization. Deng, who feared disruption of the economic reform program, proved willing to sacrifice Hu and political reform for the sake of protecting the economic reform program.

The movement for democratic reform in China then remained silenced until it suddenly erupted again in the spring of 1989. In the interim, students and intellectuals in China chaffed not only at the continued repressiveness of the regime but also at the increased economic hardship brought by the inflation. They were also rankled at the increasing evidence of widespread corruption, especially on the part of highranking government officials and their families. The best way to describe the mood of students and intellectuals is disillusionment. They were repulsed by a ruling Communist party that, in effect, had abandoned Marxism and the ideals of Mao and offered nothing worthy of commitment in their place, a government seemingly oblivious to the mounting corruption and yet impervious to demands for political change. For many of the disillusioned youth, state ideology had become irrelevant. Others looked back to Mao's era with nostalgia, not because it had been democratic, but because it at least had inspired people with high ideals and a sense of purpose. Many felt that the party had lost its moral authority to govern China. At a minimum, the students who rallied to the democratic movement insisted on accountability on the part of government leaders and an unfettered press without which accountability could not be achieved. The occasion that triggered the student demonstrations in late April 1989 was the death of Hu Yaobang on the 15th of that month. Students from several Beijing universities defied government orders by marching on Tienanmen Square in the heart of Beijing, first to commemorate Hu, who they heralded as a champion of the democratic cause, and then to demand political reforms. Students assembled daily in ever larger numbers, even as the government issued stern warnings that the demonstrations would not be tolerated. Student leaders argued that the Communist system was a failure and criticized the blatant corruption of the Communist leaders. They also insisted on democratic reforms. On their posters they demanded increased respect for human rights, release of political prisoners, a new democratic constitution, greater freedom of speech and press, and the right to hold demonstrations.[4]

Skillfully, the student leaders exploited Western press coverage, confident that the government would not risk its international prestige by the use of force against unarmed demonstrators. They also made excellent use of opportunities presented by the calendar. The first important anticipated date was May 4, when the Chinese government hoped to orchestrate a carefully planned celebration of the 70th anniversary of the student uprising in 1919, an event that gave birth to the Chinese Communist party. The students of the spring of 1989 laid claim to being the rightful heirs to that hallowed movement. By May 4, their numbers in Tienanmen Square had swollen to over 100,000, and the movement had spread to other cities. Government leaders, recognizing the powerful symbolism of the date and the challenge to their legitimacy posed by the students, considered it too dangerous to stop the demonstrations.

Another reason the government did not move to suppress the movement was the scheduled arrival of Soviet leader, Mikhail

Gorbachev on May 15. Gorbachev's visit, in its own right, was a historic event of the first order and had enormous diplomatic significance. Chinese leaders were eager to ratify the end of the Sino-Soviet feud, and they were determined not to allow the student demonstrations to undermine or interfere with these important diplomatic affairs. Nor could Deng's government afford to jeopardize good relations with the Soviet leader by the use of brutal force against the students on the eve of, much less during, his visit. Student leaders exploited the situation fully. Two days before Gorbachev arrived, 2,000 student protesters began a public hunger strike on Tienanmen Square, and on the next day hundreds of thousands flocked to the square in support, ignoring the deadline the government had issued for clearing the area. So large was the throng of protesters (probably over a million), that the welcoming ceremony for Gorbachev, which was to have been held in the Great Hall of the People adjacent to the square, had to be held instead at the airport. The students hailed Gorbachev as a true champion of democratization and argued that "not even Deng can resist the Soviet influence."[5] Deng, the dauntless author of the post-Mao reform program in China, was now lampooned by students as a stodgy old hard-liner. Gorbachev deftly managed neither to support the students nor discourage them, and gave faint praise to Chinese leaders for "opening a political dialogue with the demonstrators."[6]

There would be, however, no dialogue. No sooner had Gorbachev departed Beijing on May 18, than the government decided to crack down on the movement. On that day over one million people, including workers, flooded the square and the surrounding streets to demonstrate their support for the hunger strikes, and Li Peng gave a stern lecture to student leaders, refusing to discuss their demands and warning them against continued defiance. On the following day Zhao Ziyang, head of the party, made a predawn visit to the weakened hunger strikers, and tearfully pleaded with them to end their strike. On May 20, the government declared martial law, and Zhao resigned his party and government posts after failing to persuade Li and other hard-liners to compromise with the demonstrators.

Over the next three weeks the drama unfolding on Tienanmen Square gripped the nation and the worldwide viewing public. Students demonstrators were emboldened by the fact that the government had not taken action to enforce the martial decree and that their movement was openly embraced by large numbers of workers in Beijing and in other cities. It was precisely this fact that caused the government to crack down on the demonstrators, for it could not afford to allow the anti-government movement to spread to the working class. The protestors took heart when the troops who assembled to suppress the movement refused to open fire on the students. Emotions were fired all the more by the erection of a "goddess of democracy" statue on Tienanmen Square as a symbol of their cause. Meanwhile, as the protestors became more defiant in their demands, no longer merely calling for dialogue but rather demanding the overthrow of the government, other armies were brought into position to crush the revolt. Rumors and foreboding filled the air as troop movements in and around the city of Beijing were reported daily. Finally, under the cover of darkness, in the early hours of June 4, columns of tanks rumbled into the square and an awful massacre began. The extent of the carnage is still not known and may never be known, but estimates vary from as many as 3,000 deaths to the government's preposterous claim that no students were killed on Tienanmen Square.[7]

Much remains unclear about this dramatic turn of events. Debate continues regarding the motives or objectives of the protesters, the divisions and discord within the government and within the army, and the long-term consequences of these events, as well as the facts regarding the massacre. But it is quite clear that the government used deadly force to put an end to a popular movement, which, on the one hand, had threatened the political stability of the country and the continued rule of the Communist party, and on the other hand, had captured the hopes of millions of young Chinese and the sympathy and support of millions of people outside of China.

The Tienanmen Square massacre of June 4 was not the end but only the beginning of the government effort to suppress political opposition and restore its authority. No sooner was the shooting was over than the Chinese government employed a second tool of repression—the controlled media—to communicate to the entire nation its version of what had taken place. First came the denial of the massacre and the minimizing and rationalizing of the crack-down. The Chinese people were told that the army had heroically defended the nation against an armed counterrevolutionary rebellion. Then came the reprisals, as leaders of the "rebellion" were hunted down, and many were quickly brought to trial. Over twenty of them were pronounced guilty of treasonous acts, sentenced to death, and publicly executed. Thousands of others were imprisoned. Cowed by state power, both military and judicial, the Chinese people, including many who had seen and supported the anti-government movement, now denied any involvement in it. Next came the government's effort to correct people's thinking, a program of ideological indoctrination, which included the restoration of political ideology classes in all schools, universities and workplaces as well as the reimposition of strict censorship.

By the end of 1989, the people of China, particularly the students, remained cowed and the government remained wary. Late in 1989, when Eastern European nations were abandoning Communism and especially when the people of Romania rose up against Communist dictatorship, the hard-line regime in Beijing was on its guard against renewed political unrest on Chinese university campuses. College professors were called upon to maintain round-the-clock vigils against student activism. Nonetheless, illegal posters went up again at Beijing University, one of which read "Learn from Romania." The reappearance of such protest posters was but one indication that political tensions lay just beneath the surface of the thin veneer of political stability the Communist regime maintained in the wake of the Tienanmen Square massacre.

■ THE POPULATION AND POVERTY OF INDIA

On the other side of the Himalayan Mountains is the other Third World giant of Asia, India, a nation that shares many of China's problems, not the least of which is a burgeoning population. About one-fifth of humanity lives in South Asia, which consists mainly of the Indian subcontinent, including Pakistan and several other states bordering India. Very many of these people live in poverty. In the postwar era, India and the other heavily populated nations of this region have struggled to hold population growth in check and to elevate the standard of living, and only in the past decade have they met with moderate success in these efforts. Although they share many of the same problems, these nations have not lived in peace with one another. Hostility between India and Pakistan has flared up several times, and both countries have confronted violent internal disorders. The maintenance of large armies to deal with these problems has been a drain on the limited resources of each of these quarreling neighbors.

To speak of India is to speak of population and poverty. At the time of the partition of 1947, India's population was about 350 million, and it has grown steadily ever since at a rate of almost 3 percent a year. This meant an average annual increase of about 5 million people in the 1950s, 8 million in the 1960s, and 13 million in the 1970s. The population in the mid–1980s was estimated at over 700 million, having doubled since 1947. Moreover, about 40 percent of the Indian people are concentrated in the Ganges River Basin where the population density is among the highest in the world. Although India has eight cities with over 1 million inhabitants, over 80 percent of the Indian people still live in small rural villages. Most of these people are dreadfully poor. Their per capita income is far below—perhaps less than one-half—the national average of only $260 per year.

To feed its burgeoning population has been India's primary task, for frequently there was simply not enough food to go around. The twin aims of the Indian government, therefore, have been population control and increase of food production. Although it has tried to implement a birth control program, it has had minimal effect in rural areas. The largely illiterate villagers are suspicious of birth control, its purpose and its methods, and they cling to the age-old idea that a large family is a blessing, that it represents wealth and security. Moreover, one way Indians combat the high infant mortality rate is simply to have more children in the hope that some will survive. But even where birth control has had some effect, it did not produce an immediate decrease in population growth. Offsetting the slight decrease in the birth rate is a declining death rate. The latter is the net effect of a decreasing rate of infant mortality and an increase in life expectancy, both of which are the result of improved medical services. Thus, despite birth control efforts, the rate of population growth has not decreased significantly, and pressure of overpopulation on India's economy remains undiminished.

India has in fact attained a higher rate of economic growth (over 4 percent in recent years) than most Third World nations, but the increased production in industry and agriculture is offset by the inexorable growth of its huge population. Demographers speculate that, even if India, were to implement successfully its family planning program by the year 2000, its population would not stabilize until 2,050, by which time it would have surpassed China as the world's most populous nation, with a population of approximately 1.4 billion.

Indian food production has increased steadily since independence, but it remains inadequate. In general, the rate of increase of output has been slightly higher than the rate of population growth, but this is offset by occasional years of crop failure due to droughts or flooding. Moreover, the increased food production is not evenly distributed. Indian agriculture consists largely of subsistence farming, and it is one of the world's least efficient in terms of yield per acre. Among the reasons for this are the small size of farms, the lack of sophisticated tools and machinery, a general lack of irrigation, a tradition-bound social system, and widespread malnutrition. The last suggests a cruel cycle of cause and effect: malnutrition and disease contribute to low agricultural productivity, which in turn leads to greater poverty and hunger.

There exists in India, as in the other agrarian nations in this part of the world, a wide gulf between the wealthy landowners and the more numerous poor peasants, many of whom are landless. This great discrepancy between well-to-do farmers and the rural poor is an age-old one that is inherent in the traditional society and the farming system. The practice of dividing land among sons has contributed to making the average size family farm so small that it will not support the family, and thus the farmer is often forced to borrow money at high rates of interest in order to make ends meet. And all too often he is unable to repay the loan without selling what little land he had. The result has been a steady increase in the percentage of landless peasants in the rural population.

More recent developments, the so-called "Green Revolution" and agricultural mechanization, have produced an increase in agricultural output in India, but they have also made the gulf between rich and poor even wider and have increased rather than diminished the poverty of the majority of peasants. The Green Revolution refers to the introduction of newly developed plants, high-yield varieties of wheat and rice, and new farming techniques to grow the new type of grain.[10] In certain areas of India the wheat production doubled between 1964 and 1972, and the introduction of the new rice strains had a similar effect when introduced in the late 1960s. However, the Green Revolution turned out to be a mixed blessing at best. It benefitted only the minority of India's farmers, the wealthy landowners who could afford the new seeds and the additional irrigation works, fertilizers, and labor required to grow the new high-yield grain. The majority of the rural population—small landholders, landless peasants, and dry land farmers—lacked the capital or the means to borrow enough money to grow the new crops. Not only were they not able to reap the benefits of the increased food production, but they were actually hurt by it since the increased yield lowered the market price for grain crops and this meant a lower income for the peasant who still toiled in the traditional mode of farming. The Green Revolution thus made the rich richer and the poor poorer.

The mechanization of farming, meaning primarily the increased use of tractors, had a similar effect. On the one hand, it contributed to a rise of food production, but on the other hand, it benefitted only those who could afford or could finance the expensive new equipment, and it brought greater hardship to the poorer peasants. Specifically, the use of farm tractors greatly reduced the need for farm laborers, and by eliminating many jobs it increased the ranks of the unemployed. More and more of the impoverished villagers of India were reduced to collecting firewood and animal droppings to sell as fuel. Even progress sometimes breeds poverty.

One of the consequences of the dislocation of the landless in the countryside has been the overcrowding of Indian cities. Many of those who migrate to the cities join the ranks of the unemployed and find life little better there than in the villages they left. Large cities such as Calcutta and Bombay are teeming with hungry and homeless people, many of whom literally live and die in the streets. It is estimated that, in the mid–1980s, in Calcutta, with a population of about 11 million, there were about 900,000 people living in the streets without shelter.

■ INDIA'S ECONOMIC MODERNIZATION

India's efforts to modernize its economy and increase industrial production have met with moderate success. India has a mixed economy, whereby major industries such as iron and steel, mining, transportation, and electricity have been nationalized, that is, owned and operated by the government. The government instituted its First Five-Year Plan for economic development in 1951. Its relatively modest goals for increased industrial output were attained, and it was followed by a sequence of such five-year plans. In 1961, at the conclusion of the Second Five-Year Plan, Prime Minister Jawaharlal Nehru admitted that his country "would need many more five-year plans to progress from the cow dung stage to the age of atomic energy."[8] While some impressive large-scale, modern industrial plants have been built, most of India's industry is still small in scale and lacking modern machinery.

The overall growth rate of India's economy has been steady but yet insufficient. Since independence in 1947, India has maintained an average annual growth rate of GNP of between 3 and 4 percent.[9] One result of its modest industrial growth has been a widening of the gap between the urban rich and the poor. There is a large gap between the incomes of the educated elite, technicians, and skilled laborers in the modern sector on the one side, and the unskilled laborers and peasants in the traditional sector—not to mention the many unemployed or underemployed city dwellers—on the other.

India is handicapped by most of the problems of Third World countries: lack of capital, a difficulty in attracting foreign capital, illiteracy, and a lack of technology. To this one might add social conservatism—the weight of tradition, especially a religious tradition around which much of Indian life is centered. The remnants of the ancient caste system militate against social mobility and the advancement of all members of society. Ethnic and linguistic diversity is also an obstacle to economic modernization. Still another factor that has retarded India's economic growth is the continual "brain drain" it has experienced. Many of its best foreign-trained scientists and engineers have chosen not to return home with their talents in favor of remaining in Western countries, which provide career opportunities and creature comforts that are not matched in their native land.

One important prerequisite for economic development is the existence of a market, either a domestic or foreign. In India, the poverty of the masses means a lack of purchasing power and thus the lack of a domestic market. India strives to increase its exports of raw materials and manufactured goods in order to pay for its large volume of imports, a substantial portion of which has consisted of petroleum, foodstuffs, and industrial equipment. Given the impact of the oil crisis, and global inflation and recession, India has found it virtually impossible to maintain a favorable balance of trade. It has been unable to match the increased cost of its imports with its substantially increased exports. Over the years, its trade deficit, its need of capital to finance continued industrialization, and its periodic food shortages have forced India to rely heavily on foreign loans. In the 1950s and 1960s, India received huge shipments of food grains, mainly from the United States. However, since the late 1960s India has not needed such food relief, and it has in fact become a net exporter of food in the early 1980s. After U.S. developmental aid was terminated in 1971, the Soviet Union became India's primary source of foreign aid. India has also received substantial amounts of developmental aid and assistance from other sources, such as Japan, the World Bank, and the Asian Bank. India remains a debtor nation with an unfavorable balance of trade, but its recent economic growth has resulted in a substantially reduced annual debt.

Political stability is a very important asset for developing nations, and this is one asset that India has had. The nation has retained a functioning parliamentary system, an institution inherited from the British. It has also had prolonged rule by one dominant party, the Congress party, and continuity of leadership in the persons of Jawaharlal Nehru, who ruled from independence (1947) until his death in 1964; his daughter, Indira Gandhi, who ruled from 1966 to 1984 (except for one brief interlude); and her son, Rajiv Gandhi, who succeeded her.

Political stability in a country with such widespread poverty and with such ethnic diversity is quite a feat. After gaining independence, India's leaders have been confronted with the monumental task of binding together in nationhood the numerous subgroups of diverse ethnic and religious back-

Indian Prime Minister Rajiv Gandhi. Former pilot who succeeded his mother, Indira Gandhi, as prime minister in Oct. 1984. (*Courtesy of the Embassy of India*)

grounds. They have, for example, skillfully pacified the separatist movement of the Dravidian-language-speaking peoples of southern India. The mid-1980s did, however, witness considerable communal violence between Hindus and Sikhs, a large religious minority group in northern India, have launched a separatist movement. Their secessionist cause was dramatized by the assassination of Prime Minister Indira Gandhi in October 1984 by Sikhs, but in return they suffered bloody retaliation at the hands of angry Hindu mobs.

■ INDIA, PAKISTAN, AND BANGLADESH

India's foreign relations have not been peaceful, despite the "live and let live" neutralist policy pursued by Prime Minister Nehru in the 1950s. Nehru's efforts to exert the moral influence of India as a neutral peacemaker in the early Cold War years were noteworthy and gained him considerable international prestige, but it did little to help the country in its troubled relations with its neighbors. India's conflicts with Pakistan and China served to undermine its neutralist diplomacy and necessitated large military expenditures, which drained its meager resources.

Indian-Pakistani relations were strained from the time of partition and became rapidly worse as the two feuded over disputed territory. Both claimed the remote mountainous state of Kashmir. In 1948 and in 1949, despite United Nations efforts to keep peace, their forces clashed over this issue. India managed to secure its control of Kashmir, and it turned a deaf ear to Pakistan's continual demands for a plebiscite in Kashmir. The Pakistani claim to sparsely populated Kashmir was based on the fact that the majority of its people are Muslim, and this explains why Pakistan wished to settle the matter with a plebiscite. India's claim rested mainly on the expressed will of the local ruler of Kashmir to remain within India.

India was confronted by a more formidable foe in Communist China over still another territorial dispute in the Himalayas. Both China and India laid claim to the southern slopes of the Himalayan mountains north of the Assam plain, each staking its claim on different boundaries drawn by British surveyors in the nineteenth century in this remote mountainous area. India took the position that its claim was non-negotiable and turned down repeated diplomatic efforts by Beijing to settle the issue. In 1962, India's forces suffered a humiliating defeat at the hands of China in a brief border war.

While India was still recovering from this setback, and not long after the death of its highly revered ruler, Prime Minister Nehru, Pakistan decided to seek a military solution to the Kashmiri issue. After tensions had mounted as skirmishes along the disputed border occurred with increasing frequency, Pakistan's forces crossed the cease-fire line in August 1965, and the conflict quickly escalated into a major war. India again rallied to defeat the Pakistanis. Both sides had been fortified with modern weapons purchased mainly from the United States. U.S.-built jet fighters battled each other, some bearing Pakistani insignias and flown by Pakistani pilots, the others bearing Indian insignias and Indian pilots.

It was at this point that Indian-Pakistani conflicts began to take on important global dimensions, because each side had lined up the support of the superpowers. India rebuked the United States for supplying arms to its enemy. The United States had been selling modern weapons to Pakistan since 1954 (under terms of the Bagdad Pact), and it increased its military aid to that country after the 1965 war. Consequently, India increasingly turned to the Soviet Union, which was only too willing to provide support to a new client and extend its influence in this region. Pakistan had in the meantime found another friend, the People's Republic of China. Ironically, the supporters of Pakistan—the United States and the PRC—were bitter Cold War foes in these years.

*   *   *

Before turning to the next round of conflict, we need to take note of Pakistan's progress and problems. Pakistan was probably even worse off than India in terms of economic development, overpopulation, and poverty. Much of what was said about India's plight and the causes for it applies, in general, to Pakistan as well. But Pakistan was beset by additional problems stemming from its peculiar condition of being a nation of two separate parts. West Pakistan, where the capital was located, was separated from East Pakistan by about 800 miles of Indian territory. But the distance between the two parts was even greater culturally and politically. The people of East Pakistan were Bengalis who had very little in common, except for their Muslim religion, with the West Pakistanis who are made up of several ethnic groups, the largest of which is Punjabi.

The two parts of Pakistan were unbalanced politically in favor of West Pakistan, and this produced a sense of grievance in East Pakistan. Political and military power were concentrated in the West, despite the fact that the more densely populated East contained over half of the nation's population. East Pakistan was one of the nation's five provinces and thus had only 20 percent of the seats in the Pakistani parliament. Moreover, only about 35 percent of the national budget was earmarked for East Pakistan. The Bengalis also argued that East Pakistan was being treated as a captive market for West Pakistan. For these reasons the Bengalis in overcrowded East Pakistan felt victimized by their own government.

THE INDIAN SUBCONTINENT

Bengali frustration mounted until it erupted in late 1970, when East Pakistan was first hit by a horrible natural disaster and then a man-made disaster. In November that year, a powerful cyclone struck, followed by an enormous tidal wave and widespread flooding. This catastrophe left approximately 200,000 people dead and 1 million homeless. The lack of effective government relief measures provided irate Bengalis with further evidence of their government's indifference toward the problems of East Pakistan, thus feeding the flames of Bengali separatism. While still suffering the prolonged effects of the flooding, East Pakistan fell victim to a disaster of an entirely different kind: an assault by the military forces of West Pakistan.

The military regime of General Yahya Khan called for an election in December 1970 for a National Assembly to draft a new constitution for Pakistan and thus bring to an end some thirteen years of military rule. In the election, Sheikh Mujibur Rahman, the Bengali leader and head of the Awami League, a political party that stood for elevating the status of East Pakistan, won a large majority. General Khan and Zulfikar Ali Bhutto, head of the leading West Pakistan-based party, were shocked by the election results and conspired to block the scheduled convening of the National Assembly. Consequently, the Bengalis of East Pakistan began to stir, but their protest demonstrations were met with a military crackdown and the imposition of martial law. Sheikh Mujibur, who was solidly supported by the Bengali people, met General Khan and Bhutto for talks aimed at resolving the political crisis, but he refused to yield to their demands. As a showdown was approaching in March 1971, General Khan unleashed a military attack on East Pakistan, striking first at the leaders of the Awami League and placing Mujibur under arrest. Thus began the bloody suppression of the Bengali people in which ultimately some 3 million people of East Pakistan met their deaths at the hands of a Pakistani army of 70,000. This indiscriminate brutality in turn caused more violent resistance by the Bengalis who now demanded independence. Meanwhile, large numbers of the terrorized Bengali people began fleeing their ravaged homeland and crossed over the borders into India. Some 10 million refugees fled to India, placing a great strain on that nation's limited resources.

The military assault on East Pakistan was met by Bengali armed resistance, which took the form of guerrilla warfare, and soon the conflict became a full-fledged civil war. In December 1971, India entered into the fray and after two weeks of intensive combat, it forced Pakistan's surrender in the east. India had seized an opportunity to deliver a blow against its longtime foe by intervening on the side of the Bengalis, whose cause for independence the Indian government supported. The result, after nine months of bitter struggle and approximately a half million casualties (on all sides), was another victory for India over Pakistan and the birth of a new nation: Bangladesh.

This South Asian struggle, like most wars fought in the Third World, had an important Cold War dimension. The United States felt obliged to stick by its ally, Pakistan, and it, therefore, opposed the independence movement that created Bangladesh, despite the widely reported Pakistani brutality. During the war the United States denounced India for aggression and terminated economic aid to India. This and the support of the People's Republic of China for Pakistan caused India to strengthen its ties with the Soviet Union. In August 1971, India and the Soviet Union signed a twenty-year pact of friendship. In effect, the United States lost ground in a regional Cold War battle to its Soviet adversary. The United States delayed recognizing the new state of Bangladesh until May 1972 and delayed for about as long sending shipments of economic aid, which Bangladesh desperately needed. For its part, the PRC withheld recognition of the new nation until 1975 and all the while vetoed Bangladesh's efforts to gain admission to the United Nations.

The impact of the 1971 war was more profound on the nations directly involved. India's victory was more decisive than in previous wars with Pakistan, and its national security was greatly enhanced by the severity of Pakistan's loss as well as by its new ties with the Soviet Union. Within India, Prime Minister Indira Gandhi's popularity was immensely strengthened by success in this war, and this served her well in upcoming elections. For Pakistan, the 1971 war had a sobering effect. Now limited to what had been West Pakistan and with a population reduced by more than half, Pakistan turned to the task of rehabilitation and reorganization. Military government was ended when General Yahya Khan resigned and transferred power to Bhutto, whose Pakistan People's party had come in second in the December 1970 election. One of Bhutto's first acts was to release Sheikh Mujibur from prison and arrange his return to Bangladesh, where he was to take up rule as president of the new country. Bhutto also saw the wisdom of reducing tensions in his country's relations with India, and for that purpose he agreed to a meeting with Indira Gandhi in 1972. Indian-Pakistani relations were substantially improved by the diplomacy of the two leaders, at least until May 1974 when India successfully tested a nuclear device. By demonstrating its nuclear capacity, India established even more conclusively its position as the dominant power in South Asia, but at the same time it aroused Pakistani fears.

Bangladesh, born of disaster, has yet to overcome it. Independence produced no miracles. After the war, India ordered the return of the 10 million refugees, and when these people began pouring back into their ravaged homeland they found little that could support them. The catastrophic flood damage and war destruction had left the country devastated and unable to cope with the continuing wave of starvation, disease, and death that followed. Mujibur's government was confronted not only with a destitute people but also with crime, corruption, and general disorder. A state of emergency was proclaimed in 1974, and the once popular Mujibur was killed in a military coup in 1975. In the years that followed, political instability was prolonged by feuds between military factions contending for power.

The grinding poverty of this overpopulated land seems beyond remedy. No larger than the state of Georgia, Bangladesh is the homeland of over 90 million people (the eighth most populous nation in the world). There is simply too little land to support the swollen population. About 90 percent of the people live in the countryside, and about half of them own less than an acre of land, an amount insufficient to feed the average household of six. To make matters worse, the monsoons dump such heavy amounts of rain on this delta country that it is virtually impossible to farm the flooded land for about four months of the year. And at times the land is hit by cyclones whose winds and torrential rains cause extensive flooding and death and destruction on an enormous scale. Floods and famine, year after dismal year, appear to be the fate of Bangladesh. It is little wonder that many of the desperate people of Bangladesh flee their harsh homeland in quest for a more secure life in neighboring India. But India is itself overpopulated, especially in the state of Assam, which borders Bangladesh, and cannot support the unwanted refugees. India has in fact contemplated a most unlikely and costly strategy to keep these people from pouring into its territory: erecting a large barrier, a wire fence, around Bangladesh. Clearly there is a limit to India's neighborliness.

■ SOUTH ASIA IN THE 1980s

The decade of the 1980s brought to the Indian subcontinent a measure of economic growth, a modest reduction in the rate of population growth, and improvement in the standard of living. In both India and Pakistan, one could witness the steady growth of industry, increased urban construction, greater agricultural output, and the expansion of the small middle class. Yet both countries remained among the poorest in the world in terms of per capita GNP, which in 1987 was $300 for India and $350 for Pakistan. The abysmal poverty of peasant villagers and many city dwellers continued.

Both countries were on the threshold of breaking out of the ranks of poorest of nations. But to do this they must bring under control their population growth rates, which are threatening their economic futures. Family planning programs of past years have had scant success. As a result, family planners were hoping for a feminist revolt against the grain of societies dominated by men.[11]

Soon after coming to power in 1984, Indian Prime Minister Rajiv Gandhi nudged his country away from the system of state economic planning, which had greatly restricted imports, established over three decades earlier by his grandfather, Jawaharlal Nehru. The new policy meant a freer market, the growth of light industry, and the growth of the middle class. Indian manufactures and merchants rushed to produce goods for the expanding middle class whose buying power increased significantly. The new consumerism contributed to the continued rise in the nation's economic growth rate, which over the decade averaged about 5 percent annually.

Yet, India was still beset by such persistent problems as a gross maldistribution of wealth and an equally disproportional distribution of land. More than 300 million people—over one-third of the population—still lived below the poverty line. Wealthy landowners did not farm their land intensively, and because no thorough land reform was attempted, the productive potential of the countryside was not fully realized.

Another problem was the separatist movement of the Sikhs in the northern state of Punjab and the repressive measure Gandhi used in response to it. The Sikhs, whose religion is a mixture of Hinduism and Islam, make up about 2 percent of India's population, but they are the majority in Punjab. The brutal raid by the government security forces on the Sikh's Golden Temple in Amritsar in June 1984 left 1,200 dead and as many taken prisoner. Since then, the Sikhs have been unrelenting in their demand for an independent state to be called Khalistan, and the Indian police have been overzealous in their effort to ferret out Sikh militants, sometimes taking the law into their own hands by torturing and even murdering suspects. Thousands of Sikhs became political prisoners held with neither charges nor trials. In May 1987, after four months of escalated violence during which over 500 Sikhs were killed by security officers, Gandhi imposed direct federal rule over Punjab and ousted the elected state government of Sikh moderates.

In November 1989, the Congress party was narrowly defeated in the parliamentary election, and Rajiv Gandhi resigned as prime minister. He was succeeded by V. P. Singh, an experienced politician who led an alliance of opposition parties. Singh ran his campaign as a populist crusading against the arrogance and corruption of Gandhi's government. His earlier experience as finance minister in Gandhi's cabinet in the mid-1980s augured well for continued economic growth under his rule, but the fragile coalition on which his administration was based limited his power. The peaceful transfer of power on the basis of free elections, however, was testimony to the maturity of Indian democracy.

Pakistan, too, witnessed political change at the end of the 1980s. Through most of the decade, Pakistan remained under the rule of military strongman General Mohammed Zia ul-Haq. General Zia turned a deaf ear to critics calling for a return to civilian rule, citing the national emergency presented by the ongoing war in Afghanistan on

Pakistan's western border. The influx of thousands of refugees from that war-ravaged country strained the economy and threatened internal security. In addition to this burden, General Zia pointed to the persistent threat of Indian aggression, which remained a Pakistani obsession.

Military rule came to an abrupt end, however, in August 1988, when General Zia died in an airplane explosion—an apparent assassination—and parliamentary elections were held in November to return the country to civilian rule. The result of those elections was a stunning victory for Benizar Bhutto as the new prime minister. The 35-year-old Bhutto became the first female head of government of an Islamic state. She is the daughter of Zulfikar Ali Bhutto, Pakistan's last civilian ruler, who was deposed in 1974 and executed in 1979 by the same General Zia whom she now succeeded. After returning early in 1988 from extended exile, the British-educated Bhutto led a national movement against Zia. Her popularity carried over to the November election, in which her party won a narrow victory.

Bhutto's grip on power was tenuous from the beginning because she had only a slight parliamentary plurality and because the opposition parties, the military, and the conservative clergy all were watchful lest she make a slip. Her task was nothing less than ruling a nation beset with all the problems of the Third World and at the same time satisfying the military, who remained distrustful of her efforts to sustain democratic rule. She endeavored to steer a careful course between delivering promised increases in social spending and an austerity program required by international lending agencies for desperately needed loans. During her first year in power, her government played a key role in negotiating the terms by which the Soviet military withdrew from neighboring Afghanistan, while officially maintaining Pakistani support for Afghan rebels based in Pakistan.

■ THE FOUR TIGERS OF ASIA

Along the Asian shores of the Pacific Ocean are five prospering nations: Japan, South Korea (the Republic of Korea), Taiwan (the Republic of China), Hong Kong, and Singapore. Foremost among them as an economic power is Japan, whose economic miracle was launched in the early 1960s. (Japan will be treated in Chapter 16.) The others, sometimes referred to as "little Japans," or as the "four tigers of Asia," followed in Japan's footsteps in the 1970s and 1980s to produce their own economic miracles. Their economic performance, especially their vigorous export-oriented industrial development, together with that of

Japan, gave rise in the 1980s to such notions as the coming "Asian-Pacific century," and to the concept of the "Pacific Rim" (or alternately the "Pacific Basin") as the arena of the world's fastest economic growth and largest international trade flows. The four tigers of Asia became the source of a flood of imports into the United States and a major source of its mounting trade deficit. The U.S. trade gap with the four countries grew from $3.6 billion in 1980 to over $35 billion in 1987, an imbalance that caused strains in the relations between them and Washington.

South Korea, Taiwan, Hong Kong, and Singapore all share with Japan certain common features that account for their remarkable economic performance. They all share a Chinese historical and cultural heritage, and particularly an ingrained Confucian value system. It would appear that this philosophy—long ridiculed by the West (and by westernized Asians) as antiquated and a barrier to modern progress—is a major source of traits and attitudes that account for the high productivity of Asian workers and the efficiency of Asian management. Inculcated in the youth of those countries that share the Confucian heritage are such traits as discipline, loyalty, respect for authority, paternalism, desire for harmony, sincerity, a strong sense of duty, and respect for education. The Confucian legacy seems to be a vital ingredient for making capitalism work in these Asian nations.

There are, no doubt, other factors involved in the economic success of the four tigers, including the inspiring model of Japan and the investments and technology flowing from Japan. Still another major cause of the growth of these countries was their ready supply of relatively cheap labor. Moreover, each of these countries had authoritarian governments, which, while curbing democratic development, made economic development their highest priority and marshalled the power of the state toward that end. Their rulers centralized power and economic planning, enforced political stability (the exception of South Korea to be noted below), and mobilized human resources effectively. All four of these Asian countries, as newly industrializing countries (NICs), stressed export-oriented industrial development and took advantage of the global free trade system established by the industrialized nations of the West after World War II. They also emphasized public education, the development of technology, and birth control.[12]

The two most successful of the four tigers, South Korea and Taiwan, have several common characteristics that set them apart from the other two, Singapore and Hong Kong, which are small city-states. Both South Korea and Taiwan thrived on adversity. Both countries were highly militarized, each being confronted with threats to their security, from Communist North Korea and from the Communist mainland, respectively. The maintenance of large military establishments and the burden of large military budgets may be seen as a drag on economic development, but it seems that they also had the effect of spurring economic modernization. Moreover, the presence of a threat to the nation produced a sense of national urgency and national purpose useful to these governments and government-supported industrialists as well. One can detect in the recent historical experience of South Korea and Taiwan another similar pattern whereby authoritarian governments began to give way to democratization after the achievement of economic modernization and prosperity. Economic modernization gave rise to pluralism, particularly in the rise of an affluent middle class, which in turn demanded political liberalization and representation in the political process.

Table 13.1 Growth Rates of the Four Tigers (by percentage)

	1977–1981	1982–1986	1987	1988
South Korea	7.3	8.5	12.2	10.3
Taiwan	9.0	6.9	12.3	7.4
Hong Kong	10.8	5.9	13.5	7.1
Singapore	7.1	4.4	8.8	9.1

Sources: Bank of Japan, *Comparative International Statistics, 1988*; IMF, *International Financial Statistics, 1988*; and *The Wall Street Journal*, November 1, 1988, p. A24.

☐ South Korea

South Korea catapulted itself from the level of a miserably poor Third World nation in the 1950s to the level of a rapidly industrializing nation, which by the end of the 1980s was about to leave the category of a NIC. South Korea had suffered from the division of the Korean nation after World War II because most of the minerals and industries in the peninsula were located in North Korea, and it suffered all the more from the devastation of the Korean War in the early 1950s. Although it had at that time more paved roads and railroads (built by the Japanese before World War II) than most Third World countries, South Korea was an extremely impoverished nation. Gradually, living standards improved in the 1960s, and in the early 1970s the nation began its economic take-off. Its annual rate of economic growth rose to over 14 percent in the early 1970s, and after a brief slowdown in the early 1980s, it climbed again to the rate of 12 percent in 1986 and 1987. In 1964 the per capita GNP of South Korea was a mere $103, but by 1987 it had soared to $2,690, an incredible 25-fold increase in less than a quarter of a century. Only Japan and Taiwan matched this phenomenal record of economic growth.

South Korea's rise to economic prominence occurred during the rule of the dictatorial regimes of Park Chung Hee and Chun Doo Hwan. General Park, who came to power as a result of a military coup in 1960, dissolved the national assembly and established military rule. Three years later he resigned from the army and was elected president, but this hardly changed the character of his military dictatorship. With the help of generous economic aid from the United States and Japan, Park's government embarked on an industrialization drive led by giant state-supported industrial firms. Economic development was largely concentrated on Seoul, the capital, where living conditions improved, but poverty in the rest of the country remained endemic. Political unrest in the country continued, and in 1979, Park was shot and killed by his CIA chief.

After a brief power struggle, army General Chun Doo Hwan emerged as the new ruler of the country. Following the model of Park, Chun took off his military uniform to be inaugurated as president in September 1980 and continued military rule in civilian clothes. Korean students protested vehemently against the continuation of dictatorship, and in an uprising in the city of Kwangju in May 1980 as many as 200 student protesters were gunned down by security forces. Through the 1980s there was no letup in the student demonstrations, which at times became violent, although political repression diminished somewhat. All the while, South Korea continued to grow and prosper under the guiding hand of its new dictator.

The showcase of South Korea's emergence as a modern nation was to be the Summer Olympics in Seoul in September 1988. In anticipation of the event, there was great concern over the possible disruption of the games either by the mounting political unrest in the country or by acts of terrorism by the jealous North Koreans.[13] When President Chun rejected the pleas of opposition parties calling for new election rules to allow the direct election of the president, he was faced with still larger political demonstrations spearheaded by university students but joined now by many of the country's new middle class. Finally, to head off a bloody confrontation, which might result in the cancellation of the Olympics, Chun suddenly backed down. In June 1987, he appointed his Military Academy classmate, Roh Tae Woo, as his successor, and Roh announced a general election in December in which he would run as the ruling party's candidate for president. In that election, the first free presidential election in South Korean history, Roh won a narrow victory but only because the two popular opposition candidates, Kim Dae Jung and Kim Young Sam, split the opposition vote.

A political lull prevailed in the summer and fall of 1988 while South Korea basked in the international limelight of the Olympics. But the political rancor resumed soon afterward as Roh's opponents attacked his predecessor for corruption and demanded that he be put on trial. Meanwhile, students returned to the streets, now directing their protests at the continued presence of U.S. military forces in Korea and the Roh government's lame efforts toward seeking the reunification of Korea with the Communist regime in the North. The Roh government, however, kept its focus on managing the economy, tending to problems attendant to the nation's sudden prosperity, and readjusting its economic relations with the United States, which charged Seoul of unfair trade practices.

☐ Taiwan

The economic development of Republic of China on the island of Taiwan has been as spectacular as that of South Korea. The GNP of Taiwan rose from $8 billion in 1960 to $72.5 billion in 1986, and for most of the 1970s and 1980s it maintained double-digit growth rates. Taiwan's annual volume of foreign trade increased from $2.2 billion to $100 billion between 1969 and 1988. By virtue of its burgeoning exports it had accumulated by 1988 a foreign exchange reserve in excess of $70 billion, second in the world only to Japan. Within prosperous Taiwan, wealth is relatively evenly distributed, as all boats have risen with the tide.

Taiwan's economic success can be attributed to many factors, including (in addition to those discussed above) the infrastructure built on Taiwan by the Japanese before 1945, a quarter century of U.S. economic aid and an open U.S. import policy for Taiwan goods, an influx of highly educated Chinese from the mainland in 1949, the growth-oriented economic policies of the Nationalist government, and last but not least, the industrious Taiwanese people.

In the 1950s, a sweeping land reform was carried out and agricultural production grew steadily, paving the way for capital accumulation and investment in industrial development. By the 1960s, Taiwan's industries began shifting emphasis from producing goods for domestic consumption to export-oriented production. Lured by Taiwan's cheap and high-quality labor, U.S. and Japanese companies began making substantial investments, and Taiwanese industrialists and workers rapidly absorbed modern technology. In the late 1970s, Taiwan began making the shift to capital-intensive and knowledge-intensive industries, which paid huge dividends in the 1980s. By the end of the 1980s, electronics replaced textiles as the leading export, and Taiwan became the world's leader in microcomputers and computer parts.

Like South Korea, Taiwan's economic growth was not accompanied by political modernization; only in recent years has significant liberalization occurred. Although lauded for many years by the United States as the democratic alternative to the oppressive Communist regime on the mainland, "Free China" under Nationalist ruler Jiang Kaishek was anything but free or democratic. When Nationalist officials wrested control of Taiwan from the Japanese after World War II, they were met with resistance by the native Taiwanese, and this resistance was brutally suppressed by the Nationalist army.[14] After arriving on the island in 1949 with almost 2 million soldiers and civilian supporters, Jiang created the political myth according to which the Nationalist government (the Republic of China), now situated in the city of Taipei, remained the only legitimate government of China; and the island of Taiwan, as one province of China, had its own provincial administration. The National Assembly, for example, was comprised entirely of Nationalist party politicians who had been elected on the mainland in 1948, and it would remain without Taiwanese representation until the 1980s. In this manner, Jiang and his Nationalist party maintained thorough domination of the Taiwanese majority (then about 13 million) for the next four decades. Over these years, Jiang, until his death in 1975, and his son, Jiang Jingguo, who succeeded him, maintained the Nationalist myth and ruthlessly suppressed all opposition. Their regime remained stridently anti-Communist and remained ever vigilant against either Communist subversion or the outlawed Taiwan independence movement.

A political thaw finally occurred in the mid-1980s, made possible by the new prosperity, social change, the spread of education, and the regime's increased confidence in domestic security. In 1986, a newly formed opposition party, although still illegal, was permitted to run candidates for the National Assembly election, and it won 25 percent of the popular vote.[15] In July 1987, the Nationalist government finally lifted the martial law decree that had been in effect for 38 years, paving the way for the legalization of opposition political parties and greater freedom of speech and press. In October, the government dropped the ban on travel to Communist China, for the first time permitting its citizens to visit families on the mainland. Officially, the "Three No" policy of "no contact, no negotiations and no compromise" with the PRC remained intact, but tens of thousands quickly took advantage of the lifting of the travel ban.

Jiang Chingkuo died in January 1988, thus ending the sixty-year Jiang dynasty. He was succeeded by his vice-president, Lee Teng-hui. This represented an important change, mainly because Lee was not a mainland Chinese but a Taiwanese. Although he did not advocate independence for Taiwan, the fact that a Taiwanese was now president gave encouragement to those who did. Moreover, Lee, without a strong power base of his own, could hardly revert to the strongman type of rule characteristic of the Jiang dynasty. Instead, Lee continued the political liberalization begun by Jiang. In the December 1989 National Assembly elections the new opposition party, now a legal political party, won 40 percent of the popular vote. This was the first free two-party election in China's history, and it was conducted relatively cleanly, with 78 percent of the electorate participating.

☐ Hong Kong

The British crown colony of Hong Kong has long been a mecca of capitalism, and it too, has experienced phenomenal economic growth in the post–World War II era. Britain's "gunboat diplomacy" had pried it away from China in the nineteenth century, and it remained in British control even after the Communists came to power in China. In its early years, the PRC was too weak militarily to attempt to recover Hong Kong by force, and it eventually took a pragmatic rather than a doctrinaire view of the British presence there, deciding that it represented not a threat to China, but an opportunity to maintain profitable economic relations with the West.

The British governors of Hong Kong maintained political stability and presided over a prospering economy. Hong Kong steadily developed as a major financial, trade, and insurance center, and by the 1980s it also became highly industrialized. The thriving business environment of Hong Kong attracted huge investments from Western countries and Japan, stimulating still more its economic growth. Its average annual rate of growth was about 10 percent through the 1970s and 1980s, and rose as high as 13.5 percent in 1987. Although Hong Kong had a large number of poor people, mainly recent arrivals from the PRC, its per capita GNP reached $8,070 in 1987. The central section of the city-state became resplendent with wealth, with gleaming skyscrapers soaring above and the streets below crowded with Mercedes-Benz automobiles and free-spending shoppers.

The single threat to Hong Kong's continued prosperity and economic stability was the fact that it was scheduled to revert to Chinese rule in 1997. As early as the 1970s, when that target date was still twenty years away, both the British and the Chinese governments began to plan for the reversion. International business interests became nervous about their investments, and in order to head off a flight of capital and financial chaos, the British government was eager to secure an early agreement with the Chinese government for an orderly transition. Similarly, it was in the PRC's interest to maintain the financial strength of Hong Kong, since it played an important role in China's economic modernization.

After long negotiations, London and Beijing signed a joint declaration in 1984 providing a framework for the Chinese takeover, still thirteen years away. The agreement stipulated that Hong Kong was to retain its capitalist system while maintaining "a high degree of autonomy" as a "special administrative region" of the People's Republic for fifty years after the reversion in 1997. With this formula, the Chinese and British sought to preserve political and economic stability through 1997 and beyond. The agreement also stipulated that the ethnic Chinese citizens of Hong Kong (98 percent of the population) were to become citizens of China at the time of reversion, but that they were free to leave the colony prior to that.

The reversion agreement had mixed results by the end of the 1980s. Economic growth did not decline appreciably and foreign investments, in fact, increased dramatically in recent years.[16] But if foreign investors remained confident of Hong Kong's future, its residents were much less confident. In 1988, 50,000 people emigrated from Hong Kong (mainly to Canada, Australia, and the United States), almost twice the number who left the previous year and four times the number in 1986. This exodus of Hong Kong residents, mainly wealthy, well-educated elites, reflected a fear of Chinese rule. It caused consternation in Beijing, which has sought to reassure the people in the colony and avert the hemorrhage of wealth and talent. The bloody suppression of the prodemocracy movement in Tienanmen Square in June 1989 and the subsequent political repression carried out by the Chinese government did further damage to its credibility in Hong Kong and caused an even greater rate of emigration.

☐ Singapore

Singapore is also a city-state and it was also a former British colony, but it won its independence in 1964. Located at the southern tip of the Malay peninsula in the South China Sea, Singapore is a member of ASEAN,[17] but unlike the other ASEAN nations, its population is mainly ethnic Chinese. It is also far more wealthy than the other ASEAN nations. Under its authoritarian ruler, Lee Kuan Yew, Singapore became one of the most prosperous countries in Asia, with a per capita GNP of almost $8,000 in 1987. A combination of political stability, population growth control, high standards of education, a disciplined and skilled work force, efficient economic management, export-oriented planning, and a free market system have worked miracles for its 2.5 million people. Strategically situated at the center of the Southeast Asian sea lanes, Singapore became a conveyor belt for shipment of goods from outside the region to neighboring ASEAN countries and a major regional financial center.

Singapore's remarkable economic development is also largely due to the leadership of Prime Minister Lee Kuan Yew, whose dictatorial rule extends far beyond conventional bounds of politics and economics. Lee has endeavored to make Singapore a spotless, crime-free, morally upright and austere society, and toward that end he has taken it upon himself to dictate social and moral standards and enforce them with strict laws and strong penalties. He has, for example, decreed that men are not to allow their hair to grow long, and offenders are subject to arrest, fines, or even imprisonment. Possession of drugs, even the smallest amount, is punishable by death. Nor has Lee, who has exercised unlimited authority in Singapore since the late 1950s, allowed dissent. He has maintained that the product of the curbs on individual freedoms is not regimentation, but rather a more disciplined and productive people, whose work habits contribute to higher productivity and the betterment of all in the society.

■ DICTATORSHIP AND REVOLUTION IN THE PHILIPPINES

While the four tigers prospered and ASEAN nations began registering impressive economic growth in the 1980s, the Philippines fell behind. This island nation, once a Spanish and then a U.S. colony since 1898, had struggled since gaining independence in 1946 to sustain economic growth and maintain a semblance of democratic institutions. Under a succession of autocratic rulers, the Philippines lost ground on both fronts, especially during the 20-year-long rule of Ferdinand Marcos. When Marcos came to power in 1965, the country was developing at a pace with South Korea, Taiwan, and Singapore. When Marcos was driven from power in 1986, those nations had per capita incomes three or four times higher than that of the Philippines. By 1986, the country had a foreign debt of $27 billion, and it had been unable to make a payment on the principal of that debt since 1983. The GNP had fallen by over 25 percent since 1982, unemployment had risen to over 20 percent, and inflation to 70 percent. Corruption was rampant.[18]

At the center of mismanagement and corruption was Marcos himself. He had been elected president in 1965 as a social reformer, but he soon succumbed to the pattern of patron-client corruption common to Filipino political tradition, and he proved to be a master at it.

Governing the Philippines became so lucrative for Marcos that he made certain that he would stay in power despite a constitution that permitted only two four-year terms for president. As the end of his second term approached, he declared martial law, citing a mounting Communist insurgency and an economic crisis as the justification for cancelling elections, suspending the constitution, and writing a new one giving him broad powers. He also rounded up and jailed political opponents and critical journalists. Entrenched in power, Marcos then stole the nation blind, raking off protection payments from wealthy sugar growers and pocketing foreign aid.

Marcos promoted himself as the nation's indispensable leader, claimed to be a lawyer who had never lost a case, a heroic military officer who had never lost a battle, a lover who had won the heart of the nation's beauty queen, a great athlete and marksman, a good father, a good Catholic, and an honest and modest man. His wife, Imelda, had in fact been a former Miss Philippines, and her popularity was an added attraction in her husband's cult of power. Successive administrations in Washington turned a blind eye to what was taking place and honored Marcos as a stalwart opponent of Communism and a champion of democracy.[19] Washington remained tolerant as long as Marcos provided political stability considered necessary to protect substantial U.S. financial investments in the Philippines and to retain the two mammoth U.S. military installations in the islands, Subic Naval Base and Clark Air Base, considered vital to U.S. strategic interests in Asia. Marcos skillfully traded assurances regarding the military bases for ever larger economic and military loans from Washington.

In the early 1980s, Marcos's regime began to unravel. In 1981, he released from prison his foremost political opponent, Benigno Aquino, to allow him to go to the United States for heart surgery. Aquino, the likely winner of the 1973 presidential election had it taken place, decided to end his exile in August 1983 in order to return home and lead a movement to overthrow the dictator. He was shot to death at the Manila airport even before setting foot on the tarmac. Responding to the outrage of the Filipinos, Marcos appointed a commission to investigate the murder of Aquino. After lengthy deliberations it reported that evidence pointed to a military conspiracy reaching all the way to the chief of staff, General Fabian Ver, a cousin of Marcos. The verdict of the eight-month trial that followed was predictable: Ver and the 24 other military defendants were acquitted. Meanwhile, a vigorous opposition movement developed that regarded the fallen Aquino as a martyr and his wife Corazon a saint. While Marcos was losing credibility at home and abroad, the economy deteriorated rapidly, largely because of the flight of capital triggered by the Aquino assassination. In the hinterlands, the Communist-led New People's Army stepped up its war.

In response to mounting pressure, the undaunted dictator, who had won every political battle thus far, announced in November 1985 his decision to hold a presidential election in February 1986. Aquino's wife, Corazon, had already stated she would run against Marcos should he allow an election. The stage was now set for an election that had all the makings of a morality play. Although the 68-year-old Marcos was visibly ill, suffering from a kidney disease, and was roundly attacked by the press, he remained confident of victory and appeared to be unfazed by the enormous throngs of people who rallied in support of his opponent. Aquino, who presented herself as Cory, a humble housewife, sought to redeem the legacy of her murdered husband and called for a return to democracy, decency, and justice.[20] As election day approached, it appeared that Cory's "people power" would surely sweep her to victory, if only the elections were fair. Big business and the middle class were abandoning Marcos, and the Roman Catholic Church openly supported Aquino. Many feared, however, that the cagey Marcos, who resorted to paying people to attend his political rallies during the campaign, would find ways to rig the voting to ensure his re-election.

No clear winner emerged from the election as both sides claimed victory and charged the other with fraud. Despite indisputable evidence of election interference by pro-Marcos bullies and fraudulent vote counting by the Marcos-appointed election commission, Marcos proceeded to declare himself the winner and to plan for inauguration ceremonies.[21] Meanwhile, at the encouragement of the Roman Catholic leader, Jaime Cardinal Sin, hundreds of thousands of people went into the streets to assert their support of Aquino and demand that Marcos step down. At this point, Marcos's defense minister and high-ranking officers decided to change sides. The climax came when the pro-Marcos troops advancing toward the rebel encampments were stopped by the human wall of Aquino supporters and Catholic nuns knelt in prayer in front of the stalled tanks. At that juncture, the Reagan administration bowed to the manifest will of the majority of the Filipino people and arranged for the fallen dictator to be airlifted to Hawaii. Marcos and his wife fled the country with billions of dollars they had stolen from the Filipino people. With the help of people power, the church, and her new military allies, Cory Aquino proclaimed victory for the democratic revolution.

After the exultation over the triumph against dictatorship, the hard realities of governing the nation and restoring its shattered economy had to be faced by the new inexperienced president. Aquino moved swiftly to restore civil rights, free political prisoners, rid pro-Marcos elements from the government, and enact political reforms. She had promised land reform during her campaign, but afterward showed little interest in the problem. The power of the old oligarchy and the old economic system remained intact. Instead of "reprofessionalizing" the army, as the United States advisors called it, she promoted officers who were personally loyal to her.[22] This policy proved to be a major cause of the numerous coup attempts staged by disgruntled forces. During the December 1989 coup, U.S. forces intervened on Aquino's behalf.

The Philippines was still saddled with its enormous $27 billion foreign debt, the payment of which consumed about one-third of the country's export earnings. In 1988, the country was granted a $10 billion developmental grant from the combined sources of the International Monetary Fund and several European and Asian nations, but to little avail. Affluence for the few and misery for the many remained the dominant theme. On the eve of Aquino's fourth anniversary in power in February 1990, people power was but a distant memory. She had lost support from all segments of the population.

The status of the two large U.S. military facilities at Subic Bay and Clark Air Base remained a controversial issue, as many nationalist groups saw them as an affront to Philippine sovereignty, a social blight, and targets in a nuclear war. Aquino promised, however, not to abrogate the agreement due to expire in September 1991, but she placed clauses in the new Philippine constitution calling for freedom from nuclear weapons on its territory and requiring that any extension of the lease agreement beyond 1991 be approved by a two-thirds majority of the Philippine senate.[23] Meanwhile, she accepted an interim agreement in October 1988, by which the United States boosted its annual military and economic aid to the Philippines to $481 million a year, two and a half times that pledged in the agreement of 1983.

■ RECOMMENDED READINGS

☐ China

Hinton, William. *Fanshen: A Documentary of Revolution in a Chinese Village.* New York: Monthly Review Press, 1966.
  An enthusiastic report on Maoism at work in the countryside in the early years of the revolution.
Hsu, Immanuel C. Y. *China Without Mao: The Search for a New Order.* New York: Oxford University Press, 1982.
  A fine study of the political passage from Mao to Deng.
Meisner, Maurice. *Mao's China and After: A History of the People's Republic.* New York: Free Press, 1986.

One of the best histories of Communist China since 1949, mainly because it assesses Chinese politics on its own Marxian terms.

Schell, Orville. *In the People's Republic.* New York: Random House, 1977.
The most lucid of the many eye-witness accounts by visitors after they were welcomed to travel in China in the early 1970s.

Wilson, Dick, ed. *Mao Tse-tung in the Scales of History.* New York: Cambridge University Press, 1977.
A composite view of Mao's leadership by various scholars; among the best books on Mao.

☐ India

Barnds, William J. *India, Pakistan and the Great Powers.* New York: Frederick A. Praeger, 1972.
A classic that examines the role of outside forces on the Indian subcontinent.

Bhatia, Krishan. *The Ordeal of Nationhood: A Social Study of India Since Independence, 1947– 1970.* New York: Atheneum, 1970.
A comprehensive study of the various problems that plagued modern India in its first two decades.

Brecher, Michael. *Nehru: A Political Biography.* London: Oxford University Press, 1959.
A standard biography of Nehru.

Brown, W. Norman. *The United States and India, Pakistan and Bangladesh.* 3d ed. Cambridge, Mass.: Harvard University Press, 1972.
A comprehensive study by one of the foremost Indian specialists in the United States.

Kangas, G. L. *Population Dilemma: India's Struggle for Survival.* London: Heinemann, 1985.
An excellent up-to-date analysis of India's population problem.

☐ East Asia

Gill, Rnajit, *ASEAN Coming of Age.* Singapore: Sterling Corporate Services, 1987.

Hofheinz, Roy, Jr., and Kent Calder. *The Eastasia Edge.* New York: Basic Books, 1982.
A comprehensive account of the surging economic growth of the various East Asian countries in recent decades.

Keon, Michael. *Korean Phoenix: A Nation from the Ashes.* Englewood Cliffs, N.J.: Prentice-Hall, 1977.
Analyzes the politics and economics of Korea's remarkable modernization since the 1950s.

■ NOTES

1. Immanuel C. Y. Hsu, *The Rise of Modern China* (New York, Oxford University Press, 1983), p. 804.

2. John F. Burns, "Canton Booming on Marxist Free Enterprise," *New York Times,* November 11, 1985, A 1.

3. Deng Xiaoping, as quoted in "China Calls Rigid Adherence to Marxism 'Stupid,'" *New York Times* December 9, 1984. This piece is based on an article which appeared as a front page commentary in the December 7, 1984, edition of the *People's Daily,* the official organ of the Chinese Communist party, and it can be assumed that it was written or approved by Deng Xiaoping.

4. John Schidlovsky, "Strike Gains Momentum in China," *Baltimore Sun*, April 25, 1989.

5. Nicholas D. Kristof, "Chinese Cast Gorbachev as Champion of Democracy," *New York Times*, May 13, 1989.

6. Scott Shane, "Gorbachev Praises China for 'Dialogue' with Demonstrators," *Baltimore Sun*, May 18, 1989.

7. The Chinese government would later take the position that no unarmed students were killed on Tienanmen Square, but that a total of 300 people died in the clash between the soldiers and the rebels, and that most of the dead were soldiers.

8. .The development of these new plants that produce more grain and less stem per plant was the result of years of scientific work financed by the Rockefeller and Ford foundations. The new high-yield variety of wheat was developed in the 1950s and the high-yield variety of rice in the 1960s. Under ideal conditions, the new rice plants produce twice as much grain per acre and reduce the growing period in half so that two crops can be grown in one growing season.

9. Jawaharlal Nehru, quoted in Stephen Warshaw and C. David Bromwell with A. J. Tudisco, *India Emerges: A Concise History of India from Its Origins to the Present* (San Francisco, Diablo Press, 1974), p. 132.

10. The World Bank, *World Development Report, 1984*. India's average annual rate of growth of GNP between 1955 and 1970 was 4.0 percent and in the decade of the 1970s it fell to 3.4 percent. The rate of growth of the GNP per capita for these two periods was 1.8 percent and 1.3 percent, respectively. More recent figures indicate an economic upturn in India in the 1980s with an annual growth rate around 5 percent.

11. Steve Coll, "Burgeoning Population Threatens India's Future," *Washington Post*, January 21, 1990, p. H7.

12. The World Health Organization rated Taiwan's birth control program first among developing nations in 1989, and Singapore rated second, South Korea third, and Hong Kong fifth. The PRC was fourth. "ROC Rated Top for Birth Curbs by World Group," *Free China Journal*, December 21, 1989.

13. The Communist regime of Kim Il Sung in North Korea had resorted to terrorist attacks on South Korea, the most shocking of which was the killing of several South Korean cabinet members in a bomb attack in Rangoon, Burma, in October 1973. Speculation was rife in the South that North Korea might even demolish a dam upstream on the Han River and flood Seoul prior to or during the Olympic games.

14. In February 1947, an anti-Nationalist uprising occurred, which was suppressed with enormous violence, leaving between 5,000 (the Nationalist figure) and 20,000 (the Taiwanese figure) native Taiwanese dead. Over the years, Jiang's government forbade anyone to speak of this massacre on the punishment of death.

15. The platform of the new party, the Democratic Progressive Party, called for full implementation of democracy, welfare, and self-determination for Taiwan.

16. "New Record Set in Exodus," *Free China Journal*, December 22, 1988.

17. The six members of ASEAN (Association of Southeast Asian Nations) are Singapore, Malaysia, Indonesia, Thailand, the Philippines, and Brunei. Founded in 1967 for the purpose of developing regional cohesion and cooperation, it has remained a loosely organized group and has not developed plans for either economic or political integration.

18. Rnajit Gill, *ASEAN Coming of Age* (Singapore: Sterling Corporate Services, 1987), pp. 126–127.

19. When Vice President George Bush visited the Philippines in 1981, after nine years of martial law, he told Marcos, "We [the U.S.] love your adherence to democratic principle and to the democratic process." William J. van Heuvel, "Postpone the Visit to Manila," *New York Times*, September 8, 1983.

20. Aquino did not hesitate to point the finger of blame on Marcos charging that "Mr. Marcos is the No. 1 suspect in the murder of my husband." "A Test for Democracy," *Time*, February 3, 1986, p. 31.

21. Marcos was emboldened by U.S. President Ronald Reagan who, while noting concern about charges of election fraud, accepted Marcos's claim to victory and stated that his administration wanted "to help in any way we can . . . so that the two parties can come together." William Pfaff, "The Debris of Falling Dictatorships," *Baltimore Sun*, February 17, 1986. Pfaff criticized Reagan's view as "a preposterous proposition, wholly irrelevant to what was happening on the scene."

22. Richard J. Kessler, "The Philippines," in Peter J. Schraeder, ed., *Intervention in the 1980s: U.S. Foreign Policy in the Third World* (Boulder: Lynne Rienner Publishers, 1989), pp. 231–233.

23. The constitutional provision outlawing nuclear weapons on its territory begged the question of enforcement, because the U.S. government maintained its standard position that it would neither confirm nor deny the presence of nuclear weapons on its bases.

☐ 14

The Third World's Debt: Africa and Latin America

The 1970s saw the emergence of a phenomenon with potentially serious international repercussions, the increasing indebtedness of the Third World to the industrial First World. Traditionally, nations seeking to develop their economies have relied upon capital from abroad. This has been true, for example, of the industrial revolutions in England, the Netherlands, the United States, and Russia.[1] Foreign capital—in the form of profits from sales abroad, loans, or capital investments—has long been a catalyst for speeding up the difficult process of industrialization.

It is little wonder that the emerging, developing economies of the Third World have sought this shortcut. But until the oil crises of the 1970s the reliance on foreign money had always been kept in bounds. The money borrowed from the First World was doled out in reasoned, and at times sparse, amounts—until the surfeit of "petrodollars" (that is, money invested in Western banks by the oil-rich nations) created a binge of lending by these same banks and an orgy of borrowing by the nations of the Third World. There appeared to be no limit to the banks' willingness to extend credit and for the recipients to take it. Foreign capital seemed to promise the road out of the wilderness: rapid economic development and, with it, the ability to repay the loans. By the mid–1980s, the consequence was a staggering debt of Latin American and African nations in excess of $500 billion, a sum far beyond the capacity of most of the debtor nations to repay.[2] Many are staring bankruptcy in the face, and should they default, they threaten to take down the road to ruin the lending institutions and the international banking system itself.

■ AFRICA

The African debt has its roots in the political instability that followed independence, which resulted in frequent government turnovers, secessionist movements, and civil wars. Among the first casualties were the budding democratic institutions. Military coups became the order of the day. Political and military considerations quickly began to take precedence over economic development, for the first priority of dictatorships has always been the retention of power. As such, precious resources were diverted to the military whose main task was not so much the defense of the nation against a foreign foe, but the suppression of domestic opposition.

One consequence of political instability in Africa was the flight of Europeans who took with them their skills and capital. This was the case particularly in the new states where independence was won by force and where a legacy of bitterness and mistrust remained after the violence had subsided. Algeria, Mozambique, Angola, Zimbabwe (formerly, Southern Rhodesia), and Kenya readily come to mind. South Africa, too, has seen the flight of whites as racial tensions were beginning to mount during the early 1980s. The result of this exodus left many African nations with a badly depleted industrial base and a continued reliance on the agricultural sector. Yet, Africa's agriculture remains the world's most primitive. Most of it consists of subsistence farming where women do most of the work.

Not only does the continent's agricultural sector suffer from inefficiency but it also suffers from two additional defects that have produced catastrophic consequences: desertification and a burgeoning population. The growing deserts of Africa are the result of two factors: (1) the lack of rainfall—at times over a period of several years; and (2) overgrazing and the cutting of trees in marginal lands by the rapidly growing population. The first condition is caused by nature and is thus beyond anyone's control; the second is caused by people.

The Sahara has steadily pushed its southern frontier into West Africa. Much of the Sahel, the steppe region of the southern Sahara, has over the past two decades been claimed by the desert. The desert has also pushed toward the east, particularly into Sudan, a nation on the brink of a disaster that threatens to rival the highly publicized famines of Ethiopia where millions have perished of starvation over the past two decades. The lack of rainfall has plagued nearly all of East Africa—from Somalia in the north to the Cape of Good Hope in South Africa. In these and other parts of Africa droughts have lasted for years and the land lost to the desert will not be readily reclaimed.

Until the late 1970s, the African economies limped along, but then the roof began to cave in when a number of conditions came together. The result was that much of the continent has been bankrupted. First came the oil crisis with its accompanying rise in the cost of crude oil. The crisis had a greater impact on the poorer nations than on the industrial West, which had the means of meeting the higher payments. (Although several oil producing nations of sub-Saharan Africa, such as Nigeria and Cameroon, benefitted from the new higher price tag on oil, most suffered greatly. And when oil prices began to fall in the early 1980s, Nigeria was among the hardest hit and became saddled with mounting debts and attendant political instability.) In the West, the oil crisis contributed to a global recession, which in turn lessened the demand for raw materials. The prices for copper, bauxite (aluminum ore), and diamonds fell. Prices for agricultural exports, the result of a worldwide surplus, fell similarly. The glut of agricultural commodities played havoc with the African economies. Cacao, coffee, cotton, peanuts, and such no longer brought the prices African exporters had been accustomed to. Since 1979–1980, prices for commodity exports have declined by as much as 30 percent. Yet, the prices for goods manufactured in the West—such as machinery, tools, electronics, and weapons—continued to rise.

Appreciation of foreign currencies, particularly the U.S. dollar, has added to the dilemma. Because the debts of nations are calculated in U.S. dollars, the increasing purchasing power of the dollar in the early 1980s played havoc with the pay rate of debtor nations. Debts now had to be repaid in dollars with greater purchasing power; it meant that Third World nations had to export more. In effect, this condition has forced African governments to repay more than they have borrowed.

Africa's indebtedness to the industrial world has increased considerably during the first half of the 1980s. The poorest continent has become a net exporter of money. In 1985 alone, African nations were required to pay $7 billion to banks and governments of the developed world. On average, African nations use 25 percent of their foreign currency earnings to repay their foreign debts. They are reaching the point where they are dismantling their social and economic development plans in order to meet their debt obligations. They are, in effect, cannibalizing their economies to meet their interest payments. Hope for a future resolution of the continent's dilemma has faded.

By 1987, these African nations had amassed the largest foreign debts:[3]

Nigeria	$28.7 billion
Sudan	11.1
Ivory Coast	13.5
Zaire	8.6
Zambia	6.4
Kenya	5.9
Tanzania	4.3

Africa's foreign debt in the mid–1980s stands between $150 billion and $170 billion. As such, Africa's debt is about half that of Latin America's which is over $360 billion. But Latin America's condition, as grim as it is, is not as hopeless as that of Africa's because of its stronger economic base. Africa has reached a point where it can no longer repay its debt, nor can it borrow any appreciable sums of money. (Not surprisingly, Nigeria, a major oil exporting nation, has been able to run up the largest debt—on the basis of its projected ability to repay its obligations.) On top of this, there has been no significant foreign investment in Africa since 1979–1980. The continent is on a treadmill, pledged to come up with interest payments over an indefinite period to the industrialized West and its banks. Under such circumstances, the indebtedness to the West remains indefinite, since there is, of course, no question of making a dent in the principal (i.e., the debt itself). Predictably, African leaders are pointing an accusing finger at the international banking system.

In July 1985, the African heads of government met under the aegis of the Organization of African Unity (OAU) in Addis Ababa, Ethiopia's capital, to address this bleak situation in the hope of finding economic and political solutions. The meeting ended with a surprisingly frank declaration that most African countries were on the brink of economic collapse. The declaration placed part of the blame on an "unjust and inequitable [international] economic system," but it also acknowledged that natural calamities such as droughts, as well as "some domestic policy shortcomings," had contributed to Africa's problems.

The chair of the OAU, Tanzanian President Julius Nyerere, hinted at the creation of a defaulter's club, which promised to seek, among other things, the cancellation of government-to-government loans and the restructuring of interest rates—all for the purpose of avoiding default (national bankruptcy).

■ LATIN AMERICA

Latin America has experienced problems similar to that of Africa. The economies took sharp downward turns during the late 1970s, and the reasons were not unlike those that caused problems in Africa. Latin American nations, too, remain heavily dependent upon agricultural export. The rapid increase in oil prices in the 1970s and the drop in agricultural commodity prices produced a sharp decline in the standard of living.

Latin America has long been a region of economic promise. This has been especially the case with Brazil, a land of seemingly unlimited potential, resources, and workers. On the basis of future earnings, the Brazilian government was able to borrow huge sums of money during the 1970s, an action that later came back to haunt it. By 1987, the foreign debt of Brazil stood well over $120 billion, an amount that appears to be beyond the country's capacity to repay. The best that Brazil can do is merely make the interest payments and in this fashion avoid a declaration of bankruptcy. The country's bankruptcy would threaten the international banking system, and for this reason, despite its staggering debt, Brazil has been able to demand additional loans until the time—sometime in the distant, nebulous future—when it will be able to begin to repay the principal. In the meantime, Brazil, like many of the African countries, remains beholden to the Western banks and governments. It is a prospect that does not point to a confident future.

Argentina is another Latin American nation that has accumulated a large foreign debt. Argentina has traditionally been a nation with a strong and vigorous economy, which has made it relatively easy for its governments to borrow money from abroad. But a succession of military regimes (1976–1983) contributed to the ruination of the nation's economy. The regimes' brutality (most notably the disappearance of thousands of political suspects) and a losing war with Great Britain over the Falkland Islands in 1983 brought about the return to civilian rule in 1983. At that time, Argentina's foreign debt was thought to have been at about $24 billion—a large sum by anyone's yardstick. The new civilian government discovered, however, that the military had in fact run up a debt of twice that figure. Argentina holds the dubious distinction of having the third largest foreign debt (after Brazil and Mexico) among the developing countries, an obligation of $48 billion.

Mexico is yet another case in point. In contrast to most Third World nations, the oil shortages of the late 1970s did not initially harm Mexico's economy. Instead, the shortages appeared to work to its benefit, for Mexico's oil reserves are potentially the world's largest. It was oil that promised to solve Mexico's economic problems, caused in part by its large and rapidly growing population, weak industrial base, and inefficient agricultural system. Mexico, like Brazil, was able to borrow large sums of money in the expectation that oil shortages and high oil prices would make it possible to repay the loans. In short, Mexico borrowed against future income. At the end of 1981, Mexico's foreign debt was at about $55 billion. Four years later, that figure had risen to well above $100 billion.

In 1987, these were Latin America's leading debtors, in billions of dollars:

Brazil	$124
Mexico	108
Argentina	57
Venezuela	37
Chile	21
Peru	18
Colombia	17

■ OPEC

The reason for the rapid rise of Mexico's debt was that, by the early 1980s, a global oil glut was in the making and the bottom of the market began to drop out. The surplus was the result of conservation, a worldwide economic recession (which lessened the demand for all fuels), the discovery of new deposits (on the north slope of Alaska and in the North Sea, as well as the Mexican contribution), a worldwide increase in production once prices rose, and the cold, hard fact that even during the shortages at the pump there had always been a surplus of oil.

The oil shortages had been artificially created in the 1970s by OPEC (the Organization of Petroleum Exporting Countries), led by Saudi Arabia, the shah of Iran, and the Western oil companies. The fourteen members of OPEC include all of the oil exporting states of the Middle East: Saudi Arabia, Iran, Iraq, the United Arab Emirates, Qatar, and Kuwait. The rest are the African states of Algeria, Libya, Nigeria, and Gabon; two South American nations: Venezuela and Ecuador; and Indonesia. Equally important are the oil exporting nations that do not belong to OPEC. They include the Soviet Union (among the world's leading exporters of oil for the past decade), Mexico, Great Britain, the United States, and Canada.

In 1973 OPEC conspired to limit the supply of oil available to the rest of the world; the result was a fifteen-fold increase in prices for crude oil by the end of the decade. During the 1970s, OPEC managed to dictate the price of oil by virtue of its dominance of the market and with it its ability to create shortages. In 1979, its members controlled 63.4 percent of the world's oil market. But all this began to change during the 1980s. By 1984, the figure had dropped to 42.8 percent; by 1985, it had fallen to 30 percent.

In 1985, as their world market share continued to decline, OPEC members, desperate for oil revenues, began to break ranks by surreptitiously selling more than their allotted quotas. The most important task before OPEC in the mid–1980s, therefore, was to reestablish discipline among its members and thus to regain the means to set the price for crude oil. But this has proved to be a difficult task.

The early 1980s brought renewed competition for the petrodollar, an end to the shortages, and a return to the laws of the marketplace. The laws of supply-and-demand ruined not only OPEC, but also the prospects of several nations that had banked on a prosperity based on the sale of a scarce commodity to a world addicted to the consumption of gasoline products. As an overabundance of supply drove down the price of oil, such countries as Mexico, Venezuela, and Nigeria became saddled with large foreign debts.

For years, Mexico (although not a member of OPEC) has sought to follow OPEC's pricing levels, but in the summer of 1985 it began to establish its own pricing policy in direct confrontation with OPEC. It lowered the price of a barrel of crude oil to about $24. The Soviet Union followed Mexico's example as it too lowered its price of oil, thus placing additional pressures on OPEC. OPEC, in its turn, tried to cut back on production to reestablish an artificial scarcity, but with little impact on prices. Instead, OPEC output declined to about 14.5 million barrels per day, the group's lowest level of production in twenty years. Saudi Arabia, the linchpin of OPEC, in order to maintain the level of the price of oil, dropped its production to 2.3 million barrels a day (almost half of its quota allotted by OPEC), its lowest level since 1967. By the end of the summer, however, Saudi Arabia had joined the price-cutting war. At the meetings of OPEC oil ministers in the summer of 1985 the debates centered around a Hobson's choice, the question of whether to cut prices or production. In the end, OPEC wound up doing both.

■ INSURMOUNTABLE DEBTS

In 1985, the combined Latin American debt stood at more than $360 billion; together, Brazil, Mexico, and Argentina owed in excess of $250 billion. Africa and Latin America combined owed more than $500 billion. A default by any one of the major nations of these regions threatens to trigger an economic crisis of worldwide repercussions, the consequences of which are impossible to predict. At the least, such action promises bank failures and the slowdown of international trade. At its worst, such a development could cause the most severe economic crisis in history—a calamity that is certain to produce an extraordinary political fallout, particularly in the regions the hardest hit, namely the Third World.

Third World countries have at times raised the specter of default, but they have been at pains to avoid such a drastic measure. Instead, they have sought to meet their obligations. When in early 1987 Brazil announced a halt in its foreign debt payments, its government was careful to spell out that this was a temporary emergency measure by which it hoped to find a solution eventually. Similarly, in March 1987, after Ecuador was hit with a devastating earthquake that cut its main oil pipeline from the interior to the coast, this oil exporting nation also suspended temporarily its foreign debt payments. Third World leaders well understand that a declaration of bankruptcy is no solution. It will cut their nations adrift, incapable of borrowing additional funds and subject to economic retaliation. The consequences promise additional economic dislocation and the specter of political violence.

These nations, therefore, have taken steps necessary to meet their obligations. Yet, these measures demand putting one's economic house in order. In essence, it means the raising of taxes, which can be achieved by various means: the elimination of subsidies on food, sales taxes on fuel, a limitation on imports (particularly luxury items), and the devaluation of money. Such steps, however, promise inevitable political repercussions for they entail the lowering of the standard of living for large segments of the population. This is especially the case whenever an increase in the cost of food is the price for meeting international obligations. Public outbursts and riots in the streets have shaken governments that have sought to administer such bitter medicine. In recent years, Sudan, Tunisia, the Dominican Republic, Jamaica, Bolivia, and Argentina have all experienced the politically dangerous consequences of such actions.

The Third World is thus caught between two unpalatable choices: (1) default and with it the potential of economic ruination, which in turn will produce political unrest; or (2) compliance and political unrest. Either way, the Third World is not a place to look to for political stability, which can only exist hand-in-hand with economic progress.

The international agency that seeks to maintain the precarious balance between compliance and political stability is the International Monetary Fund (IMF). The IMF, an organization of 148 nations, is the lender of the last resort. It is the result of a conference at Bretton Woods (New Hampshire) in July 1944, at which representatives of 44 allied nations gathered for the purpose of bringing about the resumption of international trade upon the conclusion of World War II. The specific purpose for the creation of the IMF was the restoration of the system of multilateral international payments that had broken down during the Great Depression of the 1930s.

The Fund consists of a pool of money contributed by the 148 member states, of which the United States is the largest contributor. When a debtor nation proves unable to meet its international obligation, the IMF takes on the role of a financial St. Bernard and steps in in order to eliminate the specter of "non-performing" loans and with it the breakdown of the international system of payments. The IMF lends money and lines up the banks that will lend money. Without this program, the poorest nations would be cut off from the credit needed to purchase imported necessities such as food and fuel. But the IMF also insists that the recipients remain in compliance with the lending terms. The Fund here performs two functions. It lends money to shore up the international system of obligations and trade, and at the same time it holds a most powerful weapon over the heads of many governments: the threat of withholding additional funds necessary to keep impoverished societies afloat.

This second aspect of IMF involvement in a nation's economy has created much resentment in the Third World, for the Fund sometimes appears to be more interested in bailing out the private lending institutions than in helping the desperate recipient. The IMF is not alone in dealing with Third World nations, but it is the most visible and thus serves as a lightning rod for the ire of people who feel they are victimized by the developed, capitalist First World. The defenders of the IMF reply that the institution provides, first of all, much needed capital, and secondly, it merely demands a proper, although painful, treatment to restore the patient to health. The result of this arrangement is a love-hate relationship between desperate nations that need assistance and a Western, capitalist agency that provides aid and as part of the bargain insists on interfering in the internal affairs of nations. For the IMF, it is all too often but a short step from the welcome mat to becoming the target of political violence.

In September 1986, the World Bank responded to a U.S. request to play a leading role in managing the Third World debt crisis, especially in Latin America. The World Bank responded by pledging to double by 1990 the loans available to Third World nations. Officially the International Bank for Reconstruction and Development, the World Bank came out of the conference at Bretton Woods and began its operations in 1946. Its purpose is to provide financing for specific projects throughout the world. Its original working capital came from its members' contributions which put it on its feet, but the bulk of its capital comes from borrowing in the world's money markets. It operates as any bank; it has to borrow money (frequently at high rates) and it lends money at a markup. In fiscal 1986, the bank approved loans totaling $13.2 billion, a figure its officials expect to rise to $21.5 billion for fiscal 1990 to meet the Third World's debt crisis. But, as Barber Conable, the new president of the World Bank explained, this would be done in a measured way, not merely to "shovel money out for the sake of shoveling money out." The main criterion for granting new loans will be an increased accountability.[5]

The mid–1980s witnessed another phenomenon that compounded the debtors' plight, the flight of Third World capital. A case in point is Mexico, where a high rate of inflation undermined the value of money in Mexican banks. Depositors, therefore, sought safer havens, Western Europe and the United States, where the rate of inflation had been brought under control. In a decade and a half, the Third World had changed from a net importer of capital to a net exporter, a trend that only serves to widen the gap between the North and the South.

The staggering Latin American debt gave the Communist Fidel Castro of Cuba the opportunity to take center stage as the region's elder statesman. In 1985, Castro spoke several times of the need to create a "debtors' cartel" to resolve Latin America's debt obligations.[6] Oddly, Castro, the revolutionary, urged a resolution of the crisis, with the help of the United States government and the Western capitalist banks, for the purpose of avoiding the repercussions of widespread unrest. Castro wanted the cancellation and the mitigation of debts to prevent revolution. He pointed to the example of the Soviet Union, which repeatedly had written off its assistance to Cuba.

In the summer of 1985, Peru's newly elected president, Alan Garcia, declared that his nation would limit its foreign debt payments to 10 percent of its export earnings. This is the first instance whereby a debtor nation has tried to link payments to the ability to export. When in early 1987, Brazil and Ecuador suspended their payments, they took as their model Peru's argument. Other debtors are likely to find such a solution an attractive alternative to the impossible payments and domestic austerity measures demanded of them.

■ RECOMMENDED READINGS

Blair, John M. *The Control of Oil.* New York: Pantheon Books, 1976.
  A reasoned analysis of the large oil companies' control of supply and market.
Emerson, Steven. *The American House of Saud: The Secret Petrodollar Connection.* Danbury, Conn.: Franklin Watts, 1985.
  An account of the link between the U.S. oil companies and Saudi Arabia.
Harrison, Paul. *Inside the Third World: The Anatomy of Poverty.* 2d ed. New York: Penguin, 1981.
  A useful introduction by an English journalist to the realities of the Third World.
Lacey, Robert. *The Kingdom: Arabia and the House of Sa'ud.* New York: Avon, 1983.
  Another look at the oil crisis.
Sampson, Anthony. *The Sovereign State of ITT.* 2d ed. New York: Fawcett, 1974.
  By an English muckraking reporter who has written several popular books on the world of international finance. This book discusses ITT's foreign operations, particularly in Latin America.
Sampson, Anthony. *The Seven Sisters.* New York: Viking Press, 1975.
  A chronicle of the activities of the major international oil companies.
Sampson, Anthony. *The Money Lenders: The People and Politics of International Banking.* New York: Penguin, 1982.
  Sampson's latest book looks at the international banking community and its involvement in the Third World.

■ NOTES

1. Prerevolutionary tsarist Russia drew heavily upon foreign capital and foreign engineers to begin the industrialization process. Stalin's industrial revolution of the 1930s, in contrast, accomplished largely without foreign assistance, became in the early 1960s one of the models considered by a number of newly independent nations of the Third World. Their economic planners found out, however, that their economic base was so primitive, in contrast to what Stalin had inherited from the tsars, that they had little choice but to turn to economic assistance available from the industrialized First World.

2. All dollar amounts are in U.S. dollars.

3. World Bank and International Monetary Fund statistics, Michael Valpy, "African Heads of State Seek a Common Front on Foreign Debt Crisis," *Toronto Globe and Mail,* July 18, 1985, pp. 1 & 10.

4. State Department and Morgan Guaranty Trust figures, Nicholas D. Kristof, "Latin Debtors That Don't Pay," *New York Times,* February 5, 1985, p. D 1.

5. Hobart Rowen, "World Bank May Nearly Double Loans for Third World by 1990," *The Washington Post,* September 22, 1986, p. A 25.

6. Joseph B. Treaster, "Cuban Meeting Stokes Emotions on Latin Debt," *New York Times,* August 1, 1985, p. D 1.

Part 5

THE END OF THE POSTWAR ERA

During the 1980s, the Cold War took the world on a roller coaster ride, escalating in the first half of the decade and descending rapidly at the end. In the United States, the Reagan administration, which took office in January 1981, stepped up its confrontation with the Soviet Union. All the while there was a quickening pace in the nuclear arms race. The combination of the continued East-West conflict and the widening gulf between North and South produced a host of dilemmas for the world of the 1980s. Many countries of the Third World were politically unstable, and the superpowers continued to battle each other through proxies, as in Nicaragua and Afghanistan. The rise of militant Islam in Iran and Lebanon produced a powerful third ideological force in the Middle East. While the global standoff between East and West continued unabated, other power centers emerged. Japan and the European Community (EC) sustained remarkable economic growth and became new economic forces to be reckoned with.

At the end of the decade came a series of momentous events, which taken together signify the disappearance of the 45-year-long postwar world order. The Soviet Union, under a dynamic new ruler, Mikhail Gorbachev, began a program of restructuring that resulted not only in the transformation of the Communist system of that nation, but also of the Eastern European countries that were its former satellites.

The world felt the impact of the revival of Islam and its political militancy. Although long one of the world's great religions, Islam is little known by Westerners, and for that reason we have seen fit to devote the first half of Chapter 15 to an exposition of the tenets of Islam and its political dimensions. It is necessary to see that in Islam, religion and politics are inseparable and that an Islamic state is not merely a country whose established religion is Islam, but is rather a state where politics are rooted in that religion. The political power inherent in Islam became evident most dramatically in the Iranian revolution, the main topic of the remainder of the chapter. In Iran, leaders of the Shiite branch of Islam led a revolt that overthrew an U.S-supported autocrat, the shah of Iran, and brought a new order to the country, one extremely hostile toward the West, particularly the United States. In the wake of the Iranian revolution U.S. embassy officials were taken hostage, creating a major diplomatic crisis for the United States on the heels of its setback in Vietnam. In Chapter 15, we also turn our attention to the Iran-Iraq War, which drew U.S. Navy ships into the Persian Gulf, and the problem of Middle East terrorism.

The emergence of Japan and the European Community as economic superpowers is the topic of Chapter 16. One of the premier postwar success stories is the rise of Japan from the ashes of war in the mid-1940s to become the world's second economic power in the 1980s. Japan's "economic miracle" will be explained in this chapter as well as the friction that developed in its economic relations with the United States. In the 1980s, the nations of the EC made great strides in economic growth and toward the achievement of the goal of full economic integration by 1992. In this chapter, we will also examine the state of interdependence among the three economic superpowers.

In Chapter 17, we examine changes within the Communist bloc in the early 1980s. Our attention is focused initially on the crisis in Poland where a dramatic showdown between Solidarity and the Communist government took place during 1981. The subsequent military crackdown in Poland aroused Cold War passions as the United States charged not only the Polish government but Moscow as well for crushing Solidarity. We also discuss in this chapter the contrasting case of Hungary, where a quieter but nonetheless substantial change took place.

In the same chapter, we examine the Russian invasion of Afghanistan and the impact of that action on international relations and the subsequent full-fledged return of the Cold War. In response to the Soviet invasion, the Carter and Reagan administrations took a hard line toward Moscow. Tensions mounted rapidly as President Reagan charged the Soviet Union with an escalation of the arms race, with expansionism, and with intervention all around the world—in Angola, in Poland, in Nicaragua, in Cambodia, and most of all in Afghanistan.

We turn in Chapter 18 to the incredible cascade of events in the Soviet Union and in Eastern Europe at the end of 1980s. Our focus is first on Mikhail Gorbachev, the architect of the Soviet empire's radical transformation. We examine the various aspects of his program of restructuring (*perestroika*) and the problems it has encountered. Gorbachev's reforms touched off a wave of nationalistic unrest among the non-Russian Soviet republics, which threatened the unity of the Soviet Union. Chapter 18 examines this unrest as well as the upheaval in the Eastern European countries, which for more than forty years were ruled by Communist regimes that answered to Moscow. But because the shape of the post-Communist political order remains undetermined at this writing, we can relate only how the Communist governments were toppled, and must conclude, therefore, with an unfinished story.

Finally, we turn to potentially the gravest issue facing mankind: the nuclear arms race. As both cause and effect of the Cold War, the nuclear arms race has continued unabated for over forty years, but in the 1980s it became more menacing than ever, in part because of an increase in missile accuracy and a decrease in delivery time. Each of the superpowers insisted on maintaining an arsenal sufficient to deter an attack by the other side, and the deadly logic of deterrence compelled both sides to build ever more weapons and continually upgrade them. In Chapter 19, we briefly review earlier efforts at nuclear disarmament and then turn to the Strategic Arms Limitation Talks (SALT I and II), the controversy over the Strategic Defense Initiative (SDI, or Star Wars), and progress toward disarmament at the end of the 1980s. After SALT II was initialed in 1979, the United States and the Soviet Union made no progress toward nuclear arms reduction or arms limitations in the next five years; indeed, no negotiations took place during much of that time. Meanwhile, President Reagan insisted that the Soviets had gained a lead in the nuclear arms race and he vowed to retake the lead. Reagan's reading of the arms race and his arms build-up gave rise to much debate over "who is ahead?" This question is discussed in Chapter 19 as is the controversy over the SDI program launched by President Reagan in 1983. We also examine the Gorbachev peace initiative and Reagan's positive response, which resulted in a substantial lowering of tension and the first successful nuclear disarmament agreement, the intermediate nuclear forces (INF) agreement of 1988. The signing of that agreement, the continuation of disarmament talks since then, and the events at the end of the 1980s in Europe signalling the end of the Cold War era all point to the reversal of the nuclear arms race and provide hope that in the 1990s significant steps toward disarmament will be achieved.

☐ 15

Militant Islam

The Cold War after 1945 was largely a bipolar struggle between Western parliamentarianism and the Soviet variant of Communism, with much of the world simply trying to stay out of harm's way. In the late 1970s, however, a new political force emerged, militant Islam. This new political movement, steeped in the religion of Islam, sought to resurrect the world of Islam, to free it from the debilitating and overbearing influence of such outside forces as Communism, secularism, and above all the pervading Western presence. Militant Islam has left its mark throughout Islamic societies in a region that stretches, with a few minor interruptions, from the Atlantic shores of Africa to the easternmost tip of the Indonesian archipelago.

■ ISLAM: THEORY AND PRACTICE

The faith of Islam is the third of the world's great religions to come out of the Middle East. It represents to Moslems the third and last of the "true revelations" by a divinity whom the Jews call Jehovah, the Christians call God, and the Muslims call Allah.

This final revelation came in the seventh century of the Christian era when Allah spoke to His Prophet Mohammed of Mecca, Islam's holiest city, located in what today is Saudi Arabia. Mohammed had been born into a society of idol worshippers, Jews, and Christians, and he quite naturally fell under the influence of Arabia's two dominant monotheistic faiths, Judaism and Christianity. In fact, these were the starting point of Mohammed's teachings. He was always at pains to acknowledge that God had revealed himself to his prophets of another age, Abraham, Moses, and Jesus Christ among them. But he also insisted that Christians and Jews had gone astray and had ignored God's commandments and corrupted the original scriptures.

Mohammed held the view that uncorrupted Judaism and Christianity were early manifestations of Islam, literally "submission" to God. Abraham, according to Mohammed, had been the first Muslim. But since Jews and Christians had strayed from God's word, God then revealed Himself to the last in the long line of prophets, Mohammed.

Islam in this fashion became an offshoot from Judaism. Its linear relationship to the earlier faiths resembles Christianity's link to Judaism. For this reason there remain numerous significant similarities among the three faiths. At one time, Muslims, including Mohammed, faced Jerusalem while in prayer. All three religions stress justice and compassion. Islam has a heaven and a hell; God spoke to Mohammed through the Archangel Gabriel; Islam has its Day of Resurrection and Judgment,"and the hour is known to no one but God." Believers who are created "from an essence of clay . . . shall surely die hereafter, and be restored to life on the Day of Resurrection," a "day sure to come."[1]

Arabs and Jews both claim Abraham as their ancestor. The Jews descended from Abraham's second son, Isaac, born of his wife Sarah; the Arabs from the first son, Ishmael, born of Hagar, Sarah's Egyptian maid. The Bible prophesies that great nations shall descend from the two sons of Abraham. The Biblical account, however, also stresses that God renewed with Isaac the covenant he had made with Abraham, while the Muslim account makes no distinction between the sons of Abraham. Islamic scholars have argued that it is inconceivable that God would favor one son over the other. In Islamic teachings, the conflict between Jews and Muslims, therefore, becomes a family divided against itself.

The revelations to Mohammed were codified in the Koran, the holy, infallible book of the Muslims, which contains God's commands to the faithful. The Koran is as God's word, last in time and the completion and correction of all that had been written before.

A deviation from established religions is no trifling matter. It attempts, after all, to replace established faiths with one that claims to be the only true revelation from God. The results have been religious conflicts, which in the case of Islam began in Mohammed's day and have lasted centuries down to our time. Neither Judaism nor Christianity has ever recognized the validity of Islam. Western scholars have often used the insulting label of "Mohammedanism" to describe Islam, the suggestion being that it is an invention of one man rather than God's final world to humanity. And Islam, in its turn, has denied the Holy Trinity, and thus the divinity of Jesus Christ, which amounts to a demand for "the unconditional surrender of the essence of Christianity."[2]

Islam means "submission" to Allah and a Muslim is someone who has submitted to the will of God. It is thus a religion that encompasses the totality of one's existence. It is a complete way of life, both secular and religious.

There can be no separation between one's spiritual and secular existence. In an Islamic government, therefore, a believer cannot make a distinction between secular and religious law. All laws must be based on the Koran; they cannot be otherwise. And the rulers and their governments must reign according to the word of Allah. Islam is, after all, a religion of laws.

There is an elemental simplicity to the fundamental laws, the "five pillars," of Islam. They include, first and foremost, the affirmation that consists of one of the shortest credos of any religion in the world: "There is no god but God and Mohammed is the Prophet of God." All that a convert to Islam has to do is to state this credo. No other rite or ceremony is required. (The very simplicity inherent in the act of conversion explains in part why Islam today is the fastest growing religion in Africa.) Second, a Muslim is obliged to pay an alms tax (the *zakat*) of around 5 percent. Islam emphasizes the importance of charity: "Whatever alms you give . . . are known to Allah . . . and whatever alms you give shall be paid back to you in full."[3] The alms tax also has become a source of revenue for the government. Third, a Muslim must say five daily prayers facing toward Mecca. The *muezzin* (crier) calls the faithful from the minaret (a slender tower) of a mosque (or temple) at various times during the twenty-four hour cycle of the day: at sunset, during the night, at dawn, at noon, and in the afternoon. Fourth, Islam demands abstention from food, drink, and sexual intercourse from dawn to sunset during the lunar month of Ramadan. Fasting here becomes a spiritual act of renunciation and self-denial. Last, a Muslim must attempt to make at least once a pilgrimage, or *haj,* to the holy city of Mecca.

In the seventh century, following the death of Mohammed, Islam spread quickly throughout the Middle East and North Africa. With the spread of Islam came the establishment of one of the world's great civilizations, centering around the cities of Damascus and Bagdad. Yet, ultimately, this golden age of Islam gave way to a European ascendancy, which may be dated to the crusades of the Middle Ages.

In more recent times, Western powers (notably Great Britain, France, and Italy) have managed to establish their presence in the Muslim lands of the Middle East, only to find their grip weakening after World War II. Militant Islam today seeks to free the Muslim countries from the centuries-old, overbearing influence of the Christian West and to reassert the sovereignty and dignity denied to these nations in the past. Militant Islam is, therefore, a potent political and revolutionary weapon.

■ THE SHIITES AND THE SUNNIS

The most visible and radical advocates of resurgent, militant Islam during the 1970s were the Shiites, the smaller of the two main branches of Islam.

The other wing, the Sunnis, represents what is generally called the mainstream of Islam and, in fact, they make up nearly 90 percent of all Muslims. Shiites are little known in Africa among the Arabs in the north or among the blacks in sub-Saharan Africa. The same is true of southern Asia, in countries such as Indonesia, Malaysia, Bangladesh, India, Turkey, and Pakistan. The keepers of the holy places in Mecca and Medina, the Saudi family, and their subjects are mostly Sunnis. In Iran, however, nearly all Muslims belong to the Shiite branch; in fact, it has become a state religion there. The majority of the Muslims of the Soviet Republic of Azerbaijan and of Iraq are Shiites. Shiites may also be found in large numbers in all the other states of the Persian Gulf, Syria, Lebanon, Yemen, and Iraq, and in Central Asia.

The split in Islam came two decades after the Prophet's death in 632. A line of *khalifa*, or caliphs, took Mohammed's place as his deputies and successors. The first four caliphs, the Rightly Guided, were selected from the ranks of Mohammed's associates, and after that the line became hereditary. From the very outset there were strains in the Muslim community over the question of succession. There had always been those who insisted that Ali, the husband of Mohammed's daughter Fatima, was the true successor. As the caliphs became more tyrannical they increasingly appeared as usurpers. The assassination of the reigning caliph in 656 set off a civil war from which dates the open split between the party of Ali (in Arabic, *shia* means party or sect), who also was assassinated, and the main branch (*sunna* in Arabic means practice or custom). The struggle lasted until the battle of Kerbala in 681, when the Sunnis established their domination and the Shiite resistance went underground.

The struggle was both political and religious in nature. Its political content lay in the fact that the Shiites became the champions of the oppressed and the opponents of privilege and power. The Shiites have found their inspiration in the actions of Mohammed in Mecca, where the Prophet first made his mark as the advocate of the downtrodden. As such, the Shiites in Iran, for example, have always been in conflict with the throne (the government) in their attempts to recreate a social and political order in line with the teachings of the Koran. Politics and religion, in the Shiites' eyes, cannot be separated. When in 1963, the shah of Iran offered his uncompromising critic the Ayatollah Ruhollah Khomeini his freedom on condition he leave politics to the politicians, Khomeini replied: "All of Islam is politics."[4] Khomeini was the shah's most vocal critic who charged the monarch with having sold his country into bondage on behalf of U.S. interests. In 1964, Khomeini publicly refused to recognize the government, its courts, and laws. Ten days after his release in 1964, Khomeini delivered the first of a number of political speeches. Later that year he was rearrested and then exiled.[5] (Obedience to civil authority has never been a hallmark of Shiite behavior. Shiites in their challenges to entrenched political power have time and again elevated political disobedience to a religious duty.[6])

Rebellion by the powerless and oppressed more often than not ends in failure, death, and increased persecution. Suffering and martyrdom, therefore, became part and parcel of the existence of Shiites. Such an existence cannot continue without hope of deliverance. Sunnis and Shiites both accept the Prophet's promise of the return of one of his descendants who will "fill the world with justice and equity."[6] For the Shiites, however, the spirit of messianism is central to their creed. They look to an *imam,* a divinely appointed descendant of Mohammed, whose purpose is the spiritual—as well as political and at times insurrectional—guidance of the faithful.

The Sunnis, the party of custom and practice, have always stood for the continuity of the social, political, and religious order. They have emphasized consensus and obedience to civil and religious authority. The Sunnis, in contrast to the Shiites, have looked for inspiration to Mohammed's work in Medina, where he created the first Muslim state and ruled as a military commander, judge, and teacher to whom Allah's word was revealed.

■ THE REVOLUTION IN IRAN

The incomprehensible fury of militant Islam, most notably in Iran, has shocked the sensibilities of the Western world. From the end of World War II until the late 1970s, Iran stood out in sharp contrast from its neighbors. Shah Mohammed Reza Pahlavi and his country appeared to be a rock of stability in the turbulent Middle East, a bulwark against political radicalism, Islamic fundamentalism, and Soviet expansionism. It was little wonder that, even after the shah's internal position had been shaken by violent protests, President Carter could still praise him for his stabilizing influence in the Middle East. Surely, there was no solid reason to believe that the shah, still apparently a vigorous man in middle age, would not continue to rule Iran as he had in the past. Moreover, he was preparing his young son to succeed him on the Peacock Throne.

But Iran turned out to be another case of U.S. involvement in a foreign land of which few people in authority in the United States had an adequate understanding. The outward stability of the nation only masked the volatile undercurrents, which have deep historic roots. The shah had ruled for a long time, ever since 1941, but his reign had often been unstable, an uncomfortable fact that too many U.S. policy makers often conveniently overlooked. The militant clergy were a nuisance, they reasoned, but they certainly appeared to be no threat to the shah.

Successful resistance to Iran's shahs by the militant clergy over the past centuries is a constant thread that runs through Iranian history. This was particularly the case with those shahs who made deals with foreigners granting them favorable concessions at the expense of the nation as a whole. In 1872, for example, Nasir ed-Den Shah granted Paul Julius de Reuter, a British subject, such a comprehensive monopoly that the shah had, in effect, sold him the country. De Reuter received a monopoly in the construction of railroads, canals, and irrigation works, the harvesting of forests, the use of all unculti-vated lands, and the operation of banks, public works, and mines. The British leader Lord Curzon called this "the most complete and extraordinary surrender of the entire industrial resources of a kingdom into foreign hands that has ever been dreamed of, much less accomplished."[7] The clergy did manage, however, to bring about the cancellation of some of these conces-sions. In 1892, the shah faced an angry mob storming his palace and demand-ing the repeal of a monopoly granted to a British firm in the production, sale, and export of tobacco. This exercise of political power in the streets was sufficient to bring about the repeal of these concessions. But the shah's troubles persisted and, in 1896, he was assassinated. Nasir ed-Den Shah's reign points to a recurring pattern of Iranian politics: royal complicity with foreign powers, the power of the mobs in the streets, and the inability of most shahs to maintain their power. During the past 350 years, only four shahs have died natural deaths while still in possession of the throne. The rest were either dethroned or assassinated. Iran is not a likely place to look for political equilibrium.

After Nasir en-Den Shah's assassination, the practice of selling favors to foreigners—British, French, and Russians—continued. In 1906, the Iranian Parliament took away this privilege from the shah. But despite the prohibi-tion, the practice continued, contributing to a legacy of bitterness and re-sentment directed toward the ruling Qajar dynasty (1779–1925) that ulti-mately led to its demise. In its place, a usurper pronounced the creation of his own ruling house. He was Colonel Reza Khan, who subsequently crowned himself Reza Shah Pahlavi.

Years later, Reza Khan's son, the recent shah (1941–1979), attempted to identify his ruling house, the Pahlavi dynasty, with the glories of Persia's past. In 1971, he staged an elaborate ceremony in Persepolis, the ancient city of Cyrus the Great. Guests from far and wide attended the gala celebration. The shah then proceeded to date the calendar from the reign of Cyrus, symboliz-ing over 2,500 years of historic continuity.[8] He became the Shahansha (the King of Kings), the Light of the Aryans, who ruled by divine right, a man who claimed to experience religious visions.[9]

This spectacle impressed the world, but many Iranians, particularly the clergy, saw the shah in a different light. The clergy, Allah's representatives on this earth, demanded submission to their will, that is, the will of Allah. They considered the shah merely a usurper—only the second in the short line of the Pahlavi dynasty—who had been educated in the West and who had sent his own son to the West to study. Moreover, the shah's close relationship with the West, the United States in particular, was something that did not sit easily with many Iranians.

Reza Shah had not acted appreciably differently than the previous monarchs when it came to dealing with foreign powers. In 1933, he granted new favorable concessions to the Anglo-Iranian Oil Company, an enterprise that was largely controlled by the British. His close association with the British continued until World War II, when he shifted toward Nazi Germany at a time when it threatened to take the Soviet Union's oil fields north of the Caucasus along the western shores of the Caspian Sea, notably around the city of Baku. A successful German drive in that direction would have linked German-occupied territory with Iran. The upshot was the joint occupation of Iran by the Soviets (who took control of the northern part) and the British (who occupied the southern regions). The shah was then sent packing when the British and Soviets forced him to abdicate in favor of his young son, who turned out to be the second and last of the Pahlavi dynasty.

The greatest source of wealth for the Pahlavi dynasty was the country's oil. By 1950, Iran was the largest producer of oil in the Middle East. By that time Iran's own share of the oil profits had increased, but many nationalists, including many of the clergy, were not satisfied. For one thing, the Arab-American Oil Company, a U.S. concern operating in Saudi Arabia, had offered the Saudis more favorable terms. More importantly, the lion's share of the profits from Iran's natural resources still went to the foreign investors who were mostly British.

The upshot was that in 1951, Parliament, under the direction of Prime Minister Mohammed Mossadegh, challenged the shah and voted for the nationalization of the oil industry. The British, predictably, declared such an act illegal. President Truman sought to negotiate the dispute, eventually siding with the British. Mossadegh's challenge to the West found a responsive chord in Iranian society. Anti-U.S. riots and attacks on U.S. consulates and libraries in 1952 led to reprisals by the Eisenhower administration, which came to power in January 1953. In May of that year the United States government decided to put economic pressure on Mossadegh by cutting off aid and refusing to buy Iranian oil. The U.S. use of an economic weapon only inflamed the militants in Tehran, the Iranian capital. In August 1953, street riots forced the shah to flee to Rome. There he apparently came to the conclusion that his reign had ended.

But at this point the CIA, which had already been involved in actions directed against Mossadegh, moved into operation. With the help of elements in the army and others opposed to Mossadegh, the CIA managed to return the shah after only three days in exile. Demonstrations in the streets had ousted the shah; counterdemonstrations in these same streets created a political climate permitting the shah to return.[10]

The shah now owed his throne to a foreign power, something he always resented. But his ties with the United States continued to grow. Oil production and export to the West continually increased, and in the process the shah became one of the United States's best overseas customers. He then took steps to modernize Iranian society, but such a transformation always comes at a price. Modernization created a gulf between a new privileged class, which benefitted from the shah's close link with the West, and much of the rest of the country. The influx of Western technicians, engineers, military advisers, and sales representatives did not sit very well with many Iranians. The distribution of the country's enormous wealth and the attendant Westernization and modernization led to a distortion of traditional Iranian social patterns. Too many were left out and it was inevitable that the shah's actions bred resentment. Traditional Iranian self-sufficiency became a thing of the past. By the 1970s, Iran had become greatly dependent on foreign imports; it even bought food from abroad. And since Iran based much of its wealth on a one-product economy, 80 percent of its export earnings coming from the sale of oil, its dependency on the West appeared to be total.

Much of the money the shah spent abroad went for the purchase of modern military equipment, most of it U.S.-made. Between 1972 and 1978, he ordered $19.5 billion in United States arms. And the greater the oil revenues, the more weapons he bought. After 1973, about one-third of the government's spending went for armaments. This proved to be a boon for U.S. arms manufacturers, for by the end of the 1970s, one-third of all U.S. arms sales went to Iran.

The U.S. government, particularly the Nixon administration, applauded such a course: Iran, armed to the teeth, would preserve stability in the Middle East, particularly in the Persian Gulf, the waterway through which passed much of the oil on which the industrial powers depended. It was here that the "Nixon Doctrine" appeared to work best.

Nixon had first formulated his doctrine toward the end of the war in Vietnam. It was designed to permit him to exit from that war without appearing to have lost it. According to the Nixon Doctrine, the United States would arm and support a client who would do the actual fighting in support of U.S. interests. In South Vietnam the doctrine collapsed like a house of cards when its own army took to its heels. In Iran the application of this doctrine seemed to be working to perfection.

In the early 1970s, it was not clear how Iran would pay for the massive equipment the shah demanded. But good fortune intervened. October 1973 saw the fourth Arab-Israeli War conflict, the "Yom Kippur War," which led to an oil embargo by the Arab members of OPEC (the Organization of Petroleum Exporting Countries) and a doubling of oil prices. The shah took the lead in demanding this increase in the price of oil. The Nixon administration, however, saw a silver lining in all of this. The United States was now able to supply Iran with military equipment without raiding the U.S. treasury. As Henry Kissinger, Nixon's secretary of state, explained in his memoirs:

The vacuum left by British withdrawal [from Iran during the early 1950s], now menaced by Soviet intrusion and radical momentum, would be filled by a power friendly to us [the Shah's Iran,]. . . . And all of this was achievable without any American resources, since the Shah was willing to pay for the equipment out of his oil revenues.[11]

But this scenario began to fall apart in a most unexpected way when militant Islam drove the shah, a servant of the "great satan" (the U.S.), from power.

☐ The Return of Khomeini

The best known practitioner of militant Islam was the Ayatollah Ruhollah Khomeini. He identified Western civilization as Islam's enemy; an Islamic society, therefore, must be purged of it. The shah, with the trappings of Western civilization all around him, was little different than the tens of thousands of Western technicians he had invited to Iran. In the eyes of the mullahs, the Muslim clergy, the shah stood in direct violation of the history and religion of Islam.

Khomeini's denunciations of the shah at first had little effect. They were regarded merely as the ravings and rantings of an old man in exile. But as dissatisfaction with the shah's rule increased, Khomeini's sermons on cassette tapes, smuggled into Iran, began to have an effect. By January 1979, it became apparent that the shah could only maintain his throne if SAVAK (the secret police) and the army were willing to suppress with much loss of life all manifestations of discontent. Civil war loomed on the horizon. The shah, unsure of the loyalty of the army and unable to obtain a clear-cut U.S. commitment from the Carter administration, decided to leave the country. There was little else he could do. Opposition to his regime ran deep. The influx of oil money had only intensified the dissatisfaction felt by many. Corruption, favoritism, police brutality, poverty and luxury existing side by side, the lack of justice, the influence of foreigners, all contributed to the fall of the shah.

The events of 1978–1979 showed that the shah had merely given off an illusion of power, which now went to the most militant of his opponents, the Muslim clergy. The Ayatollah Khomeini returned in triumph from exile in Paris where he had been the most visible symbol of righteous, Islamic resistance to a ruler who had betrayed both his religion and his people. Iran, under the leadership of the Muslim clergy, could now be expected to experience a spiritual and national rejuvenation. There was little doubt that the support for Khomeini's regime was massive in those heady days when the shah was put to flight.

But the shah had not officially abdicated. When he left, he emphasized that he and his family were going abroad for an unspecified period. In effect,

Shah Mohammed Rezi Pahlavi, monarch of Iran, with U.S. Secretary of Defense James Schlesinger, Washington, D.C., July 26, 1973. (*AP/Wide World Photos*)

Ayatollah Ruhollah Khomeini, Shiite leader of the Iranian revolution, 1979. (*Courtesy of the Embassy of Iran*)

he promised to return.[12] It was clear that the United States preferred the shah over the anti-U.S. militants who now governed Tehran. The militants, for their part, feared a repetition of the events of 1953 when the CIA had returned the shah to power from his brief exile in Rome. Radicals, bitterly hostile to a United States government on which they blamed all of Iran's ills, were able to stir up deep emotions. Anti-U.S. street demonstrations became daily affairs, and two weeks after Khomeini had returned from exile, the first attack by militants on the U.S. embassy took place. The organizers of the attack claimed that the embassy housed the CIA. Khomeini forces at this time dispersed the attackers.

The Khomeini government initiated a concerted attack on the U.S. presence in Iran. It repealed, for example, the 1947 law authorizing a U.S. military mission in Iran. Instead of concentrating on the consolidation of power, Khomeini thus sharpened the differences between his revolution and the United States. The crucial moment came in October 1979, when the shah arrived in New York for medical treatment. To the militants in Tehran, this marked the first step of what to them was a U.S. attempt to bring the shah back to power. They never believed the shah was in need of treatment.

Thus, on November 4, a group of radical students decided to take matters into their own hands. They climbed over the walls of the U.S. compound and seized the embassy personnel, demanding that the United States dissociate itself from the shah and extradite him to Iran to stand trial. There is no evidence that Khomeini gave the order for this act, but it suited his political position perfectly since it drove political sentiments in Iran further to a radical extreme. As the symbol of the revolution, he had but little choice except to place himself at the head of it. And the extraordinary support for the students by the huge crowds who gathered daily in the square in front of the embassy ensured his open support for this radical action.

The hostage crisis came at a time when memories of helicopters lifting off the rooftop of the U.S. embassy in Saigon were still fresh in the public's eye. And, less than two months after the onset of the hostage crisis, the United States was hit with another jolt when the Soviet Union sent 80,000 troops into Afghanistan—to bail out a bankrupt Communist government, as it turned out (see Chapter 16). Together, the hostage crisis and the Red Army's invasion of Afghanistan had a dramatic impact on U.S. public opinion. The United States had lost a sphere of influence in Iran, and the Soviets had sent troops outside their postwar sphere for the first time. The U.S. loss and what appeared to be the Soviet Union's gain gave President Carter a foreign policy headache that ultimately played a major role in his defeat in 1980. Carter never worked out a satisfactory policy of how to deal with the Iranian radicals and the Soviets, and this indecisiveness cost him dearly at home.

The hostages eventually came home, but only after the 1980 election and after 444 days of captivity. President Carter had punished the Soviets by a grain embargo and a U.S. refusal to attend the 1980 summer Olympic Games in Moscow. But Carter's actions were too little and too late. He could not shake the damaging public perception that he was indecisive and a "wimp." In retrospect, it is clear that the presidential election was over long before the voters cast their first ballot. They decided to give tough-talking Republican Ronald Reagan the chance to handle the nation's foreign policy.[13]

At home, the Khomeini government set out to transform Iran according to the strictures set down in the Koran. The Islamic revolution transferred sovereignty from the shah to God. The secular parties, however, had a different vision of the future of the Iranian Republic. The upshot was a bitter conflict between the Shia clergy and its opponents. The challenge to the revolution came mainly from the numerous splinter groups on the Left—Marxists, Maoists, socialists—who feared the replacement of one dictatorship by another. When the bloodletting was over, the Islamic revolution had consolidated its power. Waves of revolutionary terror had brought about the execution of approximately 10,000 Iranians, and another half million, many of them of the professional classes, went into exile.

The revolution in Iran swept aside many of the Western influences and destroyed the old order. For all practical purposes, it ended the Pahlavi dynasty, brought about a redistribution of land, gave the nation a new constitution based on Islamic laws, and denied the United States a client in the Middle East. In addition, Khomeini's revolution threatened to spread beyond the confines of Iran. Large Shiite communities in Lebanon, Iraq, the Persian Gulf states, and Saudi Arabia have begun to look to Iran for guidance. Khomeini's revolutionary message in support of the downtrodden masses and his virulent opposition to the West have added a new and dangerous element to the Middle East. The shah, until the very end, had always felt that Communism posed the greatest danger to his throne. But with the Iranian revolution, the conflict in the Middle East ceased to be primarily a contest between Western democracy and Communism. Militant Islam, in direct challenge to the Soviet Union and the West, became another force to be reckoned with.

■ THE IRAN-IRAQ WAR

With Iran in the throes of a revolution, the government of Saddam Hussein of Iraq availed itself of the opportunity to invade Iran in September 1980. Hussein had three objectives. He sought (1) to destroy Khomeini's revolution, which he feared might spread to his subjects, most of whom, although Arabs, were Shiite; (2) to secure disputed territory at the mouth of the Tigris River, the Shatt-el Arab; and (3) to emerge perhaps as a leading figure in the Arab world.

Iraq's plan called for securing the Shatt-el Arab, capturing Iran's oil ports on the other side of the river, and crippling Iranian forces in a drive eastward into Iran. It calculated that Iran was unprepared for war because of extensive losses to the officer corps and to its pilots due to purges and desertions during the revolution. Iran, however, still had enough loyal middle-grade officers and pilots, and it rallied its people quickly to war. Because Iraqi invading forces moved too cautiously, Iran gained time to rapidly build up its Revolutionary Guard, its regular forces, from 7,000 to 200,000 men and created a new militia of more than 350,000 men. The appeal by religious extremists in Tehran for volunteers to fight the "holy war" produced a rapid mobilization, which in turn created a psychological atmosphere that benefited the extremists, who considered as Iran's mission the export of the Islamic revolution. Iran was thus able to offset Iraq's initial advantage of a better trained and better equipped army. With the two sides evenly matched, neither side was able to score a decisive victory. After Iran's

THE PERSIAN GULF STATES

counteroffensive in 1982 regained lost territory and captured almost 60,000 Iraqi troops on the battlefield, the war became a stalemate.

The United States and the Soviet Union as well as the European powers declared their neutrality in the conflict. But as the war dragged on, over forty nations supplied weapons to one side or the other, and several nations, including the United States, sold weapons to both sides. Israel and the United States both sold weapons covertly to Iran, apparently to keep the war going.[14] Israel's Defense Minister, Yitzhak Rabin, stated frankly, "We don't want a resolution of this war."[15] Iran was supported also by Libya and Syria. Iraq received financial support from Saudi Arabia and the other oil-exporting Arab states on the Gulf, all of which feared Iran's ideological revolution.

Both sides understood the importance of oil in financing the war, and each targeted the other's oil-producing and shipping facilities in the Persian Gulf. This brought in the United States, which was determined to keep the Gulf open as the passageway through which much of the Western world's and Japan's oil flowed. It accepted, in December 1986, a request of the Kuwaiti government to protect its oil tanker fleet. Kuwaiti tankers were then "reflagged"; that is, they were placed under the U.S. flag, and escorted by U.S. naval vessels. This brought the United States into direct confrontation with Iran.

The war also saw the first extensive use of chemical weapons since World War I. In March 1988, Iraq launched a chemical weapons attack on its own city of Halabaq, which was populated by Kurds, a non-Arab Islamic people hostile to Hussein's regime. The lethal chemicals killed as many as 5,000 of the city's Kurdish residents, and many Iranian troops and thousands others suffered excruciating burns. Iraq's use of chemical warfare underscored the new potential danger the world faced, "the poor man's atomic bomb," as Third World nationals called it. It brought strong worldwide rebuke, but it enabled Iraq's army to repel the Iranian offensive and roll it back.

Iraq had offered to negotiate an end to the war many times. Hussein had announced in the summer of 1987 his willingness to accept a United Nations Security Council resolution calling for an armistice, but Tehran had rejected it. Ayatollah Khomeini had his own terms for ending the war: Hussein must step down and Iraq must pay $150 billion in reparations. But after suffering a series of military setbacks, air attacks on Tehran, loss of its naval force to the United States, and a serious decline in oil profits, the Ayatollah suddenly reversed himself, announcing on July 18, 1988 that he must take "the bitter drink of poison" and accept the UN peace formula.[16]

There was no winner of the absurd eight-and-half-year–long war. Each side suffered almost a million casualties and enormous economic losses. Iraq emerged from the war with the stronger military forces. But Iran was not defeated, and its Islamic Revolution remained very much intact.

■ MIDDLE EAST TERRORISM

In the years following the 1982 Israeli incursion into Lebanon the Arab-Israeli conflict became diffused. The central issue–the dispute between the Palestinians and the state of Israel–became but one of a host of Middle East conflicts. Moreover, it had come to an impasse as neither the Israelis nor the Palestinians were able to defeat the other and both were having internal power struggles and policy debates. As a consequence of this deadlock, a new wave of terrorism became the order of the day.

Inspired by Islamic fundamentalism, and frustrated by setbacks at the hands of Israel or outside forces supporting Israel, Arab and Iranian extremists resorted to desperate, sometimes suicidal, acts of violence against the perceived enemies of Islam. To them the act of terrorism was a moral act, whatever the cost to themselves, their enemy, or for that matter, innocent parties. In some instances, they acted to redress specific grievances or to gain specific ends, such as the return of prisoners taken by Israel. To press their point, they took Westerners in Lebanon as hostages. Israeli defense forces responded in kind by bombing raids and kidnappings.

The United States, by its military intervention on behalf of the Phalangist government of Lebanon in 1983 and its naval bombardment of "enemy" strongholds in the mountains, made itself the target of terrorism. In March 1984, William Buckley, a CIA agent, was kidnapped in Beirut by the pro-Iranian Shiite group known as the Islamic Jihad and was later killed by them. In the following two years, at least twenty others–college teachers, journalists, businessmen, and priests from the United States, Britain, France, and several other countries–were taken hostage by the Islamic Jihad and other revolutionary groups in Lebanon. Lacking knowledge of the specific identity of the kidnappers or the location of the hostages, Western governments were unable to rescue them. In January 1986, Terry Waite, an envoy of the Church of England, went to Beirut in effort to negotiate the release of foreign hostages, only to be kidnapped himself by the Islamic Jihad. Since then at least six more foreigners were taken hostage, and, although several have been released, at least ten have been killed.

Exasperated by the continuing wave of terrorism and determined to stop it, the Reagan administration vowed to retaliate. It found a likely target for retaliation in Muammar Khadaffi, dictator of Libya. Khadaffi, a strident Arab extremist, had already raised President Reagan's ire for his support of the PLO and for his brash threats against the United States for trespassing in Libya's territorial waters, the Gulf of Sidra. Moreover, Khadaffi had maintained terrorist training camps in Libya and had provided financial support for Lebanese extremist groups suspected of terrorism.[17] In April 1986, a terrorist bomb ripped through a discotheque in West Berlin, killing two people, among them a U.S. soldier, and leaving 204 injured. Reagan blamed Khadaffi and ordered a punitive air attack on the Libyan cities of Tripoli and Benghazi,[18] for the purpose of killing Khadaffi. One bomb landed yards away from Khadaffi's residence, leaving him unharmed but, Khadaffi claimed, killing his adopted infant daughter. The U.S. attack, which was not supported by its European allies, was little more than an act of frustration and vengeance and was of questionable value as a deterrence to terrorism, which, in any case, continued unabated.

■ RECOMMENDED READINGS

Bakhash, Shaul. *The Reign of the Ayatollahs: Iran and the Islamic Revolution.* New York: Basic Books, 1984.
   A scholarly account of Khomeini's revolution.
Dawood, N. J., trans. *The Meaning of the Glorious Koran.* New York: Penguin, 1956.
   A valuable translation of the *Koran* for Western readers, as well as a valuable introduction to the early history of Islam, by Mohammed Marmaduke Pickthall, an English convert to the faith.
Guillaume, Alfred. *Islam.* 2d rev. ed. New York: Penguin, 1956.
   The classic analysis of the theological basis of Islam by one of the West's recognized scholars in the field.
Jansen, G. H. *Militant Islam.* New York: Harper & Row, 1979.
   An attempt to explain to Western readers the philosophic foundations of Islam and the reasons for its militant form in Iran.
Kapuscinski, Ryszard. *Shah of Shahs.* San Diego: Harcourt, Brace, Jovanovich, 1985.
   By a veteran Polish journalist, an eyewitness to the Iranian upheaval.
Kedourie, Elie. *Islam in the Modern World.* New York: Holt, Rinehart and Winston, 1980.
   Focuses on the link between Islam and Arab politics.
Rubin, Barry. *Paved With Good Intentions: The American Experience and Iran.* New York: Oxford University Press, 1980.
   An analysis of what went wrong with the U.S. scenario for Iran.
Said, Edward W. *Covering Islam: How the Media and the Experts Determine How We See the Rest of the World.* New York: Pantheon Books, 1981.
   A critical analysis, by a U.S. citizen of Palestinian descent, of how the U.S. press handled the Iranian hostage crisis.

Salinger, Pierre. *America Held Hostage: The Secret Negotiations.* Garden City, N.Y.: Doubleday, 1981.

By a U.S. journalist who was directly involved in settling the crisis.

Sick, Gary. *All Fall Down.* New York: Random House, 1985.

A member of President Carter's National Security Council presents a first-hand account of the hostage deliberations.

■ NOTES

1. N. J. Dawood, trans., *The Koran,* 4th rev. ed. (New York: Penguin, 1974), p. 220, Surah 23:14–16; p. 375, Surah, 4:87.

2. Alfred Guillaume, *Islam* (New York: Penguin, 1956), p. 38, Islam does, however, recognize Jesus as one of a long line of God's prophets.

3. *The Koran,* pp. 362–364, Surah 2:261–265, 270–277.

4. Khomeini in June 1963 when visited in prison by the chief of SAVAK. Cited in Bernard Lewis, "How Khomeini Made It," *New York Review of Books,* January 17, 1985, p. 10.

5. His exile lasted for fourteen years. In one of his speeches Khomeini denounced a law that his country's parliament had passed in October 1964 by which U.S. citizens in Iran had been granted extraterritoriality, the right to be tried according to U.S., instead of Iranian, law. Khomeini called the law "a document for the enslavement of Iran" that "acknowledged that Iran is a colony; it has given America a document attesting that the nation of Muslims is barbarous." Bernard Lewis, "How Khomeni Made It," p. 10.

6. The basis of the Shia creed, in Bernard Lewis, "The Shi'a," *The New York Review of Books,* August 15, 1985, p. 8; Shiites point to Allah's will "to favour those who were oppressed and to make them leaders of mankind, to bestow on them a noble heritage and to give them power in the land." *The Koran,* p. 75, Surah 28:5.

7. Robert Graham, *Iran: The Illusion of Power* (New York: St. Martin's, 1979), p. 33.

8. In March 1976, a dutiful parliament created the "monarchy calendar" (dating from the coronation of Cyrus the Great, 2,535 years ago) replacing the Islamic calendar (based on the date of the *hegira* (flight) of Mohammed from Mecca to Medina in 622 A.D. Ibid, p. 61.

9. "Aryans" here is in reference to the Persian- (Farsi-) speaking peoples of Iran, originally from northern India. It is an attempt to identify the shah with the nation's earliest history.

10. The operation proved to be one of the CIA's greatest triumphs. It pointed to the agency's ability to topple and create foreign governments. In the following year, the CIA overthrew, again with remarkable ease, the left-leaning government of Jacobo Arbenz in Guatemala. Once more, the CIA organized native elements, mostly Guatemalan army officers, who then deposed Arbenz. Little wonder that the CIA later thought that the overthrow of Castro in Cuba would be a minor matter.

11. Henry Kissinger, *The White House Years,* (Boston: Little, Brown), 1979, p. 1264.

12. After the shah's death in 1980, his son became the claimant to the throne and many Iranian exiles pinned their hopes on him.

13. It came as a surprise, therefore, to the U.S. public when in November 1986 it was revealed that Reagan, who for six years had bitterly denounced any and all terrorists and had vowed never to deal with any of them, was found to have paid in effect ransom to terrorists in Lebanon who were holding U.S. hostages. In the process, the Reagan administration had provided numerous shipments of weapons to the government of the Ayatollah Khomeini, which was engaged in a long and bloody war with Iraq.

14. The U.S. National Security Council officials worked out a complex, covert scheme involving the illegal sale of U.S. weapons, mainly ground-to-air missiles, to Iran through Israeli and Iranian intermediaries. Part of the profits from these sales, which totaled $1.2 million, was diverted to supply the Contra guerrillas in Nicaragua. The Reagan administration at first denied that it approved arms sales to Iran, which were illegal, but later admitted the sales, explaining that the purpose was nothing more than to strengthen "moderate elements" within Iran. Reagan, who had come to power because of the hostage crisis in Tehran during 1979–1981, became deeply troubled by the fact that he was incapable of freeing U.S. hostages in Lebanon and hoped that somehow Iranian moderates could help him. He had vowed never to negotiate with terrorists, particularly Shiite and Iranians, yet he was now arming them.

15. Quoted in Mansour Farhang, "Iran-Iraq Conflict: An Unending War Between Two Despots," *The Nation*, September 20, 1986.

16. Graham E. Fuller, "War and Revolution in Iran," *Current History*, February 1989, p. 81.

17. In October 1989, Khadaffi admitted to having bankrolled terrorist groups but added that, "when we discovered that these groups were causing more harm than benefit to the Arab cause, we halted our aid to them completely and withdrew our support." "Kadafi Admits Backing Terrorists, Says He Erred," *Baltimore Sun*, October 26, 1989.

18. Reagan provided no proof of Khadaffi's complicity. West German intelligence stated that the evidence pointed to Syria.

☐ 16

The New Economic Superpowers: Japan and the European Community

In the early 1940s, the United States and its allies were menaced by armed aggression by Germany and Japan. Less than a half century later, those two countries again posed a challenge to the United States—not a military challenge, but an economic one. After World War II, when the United States was the world's only economic superpower, it assisted West Germany and Japan in their economic recovery and provided them security. By the 1980s, however, the European Community (EC), in which West Germany is economically the strongest member, and Japan became economic superpowers, and the United States no longer stood alone. Before examining the relative economic strength of the three and the new economic relationship among them, we need to examine the remarkable economic development of Japan, the strains in its economic relations with the United States, and the emergence of the EC as an economic giant.

■ JAPAN'S "ECONOMIC MIRACLE"

Between the late 1940s and the late 1970s Japan underwent an incredible transformation. This nation, no larger than the state of California, gutted by bombs in World War II, and utterly lacking in virtually all the raw materials needed for modern industry, had grown in the space of 30 years to become the second largest economic power in the world.[1] Only the United States had a larger GNP. But Japan's industrial productivity, in terms of output per person, was already as large as that of the United States.

Japan's postwar economic recovery was rapid, but it did not occur immediately. Quite the contrary; Japan's inflation-ridden economy was in shambles and it remained that way for about three years as the people of Japan endured great hardships. In 1948, the U.S. occupation policy shifted in the direction of assisting Japan's economic recovery, and the United States began providing aid and technological assistance. Still, it was not until 1953 that Japan's economic output reached its prewar level. This resulted from U.S. assistance, Japan's own assets and hard work, and some good luck as well. The luck was the timely occurrence of the Korean War, which provided the Japanese an opportunity to sell their light industry goods to the UN forces in Korea.

U.S. economic aid and assistance to Japan came in various forms. In addition to a total of about $2 billion in direct economic aid (spread over a span of five years), the United States (1) persuaded its Western wartime allies to drop their demands for reparations from Japan, (2) pressured Japan to curb inflation and regain fiscal solvency, (3) provided Japan modern technology by making U.S. patents available cheaply, (4) opened the U.S. market to Japanese goods, (5) persuaded other countries to resume trade with Japan, (6) tolerated Japan's protective tariffs for her new industries, and (7) took up the burden of Japan's defense. The Japanese, of course, appreciated the generous assistance and took full advantage of it. Without the diligent work of the Japanese themselves, however, the economic recovery would not have been possible. Moreover, the U.S. assistance by no means accounts for the Japanese economic miracle that followed the recovery.

Japan's economy began its skyrocket growth in the late 1950s, and it kept on zooming upward through the 1960s. The average annual growth rate of Japan's GNP in the 1960s was about 11 percent, far higher than other industrialized nations. In the same period a 3 percent growth rate was considered good for the United States and other developed countries. The double-digit growth rate continued into the 1970s, until Japan's economic drive was thrown off track in 1974 by the global oil crisis. Detractors were quick to point out the fragility of Japan's economic system because of its resource dependency, and some declared that Japan's miracle was ended. But the Japanese made adjustments, reducing their oil consumption and diversifying their energy sources, and were back on track by 1976. Since then Japan's average annual growth rate has been about 4.5 percent, still the highest among the world's industrialized nations.

Japan surged past most European industrial leaders—Italy, France, and Britain—in the 1960s, and then in the early 1970s it surpassed West Germany, whose own postwar recovery was also impressive. By 1980, Japan's GNP was larger than that of the entire South American continent, more than double that of all of Africa, and more than that of France and Britain together.

By then, Japan ranked first in production in a number of modern industries. It had long been first in shipbuilding; in fact, it built more than one-half of the world's ships by tonnage since the early 1970s. It outpaced the Germans in camera production and the United States in the production of electronic equipment such as radios, televisions, sound systems, and video recorders. Japanese motorcycles left their rivals in the dust, and Japanese automobiles captured an increasing share of the world's markets, so that Japan became the world's leader in automobile production in 1980. Although not yet the largest producer of steel, it had the most modern and efficient steel industry. By 1980, Japan was poised to mount a challenge to U.S. leadership in the new, all-important "high tech" industries, especially in the computer and microelectronic chip fields.

Many in the West tended to belittle Japan's success and explain it away with self-serving excuses or outdated, if not entirely erroneous, notions—for example, Japan's cheap labor. Japan, they argued, was competitive because its people were willing to work for very low wages. This assertion had some truth to it in the 1950s and early 1960s, but not since then. Japan's wage structure reached the level of most industrial nations in the early 1970s. Another notion was that Japan's prosperity was a consequence of its free ride on defense because the United States guaranteed its security. Japan surely benefited from having a much lower level of defense spending than the United States, especially in the first two decades after World War II,[2] but this is difficult to assess. In any case, other factors were more important in explaining Japan's economic growth in the 1970s and 1980s.

■ THE BASES FOR JAPAN'S ECONOMIC GROWTH

Presented below are seven major categories of causal factors involved in the economic success Japan achieved by 1980.

1. *The government-business relationship in Japan is complementary and cooperative, rather than antagonistic.* The government, particularly the Ministry of International Trade and Industry (MITI), charted a course for the nation's economy and coordinated its industrial growth. Both government and industrial firms engaged in long-term planning, and both made use of consensus decision making. The MITI bureaucracy in Japan, with its ties to political and business leaders, steered a steady course, thereby providing policy continuity. It guided industrial development not only by targeting specific industries for growth, but also by designating other declining industries to be scaled down or even dismantled. It also targeted foreign markets on which the Japanese would concentrate their attack. In sum, the Japanese government fostered a national

consensus on the priority of economic growth and established industrial and trade policies to be pursued.

2. *The labor-management system in Japan stresses mutual harmony between the workers and management, rather than confrontation.* Japan's "life-time employment" system, with its built-in rewards for worker seniority, provided employment security to the workers who in turn developed strong identity with and dedication to their firms. This obviously benefited the industrial firm, which could count on retaining the services of its well-trained and loyal work force. Generally, management treated its work force as an investment. Worker morale and motivation were increased by various management programs, including a generous bonus system, educational benefits, housing, insurance, recreational facilities, and the like, and all this resulted in greater worker loyalty and productivity. There are labor unions in Japan, but they are organized locally (as opposed to national trade unions) and their relations with management tend to be cooperative rather than confrontational. Worker participation in management decision making and in quality-control circles also contributed significantly to the mutual benefit of employer and employee.

3. *The Japanese educational system, which is controlled by the central government, maintains uniform, high standards and is extremely competitive.* In Japan, university entrance examinations determine a person's entire future, and only the cream of the crop are admitted to the best universities, whose graduates get the best jobs. Therefore, students at all levels study intensely—incredibly so—in preparation for entrance examinations, or, as they are called in Japan, "examination hell." The result is a highly educated society with well-developed work habits. (An unfortunate consequence of such a high level of pressure on young people is a relatively high rate of suicide.)

Quality of education may be difficult to compare from one nation to the next, but it is true that, on the whole, the Japanese student receives more, if not better, education than his counterpart in other countries. The Japanese school year is sixty days longer than in the United States, and Japanese schoolchildren typically study many hours a day after school with tutors or in private schools. About 33 percent of Japanese high school graduates enter universities, compared to over 55 percent in the United States, but in Japan a higher percentage of entering students graduate from universities. The education system is centralized under the Ministry of Education, which not only provides a uniform curriculum, but also determines what subject areas in the curriculum need to be emphasized. Generally, it maintains high standards in math and science education in the nation's schools. This and the fact that Japanese universities turn out more engineers (even in absolute terms) than the United States help to explain Japan's technological progress.

4. *The Japanese aggressively sought new technology in quest of industrial rationalization and greater productivity.* The Japanese were, for example, swifter than their foreign competitors to modernize their steel plants with the most recent, efficient, and cost-saving technology. When the oxygen-burning type steel furnace was developed in Austria in the early 1960s, the Japanese quickly purchased the patents and invested a vast amount of capital to rapidly convert their plants to the new technology. They also adopted the new continuous casting process at about the same time, and the result was that within a decade they had in operation the world's most efficient and cost-competitive steel plants (to be matched only by South Korea about a decade later). This explains why the Japanese can compete with U.S.-made steel in the United States, even though they must import their iron ore and ship their finished steel across the Pacific Ocean. In this and other key industries, the Japanese have not hesitated to install the most recent technology in their plants in order to improve quality and increase production at the same time. Not surprisingly, Japan is far ahead of the rest of the world in robotics and the automation of the production line. Recent data show that Japan has twice as many industrial robots in operation than all the rest of the world combined.[3]

5. *The high rate of personal savings by the Japanese and Japan's financial and banking practices were beneficial to capital formation for economic growth.* The average Japanese saves a remarkable 18 percent of his salary, compared to about 6 percent for U.S. workers.[4] The banks in which their savings accounts are held invest in industry. Although Japanese firms are also financed by selling stock, a great portion of their capital comes from banks, which, unlike stock holders, do not insist on quarterly profits. Instead, the banks finance long-term business enterprises, which may operate in the red several years before they begin to turn a profit. The availability of this risk capital makes possible the continuous plant modernization noted above.

6. *Japan has developed superior mechanisms for marketing its products abroad.* The Japanese government, mainly MITI, established a foreign trade policy. Also, there exists in Japan comprehensive trading companies that specialize in foreign commerce. These companies have branch offices all around the world collecting data, doing thorough market research, and in numerous ways facilitating Japanese trade. They also work with MITI to arrange the most advantageous trade

agreements, secure long-term supply of vital raw materials, and direct Japanese investment abroad. Although Japan is still vulnerable because of its lack of natural resources, it has made itself much less so by becoming indispensable to resource-supplying nations both as a reliable buyer and as a supplier of technology and capital. Other nations have nothing comparable to Japan's comprehensive trading companies for conducting a large volume of foreign trade, and, in fact, foreign firms sometimes employ these Japanese trading companies to make trade arrangements with other countries.

7. *There were also certain intangible factors unique to Japan—or to East Asian countries—that contributed to economic growth.* The Japanese are served well by certain historically conditioned cultural traits, such as acceptance of authority, paternalism, a desire for harmony, loyalty to superiors, discipline, and a sense of duty and sincerity. Group consciousness prevails over individualism. Without these traits, Japan's labor-management system would hardly be possible. Additionally, there were certain historical circumstances that fortuitously benefited Japan, such as the timing of its industrial development during a period of global economic expansion. It may also be argued that Japan thrives on its own deprivation. Japan's dearth of raw materials, for example, necessitates hard work to attain, conserve, and use them efficiently. By necessity, the Japanese came to excel in industry and foreign commerce.

There were, no doubt, other factors (such as industrial rationalization or efficient organization of the industrial workplace and the rapid growth of Japan's domestic market) involved in Japan's economic performance. But these seven factors make it clear that one must look beyond such explanations as cheap labor. Japan's relatively low level of defense spending and the openness of U.S. markets also worked to Japan's economic advantage. With regard to defense spending, Chalmers Johnson has pointed out that because Japan had a very high rate of investment—capital formation exceeding 30 percent of the GNP—"the effect of low defense expenditures was negligible."[5] In any case, this factor, although not to be discounted, is relatively less important than those outlined above as explanations for Japan's success. As Japan's industrial competitiveness improved and its trade surpluses continued to increase in the 1980s, its trade partners across the Pacific added another explanation (more an accusation) for Japan's economic miracle: unfair trading practices. This charge against Japan became a recurrent theme in Japan's economic relations with the United States and other nations of the world.

■ STRAINS IN U.S.-JAPANESE ECONOMIC RELATIONS IN THE 1980S

Bilateral trade between the United States and Japan in the 1980s became the largest volume of overseas trade between any two nations in history. (Only U.S.-Canada trade, which is not overseas commerce, was larger.) Japan had a deficit in its commodity trade with the United States until 1964; that is, it exported less to the United States than it imported from the United States. From that point, it has been the reverse, with the U.S. deficit in the bilateral trade rising to $1 billion in 1972, $12 billion in 1978, $25 billion in l984, and then soaring to an astronomical $56 billion in 1987. No nation has ever had such a huge trade imbalance with its trading partner. Table 16.1 compares the U.S. trade deficits with Japan and other trading partners in 1987.

Only belatedly did the U.S. public begin to take the Japanese challenge seriously. In the late 1970s, people in the United States were caught by surprise by Japan's seemingly boundless economic growth, and began to wonder about the contrast between Japan's economic success and the recession in their own country. Many of those disaffected by the latter, especially the unemployed, began to blame their problems on Japan. In their minds the growing amount of Japanese imports and rising unemployment were directly related. In Washington, politicians were quick to respond to their plight and take up the cause of combating Japan's trade policies.

In the 1980s, "Japan bashing" became one of Washington's favorite pastimes, even though economists and government officials recognized that declining U.S. industrial competitiveness was an important cause of the trade imbalance. Consumers found Japanese products, especially cars and electronic equipment, superior and less expensive than U.S.-made products. But Japan was open to charges of unfair trade practices, such as "dumping" (selling its products abroad at a loss or at lower prices than in Japan) and protecting its own market from foreign imports by high tariffs, import quotas, and various non-tariff barriers. Some found political hay to be made by calling for "get tough" policies and economic sanctions against Japan. If the Japanese did not lower their trade barriers, they argued, then the United States must erect barriers against the flood of Japanese products. In the 1980s, President Reagan, like his immediate predecessors in the White House, opposed taking this protectionist route, knowing that it could lead to a mutually damaging trade war; instead, he put strong pressure on Japan to open its markets to U.S. goods.

Generally, Washington joined Tokyo in accentuating the positive aspects in U.S.-Japanese relations, which U.S. ambassador to Japan

Mike Mansfield liked to call "the most important bilateral relationship in the world, bar none."[6] But despite the talk of partnership and cooperation, Washington maintained pressure on Japan, which grudgingly gave in to its persistent demands. On the one hand, Tokyo agreed "voluntarily" to various trade limitations and quotas on its exports to the United States; on the other hand, Washington endeavored to pry open Japan's doors to U.S. products by removing Japan's trade barriers. In the 1960s Japan agreed to quotas on textiles, in the 1970s to limitations on steel exports to the United States, and in 1981 to a voluntary ceiling on U.S.-bound automobiles. Japan also began building automobile plants in the United States, partly in order to reduce the volume of Japanese automobile imports and partly to quiet the argument that Japanese cars rob U.S. automobile workers of their jobs.

As Washington erected trade barriers against Japan, it demanded that Japan pull down its own barriers. Since the late 1960s, Tokyo had, in fact, gradually reduced its own tariffs and quotas in order to make foreign goods more competitive in Japan, and by the early 1980s it had agreed to a schedule of tariff reductions that would by 1987 make its tariffs on industrial imports lower, across the board, than those of the United States and the European nations.[7]

Washington then pointed to remaining tariffs and quotas on agricultural imports. This was a problem area, as Japan sought to protect its farmers from foreign suppliers of such foodstuff as beef, oranges, and rice. After years of hard bargaining, the two sides managed only to achieve interim agreements gradually elevating the quotas on beef and oranges.[8] But Tokyo continued to hold out on rice, even if it meant that Japanese people would continue to pay seven times the world price for their precious home-grown rice. Still, Tokyo could respond to U.S. charges by pointing out that Japan was already by far the world's largest importer of U.S. agricultural exports.

Washington applied still more pressure on the Japanese for access to the Japanese market. It called upon Tokyo to remove various non-tariff barriers to imports and to stimulate the domestic market in Japan in order to boost sales of imported goods. Japan was charged with keeping U.S. goods out of its market through such means as restrictive licensing, excessive inspection of imports and burdensome customs clearing procedures, rigid safety standards, a uniquely cumbersome distribution system, and nettlesome purchasing regulations. The charges were certainly not groundless, but these were complicated matters involving peculiarities of the Japanese business system as well as cultural patterns, and in some cases they would be difficult to change or adjust. Only after long and difficult talks were trade negotiators able to achieve limited progress in this area.[9]

Table 16.1 U.S. Trade Deficits with Selected Areas, 1987

Total U.S. trade deficit	−$153,035,000
with Japan	−56,326,000
with the four tigers of Asia	−34,117,000
with European Community	−20,613,000
with OPEC	−12,895,000
with Latin America	−11,507,00

In 1986, the Japanese made a concerted effort to address the problems and meet the demands made of them by their critics abroad, especially regarding the demand to open more fully Japan's market to foreign competitors. Some analysts explained that the huge U.S. trade deficit with Japan was due less to trade policies than to such macroeconomic causes as adjustment of the monetary exchange rate, the increase of the U.S. budget deficit, and stimulation of Japan's domestic economy.[10] In April 1986, a panel of economic advisers headed by Maekawa Haruo, former governor of the Bank of Japan, submitted to Prime Minister Nakasone a report (the Maekawa Report) that called for the Japanese economy to shift from dependence on exports to greater reliance on domestic economic growth. To stimulate domestic consumption the panel recommended wage increases, reduction of work hours, income tax reductions, and removal of the tax exemption on personal savings accounts. The purpose of these proposed reforms was to enlarge the Japanese market for foreign goods, thereby deemphasizing export-led economic growth and reducing the trade imbalance between Japan and its trade partners. The Maekawa Report also said Japan should contribute more to resolving global problems, especially in relieving the debt burden of developing countries. Prime Minister Nakasone endorsed the Maekawa plan, stating that "Japan's future depends on this transformation" and that Japan could no longer remain a "prosperous isolated island."[11] After a meeting with President Reagan in Washington at which he vowed to implement the Maekawa plan, Nakasone made a direct appeal on television to the Japanese people to "accept foreign manufactured products in order to make your life richer and more affluent."[12] Implementation of the plan, especially regarding increasing purchases of foreign imports, was slow, however, mainly because of resistance by various groups within Japan, especially the business community. Some of the recommendations of the plan were adopted (the shorter work week and increased foreign aid, for example), but one could still hear through the end of the decade, from foreigners and Japanese leaders alike, demands that still more be done to stimulate domestic demand in

Japan and to increase its import of foreign manufactured goods.

The Reagan administration attempted another strategy to decrease the U.S. trade deficit with Japan. A monetary policy to lower the value of the dollar against the Japanese yen, it was thought, would lower the price tag on U.S. goods in Japan and raise the price tag on Japanese goods entering the United States. The dollar began its decline against the yen in 1985 when the exchange rate was 260 yen to the dollar, and continued falling until the rate leveled out at around 125 yen to the dollar in 1988. (It inched back upward to over 155 yen to the dollar in early 1990.) But for a variety of reasons, this strategy did not have the desired effect: the volume of Japanese exports to the United States did not decline; U.S. exports to Japan hardly increased;[13] and Japan's bilateral trade surplus zoomed to more than $56 billion in 1987.

The Reagan strategy had another unanticipated and undesired effect: the falling value of the dollar, in effect, lowered the cost of foreign investment in the United States, and this in combination with high interest rates in the United States attracted wealthy Japanese investors. As a result, the Japanese, who had accumulated a tremendous amount of capital from selling goods in the United States, recycled these profits and went on a buying spree, purchasing U.S. banks, companies, and real estate. Most conspicuous were the highly visible real estate acquisitions of Japanese investors in Hawaii, California, and New York City. U.S. Senator Ernest F. Hollings, an advocate of retaliatory sanctions against Japan, noted that the effect of Reagan's monetary approach was to transform the United States "into a coast-to-coast yard sale, with our assets available to foreigners at cut-rate, foreclosure-sale prices."[14]

The trade conflict between Japan and the United States heated up in 1987 when the U.S. Congress demonstrated its "get tough" policy by passing an omnibus trade bill, and the Reagan administration placed a retaliatory tariff on $300 million worth of Japanese electronic products. The 1987 trade bill, which was protectionist in its thrust, contained provisions requiring mandatory retaliation by the president against violations of U.S. trade agreements. Not only did the Japanese denounce the bill, but the Reagan administration also rejected the mandatory provisions in it. Finally in 1988, Congress passed a modified, slightly less protectionist version of the trade bill and overrode the president's veto.

Despite the efforts made by both Japan and the United States, the bilateral trade imbalance was not reduced, and the Japanese made still greater gains as an economic competitor. By 1982, Japan had won a crucial battle in the "high tech wars" when it gained a decisive edge on U.S. competitors in the production and sales of micro-chips (particularly the 64K RAM chips).[15] In the early 1980s, Japan found a booming market in the United States for VCRs (video cassette recorders), a product that, ironically, had been invented in the United States but abandoned as commercially impractical. The Japanese also won increased shares of the U.S. market for other industrial products such as precision tools, musical instruments, and power tools. Meanwhile, Japan surpassed the United States in nonmilitary research and development (R&D) expenditures, and its technological research program gained a lead on the United States in a number of new and important fields, particularly in robotics, magnetic levitation, superconductivity, fiberoptics, and high resolution television.

Japan pulled ahead of the United States in several other ways during the decade. In the mid-1980s, the United States swiftly fell from the status of the leading creditor nation in the world to the largest debtor. Japan just as swiftly became the world's leading creditor. Japan's assault on the money market in the United States in the late 1980s was breathtaking. Japan's economic expansion was no longer limited to the industrial sector, but now extended into the fields of banking and finance. By the end of the decade, 8 of the 10 largest banks in the world were Japanese; 6 of the 12 largest California banks were Japanese-owned; 20 percent of U.S. government bonds were placed by Japanese financial firms; 10 percent of the New York Stock Exchange was handled by four large Japanese companies; the top four security companies in the world were Japanese, with the largest, Nomura, being ten times larger than Merrill Lynch, the largest in the United States; and the Tokyo Stock Exchange surpassed the New York Stock Exchange in capital value and the Osaka Exchange surpassed the London Stock Exchange.[16]

The dramatic elevation of Japan's economic status raised new questions about the relative wealth of the United States and Japan. Older Japanese, clinging to outdated images, still worried about Japan's poverty, such as its paucity of natural resources, and still stood in awe of the prosperity of the United States with all its land and resources. But younger Japanese and many in the United States as well held that Japan had indeed become a rich nation and that the United States with its double deficits (trade deficit and budget deficit) and declining productivity had become a poorer nation by comparison.[17] U.S. leaders cited Japan's new wealth as the basis for insisting that Japan change its economic policies from those of a poor country, which unfairly limits access to its own market. Many in the United States berated the Japanese for not playing on a level playing field, and calling for retaliation and protectionist legislation.

The rising tide of anti-Japanese feeling and the renewed calls for protectionism in the United States caused irritation in Tokyo, and the Japanese responded with a tough-talking counteroffensive of their own. Prime Minister Takeshita, at his first press conference, called upon the United States to first get its own house in order before making demands of Japan. In 1987, "a tidal wave of frenetic and self-righteous America bashing" erupted in Japan.[18] Journalist Eto Jun published a provocative book titled *The U.S.-Japan War Is Not Over*, and the widely read intellectual journal *Bungei Shunju* carried in its June 1987 issue a series of articles under the title "It Is America that Is Wrong." Japanese political and business leaders became more outspoken in lauding Japanese economic superiority and pointing out U.S. economic inferiority. They argued that Japan was unfairly put on the defensive by Washington and made the scapegoat for the United States' own failings. They faulted the United States for such things as fiscal mismanagement, lack of long-term planning, low productivity of its workers, poor quality of its products, and deterioration of its industrial plant and technology. They argued that if Japan removed all remaining barriers to foreign imports, the imbalance in U.S.-Japan trade would scarcely be affected—a view shared by some U.S. observers as well.[19]

By the end of the 1980s, however, persistent effort by both sides did produce some progress in resolving the trade conflicts between the two countries. The bilateral trade deficit dropped from $56.3 billion in 1987 to $55.4 billion in 1988, and U.S. exports to Japan rose 34 percent in 1988 to $37.7 billion. Manufactured goods rose from 30 percent of Japan's total imports to 50 percent.[20] Japan imported more from the United States than from West Germany, France, and Italy combined.

During the 1980s, Japan also built up a large surplus ($20 billion in 1987) in its trade with the European Economic Community, where the demand for protection against Japanese imports was even stronger than in the United States.

■ THE EUROPEAN COMMUNITY

In March 1985, the European Council, whose members include the heads of the governments of the twelve member states of the European Community (EC),[21] announced its goal of a single market by 1992. It would mark the fulfillment of the goal of 1957 when the EC was founded. The European Commission, the executive branch of the EC, published a White Paper, which called for the removal of national rules and regulations, such as in banking, transport, and border controls, among others, in favor of supranational regulations. It was a mammoth task encompassing 279 areas from the rights of labor and women, to banking and insurance, agricultural subsidies, border controls, immigration, air pollution and health standards, transportation, and communication. Ultimately, sometime in the late 1990s, the EC hopes to go so far as to issue a common European Currency Unit (ECU), which would put an end to the 12 different currencies presently in use.[22]

In the late 1950s, the EC had gone a long way in breaking down many of the formidable barriers between the nations of Western Europe, but many had remained in place. Moreover, some nations, France in particular, had turned to "national solutions" to solve their economic problems, particularly those brought about by the oil embargoes of the 1970s. But in the early 1980s, several factors came together: the French and Spanish socialists, who in the past had favored governmental regulations and control of the economy, recognized the superiority of the market over a planned economy. They too began to extol the virtues of competition tied to deregulation of the economy. The EC of 1992 was the logical result of this trend to deregulation.

The first nation to take the road to 1992 was France, which at the time was no longer ruled by the nationalist Charles de Gaulle, but by the "European" Francois Mitterand. In January 1984, Mitterand became the president of the Council of Ministers of the EC and in this capacity he became a convert to European unity. His term as president of the Council, a French diplomat noted, became his "road to Damascus."[23] Helmut Kohl, the chancellor of West Germany, supported this approach as he felt that the strong German economy could only benefit by the removal of national barriers. Margaret Thatcher, the prime minister of Britain, long an apostle of *laissez faire* capitalism, had no reason to object to a free market. The main goal was to strengthen the competitiveness of Western Europe in the world market against the other great players—the United States, which in 1989 created its own free trade zone with Canada, and particularly Japan, the primary target. The Europeans resented Japan's aggressive economic expansion and its continued protection of its own domestic market. In European eyes, competition with Japan had turned into economic war.

The driving force behind European economic unification was the business elite; it was not a popular mass movement. Many, in fact, viewed the full integration process with misgivings. West Germans, for example, feared the influx of immigrants from the south. In the 1960s, West German industry had recruited a large number of workers from Turkey, Yugoslavia, and Greece, many of whom did not return home. European economic unification also bred resentment of foreigners. The EC has its own north-south division. Northern workers feared competition from southern immigrants, such as Portugal, Spain, and

Greece, where the standard of living is less than half that in the north. Labor also feared that the removal of barriers could mean relocation of businesses to countries with lower wages and social benefits. It was little wonder that "labor's sullenness contrasts with the frenzied activity of businessmen."[24]

Even before the Communist dominoes had begun to fall in Eastern Europe, the EC faced the prospect of additional members. The most recent candidate for admission was Turkey. Austria wanted to join, but its 1955 treaty with the Soviet Union barred any sort of union with a German state, be it political or economic. However, with the "new thinking" in Moscow, Austria's prospects for membership appeared brighter. Norway and Sweden discussed the pros and cons of EC membership. The new Hungarian leaders did not think there was much to discuss; Hungary ultimately must belong to the EC. And a unified Germany promised to bring a relatively strong East German economy into the EC. Should these nations join the EC, its population would grow from 322 to 422 million.[25]

The British journal *Economist* in July 1989 sought to answer the question: What is the EC building? The answer "is grander than at first seemed likely." At the end of the 1980s, the EC's competitors, the United States and Japan, increasingly took notice of the emerging structure. In Japan, industrialists "talk of little else when Europeans come to call. . . .The project has taken off more powerfully than most of these outsiders expected." The EC sought to allay fears abroad that the EC was creating a "Fortress Europe." Its communiqué of June 1988 declared that the EC "should be open to third countries and must negotiate with these countries where necessary to ensure access to their market for [European] Community exports. It will seek to preserve the balance of advantages accorded, while respecting the identity of the internal market of the Community."

"This was openness," *The Economist* explained, "but with the gloves well up." The EC toughened its rules against dumping, tightened the "rules of origin" against suspected dumpers, and uncompromisingly demanded "reciprocity" abroad. But it also underscored its commitment to international trade. After all, the total exports of its member nations (including exports to each other) amounted to 20 percent of world exports, compared to the United States with 15 percent, and Japan with 9 percent. To forestall the impact of future protectionism, U.S. and Japanese companies invested heavily in EC countries. Toyota invested $1 billion in an automobile factory in Great Britain; AT&T bought into Italtel in Italy to circumvent the rules of origin. For the Japanese, the central problem was access. Should the walls go up, Japan's global companies hoped to qualify as insiders by building industrial plants within EC nations. For this reason their direct investments in EC countries increased from $1 billion in 1984 to about $9 billion in 1989.

Since 1987, the EC cracked down on dumping by Asian firms, particularly against Japanese companies, but also against businesses operating in South Korea and Hong Kong. It drew up "rules of origin" and "local-content regulations" to determine the origin of an item of merchandise. They were meant to prevent the establishment of Asian "screwdriver plants" in Europe. The EC commission on dumping declared that "assembly is not enough to give origin" when it sought to prevent U.S.-assembled Ricoh copiers from avoiding anti-dumping rules.[26]

But the Europeans remained divided among themselves over the issue of Japanese investment. Margaret Thatcher's government has particularly welcomed Japanese investment to shore up the economy of Britain, where 100 Japanese-owned factories employ over 25,000 employees. In order to lure Japanese investments into their countries, France and Italy, which had maintained notoriously high barriers to foreign imports and investment, began to reconsider their import barriers to Japanese cars produced in Britain. But many European industrialists feared the possibility that unrestricted Japanese investments might lead to Japan's domination of whole sectors of the European economy, as it had achieved in the United States.

Table 16.2 Comparative Data on the EC, the United States, and Japan, 1987

	Population	Per Capita GNP (US$)
European Community	322,871,000	10,730
West Germany	61,200,000	14,400
United States	243,800,000	18,530
Japan	122,100,000	15,760

The EC, whose aggregate economic power is second only to that of the United States, is one of the world's three economic superpowers. The four leading members of the EC—West Germany, France, Italy, and the United Kingdom—rank third through sixth consecutively in the world in GNP. West Germany alone, with one-half the population of Japan and one-quarter that of the United States, became the world's leading exporting nation in 1988, surpassing the United States for the first time and extending its lead in 1989. West Germany's 1989 commodity trade surplus of $61 billion was equal that of Japan and was expected to exceed it in 1990.[28] In 1992, when the complete economic integration of the EC is achieved, the EC will become the world's most powerful common market, with a GNP approaching or possibly exceeding that of the United States and Canada. The 1990s promise a contest for the world's markets among three centers of economic power—the United States and Canada, the European Community, and East Asia.

■ THE NEW GLOBAL BALANCE OF ECONOMIC POWER

The simultaneous rise of Japanese and European Community economic power and the relative decline of U.S. economic power caused uncertainty in their relations and necessitated adjustments by all three in an effort to achieve a new economic balance. As recently as the 1960s, the United States alone accounted for 33 percent of the world's GNP, but by 1989 its share slipped to 20 percent. By then the U.S. current account deficit reached $125 billion, whereas Japan's surplus rose to $72 billion, Taiwan's to $70 billion, and West Germany's to $53 billion. Japan had taken on the role of the world's central banker, and West Germany played that role in Europe. At the end of the 1980s, Japan and the Asian NICs on the one hand, and West Germany and the EC on the other, were gaining momentum, whereas the United States was struggling. The massive domestic debt was a symptom that the nation was living beyond its means, consuming too much and unable to pay its bills.

Although in relative decline, the United States was still economically strong at the end of the 1980s. Its GNP was still, by far, the largest in the world, and its per capita GNP was still among the world's highest. It had recovered from a recession at the beginning of the decade and sustained a modest rate of growth during the decade. The rates of unemployment and inflation were brought under control. U.S. citizens continued to enjoy one of the world's highest standards of living, and immigrants from all over the world still came with their skills and talents looking for opportunity and a better life. On the whole, the stock market remained robust.

But there were economic woes. The strength of the stock market—a key barometer of the health of the economy—disguised serious problems. U.S. business was busier making money than making products that people use; it was moving money around laterally, but not building an economy vertically. During the 1980s, the U.S. national debt soared from $1 trillion to over $25 trillion. Linked to this burgeoning national debt was the vast increase in foreign lending to the United States; in other words, foreigners were contributing to keep the U.S. government solvent with their purchase of U.S. bonds.

The decline in U.S. industrial strength was the product of many factors including an imbalance between commercial and military priorities, lack of government planning, mismanagement by business leaders, executive greed, labor greed, lawyer greed, and other broader social problems such as declining education standards.

It is not possible to analyze all these issues here, but something must be said about the impact of military spending on U.S. economic performance and about major failures committed by U.S. business leaders. The United States has the distinction of being the only nation in the world to be one of the three economic superpowers and at the same time be one of the two military superpowers. The ongoing effort to be militarily invincible has placed a great burden on the nation's economy. The enormous U.S. defense budget, amounting to $300 billion in 1989, or 25 percent of the total budget, was a large drain on the economy. Defense spending was the largest single factor contributing to the nation's crippling debt. Although it provided employment for many U.S. workers, and although it had some spin-offs, such as commercial applications of defense-related R&D, it drew too heavily from national resources, from the pool of capital, and from the pool of engineers and technicians to allow for the nation to be industrially competitive. Because the United States spent about 30 percent of its total research money on defense projects, its spending on non-military R&D was lower on a per capita basis than that of Japan, West Germany, and other major industrial competitors. Two examples of expensive military projects that have both drained the treasury and drawn away large amounts of R&D money and talent from the commercial sector of the economy were the Strategic Defense Initiative (SDI; see Chapter 19) and the Stealth bomber. With regard to the latter, the price tag for each airplane was $500 million, and the estimated total cost of the 132 planes the Air Force requested would be $60 billion.[29]

Among the major mistakes made by U.S. business leadership were Detroit's persistence in building large gas-guzzling automobiles when the global oil crisis created the demand for scaled-down, fuel-efficient cars; the failure of U.S. steel producers to modernize their plants in the 1960s when new technology became available; and the electronic industry's failure to meet consumer demands for electronic home entertainment systems (for example, the VCR) for lack of insight and research, both in design and in marketing. The consequences of such failures as these were extremely damaging to the economic competitiveness of the United States.

Much of the discrepancy in the economic performances of Japan and West Germany on the one side and the United States on the other is to be explained by basic differences in their economic systems and in their cultures. In the United States the free enterprise ideal still lives, and business wants as little government interference in the marketplace as possible. But in Japan and West Germany, which were both later developers, the government was directly involved from the beginning of the economic modernization process in the nineteenth century, and it continues today, especially in Japan, to play a major role in determining industrial and developmental policies.[30] In the United States the idea of industrial planning—for example, government determination of industrial priorities—remains an anathema to the business community.

Japan and West Germany are much smaller nations and more dependent on the world economy. They both developed export-oriented economies, which favored developing industries that could produce exports that earn the foreign currency necessary to buy raw materials—especially important to resource-poor Japan. Thus both countries developed expertise in the conduct of foreign trade. By contrast, U.S. industries have been relatively less interested in production for export, partly because of the large domestic market. One of the more obvious cultural differences is the relatively homogenous makeup of the populations of Japan and West Germany as compared to the ethnic diversity in the United States. With less racial and ethnic diversity, they have less difficulty in achieving national unity, consensus, and cohesion. Although the work week was recently shortened in Japan, the Japanese worker—both blue collar and white collar (especially the latter)—work far more hours than do their counterparts in either the United States or Europe.[31] Relatively, the United States tends to be geared to consumption more than to production, whereas the reverse is true in Japan. The thrifty Japanese seldom use credit cards and other forms of consumer loans. Moreover, the Japanese and Germans save much of their incomes, unlike U.S. workers who tend to save much less and spend more.

A comparison between Japan and West Germany reveals still other similarities and some important differences that have a bearing on their respective economic performances. As noted above, both Japan and West Germany are impressive exporters, with the latter having a slight edge on Japan in total amount of exports. In both countries workers play a central part in industrial organization; both countries give high priority to education and to research and development; in both countries banks hold large shares in industrial companies and have powerful financial-industrial conglomerates that are difficult for outsiders to penetrate; and both countries, with their low rates of inflation and strong currencies, play a major role in the global financial system.[32]

The major difference between Japan and West Germany is that the latter is an integral member of a large and expanding economic entity, the EC. West Germany derives strength in part from its position in the EC, and the EC is strengthened by the central role played by West Germany. Japan has, however, established a dominant position as merchant and investor among the rapidly developing Asian nations. Although its economic ties with these nations remain loose by comparison to the bond forged between West Germany and the other members of the EC, Japan has a growing influence over what some have called the "yen bloc" in Asia. As Harvard economist Lawrence Summers points out, "an Asian economic bloc—with Japan at its apex, followed by the four tigers in the second echelon and the ASEAN nations in the third echelon—is clearly in the making."[33]

The growing productivity and competitiveness of Asia's Four Tigers posed a challenge to all other industrial countries, including Japan. But thus far, it is the United States that has been most affected because each of them enjoys a huge trade surplus in its bilateral trade with the United States. Their markets are no more open than Japan's, but the United States has not been able to penetrate them as well as Japan has. Japan has poured vast amounts of developmental aid and capital investment into the Asian NICs. By building industrial plants in these countries Japan has benefited from the lower labor cost and thus strengthened its international competitiveness. The NICs of Asia, especially South Korea, also represented competition to the Japanese, but Japan seems better prepared for that competition than the United States or Europe. Japan met the new challenge partly by resorting to protectionist policies and partly by making strategic adjustments in its industrial policy. For example, the Japanese chose to scale down certain industries, such as shipbuilding and textiles, conceding them, to a degree, to their newly competitive Korean and Taiwanese neighbors. Other industrial nations, which did not have industrial policies, were more vulnerable to the new competition from these countries. Japan's economic power became a concern not only to the United States but to the EC nations as well, and both found common ground in opposing Japan's economic policies. In this regard, West Germany and the EC have greater affinity with the United States than with Japan. Like the United States, EC countries believe their finished goods are kept out of Japan by its non-tariff barriers and demand that Japan stimulate its domestic market and open it to foreign-made products. They have been less tolerant of Japan than the United States. Unlike the United States, most EC nations maintained substantial tariff barriers and rigorously tried to guard against dumping.

All three economic superpowers are worried about each other's protectionist policies. Both the United States and the EC berate Japan for its nontariff barriers; Japan and EC both fear protectionist rumblings in Washington; and the United States and Japan fear that the fully integrated EC will close its doors to foreign competitors. Yet all three preach the gospel of free trade for they all know that in the long run economic nationalism runs counter to their own interests and that an all-out trade war would be devastating to all involved. Economists, who seldom find much to agree on, are in general agreement that protectionism is not the way for a nation to regain its competitive edge; refusing to buy competitive products from abroad does not result in industrial improvements but rather in higher priced and poorer quality products for consumers.

Economic nationalism, Adam Smith argued in the eighteenth century, was obsolete, but it has become all the more so since then because of growing economic interdependence and the complexity of interlocking international operations of multinational corporations. Several examples will illustrate the point. The U.S. Chrysler Corporation holds 50 percent ownership in joint venture with Mitsubishi Motors to produce cars in the United States and 15 percent interest in Mistubishi of Japan, which produces cars in Japan for Japanese and foreign markets. General Motors, Ford, and several British corporations have entered into similar joint ventures with Japanese car producers. Many "U.S.-made" or "British-made" cars have a large percentage of Japanese parts produced in Japan. Honda, the Japanese car builder, ships some of its cars manufactured by U.S. workers in Ohio to Japan. Ricoh, a Japanese firm, assembles copiers in the United States and exports some of these to Europe, and the U.S. government tried to persuade Europeans that these were U.S. exports. These examples of complicated multinational business operations suggest that simplistic protectionist schemes to keep out foreign competitors have become anachronistic.

Each of the three economic superpowers realizes the high degree of mutual dependence or interdependence in its relations with the other two. An economically and militarily strong United States has been important to both Japan and to Western Europe since World War II, and it still is. The United States has kept open for them the world's largest market. If the United States were to close its doors to Japanese goods, or as one presidential candidate (John Connally) suggested in 1980, leave all those Toyotas rusting on the loading docks in Yokohama, Japan's economy would be doomed. The Japanese government has long acknowledged its dependence on the United States, and its leaders have stated countless times that the health of the U.S. economy is vital to Japan's own prosperity. But in contrast, U.S. recognition of its dependency on Japan has been slow in coming.

By the late 1980s, Japan had become indispensable to the United States by virtue of its technological edge and its huge investments. By withholding its capital it could severely damage the U.S economy, causing the bottom to fall out of the dollar and a depression of unknown proportions. Or by withholding its micro-chips and superior tools, on which U.S. industries rely, the Japanese might cause problems for U.S. firms. But any such action would also have a detrimental or even disastrous effect on the Japanese themselves. Thus, the relationship between the two countries is one of interdependence, and each of the two countries has a great stake in maintaining that relationship.

However, U.S. economic dependency has increased in recent years while Japanese and European leverage has increased. Put another way, as long as the United States continues to run a huge deficit in both budget and trade, it is dependent on foreign investment, Japanese or European, to help pay its bills. The U.S. stock market crash in October 1987 provided evidence of both Japan's concern for the economic health of the United States and the latter's dependence on Japan. It appeared that it was in part Japan's financial intervention in the securities market that "stemmed the stock market debacle."[34]

What, then, is one to make of the foreign "buy out" of the United States? The rapid increase in foreign investment in the late 1980s, and especially the sharp rise in Japanese investments, has caused considerable alarm.[35] It should be pointed out that foreign investment in the United States is not a new phenomenon. Foreign investment, mainly from Britain, contributed substantially to the industrialization of the United States in the latter half of the nineteenth century. The United States remained a debtor nation until 1914. Since World War I, however, the United States has been, and still is, the leading foreign investor. In 1988, the United States' assets abroad were a little over $1.25 trillion, far larger than any other nation's. The problem was that the total foreign holdings in the United States rose sharply in 1988 to $1.8 trillion, leaving a net deficit of $550 billion in foreign investment transactions.

The growing foreign debt does signify a degree of dependency, but there is, nonetheless, a positive side to this influx of money from abroad. In light of the U.S. double deficits, foreign investment has been essential to keep the U.S. government solvent. Economist Herbert Stein regarded the flow of foreign capital into the United States as a benefit to both the investor, who gets high returns on the investment, and the United States, which obtains capital it needs to develop or revitalize its industries.[36] Foreigners would not invest in the United States if they perceived it as weak or if they deemed it a risky investment; on the contrary, they invested in the United States because they viewed it as strong and their investments safe and profitable.

By the end of the decade, politicians, business leaders, and journalists in the United States, Japan, and Europe had often become shrill in their criticism of the other parties in the three-way relationship. In turning up the heat on what they insisted on calling a trade war, they accentuated the negative aspects of economic ties with their rivals. Their strident rhetoric tended to drown out the voices of heads of state and diplomats (and many economists) who continued to accentuate the positive aspects of the economic ties with their trading partners and strove to resolve the differences in a spirit of compromise. In late 1989, the leading news magazine in West Germany came out with a three-part series on Japan, a scathing attack on Japanese economic policies. It lambasted Japan for a whole range of unfair trading policies and practices.[37]

At about the same time, two leading business and political figures in Japan came out with a book that, in response to years of U.S. "Japan bashing," brashly and brazenly attacked the United States for its economic failures and declared, in effect, that the United States was more dependent on Japan than the converse.[38] As suggested by the title of the book, *The Japan that Can Say "No"*, the authors asserted that the United States can no longer take Japanese cooperation for granted. The U.S. reaction to this book was understandably one of shock and outrage. Fusillades such as these served only to worsen the climate for constructive problem-solving among the three economic nations.

Western critics of Japan's economics have often noted that actions speak louder and more effectively than words. But in the case of the book *The Japan that Can Say "No"* and the reaction it has stirred abroad, words may be louder than the impressive actions of the Japanese government to rectify its economic and trade policies in 1988 and 1989. Japan has shortened the work week, increased the number of vacation days, increased domestic spending, relaxed some of the restrictions on agricultural imports, significantly increased its imports of industrial goods, launched an "internationalization" program within the country, and vastly increased its foreign aid. Moreover, it has decreased its total trade surplus over three consecutive years and reduced its trade surplus with the United States as well in 1988 and again in 1989.[39] This record of accomplishment speaks of Japan's increased endeavor to be a more responsible member of the international community.

The industrial decline and increased indebtedness of the United States and the rise of Japan and the EC as economic superpowers have, in combination, fundamentally altered the international economic structure. There now exists among the three economic superpowers a state of interdependence. The United States is clearly no longer paramount. In its effort to work its way out of indebtedness and reliance on foreign capital, the United States clearly needs the cooperation of the other two economic giants. It has more to gain from Japanese and European strength than from their weakness. Their increased economic power also gives them an increased role in international economic affairs. For example, with their strong banking institutions they are now in a position to refinance the Third World's debt.

All three economic superpowers, the United States, Japan, and the EC, play important roles in the maintenance of global economic stability. In Europe, West Germany is in a pivotal position, both as the EC's strongest member and as the one with strongest links to Eastern Europe and the Soviet Union. Japan's climb to the top has, perhaps, been too rapid for it to adjust its economic policies to new global realities. But recent changes in Japan's economic policies and performance indicate that its narrow, nationalist interests are giving way to broader international concerns and commitments. The United States remains the largest economy in the world, but it, no less than the other two, operates in a global framework of interdependence. The economic health of three economic superpowers and of the rest of the world depends in large measure on whether the three of them are able to remain constructively and cooperatively engaged in the maintenance of their interdependent partnership.

■ RECOMMENDED READINGS

Christopher, Robert. *The Japanese Mind*. New York: Fawcett, 1983.
   One of the most readable of the many new books on Japan's "economic miracle."
Frost, Ellen L. *For Richer, For Poorer: The New U.S.-Japan Relationship*. New York: Council on Foreign Relations, 1987.
   An even-handed analysis of the changing economic relationship and the perceptions the two nations have of each other.
Hofheinz, Roy, Jr., and Kent Calder. *The Eastasia Edge*. New York: Basic Books, 1982.
   A comprehensive account of the surging economic growth of the various East Asian countries in recent decades.
Johnson, Chalmers. *MITI and the Japanese Economic Miracle*. Stanford, Calif.: Stanford University Press, 1982.
   A superb analysis of the role of government in Japan's economic growth.
McCraw, Thomas K., ed., *America Versus Japan*. Boston: Harvard Business School Press, 1986.
   Consists of topical essays offering a comparative analysis of economic policies and an excellent overview and conclusion by the editor.
Prestowitz, Clyde V., Jr. *Trading Places: How We Allowed the Japanese to Take the Lead*. New York: Basic Books, 1988.
   An eye-opening interpretation of Japan's relative economic superiority by a former U.S. Department of Commerce official.
Reischauer, Edwin O. *The Japanese Today: Change and Continuity*. Cambridge, Mass.: Harvard University Press, 1986.

A masterful survey of many facets of modern Japan by one of the foremost Japanists in the United States.

Schlossstein, Steven. *Trade War, Greed, Power, and Industrial Policy on Opposite Sides of the Pacific*. New York: Congdon and Weed, Inc., 1984.

An informal but well-informed discussion of U.S-Japanese economic relations.

Vogel, Ezra. *Japan as Number 1: Lessons for America*. Cambridge, Mass: Harvard University Press, 1979.

Not only offers an explanation for Japan's economic success, but suggests ways in which the United States can learn from the Japanese.

■ NOTES

1. The size of the GNP of the Soviet Union was not known for certain, but it was generally believed in the West that Japan's GNP was as large and probably larger by 1980. Its per capita GNP was certainly much larger.

2. Since the 1950s Japan has steadily increased its defense spending so that by the 1980s it as about 6 percent of the annual budget, or 1 percent of its annual GNP. Although Japan's defense budget in absolute terms remained small compared to those of the two superpowers, it is now second only to West Germany among non-nuclear nations.

3. Robot Institute of America, *Japan 1989: An International Comparison* (Tokyo: Keizai Koho Center, 1988), p. 27.

4. This remarkably high rate of savings was accounted for in part by the government taxation laws and the relatively low pensions for Japanese workers, but other causal factors include the huge lump-sum biannual bonuses Japanese workers receive and traditional habits of saving for future security. Similar saving habits are found in other Confucian-related Asian countries such as South Korea and Taiwan.

5. Chalmers Johnson, *MITI and the Japanese Miracle: The Growth of Industrial Policy, 1925–1975* (Stanford: Stanford University Press, 1982), p. 15. Johnson points out that for a nation with a very low rate of investment, such as China, large defense expenditures do retard economic growth, but for nations where investment rates were high, such as South Korea and Taiwan, "their very high defense expenditures have had little or no impact on their economic performance."

6. John E. Woodruff, "Veteran Envoy Mansfield to Retire from Tokyo Post," *Baltimore Sun*, November 15, 1988.

7. In accordance with the Tokyo Round of multilateral trade negotiations, Japan's average tariff on industrial products would, by April 1987, be 3 percent, compared with 4.2 percent for the United States and 4.9 percent for the European Community. Japan Economic Institute, "Market Access Problems in Japan: Part II," *JEI Report*, February 12, 1982. Japan had also reduced its import quotas from 40 items in 1971 to 27 in 1976, of which only 5 were industrial products. This compared favorably with France, which restricted 27 industrial items. West Germany restricted 11 items; the United States, 6 items.

8. *The United States and Japan in 1988: A Time of Transition* (Washington, D.C.: School of Advanced International Studies, The Johns Hopkins University, 1988). After bilateral negotiations had reached an impasse on agricultural imports, Tokyo offered to place all agricultural issues on the table at the GATT (General Agreement on Trade and Tariffs) conference so long as other nations would do so. GATT determined that Japan's quotas on ten specific agricultural import items were illegal, and after first rejecting GATT's ruling because of strong opposition of the farm lobby in Japan, Tokyo announced its decision to comply in February 1988.

9. As early as January 1982 the Japanese government announced plans to take

immediate steps to eliminate 67 of 99 nontariff barriers that had been registered by foreign governments, and nine others were still under consideration. Japanese Economic Institute, "Market-Access Problems in Japan: Part II," *JEI Report,* February 1982. This article and others in subsequent issues of this publication offer detailed explanations of the extremely complex negotiations that continued between U.S. and Japanese trade negotiators on these issues through the 1980s.

10. C. Fred Bergten and William Cline, "The United States–Japan Economic Problem," Institute for International Economics, Washington, D.C., October 29, 1985.

11. Japan Economic Institute, "Maekawa Commission Report Unveiled," *JEI Report,* April 11, 1986.

12. Joseph Kraft, "Bashing Japan," *Baltimore Sun,* April 11, 1986.

13. One reason for this was that as the Japanese domestic spending increased in 1986 and 1987, the Japanese continued to prefer Japanese-made goods over U.S. imports. Also, as the dollar declined in value and the yen appreciated, all of Japan's imports—not only finished goods from the U.S. but also raw materials and components—became cheaper, and this lowered the cost of Japanese industrial production, keeping their products price competitive. Japan's industries also benefited by the fall in the price of oil in these years.

14. Ernest F. Hollings, "We're Winning the Cold War While Losing the Trade War," *Baltimore Sunday Sun,* December 17, 1989, p. 4N.

15. See Clyde V. Prestowitz, *Trading Places: How We Allowed the Japanese to Take the Lead* (New York: Basic Books, 1988), chapter 2. By August 1982, the Japanese captured 65 percent of the world market for micro-chips. In 1980, when the United States was still trying to get their 64K chip out of the lab, the Japanese had already produced prototypes of the 256K chip.

16. Richard W. Wright and Gunter A. Pauli, *The Second Wave: Japan's Global Assault on Financial Services* (New York: St. Martin's, 1987).

17. Prestowitz, pp. 10–25, expresses this view in a rather alarming way. Also see Ellen L. Frost, *For Richer, For Poorer: The New U.S.-Japan Relationship* (New York: Council on Foreign Relations, 1987).

18. For an account of Japanese America bashing in 1987 see *The United States and Japan in 1988: A Time of Transition* (Washington, D.C.: The Edwin O. Reischauer Center for East Asian Studies, School of Advanced International Studies, The Johns Hopkins University, 1988), pp. 86–88, 97–100.

19. The Japan–United States Trade Study Group, "Report of the Japan–United States Economic Relations Group," October 1981. This group was made up of the U.S. business community in Japan, the U.S. embassy, and several Japanese economic and business organizations.

20. Mike Mansfield, "The U.S. and Japan: Sharing our Destinies" *Foreign Affairs* 68, 2 (Spring 1989), p. 5; Takashi Oka, "Japan's Next Big Change," *World Monitor,* December 1989, pp. 30–31.

21. The 12 members of the EC and their years of admission, listed in order of size of GNP, are West Germany (1958), France (1958), Great Britain (1973), Italy (1958), Spain (1986), Netherlands (1958), Belgium (1958), Denmark (1973), Greece (1981), Portugal (1986), Ireland (1973), and Luxembourg (1958).

22. Presently, a citizen of an EC country on a journey to all member nations might lose 47 percent of his money changing it into local currencies. Stanley Hoffmann, "The European Community and 1992," *Foreign Affairs,* Fall 1989, p. 28.

23. Andrew Moravcsik, "Negotiating the Single Act: National Interests and Conventional Statecraft in the European Community," Cambridge, MA: Harvard University, Center for European Studies, Working Paper Series #21, n. d. [1989], pp. 14–15.

24. Hoffmann, "The European Community and 1992," pp. 35–37.

25. An increase of 100 million: Turkey, 52.6 million; Norway, 4.2 million; Sweden, 8.4 million; Austria, 7.6 million; Hungary, 10.6 million; and East Germany, 16.6 million.

26. The EC commission on dumping received about 100 complaints yearly, investigated about 40, and convicted about 15 by imposing duties. "A Survey of Europe's Internal Market," *The Economist,* July 8, 1989, pp. 36–37.

27. Steven Greenhouse, "Europe's Agonizing over Japan," *New York Times,* April 30, 1989.

28. The figures are those issued in December 1989 by the Organization for Economic Cooperation and Development (OECD); Hobert Rowen, "Bonn Next in Line as Power Center," *Washington Post,* January 7, 1990, pp. H1, H8.

29. Daniel S. Greenberg, "Two Nations Striving to Be Best," *Baltimore Sun,* December 11, 1988. President Bush's proposed budget for 1990 calls for $5.5 billion for the Stealth bomber and $4.5 billion for continued work on SDI.

30. See Johnson, *MITI,* pp. 18–23. Johnson explains that in states that were late to industrialize, the state itself led the industrialization drive. He contrasts the Japanese pattern, where the role of government in the economy has been a *developmental* function, with that in the United States, where the government's intervention in the economy was generally limited to a *regulatory* function. The U.S. government, for example, generally does not concern itself with which industries ought to exist and which are no longer needed.

31. In 1986, the average West German or French worker spent 1,650 hours on the job annually—or 75 percent of what the Japanese worker spent on the job (2,180 hours); "Reconsider Japan," *The Economist,* April 26, 1986, p. 21.

32. These points derived mainly from Jeffery E. Garten, "Japan and Germany: American Concerns," *Foreign Affairs* (Winter 1989/90), pp. 88–89.

33. The Ishihara-Morita Brouhaha," *The International Economy,* 3, 6 (December 1989), p. 49.

34. Garten, "Japan and Germany: American Concerns," *Foreign Affairs,* Winter 1989/90, p. 94.

35. Much of the alarm is focused on the Japanese, but it should be pointed out that the Japanese are a distant second to the British as the largest investor in the United States. Japan has been rising swiftly, however, and in 1989 it overtook the Netherlands as the second largest investor.

36. Everett Carll Ladd, "World's Largest Debtor," *Baltimore Sun,* July 28, 1989.

37. See the three-part series in the German newsweekly, "Der Krieg findet längst statt" ("The War Has Begun Long Ago"), *Der Spiegel,* November 6, 13, and 20, 1989. The gist of the series is that the Japanese were not interested in trade but in ambushing their competitors, not merely to gain a share of the market but to dominate certain sectors completely, and all this by unfair means, such as dumping, stealing technology, and excluding foreign competitors from their shores. According to this series, MITI does not just organize trade, it is the headquarters of a war machine, which seeks to dominate the world and dictate to it.

38. Morita Akio and Ishihara Shintaro, *"No" to ieru Nihon* (*The Japan that Can Say "No"*) (Tokyo: Heibonsha, 1989). No authorized English language publication of this book exists, but several unauthorized translations of it have appeared. Morita Akio is president of Sony Corporation and Ishihara Shintaro is a ranking member of the ruling Liberal Democratic party in Japan.

39. In 1989, Japan's total trade surplus declined 17 percent from the previous year and its surplus with the United States declined by 5.5 percent. "Japan Slashed Trade Surplus in 1989," *Baltimore Sun,* January 20, 1990, p. 15B.

□ 17

The Soviet Empire: A Beleaguered Colossus

A cursory glance at the Soviet Union's position in the world in the early 1980s revealed a powerful presence in Europe and Asia. This view was one of particular concern for the policy makers in Washington who had to confront the aspirations of the world's other superpower. Moscow's position in the arms race made it a most dangerous foe. At the same time, however, the Soviet Union was an empire with the traditional problems of an empire. It was racked by centrifugal forces threatening to cause its disintegration.

The Soviet Union's nationalities—of which about half are of non-Russian origin—were still well under Moscow's heel. The same sort of acquiescence could not be found, however, in Moscow's empire beyond its borders. Eastern Europe showed no signs of coming to terms with its subordinate status. Everywhere, with the exception of Bulgaria, the East European governments sought to move toward a position somewhere in the middle between the West and the Soviet Union. They were attempting a most precarious balancing act and the motion had to be inch by inch, as has been the case in the Hungary of Janos Kadar. A stampede, as promised by some of the hotheads of Poland's Solidarity, was not something the Kremlin was likely to look upon with an indifferent eye. In short, the East European governments sought to find their own niche within the Soviet empire.

Along its other borders, the Soviet Union again had its hands full. A hostile China tied down approximately one-third of the Soviet Army along the Soviet-Chinese border, a problem the new Soviet leader Mikhail Gorbachev understood only too well. Elsewhere, other neighbors of the Soviet Union, Turkey and Norway, remained loyal members of NATO, an alliance that showed remarkable resilience as long as the Soviet threat remained plausible. The Ayatollah Khomeini's Islamic government in Iran did not hide its distaste for the secular, atheist government in Moscow. And Afghanistan, governed by a socialist regime since the early 1970s, remained torn asunder by a bloody civil war that threatened to topple the Kremlin's clients in Kabul.

In the mid-1980s, Moscow remained proud and defiant, strong and aggressive. But it was also beleaguered by a host of problems, from restless clients along its borders, to hostile neighbors; from an economy in need of modernization, to the political and nuclear fallout from the disaster at Chernobyl. Soviet strengths and weakness were but two sides of the same coin.

■ POLAND AND SOLIDARITY

The social unrest of 1956 in Poland brought to power Wladyslaw Gomulka, who continued with the reforms that the death of Stalin had put into motion. After the end of the Second World War, Gomulka had been the champion of Poland's right to travel along its own road to socialism, but his position, a deviation from that spelled out by Moscow, earned him a lengthy prison term. After Stalin's death in 1953, it was inevitable that de-Stalinization would return Gomulka to power. When the Soviets accepted Poland's own "October Revolution" of 1956, Gomulka and his party proceeded to sort out the nation's problems. The collectivization of arable land was halted and shortly reversed when the party returned some of the land to its previous owners; the intellectuals continued their debates on Poland's past and future; the state worked out a *modus vivendi* with the Roman Catholic Church; and the lot of the workers began to improve. Within the context of Polish socialism, the reforms were significant, especially when one compares them to developments in neighboring socialist states. In this fashion, Gomulka became a politician with considerable public support.

A reform movement is fed by rising expectations. It invariably produces demands for additional reforms. But Gomulka and his party had no intention of taking the reforms to what some considered their logical conclusion, namely the abolition of the Communist party. Whatever the reforms, the changes had to be within the limits of Polish socialism. The inevitable then took place. The party sought to halt the reformist impulse. As a result, after more than a dozen years in office, the once popular Gomulka had overstayed his welcome. As the years passed, he became more and more rigid. Intellectuals and critics found it increasingly difficult to express their ideas, and social experimentation eventually came to a halt. Also, his austere economic program, which favored the interests of the state over that of the workers, caused considerable discontent.

In December 1970, just before the Christmas holidays in this most Catholic of nations, Gomulka announced a steep increase in the price of food. Riots broke out in the Lenin shipyard in Gdansk and elsewhere. Security forces used strong-arm methods and restored order after they had killed many workers. It was clear to the Communist party that Gomulka had become a liability; a change at the top was needed. The party then turned to Edward Gierek, who came from the ranks of the working class. Gierek, a former miner, caved in to the demands of the radicalized workers, particularly the miners of Silesia, and proceeded to grant them their economic demands.

Gierek's tenure coincided with Willy Brandt's *Ostpolitik*, which was marked by détente, the easing of tensions between East and West. With detente came a considerable increase in East-West trade underwritten by Western bankers. To make possible the export of Western goods to the Eastern bloc, Western banks (which held increasingly larger amounts of "petro-dollars," money deposited by the oil-rich nations) began to lend large sums of money to socialist countries. Gierek, unlike the frugal Gomulka, borrowed heavily from Western banks. In 1973, Poland owed $2.5 billion to the West; by 1982, the debt had risen to $27 billion. With the influx of Western capital and goods (machinery, grain, consumer items, and raw materials) the standard of living rose considerably during the 1970s. But the day of financial reckoning had to come.

That day came in July 1980, when the Gierek government, in order to help pay off Poland's large foreign debt, announced an increase in food prices. As in the past, such announcements produced political repercussions. This measure led directly to an unexpected and dramatic event—the birth of Solidarity.

The Communist party of Poland in the postwar era was a Russian creation and it always remained answerable to Moscow. For this reason, it lacked popular support. Economic mismanagement, police brutality, and corruption also diminished its moral authority. Resentment toward the party ran deep and it resurfaced periodically, notably in 1956 and in 1970. Work stoppages, such as at the Lenin shipyard in Gdansk and in other industrial plants throughout the nation, led to negotiations between the government and workers. The traditional tactic by the government was to buy off individual groups of workers with economic concessions.

But this time the workers refused to take the bait. Instead, they demanded a concession from the government that was nothing short of revolutionary. They demanded that a settlement would have to be with the country's workers as a whole, rather than merely with the "Lenin" shipyard workers where most of the radical activity had taken place.

This tactical position gave rise to Solidarity, a union ultimately representing 10 million people in a country of 35 million. Lech Walesa, the head of Solidarity, became one of Poland's most powerful men.

Solidarity, with the support of the vast majority of the population as well as the church, was able to wring concession after concession from the government. The attention of the world was riveted on Poland where an extraordinary spectacle was unfolding in the sixteen months following the birth of Solidarity. There, the impossible was taking place. According to Marxist ideology, Polish workers were striking against themselves, for, in theory at least, they were the owners of "the means of production," the factories. Strikes by workers against their places of employment were, therefore, both illogical and illegal. Yet this right to strike was the first and most important concession Solidarity wrenched from the state. And with it, Solidarity established its independence from the state and thus became the only union in Eastern Europe not controlled by the state.

With this independence and the right to strike Solidarity established itself as a political power to be reckoned with. Many of the 38 semi-autonomous chapters of Solidarity frequently used the right to strike, generally to correct a condition peculiar to a particular plant. The economic fate of the nation appeared to be in the hands of Solidarity. As its power grew, Solidarity moved into larger headquarters which it managed to obtain from the government. It proceeded to put out a daily, uncensored newspaper. It managed to set up book printing facilities and run a telex operation. It then wrested from the state the materials necessary to establish monuments in honor of workers whom the state had shot to death in the riots of 1956 and 1970. It gained unrestricted access to radio air waves and limited access to television. Finally, Solidarity's pressures on the government produced free local parliamentary elections with a secret ballot. In sum, Solidarity could boast of extraordinary achievements, and many of its members began to believe that the Communist state had become irrelevant.

Observers in both the West and Eastern Europe had felt that sweeping concessions such as those granted by the Polish government were impossible in an East European Communist society. But the Polish party was paralyzed in the face of Solidarity's demands. It was also deeply split. Some members openly supported Solidarity; others even quit the party to join Solidarity. Clearly, Solidarity and not the party expressed the people's will.

The party, as in the past, began to look for a savior, a Napoleon Bonaparte capable of bringing the revolution under control. It turned to a member who possessed considerable moral authority, General Wojciech Jaruzelski. Jaruzelski had risen rapidly in the ranks of the

Polish army and in 1968 he had become the Minister of Defense. In 1970, the government had placed him under house arrest for refusing to use force to suppress strikers. During the disturbances of 1976, he had acted similarly and it was at that time that he made his famous remark: "Polish troops will not fire on Polish workers."[1] Here was a man who could perhaps gain the confidence of the nation. In rapid succession, the party promoted him to prime minister in 1980 and then first secretary in October 1981. He now held what in the context of traditional European politics were the three most important positions: defense minister, head of the government, and head of the party.

Jaruzelski well understood the precariousness of his position. He held the three most important posts in the nation and yet he was unable to govern effectively. Lech Walesa, the head of Solidarity, who held no government position, clearly shared power with Jaruzelski. Another base of power, the Roman Catholic Church, supported Solidarity. On November 4, 1981, Jaruzelski met with Walesa and Archbishop Joseph Glemp, primate of Poland, to discuss the creation of

Polish Solidarity leader Lech Walesa, surrounded by supporters, Warsaw, Poland, Nov. 11, 1980. (*AP/Wide World Photos*)

General Wojciech Jaruzelski, Prime Minister, Defense Minister and First Secretary of the Polish Communist Party, addressing the United Nations General Assembly, Sept. 27, 1985. (*AP/Wide World Photos*)

a "National Front." A successful creation of such a front could institutionalize the sharing of power among the party, church, and Solidarity. But it was not to be. The party and Solidarity were unable to define what constituted a National Front.

Powerful forces in both the party and Solidarity were lining up against any attempts to share power. The hard-liners in the party had always resented the concessions granted to Solidarity and they sought to rescind them. Within Solidarity, the radicals felt there could be no coexistence with the party. One of them, Jacek Kuron, who had long been in bitter combat with the party, put it succinctly: "The essential thing is to understand that the regime has received a final blow: either it must die, or it must destroy Solidarity. There is no other solution."[2] There could be no compromises.

On Saturday, December 12, 1981, Solidarity met amid warnings by the government that "law enforcement agencies will oppose with determination any actions aimed against people's power [the Communist party], in the name of peace for citizens and public order."[3] TASS, the Soviet news agency, charged Solidarity with an attempt to seize political power. The stage was set for a showdown. At the meeting the moderates lost their influence. Solidarity's leadership then called for a national referendum on the future of the Communist party and at the same time it declared its intention to re-examine Poland's military relationship with the Soviet Union (in other words whether to leave or stay in the Warsaw Pact). Solidarity appeared to be getting ready to test the "Brezhnev Doctrine" of 1968 by which the Soviet Union reserved for itself the right to maintain its East European satellite empire.

Solidarity officials felt that the following week would be decisive. Parliament was scheduled to convene on Tuesday with the expectation that it would grant the government sweeping emergency powers. Solidarity's response to an emergency decree was to be a national strike. Thursday promised to bring about another confrontation when Solidarity expected to draw a quarter of a million people to a demonstration in Warsaw.

Over the previous sixteen months, Poland had been drifting inexorably toward this position, one which the Soviets clearly could not accept. The threat of Soviet military intervention always hung in the air. The final triumph of Solidarity or its suppression by the Red Army, with extraordinary consequences for the Warsaw Pact, appeared to be the two most plausible alternatives.

In the West, speculation ran high that the Soviet Union would interfere. But Brezhnev and his party were undecided on what course to take. They wanted Solidarity brought under control, but they knew that the cost of intervention would be high, because it promised a war between the two most important members of the Warsaw Pact. (The Soviet Union had trained and equipped the large Polish armed forces to fight NATO invaders, not the Soviet Army.)

In the middle of November 1980, the Soviet Politburo—led by an apparently reluctant Brezhnev—took steps to authorize the mobilization of Red Army troops along the Polish border. The mobilization proved to be a disaster. Reservists could not be found, others failed to answer the call, and so many deserted and went home that the authorities gave up trying to punish them. Lack of coordination and confusion added to the difficulties. All of this gave Brezhnev a chance to turn on the interventionists in the Soviet Army, and the result was a shake-up in the high echelon of the armed forces.[4] For the time being, at least, armed intervention was out of the question.

Until mid-December 1981, Solidarity continued with its challenge to what appeared to be an impotent and vacillating government which seemed to stand hopelessly against the nation and the embodiment of the nation's will. Only the Soviet Army, it seemed, could save the government of Poland. But, instead, the unexpected happened. On Sunday, December 13, the day after the Solidarity leadership had questioned the future of both the Communist party and the Warsaw Pact in Poland, the government arrested the union's leadership and declared martial law—effectively outlawing Solidarity and reestablishing the primacy of the Communist party.

The commonly held view in the West was that the Soviet Union bore direct responsibility for Jaruzelski's actions. But there was no clear proof for this. To be sure, he did precisely what the Soviet Union had demanded all along; namely he restored order. But as the head of the Polish government, the party, and the army, he had little choice. He was in no position to yield to Solidarity demands that his government and his party transfer political power to the union, for that would have meant political suicide. He also knew that either he would restore order or the Soviet Army would do it for him. Jaruzelski certainly did not relish the latter prospect.

Military law in Poland, generally attributed in the West to the Kremlin, contributed greatly to the intensification of the Cold War, particularly as it came on the heels of the Soviet invasion of Afghanistan. But the Western charge that the Communist leaders of Eastern Europe were but puppets whose strings were pulled by their masters in the Kremlin ignored the realities of East European politics. Between 1945 and 1981, Eastern Europe witnessed four major crises: the Tito-Stalin split of 1948, the events of 1956 in Poland and Hungary, the reforms in Czechoslovakia in 1968, and the rise of Solidarity in 1980-1981. In each of the first three crises, the Soviet leaders had the same complaint: why did Tito, Gomulka, and Dubcek keep the "fraternal" Communist party of the Soviet Union in the dark? The precedents established in the first three instances did not necessarily mean that Jaruzelski acted independently of Moscow when he declared martial law in December 1981. But they did raise the question whether in fact Jaruzelski was "a Russian general in a Polish uniform," a charge Jaruzelski bitterly rejected.[5]

The extraordinary gains of the previous sixteen months were now largely erased. Jaruzelski's security forces had acted with remarkable efficiency in restoring order, which astonished most observers, including Solidarity itself.[6] But Jaruzelski did not manage to win the hearts and minds of the nation. This chapter of Polish history was far from closed.

■ HUNGARY IN FLUX

At the same time that Solidarity in Poland conducted its noisy and determined challenge to the Communist party, events in Hungary proved to be no less important to the transformation of Eastern Europe.

In 1956, Janos Kadar had come to power in the wake of the bloody suppression of the Hungarian rebellion. It was the Soviet Army that had put him in power. For the next dozen years, Hungary experienced little change. The Communist party (whose official name was the Socialist Workers' party) did not experience the sporadic challenges to its authority as was the case in Poland. By the late 1960s, however, Kadar and his party began a cautious program of domestic innovation which, by East European standards, was just short of revolutionary. Throughout, however, Kadar made clear his unswerving allegiance to the foreign policy of the Soviet Union. While gradually moving away from the Soviet model at home, Kadar remained at pains to assure the Soviets that his actions did not threaten the breakup of their East European empire.

Kadar's innovations were made possible by the détente of the late 1960s, which was accompanied by an increase in trade between East and West. The relaxation of tensions also made possible experiments in small-scale capitalism. The result was a mixed economy in which the socialist sector predominated, but one in which small private businesses were permitted. Western journalists referred to this phenomenon as "goulash Communism." Hungarians called it "Communism with a capitalist facelift."[7]

Not only did the state permit the existence of small private enterprises—such as small shops, restaurants, bars, food stands, artisan shops, garages—but it in fact encouraged Hungarians to become entrepreneurs by its selling off of small and unprofitable businesses. Yet this by no means suggested a return to private enterprise as the dominant mode of economic behavior. The bulk of the economic sector—heavy industry, transportation, banking—remained in the hands of the state. Also, private businesses could not employ more than three persons. The Hungarian Communist party was far from handing the economy of the nation to what Marxists liked to call the "international bourgeoisie"; the party remained in full control.

From a rigid Marxist point of view, the Hungarian innovations were nothing short of heresy. But at no time did Karl Marx waste his time discussing the malfeasance of the man who owned a small barbershop for private gain or the peasant woman selling flowers and fruit at a street corner. When Marx wrote his *Capital* he denounced what the poet William Blake called the "dark Satanic mills" of the early industrial revolution. Kadar and his party had no intention of putting the large factories into private hands.

The boom in private enterprises started in 1980, when the government suddenly granted a large number of licenses for private industry. The result was twofold: people invested their savings and the government thus managed to pry loose accumulated savings, putting the money into circulation. All of this was soon followed by a tax squeeze that forced many of the new private enterprises out of business. The high tax rate was designed to keep the private establishments from growing too rapidly and to keep them under control. The return to capitalism had its price.

During the heyday of Solidarity in Poland, local elections gave the voters choices among the candidates, but military law ended this experiment in electoral procedures. Hungary saw a similar reform but with little fanfare, despite the revolutionary nature of the innovation. On June 8, 1985, Hungarian voters cast their ballots for representatives to Parliament and local councils in which at least two candidates ran for nearly all seats. This was the first election under a 1983 law that demanded a choice for the voters. (Multiple candidates had been permitted since the 1970s; the election of 1983, however, demanded a choice.) The law, proposed by Janos Kadar, was unique in a Soviet bloc country. It provided that each of 352 parliamentary seats must have at least two candidates, which did not include, however, the 35 seats held by "nationalist personalities," the ranking party and government leaders—such as Kadar himself. Kadar, the champion of parliamentary democracy, apparently was not willing to go so far as to put up his own safe seat for reelection.

Hungary's Patriotic Popular Front, the Communist organization in charge of conducting the elections, nominated two candidates for each Parliamentary seat in order to stay within the guidelines of the law, but in 71 districts people nominated third, and at times fourth candidates and in several cases replaced a Front candidate with one of their own choosing. The election results showed that 25 of the independent nominees won seats in the 387-member Parliament. The Communist party, however, did not expect a clash between the independent legislators and the Communists. All candidates had to sign a pledge promising to abide by the rules of a socialist society. In short, the contest remained one essentially between two socialist candidates. But there was a crack in the door and someone was certain to try and push through it.

■ THE SOVIET UNION

The reforms in Poland and Hungary began during the reign of Leonid Brezhnev, who came to power in 1964 in the wake of Nikita Khrushchev's ouster. Innovations in the economic sector which were introduced during Khrushchev's reign were quickly shelved under the conservative Brezhnev. It became clear in the mid-1970s that the Soviet Union's economy and intellectual life had entered a period of stagnation which only a change in leadership could reverse. The Soviet Union's ministries ceased publishing statistics in order not to reveal the fact that the country was falling further behind the Western nations in productivity, health care, and the standard of living. Brezhnev and the entrenched bureaucrats proved incapable of moving off dead center. Finally, after a long illness, Brezhnev died in November 1982. His successors, Yuri Andropov, who turned out to be mortally ill from cancer, and Konstantin Chernenko, who suffered from emphysema, merely served time until the Communist party of the Soviet Union elected Mikhail Gorbachev in March 1985. Gorbachev immediately took a number of highly publicized steps to transform the Soviet Union.

Gorbachev's approach did not sit well with many Western critics, for it initially consisted of Western industrial productivity grafted onto the traditional Soviet system to give Soviet society much greater room to maneuver. Still, he advocated a new openness, *glasnost*, whereby Soviet citizens and officials alike would be free to discuss not only the strengths but also the weaknesses of their society. This approach was reflected in *Pravda*, the newspaper of the Communist party, which began to cover disasters such as the nuclear accident at Chernobyl, floods, avalanches, and collisions between ships in the Black Sea. Shortly, the scope of discussion included official corruption, cover-ups, sloppy workmanship in factories, police abuse, Stalin's impact on society, and so on. A number of manuscripts, long refused by publishers in the employ of the state, were printed. Motion pictures, never before shown to the public at large, were playing to sell-out crowds. In January 1987, when a plenary session of the Central Committee refused to officially accept the principle of two candidates for Communist party offices, Gorbachev took a highly publicized trip throughout the nation to drum up support at the local level. In the context of Soviet society, Gorbachev's reforms were nothing short of revolutionary.

■ THE AFGHAN CRISIS

In December 1979, the Soviet Union sent 80,000 troops into Afghanistan. It was an act that stunned the world. For the first time since the end of World War II, the Soviet Union had sent troops into a territory which lay beyond its sphere of influence. The Soviet Union had in the past ordered its army into other nations, into Hungary in 1956 and Czechoslovakia in 1968, but the West—its rhetoric to the contrary—had tacitly recognized these nations to be within the Soviet socialist bloc. But Afghanistan was another matter.

Since 1973, the political orientation in Afghanistan had been toward the left, yet it was officially a neutral nation, a part of the Third World outside the spheres of any of the great powers. Until 1973, both the United States and the Soviet Union had jockeyed for position in Afghanistan without anyone emerging a clear-cut winner. Moreover, Afghanistan ranked far down the scale among the brass rings up for grabs for the superpowers. It was among the poorest nations on earth, with an annual per capita GNP in 1979 of $170.[8]

The Soviet invasion was an ominous sign coming at an unfavorable time for the United States. The defeat in Vietnam did not sit well with a number of people in the United States; it was, after all, the country's first defeat in war. In addition, 1979 had seen the second oil shortage of the decade. Soviet activities in Africa had already raised suspicion in Washington about Moscow's intentions. And the traumatic hostage crisis had just begun in Iran. Even in its early stages, the takeover of the U.S. embassy in Tehran pointed to the limitations of U.S. power. With one setback following another, the result was frustration and belligerence.

The U.S. response to the Soviet invasion of Afghanistan was swift, but ineffective. President Carter had to do something; if only for political reasons at home, he would have to go through the motions of responding to this example of Soviet ambition. This is not to say that the expanded Soviet military presence did not pose a potential threat to

U.S. strategic interests to the south of Afghanistan, particularly in the Persian Gulf where the U.S. fleet sought to protect the shipping lanes of oil tankers. But on the eve of the 1980 presidential election, Carter's problem was primarily of a domestic, political nature. He could not afford to stand idly by and leave himself open to the charge of doing nothing to avert the "loss of Afghanistan." A country of extraordinary poverty and industrial backwardness, a country of little significance in the international balance of power, Afghanistan suddenly took on an importance unmatched in its modern history.

There was scarcely a debate in the United States of the implications of the motivation of the Soviet action. The CIA quickly explained that the Soviet Union faced an "extremely painful" decline in oil supplies and the move into Afghanistan was intended to move the Soviet Army closer to the lucrative oil fields of the Persian Gulf. Once this motive was in place, the Soviet action seemed obvious. "Moscow is already making the point," said CIA director Stansfield Turner, "that Middle Eastern oil is not the exclusive preserve of the West."[9]

Later the CIA retracted its statement when it declared that the Soviet Union was not likely to suffer from oil shortages in the near future. In September 1983, the CIA announced that the Soviet Union's energy prospects looked "highly favorable" for the rest of the century.[10] Moreover, the CIA more than doubled its estimate of the Soviet Union's proven oil reserves, from 35 billion barrels to 80-85 billion.

A Soviet thrust through Afghanistan directed at the oil refineries of the Persian Gulf made little sense from a strategic point of view. Why take a 500-mile detour through rugged country with the prospect of getting bogged down and at the same tip off your enemy? (In the late 1940s, when the strategic planners for the Joint Chief contemplated a Soviet attack on the oil refining installations of the Persian Gulf, they had envisioned a quick and decisive act, a Soviet parachute drop on Abadan which contained the world's largest oil refinery.)

But the damage was already done by the CIA's inflammatory statements. There was to be no discussion of Soviet motives behind the invasion. The Soviet Union seemed to have chosen the right time to make its move, while the United States was preoccupied in Iran. Some in the United States viewed it as a clear example of Communist aggression and expansion and contended that unless something were done the pattern would continue elsewhere. Once again, it appeared that the time had come to draw the line and contain the Soviet Union.

Carter's options were limited. A direct military challenge to the USSR was out of the question. Few Americans would have supported such a drastic move, one that promised grave repercussions. Carter had to find, therefore, different ways by which his administration could express its displeasure with the Soviets. He wound up taking several steps. He refused to permit U.S. athletes to participate in the Soviet showcase, the 1980 summer Olympic Games in Moscow, unless the Soviets withdrew from Afghanistan. There is evidence that the Soviets were stung by Carter's boycott, for they had envisioned the Olympic Games as another stepping-stone toward legitimacy and final acceptance as one of the world's two great powers. But it was an ultimatum the Soviets ignored. They went on to hold the Olympic Games without U.S. participation, and the Soviet Army remained in Kabul. Carter then halted U.S. grain sales to the Soviet Union. But the glut on the world market in agricultural commodities meant that the Soviets shifted their orders to more reliable sources. Lastly, Carter began to look around for clients willing to help him contain the Soviet Union in Asia. Communist China and the United States were, as a result, drawn a bit closer and both began in secret to provide weapons for Afghans fighting the Soviets. The United States also provided military assistance to Pakistan, a country situated along Afghanistan's eastern borders. All told, these measures had little effect on the Soviets, who continued to beef up their forces which soon numbered over 100,000.

***

It is still not clear why the Soviet leaders took this drastic step, one that was bound to finish off the climate of détente for which Brezhnev had labored so hard and long. Perhaps Brezhnev had decided that detente was already a thing of the past. In that case, the benefits of intervention appeared to outweigh any potential losses. Another possibility was that a majority in the Politburo agreed on intervention and Brezhnev went along, as he was required by party rules. Most likely, however, neither Brezhnev nor the Politburo as a whole ever really understood the West's definition of détente, which linked improved relations with Soviet behavior. From the West's point of view, the Soviets could not expect a thaw in the Cold War and at the same time intervene in the internal affairs of another nation. In contrast, Soviet spokesmen always insisted that détente would not prevent the Kremlin from playing the role of a great power in international affairs. Détente and throwing one's weight around in the Third World, the Kremlin argued, were not antithetical.

The chief reason, however, why the Soviet Union intervened in the internal affairs of Afghanistan was apparently to bring order to a chaotic political situation in a neighboring socialist country. The Politburo, the guardian of Soviet interests and prestige, was unwilling to accept the defeat of a client. In the simple arithmetic of the Cold

War, a setback for the forces of socialism would mean a victory for capitalism. (The reverse argument, after all, was well understood and often used in the West.) Such an argument is generally motivated by a sense of the loss of prestige and image rather than rational analyses of the needs of national security. It rests largely on what conclusions others might draw from one's own misfortune.

Political instability has long been the order of the day in Afghanistan; coups and counter-coups have often followed in rapid order. A case in point was the political instability of the 1970s. In 1973, the leftist, Prince Mohammed Daoud, with the help of the military, overthrew in a bloodless coup King Zahir Shah, his cousin. In 1978, Daoud himself was ousted and killed in a second coup by the socialist People's Democratic party under the leadership of Nur Mohammed Taraki, who established closer ties with the Soviet Union. Taraki in turn was ousted and murdered in a third leftist coup carried out by Hafizullah Amin who was in power in Kabul at the time of the Soviet invasion. All this bloodletting took place in the Marxist party, the People's Democratic party.

It is here that one can find another clue to the Soviet Union's decision to invade Afghanistan. Taraki and Amin had a falling out with Taraki looking to Moscow for support and Amin apparently looking to Washington. Amin met a number of times with the U.S. ambassador, Adolph Dubs. What exactly transpired between these two men is not clear, but the Soviets feared the worst. To them, Amin was at the threshold of following in the footsteps of the Egyptian head of state, Anwar Sadat, who in 1972 ousted the 20,000 Soviet advisers in Egypt and then invited U.S. military personnel. It is possible that more than anything else the fear of an Afghan diplomatic revolution—from Moscow to Washington—prompted the Soviet invasion.[11] Seven years later, Mikhail Gorbachev, the new Soviet leader, sought an exit from Afghanistan, insisting on a guarantee that no hostile power become entrenched along the Soviet Union's southern flank.

While these leftist coups were taking place, opposition to the central government gradually increased. Such opposition has long been a central feature of Afghan politics. Local rulers in outlying regions have always jealously guarded their authority and freedom of action. But this time they had other grievances. They resented the attempts at social and economic transformation of their tradition-bound society, untouched even by colonial rule. Resentment of reform, especially when carried out with force and in direct opposition to popular will, ran deep. Amin sought to introduce education (and even co-education) for girls and the elimination of the veil and bridal dowries. The confiscation of land added fuel to the fire.

In the name of freedom, Islam, and anti-Communism, the rebels rose against the Marxist governments in Kabul which found themselves increasingly isolated from the countryside where rebellious forces were gaining in strength. Hafizullah Amin's brutal regime only made things worse and the counterrevolution threatened to doom the socialist experiment in Afghanistan. Ultimately, Amin literally waved the red flag before his enemies when he replaced the national, traditional Islamic flag of green, black, and red with one similar to those of the Soviet Union's Central Asian republics. And with it, to use an expression favored by geopolitical strategists in Moscow and Washington, the "correlation of forces" in Afghanistan threatened to shift in the West's favor. The Politburo in Moscow decided to act. Invoking the Brezhnev Doctrine of 1968 (by which the Soviet Union had taken upon itself the right to save the Communist party in Czechoslovakia from what it called a "counter-revolution"), Brezhnev and his associates sent the troops. Once again, the Soviet Army bailed out a bankrupt Communist regime. Amin was deposed and apparently killed by Soviet commandos and replaced by his rival, Babrak Karmal. The Kremlin then proclaimed that it had acted upon invitation by the government of Afghanistan.

But the removal of Amin did not placate the rebels. If anything, the rebellion against socialist Kabul only increased in strength and intensity. The new ruler of Afghanistan was correctly regarded as a Soviet puppet who promised to subjugate his nation to the interests of a foreign power. Such a prospect did not sit easily with most Afghans, many of whom remembered Stalin's brutal collectivization drive and the purges of the 1930s. In those years, many Muslims of Soviet Central Asia fled into neighboring Afghanistan where they found refuge among the local population. Soviet intervention in Afghanistan promised the repetition of history. Babrak Karmal was the creation of a foreign power bent upon the social, economic, and ideological transformation of the nation. He could maintain his position only with the backing of an occupation force.

Another plausible explanation of the Soviet invasion lies in the very ethnic makeup of the Soviet Union. It is an empire, conquered and controlled by the Russians, one that contains scores of peoples openly hostile to the Russians. Half of the country's population consists of Russians, the other half of non-Russians. The geographic division of the USSR points to this fact. Officially, the nation is a "union" of fifteen "Soviet, socialist republics," the largest of which is the "Russian Republic." The other "republics" contain Ukrainians, Belorussians, Latvians, Lithuanians, Estonians, Georgians, and others, all with their different histories, cultures, languages, and, in many instances, religions. In the West, especially in the United States, these peoples are too often lumped together under the heading of "Russians," such as "Russian athletes," and they deeply resent this erroneous characterization. One of the largest ethnic groups in the Soviet Union are the Muslims of Central Asia, peoples with long and glorious histories who only a little more than a hundred years ago fell under Russian domination.

As the Soviet Army crossed the border into Afghanistan it mobilized and used a sizable percentage of recruits from Central Asia. This step was in line with standard procedure of using the most readily available reserves. The use of such troops appeared to have an added virtue: officially, the Kremlin declared that its army had been "invited" by a beleaguered Afghan government. The Central Asian Muslim recruits, therefore, became prima facie evidence of "fraternal" Soviet assistance to the Afghan government. But this policy soon ran into trouble when the Soviet army found out that its task was the pacification of the country. The Soviet Muslims showed little inclination to fight their ethnic and religious counterparts. Some went over to the rebels; others deserted. Within three months, Soviet authorities began to change the composition of their forces. The Soviet Army in Afghanistan began to consist largely of politically more reliable Slavic troops.

The Soviet Union has one of the largest Muslim populations in the world. It contains approximately 50 million people of Muslim origin, and one estimate has it that about 75 percent of these are believers. Millions of Muslims have never bothered to learn the Russian language. To make matters worse for Moscow, the birthrate among the Russians is extraordinarily low, while that among the Muslims of Central Asia is quite high. It is clear that by the year 2000, the Russians will no longer constitute a majority in their empire. Perhaps every third draftee for the Soviet Army will come from the Muslim population. All this poses several pressing questions for Moscow. What impact will the rise of militant Islam have on this large population? (The Ayatollah Khomeini never made much of a distinction between the atheist Brezhnev in the Kremlin and the born-again Christian Carter in the White House. He condemned them both.) Dare the Kremlin, therefore, permit a successful Muslim insurgency against a Communist regime along the borders of the Soviet Union?

The Brezhnev regime repeatedly displayed an inclination to stability and order. The invasion of Afghanistan was designed to eliminate a source of potential trouble. Unfortunately for the Soviet Union, Afghanistan did not prove to be another surgical operation as was the case in Hungary in 1956 and Czechoslovakia in 1968.

***

Western reporters in Afghanistan brought back tales of heroic resistance and occasional rebel victories over government and Soviet troops. None of this was surprising, for the Afghan fighting spirit is legendary. Yet victory eluded them. Perhaps, the following can explain why.

Unlike guerrilla movements in other parts in the world, the Afghan rebels had no program of social, political, and economic reform. There was no literacy campaign (in 1979, primary school enrollment stood at 30 percent, mostly in the cities; the adult literacy rate was 15 percent), no declaration on the rights of women, no medical programs (life expectancy at birth was 36 years; in the industrial nations of the West it is twice that), no political experiments such as elected village councils, no economic enterprises such as cooperatives or shops. In short, the rebels offered no political alternative to the Marxist program of Kabul. Moreover, the rebels were deeply split into contending factions. Gerard Chaliand, a French specialist on Third World guerrilla movements, concluded that

> The current Afghan resistance movement looks [more] like a traditional revolt [against the capital] . . . than like modern guerrilla warfare. Among contemporary guerrilla movements only the Kenyan Mau Mau [of the early 1950s] are less sophisticated in their strategy and organization.[12]

The nature of Afghan resistance and its foreign supporters proved once more that politics make strange bedfellows, particularly in light of the fact that some of the rebel factions were financed by Libya's Muammar Khadaffi, the Ayatollah Khomeini of Iran, and the United States government under Ronald Reagan. This story becomes even stranger when one takes into account that the Reagan administration supported Islamic/Marxist rebels who in 1979 had kidnapped the American ambassador Adolph Dubs who then died in a rescue attempt by the Taraki government. The Islamic world faced the choice between a modern, secular society or the reinvigoration of Islam's traditions. The Afghan rebels represented neither alternative. They sought instead the preservation of a traditional society to the exclusion of the industrial revolution and all it entailed. Yet, in a strange twist of fate the United States, the standard-bearer for the industrial revolution and parliamentary democracy, became the main arms supplier for the Afghan rebels.

■ SOVIET EXODUS FROM AFGHANISTAN

Shortly after Gorbachev came to power in March 1985, he found out that it is easier to start a war than to end one. The new Soviet leader took a number of steps in an attempt to extricate his armed forces from Afghanistan. He sought to establish a dialogue with the resistance forces, only to be rebuffed. Gorbachev wanted a coalition government of Communists and members of the resistance, but too much blood had been shed to make such a solution a possibility. The Afghan rebels were not interested in sitting down with either the Soviets or their clients, against whom they had been waging an uncompromising war. The Soviet government even went so far as to suggest the return of King Zahir from his exile in Rome in hope of creating a working government. But to no avail. Gorbachev was unable to find a political solution acceptable to all sides.

The Gorbachev policy of establishing normal relations between the Soviet Union and the West demanded the withdrawal of Soviet troops from Afghanistan. At first, however, Gorbachev was unwilling to accept a military defeat along the southern flank of the Soviet Union, and for that reason he escalated the war. But the rebels were too well equipped, having received arms from a variety of sources, among them the effective U.S.-made Stinger ground-to-air missiles, which brought down numerous aircraft and helicopters. Gorbachev soon realized that only a massive increase in blood and treasure would bring victory. Yet, such a move was certain to undermine his position abroad, particularly in his dealings with the United States and China. For that reason, he shifted gears and announced that he sought the withdrawal of his army. He declared that the invasion of Afghanistan had not been merely another mistake of the Brezhnev administration, but also a sin.

But the Soviet withdrawal would not be unilateral. Gorbachev would accept a defeat of his client provided, however, that the new government of Afghanistan would not be allied with the West. The superpowers would have to cease to conduct their wars by surrogates on the fields of Afghanistan. Those were the terms of the settlement between Moscow and the Reagan administration signed on April 14, 1988. On February 15, 1989, the last Soviet troops marched out of Afghanistan, leaving a client government, led by President Najibullah, in power in Kabul.

But old habits were hard to break. Both Washington and Moscow did what they could to prop up their clients. Firepower at the cost of billions of dollars and rubles continued to pour into Afghanistan. Many in the West had expected the rapid demise of the government in Kabul, which, however, showed remarkable staying power. It managed to survive the withdrawal of the Soviet army because of the extraordinary fragmentation of Afghan society and the resistance movement in particular. In the 1950s, Prime Minister Mohammed Daoud (at that time still serving the king, Zahir Shah) had taken effective steps to form a modern, centralized state, which the civil war of the late 1970s, however, tore apart. Rural Afghanistan reverted to a state of fragmentation in which traditional kinship and religious affiliation took precedence over any attempt to create a national identification. Local leaders emerged who derived their legitimacy from the fighting men and territories they controlled. They tended to be loosely allied with one of the seven parties based in Peshawar, Pakistan. In May 1985, these parties created a wider front, the Islamic Union of Mujahedeen of Afghanistan. But only hatred of the men in Kabul held this tenuous front together. Among the leaders of these groups one could find Pushtuns, Tadzhiks, and Arabs. The alliance was dominated by Shiite fundamentalists who previously had played only a minor role in national politics; most of the mujahedeen, however, were Sunnis. Thus one side was supported by Shiite Iran, the other by Iran's mortal enemy, the keeper of the Islam's holiest of shrines, Sunni Saudi Arabia. Inevitably, they turned against each other.[13]

The rebels hoped to seize the city of Jalalabad and establish there a government. But the rural rebels, in the bitter battle with the urban population, made a major tactical error. By their indiscriminate shelling of Kabul and Jalalabad and the massacres of defectors, they left the government forces no choice but to fight to the bitter end. Although many in Afghanistan rejected the ideology of the Najibullah regime, they also rejected the policies of the Shiite fundamentalists.

The war demanded a heavy toll from Afghanistan's population of 15 million people. Approximately 1 million died during the years 1979-1989 and between 5 and 6 million became refugees in Pakistan and Iran. The political system remained a throwback to the feudal era. The official government in Kabul was still incapable of governing the outlying regions, and none of the political parties had a program for resolving the ethnic, political, and religious conflicts that were continuing to tear the nation apart. At the time of the Malta Conference in December 1989 between Gorbachev and President George Bush, Gennady Gerasimov of the Soviet foreign ministry declared that the Cold War was over, that it had been buried at the bottom of the Mediterranean Sea. In light of the events in Europe in 1989, Gerasimov's rosy outlook may have had some substance. Afghanistan, however, continued to feel the bloody impact of the rivalry between the superpowers.

■ RECOMMENDED READINGS

Ascherson, Neal. *The Polish August: The Self-Limiting Revolution* (New York: Viking Press, 1982.)
A survey of the political climate in Poland that set the stage for the rise of Solidarity.

Ash, Timothy Garton. *The Polish Revolution: Solidarity* (New York: Charles Scribner's Sons, 1984.)
Discusses the rise and fall of Solidarity.

Bradsher, Henry S. *Afghanistan and the Soviet Union* (Durham, NC: Duke University Press, 2nd ed., 1985.)
A detailed account of the events leading up to the Russian invasion.

Brumberg, Abraham, ed., *Poland: Genesis of a Revolution* (New York: Random House, 1983.)
A collection of essays by Polish activists, intellectuals, workers, party officials, clergymen, dissidents, and loyalists; the stress is on political and cultural pluralism in Poland.

Carrere d'Encausse, Helene. *Decline of an Empire:The Soviet Socialist Republics in Revolt* (New York: Harper & Row, 1978.)
An introduction to the ethnic complexity of the Soviet empire.

Chaliand, Gerard. *Report From Afghanistan* (New York: Penguin, 1982.)
A useful introduction to the history, geography, and recent politics of Afghanistan.

Garthoff, Raymond L. *Détente and Confrontation: American-Soviet Relations From Nixon to Reagan* (Washington, D. C.: The Brookings Institution, 1985.)
A military historian discusses the Soviet intervention in Afghanistan; he argues that the Soviets feared that Amin would expel their advisors and bring in U.S. personnel as Sadat had done a few years earlier in Egypt.

■ NOTES

1. "Another Bloody Sunday," *Baltimore Sun*, December 18, 1981, p. A22.

2. Michael Dobbs, K. S. Karol, and Dessa Trevisan, *Poland, Solidarity, Walesa* (New York: McGraw-Hill, 1981), p. 70.

3. John Darnton, "Leaders of Union Urge Polish Vote on Form of Rule," *New York Times*, December 13, 1981, p. 1.

4. Andrew Cockburn, *The Threat: Inside the Soviet Military Machine* (New York: Random House, 2nd rev. ed., 1984), pp. 111-114, 178-180; Michael T. Kaufman, "Bloc Was Prepared to Crush Solidarity, a Defector Says," *New York Times*, April 17, 1987, p. A9.

5. Vladimir Solovyov and Elena Klepikova, "Kudos for the General," *Baltimore Sun*, July 2, 1986, p. A15.

6. During the heady days of Solidarity, a reporter asked Walesa for his reaction should the government resort to force in an attempt to deal with Solidarity. Walesa replied that "we would ignore it."

7. Stuart H. Loory, "New Kid on the Bloc: Gorbachev's Reforms Spill into Eastern Europe," *The Progressive*, June 1987, p. 22; John Kifner, "A New Ingredient Spices 'Goulash Communism,'" *New York Times*, November 11, 1983, p. A2.

8. 1979 is the last year for which the World Bank has any figures for Afghanistan. Its level of income puts it among what the World Bank calls "low-income developing countries—that is, countries with incomes below about a dollar per person per day." The Soviet intervention and the accompanying destruction brought only greater poverty.

9. AP, "Soviets Facing Oil Crunch, CIA Director Says, *Baltimore Evening Sun*, April

22, 1980, p. A5.

10. Bernard Gwertzman, "Soviet Is Able to Raise Production of Oil and Gas, U.S. Agency Says," *New York Times*, September 3, 1981, p. A1.

11. For details, see Raymond L. Garthoff, *Détente and Revolution: American-Soviet Relations from Nixon to Reagan* (Washington, D. C.: The Brookings Institution, 1985), pp. 887–965.

12. Gerard Chaliand, *Report From Afghanistan* (New York: Penguin, 1982), p. 49.

13. For the politics of the Afghan resistance, see Bernard R. Rubin, "The Fragmentation of Afghanistan," *Foreign Affairs*, Winter 1989/1990, pp. 150–168.

☐ 18

Gorbachev and the Restructuring of Eastern Europe

After the death of Konstantin Chernenko in March 1985, the Communist party of the Soviet Union turned to Mikhail Gorbachev as its leader. The public in the Soviet Union and in the West knew little about Gorbachev, although in December 1984 he had made his successful appearance on the world's stage during his visit to London. There he behaved unlike previous Soviet visitors. Khrushchev's visit in 1955 had turned sour when he reminded his hosts ominously of his country's potentially devastating nuclear arsenal. Gorbachev did nothing of the kind. He spoke, instead, of the need to disarm and reminded the British of their wartime alliance with the Soviet Union and their losses at Coventry. Instead of the customary visit to Karl Marx's grave at Highgate Cemetery, he visited Westminster Abbey. Margaret Thatcher, Britain's conservative prime minister, concluded: "I like him. We can do business with him."

Gorbachev soon caused another stir by his speech in February 1985, in which he declared that the Soviet Union was in need of a radical transformation. "Paper shuffling, an addiction to fruitless meetings, windbaggery and formalism" will no longer do, he declared.[1] But at the outset he proved to be a careful reformer who understood that politics is the art of the possible. The then 307-member Central Committee of the party and the influential 12-member Politburo, which guides the party on a day-to-day basis, had come to power under the conservative Brezhnev. In his first speech as general secretary of the party, Gorbachev placated the right wing of his party with his reaffirmation of the old values. But as time went by, he showed that he intended to reorganize the system inherited from his predecessors; the Soviet Union, he insisted, must undergo a radical *perestroika*, or restructuring.

In the long run, Gorbachev's program was nothing short of revolutionary. Among his targets were the centrally planned industrial system and the collective farms Joseph Stalin had introduced in the late

1920s. Gorbachev ended the rigid censorship of public opinion when he set out to give non-Communists a public voice. He ended the long and debilitating conflict between the state and organized religion, ended the isolation of his country's intellectuals, invited intellectuals who had been expelled from the Soviet Union to return to their native soil, sent an unprecedented number of Soviet citizens abroad, permitted the sale of Western publications, forced the Soviet Union's conservative historians to come to grips with their history, and broke down the power of the party. He also redefined the Soviet Union's position vis-à-vis China, Eastern Europe, the West, and the Third World, and took his army out of Afghanistan. In sum, Gorbachev turned the science of Kremlinology on its head; he did what was thought no leader in the Kremlin could or would even try to do.

Gorbachev, in a sharp break with Soviet history, demanded an open and honest discussion of society's problems. To do so, he had to give society, and not just the party, a voice. *Glasnost*, from the Russian for voice, therefore, became the first order of business. The severest test of *glasnost* came early. In April 1986, an atomic reactor in Chernobyl, in the north of the Ukrainian Republic, suffered a meltdown and an explosion, spewing radioactive matter into the Belorussian Republic, Scandinavia, and then down into Germany and as far south as Italy. Soviet technology was contaminating what Gorbachev earlier had called "our common European home." In his New Year's address a few months earlier he had promised "to call things by their name." The recognition of mistakes, he said, is the "best medicine against arrogance and complacency."[2] But for the first nineteen days after Chernobyl no acknowledgment of the disaster came out of Moscow. When Gorbachev finally spoke on national television, he admitted that a nuclear plant had burned out of control.

What transpired in Moscow during those nineteen days remains unknown. Gorbachev apparently was able to make the point that the old ways would no longer suffice. Instead, "new thinking" was required. Problems must no longer be denied and officials had to be made responsible not only for their successes but also for their failures. He used Chernobyl to further weaken the conservative wing of the party, the chief obstacle to *perestroika*. At this point, the differences between Gorbachev and Nikita Khrushchev became apparent. When Khrushchev tried to implement his reforms he always shrunk back from the consequences. The result was a zig-zag course, Khrushchev's famous "hare-brained schemes." Gorbachev, in contrast with Khrushchev, repeatedly used political, natural, and man-made disasters—on the surface, setbacks—to his advantage. In the wake of Chernobyl, Gorbachev continued with the reorganization of the party, which he had begun as early as May 1985. He fired members of the old guard and replaced them with his people. The Soviet press began an open discussion of the causes and consequences of the Chernobyl disaster. What initially appeared as a setback for *glasnost* was turned to its advantage.

Artists and writers quickly tested the limits of *glasnost*. The consequence was the appearance of a veritable flood of works which had been created years ago "for the drawer" waiting to see the light of day; some had waited more than twenty years. Among them were Anatoli Rybakov's *Children of the Arbat*, a novel set in 1933–1934 at the beginning of Stalin's terror, and films such as *Our Armored Train*, a critical analysis of the legacy of the Stalin era. Periodicals openly began to discuss society's ills—poor medical care, the high incidence of traffic accidents, alcoholism, official corruption, anti-Semitism, shoddy workmanship, and the lack of quality consumer goods, among other woes.

A number of observers in the West and in the Soviet Union insisted, however, that the acid test of *glasnost* would be how the Kremlin treated the writings of Alexander Solzhenitsyn, whose novel *One Day in the Life of Ivan Denisovich* had been the literary sensation of Moscow in 1962. Khrushchev had used this exposé of the prison system to further discredit Stalin. But Solzhenitsyn refused to stop at this point. In his three-volume *The Gulag Archipelago* he laid the blame for the prison system squarely at the feet of the revered founder of the Soviet state, Vladimir Lenin, a man whose stature in the Soviet Union is no less than that of a saint. For that, for the fact that Solzhenitsyn had his works published in the West, and for other transgressions, Brezhnev had stripped him of his citizenship and expelled him from the country in 1974. Gorbachev and his Politburo initially opposed suggestions to allow *The Gulag Archipelago* to be published. Vadim Medvedev, the Politburo member in charge of ideology, explained that it undermined "the foundation on which our present life rests." But public pressure, expressed in thousands of letters and telegrams, had an unprecedented impact on Soviet cultural history. In June 1989, Gorbachev apparently told his Politburo that the decision whether to publish Solzhenitsyn should be in the hands of editors, not the party. After an absence of twenty-five years, Solzhenitsyn was reintroduced to Soviet readers.[3]

Gorbachev insisted also that Soviet society come to grips with its past. Journalists and dissident historians were quick to subject the Brezhnev "era of stagnation" (1964–1981), and in particular the Stalin legacy, to close scrutiny. The professional historians, however, dragged their heels. Too many had become comfortable with the established formulas of writing history and wanted no part of Gorbachev's "new thinking." Early in 1988, Gorbachev apparently personally intervened and purged the old editorship of all historical journals, among them the Soviet Union's most prestigious, *Voprosy istorii* (*Problems of History*). The lead article of the February 1988 issue declared that the journal's new task was to participate in the *perestroika* of the country. Articles began to discuss persons and events hitherto considered taboo—Stalin's purges of the party, the "tragedy" of collectivization in Kazakhstan by historians from that republic, the nationality problem, and others. The journal participated in the political rehabilitation of Khrushchev and victims of Stalin's purges, such as Nikolai Bukharin, and went so far as to publish Leon Trotsky's essay, "The Stalin School of Falsification of History." In the huge Lenin Library in Moscow "new" books were made available to readers—books that had been published initially decades ago by the Soviet Union's leading politicians and then suppressed by Stalin.[4]

Most writers and historians, freed from the constraints of the past, expressed distictly liberal, Western values. They supported *Memorial,* an organization in remembrance of those who had fallen victim to Stalin's purges. But *glasnost* also gave writers of anti-Western and anti-liberal persuasion a voice and showed that the nativist tradition ran deep. Another organization, *Pamiat* (Remembrance), in contrast to the liberals of *Memorial,* remembered history differently. The "Russian National-Patriotic Front Memory," *Pamiat*'s formal name, did not consider the Stalinist legacy to be the nation's main source of difficulty; it focused instead on Zionists and cosmopolitans.[5] In Pamiat's views, Stalin played the role of the good tsar, terrible but righteous, who punished the wicked and brought the nation to its military and industrial power. The debate was reminiscent of that of the nineteenth century between the Westerners and the Slavophiles, the former seeking the salvation of the nation in Western ideas, the latter in purely Russian institutions.

■ INDUSTRY

When Gorbachev first began to speak of *perestroika*, he spoke of a rapid process. Thus the third watchword for a time was *uskorenie,* or acceleration. It became clear, however, that the process of reconstruction was one of extraordinary dimensions, compounded by the fact that many managers of factories and collective farms looked upon the Gorbachev revolution with skepticism or resentment. Their opposition was largely passive. Managers and workers had learned to fulfill the plan on paper and saw few reasons to embrace a new approach that promised to punish those who failed. In the mid-1960s, Premier Alexei Kosygin had sought to reorganize the economy so that factories would have to sink or swim on their own. In 1965, *khozraschet*, or accountability, became the new slogan as Kosygin introduced with much fanfare the Liberman program, named after the economist who had proposed it in an article in *Pravda* in 1962. The conservatives, who had their hands on the political and economic levers, soon brought this experiment to a halt. The resistance to Gorbachev's *perestroika* in the late 1980s appeared to suggest that history was repeating itself.

The sociologist Tatiana Zaslavskaia found in opinion polls that Soviet citizens wanted primarily better apartments, an end to inflation, and solutions to environmental pollution. But the majority still expected the state to solve their problems; it was an attitude that had seeped into their blood.[6] Gorbachev sent a large number of people to the West, to show that there existed an alternative to the Soviet system. But to change the system, the worker must work harder and must produce goods competitively in the marketplace. In addition, Gorbachev suggested that subsidies must come to an end. But many people were comfortable with the old system, as it offered security. Early on, Gorbachev began to speak of closing down inefficient factories and raising the prices of certain goods. Much of what the state provided for its citizens it did at a financial loss: bread, milk, apartments, education, transportation, and other commodities. Gorbachev's statements hit a raw nerve. They produced a resistance to an economic *perestroika* that promised not only higher prices but also unemployment. One of the consequences of *perestroika* was the hoarding of goods that promised to cost twice as much tomorrow. The relative security of the past began to give way to an uncertain future. By early 1988, talk in Moscow of an accelerated *perestroika* became a thing of the past; the question was whether Gorbachev could reconstruct the top-heavy economy by the year 2000. *Uskorenie*, unlike *glasnost* and *perestroika*, did not make it into the *Oxford Dictionary of the English Language*.

■ FARMING

Gorbachev came no closer to resolving the agricultural problem. Agriculture, similar to industry, has been directed from the top since the late 1920s. Private farming, except that on plots made available to collective farmers, had all but disappeared in the Soviet Union. Stalin had created the collective farm system and then had neglected it.

In his speech on November 3, 1987, at the 70th anniversary of the

October Revolution, Gorbachev still defended—under pressure from his opponents on the right—the necessity of Stalin's collectivization. In October 1988, however, in a televised address, he proposed radical changes. The Communist party must rethink its position. The farmers of the Soviet Union, he insisted, must once again become "masters of their land." To achieve this, he proposed long-term leases of the land. Five months later, in March 1989, he took his case to the party's decision-making body, the Central Committee, where he presented a summary of the failure of Soviet agriculture. Between 1946 and 1953, Stalin had transferred 105 billion rubles from the agricultural sector to industry. Khrushchev and Brezhnev subsequently had spent huge sums of money to improve the productivity of the collective and state farms, but to little avail. Low productivity and an extraordinary amount of waste due to carelessness, poor transportation, and inadequate storage facilities had forced the government to purchase vast amounts of grain from capitalist nations in the West. The time had come to abandon decision making at the top and to learn from experimentation, from the United States, China, India, and the "green revolution."[7] One of Gorbachev's advisors, economist Leonid Abalkin, declared, "We are ready to borrow the best from all lands."[8]

Gorbachev did not manage, however, to abolish the collective farms. His conservative opponent in the Politburo, Yegor Ligachev, was strong enough to prevent a 180-degree turn. But on April 9, 1989, the Supreme Soviet, that is, the government, did pass a law permitting private individuals and collectives to lease land, buildings, mineral deposits, small factories, and machines from the state "for up to 50 years and more." TASS, the Soviet news agency, underlined that the law intended to promote private initiative, such as the establishment of family farms. The difficulty was in finding adventuresome entrepreneurs, *kulaks* as it were—a class that Stalin had characterized as "enemies of the working classes" and liquidated by the early 1930s. It was for this reason that Gorbachev demanded in February 1990 that farmers be able to purchase land from the state for private holding and put an end to an experiment of more than 60 years.

At the end of 1989, voices made themselves heard in Moscow complaining that Gorbachev's program was one without focus, that he did not have a concrete idea of which direction to march. Many officials, who previously had known nothing but orders from the top, found his *perestroika* unsettling. Gorbachev was quick to reply in *Pravda*. "Ready-made schemes," he declared, "were the characteristic of the Stalin era with which we have parted ways."[9] In the past, mistakes had been made precisely because the top-heavy bureaucracy had decided that success was measured on how well the directive was fulfilled; whether it made any sense had not been the issue.

What Gorbachev sought was a discussion of the ills of society and the potential remedies. But this could not be done within the context of the party alone. He needed a wider forum, which in turn would whittle away the authority of the party. The result was a new legislature, the Congress of People's Deputies,[10] which held its first Congress in May 1989. Not only were the majority of the delegates freely elected, but many were non-Communists, and Communists themselves had to compete for their positions. The weakness of the party became glaringly apparent when numerous party candidates did not receive the necessary 51 percent majority of votes, although they ran unopposed. The old guard, the *nomenklatura*,[11] was shaken by this innovation. During debates before the Congress, officials were now held responsible for their actions. For the first time since the 1920s, Soviet politicians no longer spoke with one voice.

Gorbachev not only watched without blinking an eye the demise of the Communist parties in Eastern Europe, he played a role in their downfall. But he hesitated to support the abolition of Article 6 of the 1977 Soviet constitution, which granted his party a monopoly of political power. At the end of 1989, he did not have the votes either in the party's Central Committee nor the Congress of People's Deputies to contemplate the abolition of Article 6.[12] But he did not commit himself in stone. "At the present complex stage," he stated, "the interests of the consolidation of society and . . . of *perestroika* prompt the advisability of keeping the one-party system." The party must "not concede the initiative to either populist demagoguery, national or chauvinistic currents or to the spontaneity of group interests."[13]

Many radicals supported Gorbachev as the only way to defend *perestroika* from the conservatives. But sentiment to scrap Article 6 ran deep. During his January 1990 visit to Vilnius, Lithuania, where the republic's Communist party already had legalized a multiparty system and elections, Gorbachev stated that "we must not fear a multiparty system the way the devil fears incense." The evolution of Gorbachev's position on Article 6 was completed during the extraordinary plenum of the party's Central Committee early in February 1990. After three days of debates, the party accepted the unthinkable. Lenin's legacy, the Communist party as the sole driving force in the Soviet Union, became the casualty of the February Revolution of 1990.

In the arena of foreign affairs, Gorbachev's initiatives were no less path breaking. His presence on the world's stage overshadowed that of all other statesmen. He ended the seventy-year-long conflict with the West, withdrew the Soviet Union from the battles in the Third World, led the drive for nuclear and conventional disarmament, and discarded the Brezhnev Doctrine of unilateral intervention in the affairs of other Communist nations. He insisted, instead, that the Soviet Union must live with its neighbors according to the norms of international law. In October 1989, Gorbachev went to Finland to specifically underscore this point when he stated that the Soviet Union had "no moral or political right" to interfere in the revolutionary process in Eastern Europe.

■ THE NATIONALITY QUESTION

When Gorbachev declared that things should be called by their proper names, he set into motion the discussion of the Soviet Union's nationality question. By a twist of fate, the first successful Marxist revolution had taken place in an empire that consisted of well over 100 nationalities. Many had only one thing in common, that they had been conquered by the dominant Slavs, the Russians in particular. The revolution, so ran the official interpretation, had forged a new society of peoples who now voluntarily resided in the new Soviet Union. That none had requested to secede from the Soviet Union as permitted under the constitution was proof that the new Communist consciousness had obliterated national antagonisms. The Soviet Union was one happy family of diverse nations, a point restated in Soviet publications ad infinitum.

Glasnost blew the official theory apart. The discussions revealed deep-rooted grievances on the part of all national minorities, and they were not necessarily directed against the dominant Russians, but often against each other. The national intelligentsias challenged the extreme centralization of the Moscow-imposed system and demanded greater cultural, economic, and political autonomy. Anti-Russian demonstrations also drew on workers whose standard of living had declined during Gorbachev's *perestroika*. An awareness that industrialization was destroying the environment became a major factor in publicizing nationalist grievances. Estonians complained that Moscow was polluting their land; Armenians argued that the air in their capital, Yerevan, had become a health hazard; and Uzbeks and Kazakhs charged that cotton irrigation had drained Lake Aral in Central Asia.

The discussions produced two approaches. The first was the reorganization of the relationship between the republics and Moscow. The fourteen non-Russian republics should be granted substantial economic and political autonomy. They should become, for example, the guardians of their environment. This solution envisioned strong republics with a strong center, something on the order of the Swiss model—a nation of four nationalities with four official languages. Gorbachev favored this approach, as it would keep the nation together and fit into the framework of his plan for "democratization." The difficulty lay in convincing long-suffering peoples that their best prospects were in a future democratic Soviet Union. Gorbachev's position on the nationality question acknowledged that a country as large and diverse as the Soviet Union cannot readily be administered as a monolithic whole. The Stalinist approach had to give way to "new thinking." Diversity was now held up as a positive good. One example was the legalization of the languages of the republics as official languages.

The second solution called for the dismemberment of the empire. The republics should have the right to exercise their constitutional right of secession. If adopted, it would mean a 180-degree reversal of Russian history. It is no coincidence that the Russian monarchs who were granted the appellation of "Great"—Ivan III, Peter I, and Catherine II—had earned it by virtue of expanding their empire's borders. This approach was also the most dangerous to Gorbachev's *perestroika* because he was not elected by his party to oversee the dissolution of the empire.[14]

The most difficult challenge came from the Baltic states—Lithuania, Latvia, and Estonia—where so-called Popular Fronts began to test the limits of Gorbachev's "democratization." They demanded economic autonomy, stating that they were merely supporting *perestroika;* that is, the decentralization of the top-heavy economy. They insisted on, and gained, the right to fly their old flags,   openly practice their religions, and to rewrite their histories. Their native languages gained official stature, they spoke of fielding their own teams for future Olympic games, and they declared their Communist parties independent of the party in Moscow. But then came the inevitable talk of complete secession from the Soviet Union.

The reason for the radicalism in the Baltic states may be found in their recent history. They had been part of the Russian empire for over 200 years, but after the Communist revolution of 1917, they managed to establish their independence, which, however, lasted only until 1940. On the eve of World War II, Hitler and Stalin agreed on a nonaggression pact, and for good measure decided, on the basis of a secret protocol, to divide Eastern Europe. The Baltic states fell into the Soviet sphere of influence, and in the spring of 1940 Stalin incorporated them into the Soviet Union, deported or murdered hundreds of thousands of suspected nationalists, and forbade the symbols of independence, such as the flags. Officially, however, the Baltic peoples joined the Soviet Union on their own free will.

As *glasnost* produced a critical reassessment of the Stalin era, the infamous Hitler-Stalin pact could not be ignored. After much soul-searching and hesitation, official Soviet historians finally admitted that, yes, there had been a secret protocol in violation of international law. In December 1989, the Communist party of Lithuania voted to establish its independence from Moscow, a move that spawned a four-point proposal by the mass movement Sajudis demanding (1) "freedom and independence" on the basis of the repeal of the Hitler-Stalin pact, (2) the removal of the "occupant Soviet army," (3) compensation for "the genocide of Lithuanian citizens and their exile" and environmental destruction, (4) and the establishment of friendly relations on the basis of the peace treaty of 1920 between Lithuania and the Soviet Union.[15] Gorbachev was put into the most uncomfortable position between *glasnost* and the breakup of the Soviet Union. Gorbachev and his supporters warned that the Lithuanian radicals could wreck *perestroika*.

In January 1990, Gorbachev took a highly publicized trip to Lithuania to convince the population of the dangers of secessionism. He pleaded, cajoled, and issued thinly veiled threats, all to no avail. As his limousine departed for the airport, the crowd jeered him. In Moscow, the spokesman for the foreign office, Gennady Gerasimov, remarked that the divorce between Lithuania and Russia must follow an orderly course; it could not be on the basis of Lithuania's unilateral action. Lithuanian radicals quickly replied that there had been no marriage, only an abduction and rape, and that there was nothing to negotiate. On March 11, 1990, the newly and freely elected Parliament of Lithuania unilaterally declared its independence from the Soviet Union. Gorbachev demanded that Lithuania rescind its declaration; Lithuanian independence could only be discussed within the context of Soviet law.

Not all nationalist grievances were directed against the Russians. As Lithuanians demonstrated against the Russians, the Polish minority in Lithuania demonstrated for incorporation into Poland. Nearly every Soviet republic has territorial claims against a neighbor. The Abkhazians in the western region of the Georgian Republic demonstrated against the heavy hand of the Georgians who had curbed the Abkhazians' cultural autonomy. Oddly, Georgians and Abkhazians are related; centuries ago, however, the Abkhazians fell under Turkish influence and became Muslims. They nevertheless resorted to killing each other. The highly publicized anti-Russian rally in Tbilisi, the capital of Georgia, in April 1989, in which Soviet soldiers killed twenty demonstrators, began initially as an anti-Abkhazian demonstration.

The most violent clash among Soviet nationalities, however, was the bloody conflict between the Christian Armenians and the Shiite

Muslim, Turkic-speaking Azeris. Once Gorbachev gave the Armenians a voice, they immediately demanded the return of a piece of their historic territory, which Stalin had placed under Azeri administration as far back as the 1920s. To appease the Turks, Stalin had decreed that the region of Nagorno-Karabakh, although three-quarters Armenian, should be in Azerbaidzhan. Nagorno-Karabakh was officially an "autonomous" district, but the Armenians in Nagorno-Karabakh were denied their civil rights by their ancient enemies.[16]

The history of Armenia has been marked by wars against invaders who have threatened to destroy it. Armenian national consciousness is deeply affected by the massacre of 1915 at the hands of the Turks in which 1.5 million Armenians died.[17] The Turks then drove the Armenians from their historic territory in what today is eastern Turkey. As a result, the symbol of Armenian nationalism, Biblical Mount Ararat, is in Turkey, just across the border from Yerevan.

Tensions rose in February 1988, when up to 100,000 people demonstrated in Yerevan over a period of several days against Azerbaidzhan, but also against Moscow and Communism. At the end of the month, Azeris staged a pogrom in Sumgait, a city just north of the Baku, the capital of Azerbaidzhan, in which 32 Armenians were murdered. Moscow deployed its army and internal security troops to keep continued sporadic violence at a minimum.

In June 1988, the Communist leadership of Armenia voted to regain Nagorno-Karabakh, and the Communist party of Azerbaidzhan voted to retain it.[18] For the first time, Communist parties of the Soviet Union split along national lines. The violence continued; between November 1988 and January 1989, 80 people were killed.[19] Only Moscow's intervention minimized further bloodshed, but the fear and hatred remained. After an earthquake registering 6.9 on the Richter scale destroyed much of one region in Armenia in December 1988, a number of Azeris rejoiced in the misery of their neighbors and prevented relief supplies from crossing their territory.

On January 13, 1990, a few days after Gorbachev's visit to Lithuania, the Azeri-Armenian violence erupted anew. After one of their own had been killed in an altercation with an Armenian, young Azeris went on a rampage in Baku, murdering at least 60 Armenians in a replay of the Sumgait pogrom. This massacre marked the resumption of violence between Azeris and Armenians in and around Nagorno-Karabakh. Nationalist Popular Fronts in Yerevan, Baku, and the Azeri enclave of Nakhichevan between Iran and Azerbaidzhan supplanted the Communist parties in authority. Nakhichevan declared its independence from the Soviet Union, and the mobs and Popular Front in Baku seized political power. Two days later, Gorbachev decreed a state of emergency in the Transcaucasus and, when it had no effect, on January 20 he sent the Soviet army and troops of the Interior Ministry into Baku. In a televised address he explained that he had no choice because "neither side listened to the voice of reason."[20] In the ensuing violence about 100 Azeris were killed. Azeris berated Gorbachev for his action; Armenians complained because he had not acted sooner. This time Armenians rejoiced at the deaths of Azeris.[21]

But the strongest nationalism could be Russian. Russians make up over half of the population and many of them resent the rebellious minorities. In September 1989, the United Front of Workers of Russia held its initial meeting in the Siberian city of Sverdlovsk for the purpose of defending threatened fellow Russians in the other republics. The battlefronts were shaping up.

***

The Gorbachev revolution was the product of a historical process. The social conditions that had produced support for Lenin and Stalin have undergone significant changes since 1917. The number of Soviet citizens, for example, who have a high school education or better, has increased since 1964 from 25 million to 125 million.[23] When de-Stalinization began with Khrushchev's 1956 speech, more than half of the nation's population still lived in the countryside; that figure was down to about one-quarter by the late 1980s. Gorbachev inherited a nation with a sizable and largely urbanized middle class. Soviet citizens have no personal memory of the glorious October Revolution of 1917, and increasingly fewer of World War II, the Great Fatherland War, the last great age of heroism and sacrifice. Gorbachev's generation (he was born in 1931) came to political maturity during Khrushchev's "thaw" and his attacks on Stalin. They understood their nation's ideological, intellectual, military, and economic isolation had to come to an end. *Perestroika* became a battle between reformers and the dead weight of history, the legacy that generations of tsars and commissars had bestowed on the nation.

Gorbachev's *perestroika* and "new thinking" turned the arcane science of Kremlinology upside down as he introduced one reform after another. The rigid Communist party, driven by its general secretary, was redefining its role, its position in Europe, military doctrine, economic structure, and history. Such discussions had been thought impossible. In December 1988, the West German newsweekly *Der Spiegel* named Gorbachev its "Man of the Year: Man of the Hour." Never had it bestowed such recognition on anyone before. It compared him to the Westernizer Peter the Great, the Protestant reformer Martin

Luther, and the emancipator Abraham Lincoln. In January 1990, *Time* named him the "Man of the Decade." But the applause was for a tightrope walker who had not yet reached the other side.

■ EASTERN EUROPE

In the annals of the British empire, 1759 is known as *annus mirabilis,* the "year of miracles," when the British army, seemingly doomed to suffer certain defeat, rallied to defeat the French and rearranged the map of the colonial world. The changes in Eastern Europe in 1989 were no less surprising and miraculous. When the year began, all of Moscow's satellite Communist parties appeared to be firmly in control. By year's end, however, the ring of Communist states along the Soviet Union's western borders, which Stalin had created in 1945, was no more.[24]

In 1951, Hannah Arendt declared that the Communists had found a way to stay in power forever. More recently, Jeane Kirkpatrick, who served as President Reagan's ambassador to the United Nations, restated a variation of this thesis: authoritarian governments, meaning right-wing dictatorships, were capable of reform, but totalitarian regimes, namely Communist governments, were incapable of either change or abandoning their hold on power. The events of 1989 proved them wrong. In June 1989, the Polish Communist party, for example, accepted a near 100 percent defeat in the Communist world's first free election since 1917.

The events of 1989 underscored the obvious fact that the governments of Eastern Europe had no popular support. Whenever a Communist party had shown signs of being overwhelmed by its own people, Moscow had always intervened—in East Germany in June 1953, in Hungary in 1956, and in Czechoslovakia in 1968. In 1956 and in 1981, the Polish Communist party made it clear that it could maintain control without Soviet intervention and kept Soviet troops at bay. Intervention and threats had maintained a deceptive calm.

But early in his reign Gorbachev announced that the Brezhnev Doctrine was dead, that no one had the right to impose his will on another people. He restated this position several times, as in his address to the United Nations in December 1988. Events showed that Gorbachev remained true to his word. The Communist parties in Eastern Europe now stood alone and they had to face their people without Moscow's support.

Economic factors played a large role in the events of 1989. The economies of Eastern Europe had done tolerably well in the first decade or so of Communist rule after large factories were organized and surplus labor from the countryside was used to man them. The test was whether the Communist system could raise productivity, absorb new technology, and produce a wider range of products. When it could not, the result was that every East European country in 1989 was much poorer compared to the West than it had been in the 1970s. For nearly 20 years the gap between East and West Europe had been widening, a fact that did not escape the people of the Eastern bloc. According to World Bank figures, the 1987 per capita GNP for Poland or Hungary was 14 percent of either West Germany or Sweden.[25] The Iron Curtain had ceased to be a barrier to the flow of information long ago. Nearly all East Germans, for example, regularly watched West German television—via cable, no less. The steady flow of visitors from the West gave the East Europeans a good picture of how far they had fallen behind.

□ Poland

The dam began to crack in Poland first. The events of the early 1980s showed that the vast majority of workers had supported Solidarity. It had been Solidarity and the Roman Catholic Church who spoke for the Polish nation, not the party, the creation of Poland's arch enemy, the Russian empire. In 1981, *Pravda* had made it abundantly clear that Solidarity could not replace the party in Poland as the guiding force in society. Wojciech Jaruzelski and his party had been willing to grant Solidarity numerous concessions, such as the right to strike against the state, which amounted to the de facto sharing of power between the party and Solidarity. What the party could not grant, however, was its own dissolution as Solidarity demanded. Either Jaruzelski or Brezhnev would make certain that the party would maintain its power. Jaruzelski chose the lesser of two evils when he proclaimed martial law.

Jaruzelski found out that although he could keep the party in power, he could not rule his nation without Solidarity, particularly as the economic situation continued to deteriorate. In January 1989, the party agreed to resume talks with Solidarity. The lengthy discussions at the round table led to the legalization of Solidarity in April and to the elections in June 1989.

The Polish Communist party, however, was in no mood to simply hand over power to people who it had only recently jailed. It sought to retain control of the Sejm, the Parliament, and with it the election of the prime minister, and in this fashion salvage what could be salvaged. The opposition, Solidarity, would be limited to 35 percent of the seats in the Parliament. Solidarity balked at this proposal. The deadlock in the negotiations was broken only after the government agreed to create an upper house, the Senate, which would be elected democratically. The promise of a free and competitive election outside the Communist party's control sealed the fate of the party. The Senate elections of June 4, 1989, gave Solidarity 99 of the 100 contested seats and became what Poles termed "the only known crucifixion in which the victim has nailed himself to the cross."[26] Solidarity's success in the lower house would have been scarcely less impressive, except that the Communists and their allies were still guaranteed a majority in that body. But the Communists miscalculated; they had set aside 35 percent of the seats to the opposition, but after Solidarity's smashing victory in the Senate elections, the Peasants' party, which over the past 40 years had been little more than a front for the Communists, suddenly bolted and joined the opposition. The opposition now controlled a majority of the seats and became the government. It then elected Tadeusz Mazowiecki as prime minister in August 1989,[27] the first non-Communist leader in Eastern Europe since shortly after the end of World War II. His 22-member cabinet contained nine Solidarity members and four Communists.

The legislature then elected, by the narrowest margin of one vote, Jaruzelski as president, a largely ceremonial post. Solidarity engineered the election of the Communist Jaruzelski to make clear to Moscow that Poland henceforth was a non-Communist, but not an anti-Communist or anti-Soviet, state. Mazowiecki flew to Moscow to assure the Soviet leaders that his non-Communist government did not entertain leaving the Warsaw Pact, as the Hungarian Communist party had attempted in 1956. Moreover, Solidarity would not make the mistake it had made in 1981; it refrained from any language suggesting the abolition of the Communist party, which in any case was on its way to becoming irrelevant. Gorbachev had no intention of invoking the Brezhnev Doctrine; he welcomed, instead, the political developments in Warsaw. The party remained in control of the army, as well as the police. Free elections were set for 1993, in which the party was slated to compete for positions that had been set aside for it in the elections of 1989.

Solidarity's main responsibility became the economy, a daunting task it was hesitant to tackle. Poland's foreign debt had risen from $27 billion in 1982, to $38.5 billion in 1988, an increase of nearly 50 percent in six years. Moreover, inflation of several thousand percent annually had destroyed the country's currency. The consequences were a thriving black market, the smuggling of consumer goods, and the widespread circulation of Western currencies, notably the U.S. dollar and the West German mark. Under these conditions, Solidarity, which had long opposed the Communist central planning system, became responsible for the nation's economy. It sought to introduce a market economy and integrate it into the economy of the West.

Unlike in 1981, when Solidarity was eager to seize power, many of its members showed little enthusiasm for doing so in 1989. In fact, after the elections of June, they at first were willing to allow General Czeslaw Kiszczak, the same man who as minister of the interior had jailed them in 1981, to form the government and, as prime minister, to sort out the economic mess. Solidarity began to understand that playing the opposition was easier than tackling an economy run aground on the shoals of central planning. But it was the Mazowiecki government that had to bite the bullet. It did so when it announced on New Year's Day 1990 that numerous subsidies, to which Poland's citizens had long become accustomed, would exist no more. Immediately, the price of bread rose by 38 percent and that of coal, which many use for heating, went up 600 percent. A drastic increase in gasoline and automobile insurance prices forced some Poles to turn in their license plates, as they could no longer afford to drive their prized possessions.[28] The primary movers for this drastic step were Western banks and governments, as well as the International Monetary Fund, all of which insisted that Poland must bring its fiscal house in order to justify additional aid.

☐ Hungary

In Hungary, a parallel development took place in 1989. The reform wing of the Communist party had taken control in 1988 and set out to complete what party chief Janos Kadar had put into motion—a mixed economy and tentative political reforms. It had been Kadar whom the Soviets had installed after they had crushed the revolution of 1956, and it had been his party that had begun a careful experiment with political and economic reforms. Kadar was not, however, ready to abolish the party's leading role.

In May 1988, Kadar was gently nudged aside as the leader of the party. The party then, taking a cue from Gorbachev, began to come to grips with its own recent history. The political demise of Kadar paved the way to the political, posthumous rehabilitation of his victims. For the first time since 1956, it became possible to mention in Hungary the names of Imre Nagy, Hungary's party chief at the time of the 1956 revolution, and Pal Maleter, the general who had fought the Soviet army. They had been among those who Kadar had executed and dumped face down, with their hands still tied behind their backs, in an unmarked mass grave in Budapest. Their names had disappeared from the official histories, but not from the collective memory of their nation. Their rehabilitation culminated in the solemn reinternment of Nagy and his associates, a ceremony broadcast live on television throughout Hungary in June 1989.

The reform process in Hungary, similar to the one in Poland, was controlled by the party. Other political parties were legalized and Hungarians began to reevaluate their place in the Warsaw Pact. They began to insist that their nation had always been part of Western, and not Eastern, Europe. In September 1989, the Communist party (officially the Socialist Workers' party) renamed itself as the Socialist party, and Parliament rewrote the constitution to permit a multiparty election scheduled for March 25, 1990. On October 23, on the 33rd anniversary of the demonstrations that had touched off the uprising of 1956, Parliament declared Hungary no longer a "People's Republic." It became instead the Republic of Hungary, and the red star on top of the Parliament building came down. (Earlier, Lenin's statue in Budapest had been taken from its pedestal, ostensibly for repairs; everyone knew its chances of reappearing were slim.) The newly renamed Socialist party hoped in the meantime to obtain 40 percent of the votes in the March 1990 election and form a coalition government and, should it fail, to go into the opposition.

The two rounds of elections, in March and April 1990, shattered whatever illusions the party still had of clinging to political power. The voters gave the Hungarian Democratic Forum, a populist nationalist umbrella organization with a right-of-center orientation, a plurality of 165 of parliament's 386 seats, and its leader, Jozsef Antall, set out to create a coalition with the conservative Independent Smallholder and Christian Democratic parties. The Socialist party won only 33, or 8 percent, of the 386. The Communist experiment in Hungary was over.

☐ East Germany

In the summer of 1989, Hungarian soldiers went to work to dismantle the fortifications along the Austrian border, the first example of the physical demolition of the Iron Curtain. The Hungarian government also guaranteed its citizens the right to a passport and freedom of travel and emigration. In March 1989, it had also signed a UN protocol on refugees, which obligated it not to force East Germans who sought to continue to travel to Austria to return home. This protocol, however, ran counter to the treaty of 1968 with East Berlin, which committed Budapest to return East Germans. In August 1989, Hungary's foreign minister, Gyula Horn, took sides with the UN protocol; Hungary would no longer prevent East Germans leaving for the West. Hungary, officially still a Communist country, became a hemorrhaging wound that threatened to bleed Communist East Germany, which for the first time since 1961, since the Berlin Wall was put up, was losing tens of thousands of its citizens.

The Hungarian foreign minister knew he was pulling the rug out from under Erich Honecker, the party boss in East Germany, when on September 10, 1989, his nation opened its borders. In three days, 12,000 East Germans crossed into Austria.[29] Other East Germans began to leave through Czechoslovakia and Poland. Honecker's own Warsaw Pact allies had become the road by which his people abandoned what they considered a sinking ship.

Throughout much of 1989, Honecker had made it clear that he would ride out the storm. Just because a neighbor was hanging new wallpaper, he said, was no reason why he should do the same. Article I of the East German Constitution, which granted the party the leading political role, was written in granite. But in May 1989, the voices of protest grew louder after the party had rigged the results of local elections. Church leaders, in particular, grew increasingly critical of the regime; they were joined by groups such as the New Forum. Then came the summer's exodus. But more importantly, the summer saw repeated demonstrations in many cities, notably in Leipzig, where increasingly larger crowds demanded change and insisted "we're staying here." Honecker promised "another Beijing" (in reference to the massacre of protesters there in June 1989) and ordered the security police, the despised and dreaded *Stasi*, to use "any means" to put down the "counterrevolution."

The showdown came in Leipzig on the night of October 9, 1989, one month after Hungary had become an unimpeded escape road and one day after Gorbachev's visit to East Berlin to commemorate the 40th anniversary of the creation of the East German republic. Gorbachev had come not to support Honecker, but to say good-bye to him. He reminded the East German Politburo that a leadership that isolates itself from its people will lose the right to exist. During the demonstration of October 9, the party backed down. It did not use force,[30] and nine days later the Politburo forced Honecker, who continued to insist there was no problem to resolve, to step down in favor of his protégé Egon Krenz.

Krenz's first trip as the head of the party was a visit to Moscow, where he took pains to describe himself as a disciple of Gorbachev's "new thinking." Mass protests, Krenz now insisted, were a healthy sign of change and he hinted he would make some concessions. The demonstrators, he stated, wanted "better socialism and the renovation of society." His government then lifted a one-month ban on visa-free travel to Czechoslovakia. That event essentially made the Berlin Wall—and the approximately 900-mile-long German-German border—an anachronism. On November 3, East Germans were granted the right to drive through Czechoslovakia directly to the West German border. Eight thousand East German citizens went to Czechoslovakia immediately. It was an end run around the Berlin Wall.

But the demonstrations continued. On November 6, 1989, 500,000 demonstrated in Leipzig on a cold, rainy night. There were also rallies in Dresden, Schwerin, Halle, Cottbus, and Karl-Marx-Stadt. The Dresden march was sanctioned by authorities and led by the Mayor Wolfgang Berghofer and the reformist local party chief, Hans Modrow. It was the first officially approved anti-government demonstration in the city. What only a short time previously would have been sensational concessions by the government were no longer enough. On November 8, approximately 350 East Germans per hour crossed the border into West Germany via Czechoslovakia.

On November 9, came the historic announcement that East Germans wishing to emigrate to the West could do so by applying for passports at local police stations. At the conclusion of a nationally televised news conference, a government spokesman said, "the people's police have the order to give these permits to people promptly."[31]

But the logic of revolution always demands that once changes are set into motion, halfway measures are no longer enough. The main demand was the abolition of Article I of the Constitution, which granted the party its political monopoly. The party caved in to continued public pressure and scuttled Article I on December 1. The action cleared the way for free elections, originally scheduled for May 1990. Moreover, Krenz had done his historic duty, but he suffered from a reputation of once having been a Honecker loyalist. His days at the top were clearly numbered, and the party turned to a reformer, the party chief of Dresden, Hans Modrow, as the nation's provisional prime minister until the elections. Gregor Gysi became the new head of the party, which now played for the first time a subordinate role to the government. Still, Modrow was a party functionary and tried to save as much of his party's political power as possible. The situation turned tense as people began to become weary of the continued presence of Communists at the helm of the government and the continued existence of the *Stasi*. A mob in East Berlin went so far as to storm the *Stasi* headquarters and ransack it.

In addition to the nation's political woes, the exodus continued. In early 1990, 2,000 left daily to seek their fortunes in West Germany, where the immigrants strained the nation's social net. Plants in East Germany found themselves depleted of workers. Modrow's provisional government proved incapable of dealing with these problems. The result was that the elections were moved up to March 1990.

The demise of the Berlin Wall also put the question of the unification of Germany on the agenda. Washington, Moscow, and the nations of Europe were bracing themselves for the inevitable. The remaining questions were the borders of a unified Germany and its military posture in the heart of Europe.

☐ The German Question

After the creation of the West German government in May 1949 and that of East Germany in October 1949, the division of Germany took on an aura of permanence. Officially, however, the West German government considered the question open. It treated Germany as whole, claiming to speak for all Germans. It automatically granted citizenship to any East German who made it across the border. It considered the borders of the two Germanies as well as its own existence as provisional. It did not even have a constitution, merely a temporary "basic law." Bonn was the provisional capital city of a provisional state; the true political heart of Germany was Berlin, which, for the time being, remained under the control of the victors of World War II. Lastly, according to the official West German position, the nation had been divided not merely into two, but into three parts; there was still the question of Silesia, Pomerania, and East Prussia, under Polish and Soviet "administration" since 1945.

After West German chancellor Helmut Kohl began to speak of unification in November 1989, Moscow declared that just because East Germans had been granted unrestricted access to West Germany this did not mean the automatic unification of the two Germanies. Kohl's statements received a similar cool reception in the West. The wartime allies and Europeans generally did not relish the recreation of a strong and unified Germany in the heart of the continent. Such an eventuality dredged up unpleasant memories.

There remained yet the question of the eastern border of a unified state. Officially, the war was not over because Germany had never signed a peace treaty accepting the loss of territory to Poland and the Soviet Union. Bonn had never officially accepted the border between East Germany and Poland, the Oder-Neisse Line. Legally, the Third Reich's territories as of December 31, 1937, still existed. With the emergence during the late 1980s of the new conservative West German Republican party, which openly spoke of regaining the lost regions, many in West Germany and the rest of Europe wanted to know the future territorial, political, and economic composition—and ambitions—of a unified Germany.[32]

West German historians have sought to find the answer to the riddle of the future of Germany in the lessons of the past. They turned their attention to their republic's early history, the administration of Konrad Adenauer—one which, however, does not lend itself to easy analysis. It had been Adenauer, the anti-Communist Catholic from Cologne, who had shaped the politics of West Germany. He had insisted that his government spoke for all Germans and that the Communist regime in East Berlin was an illegitimate creation of the Soviet Union. He mistrusted the Kremlin, but did not trust his own people either. He felt that in the twentieth century Germans twice had succumbed to the lure of power, to Prussian militarism in particular. Germany, in Adenauer's view, must be protected against the Russian threat from the east and from its own worst instincts. Adenauer, born on the western edge of the German Empire, therefore sought to bring his part of Germany into the community of West European nations. The German writer Heinrich Böll once remarked that Adenauer's views were typical of Germans who lived on the left bank of the Rhine, namely, that Siberia began on the other side of the river.[33] A unified, rebuilt Germany, Adenauer thought, might again pose a threat to the stability of Europe. He sought, therefore, to integrate a divided West Germany into a community of democratic West European nations.

Germany, Adenauer felt, must not be cut adrift alone in the center of Europe. To that end, Adenauer immediately rejected the Stalin note of March 10, 1952, in which the Kremlin offered a unified Germany provided it did not join NATO and remained neutral. It was Adenauer who was largely responsible for the Western rejection of the proposal without even bothering to discuss it with the Soviets.[34] He would not subordinate unification to the higher goal of integration into the Western community. Bonn would find its future in the Western anti-Soviet camp, sacrificing the possibility of a unified, independent nation in the bargain.

In 1955, Adenauer completed the process of integrating West Germany into the West European community. On May 5, West Germany became officially a sovereign state, and on the same day it joined the European Community. And on May 9, exactly ten years after the capitulation of the German army, it became a full member of NATO. In September, Adenauer went to Moscow to talk to Nikita Khrushchev. The purpose of this visit was to normalize relations between the former enemies and to bring home the 10,000 German prisoners of war remaining in the Soviet Union. Adenauer briefly raised the question of German unification, something he knew was impossible because it could be achieved only as a neutral state, which he had rejected only three years previously. Khrushchev responded predictably: "We would be fools if we were to participate in a process whereby all of Germany were to become a member of NATO and in this fashion to strengthen the forces directed against us." A week after Adenauer's return to Bonn, East Berlin and Moscow signed a treaty that underlined the division of Germany. The Kremlin recognized the sovereignty of East Germany and then formed its own military alliance, the Warsaw Pact, in which East Germany became its first line of defense.

Adenauer's visit with Khrushchev did, however, set into motion the first instance of détente between Bonn and Moscow, which despite the twists and turns in the Cold War showed a remarkable permanence. The specter of German unification raised the question, however, of whether West Germany had learned to live with both parts of Europe, with the East as well as with the West. The long process of rapprochement with the West began shortly after World War I with the Treaty of Locarno in 1925, when Germany finally accepted its borders with France and the loss of Alsace and Lorraine. World War II interrupted the process of Franco-German reconciliation, but Adenauer and French President Charles de Gaulle completed it in the early 1960s. By the outset of the 1990s, West Germany had learned one important lesson from Adenauer. It had become a responsible and the most prosperous partner of the EC. But it still faced the ratification of the loss of territory to and reconciliation with Eastern Europe—and the acceptance, once and for all, of the consequences of World War II.

☐ Czechoslovakia

The fourth Communist domino to fall in 1989 was Czechoslovakia, a nation ruled by Communists who had been put into power by Brezhnev's tanks after the crushing of the "Prague Spring" in August 1968. With the demise of the hard-liners in East Berlin, it became clear to the ruling Communist party that its days were numbered. As in East Germany, the party could not rely on Soviet intervention to prop it up. The Communist party of Czechoslovakia had to face a radicalized population alone.

The revolutionary vanguard against the old Communist regime were intellectuals and students. As long as the crowds remained relatively small—2,000 in January 1989 and still only 10,000 at the beginning of November 1989—the police were able to maintain a measure of order through arrests and occasional beatings. The workers were slow to join, mainly because they enjoyed a relatively high standard of living, something the party had concentrated its attention on since 1968. Once the workers joined the demonstrators on St. Wenceslas Square in Prague, however, the end had arrived for the party. It folded like a house of cards at the end of November 1989.

In the center of the opposition stood Charta 77, a loose union of 1,600 individuals who in 1977 had signed a petition demanding civil rights. Their spokespersons were Jiri Hajek, who had been the country's foreign minister during the "Prague Spring," and writer Vaclav Havel. Other opposition groups emerged in 1989. Since June of that year, another petition, demanding the release of all political prisoners, freedom of expression and assembly, and an independent news media circulated throughout the nation and 40,000 citizens had signed it.

On the surface, the events in Czechoslovakia followed the script written in East Germany. Demonstrations and arrests had been the order of the day until finally it became apparent that nearly the entire nation stood in opposition to the rulers. As in East Germany, it became clear that not even a bloodbath could save the old order. However, once the party agreed to abandon its ruling monopoly on November 29, 1989, events in Czechoslovakia moved much quicker and in a different direction. Havel and others took immediate steps to ensure a transformation to a new government without allowing the Communist party a continued, or even a temporary and provisional, hold on power, as in the case of East Germany and later Romania. The party, they insisted, had no right to govern the nation any longer. The party, in its turn, sought to maintain its hold on power until the scheduled elections in June 1990, but the opposition resolutely rejected the scheme. Backed by crowds of 200,000 demonstrators, it demanded, and obtained, a provisional government dominated by the opposition, until the voters could elect the country's first freely elected government since 1948.

Havel, who only earlier in the year had been arrested and jailed for anti-state activities,[35] became the new prime minister as the representative of the new Civic Forum movement. Alexander Dubcek, one of the architects of the "Prague Spring," who subsequently had been taken to Moscow in chains, became the country's new president. The formation of the new Czechoslovak government set that nation apart from East Germany and Romania, where demonstrators wondered whether the Communist parties were in fact willing to abandon their hold on political power.

At a Warsaw Pact meeting in December 1989, the five participants in the invasion of Czechoslovakia in 1968—the Soviet Union, East Germany, Poland, Hungary, and Bulgaria—formally declared the invasion to have been an "illegal action" and pledged strict noninterference in the future in each other's internal affairs. This marked the formal repudiation of the Brezhnev Doctrine. The Soviet government issued a separate statement admitting that the reasons for intervention had been "unfounded" and its decision to do so had been "erroneous."[36]

After Egon Krenz became the head of the East German Communist party, his first official state visit was the traditional call on Moscow. Havel, however, in a pointed reminder that Czechoslovakia was a part of Central and not Eastern Europe, went to Berlin—both East and West—and then to Warsaw. "It's not good-bye to Moscow," he explained, "but it's a new orientation toward West and Central Europe."[37] He then set out to negotiate the withdrawal of the Soviet troops from Czechoslovakia.

☐ Bulgaria

Next in line was Bulgaria, the most loyal member of the Warsaw Pact. The 78-year-old boss of the Communist party, Todor Zhivkov, who had been in power since 1954, showed no signs of stepping down. But his rule, particularly in the last few years, had bred widespread opposition. He was responsible for reviving in 1984 the ancient quarrel between Bulgarians and Turks when he forced the one-million-strong Muslim Turkish minority to adopt Slavic names. In May 1989, he encouraged some 310,000 Turks to emigrate. Not only did he damage Bulgaria's international standing with this action, but the exodus also wrought havoc with the nation's economy. After Zhivkov promoted his son to the Central Committee's department of culture, even his old allies deserted him. In the end his defense minister, Dobri Dzurov, his foreign minister, Petar Mladenov, and his prime minister, Andrei Lukanov, forced a meeting of the Politburo and with it the resignation of Zhivkov.

The charges against Zhivkov consisted of corruption, nepotism, and the ruination of the economy. But since Zhivkov's once-loyal lieutenants had deposed him, the question was whether any meaningful changes had taken place. The new leadership promised radical changes, economic reform plus *glasnost*. But to the increasingly larger crowds of demonstrators, Mladenov, now the new party chief, had not addressed the central issue, the party's monopoly on power.

Five days before Zhivkov fell, 4,000 members of a green movement, called *ecoglasnost*, staged a demonstration in the capital city of Sofia and gave notice that Bulgarians had become aware of the trends in neighboring countries. In subsequent weeks, as the crowds grew larger and more defiant, it became clear that the overthrow of Zhivkov was too little and too late. In a last-ditch effort, hard-liners sought to divert public attention away from political reform by organizing tens of thousands to protest against a decision by the new government that ended the assimilation campaign against the Turks.

But it was to no avail. A government commission announced that it had sufficient evidence to bring Zhivkov to trial on corruption charges. And on January 15, 1990, Mladenov and his party caved in and announced the concession that Communist parties in Warsaw, Budapest, East Berlin, and Prague had granted. The party agreed to give up its leading political role and to hold free elections.

☐ Romania

The last and least likely of the Communist dictators to be toppled in 1989 was Nicolae Ceausescu, who had came to power in 1965. Shortly thereafter, Ceausescu began to carve out a foreign policy independent of Moscow without, however, leaving the Warsaw Pact. He became known as the maverick in the Warsaw Pact as he reserved the Romanian right not to participate in the annual war games of the pact, continued to recognize Israel after the 1967 Six Day War, and refused to participate in the invasion of Czechoslovakia in 1968. In 1984, he refused to join the Moscow-led boycott of the Olympic Games in Los Angeles, where the Romanian team received a standing ovation at the opening ceremonies. The West rewarded Romania with most-favored-nation treatment and Presidents Richard Nixon and Jimmy Carter paid highly publicized visits to Bucharest, where they spared no words in heaping praise on Ceausescu.

The West rewarded Ceausescu also by ignoring the fact that his was by far the most repressive regime in the Warsaw Pact. He governed with his police force, the dreaded *securitate,* and his position appeared secure. In fact, he was able to achieve what few strongmen dare contemplate. He decided that his country must pay off its foreign debt, never mind the economic consequences of his austerity program for the Romanian people. The result was a sharp drop in the standard of living. Large amounts of food were exported, the work week consisted of six days, the price of gasoline was raised, apartments in the winter were kept at about 50 degrees Fahrenheit, electricity was strictly rationed, and hospitals were unable to purchase medicine from the West. The 24 million people of Romania, an agrarian land, were reduced to a meager diet. Pigs feet, commonly known as "patriots," remained in abundance; they were the only parts of the pig that stayed behind when the rest was exported.

Ceausescu's style was a combination of that of Stalin and the fascist Benito Mussolini of Italy. He dropped the label of "comrade" and began to call himself the *conducator,* the leader. Unlike the other leaders of Communist parties installed by the Soviet Union after World

War II, Ceausescu ruled not through his party but, similar to Stalin, through the police. The party existed merely to legitimize Ceausescu's rule. The most prominent feature of Romanian television was the glorification of Ceausescu and his wife, Elena, the second most powerful figure in the country. Their son, Nicu, was groomed to follow in his father's footsteps. Forty other family relations were on the government's payroll. Ceausescu made it clear that he intended to follow his own course, and that he would defy the changes taking place in the Soviet Union and elsewhere in Eastern Europe. In January 1989, as the Polish Communist party initiated a dialogue with the opposition, Ceausescu, who in 1968 had refused to participate in the Warsaw Pact's invasion of Czechoslovakia, now urged that the Warsaw Pact put an end to the dangerous political experiment in Warsaw. In June 1989, he sent a congratulatory message to Deng Xiaoping for crushing the Chinese student demonstrations. He made abundantly clear that he would use force to deal with his dissidents should they take to the streets. In Romania and abroad, few thought that to be a likelihood, however, in a nation where no more than three people were allowed to gather outdoors without government approval. As one party official explained: "All the systems of the world are based on reward and punishment. Ceausescu works only with punishment. It is a reward that there is no punishment."[38]

After the foreign debt had been largely repaid, the conditions in Romania did not change, however. Ceausescu continued to bleed his people when he initiated a massive building program designed to eradicate many of the symbols of Romania's past and replace them with monuments to the megalomania of the *conducator*. Fifteen thousand workmen erected the thirteen-story, 1,000-room House of the Republic in white marble on the Avenue of Socialist Victory. To make room for this palace, between 40,000 and 50,000 people had to be moved and many historic buildings had to be destroyed. Among the buildings destroyed was the sixteenth century Monastery of Michael the Brave, the ruler who in 1600 had unified Wallachia, Moldavia, and Transylvania into modern Romania. Ceausescu personally supervised the project, visiting it two or three times a week. Among Ceausescu's other projects were the razing of entire towns, many of them inhabited by ethnic Germans and Hungarians in Transylvania. Many Germans, whose towns their ancestors had built 700 years ago, left for West Germany, and Hungarians fled across the border into Hungary. Ceausescu went so far as to begin to build his own iron curtain to seal off Communist Hungary, but eventually abandoned this project. It was the city of Timisoara, in Transylvania, that lit the spark that brought the seemingly impregnable Ceausescu dictatorship down.

In early December 1989, the government decided to deport Laszlo Tokes, a little known Hungarian Protestant priest, from Timisoara. The decision touched off demonstrations forcing the government to reconsider. The concession was a victory of sorts for the people in the streets and produced an even greater demonstration on December 16. Economic considerations also played a part in the show of opposition. In October 1989, additional food items had been rationed without a guarantee that the scarce items could be found in the stores. Moreover, Timisoara contained the largest pork-processing plant in central Europe, as well as bread bakeries and other food-processing plants. It was little wonder that workers who knew nothing of Tokes, but who handled the food destined for export, joined the ranks of the demonstrators. The fall of the Communist parties in Poland, Hungary, East Germany, Czechoslovakia, and Bulgaria apparently took place without a single fatality. Romania was destined to be different. Ceausescu, who had made it clear he would follow the Chinese example, sent the *securitate* into Timisoara to gun down the demonstrators. The *conducator*, the "hero of the nation, the brilliant son of the people," began murdering his own people.[39]

The uprising might have been contained by the police, had it not continued the practice of refusing to return the bodies of those killed. People were especially bitter about the policy of not returning the bodies of those shot to death while trying to escape into Hungary. The dead of Timisoara were dumped into a mass grave on the outskirts of the city. "Give us our dead," the demonstrators demanded. Ceausescu lost control of Timisoara but vowed in a public speech to win the war against the "terrorists and hooligans" of that city.

That speech—before what appeared to be a traditionally docile crowd assembled by the authorities—proved to be a disaster for Ceausescu as it turned into an anti-Ceausescu demonstration. The revolution had spread beyond Timisoara. Ceausescu never finished the speech and fled the presidential palace. At that point, Ceausescu also lost control of the army. He had never trusted the armed forces and for good reason. After initially firing into crowds, it turned its guns onto the police, captured Ceausescu and his wife, and installed a new provisional government headed by Ion Iliescu. Iliescu, Gorbachev's classmate in Moscow in the 1950s and party boss in Timisoara in the late 1960s, had become popular with many party members for speaking out against Ceausescu's economic measures. Gorbachev had done his part for the revolution during his visit to Bucharest in 1987, when he spoke out against nepotism and for reform.

The Ceausescus were put before a military tribunal and charged with genocide, with the responsibility of murdering 60,000 Romanian citizens, as well as theft and having established Swiss bank accounts. Elena Ceausescu termed the last accusation a "provocation." The unrepentant *conducator* denied all charges and claimed to be still the leader of his nation. A firing squad ended the discussion on Christmas Day. Romanian television showed a tape of the trial and the elegantly dressed corpses of the Ceausescus.

The new government immediately followed the precedent established in other East European countries. It declared that Romania was no longer a socialist state, stocked the stores with food, reduced the work week to five days, cut the price of electricity by more than half, permitted each farm family an acre of land for private cultivation, abolished the death penalty after the Ceausescus' execution, abolished the *securitate*, and promised free elections for April 1990. It also arrested Ceausescu's closest associates, including the entire Politburo and ranking officers of the *securitate*, promising punishment for "all evildoers from the old regime." Romania, however, has never known a modern party system, a responsible political intelligentsia, or an autonomous church. Its history has been characterized, instead, by a series of despotic governments. The road to democracy promises to be long and hard.[40]

***

As 1989, the year of popular uprisings, gave way to 1990, the year of elections, the mood in Eastern Europe changed. Euphoria gave way to apprehension of the future. All states faced serious problems. Whatever democratic institutions had come into being after World War I had been destroyed by indigenous strongmen (Poland, Hungary, Bulgarian, Romania) and then by Hitler (Germany, Czechoslovakia) and Stalin. They had done nothing to teach the lessons of political tolerance. In 1989, a welter of political parties began to emerge, but only the Polish Communist party had experience in the orderly transfer of power after an election. At the beginning of 1990, crowds in East Berlin, Warsaw, and particularly in Bucharest began to take matters into their own hands and physically threatened Communists.

All nations of Eastern Europe faced nationality problems. Slovaks, for instance, always resented the Czechs. In Poland live Belorussians, Ukrainians, and Germans; in Romania, Hungarians and Germans; in Bulgaria, Turks; in Hungary, Slovaks, Germans, and Jews. The demonstrators in the streets demanded rights for themselves; the quality of East European democracy will depend on how they react to the rights of others.

The most serious ethnic problems existed in Yugoslavia, a nation of seven major ethnic regions—Slovenia, Croatia, Bosnia-Hercegovina, Montenegro, Kosovo, Vojvodina, and Serbia. After World War II, the Croat Joseph Tito sought to establish a federation in which no one people would be dominated by another, particularly by the numerically and historically dominant Serbs. The new Communist party leader Slobodan Milosevic, however, overturned in the early 1980s Tito's handiwork when he stripped the Albanian minority in Kosovo of their autonomy. In the summer of 1989, Milosevic added fuel to the fire when he led a massive Serbian demonstration into Kosovo to commemorate the 600th anniversary of a battle in which the Muslim Albanians had defeated the Christian Orthodox Serbs. The demonstration turned the Serbian defeat into a triumphant victory over their ancient enemy. It was no wonder that the violence in Kosovo continued.

But while Milosevic was trying to teach the Albanians in the southeastern corner of the nation a history lesson, the Slovenian Communist party in the northwest declared its independence of Serbia. To add to Milosevic's troubles, reformers in the capital city of Belgrade demanded that the Yugoslav Communist party follow the example of the rest of Eastern Europe—with the exception of Albania—and give up its monopoly on political power.

The Achilles heel of the new governments in Eastern Europe may well be the economy. As Soviet citizens bitterly remarked, you cannot put *glasnost* in your tea. Economic planners were seeking salvation in a return to capitalism, a road paved with opportunity, but also with dangers.

◼ RECOMMENDED READINGS

Goldman, Marshall I. *Gorbachev's Challenge: Economic Reform in the Age of High Technology.* New York: W. W. Norton, 1987.
  A discussion of the magnitude of Gorbachev's economic problems.
Gorbachev, Mikhail. *Perestroika: New Thinking for Our Country and the World.* New York: Harper & Row, 1987.
  A broad outline of Gorbachev's *perestroika.*
Medvedev, Zhores A. *Gorbachev.* New York: W. W. Norton, 1986.
  A discussion of Gorbachev's background by a dissident Soviet historian.
Schmidt-Häuer, Christian. *Gorbachev: The Path to Power.* Boston: Salem House, 1986.
  A Moscow-based West German journalist's account of how the party elected Gorbachev as its chief.
Tarasulo, Isaac J., ed. *Gorbachev and Glasnost: Viewpoints From the Soviet Press.* Wilmington, Del.: Scholarly Resources, 1989.
  A selection of Soviet views on a variety of problems.

■ NOTES

1. "On a Course of Unity and Solidarity," *Pravda,* February 21, 1985; in *Current Digest of the Soviet Press,* March 20, 1985, p. 7.

2. "In Tschernobyl 'eine glühend aktive Zone,'" *Der Spiegel,* May 19, 1986, p. 128.

3. David Remnick, "Solzhenitsyn—A New Day in the Life," *Washington Post,* January 7, 1990, p. B3.

4. B. Mironov, "Otkryvaia dver' v 'spetskhran,'" *Pravda,* September 10, 1988, p. 6.

5. Its publications dredged up, for example, the nineteenth century Russian forgery, *The Protocols of the Elder of Zion,* alleging a Jewish conspiracy.

6. Interview by Krisztina Koenen, "Warum ist die Perestroika eine Revolution, Frau Saslawskaja?", *FAZ Magazin,* June 8, 1989, pp. 54–55.

7. "On the Agricultural Policies of the Communist Party of the Soviet Union Under Present Conditions," *Pravda,* March 16, 1989.

8. Interview with Leonid Abalkin, *Der Spiegel,* April 10, 1989, p. 191.

9. Gorbachev, "Sotsialisticheskaia ideia i revoliutsionnaia perestroika," *Pravda,* November 26, 1989.

10. The old legislature, the Supreme Soviet, which traditionally rubber-stamped the party's decision, became irrelevant.

11. Literally, *nomenklatura* means the slate of names of party officials who were accountable only to the party and often served for life.

12. In December 1989, the Congress of People's Deputies, by a vote of 1,138 to 839, voted not to put this question on the agenda.

13. Gorbachev, "Sotsialisticheskaia ideia i revoliutsionnaia perestroika," *Pravda,* November 26, 1989, pp. 1–3.

14. In the summer of 1989, a third solution was briefly discussed in Moscow. It drew upon the U.S. model. The United States is the common home of all of its citizens; no portion of it should be set aside for one group or another. The difficulty with this approach is that the historic experience of the Unites States is different than that of the Soviet Union. Excepting the case of the Native American peoples, the United States is largely a nation of immigrants, who eventually forgot their native languages and in quick order became assimilated. But Soviet citizens are not immigrants; they have, instead, ancient claims to territories they inhabit and have resisted integration into a larger homogeneous society. To compound the problem, their claims frequently overlap with those of other nationalities. Russian may be the empire's *lingua franca,* but it is by no means the only language spoken, and many non-Russians never bothered to learn it.

15. The Moldavian Republic, along the Soviet-Romanian border, suffered a fate similar to the Baltic states. It, too, was brought back into the Soviet Union by the Hitler-Stalin pact. The Moldavians, ethnically related to the Romanians, have taken frequently to the streets, without, however, demanding a return to Romania as long as Ceausescu was alive.

16. Armenian-Azeri violence is nothing new. During previous internal upheavals in the Russian empire, such as in 1905 and 1918–1920, they also have fought against each other.

17. The exact number is unknown. In fact, the Turkish government still bitterly resents any mention of a massacre, denying it ever took place. It merely admits to Turkish-Armenian violence in which both suffered fatalities.

18. Gorbachev decided to maintain the status quo. Once he changed the status of Nagorno-Karabakh, he would have to consider claims emanating from nearly all other "autonomous" republics, provinces, and regions—89 in all—all multinational in composition.

19. "The Battle Lines of the Republic," *The Economist,* September 23, 1989, p. 58.

20. Transcript of address, "Soviet Chief's Address On Azerbaidzhan Fighting," *New York Times,* December 21, 1990, p. 12.

21. Esther Schrader, "Baku Refugees Celebrate Deaths of Azerbaijanis," *Baltimore Sun,* January 23, 1990, p. 4A.

22. The Russians make up 145.3 million of a population of 281.7 million; of the other Slavs, the Ukrainians, are 51.2 million strong, and the Belorussians, 10.1 million. Thus 206.6 million, or 73 percent of the population of the Soviet Union is of Slavic origin. Ukrainians and Belorussians, however, have developed over the past two centuries their own national consciousness, and many among them seek to be independent of Moscow. In sheer numbers alone the Russians have the advantage, and besides, they control the levers of power.

23. Jerry F. Hough, "Gorbachev's Politics," *Foreign Affairs,* Winter 1989/1990, p. 30.

24. The Communist parties of Yugoslavia and Albania had come to power on their own in the wake of World War II; they had not been Stalin's creation.

25. World Bank, *World Development Report, 1989* (Washington, D.C.: World Bank, 1989), p. 165.

26. "A Survey of Eastern Europe," *The Economist,* August 12, 1989, p. 10.

27. The Peasants' party with 76 seats and Solidarity with 161 seats controlled over half of the 460 seats in the Sejm. Communists controlled 173 seats, the Christian parties 23, and the Democrats 27.

28. Craig Whitney, "East Europe Joins the Market and Gets a Preview of the Pain," *New York Times,* January 7, 1990, p. E3.

29. Previously in 1989, 77,000 East Germans had left for West Germany, three quarters of them legally; "Goodbye to Berlin," *The Economist,* September 16, 1989, pp. 49–50.

30. Honecker apparently ordered the use of force against the 50,000–70,000 demonstrators, but it was never used. Who countermanded Honecker remains unclear. It may have been Egon Krenz, Honecker's protégé and the youngest member of the Politburo or, as former West German chancellor Willy Brandt believed, the Soviet military commanders; Jackson Diehl, "Leipzig's Leaders Prevent a Bloodbath," *Washington Post,* January 14, 1990, p. A36.

31. Diane Jean Schemo, "Leadership drops most restrictions," *Baltimore Sun,* November 19, 1989, pp. 2A, 8A.

32. The Republican party's chief, Franz Schönhuber, a former member of the Waffen-SS, declared in his autobiography that he was proud to have participated in Hitler's campaigns. His party's appeal rests on its opposition to foreigners in West Germany; moreover, the color of the Republican party is brown, which dredged up the memory of Hitler's brownshirts.

33. Heinrich Böll, "Adenauers Zeit und unsere Zeit," *Das Heinrich Böll Lesebuch* (Munich: Deutcher Taschenbuch Verlag, 1982), p. 312.

34. A number of West German historians subjected Adenauer's role to close scrutiny, claiming that he had missed the chance of German unification. See Rolf Steininger, *Eine Vertane Chance: Die Stalin-Note vom 10. März 1952 und die Wiedervereinigung: Eine Studie auf der Grundlage unveröffentlichter britischer und amerikanischer Akten* (Berlin/Bonn: J. H. W. Dietz Nachf., 1986). Adenauer's defenders argue that he played no role, as the Stalin note was not addressed to him but to the heads of the United States, Britain, and France.

35. In January 1989, Havel was arrested for participating in a ceremony in memory of Jan Palach, a young student who had set fire to himself in January 1969 to protest Brezhnev's invasion. One year later, in January 1990, he participated as the nation's chief of state in the ceremony honoring Palach.

36. For the statements, *New York Times,* December 5, 1989, p. A15.

37. Diana Jean Schemo, "Soviet Troops to Leave Czech Soil," *Baltimore Sun,* January 6, 1990, p. 2A.

38. Cited in William Pfaff, "Change in a Vulnerable Land," *Baltimore Sun,* December 22, 1989, p. 17A.

39. How many died remains unclear. The death toll in Timisoara ran probably into several hundreds, not the 4,500 initially reported. Mary Battiata, "State's Violence Sparked Rebellion," *Washington Post,* December 31, 1989, p. A1.

40. The first test of Romania's fledgling democracy came six months after Ceausescu's fall. The election of May 1990 gave Iliescu and his party over 80 percent of the vote, which did not sit well with university students who still considered Iliescu as a man with close ties to the old order. For eight weeks they staged a sit-in in the University Square in the center of Bucharest. On June 13, on the eve of Iliescu's inauguration as president, unarmed police cleared the square. Demonstrators retaliated by attacking the interior ministry and the central police and television stations. Five people died and 300 were injured in the violence. Iliescu apparently did not dare to use the remnants of the *securitate,* and his defense minister believed that the army's job was to protect the nation's borders, not to deal with political dissenters. Iliescu then appealed to the country's miners, the "democratic forces" as he called them, "to defend the democracy obtained by the revolution" against "fascists, extremists, and hooligans." The miners then went on a rampage, smashing the offices of opposition parties, breaking into university buildings, assaulting passers-by, and even taking their violence into gypsy neighborhoods. Not only was Iliescu's language similar to that which Ceausescu had used, but the vigilante violence was reminiscent of fascist tactics of the 1920s and 1930s.

The Nuclear Arms Race

The Cold War of the 1950s and early 1960s produced an unchecked nuclear arms race. Throughout, the United States took the lead despite the campaign rhetoric of bomber and missile gaps favoring the Soviet Union. Presidential candidate John F. Kennedy's charge against the Eisenhower administration that it had been asleep at the helm and had permitted the Soviets to forge ahead in the missile race was laid to rest shortly after Kennedy's election when the Pentagon announced a U.S. second strike capability more powerful than a potential Soviet first strike. This cold, cruel fact of the arms race, and the Soviet humiliation during the Cuban missile crisis the following year, put two items on the Kremlin's agenda, the closing of the gap favoring the United States and subsequent negotiations with Washington that acknowledged nuclear parity between the great powers.

The most immediate consequence of the Cuban missile crisis, however, was a gradual improvement in East-West relations, for both sides had faced the moment of truth when they looked down the nuclear gun barrel. Détente of the 1960s and the early 1970s produced a number of agreements between the Soviet Union and the United States to limit the nuclear arms race. The first significant agreement between the nuclear powers was a direct consequence of the nuclear showdown. It produced an agreement in 1963 on a partial nuclear test ban treaty, one that prohibited nuclear testing in the atmosphere, outer space, and on the high seas. The United States and the Soviet Union then took their nuclear weapons tests underground, thus limiting environmental contamination. More than one hundred nations signed the treaty. Notable exceptions were France (already a nuclear power) and Communist China (soon to become one when it exploded an atomic "device" in 1964).

Other agreements soon followed. They included the Outer Space Treaty (1967), which banned nuclear weapons in space and earth orbit; the Nuclear

Non-Proliferation Treaty (1967), by which the Soviet Union, the United States, Great Britain, and eighty-three other nations pledged to prevent the spread of nuclear weapons and technology; the Seabed Pact (1971), which prohibited nuclear arms on the ocean floors beyond a nation's twelve-mile limit; and the Biological Warfare Treaty (1972), which outlawed the development, production, and stockpiling of biological weapons.

■ THE SALT TREATIES

Nonetheless, the superpowers continued to add to their nuclear arsenals by developing and testing new weapons and stockpiling warheads. Toward the end of the decade, the governments of the United States and the Soviet Union saw the need for renewed efforts to control the unchecked arms race and for this reason they initiated the Strategic Arms Limitation Talks (SALT). The purpose of these talks was to limit—and eventually abolish—an unchecked, costly, and potentially deadly nuclear arms race. When the talks began during the late 1960s, both sides had more than enough to destroy the other side many times over. Unrestrained stockpiling of nuclear weapons had become an obsession and the SALT talks were meant to bring an element of control and rationality to the arms race.

The first SALT agreement was signed in Moscow in May 1972 by President Richard Nixon and Soviet party chief Leonid Brezhnev. The aim of this treaty was a modest one, a limit on the deployment of "strategic weapons." Strategic weapons consist of atomic warheads that the great powers are capable of launching from their own territories and submarines against the enemy's territory. They include the intercontinental bomber forces, intercontinental ballistic missiles (ICBMs), and submarine-launched ballistic missiles (SLBMS). SALT I was a limited agreement that did not put a dent in anyone's nuclear arsenal. It merely put a ceiling on the destructive power each side possessed. But it marked a beginning of a process of mutual consultation on one of the most pressing questions facing the world. The negotiators expressed the hope that later treaties would address the more difficult problem of reducing nuclear arsenals.

SALT I froze the existing number of land-based missiles, the ICBMs, which left the Soviet Union with an advantage in ICBMs, 1,398 to 1,052. The Nixon administration, to appease its domestic critics, argued that the agreement had prevented the build-up of the Soviet arsenal of SS-9s.[1] Moreover, the treaty also offered the United States several advantages. It ignored the questions of intercontinental bombers (in which the United States has always enjoyed a marked superiority), intermediate-range missiles in Europe (which became a major issue during the arms reduction talks of the early 1980s), and the French and British arsenals. In each instance, the United

States and its NATO allies had a decided advantage. The Soviets also accepted, if only for the time being, a U.S. advantage in the number of strategic warheads, a category in which the United States led by a ratio of two to one.

But the treaty did not address the question of limiting MIRVed missiles, a U.S. invention, where the United States held a large, if only temporary, lead. MIRV is short for multiple independently-targetable reentry vehicle, a missile capable of carrying several warheads, each with the ability of finding a different target. In other words, the missile—the expensive component—càrries a number of warheads—the less expensive components. It provides, to use a phrase out of the 1950s, "more bang for a buck." During the SALT I negotiations the United States had refused to discuss the Soviet proposal of banning MIRVed missiles, because the United States saw no reason to give away what at the time was the most sophisticated nuclear weapon either side possessed. U.S. negotiators soon had reasons to regret their decision, however.

SALT I was not expected to halt the arms race. For one thing, the treaty did not prevent the improvement in the quality of weapons, which continued to become increasingly more sophisticated. The emphasis on limiting launchers (bombers, missiles, submarines) was beginning to make less and less sense, since launchers, particularly missiles, were beginning to carry more and more warheads. And it is after all the warheads that do the damage. SALT II, which the negotiators hammered out by 1979, attempted, therefore, to limit not only launchers but also the number of warheads. This was done by placing a ceiling on missiles that could be MIRVed. By the mid–1970s, the Soviet Union had begun to deploy its own MIRVed missiles. By then, MIRVed missile technology had begun to work to the Soviet Union's advantage because the Soviet missiles were larger and more powerful than the U.S. ICBMs and thus capable of carrying up to thirty warheads. The U.S. Minuteman III missile, in contrast, carries but three warheads.

In June 1979, after years of difficult negotiations, Brezhnev and President Jimmy Carter met in Vienna to sign SALT II. The treaty placed a ceiling of 2,400 missile launchers for each side, of which only 1,320 could be fitted with MIRVs. Also, the agreement limited the number of warheads in an ICBM to ten. SALT II thus put a cap on the Soviet Union's strategic strength, its land-based ICBMs. But it also left the Soviet Union with a five-to-two advantage in the category of ICBM-launched warheads. The U.S. proponents of the treaty argued that the gap in this category would have been much wider had it not been for the treaty which, after all, limited Moscow's arsenal. The treaty also left Washington with a decided advantage in other categories, particularly in SLBMs (submarine-launched ballistic missiles).

The signing ceremony proved to be the last act of détente. By that time a climate of mutual suspicion had already set in. U.S. critics of negotiations with the Soviet Union were becoming increasingly vocal. They pointed out

---

■ GLOSSARY

ABM Anti-Ballistic Missile; a defensive missile to destroy incoming enemy missiles

ASAT Anti-Satellite Missile; a missile to neutralize satellites in earth orbit; a central component of Star Wars

ICBM Intercontinental Ballistic Missile

IRBM Intermediate-Range Ballistic Missile (such as the Pershing II and the SS-20)

MIRV Multiple Independently-targetable Reentry Vehicles; a missile carrying several smaller missiles, each capable of reaching a different target

payload destructive power of a warhead; measured in *megatonnage* (1 megaton equals 1 million tons of TNT; a *kiloton* is the equivalent of 1,000 tons of TNT); a bomb with an explosive force of about 20 kilotons destroyed Hiroshima where about 80,000 died; each U.S. strategic warhead carries an average payload of more than four megatons, or 200 times the destructive power of the bomb dropped on Hiroshima; the warheads of the Soviet Union are even larger.

SALT Strategic Arms Limitations Talks; the emphasis is on *strategic* and *limitations*

SDI Strategic Defense Initiative; the official name of Star Wars

SLBM Submarine-Launched Ballistic Missile

strategic weapons weapons capable of delivering warheads over long distances (usually over three thousand miles); they include *intercontinental* missiles, bombers, and submarine-launched missiles

tactical weapons *short-range* battlefield weapons (such as artillery shells)

theater weapons *intermediate-range* weapons for use in a specific global region, or theater (such as Europe or the Far East)

warhead Pentagon talk for a nuclear bomb (words like "bomb" tend to scare the faint-of-heart)

---

that the Soviet Union could not have it both ways: It could not have peaceful relations with the West accompanied by increased trade with Western Europe and the United States and arms limitations agreements, and at the same time support revolutionary movements in Africa and Asia. Détente, they insisted, must be tied to improved Soviet behavior. The international climate worsened when, in November 1979, the Iranian hostage crisis began, which some even blamed on the Soviet Union, followed in December by the Soviet intervention in Afghanistan. Soviet actions and the U.S. political climate drove the last nail into the coffin of détente. And with the end of détente, arms negotiators could point to no progress whatsoever during the first half of the 1980s.

Even more important than Soviet behavior abroad was the charge that détente and the SALT treaties had made it possible for the Soviet Union to pass the United States in the arms race. The most vocal critic of détente by 1980 was the Republican presidential hopeful, Ronald Reagan, who declared that a "window of vulnerability" had opened and that only one side, the Soviet Union, was engaged in the arms race. The United States, he declared, had in effect disarmed unilaterally. As a political argument, Reagan got considerable mileage out of it. But during the decade of the 1970s the United States had doubled its strategic arsenal. By the time of the presidential election year of 1980, the Soviet Union had closed the wide gap, but the United States continued to lead in the arms race. It has never been a race with one contestant.

The upshot was that détente became a casualty of the renewed Cold War. Détente had already been in trouble, but the events of 1979 finished it off. The United States Senate never ratified SALT II, in part because critics such as Reagan had hammered home the point that it was too advantageous to the Soviet Union. Once Reagan became president, however, he gave tacit recognition to the fact that the treaty had after all put a limit on the Soviet Union's strategic strength, a fact the Joint Chiefs of Staff had acknowledged when they urged the treaty's ratification, calling it "a modest but useful step."[2] For the next five years, President Reagan agreed to abide by the unratified terms of SALT II.

■ THE CORRELATION OF FORCES

Nuclear arms limitation and the ultimate goal of the reduction of such weapons has always been a process resembling a numbers game. But it has become clear that one cannot readily prove that one side or the other is "ahead" in the arms race merely by counting. What criteria does one use to determine who is ahead? What does one count? How do the weapons compare? What are the needs of the two sides? The geographic considerations? The nature of the threat each faces? The questions that may be raised are endless.

The Soviet Union has relied largely upon huge, powerful land-based ICBMs, equipped with up to ten warheads. U.S. missiles are smaller and contain smaller, but more accurate warheads. Which type is preferable? Which is more deadly? The Soviet Union, because its missiles are less accurate, has relied on the larger missiles and thus enjoys an advantage in the category known as "payload," also known as "megatonnage." (One megaton is equal to 1 million tons of TNT.) Over the past two decades, as missiles have become increasingly accurate, both sides have reduced their megatonnage. The United States, in contrast, because of its more accurate missiles, does not have the need to employ large warheads. Thus, if one focuses on the payload category, then the Soviet Union is ahead in the arms race; but if one takes into account missile accuracy, then the advantage goes to the United States.

As a consequence of the deterioration of the international climate, the Carter administration proved unable to obtain the Senate's ratification of SALT II. The failure to do so threatened to put into motion an unlimited and unchecked arms race, something that even the hawkish Reagan administration did not relish. President Reagan, therefore, agreed to abide by a treaty that he had always condemned. The result was that the arms race continued within the confines of SALT II, yet spurred on by a Cold War that promised no thaw in the near future. During the first half of the 1980s, both sides added more than 2,000 strategic warheads to their already bloated arsenals. In December 1981, the Soviet Union walked out of arms reduction talks in Geneva when it failed to halt the deployment of U.S. intermediate-range missiles, the Pershing II and cruise missiles. The talks were not resumed until March 1985. During the intervening period of forty months, both sides added approximately a warhead a day to their strategic arsenals—and this does not take into account intermediate-range nuclear weapons, which both sides continued to deploy.

The configuration of strategic forces, approximately equal in numbers, is not identical, however. The Soviet Union has put most of its eggs into one basket: 65 percent of its nuclear warheads are in land-based missiles; 27 percent are in submarines; and a scant 8 percent (an amount sufficient to destroy the United States, however) are in intercontinental bombers.

In contrast, the United States has a more balanced strategic arsenal, a "triad" of three components. The strongest leg is the submarine-based nuclear deterrent, with 51 percent of U.S. warheads in submarines; 28 percent are in the Air Force's intercontinental bomber force; and only 19 percent are in land-based missiles. As such, the United States has the more sensible balance. Should the Soviets knock out one of the triad's legs, U.S. retaliatory power would still be more than enough to provide a credible second strike deterrent. And unlike the Soviets', most U.S. warheads are not in stationary missiles on land, whose location is all too well known to the spy satellites in orbit, but are instead constantly in motion in the oceans of the world.[3]

All of this causes a problem in determining an equitable formula in the attempt to limit the arms race. The Soviet Union, with its massive land-based force, was not about to sit down to negotiate solely a reduction in land-based missiles. After all, this is where its strength lies.[4] But this is also where the Soviet Union is most vulnerable. Its missiles in the ground are inviting targets. These missiles, powerful and deadly once launched, are nevertheless slow to fire for they are propelled by a liquid fuel. The U.S. missiles, in contrast, can be fired virtually at will for they contain a solid-fuel propellant.

For this reason, the Soviet Union is moving toward the deployment of a smaller, mobile, solid-fuel intercontinental ballistic missile. Such a mobile ICBM promises to add new elements to the arms race—an increasing difficulty in verification and the ability to effect a quicker response.

By the end of 1985, the strategic balance of terror stood approximately as shown in Table 19.1.

Various studies over the past three decades have concluded that between 200 and 300 warheads can destroy the Soviet Union. An equal number can mean the ruination of the United States. The strategic arsenal both sides have is thus of a fantastic dimension. "Overkill," the ability to destroy the enemy several times over, was the stuff for comedians in the 1950s. Yet, this process of amassing more and more warheads has become institutionalized —and thus rationalized. And there is, of course, a cold logic behind it all if one seeks security in sheer numbers—in which case, neither side can ever have enough. In the mid–1980s, the United States possessed the capability of destroying the Soviet Union fifty times with its strategic arsenal alone. It is little wonder that U.S. strategic planners have run out of targets. The surfeit of atomic warheads has made possible the luxury of targeting grain elevators in the Ukraine and open fields Soviet bombers could conceivably use upon their return trips from the United States.[6] And the Soviet Union's ability to destroy the United States is no different. The pointlessness of continuously adding to one's nuclear arsenal, led Henry Kissinger to ask in 1974: "What in the name of God is strategic superiority? . . . What do you do with it?"[7]

The Europeans, and the Soviets in particular, with their record of suffering and defeat, appear to have a better understanding than most people in the United States that history is all too often tragedy. The destruction

Table 19.1   U.S. and Soviet Strategic Arsenal

Weapon Carrier	Number of Warheads	Percentage of Strategic Arsenal
United States		
1,025 ICBMs	2,125	19
36 submarines with 640 missiles	5,728	51
263 B-52 bombers, 98 of which carry 12 cruise missiles each	3,072	27
61 FB-111 bombers	366	3
Total	11,291	100
Soviet Union		
1,398 ICBMs	6,420	65
62 submarines with 924 missiles	2,688	27
173 bombers, 25 of which carry 10 cruise missiles	792	8
Total	9,900	100

Source: New York Times, October 4, 1985.[5]

wreaked by World War II, a conventional war fought with primitive weapons by today's standards, is still a recent memory. Berlin, Stalingrad, and many other cities still contain the ruins, now displayed as memorials and museum pieces, of that war. The persistence of attempts to negotiate if only a limitation to the arms race is mute tribute to the uncomfortable fact that a nuclear war cannot have winners. There will only be losers. The ruins of the Soviet Union and Germany in 1945 did not reveal which country had won the war and which had lost.

■ INTERMEDIATE-RANGE WEAPONS

The late–1970s saw the end of détente and the beginning of what has been called Cold War II. The reasons for the deterioration of relations between the Soviet Union and the West are many and are the responsibility of both sides. One factor, however, was the lack of understanding by the Soviets of the U.S. definition of détente. Détente, in the U.S. mind, was always coupled to a change in Soviet behavior. To the Soviets, however, it meant the Western acceptance of the Soviet Union as a major power, an equal of the United States—and with it an acceptance of the actions that a great power with a global role traditionally plays. After all, they argued, the Soviet Union and the United States had normalized their relations at a time when the United States was engaged in pursuing its global interests in a war against "international Communism" in Vietnam. But from the U.S. viewpoint, Soviet good behavior, particularly in Afghanistan, was a precondition to maintaining détente. The Soviet Union countered by arguing that, for them, détente was more important than Vietnam—but, for the United States, Afghanistan was more important than détente.[8] With détente at an end, the arms race began to take ominous twists and turns. The introduction of a new and increasingly more sophisticated generation of intermediate-range nuclear weapons added to the complexity of the debate on how to limit these weapons.

The strategic arsenal, originally the sole line of deterrent, was joined by shorter-range weapons whose purpose is to determine the outcome in a particular theater of war, such as the European or Pacific theater. Since the early 1960s, both sides have accumulated an extraordinarily destructive arsenal of these intermediate-range nuclear arms. Military strategists see Europe as the most likely stage where such weapons might be employed. There, the Soviets have put into place their most sophisticated medium-range missiles—the mobile SS-20s, which carry three independently-targeted warheads apiece—capable of devastating all of Europe. And the United States can reach the Soviet Union with its intermediate-range missiles—Pershing IIs and cruise missiles—launched from bases in West Germany, Great Britain, and Italy.

With the introduction of the new generation of U.S. intermediate-range missiles, the distinction between "strategic" and "tactical" missiles became increasingly blurred. What is the difference between a Minuteman missile fired from Wyoming (thirty minutes flying time to a Soviet target) and a Pershing II missile fired from West Germany (six minutes flying time)?

Until the mid–1970s, SALT talks had always focused on long-range strategic nuclear weapons. Shorter-range weapons were largely ignored until the Soviet Union began to modernize its medium-range missile arsenal in Europe and deployed a new generation of missiles, the SS-20. The SS-20 is a missile that is an improvement over the older single-warhead, liquid-fuel SS-4s and SS-5s. It has a range of over 3,000 miles, is mobile, contains three independently-targeted warheads, and is a solid-fuel missile that can be fired with a minimum of delay.

This new addition to the Kremlin's military might produced a psychological shock among the West's military strategists. The SS-20s did not change the nuclear balance of terror, but it did give the appearance of a Soviet escalation of the arms race, a perception that is largely correct.

The United States responded, predictably, with its own enhanced intermediate-range weapons in Europe, the Tomahawk cruise missile and the Pershing II. The cruise missile hugs the ground on its approach and is therefore difficult to detect. It is a slowly moving projectile with a range of 2,000 miles and thus capable of reaching the Soviet Union from West European soil. The Pershing II is a fast flying missile with a range of over 1,100 miles. Launched from West Germany, it can reach targets in the Soviet Union within six minutes. Its mobility, range, accuracy, and speed make it one of the premier weapons in the U.S. arsenal. It is a potential first strike weapon suitable for the elimination or "decapitation" of the Soviet command structures.

For the Soviet Union this round in the arms race was filled with contradictions and irony, something which all participants in this dangerous game have experienced. The United States was first to witness this strange twist of logic. The atomic bomb had given the United States the "ultimate weapon," only to subject the country to the prospect of nuclear annihilation within ten short years. Similarly, the SS-20 gave the Kremlin briefly a decided advantage in case of a nuclear exchange in Europe—provided the contest could be limited to Europe, in itself a most unlikely prospect. Within a few years, however, the U.S. counter brought about the deployment of increasingly more dangerous weapons. The result was that the Soviet Union became less secure.

The U.S. intermediate-range missiles, to be effective, had to be stationed on European soil. Presidents Carter and Reagan had their work cut out in selling this round of deployment to their NATO allies. The Europeans understood all too well that both the Soviet and the U.S. arsenal threatened to turn Europe into a shooting gallery—particulary after President Reagan said, "I could see where you could have the exchange of tactical weapons in the field [in Europe] without it bringing either one of the major powers to pushing the button."[9] The upshot was a split in the NATO alliance. All told, the United States was able to convince its European allies to accept 464 cruise and 108 Pershing II missiles, for a total of 572.[10] But public opinion in Western Europe was divided on this issue. The Europeans well understand that they are hostages of a Soviet build-up and a U.S. response.

This latest round of escalation in the nuclear arms race produced a series of ill-fated discussions at Geneva, which began in the spring of 1981. The negotiating postures of both sides were the essence of simplicity. Each sought to eliminate the other side's missiles and at the same time hold on to what they had. Such an approach to limiting or controlling nuclear armaments was a sure-fire prescription for a deadlock. Negotiators, instead of seeking compromise solutions, played to larger audiences, notably the people back home and the nervous Europeans. Propaganda and accusations of bad faith became the order of the day.

The two chief negotiators, Yuli Kvitsinsky for the Soviet Union and Paul Nitze for the United States, did manage at one point to agree on a compromise formula, their so-called "walk in the woods" proposal. It called for a rough balance between the Soviet Union's 75 SS-20s (each carrying three warheads) and the United States's 75 Tomahawk cruise launchers (each with four warheads). By this agreement, the Soviets would have had to curtail, but not scrap, the deployment of their SS-20s; while the United States would have had to forgo the deployment of its deadly Pershing IIs. The hard-liners in Moscow and Washington quickly denounced this attempt at a compromise and this round of negotiations was now dead. In December 1981, the Soviets left the conference table when the United States proceeded to deploy on schedule the first cruise and Pershing II missiles in Great Britain and West Germany, respectively.

In April 1985, about one month after the Soviet and U.S. negotiators had resumed their talks in Geneva, the new Soviet leader, Mikhail Gorbachev, announced a freeze on any further deployment of SS-20s until November 1985, provided the United States halted the deployment of its missiles. Yet, there was nothing in Gorbachev's proposal suggesting a reduction of the Soviet arsenal—whose deployment appears to have been largely completed. The Soviet gesture was too little and too late. Instead of facing 75 slow-moving cruise missiles, as proposed in the "walk in the woods," the Soviets faced 54 of the deadly Pershing IIs and 48 cruise missiles, with the prospect of more to come. And Western Europe faced 250 of the Soviet Union's 414 SS-20s. (The remainder of the SS-20s were pointed toward China and Japan, but their mobile nature made possible their redeployment.) "The Russians have all worthy targets covered," the *Baltimore Sun* commented in an editorial, "and the Americans are getting there."[11]

Soviet leader Mikhail Gorbachev and U.S. President Ronald Reagan, at Geneva for their first summit meeting, Nov. 19, 1985. (*AP/Wide World Photos*)

Radioactive substances released in U.S. nuclear bomb test, boiling skyward—shot from a plane directly overhead the blast, Bikini Atoll, July 12, 1948. (*National Archives*)

By the 1980s, the arms race had become increasingly intricate. The first two SALT talks had dealt exclusively with strategic weapons and the negotiators had the luxury of focusing on them. When talks resumed in Geneva in March of 1985 the issues were much more complex. The negotiators now sought to address three related topics—intermediate-range missiles, strategic launchers, and the U.S. program for a new defensive system, commonly known as Star Wars. The Soviets, in their turn, began for the first time to insist on counting the U.S. strike force launched from aircraft carriers off the coast of Europe, as well as the nuclear arsenals of its NATO members, Great Britain and France.

Other events were also overtaking the strategic arms limitation agreements. The two powers were on the verge of replacing older missiles with newer ones that were more accurate, carried a greater payload, or were more easily fired. The Soviets were moving toward an arsenal of land-based missiles that were less cumbersome and more efficient. The huge liquid-fueled SS-18s each carrying ten independently targeted warheads were about to be joined by smaller, yet mobile, solid-fuel missiles carrying a single warhead. The advantage of such a missile lies in its mobility and ability to be fired at will. The U.S. version of such a weapon, still in its developmental stage, has been labeled "Midgetman."

The arms race, where once the emphasis was on monster missiles and large megatonnage, has apparently adopted the slogan "small is beautiful." Over the past two decades, both sides have drastically reduced the firepower of their missiles. As missiles have become increasingly more accurate, the emphasis has switched from warheads large enough to destroy entire cities to small, but accurate warheads dubbed "silo busters." And with this development came talk of winning a nuclear war by surgical strikes that take out the other side's silos and command structures. Appropriately, this is known as "decapitation."

U.S. modernization consisted of replacing the Minutemen III missiles, each carrying three warheads, with MX missiles, each capable of carrying ten warheads, the maximum permitted under the SALT II treaty. The problem with the MX, however, has always been in finding a home for it. After considering several alternatives, the Reagan administration settled on reinforced silos previously occupied by the older Minutemen IIIs. This, however, did not solve what the president called the United States's "window of vulnerability," namely, the Soviet Union's capacity to overwhelm the U.S. land-based missile force. A sitting duck is a sitting duck no matter what species, size, or color. For that reason, the MX is not suited as a deterrent; it is, instead, a highly accurate first strike weapon and, therefore, potentially a destabilizing factor in the arms race. To alleviate public anxiety and obtain funding from Congress, Reagan renamed the MX missile the "Peacekeeper." (In White House circles it was also called the "Hallmark"—a tribute to its capabilities.)

■ STAR WARS:
THE STRATEGIC DEFENSE INITIATIVE

In March 1983, the arms race took another twist when President Reagan went public with a military research program already on the drawing board. Its purpose was to develop the means to offer U.S. land-based missiles a measure of protection in case of a nuclear exchange with the Soviet Union, particularly in an exchange in which the Soviet Union struck first with its powerful and accurate land-based missiles, notably the SS-18s. With this pronouncement, Reagan officially committed the United States to the creation of a defense against Soviet ICBMs. The research program was now no longer a scientific quest for a hypothetical defensive weapon. Instead, the government of the United States fully committed its resources to finding a technological breakthrough to neutralize hostile projectiles.

Thus far, the deterrent to nuclear war has been based on the balance of terror, that is, the assumption that neither side wants to commit suicide. It is a strategy known as Mutually Assured Destruction, better known by its acronym, MAD. And in fact, this balance of terror has kept the peace. The Soviet Union and the United States have become hostages of the nuclear arsenals pointed at them. They can neither hide, run, nor fight.

In the late 1960s, the Soviets entertained the idea of a defensive shield of their own, which, however, was unacceptable to the United States. U.S. officials pointed out to the Soviets that such an action would only invite similar measures by the United States, as well as an increase in the number of U.S. warheads. The result would be an escalation of the arms race, one that promised no security for anyone. Thus, a defensive barrier by either side would only provoke an increase in the other side's missile strength.

The United States prevailed upon the Soviet Union to abandon its missile defense program. The resultant accord, the Anti-Ballistic Missile Treaty, between the United States and the Soviet Union permitted both sides to create two limited defensive systems each, which neither bothered to develop fully. The agreement put an end to the prospect of a new element in the nuclear arms race—the building of antimissile defenses only to witness the adversary drastically increase its nuclear arsenal in order to overwhelm the defenses.

The Anti-Ballistic Missile Treaty became part and parcel of the SALT I agreement, without which SALT I would have been impossible. The U.S. military and political establishments were not about to sign an agreement with the Soviets by which the United States limited its missile strength and at the same time sat by idly as the Soviets took unilateral steps via a defensive shield to neutralize a portion of the U.S. strategic arsenal. Once the Soviets understood this, the door was opened for the ratification of SALT I and the limited Anti-Ballistic Missile (ABM) treaty. The simple, brutal deterrent of Mutually Assured Destruction remained intact.

In March 1983, eleven years after the superpowers had agreed to limit their nuclear firepower and their antinuclear defenses, President Reagan announced plans to build a highly complex system to guard the United States against a nuclear attack. With this announcement, a military research project was slated to be deployed over the next twenty-five years. Reagan had never been comfortable with arms agreements accepting Soviet parity with the United States. That and his unlimited faith in U.S. ingenuity and technical skills led him to argue for a program that, he argued, would not cause an escalation of the arms race.

Reagan's proposal, officially called the Strategic Defense Initiative (SDI) but popularly known as Star Wars, challenged the policy of Mutually Assured Destruction. It was immoral, he insisted, to rely on a military strategy predicated on the assured annihilation of the nation. He proposed instead the development of high-technology barriers to make nuclear war impossible. In fact, he went so far as to suggest that once U.S. scientists had solved the riddle of how to deal with incoming Soviet rockets, the U.S. government would hand over the secret to the Soviets. Nuclear war would then become impossible and peace would prevail. The ultimate goal, President Reagan said, was "to eliminate the weapons themselves."[12]

Star Wars played to mixed reviews. Its theoretical underpinnings cannot be readily faulted. But there are several problems in implementing a defense of such staggering complexity. First, to be effective it would have to be nearly perfect. Because 2 percent of the Soviet Union's present strategic arsenal can destroy the United States, a 90 percent efficiency in the Star Wars defense system—which according to some scientists is the best that could be gained—would not be nearly enough to protect the United States. Mutually Assured Destruction therefore would continue to prevail and the rubble would still bounce, for even 10 percent of a strategic arsenal of 10,000 warheads would destroy the other side five times over.

Star Wars, even if only 90 percent efficient, would, in effect, bring about the unilateral U.S. neutralization of a sizable portion of the Soviet arsenal, something the Kremlin is not likely to accept. Star Wars promises only to contribute to another spiral of the arms race, for the Soviets have already threatened to produce an ever-increasingly larger number of warheads. In short, the Soviets are being given the alternative of accepting U.S. nuclear superiority or of deploying enough weapons to be capable of overwhelming the Star Wars defense.

Second, there is the staggering cost. Reagan requested a budget of 30 billion (3.7 billion for fiscal 1986) for research and development during the next five years. And the figure is sure to rise in the future. There is some doubt whether the United States government, already running a record deficit of over 200 billion a year, can afford the program.

Third, there is the very complexity of the system. Star Wars calls for a new generation of sensors for the surveillance, tracking, and destruction of enemy missiles. These sensors would have to work almost flawlessly in the face of thousands of incoming warheads and decoys. The program also envisions the deployment of energy weapons consisting primarily of powerful lasers based either on the ground (and deflected by huge mirrors in orbit) or in orbit. The most crucial part of the entire program, "systems concepts and battle management," calls for an error-free computer system that instantaneously links the system's diverse elements.[13]

Fourth, ways must be found to protect the system from destruction by hostile elements. Mirrors and spy satellites in orbit are inviting targets that can readily be neutralized. They will have to be defended.

Last, the Soviet scientists are sure to work overtime to find ways over, under, around, and through any missile defense thought up by their U.S. counterparts.

In light of these obstacles, it was little wonder that Pentagon officials told Congress, which after all must come up with the money to finance all of this, that this was a long-range program of at least 25 years duration. There was talk, however, of an "interim deployment" to protect land-based missiles, presumably the MX missile. This, of course, puts first things first; civilians will have to wait. Former Defense Secretary Harold Brown wrote that "technology does not offer even a reasonable prospect of a population defense."[14]

Research in this area is not new. It has been going on in the East and in the West for a number of years. It only became public knowledge, however, in 1983. The Soviet program is of an unknown quality, although it is generally believed in the United States not to be as far advanced as the U.S. program. Until now, Star Wars has remained only a research program, but the Reagan administration has repeatedly stated that ultimately it will be implemented.

Domestic critics of Star Wars fear that it will only militarize space, add little to anyone's security, and bankrupt the government. The deployment of a space-based defense promises to produce an open-ended contest in space, because the Soviets do not have the luxury of looking upon the U.S. program with equanimity, the U.S. protestations notwithstanding that it is but a defensive system. To the Soviets, it looms as an attempt to disarm them. *Pravda* has repeatedly announced that the Soviet Union will not idly accept Star Wars. The Soviets will, therefore, join the race into space. When Reagan's secretary of defense, Casper Weinberger, was asked how he viewed the unilateral deployment of a Soviet version of Star Wars, he replied that such an act "would be one of the most frightening prospects I could imagine."[15] One should not expect the Soviets to react differently to the U.S. program. After all, as the official name of Star Wars suggests, this is a U.S. "initiative."

The debate over Star Wars in the United States has been between two fundamentally opposed camps. On the one side are the pessimists leery of the spiraling arms race, the believers in Murphy's Law. To them, Star Wars looks too good on paper. Something is bound to go wrong. On the other side are the hard-liners who seek to escalate the arms race in the expectation of beating the Soviets at this game. They are the optimists who are convinced that U.S. technology, which put astronauts on the moon, can and must win it. They reject the notion that they cannot win it. They are philosophically, and more importantly psychologically, incapable of settling for a draw. To them, parity is the same as having lost the game.

The champions of Star Wars are the same individuals who have always argued that the Soviets are outspending and outproducing the United States in the nuclear arms race. They are the philosophical heirs of those responsible for the bomber and missile "gaps," the revelation that the Soviet military budget was "far larger" than that of the United States, the claim of a U.S. "window of vulnerability," and so on. They continue to hold dear the charge, once made by candidate Reagan against the hapless Carter, that only one side has been engaged in the arms race.

But once having fired their accusations against the Soviets, the advocates of Star Wars have moved away from their starting position, which held that the Soviets were fully committed to the arms race and that Star Wars was after all merely one leg of a longer race. They have forgotten their previous arguments by which they repeatedly emphasized that the Soviets were in the race to stay, and they now minimize the Soviet contribution to the arms race. John Hawes, deputy assistant secretary of state for Politico-Military Affairs, took this logic one step further. The Soviets, he argued, would not even bother to respond to Star Wars. "The Soviets . . . have no incentive to build new missiles today . . . [because if] we find in ten years that SDI works . . . their missiles [would be] obsolete."[16] He could not understand why the Soviets would build more missiles. Similarly, President Reagan never addressed the fundamental question of how the Soviets might respond to his initiative.

Star Wars does not promise to be the arms race's equivalent of putting a person on the moon, a difficult yet manageable accomplishment. The moon did not hold suprises. It was where the mathematician knew it would be—an inert and caculable entity. Star Wars was more like climbing Mount Everest—unpredictable and dangerous. When Sir Edmund Hillary climbed the mountain he spoke of having conquered it. But his Sherpa guide, Norgay Tenzing, knew differently; he knew he had climbed the mountain only with its cooperation. If there was one thing that became clear, it was that the Soviets refused to cooperate.

Unless an agreement is hammered out, there will be no limits on what anyone does. The propulsion of the nuclear arms race into space cannot but destroy agreements that the two sides have signed over the years. One casualty will be the Outer Space Treaty of 1967, which prohibited nuclear weapons in outer space and earth orbit; another will be the Anti-Ballistic Missile Treaty of 1972. When the two powers resumed their arms limitation talks in Geneva in March 1985, the Soviet negotiators made it clear that they considered Star Wars as the paramount issue; U.S. representatives, holding the trump cards if only for the time being, did not want to discuss it.

During the 1988 presidential campaign, Vice President George Bush acknowledged that Star Wars, besides being expensive, had technological problems. By the late 1980s, it had once again become largely a research program.

■ GORBACHEV'S PEACE OFFENSIVE

One month after Mikhail Gorbachev had come to power in Moscow, the Kremlin launched its most devastating "peace offensive" of the Cold War. Gorbachev, it became eventually clear, set out determined to bring about not only a domestic *perestroika*, but one in foreign relations as well. "We will rob you of your enemy," he told the West. His proposal to freeze the deployment of Soviet SS-20 intermediate-range missiles was but his first move.

Shortly afterward the world witnessed a number of summit meetings between Gorbachev and Reagan, who had previously resolutely refused to sit down with his Soviet counterpart. Brezhnev, Andropov, and Chernenko were clearly dying men; moreover, there was nothing to talk about with the leaders of what Reagan had early in his presidency called the "evil empire." The first meeting between Reagan and Gorbachev was a get-acquainted session in 1986, in neutral Geneva, Switzerland. It led to a series of negotiations that produced for the first time a negotiated reduction of nuclear armaments on both sides. The reasons for Reagan's turnabout are not clear. Several factors seem to have played a role. First, he had been criticized at home as being the first president since 1945 who had not met with his Soviet counterpart. Second, his foreign policy appeared to be in shambles and he may have sought the opportunity to put his mark on the course of history. Third, his first meeting with Gorbachev established a good personal relationship between the two men.

The first order of business was the recent escalation of the nuclear race in the heart of Europe, the deployment of intermediate-range nuclear forces (INF) such as the U.S. Pershing II and cruise missiles and the Soviet SS-20. Gorbachev surprised the Reagan administration when he suddenly dusted off the old Western proposal, the zero-option: if the Soviet Union did not deploy its missiles, the United States would not counter with the deployment of its own rockets. Gorbachev would undo Brezhnev's error; he would take his INF forces out of Europe if the United States were to do the same. Moscow called Washington's bluff; if Reagan rejected Gorbachev's proposal of eliminating all INFs, the U.S. position would be exposed as another example of Cold War propaganda on the part of one of the superpowers.

Reagan responded positively to Gorbachev's offer. The consequence was the INF treaty of May 1988, which eliminated an entire category of nuclear rockets, those with a range between 310 and 3,400 miles. The superpowers then proceeded to dismantle the costly weapons—1,752 Soviet and 867 U.S. rockets[17]—under the watchful eyes of on-site inspectors from the other side.

Reagan was then able to turn to one of his favorite programs, namely START, the Strategic Arms Reduction Talks. Early in his presidency, Reagan had argued correctly that SALT had accomplished little. It had merely kept the nuclear arms race within certain parameters, making it possible, nevertheless, for both sides to increase their strategic arsenals. At the time of the signing of the INF treaty, the U.S. arsenal still contained 13,134 strategic warheads, the Soviet 10,664.[18] The time had come to reduce them. Reagan found a responsive partner in Gorbachev. In October 1985, Gorbachev had already proposed a 50 percent reduction of strategic nuclear forces, which would lessen the Soviet threat against U.S. land-based missiles and close what Reagan had called the U.S. "window of vulnerability." And in October 1987, at their meeting in Reykjavik, Iceland, Gorbachev had gone so far as to offer Reagan the elimination of all strategic nuclear weapons. A surprised Reagan was on the verge of accepting before his advisers interfered. They feared that a world free of nuclear weapons would leave it—particularly Western Europe—at the mercy of the superior Soviet conventional forces.

Gorbachev was not finished with his surprises, however. On December 7, 1988, he launched another volley in his peace offensive. He announced—this time unilaterally and without precondition—the reduction in the Soviet armed forces of 10 percent (500,000 soldiers), 800 airplanes, 8,500 pieces of artillery, and 5,000 tanks within two years. Included in the offer was the promise to dissolve 6 of the 15 divisions in East Germany, Hungary, and Czechoslovakia by 1991. But most important, Gorbachev included the withdrawal of assault troops and mobile bridges for crossing rivers. Gorbachev's speech marked a 180-degree turn in Soviet military doctrine as it had existed since the early 1960s. The East German party chief Erich Honecker recognized immediately what he called the "immense historical significance" of the Soviet troop withdrawal.[19] Gorbachev's speech also shocked many in the U.S. defense community; some called it another Pearl Harbor, a propaganda offensive designed to disarm the West.

On January 1, 1989, three weeks after Gorbachev's speech, the Soviet defense ministry published a secret military study dated November 5, 1946. Its subject was an operations plan purely defensive in character. The Soviet Union's defensive perimeter ran 60 to 100 miles east of the U.S. zone of occupation, near Berlin, where the civilian population was to be mobilized in support of the Soviet army. The plan was worked out by Marshal Vasili Sokolovski—the same man who in 1962 published his highly publicized book extolling the virtue of offense.[20] Sokolovski's argument of 1962 was in response to Khrushchev's whittling down of the Soviet army. Khrushchev had argued that a handful of nuclear rockets sufficed as a deterrent; the sacred Soviet army had become obsolete as a defensive force. Khrushchev's marshals needed a new rationale for their bloated army and responded that the best defense was a strong offensive capability.

Gorbachev had good reasons for releasing this document. He had recently fired the commander of the Warsaw Pact forces, General Victor Kulikov, a stubborn advocate of the offensive doctrine. He also appeared to be saying that his defensive policy was nothing new. Throughout 1987 and 1988, Gorbachev repeatedly took on the Soviet military establishment. Defense minister Sokolow became a casualty after a young West German aviator, Mathias Rust, landed his Cessna at the edge of Red Square, having flown past the vaunted air defenses of the Soviet Union. Sokolow became the first marshal in Soviet history to be pensioned off. The generals and admirals scarcely resisted. They had become casualties of the Afghan war, during which their prestige had greatly declined. *Pravda* ιand other publications carried articles and letters to the editor critical of the perquisites of high ranking officers. University students protested against serving in the armed forces.[21]

The Western critics of Gorbachev's speech of December 7, 1988, were in part correct. The first casualty of that speech was the U.S. program of "modernizing" the short-range Lance rocket, a tactical nuclear weapon. Many still feared the sizable Soviet army. The Lance II, a new rocket with a range of just under the limit of 310 miles as stipulated by the INF treaty, would not only be a deterrent but would also make possible the circumvention of the spirit, if not the letter, of the INF treaty. Lance II would give the United States in a back-handed way an INF arsenal.

But West German politics torpedoed the U.S. "modernization" program. Many in West Germany, especially the powerful Social Democratic party in opposition, insisted that the shorter-range rockets, too, must go. They had thought that the United States would not stop at merely negotiating the elimination of the INFs. The retention of these rockets signaled to them that in case of war the superpowers would try to limit the conflict to the center of Europe. "The shorter the rockets, the deader the Germans" became the West German watchword. Yet

Brent Scowcroft, President Bush's national security advisor, reacted as if nothing had changed, as if the Cold War was still in full bloom, and pressed ahead with convincing Bonn to accept the Lance II. In February 1989, Egon Bahr, the national security expert of the West German Social Democratic party, told him that the United States had no chance to deploy the missiles. If the conservative government in Bonn capitulated to U.S. pressure and accepted them, his party would win the next election and take them out.[22]

It did not help Washington that in the spring of 1989, a secret, nonsensical NATO scenario, "Wintex-Cimex 89" was made public. It envisioned a "limited" nuclear exchange whereby 17 nuclear bombs were dropped on the Soviet Union and its allies (three of them on East Germany) and Moscow somehow refrained from responding with nuclear weapons. The West German foreign minister, Hans-Dietrich Genscher, who was born in Halle, East Germany, and whose relatives still lived there, declared: "I have sworn an oath to avert harm from the German people and that includes East Germany."[23]

East German scientists joined the debate. In case of conventional war, they argued, Europe would still be contaminated with nuclear fallout. The continent contained 220 civilian reactors which, if damaged, would turn into radioactive weapons. Because of the type of fuel they used, they would emit greater doses of radiation than atomic weapons. The large concentrations of chemical plants—such as along the Rhine River in Western Europe and in the region of Halle and Leipzig in East Germany—would spill their deadly poison on humans, plants and animals. A conventional war would turn Europe into an "atomic, chemical and genetically contaminated desert." Such a war would lead to the "destruction of what the aggressor would seek to conquer and what the victims of aggression have to defend."[24]

During 1989, Gorbachev stood in stark contrast to the cautious Bush who only late in the year began to accept the idea that he, too, could play a role in affecting the course of history. Gorbachev had been the engine of change; Bush a mere spectator. The demise of the Communist parties in Eastern Europe produced a situation in January 1990 whereby Czechoslovakia,[25] Hungary, and Poland insisted that the Soviet army leave their territories by the end of 1991. An Eastern Europe without Soviet forces had become a question of when, not if, and Gorbachev, Bush suspected, would announce another level of troop withdrawals. It was at this point that Bush took the initiative and proposed the reduction of U.S. and Soviet forces to a level of 195,000 each in Central Europe. New thinking finally had come to Washington. Previously, Bush had insisted on a U.S. troop ceiling of 275,000 in

Central Europe, but budget considerations—the United States spent $150 billion a year for its troop deployment in Europe—gave the cautious Bush little choice but to take the lead. Moreover, as even the most hawkish officials in the Pentagon admitted, in the 14 months since Gorbachev's speech of December 7, 1988, the Soviet Union had dismantled its capability to invade Western Europe. Bush's speech was welcomed news in Warsaw, Budapest, Prague, and Moscow because it facilitated the Soviet army's withdrawal from its forward position in Eastern Europe. A dominant feature of the Cold War, the military confrontation in the heart of Europe, was coming to an end.

■ RECOMMENDED READINGS

Bottome, Edgar M. *The Balance of Terror: A Guide to the Arms Race.* 2d rev. ed. Boston: Beacon Press, 1986.
An excellent history of the arms race.
Cockburn, Andrew. *The Threat: Inside the Soviet Military Machine.* New York: Random House, 1983.
A sober assessment of Soviet capabilities and weaknesses.
Cox, Arthur Macy. *Soviet Roulette: The Superpower Game.* New York: Times Books, 1982.
Discusses the nature and dangers of the nuclear arms race.
Freedman, Lawrence. *The Evolution of Nuclear Strategy.* New York: St. Martin's Press, 1981.
A thorough and detailed analysis of the positions taken by the nuclear powers.
McDougall, Walter A. *The Heavens and the Earth: A Political History of the Space Age.* New York: Basic Books, 1984.
A history of the race into space.
Newhouse, John. *Cold Dawn: The Story of SALT.* New York: Holt, Rinehart & Winston, 1973.
The definitive study on SALT I.
Schell, Jonathan. *The Fate of the Earth.* New York: Knopf, 1982.
The best seller on the potential consequences of nuclear war.
Smith, Gerard. *Doubletalk: The Story of SALT I.* Garden City: Doubleday, 1980.
By the U.S. chief arms negotiator at the talks.
Soviet Military Power. Washington, D.C.: Government Printing Office, six editions, 1981–1987.
The Pentagon's assessment of the Soviet threat.
Talbott, Strobe. *Endgame: The Inside Story of SALT II.* New York: Harper & Row, 1979.
By a correspondent for *Time* whose books are the most lucid and detailed accounts of recent arms negotiations.
Talbott, Strobe. *Deadly Gambits: The Reagan Administration and the Stalemate in Nuclear Arms Control.* New York: Knopf, 1984.
As stated above.
Union of Concerned Scientists. *The Fallacy of Star Wars.* 1983.
A rejection of Star Wars as an unworkable proposition.

■ NOTES

1. SS (surface-to-surface) is the U.S. designation of Soviet missiles. As soon as a Soviet missile is tested the Pentagon assigns it a number.

2. George McGovern, "SALT II: A Political Autopsy," *Politics Today,* (March/April 1980), p 64.

3. The Seabed Pact prohibits the stationing of weapons on the ocean floor beyond a nation's 12-mile limit; it does not cover submarines that may approach the enemy's territorial waters.

4. This was the basis of Ronald Reagan's "window of vulnerability." It went something like this: the Soviet Union's land-based arsenal, which during the late 1970s had become increasingly more accurate, was capable of overwhelming the U.S. land-based missiles in their silos and with it threaten the very existence of the United States. This argument always focused on only one facet of the arms race. It ignored the fact that either of the other two legs of the U.S. "triad," the submarines and the bomber force, was more than enough to keep the Soviets honest. Reagan promised that, if elected president, he would close this window. In 1984, he declared that he had closed the window—without, however, having done anything to change reality. U.S. missiles have remained in the ground and the Soviets have continued to perfect the accuracy of their ICBMs.

5. The *New York Times,* October 4, 1985. All figures are estimates of classified information. They were compiled from Pentagon publications, the International Institute for Strategic Studies, the Arms Control Association, and the Center for Defense Information.

6. Thomas Powers, "Nuclear Winter and Nuclear Strategy," *The Atlantic Monthly,* November 1984, p. 60.

7. Lawrence Freedman, *The Evolution of Nuclear Strategy* (New York: St. Martin's, 1981), p. 363.

8. Georgy Arbatov, director of the Institute of U.S. and Canadian Studies of the Academy of Sciences of the Soviet Union, in Arthur Macy Cox (with a Soviet commentary by Georgy Arbatov), *Russian Roulette: The Superpower Game* (New York: Times Books, 1982), pp. 177–178, 182.

9. Leonid Brezhnev and Ronald Reagan, "Brezhnev and Reagan on Atom War," transcripts of statements, *New York Times,* October 21, 1981, p. 5.

10. Great Britain accepted 160 cruise missiles; West Germany, 108 Pershing II missiles and 96 cruise missiles; Italy, 112 cruise missiles; Belgium and Holland, 48 cruise missiles each. Norway, Denmark, Greece, and Turkey have rejected U.S. missiles. Turkey, by virtue of the agreement between the Soviet Union and the United States in the wake of the Cuban missile crisis of 1962, is prohibited from stationing U.S. missiles. The Greek government of Andreas Papandreou has carved out a neutralist position between the United States and the Soviet Union despite the fact that Greece is a member of NATO. Papandreou considers Turkey, a fellow member of NATO, to be a greater threat to Greece than the Warsaw Pact to the north. In Norway and Denmark, pacifist sentiment prevented the acceptance of U.S. weapons.

11. "Gorbachev's Gambit," Editorial, Baltimore *Sun,* April 10, 1985, p. A 10.

12. Ronald Reagan, quoted in "President's Speech on Military Spending and a New Defense," *New York Times,* March 24, 1983, p. A 20.

13. Star Wars "system concepts and battle management" is one of five components of Star Wars research; Wayne Biddle, "Request for Space Weapons Reflects Early Goals," *New York Times,* February 4, 1985, p. A 10. And with it the fate of the world would be in the hands (or the chips and software) of computers. "Perhaps we should run R2-D2 for president in the 1990s," declared Senator Paul Tsongas (D-Mass.) at a Congressional hearing. "At least he'd be on line all the time. Has anyone told the President that he's out of the decision-making process?" Replying to Tsongas, George Keyworth, President Reagan's science adviser said, "I certainly haven't." (George Keyworth, quoted in Philip M. Boffey, "'Star Wars' and Mankind: Consequences for Future," *New York Times,* March 8, 1985, p. A 14.

14. Harold Brown, (December 1983) quoted in ibid., p. A 14.

15. Casper Weinberger quoted in ibid., p. A 14.

16. John Hawes quoted in an interview by Kai Bird and Max Holland, "Dispatches," *The Nation,* June 1, 1985, pp. 664–665.

17. The Soviet SS–20 rockets carried three warheads each, so the Soviet Union gave up more than three times as many warheads as the United States.

18. Arms Control Association, from data supplied by the U.S. Defense Department, the Joint Chiefs of Staff, and the Arms Control and Disarmament Agency, *New York Times*, May 26, 1988, p. A12.

19. " 'Wir werden euch des Feindes berauben,' " *Der Spiegel*, December 12, 1988, p. 22.

20. "Vorstoss auf Berlin," *Der Spiegel*, February 6, 1989, pp. 136–137.

21. Christian Schmidt-Häuer, "Die Armee gerät unter Beschuss," *Die Zeit*, November 11, 1988, p. 8.

22. "Unsere Antwort wird Nein sein," *Der Spiegel*, May 1, 1989, p. 21.

23. "'Der Iwan kommt—und feste druff,'" *Der Spiegel*, May 1, 1989, pp. 23–27.

24. Wolfgang Schwarz of the Institute for International Politics and Economy in East Berlin, in a report to the East German Council of Ministers, "DDR-Wissenschaftler warnt vor Atomverseuchung Europas," *Frankfurter Rundschau*, June 21, 1989, p. 2.

25. At a meeting of the Warsaw Pact in December 1989, the five members—the Soviet Union, Poland, Hungary, East Germany, and Bulgaria—that had invaded Czechoslovakia in 1968 to crush the "Prague Spring" apologized for the invasion.

☐ Index

Abalkin, Leonid, 429
Abbas, Ferhat, 131
Abdullah, King of Jordan, 141, 144, 156
Abkhazians, 433
ABM (Anti-Ballistic Missile), 459, 468-472
Abraham, tomb of, 149, 360
Acheson, Dean, 60-62, 71, 82
Adenauer, Konrad, 79, 219-221, 444-445, 454
Afghanistan, 87-88, 182, 413-422
Africa, British departure from, 99-100, 123-126; colonialism in, 99-100, 119-122; economic problems in, 231-244, 254-256; French departure from, 126-127; foreign debt, 345-348, 351; foreign intervention in, 251-254; independence movements in, 123-125; militarization of, 247-251, 255; nationalism in, 120-121; political instability, 244-254; population growth in, 233-236; poverty in, 231-240; tribal conflict in, 245-246, 249-251; urbanization in, 236. *See also individual countries*
Afrikaner, 256-265
agriculture, in Africa, 237-240, 267; in Bangladesh, 327-328; in China, 305-306; in India, 318-320; in Latin America, 270; in the Soviet Union, 428-429; in the Third World, 237-240;
Albanians, 452
Alfonsin, Raul, 277
Algeria, battle of Algiers, 130-131; de Gaulle's policy in, 131-132; FLN, 130; French in, 126-130
Ali, 362
Allende, Salvador, 281-283
Alliance for Progress, 272
Amin, Hafizullah, 416-417

Amin, Idi, 248
Amritsar, 329
Amur River, 182, 185
ANC (African National Congress), 261, 264-265
Andropov, Yuri, 166, 412
Angola, 245-254
anti-Semitism, 138-142
apartheid, 256-265
Aquino, Benigno, 339
Aquino, Corazon, 339-341, 344
Arab-American Oil Company, 365
Arab-Israeli War (1948), 144-145
Arabs, in Algeria, 126-135; conflict with Jewish settlers, 138-144; nationalism, 100, 138, 140, 142; refugees, 144-145; wars with Israel, 144, 147-149
Arafat, Yassir, 149, 153
Aral Lake, 431
Arbatov, Georgy, 477
Arbenz, Jacobo, 89-90, 284
ARENA (National Republican Alliance), 296-297
Arendt, Hannah, 436
Argentina, economic growth, 275-277; foreign debt, 277, 349, 351; militarism, 275-277; under Peron, 275-277
Arias, Oscar, 294, 299
Armenia, 431, 433-434, 453
ARVN (Army of the Republic of [South] Vietnam), 198-200
ASAT (Anti-Satellite Missile System), 459
ASEAN, 203, 205, 337, 343, 395
Asia, colonialism in, 99-100, 103; economic development (*see individual countries*); nationalism in, 100, 104-105, 111; impact of World War II on, 12-15, 104-

105. *See also individual countries*
Assad, Hafez, 153
Aswan Dam, 86, 251
atomic bomb, building of, 16; controversy
    over U.S. use of, 16-20; dropped on
    Japan, 4, 11, 14-15; nuclear arms race,
    223, 456-473; "nuclear diplomacy," 19-
    21, 39; People's Republic of China, 180
AT&T, 390
Attlee, Clement, 107
Austria, 83, 85, 97, 390
Awami League, 326
Azerbaidzhan, 433-434, 453

Bagdad Pact, 86-87, 324
Baku, 365
Balfour Declaration, 141
Bandung Conference, 179, 185
Bangladesh, 324-328
Bantustans, 258-259, 265
Bao Dai, 188
Barcos, Virgilio, 300
Barre, Siad, 224
Baruch Plan, 21
Basic Treaty (between West and East
    Germany), 221
Basic Law (West Germany), 443
Batista, Fulgencio, 89
Bay of Pigs, 90–91
Begin, Menachem, 149, 151-152
Belgium, decolonization in Congo, 132-133;
    in Common Market, 73-75; in Congo
    Crisis, 133; in NATO, 76
Belorussians, 417
Benelux, 74
Bengalis, 324
Benghazi, 374
Ben-Gurion, David, 140, 143
Ben Tre, 197
Berghofer, Wolfgang, 442
Beria, Lavrentii, 163
Berlin, 38, 43, 73, 185
Berlin airlift, 43, 185
Berlin Wall, 184-185, 442
Bhutto, Benizar, 330
Bhutto, Zulfikar Ali, 326-327, 330
Biafran War, 250
Biological Warfare Treaty, 457
Blum, Leon, 129
boat people, 206-207
Boers, 256-257
Bohlen, Charles, 71

Bokassa, Jean-Bedel, 246-247
Böll, Heinrich, 444
Bonn, 97, 443
Bosnia-Herzegovina, 452
Botha, P. W., 261-263
Botswana, 254-255
Brandt, Willy, 35, 220-223
Brazil, economic growth, 278; foreign debt,
    348-349, 351; militarism, 278-280
Brezhnev Doctrine, 81, 173, 408, 436, 446-
    447, 457
Brezhnev, Leonid, 81, 165-166, 415, 418, 426,
    429
Britain. *See* Great Britain
Brown, Harold, 470
Brunei, 203
Bucharest, 449-450, 455
Buckley, William, 373
Budapest, 171
Buddhism, 190
Bukharin, Nicolai, 427
Bulgaria, 447-448
Bundy, McGeorge, 93
Bush, George, 223, 295, 298-299, 303, 343,
    421, 475
Buthelezi, Mangosuthu, 264-265
Byrnes, James, 21

Calcutta, 320
Cali, 300, 303
Cambodia (Kampuchea), 182-183, 199, 203-
    207, 209
Camp David Agreement, 150
campesinos, 284, 292
Canada, 76, 223, 383
Carter, Jimmy, and Afghanistan, 413-415; and
    Camp David Agreement, 150; and Iran,
    369; and Nicaragua, 287-288; nuclear
    arms policy, 461, 464; recognition of
    PRC, 216; and Romania, 448; and SALT
    II, 458;
Castro, Fidel; and Central America, 285; on
    foreign debt problem, 353, 303; as
    leader of Cuban Revolution, 89-91, 284-
    285; and Cuban missile crisis, 88-95
Ceausescu, Nicolae, 80-81, 448-451
Ceausescu, Elena, 449-450
Central African Republic, 246-247
Central Intelligence Agency. *See* CIA
Chad, 254
Chaliand, Gerard, 419
Chamberlain, Neville, 33

Chamorro, Pedro Joaquin, 287
Chamorro, Violeta, 296
chemical warfare, 372
Chernenko, Konstantin, 166, 412, 424
Chernobyl, 412, 425-426
Chile, 280-283
China, civil war in, 53-57 ; U.S. postwar
    policy in, 52-53, 55-57, 67; in World
    War II, 13-15, 52. *See also* People's
    Republic of China *and* Republic of
    China
Chinese, in Malaya, 110; in Singapore, 118;
    in Vietnam, 207
Chinese Communist Party, 52-57, 176, 306-
    309
Christiani, Alfredo, 297, 303
Christmas bombing, 200
Chun Doo Hwan, 333
Churchill, Winston, as one of Big Three, 23-
    24; colonial policy of, 105-107; defeated
    in election (1945), 38, 107; on Greece,
    41, 45; on "Iron Curtain," 42; at
    Potsdam, 38; at Yalta, 32, 37
CIA (Central Intelligence Agency), and
    Afghanistan, 414; in Angola, 253; B-
    Team, 223-224, 226; in Chile, 281-282;
    in Cuba, 90-91; estimates of change in
    Soviet foreign policy, 87; estimates of
    Soviet defense spending, 223-224, 226;
    in Guatemala, 86, 89-90; and Hungarian
    revolution, 171; in Iran, 86, 365, 368; in
    Nicaragua, 288-290; in Panama, 298-299
Civic Forum (Czechoslovakia), 446
Clark Air Base, 339, 341
Colombia, 300-301
COMECON (Council on Mutual Economic
    Assistance), 79-81
Common Market. *See* EEC
Communist bloc, consolidation of, 32-34, 42-
    44, 79-81; economic development
    within, 79-80; military strength, 173-174;
    nationalism within, 43, 80-81; and Sino-
    Soviet split, 176; under Stalin, 42-44
Conable, Barber, 353
Connally, John, 396
Confucianism, 189, 331
Congo, Belgian colonial rule of, 132;
    economy, 244; independence of, 132;
    Katanga secession crisis, 133-134; UN
    forces in, 133, 137. *See also* Zaire
Contadora Group, 289, 294
Containment Theory, 44

contras, 288-290, 293-296
Costa Rica, 294
COSVN (Communist Operations of South
    Vietnam), 199
Council of Europe, 74
Cripps, Stafford, 105
Croatia, 452
cruise missile, 463-465, 477
Cuba, in Angola, 253-254; Bay of Pigs
    invasion, 90-91; Castro-led revolution,
    89, 284-285; involvement in Central
    America, 289; missile crisis, 88-96, 179;
    ties with Soviet Union, 91; U.S.
    property in, 89, 303
Cultural Revolution, 180, 308-309
Curzon Line, 34-35
Czechoslovakia, 42, 46, 83, 172, 220-221,
    445-447

Damascus, 141
Daoud, Mohammed, 416
Dayan, Moshe, 148
de Gaulle, Charles, and African
    independence, 127; and Algeria, 131-
    132, 136-137; and China, 78; and the
    Common Market, 75-76, 78; and
    European political integration, 78, 445;
    and NATO, 77; and nuclear power, 78;
    and West Germany, 79; and U.S., 78
Deir Yassin, 144
de Klerk, Frederik W., 263-265
Democratic Party (South Africa)
Democratic Party (U.S.), 57, 59
Democratic People's Republic of Korea
    (North Korea), 56–67; creation of, 57-
    59; attack on South, 61-62; casualties in
    war, 66; cease fire, 66
Democratic Progressive Party (Taiwan), 343
Democratic Republic of Vietnam (North
    Vietnam); bombed by U.S., 194, 199-
    200; land reform in, 189; negotiation to
    end war, 198-200; and NLF, 189-192,
    196; and People's Republic of China,
    180, 202; war in South Vietnam, 187-
    188, 190-196
Deng Xiaoping, 181, 309-318
Denmark, 76
de Reuter, Paul Julius, 363-364
desertification, 237, 346
de-Stalinization, 164, 426-427
détente, 82, 97, 179, 219-225, 415, 458, 463
de Tocqueville, Alexis, 164

Diem, Ngo Dinh, 116, 188-192, 208-209
Dien Bien Phu, 114-115
Djilas, Milovan, 41
DMZ (Demilitarized Zone, Korea), 66
Dobrynin, Anatoly, 94
domino theory, 40-41, 290
drug traffic, 299-301
Duarte, Jose Napoleon, 292-293, 296-297
Dubcek, Alexander, 172-173, 446
Dubs, Adolph, 416, 419
Dulles, Allen, 86, 90-91
Dulles, John Foster, Cold War policy, 85-86;
    at Geneva Conference (1954), 116; and
    Guatemala, 90; and Hungarian revolt,
    171-172; peace treaty with Japan, 68;
    and Zhou Enlai, 213
Dutch East Indies, 110
Dutch Reformed Church, 256-257
Dutra, Eurico, 278

East Berlin, 441
East European integration, 79-81
East Germany. *See* German Democratic
    Republic
East Pakistan. *See* Pakistan
EC (European Community). *See* ECC
ecoglasnost, 447
ECU (European Currency Unit), 389, 401
EEC (European Economic Community), 75-
    76, 97; British entry into, 75-76; creation
    of, 75; and European political
    integration, 78; single market, 388-392;
    and Japan, 390-391
Egypt, and the Arab world, 145; British in,
    145, 147; Camp David Agreement, 150;
    involvement in Arab-Israel wars, 144-
    150; overthrow of monarchy, 145;
    murder of Sadat, 150; Soviet economic
    and military aid, 86-87, 145-146, 251
Egyptian-Israeli peace treaty, 150
Eisenhower, Dwight, and Cuba, 90; and
    Hungarian Revolt, 171-172; and Iran,
    365; and Khrushchev, 82-85, 88, 178,
    184; and Korean War, 66; and Suez
    crisis, 147; and Vietnam, 116, 118
Ellsberg, Daniel, 209
El Salvador, 284, 291-293, 296-297; fourteen
    families, 291
Endara, Guillermo, 299
Estonia, 432
Ethiopia, 232, 242, 244, 267
Eto Jun, 388

Europe, destruction in World War II, 12-15;
    division into East and West, 38-39, 43-
    44, 72-74; nuclear weapons in, 463-467,
    472-476. *See also* Eastern Europe;
    Western Europe; *and individual
    countries*
European Coal and Steel Community, 74
European Economic Community. *See* EEC

Falkland Islands, 277, 306-307, 345
Farouk, King of Egypt, 145
Federal Republic of Germany. *See* German
    Federal Republic
fedeyeen, 147
Five-Year Plans, China, 177
Five-Year Plans, India, 321
Five-Year Plans, Soviet Union, 161-162, 306-
    307
FLMN (Farabundo Marti National Liberation
    Front), 296-297
FLN (Front de liberation nationale), 130
FNLA (National Front for the Liberation of
    Angola), 253
Ford, Gerald, 288
Forrestal, James, 34
"four tigers," 330-338
France, at war in Algeria, 130-131; and
    Britain, 74-76, 78; colonial policy in
    Africa, 126, 251; colonial rule in
    Indochina, 111; and Common Market,
    74-76; decolonization in Africa, 126-
    127; defeat in Indochina, 114-115, 187-
    188; departure from Algeria, 131-132;
    forces in Africa, 251; *force de frappe*, 78;
    in Middle East, 140, 145; and NATO,
    76-79; and nuclear disarmament, 457-
    458; as a nuclear power, 78, 456;
    occupation zone in Germany, 38; in
    UN Security Council, 25; at war in
    Vietnam, 112-115; and West Germany,
    77-79; withdrawal from NATO, 78; in
    World War II, 12, 104
Frei, Eduardo, 281
Frondizi, Arturo, 276

Gacha, Jose Gonzalo Rodriquez, 300
Galan, Luis Carlos, 300-301
Gandhi, Indira, 322-323, 327
Gandhi, Mahatma, 107-109, 117
Gandhi, Rajiv, 322, 328-329
Gang of Four, 309
Garcia, Alan, 353

Gaullism, 77-79, 97

Gaza, 146, 153-154

Gdansk, 405

General Confederation of Labor (Argentina), 276

Geneva Agreement, 115-116, 118, 187-188, 198

Genscher, Hans-Dietrich, 475

Georgian Republic, 433

Gerasimov, Gennady, 421, 433

German Democratic Republic (East Germany), creation of, 35; demise of, 440-443; and Soviet Union, 35, 81, 85; and Warsaw Pact, 80-81, 185; and West Germany, 219-220, 443-445

German Federal Republic (West Germany), and Berlin, 43, 73; and Common Market, 74-75; creation of, 35; economic recovery, 73; and France, 77-79; and NATO, 73, 219; nuclear weapons in, 463-467, 472-476

German Question, 443-445

Germany, division of, 35, 39, 443-445; occupation of, 37-39; postwar boundaries, 34-35; and Soviet Union, 22, 29, 33-34; in World War II, 11-15, 22, 33-34. *See also* German Democratic Republic *and* German Federal Republic

Ghana, 123-124

Giap, Vo Nguyen, 114

Gierek, Edward 405

Gilpatric, Roswell, 92

glasnost, 166, 425-427

Glemp, Joseph, 407

Golan Heights, 148-149

Goldwater, Barry, 194

Gomulka, Wladyslaw, 167, 169, 404-405

Gorbachev, Mikhail, and Afghanistan, 416, 420-421; and agriculture, 428-429 arms control talks, 185, 472-476; and Eastern Europe, 426-451; and People's Republic of China, 182-183, 315; reform program of, 166, 412-413, 424-436

Goulart, Joao, 279, 285

goulash Communism, 410

Gowon, Yakubu, 250

Grand Alliance, 12, 29, 31

Great Britain, and Common Market, 74-76; and decolonization, 105, 123-124; and Egypt, 147; and Greece, 40; in India, 105-109; and Iran, 363-364; and Israel, 147; in Malaya, 109-110; and NATO, 76-77; and nuclear weapons, 20; and Palestine, 140-143; and Poland, 31-32, 38; in World War II, 11-13, 33

Great Leap Forward, 177-178, 307-308

Great Trek, 257, 259

Greece, British support of, 40; and Common Market, 97; U.S. support of, 40-41

Green Revolution, 320, 343, 429

Gromyko, Andrei, 97

Groves, Leslie, 20

Guatemala, 87, 89-90, 284

guerrilla warfare, 113, 136

Guevara, Che, 113

Guinea, 127

Gulf of Tonkin incident, 193-194

Gulf of Tonkin resolution, 194

Gysi, Gregor, 442

Habib, Philip, 151-152

Haig, Alexander, 288

Haile Selassie, 267

Haiphong, 112, 200

haj, 361

Hajek, Jiri, 446

Halle, 442, 475

Hallstein Doctrine, 219-220

Hammarskjold, Dag, 137

Havel, Vaclav, 446

Hebron, 142, 149

hegemonism, 181

hegira, 375

Helsinki Agreement, 222-223

Heng Samrin, 204

Hernández, Maximiliano, 284, 292

Herzl, Theodor, 140

high-tech industries, 379

Hindus, 105-109

Hiroshima, 15-20

Hitler, Adolf, 31-34, 128, 142, 144, 173, 220, 258, 432

Hitler-Stalin pact, 432-433

Hmong, 207

Ho Chi Minh, 111-116, 188

Ho Chi Minh City, 202

Ho Chi Minh Trail, 194

Hollings, Ernest, 386

Honda, 396

Honecker, Eric, 441, 454

Hong Kong, 336-337

Horn, Gyula, 440

Horn of Africa, 224

Houphouet-Boigny, Felix, 126-127, 267

Hu Yaobang, 313-315
Hua Guofeng (Hua Kuo-feng), 309, 314-315
Hue, 194, 197
Hungary, economic development, 410-411;
　　reforms, 410-412, 439-440; revolt, 171-
　　172; in Warsaw Pact, 80, 171, 440
Husak, Gustav, 173
Hussein, King of Jordan, 148, 153
Hussein, Saddam, 370-372
Hussein, Sherif, 141
Hussein-McMahon letters, 141

Ibo, 250
ICBMs (Inter-Continental Ballistic Missiles),
　　176, 457-458, 461-462, 467-471, 477
IMF (International Monetary Fund), 352-353
Iliescu, Ion, 450, 455
Inchon, 62
India, and Bangladesh, 324-328; border
　　conflict with PRC, 179, 323; British
　　departure from, 107-109; economic
　　growth, 318-323, 328-329;
　　ethnic/religious diversity, 324;
　　nationalism, 105; under Nehru, 321-322;
　　neutralism, 227, 323; as nuclear power,
　　327; conflicts with Pakistan, 323-328;
　　partition of, 109; population growth,
　　236, 318-320
Indian National Congress, 105-107, 322
Indochina, 111-116, 187-207
industrial growth, in China, 217, 309-312; in
　　India, 321-323; in Japan, 377-388; in
　　Third World, 240-242; in Western
　　Europe, 75, 77, 388-392; in West
　　Germany, 73; in Soviet Union, 161-162,
　　412-413, 424-436; in U.S., 22-23, 392-
　　394
Indonesia, 110, 203
INF (intermediate-range nuclear forces), 463-
　　465, 472-473
Inkhata movement, 264-265
Interim Committee, 16
intifada, 153-154
Iran, British interests in, 363-364; clergy's
　　opposition to shah, 363-364; hostage
　　crisis, 368-369; Khomeini, 367-370, 403,
　　418–419; and OPEC, 365-367;
　　revolution in, 367-370; SAVAK, 375;
　　under shah, 364-366; U.S. interests in,
　　365-367; war with Iraq, 370-373
"Iran-Contra" affair, 294
Iraq, 370-373

IRBM (Intermediate-Range Ballistic Missile),
　　459, 463-464, 472-475
Irgun Zvai Leumi, 142-144
Iron Curtain, 83
Ironsi, J. T., 250
Islam, 128-129, 359-363, 418
Islamic Jihad, 373-374
Islamic Union of Mujadaheen, 421
Israel, Arab-Israeli wars, 144-149; creation of,
　　138-144; Camp David Agreement, 150;
　　and Lebanon, 151-153; and PLO, 149-
　　153; and U.S., 147-150; West Bank
　　policy, 148-150, 154-155
Italtel, 390
Italy, and Common Market, 74-75; in NATO,
　　76; in World War II, 12
Ivory Coast, 127

Japan, allied occupation of, 47-51; and Asian
　　nationalism, 104; atomic bombings of,
　　15-19; and China, 217-218;
　　demilitarization of, 48-49;
　　democratization of, 48-51; economic
　　growth of, 305, 377-388; economic
　　relations with U.S., 392-399; emperor
　　of, 18-19, 50; military security pact with
　　U.S., 68; rearmament of, 67; surrender
　　of, 18-19; in World War II, 12, 14-15
Japanese Emperor, 18-19, 50
Jaruzelski, Woijtech, 406-410, 437-438
Jerusalem, 141, 143
Jiang Jingguo (Chiang Ching-kuo), 335-336
Jiang Kaishek (Chiang Kai-shek), and
　　Chinese Communist Party, 52, 53;
　　defeat in civil war, 53-56; U.S. support
　　of, 47, 55-56, 216-217
Jiang Quing (Chiang Ch'ing), 217, 309
Jinnah, Mohammed Ali, 107-108
Johannesburg, 260
Johnson, Chalmers, 282, 400
Johnson, Lyndon B., and détente, 220; and
　　Vietnam War, 190-198
Judea and Samaria, 149
"Just Cause," 298-299

Kadar, Janos, 171, 184, 410-411, 439
Karmal, Babrak, 417
Kasavubu, Joseph, 133
Kashmir, 323-324
Kakuei, Tanaka, 218
Katanga, 133-134, 137, 246
Katzenbach, Nicholas, 209

Kennan, George, 44, 71
Kennedy, John F., and arms control, 456; and
    Cuba, 90-95; and Khrushchev, 92-96;
    and Latin America, 272, 285; and
    Vietnam, 190
Kennedy, Robert, 94
Kent State massacre, 199
Kenya, 125, 234, 236, 242
Kenyatta, Jomo, 125, 267
Khadaffi, Muammar, 374, 419
Khalistan, 329
Khmer Rouge, 203-206
Khomeini, Ayatollah Ruhollah, 367-370, 403,
    418-419
khozraschet, 428
Khrushchev, Nikita, and agriculture, 429; and
    Austria, 83; and Cuba, 92-96; and de-
    Stalinization, 163-164; and Eisenhower,
    82, 83-85, 88, 178, 184; and Germany,
    444-445; and Hungary, 171; and Middle
    East, 87; overthrow of, 165-166, 180;
    and People's Republic of China, 176-
    180; peaceful coexistence, 83; and
    Poland, 169-170; and Soviet foreign
    policy, 86-88, 424; visits U.S., 83-85
Kikuyu, 125
Kim Dae Jung, 333
Kim Il Sung, 59, 343
Kim Young Sam, 333
Kirkpatrick, Jeanne, 436
Kissinger, Henry, on arms race, 462; and
    Chile, 282; and Iran, 366-367; and
    People's Republic of China, 213-216;
    and Vietnam, 199-200
Kiszczak, General Czeslaw, 438
Kohl, Helmut, 389
Koran, 360-361
Korea, division of, 57-59. *See also* Democratic
    People's Republic of Korea *and*
    Republic of Korea
Korean War, 57-67
Kosovo, 452
Kosygin, Alexei, 166, 428
Krenz, Egon, 441-442, 447, 454
Kubitschek, Juscelino, 278-279
kulaks, 429
Kulikov, General Victor, 474
Kurds, 372
Kuron, Jacek, 408
Kuwait, 350, 372
Kvitsinsky, Yuli, 465
Ky, Nguyen Cao, 194

laager, 263
Labor Party (Israel), 154
Labour Party (Great Britain), 14, 107
Lance II, 474
land reform, in Brazil, 279; in Chile, 281; in
    Japan, 50; in Latin America, 270, 274,
    279-282; in North Korea, 58; in People's
    Republic of China, 56, 306; in Third
    World, 237-239; in Vietnam, 189
Laos, 199, 205-207
La Prensa, 287, 295-296
latifundia, 270
Latin America, Alliance for Progress, 271-272;
    economic development in, 269-275;
    foreign debt, 348-349; militarism, 269-
    270, 274-275; population growth, 236;
    Spanish legacy, 269-270; U.S.
    intervention in, 271-272, 284-285. *See
    also individual countries*
Latvia, 432
Lebanon, 151-153
Lee Kuan Yew, 338
Lee Teng-hui, 337-338
Lehder, Carlos Rivas, 301
Leipzig, 441, 475
lend-lease, 46
Leningrad, 22
Lesotho, 245
liberation theology, 292
Libya, 289, 372
Ligachev, Yegor, 429
Likud, 153-154
Lin Biao, 178
Li Peng, 312, 314
Lithuania, 430, 432-433
Little Red Book, 308
Liu Shaoqi (Liu Shao-ch'i), 308
Lon Nol, 204, 206
London Poles, 31-32
Lublin Poles, 31-32
Lukanov, Andrei, 447
Lumumba, Patrice, 133

MacArthur, Douglas, and allied occupation of
    Japan, 48-51, 67, 70-71; in Korean War,
    62-65
Macmillan, Harold, 99
MAD (Mutually Assured Destruction), 468
Maddox, 193
Maekawa Haruo, 385
Maekawa Report, 385
Malan, D. F., 257

Malaya, Federation of, 109-110
Malaysia, 109-110, 118, 203
Malenkov, Georgi, 87, 162
Maleter, Pal, 439
malnutrition, 233
Malta Conference, 421
Malvinas. *See* Falkland Islands
Manchuria, 37, 53-54, 56
Mandela, Nelson, 261, 264-265
Manhattan Project, 20
Mansfield, Mike, 384
Mao Zedong (Mao Tse-tung), and agrarian
    reform, 305-306; anti-Soviet attitude,
    174-183; and civil war in China, 52-57;
    and Cultural Revolution, 180, 308-309;
    death of, 308-309; and founding of
    PRC, 55; and Great Leap Forward, 177-
    178, 307-308; and Jiang Kaishek, 52;
    and Khrushchev, 176-180; mass line,
    307-309; and Stalin, 174-175, 306-307
Maoism, 180, 307-309
Marcos, Ferdinand, 338-341, 344
Marcos, Imelda, 339
Marshall, George, 71
Marshall Plan, 41-42, 74, 79, 271
Marti, Augustin Farabundo
Marxism, in Africa, 224, 252-253; in Asia, 14;
    in Chile, 281; in Hungary, 410-412; in
    the People's Republic of China,
    176–178, 310; in Sino-Soviet dispute,
    176-178; in Soviet bloc relations, 170; in
    Western Europe, 14
Marxism-Leninism, 252, 308, 310
Massu, Jacques, 130-131
Matsu, 177
Mau Mau, 125
Mauritius, 254-255
Mazowiecki, Tadeusz, 438-439
McCarthy, Joseph, 57, 59, 80
McMahon, Henry, 141
McNamara, Robert, 93, 209
Mecca, 361
Medellin, 300-301, 303
Medvedev, Vadim, 426
megatonnage, 460
Mekong River, 111
Memorial, 427
Mendes France, Pierre, 128
Mengistu Haile Miriam, 224
Mexico, 236, 269, 274, 289, 303, 349
Middle East, British role in, 140-143, 147;
    French role in, 140, 147; Soviet role in,

145, 148-149; U.S. role in, 148-153
Midgetman, 467
militarism, in Africa, 231, 247-251; in
    Argentina, 276-277; in Brazil, 278-280;
    in Chile, 280-283; in Japan, 20, 50-51; in
    Latin America, 276-284, 292-293, 296-
    299
Milosevic, Slobodan, 452
minifundia, 270
Minuteman III, 458, 467
MIRV (Multiple Independently Targeted Re-
    Entry Vehicle), 457-459
missile gap, 92
MITI (Ministry of International Trade and
    Industry), 379, 381-382
Mitsubishi Motors, 396
Mitterand, Francois, 128, 136, 389
Mladenov, Petar, 447-448
Mobutu, Joseph, 248
Modrow, Hans, 442
Mohammed, 359-363
Molotov, Viacheslav, 42, 45, 85, 87, 97, 116,
    163
Monnet, Jean, 74
Monroe Doctrine, 271, 289
Moss, Ambler, 298
Mossadegh, Mohammed, 86, 365
Mountbatten, Louis, 108
Mozambique, 134, 242, 253
MPLA (Popular Movement for the Liberation
    of Angola), 253-254
Mubarak, Hosni, 153
Mujibur Rahman, Sheikh 326
Munich, lessons of, 33-34, 42, 62
Muslim League, 107
Muslims, 126-129, 127-131; in Soviet Union,
    417-418
MX missile, 467, 470

Nagasaki, 15-20
Nagorno-Karabakh, 434, 453
Nagy, Imre, 171, 184, 439-440
Najibullah, 420-421
Nakasone, Yasuhiro, 385
Namibia, 253, 267
Nanjing, 54
Nasir ed-Den Shah, 363-364
Nasser, Gamel Abdel, comes to power, 145;
    death of, 149; and Israel, 143, 145-149;
    and Suez Canal, 147; and the Soviet
    Union, 86-87, 97; and Syria, 145
nationalism, in Africa, 119-121, 123, 134-135;

in the Arab world, 140-143; in Argentina, 275; in Asia, 103-104; in Eastern Europe, 43, 173-174, 436-452; in Egypt, 147; in France, 78, 79; in India, 105, 107, 109; in Indonesia, 110; Jewish, 140, 143; in the People's Republic of China, 176; in Poland, 404-410; in Vietnam, 111-112; in Yugoslavia, 451-452; in Soviet Union, 431-435

Nationalist Army (China), 52-54, 56, 65

Nationalist China. *See* Republic of China

Nationalist Party (Republic of China), 52, 219

Nationalist Party (South Africa), 257-259

National Security Council. *See* NSC

NATO (North Atlantic Treaty Organization), creation of, 44, 76; French role in, 77-78; German entry into, 73, 77, 444-445; and nuclear weapons, 78, 464-467, 472-475

Nehru, Jawaharlal, on economic development, 321, 328; and Indian nationalism, 105, 107-109; and neutralism, 185, 323; and Pakistan, 323-324; as Prime Minister, 322

Netherlands, and colonialism, 104; in Common Market, 73-74; and Indonesian independence, 109-110; in NATO, 77; in World War II, 104

New Economic Zones (Vietnam), 203

New Forum (East Germany), 441

Nhu, Ngo Dinh, 190

NICs (Newly Industrializing Countries), 331, 392, 395

Nicaragua, 287-295, economy, 287, 295; elections (1990), 296; Sandinistas, 288-291, 293-296; Somoza family, 287-288; and Soviet Union, 288; and U.S., 287-295

Nigeria, Biafran War, 249-251; economic problems, 250, 347; foreign debt, 347; oil, 346-347; tribal conflict within, 249-251; urban growth, 236

Nitze, Paul, 465

Nixon Doctrine, 366-367

Nixon, Richard, and Cambodia, 199, 209; and Chile, 282; and Iran, 366-367; and Japan, 218, 226; and the People's Republic of China, 212–216; and Romania, 448; and SALT I, 457-458; and Vietnam War, 198-201, 203; Vietnamization policy, 198; Watergate crisis, 200, 209

Nixon shock, 218, 226

Nkrumah, Kwame, 123-124, 248-249, 252

NLF (National Liberation Front, South Vietnam), 189-193, 198-201

nomenklatura, 430, 453

Nomura, 387

Non-Proliferation Treaty, 456-457

Noriega, Manuel, 298-299

North Korea. *See* Democratic People's Republic of Korea

North, Oliver, 294

North Vietnam. *See* Democratic Republic of Vietnam

Novotny, Antonin, 172

NSC (National Security Council), role of, 71, 78; NSC-68, 59-60, 71, 82

"nuclear diplomacy," 19-20

Nuclear Test Ban Treaty, 95

nuclear weapons, arms control agreements, 21, 95, 456-460, 469; arms race, 95-96; Chinese development of, 180; in Cuba, 92-95; in Europe, 77-78, 459, 463-467, 472-476; French development of, 78, 327; Indian development of, 327; intermediate-range weapons, 463-467, 472-476, 459; proliferation of, 456-476; Soviet arsenal, 88, 95-96, 457-465; Soviet development of, 21, 49, 463; strategic defense weapons, 468-472; testing of, 456; threatened use of, 93; in Turkey, 94-95; U.S. arsenal, 88, 457-467; U.S. development of, 16, 59, 464-467

Nyerere, Julius, 252, 267, 348

OAU (Organization of African Unity), 251, 348

Obando y Bravo, Cardinal Miguel, 295

Obasanjo, Olusegun, 250

Obote, Milton, 248

October Revolution (Poland), 169-170

Oder-Neisse Line, 35, 220, 226, 443

Ogaden, 224

oil, in Alaska, 350; in Iran, 365-367; in Iraq, 372; in Mexico, 350-351; in Nigeria, 250-251; in North Sea, 250; oil crisis, 349-351, 378; OPEC, 250, 349-351; in Persian Gulf, 350, 372; in Soviet Union, 350, 414

Okinawa, 68

Olympic Games, in Los Angeles, 81; in Moscow, 415, 448; in Munich, 149; in Seoul, 333

Ongania, Juan Carlos, 277
OPEC (Organization of Petroleum Exporting Countries), 250, 349-351
Oppenheimer, Robert, 21
Ortega, Daniel, 289-290
OSS (Office of Strategic Services), 112, 130
Ostpolitik, 221
Ottoman Empire, 140-141
Outer Space Treaty, 456, 471-472

"Pacific Rim," 331
Pahlavi, Reza Khan, 364-365
Pahlavi, Shah Mohammed Reza, 363-369
Pakistan, and Afghanistan, 329-330; and Bangladesh, 324-328; creation of, 109; economic development of, 324; and India, 109, 323-329; and People's Republic of China, 324, 327; and U.S., 324, 327
Palach, Jan, 454
Palestine, British policy in, 140-142; conflict over, 139-144; Jewish immigration into, 140-141; PLO, 149–155, 289, 374; refugees from, 144-145, 148-150, 152; UN partition of, 143-144
Palestinian National Council, 154
Pamiat (Memory), 427
Panama, 283, 289, 298-299
Panama Canal, 298
Panamanian Defense Forces, 298-299
Panmunjon, 65
Park Chung Hee, 333
Pasternak, Boris, 164
payload, 459-460
PDC (Christian Democratic Party [El Salvador]), 292
peaceful coexistence, 177
Peng Dehuai, 178
Pentagon Papers, 193
People's Daily, 310
People's Republic of China (PRC), in Africa, 253, 268; creation of, 47, 55; Cultural Revolution, 180, 308-309; Deng Xiaoping, 309-318; Great Leap Forward, 177-178, 307-308; and India, 179, 323-324; and Japan, 217-218, 225-226; enters Korean War, 64-66; Mao Zedong, 177-178, 211-216, 305-309; Nixon visit to, 212-215; as nuclear power, 180, 456; and Pakistan, 324, 327; population of, 233-234, 305, 311; Tienanmen Square, 315–318; and Third World, 179; and

Soviet Union, 67, 173, 74-183; enters UN, 214, 217; and U.S., 178, 210-217
Peres, Shimon, 154
perestroika, 424-435
Peron, Eva, 276, 304
Peron, Juan, 275-277, 303-304
Peronists, 275-277
Pershing II, 461
Persian Gulf, 413-414
Peru, 353
petrodollars, 345, 350
Phalangists, 152-153
Philippines, 104-105, 203, 338-341
Phnom Penh, 206
"ping pong diplomacy," 213
Pinochet, Augusto, 282-284
Pinsker, Leon, 139
PLA (PRC People's Liberation Army), 53-54, 308
PLO (Palestine Liberation Organization), 149-155, 289, 374
Pol Pot, 204-207
Poland, borders of, 34-35; economic program, 79, 170, 404-407, 438-439; revolt in 1956, 169-170; and Solidarity, 404-410, 437-439; and Soviet Union, 31-35, 42, 79-80, 166, 168-170, 408-410; and Warsaw Pact, 80, 408-409; at Yalta, 29-33, 45; in World War II, 12-13
Politburo (Soviet Union), 97
polycentrism, 170, 174
population growth, in Africa, 234; in Bangladesh, 327-328; in India, 319-320; in Latin America, 236; in People's Republic of China, 233, 305, 311; in Third World, 233-236; in world, 233-234; urban growth, 236
Portugal, African territories of, 134, 253; and Angola, 253; and Brazil, 278; and decolonization, 134, 252; and NATO, 76
Potsdam Conference, 38-40, 57
Potsdam Proclamation, 18-19
poverty, in Africa, 242-244; in Bangladesh, 327-328; in India, 318-322; in Latin America, 270, 274, 280, 288; in People's Republic of China, 305-306; in Third World, 231-233, 236
Poznan riots, 169
Prague Spring, 173, 446
Pravda, 412, 428-429, 437, 474
protectionism, 241, 378, 383-387, 390-391, 395-398

Punjabi, 324
Pusan, 62
Putera, 110

Qajar dynasty, 364
Quemoy, 177
Quit India Resolution, 105

Rabin, Yitzhak, 372
Radio Free Europe, 171
Rawlings, Jerry, 249
Reagan, Ronald, and El Salvador, 292-293;
    and Iran, 369; and Japan, 383, 385-386;
    and Nicaragua, 288-291; nuclear arms
    policy, 460, 464-472; and Star Wars,
    468-472; and terrorism, 373-374
Red Flag, 178
Red Guards, 308
Renner, Karl, 83
reparations, World War II, 38-39
Republic of China (ROC), in civil war, 52-55;
    economic development, 334-336; and
    Japan, 217-219; Nationalist retreat to
    Taiwan, 40, 54-55; and PRC, 177, 211,
    219; PRC military pressure on, 177-178;
    in U.S.-PRC negotiations, 215-219; and
    U.S., 56-57, 69, 177, 211, 215-219
Republic of Korea (South Korea), creation of,
    58-59; economic development, 331-334;
    Korean War, 57, 60-66; U.S. military
    occupation of, 57-59
Republic of Vietnam (South Vietnam), Diem
    government, 188-190; fall of Saigon,
    200-201; NLF, 189-193; U.S. military
    involvement, 187-188, 190-201; U.S.
    withdrawal from, 200-201
Republican Party (U.S.), 57, 59, 82
Rebublican Party (West Germany), 443, 454
"responsibility system" (PRC), 309
"reverse course" (Japan), 67
revolutions, in Algeria, 127-132; in
    Bangladesh, 326-327; in Cambodia,
    203-207; in Central America, 283-285; in
    China, 52-56; in Cuba, 89-90; in Eastern
    Europe, 436-443, 445-452 (*see also
    individual countries*); in El Salvador,
    291-293, 296-297; in Greece, 40; in
    Indonesia, 110; in Iran, 367-370; in
    Korea, 58-59; in Nicaragua, 287-291; in
    Vietnam, 111-115, 189-193
Reykjavik, 473
Reza Khan, 364-365

Rhee, Syngman, 58, 66
Rhodesia, 125
Ricoh, 396
Ridgeway, Matthew, 65
Roh Tae Woo, 333-334
Rokossovsky, Konstantin, 169
Roman Catholic Church (Argentina), 276, 303
Roman Catholic Church (Poland), 170, 407,
    437
Romania, 80-81, 448-451, 455
Romero, Oscar Arnulfo, 292
Roosevelt, Franklin D., and atomic bomb, 16,
    20; in Big Three, 23, 29; on colonialism,
    104; on founding of UN, 24, 38; at
    Yalta, 19, 29-33, 37
Roosevelt Corollary, 271, 284
Rothschild, Lord, 141
Ruhr, 74
Rusk, Dean, 94, 193
Russia, anti-Semitism in, 139, 427; borders
    with Poland, 34-35; historical relations
    with China, 175; Russo-Japanese War,
    35. *See also* Soviet Union
Russians, 435, 417-418
Rust, Mathias, 474
Rybakov, Anatoli, 426

Saar, 74
Sadat, Anwar, 149-150, 416
Sahara, 346
Sahel, 346
Sakharov, Andrei, 225
Salazar, Oliveira, 134
SALT I, 457-458
SALT II, 458-460
Samrin, Heng, 204
Sandinistas, 288-291, 293-296
São Paulo, 274
Sato Eisaku, 225
Saudi Arabia, 350-351, 372
SCAP (Supreme Commander of Allied
    Powers), 48, 50-51
Schönhuber, Franz, 454
Schuman, Robert, 74
Scowcroft, Brent, 475
SDI (Strategic Defense Initiative), 469-472,
    477
Seabed Pact, 457
SEATO (Southeast Asia Treaty Organization),
    86
Secret Speech, 163-164, 168-169, 176
securitate, 448, 450-451

sejm, 437

Seoul, 333-334

Serbia, 452

Setif riot, 129-130

Shagari, Shehu, 250

Shamir, Yitzhak, 154-155

Shanghai Communique, 216

Sharon, Ariel, 152

Sharpeville massacre, 260-261

Shatt-el Arab, 370

Shevardnadze, Eduard, 97

Shiites, 361-363, 367-370, 373, 375, 421

Shultz, George, 291

Siad Barre, 224

Sidra, Gulf of, 374

Sihanouk, Norodom 199

Sikhs, 323, 329

Silesia, 220, 443

Sin, Cardinal Jaime, 340

Sinai War, 147

Sinai Desert, 147-148, 150

Singapore, 110, 118, 203, 337-338

Singh, V. P., 329

Sino-Soviet split, 174-183

Six Day War, 147-149

Slavs, 418

SLMB (Submarine-Launched Ballistic Missile), 457

Slovenia, 452

Smith, Adam, 396

Smith, Ian, 125

Smith, W. Beddell, 116, 118

Social Democratic Party (West Germany), 475

socialist imperialism, 181

Sokolowski, Marshal Vasili, 474

Solidarity, 404-410, 437-439

Solzhenitsyn, Alexander, 164, 426

Somalia, 224

somocistas, 287

Somoza, Anastasio Debayle, 287-288

Somoza, Anastasio Garcia, 287

South Africa, Afrikaner, 256-262; and Angola, 253-254; apartheid, 256-265; British role in, 257; economic growth, 263-264; foreign pressure on, 263-264; and Namibia, 253, 267

South China Sea, 206

South Korea. *See* Republic of Korea

South Vietnam. *See* Republic of Vietnam

Southern Rhodesia, 125

Soviet Union, and Afghanistan, 87-88, 413-421; in Africa, 252-254; and Angola, 253-254; and arms control, Chapter 19; develops atomic bomb, 21, 49; and Chinese civil war, 54; and Czechoslovakia, 42, 172-173, 446-447; and Cuba, 88-96; and Eastern Europe, 79-86, 167-175, 408-410, 436-452; economic developments, 161-162, 427-430; and Hungary, 171-172, 410; and India, 322, 327; Jewish immigration from, 225; and Korean War, 58-59, 61; military strength of, 81, 92-93, 226, Chapter 19; nationalities within, 431-435; and North Korea, 58-59, 61; oil reserves, 350, 414; and People's Republic of China, 67, 173, 174–183; and Poland, 409-410, 437; aftermath of World War II, 4, 11-12, 22-23; in World War II, 12, 18-19

Soweto, 261, 264

Spaak, Paul-Henri, 74

Spain, 97

Spiegel, 402, 435

sputnik, 176

Sri Lanka (Ceylon), 109

SS-9, 457

SS-18, 467-468

SS-20, 463-465, 472-473, 478

Stalin, Joseph, and China, 54; and Czechoslovakia, 42, 172-173; death of, 66, 82; and Japan, 18-19; and Khrushchev, 162-164; and Korean War, 58-59, 61; legacy of, 161-164; and Poland, 31-35, 42, 79-80; at Potsdam, 38-40; and Soviet economic development, 161-162; and Yugoslavia, 43, 45; at Yalta, 31-35

Stalingrad, 164

Star Wars. *See* SDI

Stasi, 441

Stealth bomber, 393

Steininger, Rolf, 454

Stimson, Henry, 16

Stinger missile, 420

Strategic Defense Initiative. *See* SDI

strategic hamlets, 189

Subic Bay Naval Base, 341

Sub-Saharan Africa, 119, 254-256, 346-347

Sudetenland, 220-221

Suez Canal, 148-149

Sukarno, Achem, 110

Sumgait, 434

Summers, Lawrence, 395
Sunnis, 361-363, 421
Sverdlovsk, 435
SWAPO (South-West African People's Organization [Namibia]), 253
Swaziland, 245
Sykes-Picot Agreement, 140
Syria, 145, 148, 152, 372

tactical weapons, 474-475
Tadzhiks, 421
Taipei, 335
Taiwan, 177, 179. *See also* Republic of China
Takeshita, Noboru, 388
Tanzam Great Freedom railroad, 251
Tanzania, 251-252, 267, 348
Taraki, Nur Mohammed, 416
TASS, 429
Tbilisi, 433
terrorism, 373-374
Tet Offensive, 196-197
Thailand, 203-204
Thatcher, Margaret, 389, 391, 424
theater weapons, 459, 463-465, 472-473
Thieu, Nguyen Van, 194, 200
Third World debt, 345-353
Tho, Le Duc, 199-200
Tienanmen Square, 315-318
Tigris River, 370
Timisoara, 449-450, 455
Tiran, Straits of, 147
Tito, Joseph, 43, 45, 80, 167-168, 452
Titoism, 43, 45, 80, 184
Togliatti, Palmiro, 170
Tokes, Laszlo, 450
Tokyo Stock Exchange, 387
Tonkin Gulf incident, 193-194
Tonkin Gulf Resolution, 193-194
Torrijos, Omar, 298
Trans-Jordan, 140
Transylvania, 449
tribalism, 245-246, 249-250
Tripoli, 374
troika, 163
Trotsky, Leon, 427
Trujillo, Rafael, 285
Truman, Harry, and atomic bomb, 16, 19-21; and Austria, 83; and China, 57; and Korean War, 59, 61-62, 64-65; and MacArthur, 62-64; Marshall Plan, 41-42; military spending, 82; at Potsdam, 16, 38-40; Truman Doctrine, 40-41

Tshombe, Moise, 133
Turkey, 94, 140-141
Turner, Stansfield, 414
Tutu, Desmond, 261
Twentieth Party Congress (Soviet Union), 163, 179

U-2, 88, 95, 97-98, 184
Uganda, 248
Ukrainians, 173, 417
Ulbricht, Walter, 221
Ungo, Guillermo, 292
UNITA (National Union for the Total Independence of Angola), 253-254
United Arab Emirates, 350
United Nations, and Africa, 133; and atomic energy, 21; Chinese membership, 215-216, 225; in Congo, 133-134, 137; creation of, 23-26, 37; in Dutch East Indies, 110; General Assembly of, 25; and Gorbachev, 185, 472-474; and Iran-Iraq War, 372; and Kashmir, 323; in Korean War, 58-64; limitations of, 37; in Middle East, 143-144, 147-148; organization of, 24-26; Resolution 242 (Middle East), 148; Security Council of, 24-26; Third World bloc within, 228; UN Emergency Force, 147; UNESCO (UN Educational, Scientific, and Cultural Organization), 25; UNRRA (UN Relief and Reconstruction Agency), 25; discussed at Yalta, 37
United States, in Africa, 252-253; and Angola, 252-253; and Cambodia, 199, 202; and Canada, 385; and Chile, 281-283; China policy, 52-53, 55-57, 67, 210-219; and Cuba, 89-95; and de Gaulle, 78; and Egypt, 150, 154; and Germany, 37-38, 43, 72-73, 184, 220; and Guatemala, 87, 89-90, 284; and Hungarian revolution, 171-173; and India, 322, 324, 327; and Iran, 365-369; and Israel, 147-150; and Japan, 47-51, 378, 383-388, 395-399; and Lebanon, 151-153; and NATO, 76-79, 219; and Nicaragua, 287-291, 293-296; normalization of relations with PRC, 210-217; nuclear arms talks, 21, 95, Chapter 19; nuclear arsenal, 88, Chapter 19; and Pakistan, 324, 327; grants independence to Philippines, 104; and ROC (Taiwan), 217-219, 334; and South Korea, 57-59; and Vietnam

War, 187-201; aftermath of World War
II, 3-4, 22
U.S.-Japanese Mutual Security Pact, 68
uskorenie, 166, 427-428
Ussuri River, 181, 185

Vargas, Getulio, 275, 278
Venezuela, 289, 349-350
Ver, General Fabian, 339
Verwoerd, Henrik, 261
Videla, Jorge Rafael, 277
Viet Cong. *See* NLF
Viet Minh, 112-116
Vietnam, and Cambodia, 199, 203-206;
French colonial rule, 111-112; Geneva
Accords, 115-116, 118, 187-188; impact
of war, 201-206; insurrection in South,
188-193; and People's Republic of
China, 114, 190, 203, 205, 215;
reunification under Communists, 200-
202; and Soviet aid, 203, 205; war
against French, 113-115
Vietnamization, 198
Volgograd, 164

Waite, Terry, 373
Walesa, Lech, 406-407
"walk-in-the-woods" proposal, 465
Warsaw Pact, 80-81, 173-174, 219, 408-409,
440, 448
Watergate, 200, 209
Weinberger, Caspar, 470
West Berlin, 43, 97, 184
West Germany. *See* German Federal Republic
West Pakistan. *See* Pakistan
West Bank, 148, 150, 154-156
Western Europe, Common Market, 75-76;
economic integration, 72-76, 388-392;
economic recovery, 72-76; and Japan,
390-397; military integration, 76-79; and
NATO, 76-79; and nuclear weapons,
463-465, 472-475; political integration,
72-74, 76; U.S. aid to, 41-42;
post–World War II conditions, 12-15,
72-76.
Westmoreland, William, 194-195, 197
White Paper (Great Britain, 1939), 142
White Paper (United States, 1965), 193, 209

Wilson, Woodrow, 45, 111, 284, 303
"window-of-vulnerability," 477
"Wintex-Cimex 89," 475
World Bank, 254-256, 266, 343
World Court, 294
World War II, and Africa, 119-121; atomic
bombs on Japan, 15-20; and
colonialism, 103-104; consequences of,
3-4, 11, 22; death toll, 12-15;
destruction, 12-15, 22; Grand Alliance,
12, 19, 31; holocaust, 12; Japanese
surrender, 16-20
Wyszynski, Stefan, 170

Xinjiang, 175
Xhosa, 261, 264-265

Yahya Khan, 326-327
Yalta Conference, 19, 29-39; Germany, 37-38;
Japan, 35-37; Poland, 29-35;
reparations, 38-39; UN, 37
Yalu River, 64
"yanqui imperialism," 271-272
"yen bloc," 395
Yerevan, 431
Yom Kippur War, 149
Yoruba, 250
Young Lions, 265
Yugoslavia, 43, 45, 80, 167, 184, 451-452

Zahir, Shah, 416, 420-421
zaibatsu, 67
Zaire, 133-134
zakat, 361
Zambia, 125, 232, 251
Zaslavskaia, Tatiana, 428
Zhao Ziyang, 312, 316
Zhivkov, Todor, 447-448
Zhou Enlai (Chou En-lai), at Bandung
Conference, 185; and Cultural
Revolution, 308-309; death of, 309; and
Japan, 218; and Mao, 308-309; and
Soviet Union, 178; and U.S., 213-216
Zia, Mohammed ul-Haq, 329-330
Zimbabwe, 125-126, 253
Zionists, 139-153
Zulus, 264-265

☐ About the Book and the Authors

Momentous events have occurred since *The World Since 1945* first went to press in late 1987—events in the Soviet Union and Eastern Europe that signal the end of the Cold War era. This revised edition offers a historical interpretation of these new currents, as well as of other important developments in China, Japan, the Middle East, Central America, and elsewhere.

A comprehensive yet concise study of the major political, economic, and ideological patterns in the global arena since World War II, the book—written for introductory courses in international relations or world history—serves as a corrective to often one-sided, Western-centered approaches to the salient issues of recent decades.

Wayne C. McWilliams and **Harry Piotrowski** are professors in the History Department at Towson State University.